Children and Literature

Views and Reviews

by Virginia Haviland
Library of Congress

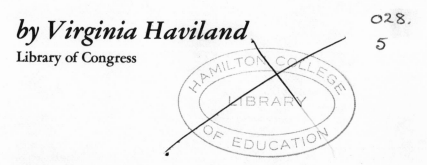
The Bodley Head Ltd.
London

First published by Scott, Foresman and Company, 1973.

This edition 1974.   ISBN 0 370 01595 9

Preface

Gathered here is a selection of essays, criticism, and statements of trends in the world of children's books, intended for those concerned with the creation, distribution, and reading of children's books. The choice of selections has been influenced in part by the compiler's experiences in teaching and the assignment of background readings in courses in children's literature. The aim has been to make readily available both the historical background and the broad range of subjects and issues covered in a library science or teacher education course in children's literature. Emphasis is less on general surveys than on the major—sometimes controversial—theories and judgments. Thus, some selections are from out-of-print and otherwise hard-to-find sources; some were written especially for this volume or expanded and updated from earlier publication; and many are "classic" essays in the field of children's literature.

The articles from previously published sources have been printed verbatim, so that in some articles only American or Continental publishers and prices current at the time of original publication are given. Therefore in this library edition of *Children and Literature* the British publishers of titles mentioned in the articles on pp. 88, 246, 250, 281, 288, 328, 400, 408 and 436 have been listed at the end of each article. The British publishers, where known, have also been added to the list of American prize winners in Chapter 12, although in some cases these editions are no longer in print.

The arrangement and number of selections allow instructors and students to use them in whatever way best fits their needs. Chapters 1 through 5 deal with the history of children's literature and basic issues, such as what makes a classic, what children read (and what they should perhaps not read), how and why one writes for children, and the illustration of children's books. Chapters 6 through 9 discuss the major genres: folk literature, fantasy (including science fantasy), poetry, fiction, history, and science. Chapter 10 presents a comprehensive study of children's literature in eight major foreign countries. Chapters 11 and 12 discuss the importance of criticism and the establishment of awards to children's literature, with lists of winners for seven major awards. Finally, each chapter is introduced by an essay which focuses the reader's attention upon the controversial issues, supplies background information, and frequently presents the views of authors we were unable, for reasons of space, to include in this volume.

Virginia Haviland

Contents

Chapter 3

Chapter 4

Chapter 1

Before the Twentieth Century

The history of books written solely for children's reading pleasure, without didacticism, reaches back only a little more than a century. If allowed freedom, children before the mid-nineteenth century did find some literary entertainments, but the uninhibited production of books designed only to amuse was indeed late. F. J. Harvey Darton called the publication of *Alice in Wonderland* in 1865 "the spiritual volcano of children's books, as the activities of John Newbery had been their commercial volcano."[1]

The first important step[2] toward a literature for children was taken by a young businessman, John Newbery, who came to London late in 1743 and, after working in other locations, opened a bookshop in St. Paul's Churchyard in 1745. In June 1744 Newbery published his first children's book, *A Little Pretty Pocket-Book*.[3] It was a simple and affectionate work aimed at providing amusement as well as instruction, a potpourri of alphabet nursery jingles, exhortatory letters which Newbery signed "Jack the Giant-Killer,"

---

1. *Children's Books in England: Five Centuries of Social Life* (Cambridge: Cambridge University Press, 1932), p.267.

2. Thomas Boreman, who published tiny books about London called *Gigantic Histories* (1738–1745), never attained the success or popularity of Newbery.

3. See *A Little Pretty Pocket-Book*, A Facsimile with an introductory essay and Bibliography by M. F. Thwaite (New York: Harcourt Brace Jovanovich, Inc., 1967), reproduced from a British Museum copy dated 1767 and issued by the Oxford University Press, 1966.

The little p Play.

HOP-SCOTCH.

FIRST make with Chalk an oblong
    Square,
With wide Partitions here and there;
Then to the first a *Tile* convey;
Hop in—then kick the *Tile* away.

RULE *of* LIFE.

Strive with good Senfe to ftock your
    Mind,
And to that Senfe be Virtue join'd.

Who

Illustration by John Newbery from *A Little Pretty Pocket-Book* by John Newbery. Courtesy of the Trustees, The British Museum.

and his "Lecture on Education, humbly addressed to all Parents, Guardians, Governnesses . . . " in which he pleaded for children's rights to read and to understand what they read. It was the antecedent of the modern storybook. Newbery's gay little flowery-and-gilt volumes and *Lilliputian*

Magazine revealed his understanding of what appeals to children and his belief that children's books should become an important part of the book trade. (Appropriately, an annual medal, presented by the American Library Association for distinction in children's books, was established in 1937 in honor of Newbery by Frederic G. Melcher, publisher, bibliophile, admirer of Newbery, and lover of children's books.)

Newbery's plea to let children read has been throughout the relatively short history of children's literature countered by a cry to let them read only what is desirable for them. To Mrs. Sarah Trimmer, an early nineteenth-century writer, editor, and reviewer, "desirable" meant religious instruction; natural history, which answered "the double purpose of amusement and information"; and tales "which inculcate the duties of childhood and youth. . . . " Novels were definitely not desirable: "[these] should not be read . . . till they [young people] are in some measure acquainted with real life. . . . " In the opinion of an advanced critic in the *Quarterly Review* of 1844, however, a selection of Scott's Waverley Novels "would be the most popular child's book in the world" and *Robinson Crusoe,* which Mrs. Trimmer did not commend, was a "masterpiece." This enlightened critic, out of step with most guardians of the age, also urged that children be given freedom in their reading, demanding only that the quality of children's books be higher, that they be a "union of the highest art with the simplest form." Didacticism, however, has not disappeared—it has merely changed from the early moral to a current social didacticism.

Another controversy which spanned many generations concerned fairy tales. In her *Guardian of Education* in 1802, Mrs. Trimmer castigated the fairy tales, saying that "the terrific images which tales of this nature present to the imagination, usually make deep impressions, and injure the tender minds of children, by exciting unreasonable and groundless fears. Neither do the generality of tales of this kind supply any moral instruction level to the infantine capacity." She found the gory violence of the early illustrations for "Blue Beard" particularly distasteful. "Cinderella" and "Little Red Riding Hood" were "perhaps merely absurd." Differing again, the *Quarterly Review* critic noted the "direct amusement" for children of "Beauty and the Beast" and "Puss in Boots" ("the *beau-ideal* of a nursery-book") and considered the 1823 edition of Grimm, with the Cruikshank illustrations to be "an exquisite book for children."

The battle of the fairy tale continued. Mrs. Gatty, in her *Aunt Judy's Magazine,* and Horace E. Scudder, in the *Riverside Magazine for Young People* and elsewhere, proclaimed the value of fairy tales. In 1888, however, Caroline M. Hewins, famous librarian of Hartford, Connecticut, found it necessary to speak out against the abridgements of great fairy tales and hero legends, which by then had appeared in many volumes. Still later, in 1895, critic Agnes Repplier took up arms against the continuing distrust of fairy tales in "Battle of the Babies."[4]

---

4. For twentieth-century developments in this controversy, see Chapter 6.

On the Care Which Is Requisite
in the Choice of Books for Children (1803)

Sarah Trimmer

Mrs. Trimmer (1741–1810) was a zealous writer for a cause—most prominently for the new Sunday Schools, an early attempt to educate the English poor. For this cause she wrote volumes of Bible stories in Sacred History *(1782–1784) and An* Easy Introduction to the Knowledge of Nature *(1782), which related religion and the natural world. Her best-known work was* Fabulous Histories *(1786), later called* The History of the Robins. *It was characteristic of her that in her introduction she took pains to explain that the conversations of Robin, Jr., Dicksy, Flapsy, and Pecksy were not real, just as she carefully noted in her review of Newbery's "entertaining and instructive"* Robin Goodfellow *that the fairies were only "imaginary beings."*

During 1778–1789 Mrs. Trimmer produced The Family Magazine *for the "instruction and amusement of cottagers and servants." Here, as in later writing, she hoped "to counteract the pernicious influence of immoral books" such as* Robinson Crusoe *and Perrault's* Histories and Tales of Past Times. *She was to become more famous for* The Guardian of Education *(1802–1806): in order to protect the young and innocent from dangerous literature, she published in it the first regular reviews of children's books.*

Formerly children's reading, whether for instruction or amusement, was confined to a very small number of volumes; of late years they have multiplied to an astonishing and alarming degree, and much mischief lies hid in many of them. The utmost circumspection is therefore requisite in making a proper selection; and children should not be permitted to make their own choice, or to read any books that may accidentally be thrown in their way, or offered to their perusal; but should be taught to consider it as a *duty,* to consult their parents in this momentous concern.

Between the ages of *eight* and *twelve years* children of both sexes may lay in a considerable stock of literary knowledge, if their school exercises are so managed as to prevent the encroachments of ornamental accomplishments at the hours which should be devoted to better purposes. Whilst the course of religious instruction, before recommended, is going on by means of the *Selection from the Scriptures,* together with the *partial reading of the Bible,* Rollin's Ancient History may be read, and some well-chosen modern Histories of England, France, &c. &c. The study of *Natural History,* that never-failing source of instruction and delight, may also be extended, by means of Books, and Museums, or private collections of natural curiosities; but in the choice of the former, particular care should be taken to provide

"On the Care Which Is Requisite" and reviews reprinted from *Guardian of Education,* 2 (1803): 407–410; 1 (1802): 430–431; and 4 (1805): 74–75.

those which are free from the general objection to books of this kind, of relating circumstances unfit for young people to be acquainted with: the occasional view of the *natural objects* which these books represent, will answer the double purpose of amusement and information. Books which treat in a general way of *Arts* and *Sciences* may also be put into the hands of children in this stage of their education; not as a regular study, but by way of assisting their ingenuity, should they discover a natural turn for simple mechanical experiments, or for any works of taste and ingenuity. But books of *Chemistry* or *Electricity,* and all that might lead them prematurely to making philosophical experiments, we would still keep from them. To the *Gardener's Dictionary* and *Calendar* they may be allowed free access, in order to instruct them to manage their little gardens, which in a family where there are boys and girls, should be the joint concern of brothers and sisters; as some parts of gardening are unfit for girls to perform.

The study of *Botany,* we would still reserve for a more advanced age. Poetry may be read and committed to memory; and select pieces in prose, such as are to be found in various collections, calculated at the same time to improve them in useful knowledge and in the art of reading aloud. Fables are also very proper for children of this age, and they are usually much delighted with them, and enter into the morals of them with surprising facility, when they relate to the common affairs of life. Some of Gay's Fables, though it is a favourite book, are too political for children. Works of fancy highly wrought, such as the Tales of the Genii, the Arabian Nights Entertainment, and the like, we would not put into the hands of young people till their religious principles are fixed, and their judgment sufficiently strong to restrain the imagination within due bounds, whilst it is led to expatiate in the regions of fiction and romance.

Novels certainly, however abridged, and however excellent, should not be read by young persons, till they are in some measure acquainted with real life; but under this denomination we do not mean to include those exemplary tales which inculcate the duties of *childhood* and *youth* without working too powerfully upon the feelings of the mind, or giving false pictures of life and manners.

Before we quit the subject of Books for Children, we must not omit to give a caution respecting those which go under the general name of *School Books,* viz. *Grammars, Dictionaries, Spelling Books, Exercise Books,* and *Books of Geography,* &c. &c. into some of which the leaven of false philosophy has found its way. In short, there is not a species of Books for Children and Youth, any more than for those of maturer years, which has not been made in some way or other an engine of mischief; nay, even well-intentioned authors have, under a mistaken idea that it is necessary to conform to the taste of the times, contributed to encrease the evil. However, there are in the mixed multitude, books of all sorts that are truly estimable; and others that might be rendered so with a little trouble in revising them; a task which we assure ourselves, the respective authors of these last-mentioned books will chearfully undertake, for *new Editions,* if they consider the infinite importance it is of, to be correct in principle, and cautious in expression, when they are writing for the young and ignorant, upon whose minds new ideas frequently make very strong impressions.

The remarks we have now made upon the different kinds of books for children, . . . will, we trust, be sufficient to guide the inexperienced mother in her choice for children under twelve years of age. . . .

An objection may probably be made to the course of reading we have recommended, as too *desultory,* but let it be remembered, that it is designed for children, who at this period of their lives are engaged in studies which require thought and application; and that, besides their stated tasks and exercises, they have the science of Religious Wisdom to call forth the exertion of their mental faculties. Young as they still are, they may look forward to a time of more leisure for the study of the Belles Lettres; therefore, it will be sufficient if a love of reading is excited.

ART. XVI—*The History of Little Goody Two Shoes, with her Means of acquiring Learning, Wisdom, and Riches.* Price 6d. Newbery.

This Book is a great favourite with us on account of the simplicity of style in which it is written, yet we could wish some parts to be altered, or omitted. It was the practice of Mr. Newbery's writers, to convey lessons to those whom they sometimes facetiously called *Children of six feet high,* through the medium of Children's Books; and this has been done in the little volume we are examining. But in these times, when such pains are taken to prejudice the poor against the higher orders, and to set them against parish officers, we could wish to have a veil thrown over the faults of oppressive 'squires and hard-hearted overseers. Margaret and her brother might have been represented as helpless orphans, without imputing their distress to crimes of which young readers can form no accurate judgment; and should these readers be of the *lowest class,* such a narration as this might tend to prejudice their minds during life, against those whose favour it may be their future interest to conciliate, and who may be provoked by their insolence (the fruits of this prejudice) to treat them with harshness instead of kindness. We have also a very great objection to the Story of *Lady Ducklington's Ghost* (though extremely well told, and as well applied) for reasons we have repeatedly given. The observations upon animals are not quite correct; and if nothing had been introduced about witchcraft, the Book would in our opinion have been more complete. However, with all its faults, we wish to see this Book continue in circulation, as some of these faults *a pair of scissors* can rectify, and the ill effect of others may be remedied by proper explanation from the parent. But amongst the numerous writers for children of the present day, who knows but some one may take in hand to give an edition of this little Work with the *proper emendations?*

ART. VIII—*Nursery Tales.   Cinderella, Blue Beard, and Little Red Riding Hood;* with coloured plates. Price 6d. each. Tabart. 1804.

These Tales are announced to the public as *new translations,* but in what respect this term applies we are at a loss to say, for, on the perusal of them we recognized the identical *Mother Goose's Tales,* with all their *vulgarities of expression,* which were in circulation when those who are now grand-mothers, were themselves children, and we doubt not but that many besides ourselves can recollect, their horrors of imagination on reading that of *Blue Beard,* and the terrific impressions it left upon their minds. This is certainly a very improper tale for children. *Cinderella* and *Little Red Riding Hood* are perhaps merely absurd. But it is not on account of their subjects and language only that these Tales, (Blue Beard at least) are exceptionable, another objection to them arises from the nature of their embellishments, consisting of coloured prints, in which the most striking incidents in the stories are placed before the eyes of the little readers in glaring colours, representations we believe of play-house scenes, (for the figures are in theatrical dresses). In Blue Beard for instance, the second plate represents the opening of the *forbidden closet,* in which appears, not what the story describes, (which surely is *terrific enough!) "a floor clotted with blood, in which the bodies of several women were lying (the wives whom Blue Beard had married and murdered,")* but, *the flames of Hell* with *Devils* in frightful shapes, threatening the unhappy lady who had given way to her curiosity! The concluding print is, *Blue Beard* holding his terrified wife by the hair, and lifting up his sabre to cut off her head. We expected in Little Red Riding Hood, to have found a picture of the wolf tearing the poor innocent dutiful child to pieces, but happily the number of prints was complete without it. A moment's consideration will surely be sufficient to convince people of the least reflection, of the danger, as well as the impropriety, of putting such books as these into the hands of little children, whose minds are susceptible of every impression; and who from the liveliness of their imaginations are apt to convert into realities whatever forcibly strikes their fancy.

Children's Books (1844)

The Quarterly Review

The appearance in the Quarterly Review *in 1844 of a lengthy unsigned critical survey was a milestone in early literary criticism. The enlightened critic (who has been identified as Elizabeth Rigby) assailed the mediocrities of the age and pleaded for imaginative rather than didactic literature. She also advocated allowing children to choose freely rather than limiting them to the "little racks of ready-cut hay that have been so officiously supplied them." In her book list she approves a number of works of folklore, classic fiction, and school books.*

The attention of our readers has already been called to a subject, to which, the more it is considered the more importance must be attached—we mean that of children's books, which, no less in quality than in quantity, constitute one of the most peculiar literary features of the present day. The first obvious rule in writing for the amusement or instruction of childhood, is to bear in mind that it is not the extremes either of genius or dullness which we are to address—that it is of no use writing up to some minds or down to others—that we have only to do with that large class of average ability, to be found in children of healthy mental and physical formation, among whom in after life the distinction consists not so much in a difference of gifts as in the mode in which they have been led to use them. In a recent article our remarks were chiefly confined to a set of books in which not only this but every other sense and humanity of juvenile writing had been so utterly defied, that the only consolation for all the misery they had inflicted, consisted in the reflection that—however silly the infatuation which had given them vogue here—they were not of English origin. We now propose casting a sort of survey over that legion for which we are more responsible—taking first into consideration the general characteristics of those which we believe to be mistaken both as to means and end—from which many who are concerned in the education of children are vainly expecting good results, and to which many who know nothing about the matter are falsely attributing them.

In this department the present times profess to have done more than any other; and it has become a habit, more perhaps of conventional phraseology than of actual conviction, to congratulate the rising generation on the devotion of so many writers to their service. Nevertheless there are some circumstances contingently connected with this very service, which may warrant us in expressing doubts as to the unqualified philanthropy of those who enter it. Considering the sure sale which modern habits of universal education provide for children's books—the immense outfit required by schools and masters, and the incalculable number annually purchased as presents, it would be, upon the whole, matter of far more legitimate surprise if either the supplies were less abundant, or the suppliers, some of them, more conscientious. Ever since the days of Goldsmith the writing and editing of children's works has been a source of ready emolument—in no class of literature does the risk bear so small a proportion to the reward— and consequently in no class has the system of *mere manufacture* been carried to such an extent.

After the bewilderment of ideas has somewhat subsided which inevitably attends the first entrance into a department of reading so overstocked and where the minds of the writers are so differently actuated, and those of the readers so variously estimated, the one broad and general impression left with us is that of the excessive ardour for *teaching* which prevails throughout. No matter how these authors may differ as to the mode, they all agree as to the necessity of presenting knowledge to the mind under what they conceive to be the most intelligible form, and in getting down as much as can be swallowed. With due judgment and moderation, this, generally speaking, is the course which all instructors would pursue; nevertheless it is to the extreme to which it has been carried that parents and teachers have to attribute the stunted mental state of their little scholars, who either have been plied with a greater quantity of nourishment than the mind had strength or time to digest, or under the interdict laid on the imagination, in this mania for explanation, have been compelled to drag up the hill of knowledge with a wrong set of muscles. Doubtless the storing up of knowledge at an age when the powers of acquisition are most ductile and most tenacious, is of the utmost moment; but a child's head is a measure, holding only a given quantity at a time, and, if overfilled, liable not to be carried steadily. Also, it is one thing to stock the mind like a dead thing, and another to make it forage for itself; and of incalculably more value is one voluntary act of acquirement, combination, or conclusion, than hundreds of passively accepted facts. Not that the faculties can be said to lie inactive beneath this system of teaching—on the contrary, the mere mental mechanism is frequently exerted to the utmost; but the case is much the same as in the present modern school of music, where, while the instrument itself is made to do wonders, the real sense of harmony is sacrificed. For it is a fact confirmed both by reason and experience, and one which can alone account for the great deficiency of spontaneous and native power—that which comes under the denomination of genius—in the schools, English and foreign, where these modes of instruction are pursued—that the very art with which children are taught exactly stifles that which no art can teach.

As regards also the excessive clearness of explanation, insisted upon now-a-days as the only road to sureness of apprehension, it is unquestionably necessary that a child should, in common parlance, understand what it acquires. But this again must be taken with limitation; for Nature, not fond apparently of committing too much power into a teacher's hand, has decreed that unless a child be permitted to acquire beyond what it positively understands, its intellectual progress shall be slow, if any. As Sir Walter Scott says, in his beautiful preface to the Tales of a Grandfather, "There is no harm, but, on the contrary, there is benefit in presenting a child with ideas beyond his easy and immediate comprehension. The difficulties thus offered, if not too great or too frequent, stimulate curiosity and encourage exertion." We are so constituted that even at the maturest state of our minds—when length of experience has rendered the feeling of disappointment one almost unjustifiable in our own eyes—we find the sense of interest for a given object, and feeling of its beauty to precede far more than to follow the sense of comprehension—or, it were better said, the belief of fully comprehending;—but with children, who only live in anticipation, this is more conspicuously the case; in point of fact they delight most in what they do *not* comprehend. Those therefore who insist on keeping the sense of enjoyment rigidly back, till that of comprehension has been forcibly urged forward—who stipulate that the one shall not be indulged till the other be appeased—are in reality but retarding what they most affect to promote: only inducing a prostration, and not a development of the mental powers. In short, a child thus circumstanced is submitting his understanding and not exerting it—a very deplorable exchange. . . .

[W]ith few exceptions, the minds of children are far more healthily exercised and generally cultivated than in a former generation. But, while gladly admitting this to be the fact, we are inclined to attribute it far more to the liberty now allowed them in promiscuous reading than to any efforts which have been made of late in their own department—far more to the power of ranging free over field and pasture than to all the little racks of ready-cut hay that have been so officiously supplied them. Children seem to possess an inherent conviction that when the hole is big enough for the cat, no smaller one at the side is needed for the kitten. They don't really care for "Glimpses" of this, or "Gleanings" of that, or "Footsteps" to the other—but would rather stretch and pull, and get on tiptoe to reach the sweeter fruit above them, than confine themselves to the crabs which grow to their level. The truth is, though seldom apprehended by juvenile book-writers, that children are distinguished from ourselves less by an *inferiority* than by a *difference* in capacity—that the barriers between manhood and childhood are marked less by the progress of every power than by the exchange of many. A mere weaker decoction of the same ideas and subjects that suit us will be very unsuitable to them. A genuine child's book is as little like a book for grown people cut down, as the child himself is like a little old man. The beauty and popularity of Lamb's "Shakspeare's Tales" are attributable to the joint excellences of both author and transposer, but this is a rare exception:—generally speaking, the way in which Froissart is cut into spoon-meat, and Josephus put into swaddling-clothes, has only degraded these authors from their old positions, without in any way benefiting the rising generation by their new. The real secret of a child's book consists not merely in its being less dry and less difficult, but more rich in interest—more true to nature—more exquisite in art—more abundant in every quality that replies to childhood's keener and fresher perceptions. Such being the case, the best of juvenile reading will be found in libraries belonging to their elders, while the best of juvenile writing will not fail to delight those who are no longer children. "Robinson Crusoe," the standing favourite of above a century, was not originally written for children; and Sir Walter Scott's "Tales of a Grandfather," addressed solely to them, are the pleasure and profit of every age, from childhood upwards. Our little friends tear Pope's "Odyssey" from mamma's hands, while she takes up their "Agathos" with an admiration which no child's can exceed. Upon the whole the idea of a book being too *old* for a child is one which rests upon very false foundations. If we do not mistake his department of enjoyment, we can hardly overrate his powers of it. With most children the taste for Robinson Crusoe will be carried out into Columbus's discoveries, Anson's voyages, and Belzoni's travels; the relish for scenes of home-life into Evelyn's Diary, Cowper's Letters, or Bracebridge Hall. With very many the easy neatness or pompous sounds of verse, from John Gilpin, or Gay's Fables, to Alexander's Feast, or Paradise Lost, have an ineffable charm. Some of no uncommon capacity are known to be smitten with the mysterious pathos of Young's Night Thoughts. But yesterday we saw one little miss sucking her thumb over Thalaba.

But to return to the present liberty of indiscriminate reading: we doubt in most cases if it be owing to any conviction of its real superiority, or whether, in the great increase of publications, and the prevailing fashion of throwing open libraries and scattering books through every room of a house, it has not rather been suffered from an impossibility of prevention. We fear, in short, that parents are far more inclined to look on this as a necessary evil than as an incidental good, and are by no means satisfied in their consciences as to the time spent in useless reading, or the risk incurred by pernicious. But may not these misgivings, like many another concerning the education of children, be traced to our giving ourselves too much credit for judgment, and them too little for discernment? As regards useless reading, so long as it does not interfere with habits of application, and powers of attention, we are but poor judges of its real amount. Children have an instinct of food which more cultivated palates lose; and many is the scrap they will pick from hedge and common which to us seem barren. Nor may the question of pernicious reading be left to its usual acceptation, more especially as what is so called deserves the epithet, not so much on account of any absolutely false principle as from a tendency to inflame the passions or shock the taste, and therefore falls innocuous on a mind where the passions are silent and the taste unformed. With the immense choice of irreprehensible works before us, no one would deliberately put those into a child's hands where much that is beautiful is mixed up with much that is offensive; but, should they fall in their way, we firmly believe no risk to exist—if they will read them at one time or another, the earlier perhaps the better. Such works are like the viper—they have a wholesome flesh as well as a poisonous sting; and children are perhaps the only class of readers which can partake of one without suffering from the other.

We are aware that a small party exists who not only deny the quality of the modern juvenile school, but go so far as to question the quality and policy of children's books altogether. Tieck, a true genius as well as a most learned man, is said never to have allowed one to enter his house. Such a mode of prevention, however, is worse than the evil itself. Juvenile books are as necessary to children as juvenile companionship, though nothing can be worse for them than to be restricted exclusively to either. Doubtless the imaginary exemption from the rules and ceremonials of general literature, which little books as well as little folks enjoy, has, as we have seen, fostered a host of works from the simply unprofitable to the directly pernicious, which would otherwise not have seen the light. But neither this nor any other consideration should forbid the cultivation of a branch of literature which, properly understood, gives exercise to the highest powers both of head and heart, or make us ungrateful to those writers by whom great powers have been so devoted. For children are not their only debtors—nor is the delight with which we take up one of the companions of our childhood entirely attributable to associations of days gone by—nor the assiduity with which we devour a new comer solely ascribable to parental watchfulness—but it is with these as with some game which we join at first merely to try whether we can play as we once did, or with the view of keeping our little playmates out of mischief, but which we end by liking for its own sake—though we do not always say so.

In truth it is good for both that the young and the old should frequently exchange libraries. We give them a world of new ideas, but they do more, for they purify and freshen our old ones. There is nothing like the voice of one of these little Mentors to brush up our better part. There is no reading from which we rise more softened in heart, more strengthened in resolution, nay, not infrequently, more enriched in information. And this brings us to a more grateful portion of our task, and one in which that general tone we were bound to observe in our deprecatory remarks may be exchanged for a more particular kind—for, considering the numbers of little volumes that have passed through our hands with a view to preparing this article, it may perhaps not seem presumptuous in us to specify modern works both of amusement and instruction which have struck us as, on the whole, most worthy of the attention of parents and teachers. At the same time the following list has been the incidental more than the intentional result of our search, and therefore professes no systematic completeness, or categorical accuracy: moreover, we doubt not that by many a reader our selection has been already anticipated. As regards also the old children's books, the much-read and roughly-treated friends of a whole little generation, whose crazy backs and soft cottony leaves have stood a greater wear and tear than any of their sprucer successors could survive—which tell not only of the times when they were devoured but of the very places—which recall the lofty bough whence the feet hung dangling at a height which now does not take them off the ground, or the pleasant nook where the little reader sat huddled up in a position which it would now be extremely inconvenient to assume—which speak of days when, engrossed in their pages, all sorrow was forgotten, and when there were no real sorrows to forget, and when even solitary confinement was borne without a murmur, if one of them could be kidnapped to share it—as regards these dearly loved books, which tell all this and much more, our impartiality of judgment might be well suspected had we not lived to see their charm extend to the hearts of the present generation as well as linger round those of the past. In our enumeration, therefore, of such works as we would most willingly see in the hands of children, we must be allowed to name many of the old school which have been superseded in circulation by works bearing no comparison with them in value, and which, though never to be forgotten by some readers, are, we have reason to know, totally unknown to others. We commence, then, with the books of direct amusement, attempting no further classification than such as the age of the child suggests.

The House Treasury, by Felix Summerly, including *The Traditional Nursery Songs of England, Beauty and the Beast, Jack and the Beanstalk,* and other old friends, all charmingly done and beautifully illustrated, which may be left to the discretion of parents. These are a grateful relief after the spiritless flippancies—the Prince of Wales's Alphabet, for instance, and other such trash of the day—while the involuntary pleasure they afford to grown up minds will go far to convince us what the delights of children really are.

Puss in Boots, with the designs of Otto Specker. We consider this as the *beau-ideal* of a nursery-book; yet it will afford much entertainment to older readers, and please all admirers of art. The engravings in the English book are even better than those in the German original.

Nursery Rhymes, Original Poems, by the Misses Taylor, of Ongar. Admirable little books. It was justly said of them by a contemporary Review, "the writers of these rhymes have far better claims to the title of poet, than many who arrogate to themselves that high appellation." Nevertheless they are too generally superseded by a tribe of very contemptible juvenile versifiers.

Æsop's Fables. There are several versions in English of this book—which furnishes more amusement to the child and wisdom to the man than almost any other we could mention. Good fables cannot be too much recommended. While other books are labouring at a fact they are teaching a principle, and that the more securely from the child's complete unconsciousness of the process.

Persian Fables, by Rev. H. G. Keene. A very wise and attractive little volume.

Gay's Fables—it is enough to name: the first we believe in date, and inferior surely to none in merit, of all the classics of the nursery.

Prince Leboo. We would wish this beautiful character to live in the hearts of all children.

German Popular Tales, translated from Grimm. An exquisite book for children, and one far surpassing in every way the many recently published German collections, for which it has mainly supplied the materials. Care should be taken to procure the original edition of 1823, illustrated by George Cruikshank—a baser edition being in circulation.

Evenings at Home, by Mrs. Barbauld and Dr. Aikin; but Mrs. Barbauld deserves the greater share of credit, as the scientific dialogues will scarce find a voluntary reader. There is a classic beauty and simple gravity in this lady's writing, which, knowing how great a favourite she is with all children permitted to posses her, shows how unnecessary as well as ungraceful is that flippant clap-trap manner now so much in vogue. We have been surprised to find the little request at juvenile libraries for this work.

Parent's Assistant, by Miss Edgeworth. Popular as Miss Edgeworth's writings were in the last generation, they deserve to be still more so now, when the beauties of her writing are more than ever wanted, and their few deficiencies, if we may say so of one to whom we owe a deep debt of gratitude, less likely to take effect. Therefore it is with the greatest pleasure that we have observed the preference evinced for her books by children who are plentifully supplied with the more showy works of her successors—all, it is needless to say, greatly her inferiors in mind and skill.

Popular Tales, by Miss Edgeworth.

Garry Owen, by the same, is a charming little piece, perhaps not so universally known.

The Child's Own Book. One of the best modern versions of old materials, and far superior to one entitled "The Child's *Fairy Library."*

Leila on the Island, Leila in England, Mary and Florence, by Miss Anne Fraser Tytler. These are excellent—especially the Leilas. Miss Tytler's writings are especially valuable for their religious spirit. She has taken a just position between the rationalism of the last generation and the puritanism of the present, while the perfect nature and true art with which she sketches from juvenile life, show powers which might be more ambitiously displayed, but cannot be better bestowed.

Mrs. Trimmer's Robins, Adventures of a Donkey. These two books have saved numerous nests from plunder, and warded off many a blow from a "despised race." They give, it is true, no precise ideas of the anatomical formation of the animals described, but they invest both the robin and the donkey with a sentiment of kindliness and humanity in the breast of a child which we are inclined to think of far more value.

Son of a Genius, by Mrs. Hofland. A very beautiful tale, and the best of this lady's numerous little books, which are mostly too much of the *novellette* style to recommend.

Hope on, Hope ever, Strive and Thrive. Both excellent—by Mary Howitt—whose children's books are numerous, but very unequal in merit, and some of them, we regret to say, highly objectionable.

Holiday House, by Miss Catherine Sinclair; a book full of mirth for children; the work of a genuinely kind, and very clever spirit.

Lamb's Shakspeare's Tales. This is a juvenile gift of the highest value. He indeed understood Shakspeare and children too.

Lamb's Ulysses. Also a beautiful specimen of art in itself.

Robinson Crusoe. No wonder that Burckhardt found the surest plan for captivating a group of wild Arabs—the children of the desert—was to translate for them a chapter of Defoe's masterpiece.

Settlers at Home, Feats on the Fiord, The Crofton Boys, by Miss Martineau. These volumes of "The Playfellow," especially the first and third, will be read with delight through every generation in a house. We purposely omit the remaining volume, "The Peasant and the Prince," which has a reprehensible purpose and tendency.

Masterman Ready, by Captain Marryat. The best of Robinson Crusoe's numerous descendants, and one of the most captivating of modern children's books. The only danger is lest parents should dispute with their children the possession of it.

May You Like It. A pathetic and fascinating volume.

Lights and Shadows of Scottish Life. We have already said a word or two on this delightful volume—the work of one of the highest and most amiable of contemporary minds—a genius which shines with equal felicity in the tender and the humorous vein. It is fast becoming a child's book.

Croker's Fairy Legends. A book quite after a child's own heart—full of dancing fun and grotesque imagery.

Elizabeth, or the Exiles of Siberia.

The Fool of Quality—a well done abridgment—in our early day highly relished by young people.

Undine, translated from the German of La Motte Fouqué—a romance for all ages.

Vicar of Wakefield.

Phantasmion, by Mrs. Henry Coleridge; a tale of fairyland, full of captivation for man, woman, and child.

Arabian Nights. We forbear to intrude our prejudice in favour of the old edition over Lane's more correct version, because we are convinced that whichever children have the pleasure of reading first will be the lasting favourite.

As regards those works which convey more direct information without any expense of interest, we may mention,

Contributions of Q. Q., by Miss Jane Taylor; a work which cannot be too highly praised; religious precepts, moral lessons, and interesting information, all given in a sound and beautiful form. Another instance of the popularity of *good writing*—this book being in high favour with children. In its present form this work is perhaps not generally known, as it was published in detached portions in the "Youth's Magazine," and the parts have only lately been collected. But many a reader is acquainted with "The

Discontented Pendulum," "How it Strikes a Stranger," &c., which appeared in separate pieces, and will be found in various selections of prose reading.

Willy's Holidays, by Mrs. Marcet.

The Boy and the Birds, by Miss Emily Taylor; a delightful little volume.

Bingley's Stories of Dogs, [*Bingley's Stories of*] *Horses,* [*Bingley's Stories of*] *Travellers,* [*Bingley's Stories of*] *Shipwrecks.* A set of works which, professing only to amuse, instruct and edify in no common degree.

Uncle Philip's Whale Fishery, of which the same may be said.

Stanley's Birds. This is by the present Bishop of Norwich—it well deserves its great popularity.

Mrs. Marcet's Conversations on Land and Water. This is so far superior to the usual class of modern books, in which it is thought necessary to give instruction a garnish of amusement, that, though drawn up in that garrulous form we so much condemn, we cannot omit to recommend it here.

Harry and Lucy, by Miss Edgeworth. It matters not how learned Miss Edgeworth may make her Harrys and Lucys, we defy her to make them dull.

White's History of Selborne, for young people. The omissions are judicious.

Peter Parley's Tales of Animals. A collection of interesting anecdotes, and very attractive to children, but the only work by the real Simon Pure we should care to see in their hands. Nor have we been more satisfied with the other writers under the same mask, which in most cases seems to have been assumed only to carry down a shallowness and flippancy of style which otherwise would not have been tolerated.

Goldsmith's Animated Nature.

Selections from the Spectator, Guardian, and Tatler, by Mrs. Barbauld. To the credit of children, this is one of their greatest delights.

Howitt's Country Boy's Book. A capital work, and we are inclined to think his best in any line.

Stories for Children from the History of England, by Mr. Croker. This skilful performance suggested the plan of Sir W. Scott's

Tales of a Grandfather.

Southey's Life of Nelson.

Mutiny on the Bounty.

Lives of the Admirals.

The (abridged) *Life of Columbus,* by Washington Irving.

Hone's Every-Day Book. Excessively interesting to children from the earliest ages.

Sketch Book.

Bracebridge Hall.

Fragments of Voyages and Travels, by Captain Basil Hall.

The Waverley Novels.

We should think a selection of these, with some of the prints *representing realities* from the Abbotsford edition, would be the most popular child's book in the world; and the drawing-room set would last a good while longer.

Works of a more directly religious cast:—

Watts's Hymns,

Hymns for Infant Minds, by the Misses Taylor of Ongar,

Mrs. Hemans's Hymns for Childhood. These are all that can be required for the exercise of early piety, and three more beautiful little works cannot be desired.

Child's Christian Year.

Tracts and Tales, and

Sacred Dramas, and other writings, by Mrs. Hannah More.

Agathos, and other tales, by Archdeacon Wilberforce. These are indeed the works of a master. Their success can surprise no one.

The Distant Hills,

Shadow of the Cross. Two beautiful little allegorical works, of which a child can make no false application. The explanatory dialogues at the close of each will be found of the utmost utility.

Gospel Stories, by Mrs. Barrow. This is not to be confounded with the mob of little books bearing similar titles: it is a very remarkable specimen of skill, and treats some of the most difficult passages in Gospel History with a clearness that may guide and help many an experienced parent in the instruction of her children.

Ivo and Verena. A most impressive little volume.

Loss of the "Kent" East Indiaman. A lesson to young and old.

Burder's Oriental Customs.

Translations from Fénélon.

Keble's Christian Year.

Pilgrim's Progress. The sooner read the better.

. . . In the list thus offered, it would be absurd to imagine that all have been mentioned that are worthy of attention. As we said before, we offer what has indirectly presented itself to us, more than what we have directly sought for. The aim, also, has been more to contract than to expand—to the exclusion of many works highly respectable in ability, but too similar and numerous to be distinguished. Being also convinced by experience, that it is the out of school reading which equally leaves the deepest impression on the child, and gives the greatest licence to the writer, it is this branch of juvenile books to which our chief attention has been devoted. As to the works of an older kind fitted for children's reading, we need hardly remind those concerned in their welfare, that Homer, Shakspeare, Milton, and Addison, are enjoyable and appreciable from a very early age, and that the child's store of such reading is one of the richest legacies the adult can inherit. And in an age when, by a strange perversity of reasoning, a twofold injury, both in what is required and what is withheld, is inflicted upon children, it behoves us the more to supply them with those authors who, like old plate, though their pattern may go out of fashion for a season, yet always retain the same intrinsic value.

Upon the whole, we should be happy if, by calling attention to the real excellence and beauty of a genuine child's book, we could assist in raising the standard of the *art* itself—the only effectual way, it seems to us, of checking the torrent of dressed-up trumpery which is now poured upon the public. For on taking a retrospective view of the juvenile libraries of the day, it is very obvious that there are a set of individuals who have taken to writing children's books, solely because they found themselves incapable of any other, and who have had no scruple in coming forward in a line of literature which, to their view, presupposed the lowest estimate of their own abilities. Nor has the result undeceived them—on the contrary, they write simple little books which any little simpleton can understand, and in the facility of the task become more and more convinced of its utter insignificance. The whole mistake hinges upon the slight but important distinction between *childish* books and *children's* books. The first are very easy—the second as much the reverse—the first require no mind at all—the second mind of no common class. What indeed can be a closer test of natural ability and acquired skill than that species of composition which, above all others, demands clearness of head and soundness of heart, the closest study of nature, and the most complete command over your materials? A child's book especially requires that which every possessor of talent knows to be its most difficult and most necessary adjunct, viz. the judgment evinced in the selection of your ideas—the discretion exercised in the control of your powers. In short, the *beau-ideal* of this class of composition lies in the union of the highest art with the simplest form; and if it be absurd to expect the realisation of this more frequently in children's books than in any other, it is quite as absurd to attempt to write them without keeping it in any way in view.

Aunt Judy's Magazine (1866)

Margaret Gatty

Mrs. Gatty (1809–1873) established Aunt Judy's Magazine *(1866–1885) as a place in which to publish the stories of her daughter, Juliana Horatia Gatty (better known as Mrs. Ewing) and based the magazine's name on her daughter's nickname. In December of its first year she published enthusiastic reviews of Lewis Carroll's* Alice *and Andersen's* What the Moon Saw and Other Tales. *Both of these authors were also contributors to the magazine, as was Mrs. Gatty, whose popular children's books had an educational purpose, but "pleasure was to be the means." For example, her educational series,* Parables from Nature *(1855–1871) presented fables based on the real world of nature.*

The sweet old salutation, "You're as welcome as the flowers in May," comes into our head as we pen the first lines of this magazine, which is intended for the use and amusement of children. Accordingly, on this our first appearance, our May-day of opening, as it were, we look wistfully to the young folks for whom we have catered, craving a welcome like that they always give the flowers. We cannot wish a warmer—for they take them to their heart! They scatter and squander them, it is true; gather them into posies only to fling them away; make wreaths of them for their hair, and garlands for their necks; even turn some into balls to pelt each other withal: but all the time they love and enjoy them with a freshness of affection grown-up people seldom, if ever, feel. Or if any one does, we say of him at once, that he is as fond of flowers as a child.

Quite as hearty and universal a welcome it would be folly, of course, to expect. Only God's works can call out such emotions—so warm, so wide-spread, and so lasting. But a welcome, and a kindly welcome, we have tried to deserve, and cannot but hope for. Whether we have laboured skilfully, as well as earnestly, the children will decide; but our honest endeavour and wish have been to provide the best of mental food for all ages of young people, and for many varieties of taste; and we trust the means will not be found wanting.

That our young readers may know, however, not only what this number affords, but what they will have to expect of us in future, we will enter into a few particulars.

Stories, we need hardly say, will form a staple commodity in our bill of fare—and those of various sorts, to suit the requirements of various ages. And included under this head will occasionally be some tale of allegorical or parabolic teaching for those who enjoy such writing.

"Introduction" and review reprinted from *Aunt Judy's Magazine for Young People,* 1 (1866): 1, 123.

Alice's Adventures in Wonderland. By Lewis Carroll: with Forty-two Illustrations by John Tenniel. (London: Macmillan & Co.)

Forty-two illustrations by Tenniel! Why there needs nothing else to sell this book, one would think. But our young friends may rest assured that the exquisite illustrations do but do justice to the exquisitely wild, fantastic, impossible, yet most natural history of "Alice in Wonderland." For the author (Mr. Lewis Carroll, of course—you see his name on the title-page, do you not?) has a secret, and he has managed his secret so much better than any author who ever "tried on" a secret of the same sort before, that we would not for the world let it out. No; the young folks for whom this charming account is written must go on and on and on till they find out the secret for themselves; and then they will agree with us that never was the mystery made to feel so beautifully natural before.

Of Mr. Tenniel's illustrations we need only say that he has entered equally into the fun and graceful sentiment of his author, and that we are as much in love with little Alice's face in all its changes as we are amused by the elegant get up of the white rabbit in ball costume, the lobster quadrille on the sands, or the concourse of animals fresh from the "Pool of Tears" drying themselves in the mouse's most dry historical memories.

The above hints will probably make "parents and guardians" aware that they must not look to "Alice's Adventures" for knowledge in disguise.

Books for Young People (1867)

Horace E. Scudder

Editor of the highly praised Riverside Magazine for Young People
(1867–1870) and later of the Atlantic Monthly, *Horace E.
Scudder (1838–1902)
believed in the application of true criticism to children's books. Alice M. Jordan
considered him to be "... one of the two most discriminating editors a children's
magazine ... ever had," one who played "a fundamental part in the establishment
of a sane attitude toward children's books and readings."[1] Indicative of this attitude
is a statement he made in his Lowell Institute Lecture Series: "... it is quite safe to
say that the form in which childhood is presented will still depend upon the sympathy
of imaginative writers with the ideal of childhood and that the form of literature for
children will be determined by the greater or less care with which society guards the
sanctity of childish life."[2]*

*Scudder's importance in the history of children's literature rests upon numerous
contributions, such as his column in the* Riverside, *"Books for Young People," in
which he expressed advanced views on children's reading; his publication, also in the*
Riverside, *of a series of stories by Hans Christian Andersen (1868–1870) before
they appeared in Denmark or England;[3] his editorship of Houghton, Mifflin's*
Riverside Literature Series for Young People; *his anthology* The Children's
Book;[4] *and his popular series of stories about the Bodley family and their travels
around New England, England, Holland, and Denmark. His anthology was
highly praised by Caroline M. Hewins: "A child who has it for a companion
knows the best that has been written in English for children."[5]*

It may seem suicidal, but we begin this series of informal notes, intended
for children's elders, with the remark that children have too much reading
nowadays. Any one who recalls his resources of reading among books
designed expressly for children forty, thirty, or even twenty years since,
will see that not only has the style of such books changed, but there has
been increased fertility of production, and the signs all point to a still
greater fruitfulness. A literature is forming which is destined to act

---

"Books for Young People" by Horace E. Scudder reprinted from *Riverside Magazine for
Young People,* 1 (January 1867): 43–45.

1. *From Rollo to Tom Sawyer* (Boston: Horn Book, Inc., 1948), p. 40.

2. Published as *Childhood in Literature and Art, with Some Observations on Literature for Childhood*
(Boston: Houghton Mifflin Company, 1894), p. 245.

3. Correspondence from Andersen to Scudder contains a compliment on Scudder's excellent
knowledge of Danish, which he had learned in order to ensure good translation. See Jean
Hersholt and Waldermar Westergaard, *Hans Christian Andersen's Correspondence with Horace
Scudder* (Berkeley: University of California Press, 1949). For Scudder's essay on Andersen, see
Chapter 2, below.

4. (Boston: Houghton Mifflin Company, 1881).

5. *Books for Boys and Girls,* 3rd ed., rev. (Chicago: American Library Association Publishing
Board, 1915), p. 64.

powerfully upon general letters; hitherto it has been little disturbed by critics, but the time must soon come, if it has not already come, when students of literature must consider the character and tendency of *Children's Letters;* when all who have at heart the best interests of the Kingdom of Letters must look sharply to this Principality. It is idle to complain of the present abundance of children's books, as if somebody were to blame for it; it is worse than folly to look upon it with contempt. No faithful student can fail to see that there is a new movement in literature, and that the present state of the book-market is not the result to some conspiracy on the part of authors and publishers.

At some future time we hope to offer suggestions as to the meaning of this movement; just now our purpose is more directly practical. Children have too much reading, and the fault is not theirs but their elders'. We have not become accustomed to the new order of things, and it serves our indolence in managing the young, to still their noise with a book, and relieve ourselves of a burden by placing them under the care of some livelier, though silent companion. A child's mind is awaking into a restless inquiry, and we administer a soothing draught in the shape of an entertaining story. The spell works for a time, we get more comfort; and so we always keep the *book* by us, just as a lazy and foolish nurse is never without a mysterious bottle. Perhaps it would be fairer to say that we treat the young as we treat ourselves, for do we not take books as opiates?—reading them not to satisfy or stimulate thought, or even to produce generous pleasure, but to stifle restless dissatisfaction with ourselves, to stave off the necessity of doing something, and at the best, to get rid of ourselves. Besides, we are somewhat in the condition, with respect to our reading, in which we find children placed,—embarrassed by the incessant demands laid upon us by publishers, who act as if they were apostles, and held us morally responsible if we did not buy their books; by critics, who appeal to our instinct for good bargains, assuring us that the first paragraph alone is worth all the price of the book; and by friends, who look surprised if we do not happen to have read what they have chosen to read. We have not yet become used to the multiplicity of books combined with increased facility of intercourse, and are still laboring under the delusion that we ought to be ashamed of ourselves if we have not read the latest poem or novel, or are unable to join in society-talk upon the last witty book. We make the apology that we have been much pressed of late, as if doing our work were rather a poor excuse; and deprecate scorn by assurances that we hope to find leisure soon to read—what will then have been forgotten by others, and when we shall be in equally disgraceful arrears over some other piece of literature.

The modern magazine offers a great relief to the overburdened reader, by making him, with great economy, familiar with the latest subject that is talked about, and giving him a taste of the reading in vogue at the time, so that he need not grow too old-fashioned, and chat about Walter Scott with those who only know Trollope. It is one step toward the simple system of choosing our constant reading matter from what is best in literature, and not necessarily from what is latest, though some still seem to think that books, like breakfast-cakes, are good only when hot; and, indeed, such books as will not keep are about as good as breakfast-cakes, producing as instantaneous inflation and as inevitably an aching void afterward. Magazines for young people, in the same way, have this in their favor, that they are substitutes for many books; the freshest and most enjoyable literature can be given there in compact form, with all the seduction of an expected weekly or monthly arrival, and so that hunger for mere reading, which they share with their elders, can be appeased at no great cost of time and attention.

But the magazine at its best does not supply the want in reading for the young, and a multiplication of magazines makes matters worse. What shall we give our children to read? is the constant cry of anxious parents, as they stand in despair before the counters in the bookstores, turning over the demure or gaudy books which profess to be the latest and best. But what is it to a child whether a book was first published in hot haste this Christmas or has lain on the counter for a year, and is now, may be, rather dull in cloth beside its new companions, though then it was thought brilliant enough? We may as well discard at once all such unnecessary considerations as when a book was published, or where it was published, and come right at the gist of the matter, and ask if it is *good*,—good in itself and adapted to the reader for whom we are buying it.

There is one other suggestion for the buyer in the thought that the ordinary classification of "books for young people" is a very recent one, and that some very excellent people have grown up with delightful recollections of their childhood who never, after they left the nursery, read books designed expressly for children, and yet were not starved intellectually; perhaps the field of selection then might be widened by taking in the books which they had to read, and inquiring what there was for children before books were made expressly for them. By and by, if we mistake not, the parent in search of reading for children would make the discovery that, instead of one poor little corner of literature being fenced off for the little lambs, planted with tender grass which was quickly devoured, and with many medicinal but disagreeable herbs which were nibbled at when the grass was gone, the whole wide pasture land was their native home, and the grass more tender where fresh streams flowed than it possibly could be in the paddock, however carefully planted and watched.

But to leave fables, though that is a natural way of talking on this subject, we propose in these notes to treat of Books for Young People, giving to that term the very broadest sense. We shall not make a Retrospective Review, and notice only such as have been published twenty years and still live, yet we shall esteem it a real pleasure to remind parents of books which we may think have grown a little old-fashioned, but which have the freshness of young life about them; and we shall attempt gradually to collect the names of really valuable books which are not likely soon to die and are worth reading over and over again. We shall pay no very close attention to the line which divides books written for the young from books written for the old; but, making a survey of literature, single out those writings which are worth giving to a child, and for an acquaintance with which he will always hold us in grateful remembrance.

We said on beginning that children had too much reading nowadays, not that there was too much reading matter at the disposal of children. The distinction is a simple one. If we select for children with real care, there will always be a check upon idle reading; but if we let them gather what they like from Sunday-school, day-school, and public libraries, and only cast our eyes over the books to see that they have no wicked-looking words in them, we may expect to see them grow up listless readers, with a taste spoiled for the richest and finest literature by being satiated with leanness. Above all, there is great virtue in reading to the young, rather than leaving them to silent reading. We are getting into a sort of sociability which consists in a household sitting in the evening round a table, very likely with backs all to the light, for the sake of saving weak eyes, each reading to himself,—

"All silent, and all"—

Of all people, children should be spared this refinement of civilization. If we would only consider the subtle strengthening of ties which comes from two people reading the same book together, breathing at once its breath and each giving the other unconsciously his interpretation of it, it would be seen how, in this simple habit of reading aloud, lies a power too fine to analyze, yet stronger than iron in welding souls together. To our thinking, there is no academy on earth equal to that found in so many homes, of a mother reading to her child.

Class Literature of the Last Thirty Years (1869)

Charlotte Yonge

Known for creating the girl's story in England, though acknowledged to be no competitor for Louisa May Alcott, Charlotte Yonge (1823–1901) wrote over a hundred books for adolescents and young women as well as much literary criticism. As editor (1851–1893) of The Monthly Packet, *an Anglican dominated magazine for girls, she gave regular advice on what books to choose. Here appeared serially the first of her family stories,* The Daisy Chain *(1856), and* The Little Duke *(1854), the most famous of her numerous historical stories. Among her works of criticism is the three-part "Children's Literature in the Last Century," which included "Nursery Books of the Eighteenth Century," "Didactic Fiction," and "Class Literature of the Last Thirty Years."[1] (Only the conclusion is reprinted here.) In* What Books to Lend and What to Give[2] *Miss Yonge compiled a classified selection of 955 books for a parish library. Setting forth her criteria in the introduction, she annotated the books listed with forthright comments, such as this for* Treasure Island: *"it brings the reader into rough company, among a good many horrors."[3]*

After all, our conclusion as to children's literature is a somewhat Irish one, for it is—use it as little as possible; and then only what is really substantially clever and good. Bring children up as soon as possible to stretch up to books above them, provided those books are noble and good. Do not give up such books on account of passages on which it would be inconvenient to be questioned on. If the child is in the habit of meeting things beyond comprehension it will pass such matters unheeded with the rest. We believe no child was ever contaminated by "The Fairy Queen," "Don Quixote," "The Vicar of Wakefield," or "The Arabian Nights." The only things to put out of its way are those that *nobody* ought to read, certainly not its mother. And if father or mother will take the pains to lead and sympathise with the child's tastes, encouraging but not overruling, they will find their palate curiously adapting itself to judge for and with the child, and will enjoy a fresh feast of all the old favourites of their lives. It seems like a sacrifice, but it is one worth making, and it proves all pleasure.

"Class Literature of the Last Thirty Years" by Charlotte Yonge reprinted from *Macmillan's Magazine*, 20 (September 1869): 456.

1. Republished in *Signal*, No. 2–4 (Stroud, Glos., England: The Thimble Press, May & September 1970, January 1971).

2. (London: National Society's Depository, 1887).

3. See also Kathleen Tillotson, "Charlotte Yonge as a Critic of Literature," in *A Chaplet for Charlotte Yonge* (London: Cresset Press, 1965).

Children's Magazines (1873)

Mary Mapes Dodge

Recognizing Mrs. Dodge's inspired editorship of St. Nicholas, *Alice M. Jordan wrote: "Behind the making of such a magazine . . . there had to be a creative personality. . . . The early seventies was an arid time for children's books, no less than for literature in general, save for the small group of New England writers. Parents were worried, too, about the prevalence of dime novels, but a sufficient body of suitable literature for children was not yet in sight. It took vision to see a future for a new magazine which should aim to please children rather than their elders, a bright and gay magazine with many pictures by the foremost artists."*[1] *Vision and a creative personality Mrs. Dodge (1831–1905) certainly had. She had written the immediately successful* Hans Brinker; or, The Silver Skates *(1865) and many other stories, articles, and poems. While working for* Hearth and Home *magazine in 1873, Mrs. Dodge was asked by Scribner's to edit a children's magazine; from then until her death she edited* St. Nicholas, *soon recognized as the greatest magazine for children. In it appeared such classics as Louisa May Alcott's* Eight Cousins *and* Under the Lilacs, *Howard Pyle's* Otto of the Silver Hand *and* The Story of King Arthur, *and Rudyard Kipling's* Jungle Book *and* Just So Stories.

Sometimes I feel like rushing through the world with two placards—one held aloft in my right hand, BEWARE OF CHILDREN'S MAGAZINES! the other flourished in my left, CHILD'S MAGAZINE WANTED! A good magazine for little ones was never so much needed, and such harm is done by nearly all that are published. In England, especially, the so-called juvenile periodicals are precisely what they ought not to be. In Germany, though better, they too often distract sensitive little souls with grotesquerie. Our magazines timidly approach the proper standard in some respects, but fall far short in others. We edit for the approval of fathers and mothers, and endeavor to make the child's monthly a milk-and-water variety of the adult's periodical. But, in fact, the child's magazine needs to be stronger, truer, bolder, more uncompromising than the other. Its cheer must be the cheer of the bird-song, not of condescending editorial babble. If it *mean* freshness and heartiness, and life and joy, and its words are simply, directly, and musically put together, it will trill its own way. We must not help it overmuch. In all except skillful handling of methods, we must be as little children if we would enter this kingdom.

If now and then the situation have fun in it, if something tumble unexpectedly, if the child-mind is surprised into an electric recognition of comical incongruity, so that there is a reciprocal "ha, ha!" between the printed page and the little reader, well and good. But, for humanity's sake,

"Children's Magazines" by Mary Mapes Dodge reprinted from *Scribner's Monthly,* 6 (July 1873): 352–354.

1. Alice M. Jordan, *From Rollo to Tom Sawyer,* p. 132.

let there be no editorial grimacing, no tedious vaulting back and forth over the grim railing that incloses halt and lame old jokes long ago turned in there to die.

Let there be no sermonizing either, no wearisome spinning out of facts, no rattling of the dry bones of history. A child's magazine is its pleasure-ground. Grown people go to their periodicals for relaxation, it is true; but they also go for information, for suggestion, and for to-day's fashion in literature. Besides, they begin, now-a-days, to feel that they are behind the age if they fail to know what the April *Jig-jig* says about so and so, or if they have not read B—'s much-talked-of poem in the last *Argosy*. Moreover, it is "the thing" to have the *Jig-jig* and *Argosy* on one's drawing-room table. One must read the leading periodicals or one is nobody. But with children the case is different. They take up their monthly or weekly because they wish to, and if they don't like it they throw it down again. Most children of the present civilization attend school. Their little heads are strained and taxed with the day's lessons. They do not want to be bothered nor amused nor taught nor petted. They just want to have their own way over their own magazine. They want to enter the one place where they may come and go as they please, where they are not obliged to mind, or say "yes ma'am" and "yes sir,"—where, in short, they can live a brand-new, free life of their own for a little while, accepting acquaintances as they choose and turning their backs without ceremony upon what does not concern them. Of course they expect to pick up odd bits and treasures, and to now and then "drop in" familiarly at an air castle, or step over to fairy-land. They feel their way, too, very much as we old folk do, toward sweet recognitions of familiar daydreams, secret goodnesses, and all the glorified classics of the soul. We who have strayed farther from these, thrill even to meet a hint of them in poems and essays. But what delights *us* in Milton, Keats and Tennyson, children often find for themselves in stars, daisies, and such joys and troubles as little ones know. That this comparison holds, is the best we can say of our writers. If they make us reach forth our hands to clutch the star or the good-deed candle-blaze, what more can be done?

Literary skill in its highest is but the subtle thinning of the veil that life and time have thickened. Mrs. Browning paid her utmost tribute to Chaucer when she spoke of

> "—his infantine
> Familiar clasp of things divine."

The *Jig-jig* and *Argosy* may deal with Darwinianism broadly and fairly as they. The upshot of it all will be something like

> "Hickory, dickery dock!
> The mouse ran up the clock.
> The clock struck one
> And down she ran—
> Hickory, dickery dock!"

And whatever Parton or Arthur Helps may say in that stirring article, "Our Country today," its substance is anticipated in

"Little boy blue!
    Come, blow your horn!
The cow's in the meadow
    Eating the corn."

So we come to the conviction that the perfect magazine for children lies folded at the heart of the ideal best magazine for grownups. Yet the coming periodical which is to make the heart of baby-America glad must not be a chip of the old Maga block, but an outgrowth from the old-young heart of Maga itself. Therefore, look to it that it be strong, warm, beautiful, and true. Let the little magazine-readers find what they look for and be able to pick up what they find. Boulders will not go into tiny baskets. If it so happen that the little folks know some one jolly, sympathetic, hand-to-hand personage who is sure to turn up here and there in every number of the magazine or paper, very good: that is, if they happen to like him. If not, beware! It will soon join the ghosts of dead periodicals; or, if it do not, it will live on only in that slow, dragging existence which is worse than death.

A child's periodical must be pictorially illustrated, of course, and the pictures must have the greatest variety consistent with simplicity, beauty and unity. They should be heartily conceived and well executed; and they must be suggestive, attractive and epigrammatic. If it be only the picture of a cat, it must be so like a cat that it will do its own purring, and not sit, a dead, stuffed thing, requiring the editor to purr for it. One of the sins of this age is editorial dribbling over inane pictures. The time to shake up a dull picture is when it is in the hands of the artist and engraver, and not when it lies, a fact accomplished, before the keen eyes of the little folk. Well enough for the editor to stand ready to answer questions that would naturally be put to the flesh-and-blood father, mother, or friend standing by. Well enough, too, for the picture to cause a whole tangle of interrogation-marks in the child's mind. It need not be elaborate, nor exhaust its theme, but what it attempts to do it must do well, and the editor must not over-help nor hinder. He must give just what the child demands, and to do this successfully is a matter of instinct, without which no man should presume to be a child's editor and go unhung.

Doubtless a great deal of instruction and good moral teaching may be inculcated in the pages of a magazine; but it must be by hints dropped incidentally here and there; by a few brisk, hearty statements of the difference between right and wrong; a sharp, clean thrust at falsehood, a sunny recognition of truth, a gracious application of politeness, an unwilling glimpse of the odious doings of the uncharitable and base. In a word, pleasant, breezy things may linger and turn themselves this way and that. Harsh, cruel facts—if they must come, and sometimes it is important that they should—must march forward boldly, say what they have to say, and go. The ideal child's magazine, we must remember, is a pleasure-ground where butterflies flit gayly hither and thither; where flowers quietly spread their bloom; where wind and sunshine play freaks of light and shadow; but where toads hop quickly out of sight and snakes dare not show themselves at all. Wells and fountains there may be in the grounds, but water must be drawn from the one in right trim, bright little buckets; and there must be no artificial coloring of the other, nor great show-cards about it, saying, "Behold! a fountain." Let its own flow and sparkle proclaim it.

The History of Children's Books (1888)

Caroline M. Hewins

Famous administrator of the early Hartford, Connecticut, Public Library, which pioneered in service to children, Caroline M. Hewins (1846–1926) is also notable for her numerous critical articles on children's reading and as a pioneer in the making of selective book lists.[1] Of her criticism, "The History of Children's Books" and the prefaces to sections within the book lists are especially important. (Indicative of her courage and good critical sense was her refusal to remove the then controversial Tom Sawyer from the children's library.) Miss Hewins' book lists have proved invaluable to librarians and booksellers. In 1946 Frederic G. Melcher, who used them in his early years as a bookseller, established in her honor the annual Caroline M. Hewins Lectureship in children's literature.[2]

It is hard to imagine a world without books for children. There have been children's stories and folk-tales ever since man first learned to speak. "Many of them," in Thackeray's words, "have been narrated, almost in their present shape, for thousands of years since, to little copper-colored Sanscrit children. . . . The very same tale has been heard by the Northmen Vikings, as they lay on their shields on deck; and by the Arabs, couched under the stars in the Syrian plains, when the flocks were gathered in, and the mares were picketed by the tents." Children's books, however, are a late growth of literature. Miss Yonge says, "Up to the Georgian era there were no books at all for children or the poor, excepting the class-books containing old ballads, such as Chevy Chase, . . . and short tales, such as The King and the Cobbler, Whittington and his Cat." We shall nevertheless see that there were English books for children (and it is with no others that we have to deal) long before this time. . . .

The tendency in the United States had been . . . to reprint English books, either exactly, or with very slight modifications to suit republican taste. From Franklin's little volumes of Bunyan, which he sold to buy some small chapmen's books, a historical collection, his Plutarch, Defoe, and Spectator, there was little change to the end of the century, when Buckingham, the Boston printer, had, besides the last-mentioned work,

---

"The History of Children's Books" by Caroline M. Hewins reprinted from *Atlantic Monthly,* 6l (January 1888): 112, 125–126.

1. The first book list was published under the title "Books for the Young, a Guide for Parents and Children" in *Publisher's Weekly* (New York: R. R. Bowker Company, 1882); later editions were published by the American Library Association.

2. See also Caroline M. Hewins' *A Mid-century Child and Her Books* (New York: Macmillan Company, 1926); also included with Jennie D. Lindquist's Hewins Lecture, "Caroline M. Hewins and Books for Children," in *Caroline M. Hewins, Her Book* (Boston: Horn Book, Inc., 1954).

Robinson Crusoe, Goody Two Shoes, Tom Thumb, Michael Wiggles-worth's Day of Doom, a file of almanacs, Gulliver's Travels, The History of the Pirates, the Vicar of Wakefield, Tristram Shandy, Tom Jones, and Junius. But school-books were scarce and dear during the Revolution, and Noah Webster, foreseeing that works like Dilworth's New Guide to the English Tongue, probably intended for charity schools, would not long be useful in a new country, published his Grammatical Institute, containing a little general information for country boys and girls who had few books, and later his typical New England spelling-book.

Dr. Holmes tells how much more New England boys and girls used to hear, in books, of English birds, and flowers, and games, and social customs, than of their own, and how he used to find himself in a strange world, "where James was called Jem, not *Jim,* as we heard it; . . . where naughty school-boys got through a gap in the hedge, to steal Farmer Giles's red-streaks, instead of shinning over the fence to hook old Daddy Jones's Baldwins; where Hodge used to go to the alehouse for his mug of beer, while we used to see old Joe steering for the grocery to get his glass of rum; . . . where there were larks and nightingales instead of yellow-birds and bobolinks; where the robin was a little domestic bird that fed at table, instead of a great fidgety, jerky, whooping thrush." The time was now coming when as distinctively American characteristics would be found in stories and books of amusement as in Webster's school-books. We owe the change to one man, Samuel Griswold Goodrich, born in Ridgefield, Connecticut, in 1793. His father was a clergyman, who had, for the time, a large collection of theological books, but few others. The son says, "When I was about ten years old, my father brought me from Hartford Gaffer Ginger, Goody Two Shoes, and some of the rhymes and jingles now collected under the name of Mother Goose, with perhaps a few other toy books of that day. These were a revelation. Of course I read them, but, I must add, with no real relish." A little later, one of the boy's companions lent him a book with some of the popular fairy and giant tales, which inspired him with such horror that his mother was obliged to tell him that they were not true, but invented to amuse children. With fine scorn and the true matter-of-fact Parley spirit, the child replied, "Well, they don't amuse me." He grew up with the belief that the children's books of the day were full of nothing but lies and horrors, exciting those who read them to crime and bloodshed. At twelve, however, he was delighted with Robinson Crusoe, and a translation of one of Madame de Genlis's tales, explaining certain marvels by simple physical causes. He read, too, The Shepherd of Salisbury Plain, and twenty years later, while telling Hannah More how he had enjoyed it, formed the idea of the Parley Tales. In 1827, he published the first of them,—Tales of Peter Parley about America. In the next thirty years he wrote or edited more than a hundred volumes, most of them for children or schools, told in a pleasant and familiar style. A middle-aged reader can hardly see his little History of the United States, with chapters on Central and South America, without recognizing as the source of many ideas useful in later life the hideous little woodcuts of the Pilgrims landing in a snow storm, the Dustin family attacked by Indians, the burning of Schenectady, or Captain Waterton on the cayman's back. It is just possible that true tales of Indian barbarities may impress a sensitive child with as great a sense of horror as legends of giants, but Peter Parley seems never to have thought so. In his mind, if a thing was true, it was right; if false, it was wrong. He speaks with scorn, in his autobiography, of attempts to revive the old fairy-tales, and treats Halliwell's edition of the nursery rhymes of England as if it were beneath notice. His mind was essentially prosaic, but he did a great work in simplifying history, geography, and books of travel for children.

Jacob Abbott published his Young Christian in 1832, and from that time until his death, in 1879, was constantly writing for young people. Who is not grateful, notwithstanding late irreverent burlesques, for the simple pictures of happy child-life in the Rollo, Lucy, Jonas, and Franconia books? Old-fashioned as they seem now, they are so full of common sense, and have so clear an idea of children's relations to each other and their elders, that some of them should be on every child's bookshelves. The young people of fourteen or fifteen, like Beechnut and Mary Bell, who act as guides and teachers to children a few years younger, are remarkably mature, and have a wonderful development of reason, judgment, and knowledge of child-nature; but their advice is always good, and worthy of remembrance. Then, too, these are distinctively New England story-books. The children go sleighing and coasting, walk on snowshoes, pop corn, roast apples, and do a thousand things such as country boys and girls delight in. They learn, too, to use their eyes in traveling, and many a grown-up man or woman of to-day, who cannot tell why London or Paris looks so familiar, is indebted to Rollo in Europe for knowledge absorbed so long ago that its source has been forgotten.

Between 1840 and 1850, a German influence was felt in children's books. Grimm's tales had been translated before, but Gammer Grethel and little stories of real life came on the scene. Illustrations and type began to be better. Soon after 1850, really beautiful colored pictures were to be seen in books for children, published on both sides of the Atlantic. Hans Andersen was by this time well known to English-reading children. The reign of fairy-tales had begun again with the study of folk-lore.

With fairy-tales and hero-legends rewritten and simplified for children, with history told in story-form, there is only one danger,—that young readers will be satisfied with abridgments, and know nothing in later years of great originals.

Battle of the Babies (1895)

Agnes Repplier

Among Agnes Repplier's (1858–1945) several volumes of learned, witty pieces is Essays in Miniature, which includes "Battle of the Babies," a trenchant answer to the persistent distrust of fairy tales. Here she states, "That which is vital in literature or tradition, which has survived the obscurity and wreckage of the past, whether as legend, or ballad, or mere nursery rhyme, has survived in right of some intrinsic merit of its own, and will not be snuffed out of existence by any of our precautionary or hygienic measures."

A warfare has been raging in our midst, the echoes of which have hardly yet died sullenly away upon either side of the Atlantic. It has been a bloodless and un-Homeric strife, not without humorous side-issues, as when Pistol and Bardolph and Fluellen come to cheer our anxious spirits at the siege of Harfleur. Its first guns were heard in New York, where a modest periodical, devoted to the training of parents, opened fire upon those time-honored nursery legends which are presumably dear to the hearts of all rightly constituted babies. The leader of this gallant foray protested vehemently against all fairy tales of a mournful or sanguinary cast, and her denunciation necessarily included many stories which have for generations been familiar to every little child. She rejected *Red Riding Hood,* because her own infancy was haunted and embittered by the evil behavior of the wolf; she would have none of *Bluebeard,* because he was a wholesale fiend and murderer; she would not even allow the pretty *Babes in the Wood,* because they tell a tale of cold-hearted cruelty and of helpless suffering; while all fierce narratives of giants and ogres and magicians were to be banished ruthlessly from our shelves. Verily, reading will be but gentle sport in the virtuous days to come.

Now it chanced that this serious protest against nursery lore fell into the hands of Mr. Andrew Lang, the most light-hearted and conservative of critics, and partial withal to tales of bloodshed and adventure. How could it be otherwise with one reared on the bleak border land, and familiar from infancy with the wild border legends that Sir Walter knew and loved; with stories of Thomas the Rhymer, and the plundering Hardens, and the black witches of Loch Awe! It was natural that with the echoes of the old savage strife ringing in his ears, and with the memories of the dour Scottish bogies and warlocks lingering in his heart, Mr. Lang could but indifferently sympathize with those anxious parents who think the stories of Bluebeard and Jack the Giant Killer too shocking for infant ears to hear. Our grandmothers, he declared, were not ferocious old ladies, yet they told us

"Battle of the Babies" reprinted from *Essays in Miniature* by Agnes Repplier (Boston: Houghton Mifflin Company, 1895. London: Gay and Bird, 1893).

these tales, and many more which we were none the worse for hearing.
"Not to know them is to be sadly ignorant, and to miss that which all
people have relished in all ages." Moreover, it is apparent to him, and
indeed to most of us, that we cannot take even our earliest steps in the
world of literature, or in the shaded paths of knowledge, without encountering suffering and sin in some shape; while, as we advance a little
further, these grisly forms fly ever on before. "Cain," remarks Mr. Lang,
"killed Abel. The flood drowned quite a number of persons. David was not
a stainless knight, and Henry VIII. was nearly as bad as Bluebeard. Several
deserving gentlemen were killed at Marathon. Front de Bœuf came to an
end shocking to sensibility, and to Mr. Ruskin." The *Arabian Nights,
Pilgrim's Progress, Paul and Virginia*—all the dear old nursery favorites
must, under the new dispensation, be banished from our midst; and the
rising generation of prigs must be nourished exclusively on *Little Lord
Fauntleroy,* and other carefully selected specimens of milk-and-water diet.

The prospect hardly seems inviting; but as the English guns rattled
merrily away in behalf of English tradition, they were promptly met by an
answering roar from this side of the water. A Boston paper rushed gallantly
to the defense of the New York periodical, and gave Mr. Lang—to use a pet
expression of his own—"his kail through the reek." American children, it
appears, are too sensitively organized to endure the unredeemed ferocity of
the old fairy stories. The British child may sleep soundly in its little cot after
hearing about the Babes in the Wood; the American infant is prematurely
saddened by such unmerited misfortune. "If a consensus of American
mothers could be taken," says the Boston writer, "our English critic might
be infinitely disgusted to know in how many nurseries these cruel tales must
be changed, or not told at all to the children of less savage generations. No
mother nowadays tells them in their unmitigated brutality."

Is this true, I wonder, and are our supersensitive babies reared perforce
on the optimistic version of Red Riding Hood, where the wolf is cut open
by the woodman, and the little girl and her grandmother jump out, safe and
sound? Their New England champion speaks of the "intolerable misery"
—a very strong phrase—which he suffered in infancy from having his nurse
tell him of the Babes in the Wood; while the Scriptural stories were
apparently every whit as unbearable and heart-breaking. "I remember," he
says, "two children, strong, brave man and woman now, who in righteous
rage plucked the Slaughter of the Innocents out from the family Bible."
This was a radical measure, to say the least, and if many little boys and girls
started in to expurgate the Scriptures in such liberal fashion, the holy book
would soon present a sadly mutilated appearance. . . .

I believe it is as well to cultivate a child's emotions as to cultivate his
manners or his morals, and the first step in such a direction is necessarily
taken through the stories told him in infancy. If a consensus of mothers
would reject the good old fairy tales "in their unmitigated brutality," a
consensus of men of letters would render a different verdict; and such men,
who have been children in their time, and who look back with wistful

delight upon the familiar figures who were their earliest friends, are entitled to an opinion in the case. How admirable was the "righteous rage" of Charles Lamb, when he wanted to buy some of these same brutal fairy stories for the little Coleridges, and could find nothing but the correct and commonplace literature which his whole soul abhorred! "Mrs. Barbauld's and Mrs. Trimmer's nonsense lay in piles about," he wrote indignantly to papa Coleridge, "and have banished all the old classics of the nursery. Knowledge, insignificant and vapid as Mrs. Barbauld's books convey, must, it seems, come to a child in the shape of knowledge; and his empty noddle must be turned with conceit of his own powers when he has learnt that a horse is an animal, and that Billy is better than a horse, and such like; instead of that beautiful interest in wild tales which made the child a man, while all the time he suspected himself to be no bigger than a child."

Just such a wild tale, fantastic rather than beautiful, haunted Châteaubriand all his life—the story of Count Combourg's wooden leg, which, three hundred years after its owner's death, was seen at night walking solemnly down the steep turret stairs, attended by a huge black cat. Not at all the kind of story we would select to tell a child nowadays. By no means! Even the little Châteaubriand heard it from peasant lips. Yet in after years, when he had fought the battle of life, and fought it with success; when he had grown gray, and illustrious, and disillusioned, and melancholy, what should come back to his mind, with its old pleasant flavor of terror and mystery, but the vision of Count Combourg's wooden leg taking its midnight constitutional, with the black cat stepping softly on before? So he notes it gravely down in his Memoirs, just as Scott notes in his diary the pranks of Whippity Stourie, the Scotch bogie that steals at night into open nursery windows; and just as Heine, in gay, sunlit Paris, recalls with joy the dark, sweet, sombre tales of the witch and fairy haunted forests of Germany.

These are impressions worth recording, and they are only a few out of many which may be gathered from similar sources. That which is vital in literature or tradition, which has survived the obscurity and wreckage of the past, whether as legend, or ballad, or mere nursery rhyme, has survived in right of some intrinsic merit of its own, and will not be snuffed out of existence by any of our precautionary or hygienic measures. We could not banish Bluebeard if we would. He is as immortal as Hamlet, and when hundreds of years shall have passed over this uncomfortably enlightened world, the children of the future—who, thank Heaven, can never, with all our efforts, be born grown up—will still tremble at the blood-stained key, and rejoice when the big brave brothers come galloping up the road. We could not even rid ourselves of Mother Goose, though she, too, has her mortal enemies, who protest periodically against her cruelty and grossness. We could not drive Punch and Judy from our midst, though Mr. Punch's derelictions have been the subject of much serious and adverse criticism. It is not by such barbarous rhymes or by such brutal spectacles that we teach a child the lessons of integrity and gentleness, explain our nursery moralists, and probably they are correct. Moreover, Bluebeard does not teach a lesson of conjugal felicity, and Cinderella is full of the world's vanities, and Puss in Boots is one long record of triumphant effrontery and deception. An honest and self-respecting lad would have explained to the king that he was not the Marquis of Carabas at all; that he had no desire to profit by his cat's ingenious falsehoods, and no weak ambition to connect himself with the aristocracy. Such a hero would be a credit to our modern schoolrooms, and lift a load of care from the shoulders of our modern critics. Only the children would have none of him, but would turn wistfully back to those brave old tales which are their inheritance from a splendid past, and of which no hand shall rob them.

Chapter 2

Of Classics and Golden Ages

Time has allowed historians and critics to speak firmly of landmarks in the first golden age of children's literature—those last years of the nineteenth and first two decades of the twentieth century. Such universally heralded giants as Carroll, Andersen, Grahame, and Potter broke ground with new genres (and stimulated waves of imitators). Providing tested measuring-sticks, this era set standards for critics.

It is only judicious speculation, however, to claim that a work from the "second golden age" (the period beginning with 1918) is a classic, for in the ever-changing climate of the literary world such a claim will be long debated. Furthermore, hours of debate can and have been devoted to reviewing the "greats" of yesterday and examining claims that the "second golden age is now." Here for the pondering is a selection of views on greatness, beginning with the question, "What makes a classic?"

Children's Classics

Alice M. Jordan

A contemporary of Anne Carroll Moore and Caroline M. Hewins (her later career), Alice M. Jordan (1870–1960) began work as a children's librarian in the Boston Public Library in 1902 and was Supervisor of Work with Children from 1917 until her retirement in 1941. Miss Jordan served also as book editor for the Horn Book Magazine *(1939–1950) and wrote numerous articles published in it. These were brought together in her book* From Rollo to Tom Sawyer, *the title paper being the first Caroline M. Hewins Lecture, delivered in 1947. As editor of children's books at Macmillan's, Louise Seaman Bechtel relied upon the "sane, humorous, learned"[1] Miss Jordan to criticize manuscripts. Miss Jordan's knowledge of her field also greatly enriched her teaching of children's literature at the Library School of Simmons College and in the training program of the Boston Public Library. The following piece is Miss Jordan's introduction to a book list (published by the* Horn Book Magazine) *which since its first printing has been several times revised and is still available.*

Riding on a subway car from Cambridge to Boston one day was a man who was dissatisfied with the behavior of his watch. He shook it gently, then lifted it to his ear for confirmation of what his eye told him, as we all do in similar circumstances. Beside him was seated another man, a stranger, who leaned toward him with the words, "I told you butter wouldn't suit the works." Quick as a flash came back the answer, "It was the best butter." That was all, but each man settled back with the pleasant sense of an unexpected meeting with a member of his own fraternity, as it were.

Perhaps no other book for children is so generally called a classic as *Alice's Adventures in Wonderland*. It delights us when we are young, it is cherished, reread and quoted for its philosophy and humor when we are old. There are so many apt conversations in it, so many occurrences called to mind in our everyday life, so many characters reminding us at times of ourselves or our friends. Always there is the sweet wholesome laughter that follows the inconsequential turn of events in that book and in *Through the Looking-Glass*. To miss such a book when the time for it is ripe is to suffer a real loss in one's store of mental treasure. Then, too, as Marie Shedlock, the wise Fairy Godmother, believed, no other story is as effective in educating children in an appreciation of humor. *Alice in Wonderland* without the Tenniel drawings seems to most of us to be shorn of its perfect accompaniment, so we scan each new edition with stern scrutiny and a

"Children's Classics" by Alice M. Jordan from *Horn Book Magazine,* 23 (February 1947): 3–9. Reprinted by permission of Horn Book, Inc.

1. Louise Seaman Bechtel, *Books in Search of Children* (New York: The Macmillan Company, 1969. London, Hamish Hamilton Ltd., 1970).

feeling that he is indeed a daring person who thinks he can interpret Lewis Carroll better than John Tenniel did.

What makes a book a classic? In a discussion of Greek epics Gilbert Murray has written some cogent, arresting words, as applicable to children's books as to world masterpieces. That which lives, becomes classical, he says.

> Intensity of imagination is the important thing. It is intensity of imagination that makes a poet's work "real," as we say; spontaneous, infectious or convincing. Especially it is this that creates an atmosphere; that makes us feel, on opening the pages of a book, that we are in a different world, and a world full of real beings about whom, in one way or another, we care. And I suspect that, ultimately, the greatness of a poem or work of imaginative art depends mostly upon two questions: how strongly we feel ourselves transported to this new world, and what sort of world it is when we get there, how great, or interesting, or beautiful.

Take the four great books, not written for children but adopted by them and universally counted among the books to which they should all, at one time or another, be exposed—*Robinson Crusoe, Gulliver's Travels, Don Quixote* and *Pilgrim's Progress.* They are not all liked by all children, but how real are their worlds, and how thoroughly a reader enters into them. In *Books, Children and Men,* Paul Hazard writes illuminatingly of their appeal to children.

Until a book has weathered at least one generation and is accepted in the next, it can hardly be given the rank of a classic and no two people are likely to be in full agreement as to what should be included in a list of them. From time to time conditions have been such that publishers have been obliged to allow many standard books to go out of print; it is a heartening thing to note how they are coming back. Such a profusion of new editions of children's favorites in attractive dress, at surprisingly low prices, gives an encouraging lift to the cause of good reading. If a purchaser really wants to secure a well-made classic, he is well able to do so now.

Form has much to do with the permanence of a book. Some of the books written for children have a charm of style that insures their acceptance as literature in the best sense of the word; *Andersen's Fairy Tales, A Child's Garden of Verses, The Wind in the Willows* are outstanding examples of books that rank high for the quality of their writing. Simplicity and sincerity are important factors. No book that is merely clever, or devised with the tongue in the cheek or an over-the-shoulder glance at an audience of grown persons, will be more than evanescent in the affections of children. Such books may have a temporary popularity, but they fade away quickly.

The lasting appeal of the fairy tale is proof that children do not change essentially through the years. If the fairy-tale world is not a great one, it is a thoroughly interesting one to the majority of us at a certain stage in our development. Opportunity to know the best books of the past must be provided by older people who are associated with children. Often the most rewarding introduction is made by reading aloud in the home, or by leaving attractive editions where they may be discovered. For the sense of discovery brings a joy of its own.

So it is the children who make the final decision as to the vitality of books written for them. The little girl who said of *Alice in Wonderland*, "This is the sort of thing that glees my heart," knew the touchstone. And though we may feel that since *Mary Poppins* "glees" so many hearts she is well on the road to rank as a classic, only time will tell whether her world will continue to be one into which another generation will love to enter as today's children do.

There is plenty of room for nonsense in our chosen list, which must include *Mother Goose* and Lear's *Nonsense Books.* The first is traditional verse which, possessing perfect rhythm and the simplicity of early childhood, has delighted countless nurseries in the English-speaking lands; the second, an early break from didacticism and unimaginative dullness.

High adventure is an irresistible magnet drawing readers to travelers' wonderful tales, deeds of daring and brave encounters. Even stories of home life belong among the adventure classics, if the characters ring true and have vitality as *Tom Sawyer* and *Huckleberry Finn* have.

Few are the books so surely associated with a single illustrator that there is not room for a new interpretation to appeal to modern moods. Howard Pyle's books are among the few. His *Merry Adventures of Robin Hood*, his *Story of King Arthur*, are inseparable from the drawings by which he gave play to the "pleasure of spirit" he felt in creating those incomparable books. The new edition of his *Robin Hood*, with fresh plates from the original drawings and new type, ought to bring great enjoyment to many young readers.

Yet a book of glowing facets sometimes reflects a new light when illustrated freshly by one to whom it has genuine significance and who has the trained hand to set down his concepts in contemporary terms.

Looking back over the past forty years on the production of children's books, we conclude that the books illustrated by the Rhead brothers, published by Harper, started the fashion of bringing out famous children's books in a uniform edition. *Robinson Crusoe* was the first published, followed by *Swiss Family Robinson, Tom Brown's School Days* and *Gulliver's Travels.* These have had a long usefulness, but it is plain that no one artist can be temperamentally fitted to do justice to widely diverse subjects, nor is it desirable that he should be. Collections of books with identical shape and binding, and with the same type of pictures, have a deadening effect on home and library shelves. Children's classics deserve individual treatment, a fact of which relatives and friends of children should be definitely aware.

Two specially important editions which have long held high place in children's libraries are Scribner's Illustrated Classics and Macmillan's Children's Classics. For the first of these, N. C. Wyeth painted many of his splendid pictures, beginning with those for *Treasure Island,* which have

Robin Hood · meeteth · the · tall
· Stranger · on · the · Bridge

Illustration by Howard Pyle from *The Merry Adventures of Robin Hood* by Howard Pyle. Reproduced by permission of Charles Scribner's Sons. British edition published by Tom Stacey, London, 1971.

never been surpassed by the work of later artists.

For *Arabian Nights,* in the same series also, Maxfield Parrish made his beautiful, dramatic illustrations that reflect the splendor and richness of the East, with its fountains and golden palaces, its sorcerers and magicians. "Nowhere in the whole realm of literature," writes Kate Douglas Wiggin in her Introduction to this edition, "will you find such a Marvel, such a Wonder, such a Nonesuch of a book; nowhere will you find impossibilities so real and so convincing." And she warns against rearing children who have never fallen under its spell. Not many of the Arabian Nights tales are included in this colorful volume. To find a wider selection children may be directed to the standard translation, edited by Andrew Lang, which has been republished in a better form than that in which it originally appeared, with larger type and the substitution of several more popular tales for others not so well liked by children.

It was early in the twenties that the Macmillan Company began to reissue some of their favorite publications as a series of Children's Classics. These were warmly welcomed by book buyers for the high quality of their workmanship and they continue to be counted among the most satisfactory editions. George MacDonald's lovely fairy tales were republished in this series. *At the Back of the North Wind,* with its rare beauty and spiritual significance, appeals strongly to many impressionable children. Here is the intensity of imagination mentioned by Professor Murray; here there are mystery and poetry, a deep love for animals and the varying aspects of Nature, a two-world consciousness. Chesterton was a profound admirer of *At the Back of the North Wind* and *The Princess and the Goblin,* which he called the most lifelike of all the stories he had read.

There are several other fairy tales of the Mid-Victorian period which bring lasting pleasure to the children of today. *The King of the Golden River,* by John Ruskin, is a vigorous Old World legend, reissued in the Rainbow Classics with a particularly happy choice of illustrator in Fritz Kredel. Thackeray's *The Rose and the Ring,* famous Christmas pantomime loved for its humor, Mrs. Craik's *Little Lame Prince,* with its wonder and mystery; these never become too old-fashioned to please children with their simple lessons.

Andersen's Fairy Tales are among the literary masterpieces, not to be missed in childhood, yet not for the earliest fairy-tale age. Their best introduction is through storytelling or reading aloud. The edition should be chosen for the integrity of its translation; the illustrations should not be of the "pretty-pretty" type.

In our own time there has been published a creative piece of writing that is unquestionably destined for long life, a book we are willing to accept now as a classic for young and old—Kenneth Grahame's *The Wind in the Willows.* When you have once felt its magic, you need no argument, no prophecy of its enduring quality; you only hasten to share its poetry, its beauty and humor with a child who will love it.

About one hundred years ago, Hawthorne made his own version of what he termed immortal fables. He thought that by their indestructibility "they are legitimate subjects for every age to clothe with its own garniture of manners." Hawthorne's stories are more romantic than Greek in form, but no later versions have wholly taken their place. The beauty of their English places them among Hawthorne's choicest books, and children turn again and again to the *Wonder Book* and *Tanglewood Tales*.

Three realistic stories challenge us to give reasons for their continued popularity, their repeated appearance in any group of children's classics, their never failing inclusion in reading lists for girls: they are *Hans Brinker, Little Women* and *Heidi*. When they were written, they were unique, but now later writers have followed their established patterns without superseding these loved books. If the worlds they create are neither great nor beautiful, they are real and interesting to the readers and the stories are about characters for whom children have a warm affection. The choice of Hilda van Stockum, who knows Holland well, as illustrator of *Hans Brinker* in Rainbow Classics is a fortunate one. Before *Little Women,* there was practically no spontaneity in American stories for girls. Natural family life, with characters for whom we care, has made *Little Women* loved for three, possibly four generations, in spite of its sentimentality and doubtful English. In the portrait of Jo March, Louisa Alcott shared with her readers her own brave and cheerful struggle against difficulties that girls can understand; that is what makes the book so real. Sentimental, why not, at the age when it is read? If family life is going to disappear, as we are sometimes told it is, all the more reason for holding on to this book. And Heidi—who can say just why that little Swiss girl lives so vividly in many hearts?

Over the years the store of treasure for the reading of American children has rolled up, adding here and there bright gems from the Old World: Andersen from Denmark, Grimm's *Tales* from Germany, *Pinocchio* from Italy, the *Wonderful Adventures of Nils* from Sweden, *The Wind in the Willows* from England. Foundation for the growth of discriminating literary taste lies within the covers of such as these famous books, which open shyly the door of imagination, enchant by their poetry and humor, make us freeholders in a country where animals are as much at home as we are, or simply give visions of unguessed worlds of adventure and friendship.

Ancient and Modern

Times Literary Supplement

The making of book-lists is a fascinating, insidious, and fundamentally unsound occupation. An attempt has recently been made to draw up a list of *The One Hundred Best Books for Children (Sunday Times,* 1s. 6d.) What could possibly be a more profitless—or more pleasurable—parlour game? The very phrase, "the One Hundred Best Books for Children," is question-begging. Why should all children be lumped together in this indiscriminate manner? It would almost be as sensible, or as senseless, to try to compile a list of one hundred best books for grown-ups. True, the list classifies children into age-groups, but even so there still remain fundamental differences of taste and intelligence, of education and background. If such a list is to be of any practical value its limits must be much more clearly defined.

Some seventy years ago a successful author of children's books compiled just such a list, deliberately limited to books that should appeal to one particular type of child. In 1887 Miss Charlotte Yonge published a pamphlet intended to help with the selection for books for a parish library. She was well ahead of her time in her insistence that every country parish should be provided with a library and that such a library should contain a section devoted entirely to the needs of the village children. She would have liked to see a library in every village school and so interested was she in this question that more than half of her pamphlet, *Books to Lend and Books to Give,* is devoted to lists of books for children's reading.

Although her list was compiled specifically with a view to the scholars in a village school, Miss Yonge included a section characteristically entitled "Drawing-Room Books," intended for those other children who came down to the drawing-room for an hour after tea to listen to Mamma or Papa reading aloud. It is curious to notice that the modern list is obviously intended for the present-day equivalent of "the drawing-room child." Children's books have always tended to be upper-class in outlook. In Victorian days a few moral tales were deliberately aimed at the children of the poor, but stories intended for amusement rather than for edification have almost invariably been written with an upper-class background. Although the system of universal education has enormously enlarged the potential circle of child-readers, even to-day, in a society far more egalitarian than any Miss Yonge ever dreamt of, many children's books, unlike children's radio and television programmes, still presuppose a familiarity with such things as ponies, sailing-boats and boarding schools.

To borrow a phrase from Miss Yonge, the books in the modern list "deal in general with a way of life, with pursuits, allusions and temptations, so much out of the line of the ordinary clients of the parish library that we do not recommend them for that purpose."

The difference in the type of child-reader must be borne in mind in any comparison between the two lists, and so too must the restriction confining the modern list to books actually in print to-day. If this limitation could have been abolished the number of books common to both lists would assuredly have been much larger. Nevertheless a comparison between the two lists just as they stand is certainly amusing and possibly instructive. To turn from the one to the other is to leave a brightly-lit modern bookshop, clean, gay, and attractively arranged, but to the eye of nostalgic middle-age, ever so little lacking in romance, for the gloom of a garret stacked high with books banished long ago from nursery and schoolroom shelves. The tarnished gold titles are barely legible beneath their coating of dust. *Little Suzy's Six Birthdays, The Star in the Dust-Heap* (almost too apt a title, this), *Regent Rosalind, A Diller, A Dollar, a Ten O'Clock Scholar*—who now alive remembers any of these nursery stories? But every so often the patient explorer comes upon treasure-trove from his or her own childhood. Here is *Little Meg's Children* side by side with Miss Martineau's *Feats on the Fjord* and *The Crofton Boys*. Here is de la Motte Fouqué's *Sintram*, which Miss Yonge herself loved and quoted in so many of her books. Here is *The Swiss Family Robinson*—"the adventures are unfortunately more charming than possible" is Miss Yonge's comment—and, going farther back in time, here are five little books by Maria Edgeworth, including *The Parent's Assistant* and that unkindest of tales, *Rosamund and the Purple Jar*. Best of all, here is a story about the young Grinling Gibbons which once beguiled the appalling tedium of needlework classes. Its curious title, *The Carved Cartoon*, has been forgotten these forty years or more.

Thirteen books only are to be found both in garret and bookshop, in Miss Yonge's list and in the modern one. Of these a surprising proportion are books such as *Tanglewood Tales* and Kingsley's *Heroes,* the stories of the *Iliad* and the *Odyssey* retold for children, and tales of King Arthur and his knights. Grown-ups have always supposed such books to be excellent and indeed essential reading for children, but the suspicion inevitably arises that they would not figure quite so conspicuously in any list compiled by the children themselves. Nevertheless, here they are alongside those undoubted favourites, the fairy stories of Grimm and Hans Andersen. With the fairy stories Miss Yonge (but not the moderns) includes *The Arabian Nights*. She declares that children should not be allowed to grow up ignorant of Aladdin and Sindbad and Ali Baba, adding the comment, "It is remarkable that Hannah More thought even the old uncastigated translation from the French more wholesome reading for young people than contemporary tales of character, perhaps because less tending to introspection." Presumably the translation from the French was slightly more "castigated" than Sir Richard Burton's version.

Tom Brown's School-Days, Treasure Island, The Water Babies, Alice in Wonderland—nobody is surprised that children should still read and love these favourites as children read and loved them seventy years ago. It is, however, a little strange to find that *The Children of the New Forest* is still popular and that Jules Verne's *Twenty Thousand Leagues Under the Sea* has not been displaced by more up-to-date "science fiction." Henty is supposed to be forgotten, but he, too, must be credited with a double appearance because, although different books occur in each list, his stories are so much alike that the variation in title hardly counts. It is pleasant to know that to-day's children, like their parents and grandparents before them, enjoy the stories of Mrs. Ewing, but the happiest surprise of all is to find a long-forgotten favourite, *Hans Brinker or the Silver Skates,* still in print and still apparently at the height of his popularity.

Pilgrim's Progress is the worst and most glaring omission from the modern list. It might be argued that this is not a child's book, but the fact remains that it has been the joy and delight of English-speaking children for more than three hundred years. In Miss Yonge's words, "in spite of its peculiarities the king of allegories must be admitted." Significantly enough, while Miss Yonge devoted four whole sections to religion not a single religious book appears in the modern list. The beginning of the present century saw the publication of some of the most attractive "Sunday books" ever written. William Conton's *Child's Book of Saints,* for instance, or Florence Converse's *House of Prayer,* or Father Hugh Benson's *Child's Rule of Life.* Many, if not most, of these are still in print. The best of to-day's religious books for children—and most of them are very good indeed—consist simply of well-chosen and well-illustrated extracts from the Bible. As such they hardly qualify for inclusion but someone might have spared a thought for the Roman Catholic *Six O'Clock Saints* series, which in style, in humour and in fantasy might well be described as the Just So Stories of the Church.

The real *Just So Stories* are one of the especial delights of the modern list, together with *Puck of Pook's Hill* and *The Jungle Book,* which is described as "the first really original modern children's book." Where children's books are concerned Kipling is the peculiar pride and glory of the twentieth century. After him, but a long way behind, come E. Nesbit and Arthur Ransome. The works of these three authors, together with a few individual books such as *The Wind in the Willows* and *The Secret Garden,* make it possible to argue that the twentieth century has produced books for children at least as good as those of the Victorian age.

Apart from these three authors the strength of the modern list lies in the sections entitled "Nursery Rhymes and Picture Books" and "Animal Stories." Victorian toddlers had to do without Peter Rabbit and Babar and

Illustration by Rudyard Kipling from "How the Camel Got His Hump," from *Just So Stories* by Rudyard Kipling. Courtesy The Newberry Library. First British edition published by Macmillan, London, 1902.

Winnie-the-Pooh and even Little Black Sambo, whose date of publication is surprisingly late. They could, of course, enjoy nursery rhymes and simple verses illustrated by Caldecott, Walter Crane and Kate Greenaway, but Miss Yonge omits any mention of these charming picture-books, which are rightly included in the modern list. Perhaps she considered them too "refined" for the Infant School.

Much more inexplicable is her omission of that beloved book *Black Beauty*, prototype of all animal stories for children. Her "Natural History" section includes a few tales of animal life, but it is mostly devoted to such titles as *Wild Animals of the Bible*, *Homes without Hands*, or *The Herb of the Field*. By contrast the modern list is rich indeed. As well as *Black Beauty* and *The Jungle Book* it includes *Jock of the Bushveld* and selections from Ernest Thompson Seton, together with more modern favourites such as Bambi, Grey Owl, and *The Yearling*.

The three great champions of the Victorian age are all women, Miss Louisa M. Alcott, Mrs. Molesworth, and Miss Yonge herself, with Mrs. Ewing a short head behind. Curiously enough, Miss Yonge's list includes *Under the Lilacs*, a very second-rate example of Miss Alcott's genius, but omits that most persistent of best-sellers, *Little Women*. Such an omission is inexcusable; *Little Women* has been translated into more than a dozen languages, and even to-day, ninety years after publication, it remains the most popular of all stories for girls. As the modern list has it, "Meg, Jo, Beth and Amy, in their simple home at Concord, have been hostesses to children all over the world."

If Miss Alcott's masterpiece is unaccountably missing from Miss Yonge's list Mrs. Molesworth's stories are as unaccountably missing from the modern one. Several of her books have recently been reprinted. Miss Yonge gives *Four Winds Farm* as an example of what she describes as "the dream-like tales." Of Mrs. Molesworth in more down-to-earth mood she surprisingly chooses *Hermy* and a little-known story, *The Abbey by the Sea,* which she describes as "perhaps a little too ideal but refining."

Like Mrs. Molesworth, Miss Yonge herself is missing from the modern list. She has been badly treated in the matter of new issues, but it is strange that no one thought to include the modern edition of *Countess Kate* with its entrancing illustrations by Gwen Raverat. Unless parents and grandparents have been wise enough to cherish their own copies present-day children must do without such delights as *The Daisy Chain* or *The Chaplet of Pearls*. Saddest of all is the absence of *The Little Duke,* which nowadays is only to be found in an American edition or in abridged form as a School Reader. Surely some enterprising publisher this side of the Atlantic might give us back young Richard of Normandy hidden in his truss of hay.

Miss Yonge was a pioneer of the historical tale for children. In her own childhood her favourite reading had been the Waverley Novels, and it is not surprising that the section of her list which is headed "Historical Tales" should be a peculiarly well-chosen one. In this section the only book common both to her list and to the modern one is *The Prince and the Pauper.* She was convinced that a child should be given books and ideas beyond rather than below its comprehension; "a child's reach should exceed its grasp" might almost have been her motto. As well as some dozen of Scott's novels, her list of historical stories suitable for children's reading includes books by such authors as Bulwer Lytton, Harrison Ainsworth, Kingsley and G. P. R. James. With surprising perspicacity she even admits *John Inglesant,* a book which only the most enlightened would regard as suitable fare for the very young.

Miss Yonge knew very well that children can appreciate what they cannot understand. It is impossible to make a satisfactory book-list for children that does not include books written for grown-ups. The really serious weakness of the modern list lies in the fact that it includes only books specifically written for children, that is to say, books which grown-ups think suitable for children to read. But the children themselves prefer unsuitable books. They like to read about grown-ups rather than about their own contemporaries, a preference which is not altogether to be discouraged. As Miss Yonge remarked somewhat ungrammatically in another context, "people sometimes learn best from what does not profess to be about their own life." A list drawn up by a reasonably intelligent eleven-year-old would certainly include some such titles as *The Adventures of Sherlock Holmes, The Prisoner of Zenda, David Copperfield, The Thirty-nine Steps, Seal Morning* and *Jane Eyre*. Miss Yonge would have been the first to applaud such a selection. To quote the words of her own Ethel May, herself an omnivorous and very precocious reader, "One ought to know all good things with familiarity before one can understand, because understanding does not make you love."

Hans Christian Andersen

Horace E. Scudder[1]

As Overbeck and his school returned to the religious art which preceded the Renaissance, so Thorwaldsen, like Canova and lesser men, turned back to Greek art, and was working contemporaneously with Overbeck at Rome in a very different temper. To him the central figure of Christianity was not a child in its mother's arms, but a strong, thoughtful man; for childhood he turned to the sportive conception of Amor, which he embodied in a great variety of forms. The myth appealed, aside from the opportunity which it offered for the expression of sensuous beauty, to his northern love of fairyland. His countryman, Andersen, tells us how, when they were all seated in the dusk, Thorwaldsen would come from his work and beg for a fairy-tale.

It is Andersen himself who has made the most unique contribution not only to the literature which children read, but to that which is illustrative of childhood. He attained his eminence sheerly by the exhibition of a power which resulted from his information by the spirit of childhood. He was not only an interpreter of childhood; he was the first child who made a real contribution to literature. The work by which he is best known is nothing more nor less than an artistic creation of precisely the order which is common among children.

It is customary to speak of his best known short stories as fairy tales; wonder-stories is in some respects a more exact description, but the name has hardly a native sound. Andersen himself classed his stories under the two heads of *historier* and *eventyr;* the *historier* corresponds well enough with its English mate, being the history of human action, or, since it is a short history, the story; the *eventyr,* more nearly allied perhaps to the German *abenteuer* than to the English *adventure,* presumes an element of strangeness causing wonder, while it does not necessarily demand the machinery of the supernatural. When we speak of fairy tales, we have before our minds the existence, for artistic purposes, of a spiritual world peopled with beings that exercise themselves in human affairs, and are endowed in the main with human attributes, though possessed of certain ethereal advantages, and generally under orders from some superior power, often dimly understood as fate; the Italians, indeed, call the fairy *fata.* In a rough way we include under the title of fairies all the terrible and grotesque shapes as well, and this world of spiritual beings is made to consist of giants, ogres, brownies, pixies, nisses, gnomes, elves, and whatever other creatures have found in it

"Hans Christian Andersen," by Horace E. Scudder reprinted from *Atlantic Monthly,* 36 (November 1875): 203–234. Also in *Childhood in Literature and Art* by Horace E. Scudder (Boston: Houghton Mifflin Company, 1894), pp 201–216.

1. For biographical information about the author, see p. 21.

Hans Christian Andersen papercutting courtesy the Hans Christian Andersen Museum, Odense, Denmark.

a local habitation and name. The fairy itself is generally represented as very diminutive, the result, apparently, of an attempted compromise between the imagination and the senses, by which the existence of fairies for certain purposes is conceded on condition they shall be made so small that the senses may be excused from recognizing them.

The belief in fairies gave rise to the genuine fairy tale, which is now an acknowledged classic, and the gradual elimination of this belief from the civilized mind has been attended with some awkwardness. These creations of fancy—if we must so dismiss them—had secured a somewhat positive recognition in literature before it was finally discovered that they came out of the unseen and therefore could have no life. Once received into literature they could not well be ignored, but the understanding, which appears to serve as special police in such cases, now has orders to admit no new-comers unless they answer to one of three classes: either they must be direct descendants of the fairies of literature, having certain marks about them to indicate their parentage, or they must be teachers of morality thus disguised, or they may be mere masqueraders; one thing is certain, they must spring from no belief in fairy life, but be one and all referred to some sufficient cause,—a dream, a moral lesson, a chemical experiment. But it is found that literature has it own sympathies, not always compassed by the mere understanding, and the consequence is that the sham fairies in the sham fairy tales never really get into literature at all, but disappear in limbo; while every now and then a genuine fairy, born of a genuine, poetic belief, secures a place in spite of the vigilance of the guard.

Perhaps nothing has done more to vulgarize the fairy than its introduction upon the stage; the charm of the fairy tale is in its divorce from human experience; the charm of the stage is in its realization, in miniature, of human life. If the frog is heard to speak, if the dog is turned before one's eyes into a prince, by having cold water dashed over it, the charm of the fairy tale has fled, and in its place we have only the perplexing pleasure of legerdemain. The effect of producing these scenes upon the stage is to bring them one step nearer to sensuous reality, and one step further from imaginative reality; and since the real life of fairy is in the imagination, a wrong is committed when it is dragged from its shadowy hiding-place and made to turn into ashes under the calcium light of the understanding.

By a tacit agreement fairy tales have come to be consigned to the nursery; the old tools of superstition have become the child's toys, and when a writer comes forward, now, bringing new fairy tales, it is almost always with an apology, not for trespassing upon ground already occupied, but for indulging in what is no longer belief, but make-belief. "My story," he is apt to say, "is not true; we none of us believe it, and I shall give you good evidence before I am done that least of all do I believe it. I shall probably explain it by referring it to a strange dream, or shall justify it by the excellent lesson it is to teach. I adopt the fairy form as suited to the imagination of children; it is a childish thing, and I am half ashamed, as a grown person, to be found engaged in such nonsense." Out of this way of regarding fairy tales has come that peculiar monstrosity of the times, the scientific fairy tale, which is nothing short of an insult to a whole race of innocent beings. It may be accepted as a foregone conclusion that with a disbelief in fairies the genuine fairy tale has died, and that it is better to content ourselves with those stories which sprang from actual belief, telling them over to successive generations of children, than to seek to extend the literature by any ingenuity of modern skepticism. There they are, the fairy tales without authorship, as imperishable as nursery ditties; scholarly collections of them may be made, but they will have their true preservation, not as specimens in a museum of literary curiosities, but as children's toys. Like the sleeping princess in the wood, the fairy tale may be hedged about with bristling notes and thickets of commentaries, but the child will pass straight to the beauty, and awaken for his own delight the old charmed life.

It is worth noting, then, that just when historical criticism, under the impulse of the Grimms, was ordering and accounting for these fragile creations,—a sure mark that they were ceasing to exist as living forms in literature,—Hans Christian Andersen should have come forward as master in a new order of stories, which may be regarded as the true literary successor to the old order of fairy tales, answering the demands of a spirit which rejects the pale ghost of the scientific or moral or jocular or pedantic fairy tale. Andersen, indeed, has invented fairy tales purely such, and has given form and enduring substance to traditional stories current in Scandinavia; but it is not upon such work that his real fame rests, and it is certain that while he will be mentioned in the biographical dictionaries as the writer of novels, poems, romances, dramas, sketches of travel, and an autobiography, he will be known and read as the author of certain short stories, of which the charm at first glance seems to be in the sudden discovery of life and humor in what are ordinarily regarded as inanimate objects, or what are somewhat compassionately called dumb animals. When we have read and studied the stories further, and perceived their ingenuity and wit and humane philosophy, we can after all give no better account of their charm than just this, that they disclose the possible or fancied parallel to human life carried on by what our senses tell us has no life, or our reason assures us has no rational power.

The life which Andersen sets before us is in fact a dramatic representation upon an imaginary stage, with puppets that are not pulled by strings, but have their own muscular and nervous economy. The life which he displays is not a travesty of human life, it is human life repeated in miniature under conditions which give a charming and unexpected variety. By some transmigration, souls have passed into tin-soldiers, balls, tops, beetles, money-pigs, coins, shoes, leap-frogs, matches, and even such attenuated individualities as darning-needles; and when, informing these apparently dead or stupid bodies, they begin to make manifestations, it is always in perfect consistency with the ordinary conditions of the bodies they occupy, though the several objects become by this endowment of souls suddenly expanded in their capacity. Perhaps in nothing is Andersen's delicacy of artistic feeling better shown than in the manner in which he deals with his animated creations when they are brought into direct relations with human beings. The absurdity which the bald understanding perceives is dexterously suppressed by a reduction of all the factors to one common term. For example, in his story of The Leap-Frog, he tells how a flea, a grasshopper and a leap-frog once wanted to see which could jump highest, and invited the whole world "and everybody else besides who chose to come," to see the performance. The king promised to give his daughter to the one who jumped the highest, for it was stale fun when there was no prize to jump for. The flea and the grasshopper came forward in turn and put in their claims; the leap-frog also appeared, but was silent. The flea jumped so high that nobody could see where he went to, so they all asserted that he had not jumped at all; the grasshopper jumped in the king's face, and was set down as an ill-mannered thing; the leap-frog, after reflection, leaped into the lap of the princess, and thereupon the king said, "There is nothing above my daughter; therefore to bound up to her is the highest jump that can be made: but for this, one must possess understanding, and the leap-frog has shown that he has understanding. He is brave and intellectual." "And so," the story declares, "he won the princess." The barren absurdity of a leap-frog marrying a princess is perhaps the first thing that strikes the impartial reader of this abstract, and there is very likely something offensive to him in the notion; but in the story itself this absurdity is so delightfully veiled by the succession of happy turns in the characterization of the three jumpers, as well as of the old king, the house-dog, and the old councilor "who had had three orders given him to make him hold his tongue," that the final impression upon the mind is that of a harmonizing of all the characters, and the king, princess, and councilor can scarcely be distinguished in kind from the flea, grasshopper, leap-frog, and house-dog. After that, the marriage of the leap-frog and princess is quite a matter of course.

The use of speaking animals in story was no discovery of Andersen's, and yet in the distinction between his wonder-story and the well-known fable lies an explanation of the charm which attaches to his work. The end of every fable is *hæc fabula docet,* and it was for this palpable end that the fable was created. The lion, the fox, the mouse, the dog, are in a very limited way true to the accepted nature of the animals which they represent, and their intercourse with each other is governed by the ordinary rules of animal life, but the actions and words are distinctly illustrative of some morality. The fable is an animated proverb. The animals are made to act and speak in accordance with some intended lesson, and have this for the reason of their being. The lesson is first; the characters, created afterward, are, for purposes of the teacher, disguised as animals; very little of the animal appears, but very much of the lesson. The art which invented the fable was a modest handmaid to morality. In Andersen's stories, however, the spring is not in the didactic but in the imaginative. He sees the beetle in the imperial stable stretching out his thin legs to be shod with golden shoes like the emperor's favorite horse, and the personality of the beetle determines the movement of the story throughout; egotism, pride at being proud, jealousy, and unbounded self-conceit are the furniture of this beetle's soul, and his adventures one by one disclose his character. Is there a lesson in all this? Precisely as there is a lesson in any picture of human life where the same traits are sketched. The beetle, after all his adventures, some of them ignominious but none expelling his self-conceit, finds himself again in the emperor's stable, having solved the problem why the emperor's horse had golden shoes. "They were given to the horse on my account," he says, and adds, "the world is not so bad after all, but one must know how to take things as they come." There is in this and other of Andersen's stories a singular shrewdness, as of a very keen observer of life, singular because at first blush the author seems to be a sentimentalist. The satires, like The Emperor's New Clothes and The Swiftest Runners, mark this characteristic of shrewd observation very cleverly. Perhaps, after all, we are stating most simply the distinction between his story and the fable when we say that humor is a prominent element in the one and absent in the other; and to say that there is humor is to say that there is real life.

It is frequently said that Andersen's stories accomplish their purpose of amusing children by being childish, yet it is impossible for a mature person to read them without detecting repeatedly the marks of experience. There is a subtle undercurrent of wisdom that has nothing to do with childishness, and the child who is entertained returns to the same story afterward to find a deeper significance than it was possible for him to apprehend at the first reading. The forms and the incident are in consonance with childish experience, but the spirit which moves through the story comes from a mind that has seen and felt the analogue of the story in some broader or coarser form. The story of The Ugly Duckling is an inimitable presentation of Andersen's own tearful and finally triumphant life; yet no child who reads the story has its sympathy for a moment withdrawn from the duckling and transferred to a human being. Andersen's nice sense of artistic limitations saves him from making the older thought obtrude itself upon the notice of children, and his power of placing himself at the same angle of vision with children is remarkably shown in one instance, where, in Little Klaus and Big Klaus, death is treated as a mere incident in the story, a surprise but not a terror.

The naïveté which is so conspicuous an element in Andersen's stories was an expression of his own singularly artless nature. He was a child all his life; his was a condition of almost arrested development. He was obedient to the demands of his spiritual nature, and these led him into a fresh field of fancy and imagination. What separates him and gives him a distinct place in literature is, as I have said, that he was the first child who had contributed to literature. His very autobiography discloses at every turn this controlling genius of childhood, and the testimony of his friends confirms it.

Now that Andersen has told his stories, it seems an easy thing to do, and we have plenty of stories written for children that attempt the same thing, sometimes also with moderate success; for Andersen's discovery was after all but the simple application to literature of a faculty which has always been exercised. The likeness that things inanimate have to things animate is constantly forced upon us; it remained for Andersen to pursue the comparison further, and, letting types loose from their antitypes, to give them independent existence. The result has been a surprise in literature and a genuine addition to literary forms. It is possible to follow in his steps, now that he has shown us the way, but it is no less evident that the success which he attained was due not merely to his happy discovery of a latent property, but to the nice feeling and strict obedience to laws of art with which he made use of his discovery. Andersen's genius enabled him to see the soul in a darning-needle, and he perceived also the limitations of the life he was to portray, so that while he was often on the edge of absurdity he did not lose his balance. Especially is it to be noted that these stories, which we regard as giving an opportunity for invention when the series of old-fashioned fairy tales had been closed, show clearly the coming in of that temper in novel-writing which is eager to describe things as they are. Within the narrow limits of his miniature story, Andersen moves us by the same impulse as the modern novelist who depends for his material upon what he has actually seen and heard, and for his inspiration upon the power to penetrate the heart of things; so that the old fairy tale finds its successor in this new realistic wonder-story, just as the old romance gives place to the new novel. In both, as in the corresponding development of poetry and painting, is found a deeper sense of life and a finer perception of the intrinsic value of common forms.

This, then, may be taken as the peculiar contribution of Andersen: that he, appearing at a time when childhood had been laid open to view as a real and indestructible part of human life, was the interpreter to the world of that creative power which is significant of childhood. The child spoke through him, and disclosed some secrets of life; childhood in men heard the speech, and recognized it as an echo of their own half-forgotten voices. The literature of this kind which he produced has become a distinct and new form. It already has its imitations, and people are said to write in the vein of Andersen. Such work, and Andersen's in particular, presents itself to us under two aspects: as literature in which conceptions of childhood are embodied, and as literature which feeds and stimulates the imagination of children. But this is precisely the way in which a large body of current literature must be regarded.

Lewis Carroll

Walter John de la Mare

Peculiarly well suited to analyze the earlier poet and creator of make-believe, Walter de la Mare (1873–1956) pictures how it was that "the child" showed so clearly "the father-to-be of the man" who could write Alice. *He examines also "the division" between Dodgson and Carroll, "these two strange collaborators," and Carroll's phenomenal ability to establish "rational poise in a topsy-turvy world." Among de la Mare's works long enjoyed by children are* Songs of Childhood *(1902),* Peacock Pie *(1913),* Broomsticks and Other Tales *(1925),* Animal Stories *(1940), and* Bells and Grass *(1941).*

The following article appears with a biographical section on Carroll omitted.[1]

Every century, indeed every decade of it, flaunts its own little extravagances and aberrations from a reasonable human standard. Passing fashions in dress and furniture, in plays, music and pictures, and even in ideas and sentiments, resemble not only the caprices of our island climate, but also the extremes made manifest in English character, both of which in spite of such excesses yet remain true to a more or less happy medium. And so too with literature.

The Victorian age was rich in these exotics. It amuses us moderns, having dried and discoloured them, to make little herbariums of them. We may even be on easier terms with the great writer of the Eighties if, for symbol, he wears whiskers, though less so perhaps with feminine dignity trailing a crinolette. But there is one Victorian wild flower which makes any such condescension absurd—and it is called Nonsense. Unlike other "sports" of its time, this laughing heart's-ease, this indefinable "cross" between humour, fantasy and a sweet unreasonableness, has proved to be a hardy habit and is still living and fragrant. And we discover it suddenly in full bloom under the very noses of Martin Tupper and Samuel Smiles. . . .

But even M. Emile Cammaerts in his *Poetry of Nonsense*—a little book as rich in appreciation and interest as it is original in theme—has been able to cite very few specimens of true Nonsense of a date prior to the Nineteenth Century. And the practice of the art seems to be as clearly localised in space as it is in time. The French word *non-sens* has not this particular *nua*nce and the German *un-sinn* is in meaning, I gather, to madness nearer allied.

Its acknowledged masters in English literature were two in number. Two years after the appearance in 1810 of Jane Taylor's *Hymns for Infant Minds* Edward Lear came into the world. He was followed eighteen years later, and two years after the death of Charles Lamb, by Charles Lutwidge

"Lewis Carroll—A Biography" by Walter de la Mare from *Fortnightly Review*, 132 (September 1, 1930): 319–321, 325–331. Reprinted by permission of Contemporary Review Co. Ltd.

1. See also Roger Lancelyn Green, *Lewis Carroll* (London: The Bodley Head, 1960; New York: Henry Z. Walck, Inc., 1962); Leonard Clark, *Walter de la Mare* (London: The Bodley Head, 1960; New York: Henry Z. Walck, Inc., 1961); and *Horn Book Magazine, A Walter de la Mare Issue* (1957).

Dodgson, who having latinised his Charles and transmogrified his Lutwidge, was destined at last to be known, and beloved, all the world over by
his pen-name Lewis Carroll.

Lear's first *Book of Nonsense* was published in 1846, a year after the death
not only of the author of *The Ingoldsby Legends* but also of Thomas Hood, a
poet who because, perhaps, he was also a punster, has not even yet had his
due. *The Rose and the Ring* followed in 1855. Hood, like Lear and
Thackeray, could fit pictures to his rhymes as amusing as themselves, but
Lear was an artist by profession. He contributed the handsome plates to one
of the earliest of the lavishly illustrated English books about birds; and it is
as appropriate that its title should have so alluring a flavour as *The Family of
the Psittacidae* as that the first published pamphlet in which Dodgson
collaborated with his *alter ego* should have been called *The New Method of
Evaluation as Applied to II.*

Lear left this world—much the poorer by his absence—in 1888; four
years after Calverley. Lewis Carroll, the veritable pied piper, having visited
"valleys wild" on his way from Hamelin, vanished from its ken in the
Eighties, while Dodgson himself lived on until a year after Queen Victoria's
second Jubilee.

The rich sheaves of pure Nonsense had by then been garnered. While
The Hunting of the Snark was of 1876 and Prince Uggug had edged into being
at Hatfield to amuse Princess Alice in 1872, by 1889, when *Sylvie and Bruno*
was published, another order of nonsense was in flower. *The Green
Carnation* and *The Yellow Book* are symptomatic of a very different and a
wholly adult species. Satire and parody in themselves are mortal enemies of
true Nonsense; and though such sallies as "On an occasion of this kind it
becomes more than a moral duty to speak one's mind. It becomes a
pleasure"; or "A little sincerity is a dangerous thing, and a great deal of it is
absolutely fatal"; or "Punctuality is the thief of time"—though pleasantries
of this nature may faintly echo (and may even have been inspired by)
Humpty Dumpty, Oscar Wilde would not perhaps have greeted the kinship
with a cheer, and Humpty Dumpty, quite apart from his setting, conversed
in a far less worldly English.

As compared with wit, too, Nonsense, in M. Cammaerts' metaphor, is
what bubble is to needle, though wit itself is powerless to prick the bubble.
Twinkling on in its intense inane, it is as far out of the reach of the
ultracommonsensical, the immitigably adult and the really superior as are
the morning stars. That flat complacent veto—"This is nonsense!" (in the
cast-iron sense of the word), while intended as a sentence of death, means
little more than "We are not amused."

But what *is* this Nonsense? How does it differ from the merry, the
comical, the frivolous, the absurd, the grotesque and mere balderdash?

In what does it consist?

> They hunted till darkness came on, but they found
>   Not a button, or feather, or mark,

> By which they could tell that they stood on the ground
>   Where the Baker had met with the Snark.

That unfortunately is the position. None the less a glance at *Alice in Wonderland* with its bright full moon of Nonsense for lantern, may help to enlighten it a little. . . .

There is a well-known story to the effect that Queen Victoria, captivated by *Alice in Wonderland*, sent for the rest of its author's works, and was thereupon presented with copies of *The Condensation of Determinants*, and *A Syllabus of Plane Algebraical Geometry*. Dodgson himself in one of his books denied that there was any truth in it. It is none the less remarkable that the author of a book so remote from the realm of phantasy as *Leaves from a Journal of our Life in the Highlands* could and did share her delight in *Wonderland* with the youngest of her subjects. But here is precisely its supreme achievement. It is, in the words of Sir Walter Besant, one of the very few books in the world "which can be read with equal pleasure by old and young. . . . It is the only child's book of nonsense that is never childish." And not only that: it admits us into a state of being which until it was written was not only unexplored but undiscovered. Nevertheless like other rare achievements it was the fruit apparently of a happy accident. For once in a while the time and the place and the loved one came together.

On the afternoon of July 4th, 1862, in the Long Vacation, a minute expedition set out from Oxford up the river to Godstow. It returned laden with a treasure compared with which that of the *Golden Hind* was but dross. It consisted of Canon Duckworth, then a tutor at Christ Church and the "duck" in the story itself, of Dodgson, and the three little Liddells, whom Dodgson had nicknamed Prima, Secunda and Tertia. They were, each in her own degree, members of a happy band of children who were the delight and solace of Carroll's long years at Christ Church. A few of them remained his intimate friends. But in general they reigned in turn as briefly as the Aprils that have followed one another throughout the centuries. He collected them wherever he had the good fortune to find them, especially, so it seems, at the sea-side and in railway trains. It is related that, bound for the beach, he would leave his lodgings at Eastbourne armed not only with puzzles but with a supply of large safety pins, in case any little girl intent on paddling should be in need of one. Unlike most other dons, he provided not cakes or goodies for their entertainment in his "large, lofty and extremely cheerful-looking study," where he insisted on keeping all his furniture and carpets in precise alignment, but a musical box, toys and an old Woolly Bear, not to mention home-made devices for lighting his gas and for boiling his kettle. In London he took them to plays and pantomimes, and blessed any small actresses who shone behind the footlights with a like generosity and kindness. However brief the reign of these (occasionally fractious) little princesses, he was faithfully fickle to one and all of them—each in turn. Not so with small boys. Bruno may be a compound of imp, elf and infant Samuel, but for small boys in general

Dodgson and even Carroll professed an aversion "almost amounting to terror". But then, as Mrs. Meynell has pointed out, small boys in Art have never been neglected. It was Carroll's prerogative "to make great amends to little girls".

Of the three children who accompanied him to Godstow that afternoon, it was Secunda—Alice Pleasance Liddell—"courteous, trustful, wildly curious . . . loving as a dog and gentle as a fawn", who was destined as "Alice" to be immortal. She was the mistress jewel in his carcanet. They paddled on; Duckworth was stroke of the "pair", Dodgson bow, and *Alice's Adventures Underground* were told, on and on, over stroke's shoulder to Secunda who, with her sisters, and robes in lap, sat at the tiller. "Yes," the skipper agreed, on the question being put to him, "I am inventing as we go along." Carroll was then thirty, Blake being two years older when *Songs of Innocence* was published.

Now afternoons in July, if fair and cloudless, are apt to be narcotic. The rhythm of sculling quiets the mind and sets the workaday wits drowsing. The low secret chuckle of the water, the lovely light on its surface, rimpling up into those three rapt little faces, would have decoyed any imagination into activity. And Carroll's voice flowed gently on to the accompaniment of the clucking of the river, the dipping swallows and the faint stir of the wind in the branches at the water side.

It was at Duckworth's suggestion that he laboured on into the small hours that evening, pen and paper for company and midnight oil for illumination. "His memory was so good," said his friend, "that I think the story as he wrote it down was almost word by word the same as he had told it in the boat." The *MS.* was bestowed on the Deanery, and here Henry Kingsley chanced on it. Why should such a treasure remain hidden under a bushel? He urged Mrs. Liddell to persuade its author to publish it, and suggested Tenniel as illustrator. *Alice's Hour in Elfland* having been discarded as a title, it appeared exactly three years afterwards, and in spite of its temporary withdrawal from circulation owing to the poor reproduction of its pictures, it instantly captivated the sedate Victorians and has never since suffered the faintest eclipse.

There are variants of this account. But what they all have in common is evidence that the tale, rhymes and all, and "finished" to the finest edge of craftsmanship, seems for the most part to have floated into Carroll's mind as spontaneously as did one of the best lines in English verse: "For the Snark was a Boojum, you see." "Every word of the dialogue," he said, "came of itself." And though he confesses elsewhere that his "jaded muse was" at times "goaded into action . . . more because she had to say something than because she had something to say", and that he despatched Alice down the rabbit hole not knowing in the least what was to become of her; and though, whenever the crystal wellspring ceased to flow, he could always pretend to fall fast asleep (whereas of course he had actually come wide awake)—all this little affects the marvel, and is interesting mainly because Dodgson in *Sylvie and Bruno* expressed his contempt for any writing that was chiefly the result of taking pains. He maintained that all such writing cannot but remain unimpassioned and uninspired.

What, then, of the scorned delights, and the laborious days; what of the loading of every rift with ore; and that midnight oil in the study of Christ Church? Are these the sighs of a Dodgson weeping over a lost Carroll? Or was it merely that, with advancing age, he himself, like most elderly writers, when recalling the light that shone upon their youthful achievements and the dews that dropped on them from heaven, forgot the care, the patience and the pains? Yet another marvel is that *Wonderland* should have been followed by so consummate a sequel as *Through the Looking-Glass*. They are twin stars on whose *relative* radiance alone literary astronomers may be left to disagree.

Both stories have a structural framework—in the one playing cards, in the other a game of chess, the moves in which Dodgson afterwards punctiliously justified. These no doubt suggested a few of his chief characters, or rather their social status; but what other tale-teller could have made Carroll's use of them? All that he owed to the device of the *Looking-Glass,* except that it is one which has perplexed and delighted child, philosopher and savage alike, is that the handwriting in the story is the wrong way round, and that when Alice wished to go forwards she had to walk backwards—a method of progression that is sometimes of service even in life itself. Both stories, too—and this is a more questionable contrivance, particularly as it introduces a rather sententious elder sister—turn out to be dreams; and one little girl I know of burst out crying when the awakening came. . . .

It is, however, their rational poise in a topsy-turvy world (a world seen upside-down, as M. Cammaerts says, and looking far more healthy and bright), that gives the two tales their exquisite balance. For though laws there certainly are in the realm of Nonsense, they are all of them unwritten laws. Its subjects obey them unaware of any restrictions. Anything may happen there except only what can't happen *there.* Its kings and queens are kings and queens for precisely the same reason that the Mock Turtle is a Mock Turtle, even though once he was a real Turtle—by a divine right, that is, on which there is no need to insist. A man there, whether he be Tweedledum or the Carpenter or the White Knight, apart from his being a gentleman so perfect that you do not notice it, is never "a man for a' that," simply because there isn't any "a' that". And though "morals" pepper their pages—"Everything's got a moral if only you can find it"—the stories themselves have none. "In fact," as Carroll said himself, "they do not teach anything at all".

Instead, they stealthily instil into us a unique state of mind. Their jam—wild strawberry—*is* the powder—virgin gold-dust—though we may never be conscious of its cathartic effects. Although too Carroll's Nonsense, in itself, in Dryden's words, may be such that it "never can be *understood*", there is no need to understand it. It is self-evident. Besides, haven't we, like the Red Queen herself, heard other kinds of nonsense, and in very sober spheres, "compared with which *this* would be as sensible as a dictionary"? It lightens our beings like sunshine, like that divine rainbow in the skies beneath which the living things of the world went out into radiance and freedom from the narrow darkness of the Ark.

And what, for example, even from a strictly conventional point of view, is unusual, unpractical, amiss in the Duchess's kitchen. She is gracing it with her presence, and these are democratic times; she is nursing a baby, and *Noblesse oblige;* and the kitchen is full of smoke, which Victorian kitchens often were. What do we expect in a kitchen? A cook, a fire, a cat, and a cauldron with soup in it. It is precisely what we get—and, to give it flavour, someone has been a little free with the pepper. The cook, it is true, is throwing frying-pans and saucepans at her mistress, but nowadays there's many a lady in the land who would forgive the fusillade if only she could secure the cook. As for the Duchess's remarks, they are as appropriate as they are peremptory. And do we not expect the high-born to be a little high-handed. Alice enquires why her cat grins like that.

"It's a Cheshire cat," she says, "and that's why."

Alice smiled that she didn't know cats *could* grin.

"They all can," said the Duchess, "and most of them do."

Alice didn't know of any that did.

"You don't know much," said the Duchess, "and that's a fact."

So far, so practical. But it must not be forgotten that this "large kitchen" into which nine-inch Alice had so unceremoniously intruded belonged to a little house in a wood only about four feet high, nor that the Duchess's grunting infant as soon as it breathes the open air in Alice's arms turns placidly into a small pig. And that, except metaphorically, children don't do. Not in real life, that is. Only in *dreams.*

And it is here that we stumble on *the* sovereign element in the *Alices.* It consists in the presentation of what is often perfectly rational, practical, logical, and, maybe, mathematical, what is terse, abrupt and pointed, in a state and under conditions of life to which we most of us win admittance only when we are blessedly asleep. To every man his own dreams, to every man his own day-dreams. And as with sense, nonsense and un-sense; as with me, you and a sort of us-ishness; as with past, future and the all-and-almost-nothing in between; so with Greenwich time, time and *dream* time; good motives, bad motives, and dream motives; self, better self and dream self. Dreaming is another state of being, with laws as stringent *and* as elastic as those of the world of Nonsense. And what dream in literature has more blissfully refreshed a prose-ridden world than the dream which gently welled into Dodgson's mind that summer afternoon, nearly seventy years ago, when, oars in hand and eyes fixed on little Alice Liddell's round-orbed countenance, the Lewis Carroll in him slipped into Wonderland.

Who can say what influences one silent consciousness may have upon another? May it not be to some magical suffusion and blending of these two, the mathematician's and the child's, that we owe the *Alices?* Even the technical triumph of the two books consists in having made what is finally

declared to be a dream actually and always *seem* to be a dream. Open either
of them at random; ask yourself any one of the questions on the page
exposed; endeavour to find an answer not merely as apt and pungent as are
most answers of the *Alice* order, but one that will at the same time fret by
not so much as a hair's breadth the story's dream-like crystalline tissue: and
then turn back to the book for *Carroll's* answer. That alone, though a trivial
one, will be proof enough of the quality of Carroll's genius.

And what of the visionary light, the colour, the scenery; that wonderful
sea-scape, for example, in *The Walrus and the Carpenter,* as wide as Milton's
in *Il Penseroso*—the quality of its sea, its sands, its spaces and distances?
What of the exquisite transition from one setting on to another in a serene
seductive discontinuity in—for but one example—the chapter entitled
"Wool and Water"?

As for the relation between the world of our dreams and the world of our
actual, our modern oneirocritics have their science, but the lover of the
Alices is in no need of it. What relation any such dream-world has to some
other state of being seen only in glimpses here and now may be a more
valuable but is an even less answerable question. In any case, and even
though there are other delights in them which only many years' experience
of life can fully reveal, it is the child that is left in us who tastes the sweetest
honey and laves its imagination in the clearest waters to be found in the
Alices.

How the books fare in translation I cannot say. It would be insular, in any
case, since their nonsense is solely their own, to flatter ourselves overmuch
that it is not only English of the English but how strangely verdant a
Victorian oasis amid such quantities of sand! May that nonsense in all its
varieties continue to blossom like the almond tree, for the oaks of the forest
will flourish none the less bravely in its floral company. Indeed there are
times and crises in affairs not only personal, but public, political and even
international, when the following tribute from M. Cammaerts may first
serve for a solace and then for a solemn warning:

> The English, he says, speak, in an off-hand way, of "possessing a
> Sense of Humour" or of not possessing it, little realising that this
> sense, with the meaning they attach to it, is almost unique in the
> world, and can be acquired only after years of strenuous and
> patient effort. For many foreigners, Einstein's theories present
> fewer difficulties than certain limericks. . . .

Than certain limericks! We can at need, that is, while still we keep the mint,
dole out these precious coppers whensoever the too too intellectual alien
becomes a little too superior; while for our own precious island currency we
can treasure the gold of the crystal-watered land of Havillah—Carroll's and
the *Alices'*. And if at any time we ourselves need an unfaltering and
unflattering looking-glass, which is not unseldom, there is always the
Cheshire Cat.

Views and Reviews on Louisa May Alcott

The Nation

Miss Alcott's literary success seems to be very like that achieved by her favorite, "Jo," in this pleasant little story. She has not endangered her popularity by any excessive refinement, nor by too hard a struggle after ideal excellence in her work. Her book is just such a hearty, unaffected, and "genial" description of family life as will appeal to the majority of average readers, and is as certain to attain a kind of success which is apt enough fatally to endanger its author's pretensions to do better work in future. Meantime, "Little Women" is entertaining reading, and, as far as its moral lesson goes, may safely be put into the hands of young people, and will be likely, too, to give their elders a certain pleasure.

. . .

It is sometimes affirmed by the observant foreigner, on visiting these shores, and indeed by the venturesome native, when experience has given him the power of invidious comparison, that American children are without a certain charm usually possessed by the youngsters of the Old World. The little girls are apt to be pert and shrill, the little boys to be aggressive and knowing; both the girls and boys are accused of lacking, or of having lost, the sweet, shy bloom of ideal infancy. If this is so, the philosophic mind desires to know the reason of it, and when in the course of its enquiry the philosophic mind encounters the tales of Miss Alcott, we think it will feel a momentary impulse to cry Eureka! Miss Alcott is the novelist of children—the Thackeray, the Trollope, of the nursery and the school-room. She deals with the social questions of the child-world, and, like Thackeray and Trollope, she is a satirist. She is extremely clever, and, we believe, vastly popular with infant readers. In this, her latest volume,[1] she gives us an account of a little girl named Rose, who has seven boisterous boy-cousins, several grotesque aunts, and a big burly uncle, an honest seaman, addicted to riding atilt at the shams of life. He finds his little niece encompassed with a great many of these, and Miss Alcott's tale is chiefly devoted to relating how he plucked them successively away. We find it hard to describe our impression of it without appearing to do injustice to the author's motives. It is evidently written in very good faith, but it strikes us as a very ill-chosen sort of entertainment to set before children. It is unfortunate not only in its details, but in its general tone, in the constant ring of the style. The smart satirical tone is the last one in the world to be used in describing to children their elders and betters and the social mysteries that surround them. Miss Alcott seems to have a private understanding with the youngsters she depicts, at the expense of their pastors and masters; and her idea of

First review reprinted from *The Nation*, 8 (May 20, 1869): 400. Second review, attributed to Henry James, reprinted from *The Nation*, 21 (October 14, 1875): 250–251.

1. *Eight Cousins.*

friendliness to the infant generation seems to be, at the same time, to initiate them into the humorous view of them taken by their elders when the children are out of the room. In this last point Miss Alcott does not perhaps go so far as some of her fellow-chroniclers of the nursery (in whom the tendency may be called nothing less than depraved), but she goes too far, in our opinion, for childish simplicity or parental equanimity. All this is both poor entertainment and poor instruction. What children want is the objective, as the philosophers say; it is good for them to feel that the people and things around them that appeal to their respect are beautiful and powerful specimens of what they seem to be. Miss Alcott's heroine is evidently a very subjective little girl, and certainly her history will deepen the subjective tendency in the little girls who read it. She "observes in a pensive tone" that her health is considered bad. She charms her uncle by telling him, when he intimates that she may be vain, that "she don't think she is repulsive." She is sure, when she has left the room, that people are talking about her; when her birthday arrives she "feels delicate about mentioning it." Her conversation is salted with the feminine humor of the period. When she falls from her horse, she announces that "her feelings are hurt, but her bones are all safe." She certainly reads the magazines, and perhaps even writes for them. Her uncle Alec, with his crusade against the conventionalities, is like a young lady's hero of the "Rochester" school astray in the nursery. When he comes to see his niece he descends from her room by the waterspout; why not by a rope-ladder at once? When her aunts give her medicine, he surreptitiously replaces the pills with pellets of brown-bread, and Miss Alcott winks at the juvenile reader at the thought of how the aunts are being humbugged. Very likely many children are overdosed; but this is a poor matter to tell children stories about. When the little girl makes a long, pert, snubbing speech to one of her aunts, who has been enquiring into her studies, and this poor lady has been driven from the room, he is so tickled by what would be vulgarly called her "cheek" that he dances a polka with her in jubilation. This episode has quite spoiled, for our fancy, both the uncle and the niece. What have become of the "Rollo" books of our infancy and the delightful "Franconia" tales? If they are out of print, we strongly urge that they be republished, as an antidote to this unhappy amalgam of the novel and the story-book. These charming tales had, relatively speaking, an almost Homeric simplicity and "objectivity." The aunts in "Rollo" were all wise and comfortable, and the nephews and nieces were never put under the necessity of teaching them their place. The child-world was not a world of questions, but of things, and though the things were common and accessible to all children, they seemed to have the glow of fairy-land upon them. But in "Eight Cousins" there is no glow and no fairies; it is all prose, and to our sense rather vulgar prose.

A Masterpiece, and Dreadful

Brigid Brophy

An English novelist, essayist, playwright, and critic, Brigid Brophy is a witty and lucid writer. She has been accused by some reviewers of an excessive allegiance to Freudian psychology and of overdocumentation in her nonfiction, but her fiction is generally considered to be exquisitely and tautly written. She is a regular contributor to the New Statesman, *the* Sunday Times, *and* London Magazine, *but has little faith in the ultimate effectiveness of any formal criticism, feeling that the public is determined to believe that critics are frenzied destruction-maniacs. Perhaps to confirm that opinion, Miss Brophy, her husband (Michael Levey), and a friend (Charles Osborne) collaborated to "blast" fifty classics in* Fifty Works of English and American Literature We Could Do Without *(1967). Among her novels are* Flesh *(1962),* The Finishing Touch *(1963), and* The Snow Ball *(1964).*

Who's afraid of Louisa M. Alcott? Well, Louisa M. Alcott, for one; and for another, me.

I'm afraid of her in a quite straightforward way—because she makes me cry. Being myself an almost wholly unsentimental writer, I'm not a bit afraid of her example, which doesn't tempt me. It's not as a writer but as a reader that I fear her.

Her own fear of herself was, however, more ambiguous. She is, I suppose, of all writers, the one whose name *means* sentimentality; and yet sentimentality is what she and her characters most dread. Indeed, the very reason why Josephine March preferred to be known as Jo (and I would guess the nickname was the final simple stroke which turned her into one of the classic characters of popular-cum-nursery culture, up there with Sherlock Holmes and Little Miss Muffet) is that she found the name Josephine "so sentimental."

I was driven back to Louisa M. Alcott, whom I hadn't read since I was 14, by the revival on B.B.C. television of the old film of "Little Women." The film brought back enough memory of the text for me to think that it was sticking fairly *reverently* to Alcott situations and dialogue—which I soon afterwards confirmed by getting hold of the book or, rather, books; the film is in fact taken from "Little Women" and "Good Wives."

Having re-read them, dried my eyes and blown my nose (it is itself a sentimentality that this less dignified aspect of weeping is so seldom mentioned: one day I shall go through the fiction in the public library and to every "His eyes filled" add "so did his nose"), I resolved that the only honorable course was to come out into the open and admit that the dreadful books are masterpieces. I do it, however, with some bad temper and hundreds of reservations.

For, of course, to admit sentimentality at all is to play with fire. Sentimentality is always doing something of which art can stand only very small and controlled amounts—bursting out of the conventions of art and making a direct appeal (all art makes an oblique one) to real life. Sentimentality is always playing on your experience of real drowned kittens and real lost mothers—or, worse still, playing on your real dread of losing kittens or mothers. The weepiest of trashy movies is the one which throws in a moment or two of genuine newsreel. And then, having invoked the morality of the real world, sentimentality does the one thing neither morality nor art can stand for—it is hypocritical.

The true artistic impulse is, largely, cruel—or at least relentless. To bring a novel, for instance, to a climax, the artist must drive the situation, and probably the characters, to extremes. He harries his *donnée* until it falls apart and its logical structure is pitifully exposed. The sentimentalist, on the other hand, is a non-artist who won't take the responsibility of being ruthless. He won't drive his situations to the point of artistic inevitability. Instead, he appears to hold his hand in compunction. He resigns himself— much too soon—to the will of God; but covertly he is manipulating the will of God to suit what he is too hypocritical to admit is really his own taste.

Hundreds of fictional infants were, so to speak, raped on their deathbeds by Victorian anecdotalists—both novelists and painters—in order to pro- cure for author and audience the pleasure of destroying an innocence, but in such a way that the pleasure could pass for the quite innocent, the even creditable, enjoyment of feeling a spasm cross the eyelids. Even now one cannot stand quite indifferent beside those deathbeds. I think Oscar Wilde said that no man of feeling could read the death of Little Nell without laughing. But the unwitty and much more terrible truth is that no one can read it without crying. Dickens has made the illegitimate appeal to real life and no matter what ludicrous nonsense he makes of the death of Little Nell, the death of children *is* sad.

The sentimentalist always breaks the rules of art and frequently those of morality. The most unforgivable of all the occasions when sentimentality has burst through the artistic conventions is the one when Peter Pan bursts through the proscenium and invites the audience to keep Tinker Bell alive by affirming that they believe in fairies. That the audience consists of children is the ultimate sentimental immorality.

When Theseus calls the lovers' account of what took place in that wood near Athens "antique fables" and "fairy toys," Hippolyta objects that their story "More witnesseth than fancy's images, And grows to something of great constancy." So it does: to a fairy tale genuinely imagined (and therefore genuinely and poetically moving), which is to be believed utterly—but strictly in the realm of the imagination. But Peter Pan's telling the audience that Tinker Bell "thinks she could get well again if children believed in fairies . . . If you believe, clap your hands!" is moral torture inflicted by a wanton—but highly skilled—sentimentalist. Ours is a paradoxical society which dreads that one of its children might come on the charming, sentimentality-free little tale "Fanny Hill" and yet for decades put on "Peter Pan" at the very times of day and year when it was most likely to be seen by children. (Unless our winter holiday in fact celebrates not Christmas but the Slaughter of the Innocents?)

Not that I am supporting censorship, even for "Peter Pan," though if I could see any sense in censorship at all, "Peter Pan" would be my first and probably only candidate. I just think we ought to treat "Peter Pan" as a play for adults, as we already sensibly do its runners-up as sentimental masterpieces for the theater, "Private Lives" and "Who's Afraid of Virginia Woolf?"

It would certainly be unkind to deprive adults of "Peter Pan," because as a piece of craftsmanship it is perhaps the most highly skilled job in the repertory, and is therefore capable of giving pleasure to two groups which more usually fail to agree on anything. For, incongruously enough, it is on works of literary craftsmanship that highbrow and lowbrow can often meet. Really, of course, they are at cross purposes. The lowbrow cares nothing for technique as technique, and probably doesn't even notice it as such. All he wants is a good read at or a good cry over a good story; and he wants to have that without subjecting himself to the subversive effect—whether of society or of individual emotions—which is inherent in all good works of art. The highbrow, on the other hand, studies technique in order to pick up tips, which he intends to put to use in better appreciating or even better practising the subversiveness of art. But though they are at cross purposes and the lowbrow wouldn't approve of the highbrow's purpose if he knew of it, both highbrow and lowbrow (the two cultures which we are really divided into) are glad, through simple good will, of any meeting place. They could go further and find worse rendez-vous than Louisa M. Alcott.

You can measure Alcott's technical skill by asking any professional novelist how he would care to have to differentiate the characters of four adolescent girls—particularly if he were confined to a domestic setting, more-or-less naturalism and the things which were mentionable when Alcott wrote. Greater scope in at least the first and last of these departments has not prevented more than one recent novel from making a hash of almost the identical technical problem. Alcott, of course, triumphed at it (that is why we have heard of her), incidentally turning out for one of her four, Meg, a brilliant portrait of the sort of girl whose character consists in having no character. Girls of this sort are the commonest to meet in life and the rarest in literature, because they are so hard to depict (the problem is a variant of the old one about depicting a bore without being boring).

Whereas Meg was a commonplace of Alcott's own—or any—time, in Amy she actually showed sociological prescience. Or rather, I think, it showed despite her. Try as she would to prettify and moralize, she could not help making Amy the prototype of a model which did not become numerous in the United States until the 20th century—the peroxided girl-doll golddigger. Of course, it's Amy who gets Laurie in the end (he's rich, isn't he?); she's had "Good pull-in for Laurie" emblazoned on her chest from the moment it began to bud.

With Beth, I admit, Alcott went altogether too far. Beth's patience, humility and gentle sunniness are a quite monstrous imposition on the rest of the family—especially when you consider at what close, even cramped quarters they live (two bedrooms to four girls); no one in the household could escape the blight of feeling unworthy which was imposed by Beth. I concur in the judgment of the person with whom I watched the film (and who wept even more than I did) in naming her Black Beth. (I also concur in his naming Marmee Smarmee.) I think Louisa Alcott may herself have had an inkling that in designing a fate for Beth she was inspired by revenge. She seems, perhaps through suspicion of her own motives, to have faltered, with the result that she committed the sort of blunder only a very naive technician would fall into and only a very self-assured one could, as she does, step out of in her stride. She brings Beth to the point of dying in "Little Women," and then lets her recover; whereupon, instead of washing her hands—as not ruthless enough to do it—of the whole enterprise, she whips the situation up again in "Good Wives" and this time does ("As Beth had hoped, 'the tide went out easily' ") kill her off.

As for Laurie: well, of course Laurie is awful, tossing those awful curls; yet though I will go to my death (may the tide go out easily) denying that Laurie has a millionth part of the attractions he thinks he has and the girls think he has, I cannot deny that he is lifelike. If you want to see the romanticized implausibility which even an intelligent woman of the world (and great novelist into the bargain) could make of a curly-haired young man, look at George Eliot's Will Ladislaw.   Laurie by contrast is—if awful—probable.

In the most important event affecting Laurie, the fact that Jo refuses him, Alcott goes beyond verisimilitude and almost into artistic honesty. No doubt she found the courage for this, which meant cutting across the cliché-lines of the popular novel and defying her readers' match-making hopes, in the personality of Jo. Jo is one of the most blatantly autobiographical yet most fairly treated heroines in print. All that stands between her and Emma Woodhouse is her creator's lack of intellect. Alcott is not up to devising situations which analyze and develop, as distinct from merely illustrating her characters.

And, in fact, absence of intellectual content is the mark of the sentimental genre; conversely, it is because of her intellect that Jane Austen is never sentimental. I think, incidentally, that the word "sentimental" may have been in bad repute with Louisa Alcott because in 1868 it still wore 18th-century dress. And the reason, of course, why the 18th-century sentimental mode, unlike the 19th-century one, no longer works on us is that the 18th-century was so double-dyed intellectual that it couldn't put aside intellect when it took out its handkerchief; its many attempts to be affectingly simple were made self-conscious and absurd by its (perfectly correct) suspicion that it was being a simpleton.

As sentimentalists go, Louisa M. Alcott is of the gentler and less immoral sort. Beth's is the only really lushed-over death (the canary who dies in Chapter XI of "Little Women" is virtually a throw-away); on the whole, Alcott prefers to wreak her revenges on her characters by making them unhappy in their moments of happiness. (They make it easy for her to do so, through their own proneness to sentimentality.) Even here, one can morally if not esthetically justify her. It's all, so to speak, between consenting adolescents. All four girls are quite masochists enough to enjoy what she does to them.

I rest on Louisa M. Alcott my plea—hedged about with provisos, reduced, indeed, to a mere strangled sob—that we should recognize that, though sentimentality mars art, craftsmanship in sentimentality is to be as legitimately enjoyed as in any of these genres (thrillers, pornography, ghost stories, yarns, science fiction—whichever way your taste lies) which, because they suppress some relevant strand in artistic logic, are a little less than literature. The spasm across the eyelids is not inherently more despicable than the *frisson* of the supernatural or the muted erotic thrill imparted by a brilliant sado-erotic literary craftsman like Raymond Chandler. It is, however, more dangerous. One should take to heart this stray little fable by Kierkegaard (whose personality is, indeed, to be taken to heart in all contexts): "In itself, salmon is a great delicacy; but too much of it is harmful, since it taxes the digestion. At one time when a very large catch of salmon had been brought to Hamburg, the police ordered that a householder should give his servants only one meal a week of salmon. One could wish for a similar police order against sentimentality."

Puppet's Progress: Pinocchio

Martha Bacon

A New England author of fiction for young people, Martha Bacon has written Puritan Promenade *(1964),* Sophia Scrooby Preserved *(1968), and* The Third Road *(1971). Jill Paton Walsh, in a review in the* New Statesman, *says of the second: "There is no trace of the heavy-footed, socially aware agony of the 20th century contemplating the sufferings of the oppressed; instead there is the 18th century's casual blend of tenderness and brutality, with an ever present and elegant wit."*[1]

Pinocchio is ninety years old this year, going strong and showing no hint of age. His nose still changes, of course, with every reading of the story that has charmed millions of children and many of their elders. Here is a birthday salute to the hardy splinter, to his creator, Carlo Collodi, and to the rest of that breed of men and women who write stories that, unlike the children they are written for, do not grow old.

What manner of man—or woman—sits down and deliberately writes a book for children? One would suppose that he or she would have had some first-hand experience with youngsters, coupled with a keen sense of what is suitable, pleasant, and instructive. But three of the greatest writers for children, whose contribution stands unquestioned, were all eccentric bachelors.

If we study the lives of Hans Andersen, Lewis Carroll, and Carlo Collodi, we find it impossible to picture them as fathers, or even baby-sitters. Hans Andersen was a wandering minstrel of a man, a gawky, sensitive crybaby, scarcely to be trusted to cross a street alone. Lewis Carroll was an intense neurotic, obsessed with night fears, a nervous stutterer, who had difficulty sustaining the most ordinary adult relationships. Carlo Collodi, the author of *Pinocchio*, was a school dropout, a knock-about journalist, hack playwright, odd-jobber on the fringes of literature, possibly the father of an illegitimate child but too scatterbrained apparently even to have been sure about this. At all events he eschewed marriage and legal heirs, finding fulfillment late in life in his dream child.

Yet these writers produced great symbols of their times for their own age and for generations to come. They were men who seem to have made concessions to the world, rather than an adjustment to it. They evaded

"Puppet's Progress: Pinocchio" by Martha Bacon from *Atlantic Monthly*, 225 (April 1970): 88–90, 92. Copyright © 1970 by The Atlantic Monthly Company, Boston, Mass. Reprinted by permission of The Atlantic Monthly and the author.

1. *New Statesman*, 81 (June 4, 1971): 778.

everything but greatness. Andersen was scarred and shaped by Protestant Denmark in the same climate that brought forth Sören Kierkegaard in *Fear and Trembling*. The clammy fingers of Puseyism, the glow of the Victorian drawing room, and the cold wind of modern mathematics disfigured and disciplined Lewis Carroll. Collodi, a runaway seminarian, heard the call of Guiseppe Mazzini, found an obscure place in the annals of the Risorgimento, and hoped to write in the pedantic tradition of the previous century.

To write a great book for children—as opposed to an amusing, commendable, or useful book—evidently requires a volatile mixture of contradictions in the personality and a wide measure of irresponsibility. The foregoing is not to suggest that such people are not concerned with morality. But moral earnestness is skeletal to their work. They are priests in harlequinade, moralists in motley. Almost against their wills their sermons are entertainments. Collodi set out, at the urging of his publishers, to write a book for Italian children which should celebrate diligence, deplore idleness, and convey the idea that man is rationally happy only through work. He sought to caution the Italian child that pleasure-seeking leads to misery and a donkey's grave. He succeeded in writing a wry, elegant, comic, and wistful book, as universal as *Pilgrim's Progress*, which it resembles in structure, as Tuscan as a terraced vineyard and antic as the commedia dell'arte, which informs it.

Pinocchio was first published in 1880, but at the time of its appearance nothing like it had been seen in Italy, and the art of writing for children—considered as an art—was new by any standards. Although Voltaire was three years old when Perrault brought out his collection of tales in 1697 and presumably grew up with *Cinderella* and *Puss in Boots*, there was little in the Age of the Enlightenment to encourage flights of the imagination, especially in the young. The eighteenth century opened with a glimpse of fairy lands forlorn and closed with the undying fall of Blake's *Songs of Innocence*, but these peaks of joy and beauty were almost entirely surrounded by the wastes of pedagogy. The purpose of most eighteenth-century writers for children was propaganda, and to this end they harnessed meager talents to the tumbrels of solid use, discarding at a blow both fact and fancy in favor of reason and expediency.

Young people learned to be contented in the condition to which God had called them from the sublime Mrs. Hannah More. In the most appalling of all her appalling works, *The Shepherd of Salisbury Plain*, a family of heaven knows how many starving children cheerfully resign themselves to a diet of potatoes and water, while the author approves, for hundreds of pages, of both their situation and their behavior. Children learned from Maria Edgeworth to make wise choices and to prefer useful objects to gawdy ones. Young Rosamond foolishly spends her money on a beautiful purple jar instead of a pair of shoes, which she happens to need. When she arrives home with her trophy she discovers that it is not purple at all but merely seems so, having been filled with purple liquid. So poor Rosamond, a sadder, wiser, girl, finds herself with no shoes and a plain glass jar. As one wanders through these wastelands one scarcely wonders that throwing eggs at grownups in pillories was a popular recreation two-hundred-odd years ago.

In fairness to these people, we must admit that for all their sanctimonious mewling, their trash served as compost. And as one century slipped into another, people of genuine talent began to find a new form of art. From Denmark came a set of tales as luminous as a display of northern lights. The authors of countless tracts and moral tales lay buried, and the Snow Queen, Alice in Wonderland, and Pinocchio danced on their graves.

Pinocchio is as firmly rooted in Italian culture as Alice is in the English. He looks back to Dante and *Orlando Furioso,* forward to Pirandello and Federico Fellini. He is a descendant and an ancestor. He emerges from a log of wood and becomes a *"ragazzo per bene"* (a real boy). He faces death by fire, by hanging, and by drowning, and achieves at last the human condition, the unification of the flesh with the spirit. The consummation was no more than that which his author asked for his country.

Carlo Collodi was born Carlo Lorenzini in Florence in 1826, the son of a professional cook and a young woman who was lady's maid to the Marchesa Ginori Lisci. Young Carlo was bright and engaging, and the Ginori family was benevolent, and the Marchesa took pains to see that the attractive urchin should not waste his brio on the secular life. Carlo was clapped into the nearest available seminary, where by his own account he bedeviled the fathers until at the age of sixteen he went over the wall. Through this gesture the church lost a priest but the country acquired a journalist. Lorenzini remained a scribbler for the rest of his fairly long life, with intervals of soldiering in the first and second wars of independence. He wrote blood-and-thunder comedies, "mortal sins in five acts" as he called them, and served as theater censor for the provisional government of Tuscany in 1860.

Lorenzini took the name of Collodi from the Castello Collodi in Valdineme, a place which had caught his fancy. His affairs prospered in a mild way. He became an editor of the Tuscan dictionary, was rewarded for his services and made a knight of the Star of Italy. In the 1870s he came under the influence of Felice Paggi, a vigorous and imaginative man, one of the first people to see the possibilities of textbooks as an industry. He had published Italian versions of Perrault and Mme. D'Aulnoy, and he urged Collodi to turn his attention to children's books, a commodity in which Italy was notably lacking.

Collodi obliged his friend by writing the *Gianettino,* in imitation of the *Gianetto* of Paravicini. The *Gianettino* is of no more interest than its eighteenth-century prototype, and Collodi followed it with other negligible work, *Minnuzolo* and *Occhi e Nasi.*

But his work within the pedantic tradition served to show Collodi his mistakes. "The brighter the child," he observed, "the fewer adults it will question and the more it will try to find out for itself." He abandoned tedious explanations, ceased to imitate, and turned to a celebration of his

Italy, its virtues and its flaws, its landscape, festivals, poverty, people, and puppets, its laws and legends.

Collodi was fifty-four when he wrote the epic of the marionette. He had fought two campaigns against the Austrian domination, his mind had been formed by his association with the makers of Risorgimento, and he understood completely the implications of the new industrialism which would bring the young nation abreast of the modern world. *Pinocchio* is a children's story, but it is also a political comment, an interpretation of history, a document of man's search for his soul, and a sign of the shape of things to come.

As a children's story *Pinocchio* is quite matchless. The line is true as Giotto's, and the language is light as thistledown. The theme is probably the one which children most favor, the search by children for parents and by parents for children, a search which in this case ends in success and reunion. Like all good writers for children, Collodi lets his hero sin, suffer, and triumph strictly on his own recognizances and permits only minimal intrusion by the adult world. No book, to be sure, was ever harmed by a wicked uncle or Satan, but any gifted writer knows that adults or Olympians must be kept in their place—in the first chapter and the last.

Collodi manages his father figure beautifully. Gepetto, nicknamed Polendina because of his yellow wig—the color of cornmeal—appears a fully rounded character, crotchety, warmhearted, cynical, and selfless. He carves the puppet from a piece of wood, clothes him in scraps, and makes a little cap of bread dough for him. He embraces the marionette as a son and names him for a family of his acquaintance, Pinocchio: "Everyone in the family, Pinocchio father, Pinocchia mother, and Pinocchi all the sons and daughters: they all did well in life; the richest of them begged for a living." He pawns his jacket to buy his son an alphabet book, and the marionette, after passionate protestations of affection and promises of good behavior— he took to lying upon emerging from the log of wood from which he was carved—runs away in search of pleasure and excitement. He finds plenty of both, and we never encounter Gepetto again until Pinocchio discovers him inside the belly of the sea monster. By this time he has almost ceased to be a parent and is but a pathetic dotard, entirely dependent on the marionette. The reunion is partly effected now, but it is not complete until the final chapter when the magic change takes place. "Through labor and through hope" Gepetto renews his youth and finds himself the happy father, not of a puppet, but of a beautiful boy with chestnut curls and sparkling blue eyes—a boy of roses. To be a human child is to Pinocchio what the Celestial City is to Bunyan's Christian.

Like the damned as seen from heaven, the marionette lies, a discarded husk, in a corner, and the living father embraces the living son, while blessings rain upon the house. The fairy with azure hair who has watched over and disciplined Pinocchio, as Beatrice watched over and disciplined Dante, has shown herself not dead but a living presence, and in a most practical and Tuscan manner. She has paid back the forty soldi which Pinocchio earned for her during the course of his metamorphosis from puppet to person.

As a political allegory *Pinocchio* makes an unequivocal statement. Collodi believed that two imperatives must govern the mind and spirit of Italy: the republican idea and the necessity for sacrifice and work. Mazzini himself never wrote a more commanding call to republican sentiment than the opening sentences of *The Adventures of Pinocchio:*

> Once upon a time there was—
> A king! my little readers will say at once.
> No, boys and girls. You are wrong. Once upon a
> time there was a piece of wood.

Nowhere in *Pinocchio* do we find the traditional nobility of the fairy tale. The story is about the common people of Italy, the cobblers and carpenters, the puppeteers and circus touts, the fishermen and farmers, the dogs and donkeys, the cats and crickets, the fishes of the Mediterranean, and the leaden-eyed boys who slouch at street corners to prey upon and corrupt the unwary. The book rings with the salty speech of Tuscany, and its characters live with its sardonic proverbs.

The only "personage" in the book is the fairy with azure hair, the enchanted being who has lived many thousands of years in the neighborhood of Pinocchio's adventures, and she is not a mortal maiden. Even she does not maintain at all times an exalted station in life, although she occasionally resides in a castle. She is served by a veritable zoo of queer animals, snails, jackdaws, rabbits, and she is at home in the humble guise of a peasant girl, her beautiful, blue locks neatly plaited, and once she takes the form of a little blue goat. The only official to intrude on the narrative is a judge, and he is an ape who in a fit of legal logic condemns Pinocchio to prison for having been robbed by the fox and the cat. He subsequently refuses to let the marionette out of prison on the grounds that only criminals can be released under the duke's decree of amnesty and Pinocchio is innocent of any crime.

In Collodi's book the highest level to which the human spirit may rise is humanity itself. The transcendent flaw in this spirit, as Collodi saw it, was pleasure-seeking. Pleasure is not happiness and pleasure is the business of puppets, but the business of men and of the Risorgimento was work, and it is through work alone that puppets become men.

"Open a school," cried Collodi, "and you will close a prison."

The foregoing describes the political atmosphere of Collodi's book, but if allegorical interest were its only merit it would have long been relegated to the remaindered list. *Pinocchio* is more than a puritan sermon by a conscientious patriot. It is a fragment of the commedia dell'arte. And for all that he reforms, ceases his lies and his follies, and learns wisdom and thrift, Pinocchio is Harlequin.

"Harlequin," says Professor Allardyce Nicholl, "exists in a mental world wherein concepts of morality have no being and yet despite such absence of morality, he displays no viciousness." The description fits Collodi's hero to his wooden fingertips. Harlequin haunts Italy and occurs like Buddha from time to time in one incarnation or another, and Pinocchio is one of them.

Who is Harlequin? Some say that he is the spirit of the night, Hellequin, cousin to the devil, but time has robbed him of his satanic qualities. He is one of the foremost characters to animate the commedia dell'arte. The commedia dell'arte is, we are told, dead. Even in Italy the theater is a written thing which actors study and then recite. They are no longer required to create the play which they perform, and yet it appears that the Italian theater has never quite forgotten its merry and irresponsible infancy. The titles of many of Luigi Pirandello's plays wistfully recall it: *Tonight We Improvise, Six Characters in Search of an Author, Right You Are If You Think You Are, As You Desire Me* bear witness to the influence of the theater of the cathedral square and the back alley. It is apparent also in the improvisations which occur in many recent Italian films, and the film art indeed owes some of its vocabulary to the commedia. The word scenario originally described a rough outline of the plot upon which a group of actors would improvise.

A vivid artistry was lavished on the commedia, and from records kept by individual actors we can learn something of its voice. It bears some resemblance to aria and recitative in opera, but it keeps the rhythm of common speech, the short sentence, and the quick riposte. It is with this voice that Pinocchio speaks:

"Good morning. Master Antonio, what do you do on the floor?"
"I am teaching the ants their alphabet."
"Good for you."
"What has brought you to me, Father Gepetto?"
"My legs. You must know that I've come to ask a favor."

It pours forth without benefit of intellect and is saved by brio, by dancing, tumbling, handstands, and snatches of music. Like Harlequin, Pinocchio never thinks before he speaks. He hasn't time. The book gives the effect of improvising itself. Pinocchio is a commedia character to the end of his long nose, which grows alarmingly whenever he starts to deal in falsehoods. His nose and the indestructible cricket are his conscience, and he can never escape them.

When Collodi wrote *Pinocchio* he was determined that no mention of religion should be made in the text. He was devout, and like Lewis Carroll he had a morbid dread of anything approaching irreverence. There should be no allusion to the Deity or to the Mother of God or her Son. But how remarkable is Mary, Star of the Sea, especially in Italy? Every Italian child wakes and sleeps, plays and works under the veil of the Madonna. With her magnificent hood of azure hair she sanctifies Pinocchio in the role of the fairy. She mothers him, nurses him when he is ill, rescues him from assassins, and punishes him as a wise and just mother punishes. She teaches patience, fortitude, and resignation, and rewards him in the end with her fragrant but invisible presence in his apotheosis. She is the great lady, the Madonna Coronata in her castle and the peasant Madonna of the hill towns. She is the suffering Madonna, full of animal grief, who stands on the rock when Pinocchio is engorged by the great fish. She is the blue and worshiped Italian sky.

When Federico Fellini made his remarkable film *La Dolce Vita*, he could not, whether or not he intended to, escape Collodi's story. He preaches the same sermon and makes use of both the devices and the symbols which inform Collodi's work. The film begins with the puppet Christ carried over the rooftops of Rome and continues as a polemic delivered against idleness, lies, corruption, both sexual and spiritual, and above all pleasure for pleasure's sake. Marcello, the hero, is a Harlequin, open-handed, irresponsible, changeless, a puppet whose strings are pulled by fear and lust. He is an undutiful son, a faithless lover, a gull, the prey of any fox or cat who can catch him. He is not evil, and he is aware of what a man ought to be but lacks the will to be one himself. We see Marcello in the final sequence of the film, about to be engulfed by the sea monster of sensation, a dead, single-eyed, and shapeless thing. Marcello sees but he cannot hear the *fanciulla,* the young girl, Paolina, who is desperately and vainly trying to recall him to her side.

It is "the sweet life," Fellini tells us, which could destroy the republic, not crime, but acedia, the deadly sin of sloth. This is the rot which besets Harlequin, Pinocchio, Marcello. In Fellini's film, Steiner, the musician, sees it and kills himself and his children rather than submit to it.

Harlequin, Child of the Sistine Chapel, Pinocchio stands at the center of Italy, "the terrible puppet of her dreams," a character forever "in search of an author."

At 75, Heidi Still Skips Along

Elizabeth Enright

Beginning her career as an illustrator, Elizabeth Enright (1909–1968) has written much-praised short stories for adults as well as a wide range of beloved children's books, illustrated by herself. Among the latter are Thimble Summer *(1938), which won the 1939 Newbery Medal,* The Sea Is All Around *(1940), the family series beginning with* The Saturdays *(1941),* Gone-Away Lake *(1957) and* Return to Gone-Away *(1961),* Fantasies, Tatsinda *(1963), and* Zeee *(1965).*

One reason I loved Heidi as a child was because I felt that I had a proprietary interest in her. My mother, Maginel Wright Enright, had illustrated one of the editions of her story and I, though older than Heidi and younger than her friend Clara, had posed for both of them in her drawings. This was not unusual; I was the household model and posed for everything, sometimes as a boy, once even as a dog. I must have been more of a trial than a convenience, whining, itching, twitching and making things difficult generally, but when the picture was finished and printed in a real book I often felt a certain proud identity with the character portrayed, and this was particularly true of Heidi, whom I admired. I read her story over and over, and I was only one of thousands who did the same (though *they* had never had a share in her creation, as I had), and who do so to this day.

That small girl, whom we all first met scrambling up the mountain path at the heels of her impatient aunt, is 75 years old this year; and since she shows none of the usual signs of aging and fading she may reasonably be considered an immortal. Her story has been read in many languages and countless copies—sales in this country alone have been in the millions. Her name is almost a household word.

Still, of her author, Johanna Spyri, little is known. She was born Johanna Heusser in Hirzel, near Zurich, on July 12, 1827. Her father was the village doctor and her mother a poet. There were six brothers and sisters and two young cousins in that house. Their childhood was a happy one, with many trips to the high village of Maienfeld where they played by brooks in upland pastures and lunched at the herdsman's hut.

Johanna married Bernhard Spyri, the town clerk of Zurich. Her stories were first told to her little boy and were later sold to earn money to help the refugees who poured into Switzerland during the Franco-Prussian war. "Heidi" was published in 1880, under the alarming title of: "Heidis

"At 75, Heidi Still Skips Along" by Elizabeth Enright from *The New York Times Book Review*, pt. 2, v. 59 (November 13, 1955): 42. © 1955 by The New York Times Company. Reprinted by permission.

Lehr-und Wanderjahre: eine Geschichte fuer Kinder und auch fuer Solche welche die Kinder lieb haben." It was first translated into English in 1884 and was immediately successful. The sequels, "Heidi Grows Up," and "Heidi's Children," were never as popular and are now forgotten; but the original Heidi, the dark-haired girl who wore all the clothes she owned to save her aunt the bother of carrying them, is just as vigorous and as interesting to children today as she was to their grandparents.

Why is it? In an era when so much children's literature was burdened with dead dialogue and moral content, the freshness of this story must have come as a breath of mountain air; today, Heidi holds her own with carefree heroines of any of the best modern children's books because she is real. Through all the grind and clatter of awkward translations her character continues to ring true. She is good-natured and sensible, never dull. Escaping from the aunt, she intelligently takes off her dresses, shoes and stockings (knitted); and in her petticoat, barefooted, hops nimbly up the rocks with Peter the goatherd and his flock. And Peter is real, so are the goats.

The author (who died in 1901) did not escape some of the literary conventions of her day. In the fiction of that period one of the principal characters always had to be an invalid (a few years earlier one of the principal characters, preferably a child, always had to die), somebody else had to be rich, and another, or others, had to be very poor. All these requirements were filled in "Heidi"; but the invalid, fortunately, gets well and walks on her own two feet; the rich people spend their money wisely by giving everybody presents, and the poor are suitably benefited and grateful. And over and above the action of the characters tower those other mighty characters, the mountains, with their fiery snowfields and high pastures all jeweled with rock-roses and gentians. For a child who has never seen it, a new land is created: high, airy, exciting. His inward ear can hear that world of bells and brooks; his imagination's eye can scan the deeps or see the eagle in the air.

Reading about Heidi and Peter eating their lunch on the mountainside is enough to make anybody hungry, and many a child has developed a sudden taste for cheese after reading this book. And then what could be cozier to think about, to imagine oneself in, than that little bed of hay under the eaves? There Heidi and the reader look through the round window at a thousand stars, just as if, as Clara says, one "were driving in a high carriage straight into the sky." One can hear the great soft roaring of the wind in the old fir trees by the hut. . . .

As a child, I remember, I never felt uncomfortable about the Alm-Uncle. He seemed to me too forbidding and austere, and I did not really like him after his conversion to kindliness. I seem to have missed the point that he had been a gay blade in his youth, loving wine and high-living, squandering his money and at last retiring to the Alm-hut, stung by the criticism of his neighbors, to live a life of solitary misanthropy. I suppose, being a child, that I viewed such reckless behavior by an adult as pure wickedness, whereas now I can look on his derelictions with a tolerant eye. I used to feel that Fraulein Rottenmeier, the governess-housekeeper, was entirely evil; now I see that she was a humorless fool with an unhealthy passion for authority. Perhaps she was the daughter of a Prussian officer. Who knows?

About Heidi I had no misapprehension. I recognized her as a girl like myself: better, more sensible and generous, praying oftener (much oftener), but nevertheless a real child whom I would have liked for a companion, and whose marvelous playground I wished had been my own.

After her marriage Johanna Spyri lived for many years in Zurich, but she never lost her longing for the mountain valleys with their bells and birds, and probably it is just this quality, this longing to relive, by describing, the brightest morning-moments of childhood, that gives the story its share of authentic power. Reading it we can almost know what it was like to see the snowfields catching fire, or hear the night wind combing through the firs.

The Early Record

Elizabeth Nesbitt

Long associated with the Carnegie Library in Pittsburgh (as children's librarian, director of its famous storytelling program, head of the library's work with children, and teacher in the Carnegie Library School), Elizabeth Nesbitt is also well known for her numerous publications,[1] including part three of A Critical History of Children's Literature *and a monograph on Howard Pyle. She presents in "The Early Record"[2] a summing up of the first "golden age" of children's literature.*

When the Carnegie Library of Pittsburgh opened in 1895, the idea of library service to children was gaining recognition as an essential part of total library service to the community. During the years between 1895 and 1900, work with children was established as a vigorous and vital part of public library development in the United States.

The history of the development of this phase of library work and of the pioneer librarians who so competently carried on the development is in itself a fascinating study. Of equal interest is the realization that these librarians, who did so much to make children's work the "classic success of the public library,"[3] as it was later to be called, would have been helpless had they not had available the essential tool of their profession, a body of books for children which fully deserved the title of literature.

The shelves of the children's rooms which were opened in public libraries from coast to coast in the last five years of the nineteenth century contained books which were to be proven immortal. In the first two decades of the twentieth century, so many more books of permanent beauty and significance were written for children that this period has been called the first golden age[4] of children's literature.

Such a phenomenon in literary history does not occur without cause, and the cause of the phenomenon is as important as are the results. In 1865,

---

"The Early Record" by Elizabeth Nesbitt from *Horn Book Magazine,* 47 (June 1971): 268–274. Reprinted by permission of Horn Book, Inc.

1. See her Anne Carroll Moore Lecture, "Book Selection: Its Perplexities and Pleasures," in *The Contents of the Basket, and Other Papers on Children's Books and Reading,* Frances Lander Spain, ed. (New York: New York Public Library, 1960); Cornelia Meigs, et al., *A Critical History of Children's Literature,* rev. ed. (New York: The Macmillan Company, 1969. London: Collier-Macmillan, 1970; and *Howard Pyle* (London: The Bodley Head; New York: Henry Z. Walck, Inc., 1966).

2. Talk delivered for the Seventy-fifth Anniversary of The Carnegie Library of Pittsburgh at its *Fall Festival of Children's Books,* October 30, 1970.

3. Robert D. Leigh, *The Public Library in the United States* (New York, Columbia University Press, 1950), p. 100.

4. Alice M. Jordan, *From Rollo to Tom Sawyer and Other Papers* (Boston, Horn Book, Inc., 1948), p. 146.

Alice's Adventures in Wonderland had been called a "spiritual volcano of children's books."[5] It definitely was a spiritual volcano, because it is a book written with no purpose other than that of giving pleasure and delight. As such, it marked the passing of the Age of Reason, which had dominated the literary scene in England and America. The Age of Reason had a particularly disastrous effect upon children's books, since in this field it took the form of thorough didacticism—so thorough as to become ridiculous and therefore unconvincing. On the positive side this passion for didacticism proved two things—that a book written with ulterior motives may be a good treatise, but never literature, and that the qualities of potentially good writers are rendered negative when didacticism is dominant. Nothing written for children during the didactic period was considered acceptable unless it taught a lesson. The chief criterion by which a book was judged was that of usefulness; unless it could be proven to be good for something, it was good for nothing. This obviously ruled out the qualities of imagination and wonder, which are nonutilitarian and therefore valueless. The human race is so constituted that when an idea or theory reaches a point of absurdity, a reaction sets in, and the pendulum swings, usually to the opposite extreme. The resulting revolt may be partly good or partly bad, or wholly good or wholly bad. In the case of children's books, the romantic revolution in literature produced books of memorable quality and variety.

What has been said is, of course, an oversimplification of the situation which led to the creation of so many children's books of lasting beauty and import and appeal. Integrated with the general rebellion against the excesses of the didactic era were several factors of importance: the realization that childhood is a way of life as well as an age of life; that a child is a being in his own right, and not a miniature adult; that as a child, he should not have the preoccupations of adults forced upon him, especially since to a child, most such preoccupations are unimportant and time wasting. And there was a long overdue recognition of the limitless value of the imagination and of the sense of wonder, which are the natural possessions of children until and unless they are atrophied by the unwise neglect or interference of adults. The appreciation of the beauty which can be brought to life by the creative imagination was sharpened by the growing interest in folk literature and in the modern fairy tale. *Grimm's Fairy Tales* had been translated and published in England between 1823 and 1826, and the stories of Hans Christian Andersen appeared in English translation in 1846.

The best of the books available to the children of the late 1800's resulted from these changing patterns of thought and from the fact that men and women of creative talent began to write for children, and to write with pride in giving their best. It is true that there were some books, like

5. F. J. Harvey Darton, *Children's Books in England: Five Centuries of Social Life* (Cambridge, Cambridge University Press, 1958), p. 267.

Kingsley's *The Water-Babies,* which had remnants of the Didactic Age clinging to them, but these were transition books, unable to completely abandon the old, but prophetic of the new in their qualities of imagination, of story telling, and of excellent writing. But there were also books wholly of the new era, such books as had never been written before: for example, *Alice in Wonderland,* with its unfettered imagination, its originality, its logical illogicalities which contribute in no small part to the supreme nonsensical quality of the book; the nonsense verse of Edward Lear, unsurpassed even now, for there is nothing so rare as nonsense which seems to make sense; George Macdonald's books, *The Princess and the Goblin, The Princess and Curdie, At the Back of the North Wind,* fairy tales with an unique quality of enchantment which lingers in the memory long after the details of the story have been forgotten. And there was Dinah Mulock Craik's *Adventures of a Brownie,* with its enticing combination of real children in the real world and a brownie from the folk world, as well as the fantasies of Mrs. Molesworth, notably *The Cuckoo Clock* and *The Tapestry Room.* In the latter, as Anne Thaxter Eaton has said in *A Critical History of Children's Literature,* the author expertly re-creates the strange, almost magic attraction which things have for children, things such as a cuckoo clock or a storied piece of tapestry. Authentic realism and a variety of theme and background were found in the tales of Mrs. Ewing, in *Heidi,* in *Hans Brinker, or the Silver Skates,* in *Little Women,* and in *The Adventures of Tom Sawyer.* Mark Twain's novel is a genuinely classic book, a story told by a master storyteller, with vividly portrayed characters that step living from the pages; the book has regional and period background drawn with a sure touch, humor of a quality all too rare, constant action and adventure. Stevenson's *Treasure Island* exemplified romance and adventure in their purest forms. There were retellings of myths and legends in Hawthorne's *The Wonder-Book and Tanglewood Tales,* Kingsley's *The Heroes,* and in Pyle's *The Merry Adventures of Robin Hood.* And there was the emergence of the true picture book in the work of Walter Crane, Kate Greenaway, and of Randolph Caldecott, the greatest of these three.

These books and others like them revealed that an original, creative mind is no less original and creative when it produces literature for children than it is when it produces literature for adults. They demonstrated that literature for children is not only a literature in itself, but that it belongs to and enhances the total literature of a country. What would English literature be without *Alice in Wonderland* or American literature without *Tom Sawyer?* They proved that an audience of children is a challenging, discriminating, and responsive audience, deserving of the best. They established the fact that to write a great book for children is to win lasting honor. Many writers for children have felt as Howard Pyle[6] did when he wrote:

---

6. Charles D. Abbott, *Howard Pyle; A Chronicle* (New York, Harper, 1925), p. 131.

My ambition in days gone by was to write a really notable adult book, but now I am glad that I have made literary friends of the children rather than the older folk. In one's mature years, one forgets the books that one reads, but the stories of childhood leave an indelible impression, and their author always has a niche in the temple of memory from which the image is never cast out to be thrown into the rubbish-heap of things that are outgrown and outlived.

We have become so accustomed to having at hand for the taking a large collection of children's books of true merit that it is difficult for us to realize the impact of these revelations of seventy-five years ago. A list of names of those who, in the early years of the twentieth century, were inspired by these earlier writers may be the best proof of the force of the impact: Howard Pyle (most of whose work was done after the turn of the century), Beatrix Potter, Kenneth Grahame, Rudyard Kipling, E. Nesbit, James Barrie, Walter de la Mare, William Henry Hudson, Leslie Brooke.

From such a galaxy of names, it is undoubtedly foolhardy to attempt to select one or more as preeminent. If the temptation to do so proves irresistible, a good case could be made for the choice of Howard Pyle and Beatrix Potter and Leslie Brooke.

Howard Pyle is deserving of special mention not only because of the versatility, the quality and the beauty of his writing and of his illustration, but also because of the influence his work had upon others of his own time and of the present. He was a man, an artist, a writer of the highest integrity, passionately devoted to the pursuit of excellence. His imaginative power was of a high order, and his sensitivity to beauty and to the significance of beauty enabled him to draw word pictures as vivid as are his illustrations— word pictures somehow underlined with a sense of mystery, of wonder, and of elusive meaning. The romanticist in him attuned him to the spirit of folk tale, legend, and the romances of chivalry. The realist in him imbued his realistic stories with authenticity of background and of detail, with vigor and vitality and action. And always he was a master storyteller. The variety and extent of his work is astounding. No less astounding is the consistent excellence of his writing and his illustration. After his death in 1911, it was said of him, "We shall not see his like again."

The selection of Beatrix Potter can be justified in so many ways. She is totally without the faults so easily incurred in writing for very small children. Her imaginative power, her creative talent are never diluted by the trivialities of shallow fancy, by mere inventiveness and ingenuity. But her greatest gift to children and to the world of literature is her demonstration that books for little children can be written in a pure and beautiful English style, and that they can be concerned, in their own miniature way, with the imperishable verities of life, with the humor and the pathos of living.

Leslie Brooke's picture books are in the great tradition established by

Randolph Caldecott. One of the aspects of the present-day production of children's books is the expansion of the picture book into a great variety of content and of form of illustration. But the standards of conception and execution set by Randolph Caldecott and Leslie Brooke have not been surpassed. Both Caldecott and Brooke possess the lovely quality of gentle and endearing humor, the faculty which allows the imagination to play with the content of the story or rhyme being illustrated, the mastery of the right kind and amount of detail, the ability to picture beauty in background and setting, and yet keep background and setting unobtrusive. These qualities are still the essential traits of a true picture book.

The selection of Howard Pyle, Beatrix Potter, and Leslie Brooke as pacemakers can be justified, but both the selection and the justification are underlined with trepidation. For the truth of the matter is that each of the writers of the late nineteenth and early twentieth centuries whose work brought literature for children to the attention of the world endowed that literature with singular gifts.

Kipling's compelling and unique stories, his command of English style, his sense of atmosphere and place, his feeling for drama; the wealth of beauty, of fun, of nonsense, of seriousness, the ever-changing style and mood of Grahame's *The Wind in the Willows;* E. Nesbit's blending of realism and fantasy, her fresh, unjaded invention, her gay humor, her delightful child characters and equally delightful supernatural characters; the whimsical charm of *Peter Pan;* the unearthly and elusive beauty of De la Mare's prose and poetry; the stern and awe-inspiring beauty of Hudson's *A Little Boy Lost*—all these have given to children's literature an inextinguishable splendor.

There were others who played no small part in the enrichment of books for children. Notable among these were the retellers of folk tales, of myths, of ballads and romances, of the magnificent epics and sagas of Greece, of Persia, of Ireland, and of Iceland. These retellers were men and women who knew and loved the original materials with which they worked, who had equal respect for the materials and for the children who would read their retellings, and who believed that children could be lifted to the level of greatness. As a result, they set standards of excellence in the difficult art of retelling folk literature. Their books not only opened the minds of children to an apprehension of great world literature, they also gave to the art of storytelling a richness of source materials which stimulated both storyteller and audience.

In the late 1800's, there was also apparent the beginning of an interest in children's books from countries other than England and America, manifested by translations into English of such books as *Heidi, The Wonderful Adventures of Nils,* and *The Adventures of Pinocchio.*

One evening in late summer, I was thinking about these writers. I wondered what I would name as their greatest gift, were I called upon to make such a decision. It had been a day of alternating storm and sunshine, with dark clouds wind-driven across the sky. At sunset, the clouds had gathered in the west. Between and behind the clouds, as the sun sank lower, the sky became a lake of gold, so dazzling that it was almost impossible to look at it with the naked eye. Across the slate gray of the clouds and across the brilliance of the sky flew great flocks of birds. The physical beauty of that sunset was stunning. Even more overpowering was the sense of something significant, some mysterious, intangible meaning behind the beauty of color and form. I thought of Howard Pyle's description of an astonishingly similar evening sky, that word picture of his which begins with the lovely phrase[7] "Now toward the slanting of the day. . . . " I remembered the extraordinarily vivid word pictures in *The Wind in the Willows* which capture not only the outward aspects of the changing seasons, but also the spirit, the essence, of each season. I recalled the strange, lovely quality of Selma Lagerlöf's description of the great crane dance; I felt again De la Mare's uncanny power to reveal that the beauty of this world is an indication of a greater, more infinite beauty. Sometime later, I watched on television the preview of a series of special programs (Kenneth Clark's "Civilisation") dealing with the history of Western civilization. This description and the title of the series give no indication of the exciting and inspiring nature of the contents of the programs, which are concerned with the achievements of man and which arouse in the viewer a feeling of awe and wonder as he perceives the greatness of which man is capable. In fairness, it should be added that the commentary by the British art-historian, Lord Kenneth Clark, and at the end of the preview, his summary of those things in which he believes, are in no small degree responsible for the sense of exhilaration conveyed by the program. About this time too, I began to reread a hoard of articles which had been clipped and kept because I had been impressed with what they had to say. As I read them one after the other, I discovered that, different though they might be in content and approach, ultimately they seemed to be asking the same question or sounding the same warning. One asks what will happen to a civilization if it loses its capacity to dream and to dance. Another says that once we were young enough to wonder and asks "what have we grown into?" Another, and it should be noted that this article is by a man versed in the field of science, warns that in our preoccupation with the cleaning up of our physical surroundings, we must not neglect the need to nourish the most precious resource we have, the human spirit. Still another points out that art, whether it be the art of nature, or art created by man, is the only thing that sustains faith in Humankind.

And so the singular beauty of that sunset, the memories of books read and loved, the television programs which revealed the heights to which man may rise, the concerns voiced by the writers of the articles—all these

---

7. Howard Pyle, *The Story of King Arthur and His Knights* (New York, Scribner, 1903), p. 83.

separate and very different experiences began to converge upon one point and finally brought me to one conclusion. In the past the best writers of children's books all had something to say and they said it surpassingly well. But they did more than this. They permitted children to dance and to dream, to laugh and to cry, to stand in awe before the miracles of nature and before the greatness of man, to be challenged by the mystery of human destiny. In short, they protected and nourished the capacity for wonder inherent in children. This is their greatest gift, the most sustaining bequest any age can bestow upon its children.

A Second Golden Age?
In a Time of Flood?

Virginia Haviland

Children's Book Specialist for the Library of Congress, teacher of children's literature, reviewer of children's books for the Horn Book Magazine, *Virginia Haviland is also author and editor of books, bibliographies, and articles on children's literature. Among her books are a series of national folk-tale collections from France, Germany, Japan, Czechoslovakia, Sweden, and Russia.[1] This article is based on a talk delivered for the Seventy-fifth Anniversary of The Carnegie Library of Pittsburgh at its Fall Festival of Children's Books, October 1970.*

Elizabeth Nesbitt has brilliantly defined the essential, durable qualities that distinguished the writers of genius who added so much to children's literature at the turn of the century. . . . It is now our concern to consider whether they have been matched in recent decades.

In 1965, concluding his evaluation of children's literature in his book, *Written for Children: An outline of English children's literature* (Lothrop), John Rowe Townsend, English critic-author, asserted that "The second golden age is now" (the first, as he stated, having been the half century before 1914). On publication, Mr. Townsend's assertion was immediately challenged. Five years later, I was glad to be able to ask him whether he still finds this to be a golden age.[2] He declared that he does and added that there are a greater number of good writers than ever before. "We have pulled up a lot in the last few years," he said. Similarly, for us to take sides in the controversy—to decide whether or not we have been enjoying a renaissance of greatness in a second golden age—we must look at achievements and trends during the decades since World War I, considering American, British, and translated works together.

It is natural, I think, to speculate on the reasons why certain kinds of books are published during any period and on the specific incentives operating during the period under consideration. We can see that in recent decades new external forces have strongly affected the *quantity* of children's books; we cannot say their *quality,* for creative work can go on without such incentives.

One external force was the allotment of federal moneys to schools and libraries which increased the already great institutional support of American

"A Second Golden Age? In a Time of Flood?" by Virginia Haviland from *Horn Book Magazine,* 47 (August 1971): 409–419. Reprinted by permission of Horn Book, Inc.

1. See, for example, *Favorite Fairy Tales Told in France,* illustrated by Roger Duvoisin and *Favorite Fairy Tales Told in Germany,* illustrated by Susanne Suba (Boston: Little, Brown and Company, 1959. London, The Bodley Head Ltd., 1967 and 1969).

2. In his introduction to *A Sense of Story,* Mr. Townsend refers (p. 10–11) to an English essayist on Philippa Pearce *(Use of English,* Spring 1970) who declared that "ours is the golden age of children's literature" and adds, "a view with which I agree, although the figure of speech grows wearisome. . . ."

children's book publishing. Also, new kinds of book promotion—Book and Library Weeks and festivals, prizes in increasing numbers and variety, and institutes and seminars for the study of children's literature—have publicized children's books and focused critical attention upon them. And internationalism has become a greater influence, nourished by new systems of communication and by the increased trend toward copublishing.

Social forces have, of course, affected the content and style of books. But neither commercial nor social pressures are responsible for most of our enduring books, the kind to which we feel future decades may look back to as belonging to a golden age. If we are to call these years "golden" for children's literature, it has to be because we find distinction in the creative works that came into existence in spite of pressures. We can, indeed, look to a solid core of luminaries, however much we seem surrounded by mass-produced mediocrity. (The first golden age had its mediocrities, too.)

In addition to literary facility and imagination, various forces have always operated to generate good writing for children. A basic one is the consuming urge to write in authors who have something they must say, and among such writers are those who turn from adult to children's literature when what they have to say is best said in children's literature. C. S. Lewis, who wrote for both adults and children, said in his essay "On Three Ways of Writing for Children," that he wrote for children because he found this the best art-form for saying what he wanted to say.

In her survey, Elizabeth Nesbitt included a number of all-around geniuses who wrote both for adults and children: Kipling, Macdonald, and Hawthorne, among others. To such a list of versatile, creatively independent authors, we can add more recent writers of fiction who have not limited their attention to an audience either of adults or of children. Among them have been Walter Edmonds, Rachel Field, and Esther Forbes; John Masefield and Carl Sandburg; Elizabeth Coatsworth, Elizabeth Enright, E. B. White, and Rumer Godden; Eilís Dillon and Paula Fox—all genuine writers, unaffected by pressures from without.

Another creative force which produces convincing and honest children's books is found in an identification with childhood, or, at least, in an instinctive understanding of children. The obvious identification with childhood that was so notable in the success of Hans Christian Andersen and Beatrix Potter is to be found, although with vastly different expression, in the writing of Laura Ingalls Wilder, Meindert DeJong, William Mayne, and Maurice Sendak.

And the critical attention given to American books in other countries could be a useful guide in searching for excellence. *Island of the Blue Dolphins* (Houghton) and *The Wheel on the School* (Harper) have won German prizes, as have our picture books, *The Happy Lion* (McGraw) and *Swimmy* (Pantheon). *The Story of Doctor Dolittle* (Lippincott) has won an Italian prize. And best of all, Meindert DeJong and Maurice Sendak[3] have

---

3. And, in 1972, Scott O'Dell.

won Hans Christian Andersen medals, while Elizabeth Coatsworth and
E. B. White were strong candidates in the years of their nomination for the
same honor.

A special supplement to a new educational publication from Cambridge,
England, entitled *Where,* has a series of pieces about leading authors by
well-known critics including Margery Fisher and Edward Blishen. These
sketches of modern giants direct attention first to E. B. White, Wanda Gág,
and Meindert DeJong, along with Philippa Pearce and Leon Garfield, and
then, in shorter pieces, to Laura Ingalls Wilder and Elizabeth Enright, along
with two Frenchmen—René Guillot and Paul Berna—and seven more
English writers: Alan Garner, C. S. Lewis, William Mayne, Mary Norton,
K. M. Peyton, Rosemary Sutcliff, and John Rowe Townsend. (To which I
would have felt compelled to add the names of Lucy Boston, P. L. Travers,
and Henry Treece.) Representing a variety of genres, these authors form an
immediately arresting combination.

American writers lag far behind the British in the writing of historical
fiction, but *Johnny Tremain* (Houghton) by Esther Forbes has indeed
traveled well, and we can claim Erik Haugaard (although he writes from his
home in Denmark). For us at least, it seems certain that Elizabeth George
Speare's *The Witch of Blackbird Pond* (Houghton), Irene Hunt's *Across Five Aprils*
(Follett), and Scott O'Dell's *Island of the Blue Dolphins* (Houghton) will live. But
consider the modern British contribution to historical fiction: Rosemary Sutcliff
deals with early Britain; Henry Treece, with prehistory and the Vikings; Hester
Burton and Ronald Welch, with later centuries; and Leon Garfield, Cynthia
Harnett, and K. M. Peyton, among many, write distinctive period stories.

However, most of all, it has been fantasies and editions of folklore that
have survived through generations of reading by the young. In a recent
richness of fantasy, England has by no means fallen behind the accomplishments of the first golden age that opened with Carroll, Kingsley, Lear, and
Macdonald, and continued with Kipling, Grahame, and E. Nesbit. Perhaps
because of their long heritage and love of folklore and poetry it is natural
that British writers should have developed a unique felicity in this genre.
Whether in the style of a quest, the creation of a whole new world, the use
of folk-tale motifs, or in fantasy about animals or space, English writers
have shown genius. Recent English writers of fantasy include Lucy Boston
and Rumer Godden, Philippa Pearce with her masterpiece *Tom's Midnight
Garden* (Lippincott), Alan Garner, and Pauline Clarke with her *The Return of
the Twelves* (Coward), following upon De la Mare, P. L. Travers, Mary Norton, C.
S. Lewis, and J. R. R. Tolkien. He who is acquainted with anything of children's
literature today knows *The Hobbit* (Houghton), *The Borrowers* (Harcourt), *Mary
Poppins* (Harcourt), and the Narnia books. Here is where we can shout "golden
age."

And we can include American writers, too, with E. B. White at the top of
the list; *Charlotte's Web* (Harper) is as moving a fantasy as there is. Mr.
White has again successfully combined naturalistic elements of animal life

with make-believe in his new *The Trumpet of the Swan* (Harper). Other long-loved animal fantasies must include Robert Lawson's *Rabbit Hill* (Viking) and Hugh Lofting's stories about Doctor Dolittle. We salute William Pène du Bois for highly original fantasies wholly unlike anything else, and we recognize the proven popularity of Madeleine L'Engle's *A Wrinkle in Time* (Farrar) and Lloyd Alexander's Prydain cycle beginning with *The Book of Three* (Holt). The last five authors mentioned are all Newbery Medal-winners, and Mr. White is a winner of the significant Laura Ingalls Wilder Medal for a lasting body of work. For wholehearted enjoyment, and critical acclaim as well, there are Edward Eager's *Half Magic* (Harcourt) and Beverly Cleary's *The Mouse and the Motorcycle* (Morrow), and their sequels. For older readers of fantasy, Jean Merrill has written a brilliant fable for our times, *The Pushcart War* (W. R. Scott). Altogether, a rich harvest.

Filling a special place in modern children's literature and contributing to an enduring body of work is science fiction. As Peter Dickinson, an Englishman writing for adults *and* young people, says, this genre has the "virtue of embodying abstract notions, allowing you to look beyond the everyday." Thus, in the imaginative, controlled writing of John Christopher, Andre Norton, Ben Bova, and a few others, one sees a highly creative handling of philosophical ideas and social problems. "Pollution," said Mr. Dickinson in an Exeter conference talk, "has been the current language of science fiction for twenty years."

In recent years, the use of myth and legend in the framework of fantasy has been striking. Alan Garner,[4] who won the Carnegie Medal and passionate admiration from discriminating readers young and old for his story *The Owl Service* (Walck), used as a springboard the Welsh myths which he found in *The Mabinogion*. He likes using mythology in his writing, he says, because "you find that over the millennia myth contains crystallized human experience and very powerful imagery. This imagery is useful for a writer if he uses it responsibly."

As creators of the shorter literary fantasies often borrowing from folklore, we have seen Hans Christian Andersen and Howard Pyle, Frank Stockton and Lawrence Houseman, followed by Eleanor Farjeon and Walter de la Mare, and in England today by Barbara Leonie Picard and Joan Aiken.

A fresh gathering and retelling of folk tales from all corners of the globe has provided us with a steady stream of volumes attractively presented for storytellers and child readers. Some of today's more distant gathering of tales has been done by Peace Corps workers, our contemporary counterparts of those nineteenth-century missionaries who gathered folklore. Other government workers and American residents abroad also have been gathering tales from local storytellers in Vietnam and in parts of Asia, as

---

4. See note 6, below.

well as in Africa. Harold Courlander's many collections from Africa, Indonesia, and the West Indies have been models of good storytelling and fully documented sources.

But without traveling to remote areas, literary retellers have contributed something important in rendering anew the familiar tales. On this side of the Atlantic we look to Wanda Gág for her telling of Grimm; to Olivia Coolidge for her dealing with the Greek and Norse myths; to Dorothy Hosford, who added to our living volumes of myth and saga from the Norse; to Joseph Gaer for his versions of Asian tales. In England today Rosemary Sutcliff and the poet Ian Serrailier are giving new shape to legendary tales of the British Isles. Recently, a number of full-length books have extended the stories of individual mythical heroes, reworking the inherited literature as Eleanor Farjeon and Padraic Colum did in extending the Cinderella story and as opera, ballet, and other art-forms have done.

It is in picture-book form, however, that we have had a phenomenal modern use of the folk tale, though the picture-book folk tale, of course, is not a new idea. Randolph Caldecott and Leslie Brooke provided irresistible picture-book treatments of traditional material that will endlessly enrich our literature for small children. But to name modern artists who have notably contributed to this veritable flood of picture books with their conceptions of traditional tales and rhymes is to recite the roster of many distinguished modern illustrators: Felix Hoffman of Switzerland (an artist of many talents); our own Caldecott Medal-winners Marcia Brown, Maurice Sendak, Roger Duvoisin, Nonny Hogrogian, Evaline Ness, Barbara Cooney, and Uri Shulevitz, as well as Wanda Gág, Margot Zemach, Peter Spier, and Adrienne Adams; and from England—Brian Wildsmith, Raymond Briggs, William Stobbs, and Edward Ardizzone.

The picture-book field has been served and is still being served particularly well for the very young by original nonsense and make-believe. The Beatrix Potter books have been joined by latter-day dressed-up-animal fantasies for small children, which are among the best told and most loved stories for children. *Little Bear* (Harper) has proved itself in many countries and the Hobans' Frances books and the Duvoisins' Happy Lion picture books have gone all over the world. A new I Can Read book, Arnold Lobel's *Frog and Toad Are Friends* (Harper), has an imaginative quality similar to that of *Little Bear,* and reaches both the very young listeners and the beginning readers for whom this series is intended. And there is the 1970 Caldecott Medal-winner, William Steig's *Sylvester and the Magic Pebble* (Windmill/Simon). Its dressed-up donkeys and pigs are loved by American children and, already, as we have heard, by Japanese children for its plot and lively pictures. Raymond Briggs has also provided well for the youngest listener in his picture book *The Elephant and the Bad Baby* (Coward), a story by Elfrida Vipont which she had often told to her own children and grandchildren. And then there is that new stream of highly original animal nonsense books without words: *The Adventures of Paddy Pork* (Harcourt), *Rosie's Walk* (Macmillan), and *Frog, Where Are You?* (Dial).

But how few books there are for the small child which combine storytelling, a sense of compassion, and pictures that can be lingered over—books with that perfect unity of words and illustration that makes a true picture book. I was cheered recently to hear that one highly praised though very young artist had declined to illustrate a picture-book manuscript, because, he said, "It was just untouched by human love." A good description, his editor comments, of a "lot of manuscripts and a lot of published books, too, alas!"

In the international big business created by picture books in the last decade we have seen too many mistakes: books with lush, full-color, sophisticated artwork, printed abroad for co-publishing deals. But, at the same time, I agree with Julia MacRae's view of the advantages of international cooperation. Like other editors, she sees these advantages from the point of view of a regular involvement in the flow of books between England, the United States, Switzerland, Japan, and other countries successful in this kind of publishing. Despite the danger of blandness due to tailoring a picture book to make it safe for all the countries involved, Miss MacRae sees the real advantage: being able to share with children all over the world picture books created by a "galaxy of names in the new golden age of the picture book."

We recognize that in the earlier golden age, England furnished us with picture books that were destined to become classics in the English-speaking world. Later, we sent our American picture books to England. But today again the English have a number of distinguished artists at work, stimulated or at least recognized by England's Kate Greenaway Medal for illustration, first presented in 1956. Miss MacRae's accolade to modern picture books is echoed for England in *Graphis,* an international journal for the graphic arts, where in 1967 two other English commentators, Judy Taylor and John Ryder, contributed an article on "Children's Book Illustration in England." They noted that "In the past five years English children's book publishing seems at last to have begun to loosen the shackles of American domination of their picture-books. . . . "

In spite of reservations, we can agree that both in England and in the United States, we are indeed in a renaissance of children's book illustration. In *Illustrators of Children's Books: 1957–1966,* Ruth Giles Lontoft remarks that "in the past ten years illustrated children's books have been unsurpassed in both quantity and quality by those of any other period of similar duration."

It is too soon to evaluate the possible influences and contributions from the so-called "realistic" fiction of today, but we cannot avoid giving it attention. Children's books, like adult books, have always reflected the times in which they have been created. Today, they project the restlessness and extreme reactions of an age of materialism and insecurity. Happily, however, in spite of a new load of didacticism, we can find writing with vitality by authors who have preferred not to deal with fantasy or with safer periods in the past. Arresting examples are *Queenie Peavy* (Viking) vividly created by Robert Burch; *Harriet the Spy* (Harper); and stories by Paula Fox and Betsy Byars who both handle the problems of variously disadvantaged or harassed children with a depth and wholeness that make their treatments meaningful. The keen perception of childhood by such writers, and their resistance to standardization and to a narrow focusing on social cause, special environment, or personal problem suggest that their books may live. Elizabeth Enright's earlier Melendy and Gone-Away stories and Eleanor Estes' *The Hundred Dresses* (Harcourt) and her Moffat books with their gentle activities and environments, have shown the strength necessary for survival. In Laura Ingalls Wilder's Little House books, in Meindert DeJong's stories, and in Kate Seredy's *The Good Master* (Viking), adults as well as children play important roles, and the relationships drawn between children and adults contribute to a wholeness that is part of the books' success.

I do question the narrowly centered case-study stories and must blame adults who buy these books for thus endorsing pressures put upon the publishers. And I often ponder to what degree children are different today, and ask: Are we being governed by a belief that children are so sophisticated and so accustomed to violence and knowledge of social vices that there are radically new reader interests? How much change must we allow for? Do children only appear to be more sophisticated? Or do they not still want to read for fun, for enjoyment, and for inspiration?

Aware of these questions, I was caught up sharply when I heard Deputy Minister of Culture, N. J. Mokhov speak in the Soviet Union this past summer on "Libraries as a Means of Education and Enlightenment" (in the U.S.S.R., libraries are considered to be a great power for children's education). In his paper, Mr. Mokhov stated that "children become 'grown-up' early due to the conditions of life itself, including television, cinema, and radio." And, he added, "children are increasingly becoming too grown-up for children's books. . . . "

Perhaps you read in Maia Wojciechowska's recent *Don't Play Dead Before You Have To* (Harper) the complaint of a teen-age baby-sitter to a little boy in a home without television. "So what am I supposed to do with you, kid?" he shouts. "Do you realize that I haven't spent one single solitary evening without a television since I was born?"

Soon after reading *Don't Play Dead Before You Have To,* I came to John Steptoe's second handsomely illustrated picture book, *Uptown* (Harper)—a volume labeled for the four- to eight-year-olds. In this, two school children of Harlem discuss what they will be when they are grown up, including and dismissing in their dialogue the possibilities of becoming junkies or policemen. Mr. Steptoe says of his work, "This isn't the type of book that some people want their children to read. But it is the way that some people's children have to live." To what age group belongs such a picture book or such a book as the recent picture-book presentation of an autistic child?

Again, we can ask whether preadolescent children will be able properly to interpret a searing indictment of a society which sympathizes with purse snatching by abjectly poor children moved from Appalachia to Chicago? Or the case of the eleven-year-old poor little rich boy in a story of retardation at school caused by neglect at home—a story that leaves the tearful boy and the reader as despairing of his world at the end of the book as at the beginning?

After reading these in all too close succession, I came up wondering what had gone wrong. Are authors being pressured, being encouraged to "tell it like it is" with no holds barred? My quibble is not so much with subject matter, however: Children can cope with reading about problems they are well aware of, including drugs and sex, and they can enjoy reading case studies if the storytelling is strong, the characters and background not limited, and the facts presented with truth. Just as we must not contribute to pressures put upon the author, we must not condemn him out of prejudice, but rather attempt to understand his intent.

It may be that the producers of these books are trying to provoke thought and discussion by airing the evils of today's society in fiction for children. The American editor of the story about the poor little rich boy wrote me that he believes the main contribution his book will make is to cause children to *think*—because, he says, "one doesn't have the comfort which comes when an author makes it clear through his main character and his plot that he values certain things, and that these things will triumph in the end. It is ambiguous, paradoxical, sometimes unsettling—as much of life is."

Julia MacRae has said:

> [I]t is from America that much of the most interesting and provocative writing is coming at the moment, some of it perhaps too powerful for the present climate in Britain. We are still concerned by the question of what is, or is not, suitable for children and it is not a question which can be answered irresponsibly or overnight. We know that children need and want . . . emotional honesty and characters with whom they can readily identify in works of imaginative literature. . . .

It is tempting to line up three final quotations, from authors who are also parents, and I do this because they hold such varying points of view. First, from Joan Aiken,[5] in a talk presented in England in 1969:

> I can see that in such an increasingly threatened and frightening world as ours now is, children, probably more than ever before, need to be given real values and sustaining ideas and memories that they can hold on to and cherish.

---

5. See note 6, below.

Another side of the argument is represented by such critics as Julius Lester, who said in a piece entitled "The Kinds of Books We Give Children: Whose Nonsense?" *(Publishers Weekly,* Feb. 23, 1970):

Unfortunately, there aren't many children's books as ruthlessly honest and painful as *Harriet and the Promised Land* (Windmill/ Simon) [that brief picture-book presentation of Harriet Tubman]. Too many of us feel that children are to be protected and sheltered from pain. Yet, they live close to it and perceive it every day. And not to acknowledge its existence is really to leave them unprotected and unsheltered.

John Rowe Townsend, whose stories deal skillfully, honestly, and sharply with the underprivileged child of the inner city, states:

We are not trying to protect from life children who are not suffering deprivations and discrimination. They should read about them and not be shielded—up to the point that they can understand. But burdening them with social and psychological problems may be too great a burden.

In this confusion, we must admit that children are not alike; they do not all have the same needs. We cannot therefore make sweeping generalizations about "relevance," or prescribe problem literature for the child, but only insist on honesty and compassion, and a show of some degree of faith and hope in the resolution of the human plight. In library service we are aiming as never before to recognize differences in cultural background, reading readiness, and attitudes to life, endeavoring to make reading a part of all young lives, through a universal library service, with a book production that attempts to meet the needs of every socioeconomic area. As we admit these purposes, we must admit that the literature designed to serve such needs is likely to relate little to the question of a golden age.

I agree with author Leon Garfield,[6] who sets his problem stories in the past because, he says, he finds "the social aspects of contemporary life too fleeting to grasp imaginatively before they are legislated out of existence. And anyway," he continues, "I don't think the novel is as suited to coping with them as is the television documentary or the newspaper. It was once, but not now. . . . Fortunately for the novelist," he adds, "human nature is more constant than fashion."

If we are depressed by some of these signs of our times, and unready to shout too loudly about a golden age, we must take cheer from the positive achievements and trends that affect the status of children's books. For

---

6. Quoted from *Children's Literature in Education,* Volume I, No. 2, July 1970, St. Luke's College, Exeter, England (APS Publications, Inc.): Alan Garner, "Coming to terms"; Joan Aiken, "A thread of mystery"; Leon Garfield, "Writing for childhood."

example, efforts have been made both in the United States and in England to insist that children's literature is part of the mainstream of literature. Aware, then, of some advance in the status of children's literature and convinced of creativity in important areas, I feel we are justified in backing Mr. Townsend when we agree with him that we are in the "second golden age" of children's literature.

British editions of books mentioned with their American publishers in this article:

John Rowe Townsend. *Written for Children: An Outline of English Children's Literature.* J. G. Miller, revised edition Kestrel.
Scott O'Dell. *Island of the Blue Dolphins.* Longman/Kestrel.
Meindert DeJong. *The Wheel on the School.* Lutterworth Press.
Louise Fatio and Roger Duvoisin. *The Happy Lion.* Bodley Head.
Leo Lionni. *Swimmy.* Dobson.
Hugh Lofting. *The Story of Doctor Dolittle.* Cape.
Esther Forbes. *Johnny Tremain.* Longman/Kestrel.
Elizabeth George Speare. *The Witch of Blackbird Pond.* Gollancz.
Irene Hunt. *Across Five Aprils.* Bodley Head.
Philippa Pearce. *Tom's Midnight Garden.* Oxford University Press.
Pauline Clarke. *The Twelve and the Genii* (published in U.S.A. as *The Return of the Twelves).* Faber.
J.R.R. Tolkien. *The Hobbit.* Allen & Unwin.
Mary Norton. *The Borrowers.* Dent.
P.L. Travers. *Mary Poppins.* Collins.
E.B. White. *Charlotte's Web.* Hamish Hamilton.
E.B. White. *The Trumpet of the Swan.* Hamish Hamilton.
Robert Lawson. *Rabbit Hill.* Harrap.
Madeleine L'Engle. *A Wrinkle in Time.* Longman/Kestrel.
Lloyd Alexander. *The Book of Three.* Heinemann.
Edward Eager. *Half Magic.* Macmillan.
Jean Merrill. *The Pushcart War.* Hamish Hamilton.
Alan Garner. *The Owl Service.* Collins.
Else Holmelund Minarik. *Little Bear.* World's Work.
Arnold Lobel. *Frog and Toad are Friends.* World's Work.
William Steig. *Sylvester and the Magic Pebble.* Abelard-Schuman.
Elfrida Vipont. *The Elephant and the Bad Baby.* Hamish Hamilton.
John Strickland Goodall. *The Adventures of Paddy Pork.* Macmillan.
Pat Hutchins. *Rosie's Walk.* Bodley Head.
Louise Fitzhugh. *Harriet the Spy.* Gollancz.
Kate Seredy. *The Good Master.* Harrap.

Chapter 3

Children: Their Reading Interests and Needs

What should children read? Should they read what adults believe will stimulate their intellect, stir their imagination, develop their sense of humor, strengthen their morals, further their understanding of themselves and others, or simply what they most enjoy reading? Arguments about these questions are endless. Book selectors aware of the issues, the opinions, and the standards of excellence of experts in the field of children's literature will formulate their own criteria for selection.

While succeeding chapters of this book will deal with standards of excellence for various genres, this chapter will present general areas of controversy. Some controversies—such as whether a book should promote certain values and whether children should have the right to freely choose their own reading matter—have been long debated. Contemporary authors indicate that these issues have not been resolved over the past century and a half.[1] Margery Fisher finds it necessary to remind book selectors that "we should not *expect* children's stories to be sermons or judicial arguments or sociological pamphlets. As independent works of art they must be allowed to appeal to the imagination, the mind, and the heart on their own terms."[2] And John Rowe Townsend points out a very basic and important fact:

1. See Chapter 1 for nineteenth-century views on these two issues.
2. "Rights and Wrongs," American Library Association, *Top of the News,* 26 (June 1970): 373–391.

. . . neither morality nor magnificent invocations will make a work of art live if the breath of life is not in it. . . . Quality publishing for children is governed by a complex social-institutional-economic equation which replaces the law of supply and demand; and as the result the adults are uniquely able to procure on the child's behalf not so much the thing he wants as the thing they feel he ought to have. . . . Now is the time to recognize just what we are doing and consider the dangers we run. The first danger is an obvious one: the child opts out of the whole procedure and reads comics or nothing. He has, after all, the ultimate veto. . . . [3]

Peter Dickinson, in "A Defence of Rubbish," presents another aspect of the freedom vs. censorship issue. He argues that children should be allowed to read rubbish—what, to the adult, has no visible value. They should have a whole culture, not just the "plums," and they will, by reading good and bad literature, "learn the art of comparison, and subconsciously acquire critical standards." But can we be sure this will happen and can children afford to waste the limited time they have for free reading?[4] Is it not the adult's responsibility to make it possible for the child to find and enjoy the best? Shall we not always be right in stressing that children know what they like but *not all that they are capable of liking?*[5]

Another area of controversy concerns presenting subjects which may be frightening, traumatic, or not relevant in terms of the real world in which the child lives. From differing viewpoints, Julius Lester, in "The Kinds of Books We Give Children: Whose Nonsense?" and Nicholas Tucker, in "Books That Frighten" (reprinted here), argue against our overprotection of children. To shield children from what is painful and frightening, says Lester, is to "make them emotional and spiritual amputees. They see the pain and feel it themselves quite often, yet we tell them that it does not exist, that they're too young to understand, that they shouldn't worry about it" when we should be teaching them "not only what the reality is and how one survives in it, but, how one can begin to change it."[6] Lester's argument

3. "Didacticism in Modern Dress," *Horn Book Magazine,* 43 (April 1967): 159–164.

4. See Joan Aiken's reference to "Filboid Studge" in "Purely for Love," p. 149.

5. For analyses of the lure of series fiction see Selma G. Lanes, *Down the Rabbit Hole* (New York: Atheneum Publishers, 1971), pp. 128–145 and Wallace Hildick, *Children and Fiction* (London: Evans Brothers, Ltd., 1970; New York: The World Publishing Company, 1971), pp. 96–101, 117. Hildick objects to the "total drizzly thinness" in the Bobbsey series and to the serial strip cartoon which "tends to restrict, cramp, nullify." For viewpoints on the one-time "fifty-center" series, see "For It Was Indeed He," *Fortune,* 9 (April 1934): 86–89, 193–194 and Arthur Praeger, *Rascals at Large* (Garden City, N.Y.: Doubleday & Company, Inc., 1971). See also "Edward Stratemeyer and His Book Machine," *Saturday Review,* 54 (July 10, 1971): 15–17, 52–53 and "The Secret of Nancy Drew—Pushing Forty and Going Strong," *Saturday Review,* 52 (January 25, 1969): 18–19, 34–35.

6. "The Kinds of Books We Give Children: Whose Nonsense?," *Publishers' Weekly,* 198 (February 23, 1970): 86–88.

applies generally to all children, but he is speaking particularly about black children. Augusta Baker's "Guidelines for Black Books: An Open Letter to Juvenile Editors" (reprinted here), and David Elkind's "Ethnicity and Reading: Three Avoidable Dangers,"[7] present other views on making books relevant to black children. Because "we have so little concrete data as to what is 'degrading' and what is 'egalitarian,' " says Elkind, "decisions in those regards are often made on a personal and arbitrary basis."

Finally, there is controversy over whether classics should be adapted for quicker and easier absorption. In the last two selections in this chapter, Frances Clarke Sayers refutes Walt Disney's vulgarizing of classics in films, and Margery Fisher comments on book adaptations and abridgments, noting that sometimes a classic is improved by abridgment.[8]

Above and beyond the debating, there is an unassailable creed for all who are guardians of the young, stated by John Rowe Townsend in his Arbuthnot Honor Lecture: " . . . we would wish every child to experience to his or her full capacity the enjoyment, and the broadening of horizons, which can be derived from literature."[9]

---

7. "Ethnicity and Reading: Three Avoidable Dangers," in *Reading, Children's Books, and Our Pluralistic Society*, compiled and edited by Harold Tanyzer and Jean Karl (Newark: International Reading Association, 1972), pp. 4–8.

8. See also Rumer Godden's "An Imaginary Correspondence," p. 133–139, and Hildick (note 3) on the barbaric treatment of classic prose works in the comic-strip medium.

9. "Standards of Criticism for Children's Literature," *Top of the News*, 27 (June 1971): 373–387.

A Defence of Rubbish

Peter Dickinson

A regular verse contributor to Punch, *Peter Dickinson is also an award-winning author of adult crime novels and of successful books for young people. These last include a trilogy of futuristic science fantasies—*The Weathermongers *(1969),* Heartsease *(1969), and* The Devil's Children *(1970)—and a present-day, witty story of adventure,* Emma Tupper's Diary *(1971).*

The danger of living in a golden age of children's literature is that not enough rubbish is being produced.

Nobody who has not spent a whole sunny afternoon under his bed rereading a pile of comics left over from the previous holidays has any real idea of the meaning of intellectual freedom.

Nobody who has not written comic strips can really understand the phrase economy of words. It's like trying to write *Paradise Lost* in haiku.

At the August conference in Exeter I made a few remarks about rubbish. These turned out to be the most interesting part of an otherwise rather frivolous and incoherent lecture. What follows is an attempt to provide a serious defence of the position I then took.

I have always believed that children ought to be allowed to read a certain amount of rubbish. Sometimes quite a high proportion of their reading matter can healthfully consist of things that no sane adult would actually encourage them to read. But I had not, until people started asking me what I really meant, attempted to defend my position or to think it out in any detail.

Definition: by rubbish I mean all forms of reading matter which contain to the adult eye no visible value, either aesthetic or educational.

First I believe that it is very important that a child, or anybody for that matter, should have a whole culture—at least one whole culture—at his fingertips. We make no objection now to those adults who spent their youth going two or three times a week to the cinema regardless of the merit of the films shown. They have the whole of the Golden Age of the flicks at their fingertips down to the last most trivial B film and it has immensely enriched their life and their outlook in a way which a diet which consisted solely of plums could not possibly do. Nowadays one can say the same about the pop song culture. There is good stuff on the discs, mixed in with an enormous amount of trash, but both of these are necessary to a child who

From "A Defence of Rubbish" by Peter Dickinson from *Children's Literature in Education*, no. 3 (November 1970): 7–10. Reprinted by permission of the author.

is taking a serious interest in pop. The child may not realize that the interest is serious but when he grows up he will then find, with luck, that it has been and that he is the better for it. As one teacher expressed it to me at the conference, it is vital that children should have "all that stuff churning around in there" and he rubbed his belly.

Second it is also especially important that a child should belong, and feel he belongs, to the group of children among whom he finds himself and he should feel that he shares in their culture. Inevitably the group interest will be mostly rubbish. For instance, my son at the moment reads two football comics a week. I love comics, but by the standard of comics these are not much cop. Even so I do not discourage him because this gives him that essential sense of belonging to a group. To remove these comics or to attempt to discourage their reading in any way would be a socially divisive move. A child should feel that he is an individual; but he must not, if possible, feel that he is somehow set apart, especially by family taboos which are not shared by the families of the group to which he belongs. Obviously one can carry this point too far, but in the case of things like football comics I am sure that laissez faire is the only sensible attitude.

Third I am convinced of the importance of children discovering things for themselves. However tactfully an adult may push them towards discoveries in literature, these do not have quite the treasure trove value of the books picked up wholly by accident. This can only be done by random sampling on the part of the children, and it is inevitable that a high proportion of what they read will be rubbish, by any standard. But in the process they will learn the art of comparison, and subconsciously acquire critical standards, so that in the world they are discovering—even in the world of football comics—they will begin to work out why one strip is "better" than another and seems more fascinating and is more eagerly looked forward to than another. They may even argue about this with their friends and so make the beginning of an effort at rationalizing their appreciation or dislike of cultural objects.

Fourth comes a psychological point. Children have a very varying need of security, but almost all children feel the need of security and reassurance sometime. For instance, in those families where boys are sent away to boarding school it is often very noticeable that, in the first week of the holidays, the boys do not read just the books they read last holidays, but books off their younger brother's bookshelves. One can often tell how happy or insecure a child is feeling simply by what he is reading. And sometimes he may need to reread something well known but which makes absolutely no intellectual or emotional demand. Rubbish has this negative virtue, and I would be very chary of interfering with a child who felt an obvious need of rubbish.

My fifth point is more nebulous. There is no proof, or even arguing about it. But I am fairly sure in my own mind that a diet of plums is bad for you, and that any rational reading system needs to include a considerable amount of pap or roughage—call it what you will. I know very few adults who do not have some secret cultural vice, and they are all the better for it. I would instantly suspect an adult all of whose cultural activities were high, remote and perfect.

Sixth, it may not be rubbish after all. The adult eye is not necessarily a perfect instrument for discerning certain sorts of values. Elements—and this particularly applies to science fiction, about which I was talking at the conference—may be so obviously rubbishy that one is tempted to dismiss the whole product as rubbish. But among those elements there may be something new and strange to which one is not accustomed, and which one may not be able to assimilate oneself, as an adult, because of the sheer awfulness of the rest of the stuff; but the innocence—I suppose there is no other word—of the child's eye can take or leave in a way that I feel an adult cannot, and can acquire valuable stimuli from things which appear otherwise overgrown with a mass of weeds and nonsense.

I am not of course advocating a total lack of censorship. I have no doubt in my own mind that there are certain sorts of reading which are deleterious, and from which a child should be discouraged. Rubbish does not have this quality. It has absolutely no quality. It is negative.

Nor am I advocating that children should be *encouraged* to read rubbish. None of the ones I know need much encouragement. All I am asking is that they should not be discouraged from reading it.

The question remains of the children whose diet appears to consist solely of rubbish. Obviously, as far as possible, they should be slightly weaned. But not totally weaned. And besides, if they did not have this diet they would not be reading at all, and in a verbal culture I think it is better that the child should read something than read nothing. And perhaps, long after the child is out of the hands of parents or teachers, the habit of reading—even the habit of reading rubbish—may somehow evoke a tendency to read things which are not rubbish. I know two or three of my contemporaries who were, by cultural standards, total philistines in their boyhood; but they used to read a considerable amount of rubbish and have now, from the habit of reading, become considerably more literate than I.

Books That Frighten

Nicholas Tucker

Formerly an educational psychologist for the Inner London Education Authority, now a lecturer in developmental psychology at Sussex University in England, Nicholas Tucker is well-qualified to discuss the effects of nursery rhymes on children. He has written extensively on nursery rhymes and is the compiler, with Trevor Stubley, of Mother Goose Lost *(1971), which includes traditional nursery rhymes not popular in their day.*

From nursery rhymes upwards, children's reading tastes have suffered periodic attack. Moralists in the 19th century, according to Meredith, "traced the national taste for tales of crime to the smell of blood in our nursery rhymes"; and in post-revolutionary Russia stories that treated household pests, like flies, with affection, or like *Baron Munchausen* dealt with the impossible, were also condemned as irresponsible. Children's stories have been accused of many other things: Mrs. Trimmer, writing in 1806, branded Cinderella as "a monster of deceit," and accused the general story of painting "some of the worst passions that can enter into the human breast, and of which little children should, if possible, be totally ignorant, such as envy, jealousy, a dislike of mothers-in-law and half sisters, vanity, a love of dress, etc, etc."

More recently, it has been the horrific aspect of nursery lore that has tended to upset some parents. Rhymes that refer to whipping or death have dropped out of many anthologies; some have even been rewritten:

> Ding dong bell, Pussy's at the well.
> Who took her there? Little Johnny Hare.
> Who'll bring her in? Little Tommy Thin.
> What a jolly boy was that to get some milk for pussy cat,
> Who ne'er did any harm, but played with the mice in his father's barn.

The intention here is not just to protect pussy cats from naughty boys; in the last line pussy herself is unnaturally reformed too.

CHILDREN PRODUCE THEIR OWN HORROR

But since the psycho-analytic discoveries of Freud and more particularly Melanie Klein, it seems probable that young children produce their own horrific fantasies and nightmares—which may be about anything from murder and mutilation to incest or cannibalism—whether they have read frightening books or not. There are good reasons for this: the young child

"Books That Frighten" by Nicholas Tucker from *Where*, Supplement 15, *Books for Children* (1969): 10–12. Reprinted by permission of the Advisory Centre for Education.

feels both love and hate, joy and rage, and many of his aggressive destructive fantasies will centre around the necessary frustrations of his early feeding experiences—hence the oral emphasis. Such fantasies can help release tension in the child but can also threaten to overwhelm him, especially since he tends to project them onto fantasy figures such as witches or ogres who then come back to haunt him.

If this picture is accepted, and it has been well summarised by a psychotherapist, P. M. Pickard, in her generally fascinating book *I Could a Tale Unfold,* then it will be seen that books which do not ignore frightening topics, but give them their place—neither too large nor too small—in the general run of things can help rather than corrupt children. They will learn from them that they are not the only ones to have these feelings, and can listen cathartically and therefore without guilt to stories of other people killing, devouring, hating or envying.

Even more important, they can see that such feelings in the stories are not necessarily annihilating, but can be thwarted or manipulated towards a happy ending. Thus Jack is able to kill the giant and steal his money too, just as a child will have to learn to overcome the beast within him while stealing from it the vitality that it can provide. Not surprisingly, many children have a more than sneaking sympathy for the giant, the Daleks on TV or monsters in films, even though they know that such things must be beaten in the end. Later on, roughly between the ages of seven and 11, although in all these age groupings there are bound to be children who are exceptions, they will wish to test themselves out through fiction against other more realistic fears, such as abandonment and rough treatment or parental strain, bereavement and wicked step-parents. Like Rumplestilt-skin, frightening things tend to lose a lot of their power when they are brought out into the open and named.

When should this best be done? A two-year-old child, who has neither the vocabulary nor the experience to get much out of reading, usually prefers to play out his fantasies, and will beg Daddy to be a giant over and over again, however terrified his shrieks may seem. Later, roughly between three and six, a child is more verbal but still living a life that is midway between reality and fantasy. Dreams have as much face value as anything that happens during the day. So he will require stories that bring in both these aspects of his experience. He will want to learn more about the tangible reality he is beginning to recognise and will therefore turn to books set in and about families and their possessions, as in the *Topsy and Tim* series. At the same time, as I have already said, he will need to explore some of his frightening fantasies in a way that can lead to their modification and eventual control. So he may turn to another Tim: the storm-battered and perpetually lost, abandoned but always eventually found boy-hero created by Edward Ardizzone.

Nursery rhymes, like Punch and Judy, which among other things can deal very briskly with a whole range of primitive behavior, from chopping off heads to throwing old men downstairs, can particularly relieve a child by ventilating some of his most violent fantasies. On the other hand, if these are repressed in guilty isolation, it can sometimes lead to a great anxiety within the individual. Henceforth, even by being able to sing or recognise some of these rhymes for himself, the child will have gained that much more control over the material within them, other things being equal, of course. Too much horror or sadness at this age, though, as is found for example in some of the long-drawn-out Victorian versions of *Babes in the Woods,* can be self-defeating in that it produces more anxiety than it relieves. When very young and without strong defences, children want the dark side of things put in its place, not raised to new levels of realism or emphasis.

HOW WE CAN HELP

At this stage, a parent can help a child get through his natural confusion between reality and fantasy not by ignoring fantasy altogether, since it plays an essential part in any child's development, but by helping a child to sort out which is which. Thus we let him play with real things, and try to give reasonably sensible answers when he wants to know how something works. With imaginative material, though, there is often a clue in the tone of voice, or in the very nature of the presentation itself—whether it is the use of song, rhyme or even "Once upon a time"—that indicates to the child that this is something less valid, but different. Of course this distinction is sometimes blurred, but parents who continually insist upon whimsical explanations for factual matters but tell stories of ghosts and ogres with eye-popping realism should not be altogether surprised if this to some extent saps their children's confidence.

When, however, a child can broadly separate reality from fantasy, he is then ready to suspend his new-won disbelief and go hunting and being hunted by quite real-sounding and horrible ogres and witches with the best of them. His fantasies will still be about feelings that are important to him, even if he no longer believes in their face value; as Kornei Chukovsky says in his marvellous book *From Two to Five,* he will continue to make mud pies even though he won't try to eat them. He will still not be at the stage when he wants undiluted horror to test himself out, but he will certainly like books that have real pace and tension. Thus he will be able to take ogres who suck blood in Grimm, monsters that crack bones in *The Arabian Nights,* and the complete goblin underworld of J. R. R. Tolkien, so long as everything is safely resolved by the end.

What books, then, will be positively harmful at this age, before the child is ready to really test himself out on the most gruesome ghost stories, tough comics and illegally-entered X films? Although he may have a firm footing in reality, there are still some books that by the very force and vividness of their detail can overcome his defences and make him dread the light going out and the bad dream.

This is particularly true of pictures in books. When a child reads a text, he of course provides his own mental pictures for it. Thus a fearful child, when reading *The Tinder Box,* may render it manageable by imagining the dog with saucer eyes as quite a modest little thing. Yet a picture showing the dog as undeniably huge and terrifying is another matter, and some of children's worst memories of books are about pictures rather than texts. For a child, too, it really can be a matter of once seen never forgotten, since it has been estimated that at least 60 per cent of children have at some time the power to remember a picture seen only for a short time in quite astonishing and lasting detail, as if he could still quite literally see it in his mind's eye—a phenomenon known as eidetic imagery.

The 19th century was particularly rich in horrific illustrations, producing for example, far nastier pictures for *Foxe's Book of Martyrs* than anything the 16th century could think up. Perhaps the most famous example of this is still *Struwwelpeter,* having sold at least 200,000 copies in this country alone, with an extra spurt around the time when horror comics were debated in Parliament in 1955, when *Struwwelpeter* was invoked by both sides in the argument. Certainly around 1845 one can understand its popularity, since it was at least lively compared with the very dull moralistic children's books that had come before. But these days I think the story about the "great long red-legged scissor-man" who cuts off thumbs and leaves poor Conrad desolate and bleeding, his truncated (or should one say castrated?) hands hanging limply by his side, if left lying around could well provide one of childhood's nastier memories.

The Beardsley-type drawings of Arthur Rackham to illustrate fairy stories also seem to me to be unnecessarily repulsive. So often his characters, even the "good" ones, peer out of the dark embellished with carbuncles, thin dripping noses, gnarled and deformed limbs, cracking skin and tusk-like teeth. Like the forest scene in Disney's *Snow White,* his trees sprout clutching misshapen arms and hideous chuckling faces, effective but also rather gratuitous in their seeming desire to frighten children at all costs.

Recently objections have been made to Maurice Sendak's *Where the Wild Things Are,* but this seems to me a quite different case. Sendak's monsters are essentially amiable grinning things, easily tamed and if anything rather ridiculous. All the aggression is centred around Max, the little boy hero, with whom the Wild Things can hardly compete.

UNNECESSARY NASTINESS?

There are also those stories that, while not illustrated, dwell on certain details with such lingering and even gloating effect that this too can become difficult to forget for a child who is not yet ready for them. One of the hoariest of these is the nursery jingle recorded by the Opies in *The Oxford Dictionary of Nursery Rhymes.* It is about a "lady all skin and bone" who sits by a churchyard. Soon:

> On looking up, on looking down,
> She saw a dead man on the ground;

And from his nose unto his chin,
The worms crawled out, the worms crawled in.[1]

The whole thing immemorially ends with a piercing scream from the narrator. The Opies record that Southey, in tears, used to beg his family not to proceed, and another correspondent in 1946 mentions how these verses "scared us so much as children, we fastened the leaves together." One can see why.

Although young children can take some horror, there is a difference between a story containing a ghost and a *ghost story*. One mentions fears, the other aggrandises them.

Some parents may object to passages from Grimm, such as the time when the ogre first cuts his own daughters' throats and then devours them. Then there is *Sinbad the Sailor,* where the monster first puts his foot upon the shipmaster's neck, breaks it, then thrusts a long spit through him, roasts him and then separates the joints "as a man separates the joints of a chicken." He then eats the flesh, and after gnawing the bones, tosses them to the side. Later, of course, Sinbad and his men blind him by forcing two red-hot iron spits into his eyes "with all their might." "Verily," Sinbad goes on, "every death we witness is more horrible than the preceding one." Many parents will agree, but passages like this, or the one in the recently re-issued *Brown Fairy Book* by Andrew Lang, where a beautiful girl is first whipped and then made to eat dog manure, are still fundamentally a question of taste. Parents who do not like them had better not read them out, since they will make their feelings clear in the tone of their voice and thus make the whole matter worse. But at the same time it would be a pity to get over-protective about *The Arabian Nights* altogether; there are some gruesome bits in *Ali Baba* too, but nothing like as circumstantial as *Sinbad,* and surely within most normal children's (and parents') powers of assimilation.

Some great writers can create an overpowering effect just with one story. Many children have been permanently frightened of blind men because of Blind Pew, the idea of madness because of *Jane Eyre,* and just about everything because of Edgar Allan Poe. Sometimes parents may be at fault by trying to plunge their children into classics too early, but situations like this are bound to happen sometimes, and can best be modified by discussion afterwards rather than censorship before.

A PSYCHOLOGICAL TRAUMA?

What about stories that are supposed to create a psychological trauma? I have heard *Cinderella* referred to as encouraging boot-fetichism; *Alice in*

---

1. "On Looking Up, On Looking Down" from *The Oxford Dictionary of Nursery Rhymes,* edited by Iona and Peter Opie. Copyright 1951. Reprinted by permission of The Clarendon Press, Oxford.

Wonderland and Tom up the chimney in *The Water Babies* to be about the birth process, and the Three Blind Mice to be directly about the castration complex, so much so that there is now a re-written version where the farmer's wife is made to "cut them some cheese with a carving knife." There may be some truth in these assertions, and it is silly to read Alice or indeed any story to children who, among other things, are simply too young to appreciate it anyhow. But fundamentally if children are psychologically upset by these things, then their anxieties must be very near the surface. In the same way, the present spate of books about social problems like illegitimacy, divorce, adoption and race will probably only deeply affect those who are already affected by them, and whether this will be in a good or a bad sense will depend upon the child and the quality and motivation of the book itself, not the problem it chooses to discuss.

As always, the parent is left with no very clear guide but instinct and his feeling for his children on what or what not to read to them. If he is over-protective, the very act of avoiding fear in literature can eventually leave the child more exposed than he should be both to himself as well as to reality. If the parent throws them in at the deep end straight away, then again he may not give them time to build up adequate defences and controls. The best guide of course is the child himself. If reading aloud is an intimate unhurried occasion, and if there is time to talk about it afterwards *before* going straight to bed where a child really does mull over things, the parent may soon find out if he has gone a little too far. On the other hand, if the child fidgets during reading and looks longingly round for his comics, then the parent may have to step up the pace a little, even if this may involve the mild bruising of some of his own sensibilities. This should not have to happen though, since some of the best writers for the young these days are also the most exciting.

The final dilemma, of course, is that one wants children to be horrified by some things, but that it is not really fair on the child to encourage this type of horror too early. Thus when topics like the Moor murders or Nazi atrocities suddenly crop up, I think it important not to attempt to laugh them off into indifference. Children should be told the truth, or else they will hear different versions rather than nothing at all, and they should see how their parents feel about such things. But we must also be careful to spare some of the detail and not dwell upon such things with young children, since this could lead to a feeling of insecurity as well as horror. So long as they feel their parents are in control and are there with the time to give comfort and warmth when things or books are upsetting, then a child has a sure enough base to begin to see things as they really are. Some books, among many other things, can help him in this too, as well as sometimes having the far more positive role of making him want to do something about it, and having some idea of what to do.[2]

---

2. Mr. Tucker has also discussed the effects on young children of some frightening moments in Walt Disney's films in *New Society,* 4 April 1968.

Guidelines for Black Books:
An Open Letter to Juvenile Editors

Augusta Baker

Augusta Baker is Coordinator of Children's Services for the New York Public Library, lecturer, storyteller and teacher of storytelling, and compiler of The Talking Tree and Other Stories *(1955) and* The Golden Lynx and Other Stories *(1960). She is also editor of* The Black Experience in Books for Children *(1971), published by the New York Public Library as a revision of its* Books About Negro Life for Children. *This article is based on a speech given at a membership meeting of the Children's Book Council, Inc., May 8, 1969.*

One of my pet irritations today is the whole idea that the great interest and upsurge in books about black life has just come along. 1937 and 1938 were the years when the interest in this whole subject was born. We realized then there was a great need for this kind of material. I worked in Harlem just opposite a public school, and I hadn't worked there very long before I realized that the boys and girls, all Negro boys and girls, knew three people—Frederick Douglass, Booker T. Washington and George Washington Carver. And that was it. When we gave book talks about Phyllis Wheatley, Robert Smalls and others, these children had no idea who these people were. We thought that they certainly should have books which would introduce them to the important people in their own heritage. It goes without saying that if the Negro boys and girls didn't know about these people, white children did not know either. Some of them had not even heard of Frederick Douglass, George Washington Carver and Booker T. Washington. So the need was recognized as early as the 30's.

At that time, at Countee Cullen Regional Branch, which was then 135th Street Branch, we set up a model collection. In order to do this we had to think about criteria. We couldn't just pick up one book after another and say, "Well, I like this book, so this book should go in. I don't like this book so out it goes." We had to work with some kind of guidelines. Since then, we've added a few more. We can afford, now, to add "quality." We absolutely couldn't consider "quality" in 1939, 1940, 1941, because we really had very few books to meet our general criteria. However, we still use the same guidelines today.

We selected illustrations as the first one, because as we watched our boys and girls in the library, we realized that they went to the shelves, took down a book and looked at it carefully. They looked at the illustrations, before they did any reading. Children, today, approach books the same way. We do want the illustrations to be attractive. We do not want these Negro boys and girls to look like white children with brown wash or black wash spread over them. We want them to have the features, to have the distinction, to have the attraction that one finds among Negro boys and girls. Let the characters be natural.

Our next criterion is a matter of language. We discarded the books that were so full of dialect that you couldn't understand them. Rarely do we find a book today where the dialect is author-created, but imagine what we ran across in those days! There were plantation stories then, with all these little children playing together, born and raised on the same plantation. A great deal was made in the beginning of the book of the fact that both the black children and the white children were born on and never left the plantation, and were raised together by "Mammy." Then you'd come to the dialog. The white children would speak as if they had Ph.D.'s from Oxford, but you couldn't understand one word the little black children were trying to say because you were bogged down in the "deses" and "doses." We don't come across too much of this today. When we do we're naturally upset about it. We watch more for this kind of dialect when we read the stories where the locale is West Indian. Some of the editors are having problems with the West Indian speech, which is a very distinct pattern of speech. Regional vernacular is fine, but if you use it, then all of the characters should speak the same way. If they all came from the same place, with roughly the same economic standing and the same general education, they're going to speak pretty much the same way. So we still look for this—consistency in speech patterns.

There is no place for the hero of a story to use derogatory terms. One of the last disagreements we had with some people was about what constituted a derogatory term. I think the last word we really gave up was "pick-a-ninny" because this, for so long, was "a term of great affection." Other terms, such as "darkie" and "nigger" were dropped without too great a problem, but it took a little doing to give up some of those other "affectionate" terms. Gradually, we got this point across. There is never an excuse for such words to appear editorially or for the author himself to think this way. If a book is historical in background, however, it must be true to the times. In Hildegarde Swift's "Railroad to Freedom," she explains to the boys and girls that she uses certain words because they are historically accurate. When the patroller, who has been chasing the escaped slave, catches Harriet Tubman, he does not say, "And now, Miss Tubman, will you please return to the plantation with me?" He is apt to use more "colorful" language. So that when we're looking at the books, we recognize this. It's just the same with the realistic stories of today. You have the pattern of speech that one finds in the streets, and this is part of the atmosphere of the story. We try very hard, though, to make sure that the hero doesn't use this kind of language indiscriminately. There still is this criterion to be applied. There still is a feeling about the use of this kind of language and its indiscriminate use.

THEMES AND ATTITUDES

Another general criterion is theme. In the late 1930's and in the 1940's, when we reached theme, we really had reached a barrier. If we had applied the criteria of today, where we now expect a full picture of Negro life, we wouldn't have had any books. We did have about 40 books in the James Weldon Johnson Memorial Collection, but in all of those books, the Negro was portrayed in some kind of servile position, and it was unheard-of to portray a black man as anything other than a servant. This just wasn't done. Since that time, of course, children's editors have taken care of that problem, but we never have had as wide a range of social life portrayed in children's books as there should be.

I'm sure that juvenile editors must be absolutely deluged with manuscripts on the current scene. This always happens when the public says, "we *need* something." But perhaps editors will keep in mind some guidelines when they are wading through all those manuscripts—good, bad and indifferent. I think, first of all, the characters should be just people and circumstances should be normal circumstances. In stories about city life I am pleased to see children of all sizes, shapes and colors. I would hope that situations would be normal situations. I would hope that we would not take a manuscript and go through every third page and paint one child and every fourth family black to integrate the book. Where it is a normal situation or there is a normal reason for there to be a black family with the white families, fine. Sometimes however, we lose track of this, and the upper most thing in our minds is to get that book integrated. We still do not have to be afraid to publish a few stories that aren't integrated, especially if the integration is artificial. If it's a normal part of life for the families and children in the book to be all kinds of families and all kinds of children, fine. This is as it should be.

Older editors will remember that there was a time when realistic fiction was one of the hardest subjects to get published. Back in the old days the nonfiction was strong, the fiction had to be very pleasant. Follett had the courage to publish Lorenz Graham's "South Town," but there were many who thought that the children weren't quite ready for this kind of story. Now, we have a number of good, realistic stories but we still need more realistic books. I have a feeling that we have not quite moved into the area of what I call "an unhappy ending." I believe some of the ghetto stories, some of the very realistic stories, are very good—until we come to the end. Something happens, and perhaps it's that we do not really carry that realism to the end. The thing which impressed me with "Edgar Allen" was that the author made no attempt to give it a they-lived-happily-ever-after ending. "Edgar Allen" is based on the truth and the author had the courage not to twist that truth. I would hope, too, for books about a Negro family that does not necessarily find itself in the slums. There's still room for stories on all levels, all facets, of black life; all black people are not in the ghettos and slums.

It is interesting how stories come along in waves. It seems that right now we're on a "foster home kick." This is fine, if the author really knows about what he is writing. The person who writes realistic fiction must be inside, writing about life, rather than outside, looking in on it. Then he has written a book which youngsters will say really has soul, as opposed to a book which just doesn't quite make it. This requires fine writing, along with the other criteria.

A guideline for imports: these are the books which we must examine very carefully and which we must read and reread. Many of the books which are published first abroad reflect certain attitudes that we would hope to eliminate. These attitudes sometimes are so subtle that, in a very quick, cursory reading, you may miss them—the books on Africa, for instance. Illustrations are an important matter. A book came across my desk a few days ago and from a quick glance, the text seems to be all right. The illustrations, however, leave something to be desired. I feel that, if we apply certain criteria to the work of our own illustrators, we have no right to accept less than that when the illustrations have been made by someone abroad. Several books have now come across my desk with illustrations that, had the book originated in America with an American artist, would be considered bordering on the stereotyped. If the illustrations border on the stereotype for an American artist, they border on the stereotyped for all artists, even very famous and well-known ones.

Guidelines for reissues and reprints of our own old titles: these should be read very, very carefully, in the light of today's thinking. Editors should not be over-influenced by the importance of the author. After all, there are many authors whose whole outlook on life has changed in the last 20 or so years. These people have grown, they have changed their attitudes, they are influenced by social life around them just as we are; so, it might even be doing a disservice to them to reissue some of those books.

The books on the history of the black man, the books on civil rights and nonfiction in general are good. They are so numerous that we now apply literary standards to them. This is something that we did not do a number of years ago. If the attitude was right, if the book said what we really wanted it to say, that was sufficient. Now we ask that the nonfiction book meet the same literary standards as all our other books. It should be lively and entertaining rather than encyclopedic.

AUTHORS AND ILLUSTRATORS

About black authors and illustrators: like white authors and illustrators, they are not all good. I had an agent call my office recently. She had called several children's librarians and they had referred her to me. She identified herself and said, "It is very, very necessary for me to get two things. I need some manuscripts on black life and black children; and, more than that, I very badly need some books where the authors are black. I could sell them overnight!" She hesitated and then she said, "Mrs. Baker, I wonder if you would consider writing a book." Well, we had a little session about respecting the rights of children to have good books and not to have quite so many of these contrived books. Children don't care whether the author is green, lavender or what. They won't read badly written, contrived books. Of course, talented black authors and illustrators should be encouraged. I believe they *will* come to the fore, that they *will* be encouraged to produce good books because there is great talent there. It simply needs to be found, and nurtured. Many editors have taken black illustrators and turned them loose and said, "Create. You can create any way you want, you don't have to create black." We know Alvin Smith and others like him who are marvelous illustrators working with general themes. I'm very, very excited right now to have seen the jacket of Countee Cullen's "Lost Zoo," a beautiful sensitive book written by a black poet who wasn't even thinking about race when he created this book.

Another area is one I call "books dealing with the black child's own feelings and emotions." We are getting a number of these books. Sometimes, I don't know whether these are books for children or about children, but we have received some very interesting ones. "It's Wings That Make Birds Fly" (*Pantheon*) is a very, very sensitive book in which the author records the words of a black child. "The Way It Is" (*Harcourt*) is also very interesting. It is composed of photographs taken by a group of teenagers with their own descriptions of the photographs as text. I think each one of these books really has to be dealt with individually. They are so different. Some are very good and some simply aren't. I take a good hard look at the concept books, such as "Color Me Brown" and "Black Is Beautiful," that attempt, I suppose, to make the very small child aware of this kind of thing. These must be written very well. Editors must be very critical when they get this kind of manuscript. They must make sure that it is well done and that it is going to reach the age group for which it is intended—and that it is *for* children and not *about* them.

I think the books must be worth reading. I think that is the very first criterion of all. A book has to be about people who are individuals with character and who really come alive. I keep Anne Carroll Moore's books on my desk, and when I need a little sustenance, I very often go back and reread them. In one of her books she tells about a young author who came to see her because she was disturbed about whether she was writing the right kind of books for children. I think Miss Moore's answer holds for all of us today. She told this young woman: "I think you have the biggest chance in the world, if you keep straight on working and appraising everything you do on the basis of sound criticism. Writing for children, like daily living with them, requires a constant sharpening of all one's faculties, a fresh discovery of new heights and depths in one's own emotions. The saving conviction is that children have as many and as varied tastes in reading as grown-ups. In the matter of their reading, I think that they have more sense since they are entirely unconcerned with other people's opinions of books. When they are bored, they stop reading the book. 'I didn't like that book' is reason enough and it admits of no argument." If we think about the child who is going to decide whether this book is read or not read, we will come out on the right track whether we are writing about whites or blacks.

Walt Disney Accused

Frances Clarke Sayers

Frances Clarke Sayers has a wide reputation—as former head of work with children in the New York Public Library (succeeding Anne Carroll Moore), storyteller, teacher of children's literature, writer of children's books and of books, articles, and speeches about children's literature. She also aided, through a survey and report on children's books in the Library of Congress, in the establishment of the Children's Book Section in 1963. Among her many publications are Anne Carroll Moore: A Biography *(1972) and* Summoned by Books *(1965), a collection of her published pieces. Most famous of these is perhaps her "Lose Not the Nightingale." Among her children's books are* Bluebonnets for Lucinda *(1934),* Mr. Tidy Paws *(1935), and* Tag-along Tooloo *(1941).*

In the spring of this year [1965] Max Rafferty, California's Superintendent of Public Instruction, wrote an article praising Walt Disney as "the greatest educator of this century." Frances Clarke Sayers challenged Dr. Rafferty's stand in a letter to the Los Angeles *Times,* which we reprint with Mrs. Sayers' permission.

It is a pity, in this fairest of springs, to break into the idyllic world of Dr. Max Rafferty and Walt Disney with a blast of anger, but it must be done.

I, too, am an educator, and because I am, it will take more than "a spoonful of sugar to make the medicine go down"—the medicine of Dr. Rafferty's absurd appraisal of Walt Disney as a pedagogue.

Mr. Disney has his own special genius. It has little to do with education, or with the cultivation of sensitivity, taste, or perception in the minds of children.

He has, to be sure, distributed some splendid films on science and nature, but he has also been a shameless nature faker in his fictionalized animal stories.

I call him to account for his debasement of the traditional literature of childhood, in films and in the books he publishes:

He shows scant respect for the integrity of the original creations of authors, manipulating and vulgarizing everything for his own ends.

His treatment of folklore is without regard for its anthropological, spiritual, or psychological truths. Every story is sacrificed to the "gimmick" (Dr. Rafferty's word) of animation.

The acerbity of *Mary Poppins,* unpredictable, full of wonder and

"Walt Disney Accused" by Frances Clarke Sayers and Charles M. Weisenberg from *Horn Book Magazine,* 40 (December 1965): 602–611. Copyright © 1965 by Horn Book, Inc. Reprinted by permission of the authors and *Coast Magazine.*

mystery, becomes, with Mr. Disney's treatment, one great marsh-mallow-covered cream puff. He made a young tough of Peter Pan, and transformed *Pinocchio* into a slapstick sadistic revel.

Not content with the films, he fixes these mutilated versions in books which are cut to a fraction of their original forms, illustrates them with garish pictures, in which every prince looks like a badly drawn portrait of Cary Grant, every princess a sex symbol.

The mystical Fairy with the Blue Hair of the *Pinocchio* turns out to be Marilyn Monroe, blonde hair and all.

As for the cliché-ridden texts, they are laughable. "Meanwhile, back at the castle . . . "

Dr. Rafferty finds all this "lone sanctuaries of decency and health." I find genuine feeling ignored, the imagination of children bludgeoned with mediocrity, and much of it overcast by vulgarity. Look at that wretched sprite with the wand and the over-sized buttocks which announces every Disney program on TV. She is a vulgar little thing, who has been too long at the sugar bowls.

Frances Clarke Sayers
Senior Lecturer, School of Library Service
and Department of English, UCLA

The controversy culminated in an interview with Frances Clarke Sayers, conducted by Charles M. Weisenberg, Public Relations Director of the Los Angeles Public Library. The interview was published in the August issue of *F. M. and Fine Arts* and is reprinted here with permission of Mrs. Sayers, Mr. Weisenberg, and *F. M. and Fine Arts*.

CMW: *Your criticism of Walt Disney has created a considerable stir among Los Angeles parents and educators, many of whom feel that twenty-five million children's books published by his companies are bringing good literature and culture to the young people of the twentieth century.*

SAYERS: I think the number of books published by Mr. Disney has nothing to do with whether or not he is bringing literature to children. That judgment has got to be based on quality rather than quantity. It's the same old problem that continually plagues American culture. I would rather have children playing their own games out of doors in the sunlight than getting the misrepresentation of literature as given by Walt Disney.

CMW: *I wonder if we might look at what he is giving them in rather specific terms. I'm talking about Walt Disney's use of folk tales and his reinterpretations of standard children's literature. In terms of quality and style, to what do you object?*

SAYERS: I find almost everything objectionable. First let's take the folklore. One of the great faults he has is to destroy the proportion in folk tales. Folklore is a universal form, a great symbolic literature which represents the folk. It is something that came from the masses, not something that is put over on the masses. These folk tales have a definite structure. From the folk tale, one learns one's role in life; one learns the tragic dilemma of life, the battle between good and evil, between weak and strong. One learns that if he is kind, generous, and compassionate, he will win the Princess. The triumph is for all that is good in the human spirit. There is a curious distortion of all these qualities in Disney's folklore. He does strange things. He sweetens a folk tale. Everything becomes very lovable. In *Cinderella,* for example, the birds are too sweet, and a great deal of attention is paid to the relationship of Cinderella to the birds and the mice. You realize this technique gives animation a chance to operate, but it destroys the proportion and purpose of the story, the conflict and its resolution. Folk tales are so marvelous in structure and symbolism that this distortion of the elements is particularly bad.

CMW: *But aren't folk tales currently being criticized because they are terribly gory, and doesn't Walt Disney eliminate the gore?*

SAYERS: He eliminates it on one hand, but on the other, he will accentuate it. In *Snow White,* for example, he makes a sentimental world where the little animals are all so cute, so curved, so soft; and then on the other hand, the villainess is depicted with such exaggerated realism that many children lose the whole point of the story in their concern over the terrible witch. The difference is partly between something that is heard and something that is seen. When a child reads about a witch, a child knows immediately that a witch is evil. But when he sees the terrible witch in detail, it has greater impact. It's as if a musician were playing and simply distorting the music by making it loud where the composer called for it to be soft, and by playing the whole thing out of key with no respect for the mood or the message or the markings of the composer.

CMW: *You talk about the message. Isn't it true that in Disney books good always triumphs? Don't we always get a moral lesson before we're done?*

SAYERS: That's another thing he does, always making it so obvious. In *Pinocchio,* which is one of the children's classics, he labels everything. He leaves nothing to the imagination of the child. In the original story of *Pinocchio,* there is a cricket. The cricket gives Pinocchio good advice, to which he pays no attention. In the Disney book, it's labeled that this cricket is the conscience of the child. That's sort of overworking the idea.

CMW: *Are you saying Disney restricts the child's need to think as a child does when he reads the more traditional versions?*

SAYERS: Yes; precisely. Disney takes a great masterpiece and telescopes it. He reduces it to ridiculous lengths, and in order to do this he has to make everything very obvious. It all happens very quickly and is expressed in very ordinary language. There is nothing to make a child think or feel or imagine.

CMW: *Another book that comes to mind, perhaps the one that is receiving the most current attention, is* Mary Poppins. *I noted there are several editions put out by Disney, apparently aimed at different age levels. Do you feel there is an attempt being made to bring stories like* Mary Poppins *down to children who are really not ready for them?*

SAYERS: I think Mr. Disney is basically interested in the market. He sees this all as a means of reaching a wider audience. With *Mary Poppins,* again, I'm talking of the book as it was originally conceived; in this form it is one of the most creative, imaginative and original efforts in the field of children's literature. In an effort to reach all the children, Disney belittles them. *Mary Poppins* is a story that almost anyone would be interested in from the age of four to eighty. It could be read aloud to a child of four. Like all great books, it is without age limits. What I deplore about Mr. Disney is his tendency to take over a piece of work and make it his own without any regard for the original author or to the original book.

CMW: *Then he takes a book like* Mary Poppins *or* Treasure Island *and simplifies it. Might not the child be introduced to the book at too early an age and then not bother with it later because he thinks he has read that book?*

SAYERS: This would be a great loss. The same problem exists in certain rewriting of the classics in order that everyone can read them. You know, some educators believe in this. They believe that it is important for a child who has no skill in reading to read a rewritten *Treasure Island* or a rewritten *Tom Sawyer* so that he can have the book. I think that this is a false concept of education because all children have in the rewritten edition is the plot, and the plot is the least important part of a great book. Much of the book—the atmosphere, the feeling, the emotion, the language, the skill and artistry of the writer—is lost. It's like reading the *Reader's Digest.* When you ask someone if they read such and such a book, they will never say, "Yes, I have read it." They will say, "I read the *Reader's Digest* edition," because, as adults, they know the difference. Many educators say that it's better that they at least know that such a book exists. I don't agree. There is no reason why good books should be lowered or lessened to meet the demands of people who are not ready or interested enough to make the effort to read.

CMW: *What about the children who are not ready to read quality literature; isn't Disney fulfilling a need?*

SAYERS: There are books for such children and I don't think Disney has any place in that field. It seems to me that it's a matter of merchandise with Mr. Disney. He is seeking that which sells quickly and easily to the mass market. What I deplore is that such books seem to show so little respect for the imagination of a non-reading child and so little respect for the capacity of a reading child.

CMW: *Let's turn to art and matters of illustration. What about Disney's art? You spoke of his illustrations of the witches being particularly devastating and his illustrations of the birds being too sweet; how would you rate the artistic or aesthetic quality of the drawings of the Disney books in comparison with what is available in other children's books?*

SAYERS: Here again I think that a major crime has been committed. In the first place, you cannot attribute these pictures to any one artist; the pictures in the books are done by the Disney staff. The minute you have a collective illustration, you lose one of the great qualities of an illustrator, which is his own style, his own conviction. In every book, you get the "Disney look." The simpering female, the badly drawn prince, a cartoonish nature, and a lack of respect for the anatomy of animals. This is a particularly tragic aspect of Mr. Disney's books because the illustrations in children's books, especially in America during the last twenty-five years, have made a golden era in picture books. Some of our finest artists—not only our great illustrators, but the great artists, men and women whose pictures hang on the walls of museums—have illustrated books for children. Each book is a separate and individual experience, and the children who have access to these books are learning about all the subtleties of art and subtleties of appreciation and enjoyment.

CMW: *What do you say to those who say that the cartoon style of drawing is really a form of American art and that you simply aren't willing to accept it?*

SAYERS: I'm willing to accept certain cartoons. I just can't accept Disney. I have been accused of being the sort of person who would take the blanket away from Linus in *Peanuts* because I object to Walt Disney. I think that *Peanuts* is absolutely perfect in its conception and in its drawing. It is so close to children and so close to the universal experience. It isn't that I'm anti-cartoon. Some of our great picture book artists, Robert McCloskey, for example, have the same marvelous stern, sharp lines; the same beautiful control of line, strong and definitive; and the ability to exaggerate certain aspects of a person. These are the makings of a fine cartoonist. Here again, I think there's a quality of muddy color in Disney pictures, mushy outlines and nebulous design.

CMW: *There's another aspect of a book that I think we should cover. We've talked about literary style; we've talked about illustrative styles; but how about things like characterization? Do you find significant differences in the characterization of people and creatures in the Disney version of standard children's works and folk tales?*

SAYERS: Yes. Disney seems to think that the names he gives creatures are better than the names the original author gave them. A pertinent example is in *Pinocchio*. There is one chapter in *Pinocchio* in which he goes to a land where there are no schools and no tasks to be done—every child's ideal of how the world should be. Let me tell you how Carlo Lorenzini, the author of this book, describes the land where they do nothing but play.

"The population was composed entirely of boys. The oldest were fourteen, and the youngest scarcely eight years old. In the streets there was such merriment, noise, and shouting, that it was enough to turn anybody's head. There were troupes of boys everywhere. Some were playing with nuts, some with battledores, some with balls. Some rode velocipedes, others wooden horses. A party were playing at hide-and-seek, a few were chasing each other. Boys dressed in straw were eating lighted tow; some were reciting, some singing, some leaping. Some were amusing themselves with walking on their hands with their feet in the air; others were trundling hoops, or strutting about dressed as generals, wearing leaf helmets and commanding a squadron of cardboard soldiers."[1]

It's true that there are some old-fashioned toys mentioned here, but this is a description of a world from a child's point of view. The boys are amusing themselves with boylike games. Now, here's what Disney does with this same country.

"One day, down in Tobacco Lane, Jiminy came upon Pinocchio puffing on a corncob pipe; Lampwick had a big cigar; Jiminy lost his temper and shook his little fist angrily. 'This has gone far enough; throw away that pipe; come home this minute.' Pinocchio looked sheepish, but Lampwick began to snicker; 'Don't tell me you're scared of a beetle,' he said."

And then there's an illustration of Pinocchio smoking the pipe and Lampwick playing at billiards. The description of Lampwick is supposed to be childlike, and these are the games that they play: billiards and smoking pipes.

CMW: *Some might say that Disney has updated the story and introduced a degree of sophistication that is necessary in the twentieth century.*

SAYERS: I don't think it is necessary. What if a child does meet a game he's not known before? What if he doesn't know what battledores are? There are other things mentioned here such as

---

1. From *Pinocchio* by Carlo Lorenzini (J. B. Lippincott Co., 1948).

hide-and-seek, balls, strutting about wearing hats, whistling and shouting. I think the truth is that Walt Disney has never addressed himself to children once in his life—never. This material is made to reach an adult audience. This is the whole trouble. Everything is made to reach everyone, and in order to reach everyone, he must introduce the Hollywood touch. Every illustration of a girl in Disney's books looks like the Hollywood queen and every picture of the hero looks like a badly drawn Cary Grant. Obvious symbols of an adult world.

CMW: *Mr. Disney is a free enterprise agent in a very competitive line. Do you feel that Mr. Disney has any responsibility or obligation to preserve the traditional or the original? Does he have any responsibility or obligation to further what would be considered quality literature?*

SAYERS: I feel that anybody who addresses himself to children has a responsibility, and that responsibility is to make available to children the very best that has ever been produced and to sustain the distinction of what has been produced. Everybody in the popular entertainment field or in the popular arts has a responsibility. It's not that I want everybody to be precious or snobbish; it's that I want everybody to be sincere. They should present what is individually their own point of view instead of taking someone's point of view and distorting it and even profaning it.

CMW: *Are we making a distinction here between destroying or profaning something and simply modernizing it? In the last fifty years the American language has changed enormously. Is there a distinction here between the destruction of something and the updating or modernizing of it to make it more acceptable?*

SAYERS: I've heard people ask, What's so sacred about a classic that you can't change it for the modern child? Nothing is sacred about a classic. What makes a classic is the life that has accrued to it from generation after generation of children. Children give life to these books. Some books which you could hardly bear to read are, for children, classic. *Black Beauty* is dated, Victorian, and a tear jerker, but it has an enduring life because when you read *Black Beauty*—you feel like a horse. This is the quality that must be preserved, that makes a classic. A lot of people living in an ivory tower saying a book is a classic doesn't make it one. To be a classic means that it has enduring life which is given to it from its readers.

Now, on this matter of updating and changing the language. As a teacher at the university level, I see that one of the great lacks in the modern college student is a knowledge of the past. He lives in a kind of vacuum between birth and death with very little relationship to anything that has gone on before. I think you can overdo this updating. If something seems dated to you, then it's dated and you don't have to read it. But there will be many children who do like it. Children always ask Mother to tell about the olden times when she was little. There is a genuine interest in olden times with old language, with the language of Howard Pyle in his King Arthur stories and *Robin Hood.* We're caught in the pace of modern living—this emphasis on the "quick take," on the magazine that says it will take you eight minutes to read an article. It seems to me that here is a tendency that ought to be denied in part. Certain children do read in the past; they love the old language; they love the sound of words. I don't think it's good enough to say something is better because it is updated and modern.

CMW: *You talk about the "quick take"; are you suggesting that the kind of rewriting that Disney engages in accustoms young children to wanting everything that way? And that their future reading might also be limited by this background?*

SAYERS: Precisely. That's it exactly. If everything is made so obvious that it asks nothing of the readers, then after a while, their ability to respond is atrophied. And they grow up as young people unable to take anything from a printed page, or they become bored because they haven't discovered the nuances, the differences of opinion, the differences of approach between one author and another. Children can be trusted to skip what they don't like in a book. That's perfectly all right. But to have it all reduced to the supposedly twelve-year-old mind of the adult public is what I object to. I think the great skill of the animators in the Disney films and the control of all the techniques of animation and drawing are interesting in themselves; but they should be subordinate to the material, and I think that, too often, they are not.

CMW: *In all honesty, do you think quality children's literature is marketable to a mass audience in America today?*

SAYERS: I think you can find the answer to that in the public libraries all over the country. The folk tales, the fantasy, the fiction, as well as the great and wonderful field of non-fiction, circulate by the millions. These books are marketable because children consume them.

CMW: *Walt Disney has been praised by a great many people. One of them was Max Rafferty, Superintendent of Public Instruction in California. Not too long ago, he wrote a column about Walt Disney in which he called him a great educator. He said: "Disney's live movies have become lone sanctuaries of decency and health in the jungle of sex, sadism and pornography created by the Hollywood producers. His pictures don't dwell on dirt; they show life as something a little finer than drunken wallowing in some gutter of self-pity. The beatniks and degenerates think his films are square. I think they're wonderful."*

Couldn't this quotation perhaps be applied to the books of Walt Disney? Aren't his books also an oasis in a field of smut that fills the newsstands from one end of the city to another?

SAYERS: I once heard Jessamyn West give a marvelous address at an American Library Association meeting in which she said there was only one kind of dirty book, and that was a book which falsified life. I think Disney falsifies life by pretending that everything is so sweet, so saccharine, so without any conflict except the obvious conflict of violence. I think that even in the lines of Mother Goose you find an element that is in all great literature, and that is the realization that in life there is a tragic tension between good and evil, between disaster and triumph, and it isn't all a matter of sweetness and light. The first people to know this intuitively are the children themselves. In my experience as a children's librarian in the public libraries in New York City, I've had children come to tell me things that happened in their homes that are as tragic and as dreadful as anything that ever appeared in a book. We can't make them think everything is sweet and lovely. This, I think, is the tragic break in Disney. He misplaces the sweetness and misplaces the violence, and the result is like soap opera, not really related to the great truths of life. It's set up so that you can sit there quietly and take on *Peyton Place* and all that utter nonsense without really feeling a thing.

CMW: *By way of closing I'd like to look to the positive side of children's literature. You've talked about the inadequacy of Disney's illustrations, but who are the good or even great illustrators? Who can reach the child of today with drawings that have the quality you think should be found in a children's book?*

SAYERS: Robert McCloskey—we've already spoken of him. Maurice Sendak is an outstanding illustrator. There is Marcia Brown, who's doing marvelous illustrations in wood blocks, who changes her style for every book she illustrates. When she illustrated *Cinderella* she went into a French period because the earliest version of that story was a French version. Here in Los Angeles we have Taro Yashima, the great Japanese illustrator of children's books. There are hundreds of them, really: Louis Slobodkin, the sculptor, who makes children's picture books; James Daugherty, a famous muralist, whose *Andy and the Lion* is a great classic of picture books—it's the old story of Androcles and the Lion which he's turned into a piece of Americana.

CMW: *Do you distinguish between the Disney work we've been talking about and the Mickey Mouse material?*

SAYERS: Yes. I remember vividly the *Three Little Pigs,* one of the early animated films of Disney which I thought was absolutely enchanting, and the Donald Duck and Mickey Mouse stories. In the early days I found them most original and pleasing. What I am eager for people to do is to realize that in his own medium Walt Disney has made a great contribution to the humor of the world. What I object to is his treatment of traditional literature and of the great books of childhood.

CMW: *Do you have an objection to the contemporary Donald Duck and Pluto and other standard characters that he himself has created?*

SAYERS: On the screen, no. That's what they were created for and that's where they should be enjoyed. What I do object to is the milking of everything. For instance, that terrible organization of children, The Mouseketeers, which makes me cringe. It's making everything a gimmick. In the early days and in certain other films, Disney is a master in his own field. I just would like to have him stay in that field and not attempt to impose his particular gifts on the literature and the arts of children.

CMW: *What do you say to those people who say you are tearing down and attacking a great American? Walt Disney has become more than just a man, hasn't he? He's almost a household word. The Walt Disney imprint is accepted far and wide as a sign of quality, and certainly the Disney imprint is accepted immediately as something good for children.*

SAYERS: You're like the manager of a radio station who said to me, "It's like attacking motherhood to attack Walt Disney." Just let me say that I am attacking Walt Disney in relation to children's literature, not in relation to many other things that he has done. I think he is a genius in many ways. To the people who think that I am tearing down an American institution, that he is a great educator, and that he is a great patron saint of childhood because he's put these books into his pictures, I have just one thing to say to those people: If you read *Mary Poppins,* you will see what has happened to it in the film. If you read *Treasure Island, Alice in Wonderland,* and *The Wind in the Willows,* you will see for yourself how Disney has destroyed something which was delightful, which was an expression of an individual mind and imagination. I would say that before you condemn anyone who attacks Disney, read the original classics and compare. Form your own opinion. We all have that right.

Signs of the Times

Margery Fisher

Margery Fisher was England's first recipient, in 1966, of the Children's Book Circle's Eleanor Farjeon Award for distinguished service in the world of children's books. She is also notable as a critic—especially for Growing Point, *for which she almost single-handedly writes the reviews—and as a lecturer. In 1970 Mrs. Fisher gave the first May Hill Arbuthnot Honor Lecture.[1] She is author of* Intent Upon Reading *(1961) and* Matters of Fact *(1972).*

Johann Wyss *The Swiss Family Robinson* Collins £1•05(21s) Abridged by Audrey Butler. Ill. Gay Galsworthy. 182 pages. $8^3/_4 \times 6^1/_4$.

R. D. Blackmore *Lorna Doone* Collins £1•05(21s) Abridged by Olive Jones. Ill. Pauline Baynes. 216 pages. $8^3/_4 \times 6^1/_4$.

George Macdonald *The Princess and the Goblin. The Princess and Curdie* Collins £1•05(21s) Abridged by Olive Jones. Ill. William Stobbs. 200 pages. $8^3/_4 \times 6^1/_4$.

Charles Dickens *Great Expectations* Collins £1•05(21s) Abridged by Rosemary Manning. Ill. Gareth Floyd. 217 pages. $8^3/_4 \times 6^1/_4$.

Perhaps the first essential when one is reviewing a literary abridgement is to declare an interest. I must therefore admit that while I enjoyed the Swiss Fam. as a child I didn't go back to it again and again and it does not hurt me to see some of its longueurs disappearing. Besides, Wyss's story as we have it has always been a bit of an editorial hotch-potch and an abridger can hardly be said to be treading on sacred ground in making it over once more, especially if she is, as in this case, abridging her own translation. *The Swiss Family Robinson* is not a great literary work. It has been loved in many families, but for its absurdity, its endless Robinsonian inventiveness and for that never-a-dull-moment flair that livens so many unliterary books. These qualities are actually enhanced by abridgement; spared paternal disquisitions and offered only a sprinkling of topographical description, the reader is dragged at tremendous speed from one thrill to another. The Robinsons have barely noticed a housekeeping lack or an impending danger when the solution is at hand—passively, with the discovery of an edible root or a safe tree, or actively, with the arrival of a tameable onager or a female castaway who can ensure the continuance of the human race in this island paradise. With the neat and attractive production of the series and the dramatic pictures, this edition is likely to become the Best Buy among those currently available.

"Signs of the Times" by Margery Fisher from *Growing Point,* vol. 9, no. 7 (January 1971): 1662–1666. Reprinted by permission of the author.

1. "Rights and Wrongs," *Top of the News,* 26 (June 1970): 373–391.

The interest I have to declare in regard to *Lorna Doone* is a negative one. I have tried four or five times in my life to get through this novel, always in vain. Having read the strongly limned tale that emerges from Olive Jones's pruning I can see its virtues and indeed the point of marketing a well-produced, agreeable edition of a story surprisingly modern in tone. Perhaps "surprising" is not the right word, in view of the elegant, forthright and vivacious dialogue to be found in so many Victorian novels. Moreover, most novelists of the period had a zest for Chinese-box plots that called for, and found, conspicuous skill in narrative. But though I was hardly surprised to find what a good story *Lorna Doone* was, and ashamed at not discovering this years ago, I have not the courage to put the abridgement to the test by reading the original and finding just what has been cut. I cannot feel the book is sacrosanct but have no grounds for being dogmatic on the subject.

As a general rule I am sure that children need to be aware of the feel of a period other than their own, and novels provide one of the best ways of developing that sense of the past which is hard to acquire consciously. This is relevant to the skilful tape-joining that has compressed the history of Gwyntystorm into one volume. Olive Jones's excisions in *The Princess and the Goblin* and its sequel are of several kinds. First and simplest are the cutting of a few heavy Latinisations no longer current. The only one of these I am really sorry to lose occurs in *The Princess and Curdie* in that cumulative description of the animals driving the wicked townspeople out of doors. Into howling wind and rain they rush, but as George Macdonald puts it, "Thither also were they followed by the inexorable avengers." The phrase locks the whole magnificent paragraph together; lose it, and you lose its clanging momentum. Apart from single words, a great number of relatively unimportant repetitions and bridging passages have been taken out so that the story (besides costing less to print) is brought nearer to the modern fashion for streamlined narrative. Most of these small cuts are inoffensive taken one by one: looked at as a whole, they speed up the story at the expense of the ample, discursive tone that is integral to the books. As I do not agree with the general editor of the series that children will not read long, discursive stories any more (though George Macdonald is better read aloud anyhow), I think these cuts are a pity. Children can skip if they want to, but the stories are not over-long and certainly not difficult to read.

Then, many of these cuts remove clues to states of mind, so that their accumulated effect is to emphasise the *adventure* aspects of the stories and to weaken their *emotional* force. In the first book a short chapter has been entirely omitted in which Irene, after her first sight of the old lady spinning in the tower, goes again to look for her in vain. The chapter does not forward the plot but it does slow down the narrative so that the reader can feel something of the way the seriousness of the encounter drives in upon the little girl. Again, in *The Princess and Curdie,* small cuts at the beginning curtail the author's careful analysis of Curdie's state of mind, the to-and-fro of his conscience and the way his boyish sensitiveness is sharpened by his second meeting with the "great-grandmother." George Macdonald is plotting the growth of a soul in these two books and it is craven to try to lessen the force of this theme in case children may be put off by it.

Apart from the small indications of feeling that I have mentioned, a good many of the author's own moral comments have been cut out, though they are part and parcel of the story. At the beginning of *The Princess and Curdie* the miner's boy is back at work, having refused to leave his parents for a position in the King's household. His parents reflect sadly on the opportunity lost and George Macdonald adds his word to theirs:

> He might soon have been a captain, they did believe! The good, kind people did not reflect that the road to the next duty is the only straight one, or that, for their fancied good, we should never wish our children or friends to do what we would not do ourselves if we were in their position. We must accept righteous sacrifices as well as make them.

The revised version ends mundanely "It would have been such a fine thing for him and them, too, they thought, if he had ridden with the king's train." But the moral after-word is important. It points forward to the purpose of what is to come and suggests that it is more than a simple adventure. We don't write like this now; but we have our own way of stating a moral. George Macdonald's book deserves to be read in context. The abridger has cut out almost all the side-remarks about evolution and religion and in particular a long sardonic chapter in the second book describing how the discomfited councillors try to develop new religio-political philosophies to put themselves back in power. Passages like these usefully reflect the preoccupations of the time.

Another section of abridgment is connected with Victorian social prejudices. Many of the conversations between the Princess and her nurse Lootie have been cut or severely pruned; part of the description of Curdie as being neither "clownish or rude" has gone; so have Lootie's apprehensive remarks about punishment from her royal employers; so has a passage describing Curdie's mother with her hands "hard and chapped and large" through working for her family; so have passages describing how Curdie is ill-used by the palace servants. One suspects that a sense of social shame has been operating here as much as a desire to remove a required number of words. But these stories were written within a conception of class different from our own, and one that children should know and appreciate.

The alteration to the end of *The Princess and Curdie* perhaps epitomises the skilful but I think mistaken editing of the two books. Olive Jones's version ends "Irene and Curdie were married. The old King died, and they were king and queen." This is not a climax but an anti-climax. It negates the moral point of the story and peculiar melancholy of the whole disquisition on good and evil. George Macdonald allows his readers a moment of optimism, but after Irene and Curdie have died the country once more succumbs to greed and the final paragraphs, superb in rhythm and pictorial strength, indicate that it is not the fortunes of our hero and heroine that matter finally but the eternal fight. "All round spreads a wilderness of wild deer, and the very name of Gwyntystorm has ceased from the lips of men." If we left children alone I believe they would choose this ending in preference to the bad one in the abridged edition. Not all children will read, or will enjoy, the writings of George Macdonald. Why should they? But if they want to try, they should try him unadulterated. It is not for us to pick over books as great as these, to bring them into line with taste that is itself ephemeral, any more than it was reasonable for Garrick to bring Shakespeare in line with mid-eighteenth-century taste by supplying a happy ending to *King Lear*.

Rosemary Manning's expert handling of *Great Expectations* has resulted in a story eminently suitable for children, clear (mostly) in plot and with the central character's state of mind carefully filleted and brought out of its particularly Victorian murk of symbolic introspection. Leaving aside for the moment the question of whether this was worth doing, let me suggest one or two of the results of the treatment. In the Foreword the general editor suggests that serialisation perhaps encouraged authors "to write more words than strictly necessary and to drop in a new minor character whenever they ran short of material." In cutting *Great Expectations* Rosemary Manning has dispensed with almost all of Mr. Wopsle, most of Mr. Pumblechook, a lot of Biddy and of Jagger's mysterious servant Molly. Mr. Wopsle's posturings at the village school and later on the boards in London are certainly self-indulgent from the point of view of narrative and except in one instance, when his warning to Pip that he is being followed does heighten the tension of the Magwitch-Compeyson sub-plot, this clownish man does not further the action. But he gives Dickens the opportunity to enlarge once more on two institutions on which he is always worth reading, and what a pity for anyone to miss the inspired idiocies of the Hamlet performance when Pip wished Mr. Wopsle's "curls and forehead had been more probable" and when the absurd actor "died by inches from the ankles upward." The hypocritical Mr. Pumblechook is another matter. His insistence that he is Pip's secret benefactor adds welcome comic relief to the dark moments in the story; there is a flavour in this character, especially in his mouthings at Mrs. Gargery's funeral, which is needed in the book and is typical of its period. The shortening or omission of several of Pip's heart-to-heart talks with Biddy and much of the material brutality of Mrs. Gargery means that Pip's social attitudes, especially towards Joe Gargery, his snobbery and its many unhappy results, are offered too suddenly to the reader and without enough period psychology, if I may so describe it, to help him to understand this very Victorian situation. It is hardly fair to Dickens to simplify Pip so much; certainly it seems unwise to cut so many of his soliloquies, for his changes of heart come upon one now too quickly for them to seem anything but superficial. As regards the plot, the cutting of much talk between Miss Havisham's scheming relatives, of a conversation Pip and Biddy have about Orlick and of Pip's musing about Molly all make the course of events less easy to follow and impossibly abrupt. Indeed, some of the adapter's contrivances are very lame. If we are not to have Mr. Trabb measuring Pip for his departure to the metropolis, it would have been better not to keep him to the extent of a sentence or two, and in the case of the first appearance of the Pockets at Miss Havisham's house, words have been inserted that Dickens never wrote (harmless, possibly, but outside the abridger's brief). The effect of truncation is perhaps most clearly seen at the close of the vital chapter where Pip is confronted with the truth about his parentage and his benefactor. Magwitch has retired for the night. Pip muses (in the shortened book):

> Miss Havisham's intentions towards me, all a mere dream; Estella not designed for me; I only suffered in Satis House as a convenience, a sting for the greedy relations, a model with a mechanical heart to practise on when no other practice was at hand; those were the first smarts I had. But, sharpest and deepest pain of all—it was for the convict, guilty of I knew not what crimes, that I had deserted Joe.

There follow, in the original, three paragraphs in which Pip gives way to his fears of this alarming visitor. "In every rage of wind and rush of rain I heard pursuers"; in a passage of overwrought prose we get inside Pip's mind and the light-dark composition of the story that carries so much to the reader insensibly is established once more. By firelight Pip examines the features of the convict and after an uneasy sleep he wakes to find "the candles were wasted out, the fire was dead, and the wind and rain intensified the thick black darkness." It is not only by what is stated that Dickens's meaning is conveyed; he needed these paragraphs, and so do we all.

Great Expectations in its cut form is certainly put within the reach of more children, or young people, than before. But must they necessarily read the book when they are young? Why can they not wait till they are in a state to take Dickens whole, with all his divagations, his sentimentality, his serialisation devices, and to have as well his full grotesque humour, his cruel perception of human weakness, the superb phrases he tosses into the baldest piece of narration. The assumption behind this edition is that once children have been wooed by an easy-to-read version they will proceed, sooner or later, to the uncut novel. I doubt it. It seems more reasonable for them to meet this and other stories by Dickens first in a dramatised form. Rosemary Manning's version is really a reader's substitute for a television serial and I am sure we don't need both. Children are more likely to read "the book of the play" than to move from a book of 19 chapters to the same book with 59. It is hardly likely that we can persuade them to do so by stressing that they will then discover the "real" Dickens. They must discover the real Dickens at once or not till they are fit for him—or even, not at all. It is less unfortunate to miss him entirely than to meet him with a crew-cut in our own century.

Chapter 4

Writers and Writing

The how and why of writing for children are questions pondered by many authors, some of whom have turned from an adult audience to the young.

How does one write for children? Rumer Godden in "The Writer Must Become as a Child" states that the famous books "never . . . have a big plot written down, but a little plot written up. . . . The words themselves are expressive almost to onomatopoeia and they are often long words. . . . Children's books . . . must sound well; they will be read aloud and the words must bind into a rhythmic whole as in a poem, a rhythm that matches the subject. . . ."[1] E. B. White agrees: "You have to write up, not down. . . . Children . . . love words that give them a hard time, provided they are in a context that absorbs their attention." (See "On Writing for Children," in this chapter.)

Does an author write differently for children than for adults? In "Happy Endings? Of Course, and Also Joy" (reprinted in this chapter), Natalie Babbitt sees only one real difference "where emotional themes are concerned;" while Paula Fox, quoted in John Rowe Townsend's *A Sense of Story*, suggests that she sees no sharp difference: "What applies to good writing is, I think, absolute, whether for children or grown-ups or the blind or the deaf or the thin or the fat. . . . I am just starting another children's

---

1. *New York Times Book Review,* pt. 2, v. 59 (November 14, 1954): 1, 28.

book and another novel—and I hope I shall remember which is which."[2]
Leon Garfield, who believes that themes and language have nothing to do
with the difference between books for adults and for children, says in the
Horn Book Magazine:

> . . . at no time did I ever think of writing for any particular
> audience, children or otherwise. I do not believe anybody ever
> has. Certainly Philippa Pearce—probably our best children's
> writer—does not; nor, I fancy, do Rosemary Sutcliff, Alan
> Garner, William Mayne. One writes so that children can under-
> stand, which means writing as clearly, vividly, and truthfully as
> possible. Adults might put up with occasional lapses; children are
> far less tolerant. They must never be bored; not for an instant.
> Words must live for them; so must people. That is what really
> matters, and it entails believing entirely in what one writes and
> having a real urgency to convince the reader that it is absolutely,
> utterly true.[3]

Why write for children? Isaac Bashevis Singer, winner of the National
Book Award for children's literature, has turned to children's books
because, he says, he finds satisfaction in the young audience and believes
that "if literature for adults is destined for revival it will come from
literature for children."[4]

Who should write for children? In one of the selections in this chapter,
Joan Aiken suggests that it is perhaps dangerous to allow just anyone to
write for children.

> Writing anything for children unless one has a strong, genuine
> impulse not only to write at all but to write that particular
> thing . . . is every bit as wicked as selling plastic machine-gun
> toys, candies containing addictive drugs, or watered-down penicil-
> lin. . . . Really good writing for children should come out with
> the force of Niagara; it ought to be concentrated; it needs to have
> everything that is in adult writing squeezed into a smaller com-
> pass . . . the emotional range ought to be the same, if not
> greater.[5]

---

2. (Philadelphia: J. B. Lippincott Company, 1971. Harmondsworth: Longman Young Books,
1971, now Kestrel Books).

3. "And So It Grows," *Horn Book Magazine*, 44 (December 1968): 668–672.

4. " 'I See the Child as a Last Refuge,' " *New York Times Book Review*, pt. 2 (November 9,
1969): 1, 66.

5. See also Philippa Pearce, "Writing a Book," *Horn Book Magazine*, 43 (June 1967): 317–327.

An Imaginary Correspondence

Rumer Godden

Since 1946 Rumer Godden has written both children's stories and adult fiction, beginning with The Dolls' House *(1948) and including in a long line of successes* The Mousewife *(1951),* Impunity Jane *(1954),* Miss Happiness and Miss Flower *(1961), and* Little Plum *(1963). Some of her adult fiction also centers on children:* An Episode of Sparrows *(1955) and* The River, *which was so remarkably well filmed. Rumer Godden has written critiques of Hans Christian Andersen and Beatrix Potter and much about the business of writing. She has also written poetry and translated from the French Carmen B. De Gasztold's poems in* Prayers from the Ark *(1962) and* The Creatures' Choir *(1965).*

An imaginary correspondence between Mr. V. Andal, editor of the De Base Publishing Company, Inc., and the ghost of Miss Beatrix Potter,[1] using the word *ghost* in its old meaning of soul or spirit. She would be shocked to its depth if she knew some of the things that are going on nowadays in the world of children's books.

Mr. V. Andal to Miss B. Potter.

January 18, 1963

Dear Miss Potter:

I am editing for the De Base Publishing Company, Inc., an unusual series of books aimed at beginning readers. The general title is "Masterpieces for Mini-Minds," and the series will consist of reissues, in a modern production, of famous books that have become classics for children, so that the first reading of the very young will also be an introduction to their own great authors. We are approaching, among others, Hans Andersen, Edward Lear, Lewis Carroll, George Macdonald, Anna Sewell, and Andrew Lang.

The works will be produced whole and entire, though with certain modifications to the text to make them suitable for children of 1963: with this in view we have decided on a limited vocabulary of 450 different words. I have had a list of words prepared by a trio of philologists and I would be glad to send it to you if you are interested. Other words may be added as long as they are within the grasp of a reader from 5 to 8.

"An Imaginary Correspondence" by Rumer Godden from *Horn Book Magazine,* 38 (August 1963): 197–206. Reprinted by permission of Curtis Brown, Ltd. Copyright © 1963 by Rumer Godden.

1. Some of Beatrix Potter's remarks are taken from her letters.

Mr. Al Loy, our president, has authorized me to pay an advance of $3,000 against royalty upon receipt of an acceptable manuscript along the lines indicated. In addition to the advance, there should be continuing payments, for the books will have, besides quality writing, the collaboration of the best illustrators and should enjoy a huge sale.

I hope you will be one of the contributors to this project. If you like to edit your own book, I will be delighted to send you the word list, from which departures can, of course, be made (as long as they come within this age range). If you would rather we edited, this will be undertaken with the utmost care and the De Base Company will be pleased to send you a check for $3,000 as soon as I forward your work.

Cordially,
V.Andal

I send you Hans Andersen's "Ti-ny Thum-my" to see. (Originally issued as "Thumbelina," and I think now much improved.)

Miss B. Potter to Mr. V. Andal

26th January, 1963

Dear Mr. Andal,

Thank you for your letter. That a request for a fresh issue of my books should reach me after so many years is heartening. The cheque you offer is certainly generous; there are several acres round Sawrey that could with advantage be purchased and given to our National Trust. Publication with another firm would vex my old publishers very much, and I don't like breaking with old friends, but possibly we might arrange to have something published on the American market that would not interfere with my normal sales.

I presume you will want *Peter Rabbit*. I believe my attitude of mind towards my own successful publications has been comical. At one time I almost loathed Peter Rabbit, I was so sick of him. I still cannot understand his perennial success. I myself prefer *The Tailor of Gloucester*, and send you both books to see.

Yours sincerely,
Beatrix Potter

N.B. My books are illustrated by myself.
N.B. I do not understand your second paragraph. How can a work be "whole and entire" if it is modified? How can a philologist, however gifted, know what words I need? Perhaps I have misunderstood you.

Illustration by Beatrix Potter from *The Tailor of Gloucester* from the original manuscript by Beatrix Potter. Copyright © Frederick Warne & Co., Ltd., 1968; reproduced with their permission.

Mr. V. Andal to Miss Potter

February 4, 1963

Dear Miss Potter:

I hasten to thank you for "Peter Rabbit," a most charming tale, and am sure that, when made larger (it must be enlarged—people like to get their money's worth) and given good illustrations, it will make a magnificent book for our series; we shall have our reader's report in a day or two when I shall write to you again. "The Tailor of Gloucester" I have, for the moment, put aside. It has an old-fashioned air about it that might puzzle a child, but perhaps it might be reissued as a "period piece." The words would need a great deal of simplification: "worn to a ravelling"—what could a child make of that?

I am sorry my letter was not clear. The modifications about such words are only those needed to make language more assimilatory to the children of today. In this connection, we believe the advice of our philologists is of value; they are often able to help an author to put his, or her, delightful thoughts into plain words—simple enough for a child to understand.

Yours very sincerely,
V. Andal

Miss Potter to Mr. V. Andal

10th February, 1963

Dear Mr. Andal,

Again I do not understand. What do you mean by "reader's report"? when I sent the manuscript of *Peter Rabbit* to Mr. Warne, my original publisher, he read it, made up his mind he liked it, accepted it, and that was settled. Do you really need other people to do this for you? It seems to me a fuss over a very small matter.

I have too much common sense to think that *Peter Rabbit* could ever be magnificent: he is an ordinary small brown rabbit. Nor do I like the idea of the book being enlarged. I have never heard that size was a guarantee of quality, and must point out that my books were made small to fit children's hands, not to impress the grownups.

As for the philologists: if an author needs help in putting thought into plain and simple words he, or she, should not try to be an author. It would seem to me you are in danger of using "simple" in the sense of mentally deficient. Are children nowadays so much less intelligent than their parents?

I have been told I write good prose. I think I write carefully because I enjoy my writing and enjoy taking pains over it. I write to please myself; my usual way is to scribble and cut out and write it again and again. The shorter, the plainer—the better. And read the Bible (unrevised version and Old Testament) if I feel my style wants chastening.

Yours sincerely,
Beatrix Potter

N.B. My books, as I said, *are* illustrated.

Mr. Andal to Miss Potter

February 19, 1963

My dear respected lady:

While disliking having to cross swords with someone as eminent as yourself, I really must enlighten you to the fact that the Old Testament, as reading, is almost totally out of date, not only for children but adults. It has been replaced by the epic screen pictures which, sequestered as you are in your native Cumberland, you may not have seen. These movies are money-spinners, which is heartening as it endorses our belief that there is life in old tales yet—if properly presented. (One of our "masterpieces" is Genesis, retold in uno- or duo-syllable words.)

Mr. Warne could perhaps make his own decision to publish an important manuscript (which is what we want to make "Peter Rabbit" in this new illustrated edition), but that was years ago. Publishing nowadays is such a costly business that we need expert advice. Properly handled, in attractive wrappers, perhaps packaged with one or two others, and well advertised, books for juveniles can become really big business, which is why I hope you will consider carefully our reader's report and let us guide you.

Your well-wisher,
V. Andal

Miss Potter to Mr. Andal

22nd February, 1963

Dear Sir,

I am not "eminent" as you call it but a plain person who believes in saying what she thinks.

Your publishing would not be so costly without all these "experts" and elaborate notions; indeed, your last letter reads as if you were selling grocery, not books. In my day, philologists kept to what is their real work: to enrich a child's heritage of words—not diminish it.

Yours faithfully,
Beatrix Potter

N.B. The illustrations in my books are integral with the text. They may *not* be separated.

Mr. Andal to Miss Potter

March 7, 1963

Dear Miss Potter:

It is with pleasurable anticipation that I send you our detailed reader's report. It has taken a little time to get it—some work was necessary—but, as you will see, apart from some words in the text, some details of plot, new illustrations, fresh names and a larger size for the book, very little has had to be changed.

I very much hope you will co-operate in helping us to bring this classic little book within reach of our children.

Awaiting your favorable reactions,
Again yours cordially,
V. Andal

REPORT AND RECOMMENDATIONS FOR MODERNIZATION OF TEXT AND
ILLUSTRATIONS OF "PETER RABBIT" BY BEATRIX POTTER

"Mother" must read "Momma" throughout.

p. 45	". . . some friendly sparrows . . . flew to him in great excitement, and implored him to exert himself."	Not all children will be able to identify sparrows; suggest the more general "bird-ies"; last five words especially difficult; suggest "to try again" or "try harder."
p. 52	"Kertyschoo" for sneezing	Unfamiliar. "Tishoo" is more usual.
p. 58	"Lippity lippity"	Not in the dictionary.
p. 69	"Scr-r-ritch"	Might confuse.
Same page	"Scuttered"	Onomatopoeia, though allowable, should not distort a word. Unfamiliar again. Suggest "ran away and hid," which has the advantage that three out of the four words have only three letters.
p. 80	"Camomile tea"	Not in use now. Suggest "tranquilizer" or "sedative."

As well as word limitation, the De Base Publishing Company has decided to use a certain "thought limitation" so that parents may entrust their children's reading to us with complete confidence. In this connection:

p. 10   We do not think father should have been made into rabbit pie. Mr. McGregor is altogether a too Jehovah-like figure. We want children to *like* people rather than have that out-of-date respect. They must not be left thinking that a little rabbit can be blamed for trespassing and stealing: it was, rather, that he was deprived of lettuce and radishes. Mr. McGregor must be made a sympathetic figure.

ILLUSTRATIONS

We now have a report from our art panel, and though these illustrations have charm we believe fresh ones should be used. The rabbits' furniture and clothing are out of date; i.e., the red cloaks used by Flopsy, Mopsy and Cottontail; the length of Mrs. Rabbit's skirts; the suspended pan and open cooking fire on p. 81. We therefore propose to commission a young Mexican artist who specializes in vivid outline drawing. (Less expensive to reproduce.)

NOMENCLATURE

Our bureau reports that while "Peter" is familiar to most children, Flopsy, Mopsy and Cottontail must be retitled.

Cable from Miss Potter to Mr. Andal, March 12, 1963

RETURN PETER RABBIT AT ONCE

Mr. Andal to Miss Potter

March 13, 1963

Dear Miss Potter:

We are sorry you have taken this attitude, which I confess seems to us unrealistic and does not take into account public opinion (supported by our own careful poll statistics). We are having much the same reaction from Mr. Edward Lear. We saw a charming first version[2] of his poem, "The Owl and the Pussy-Cat," which then had the lines:

They sailed away
For a year and a day
To the land where the palm tree grows.

and:

They dined on mince
and slices of quince
which they ate with a silver spoon.

lines quite innocuous and satisfactory; but now he has come up with "bong tree" for the first lines, and "runcible spoon" for the second, words not only unusual but not even in the dictionary.

As he insists on keeping these we have had to return his manuscript as, at your own request, we are returning yours. We can only tell you that it is our opinion, formed by expert advice, that in its present form, parents, teachers and children will not buy, nor understand, nor like "Peter Rabbit."

Yours respectfully,
V. Andal

Miss Potter to Mr. V. Andal

24th March, 1963

Seven million have. I rest in peace.

---

2. The lines that follow are authentic and are in the first draft of "The Owl and the Pussy-Cat."

On Writing for Children

E. B. White

Staff member and writer for the New Yorker Magazine, *E. B. White has been called humorist, philosopher, and, by Irwin Edman, "our finest essayist, perhaps our only one." While producing a stream of satirical essays, editorials, and poems [collected from the* New Yorker *and other magazines in* One Man's Meat *(1950) and* The Second Tree from the Corner *(1954)], Mr. White created beloved stories for children:* Stuart Little *(1945) and* Charlotte's Web *(1952). Later came* Trumpet of the Swan *(1970). In 1970 he won the Laura Ingalls Wilder Medal for the first two of these and the National Medal for Literature in 1972 for his total body of work.*

When E. B. White was once asked if there was any shifting of gears in writing books for children, he replied:

Anybody who shifts gears when he writes for children is likely to wind up stripping his gears. But I don't want to evade your question. There *is* a difference between writing for children and for adults. I am lucky, though, as I seldom seem to have my audience in mind when I am at work. It is as though they didn't exist.

Anyone who writes *down* to children is simply wasting his time. You have to write up, not down. Children are demanding. They are the most attentive, curious, eager, observant, sensitive, quick, and generally congenial readers on earth. They accept, almost without question, anything you present them with, as long as it is presented honestly, fearlessly, and clearly. I handed them, against the advice of experts, a mouse-boy, and they accepted it without a quiver. In *Charlotte's Web,* I gave them a literate spider, and they took that.

Some writers for children deliberately avoid using words they think a child doesn't know. This emasculates the prose and, I suspect, bores the reader. Children are game for anything. I throw them hard words, and they backhand them over the net. They love words that give them a hard time, provided they are in a context that absorbs their attention. I'm lucky again: my own vocabulary is small, compared to most writers, and I tend to use the short words. So it's no problem for me to write for children. We have a lot in common.

"On Writing for Children" by E. B. White from "The Art of the Essay," *Paris Review,* no. 48 (Fall 1969). Reprinted by permission of The Paris Review.

Purely for Love

Joan Aiken

Daughter of poet Conrad Aiken, Joan Aiken is, according to John Rowe Townsend, "one of the liveliest and most exuberant of today's writers for children." Her novels range from adult whodunits to the teen-age mystery story, Night Fall *(1971), and a line of fast-paced period adventures for children. The latter include* The Wolves of Willoughby Chase *(1963),* Black Hearts in Battersea *(1964),* Nightbirds on Nantucket *(1966), and* The Cuckoo Tree *(1971), all slightly connected through the characters. In* The Whispering Mountain *(1969) Joan Aiken has combined parody of a Welsh legend and picaresque adventure to produce a very different and humorous story and a Carnegie Medal honor-winner. Her writings also include collections of short stories, such as* Smoke from Cromwell's Head *(1970) and, for younger children,* A Necklace of Raindrops and Other Stories *(1969). In 1969 she won the* Manchester Guardian Award *and in 1971 gave the annual Children's Book Week lecture at the Library of Congress.*

To begin this rambling series of disjointed meditations, questions without any answers and impracticable suggestions, I am going to give a couple of quotations whose relevance can probably be guessed. Here is the first:

' "Do you know where the wicked go after death?"

"They go to hell," was my ready and orthodox answer.

"And should you like to fall into that pit and be burning there for ever?"

"No, Sir."

"What must you do to avoid it?"

I deliberated a moment; my answer, when it did come, was objectionable. "I must keep in good health and not die."

"How can you keep in good health? Children younger than you die daily. . . . Here is a book entitled *The Child's Guide*; read it with prayer, especially that part containing an account of the awfully sudden death of Martha G—, a naughty child addicted to falsehood and deceit." . . .

"I am not deceitful: if I were, I should say I loved *you*; but I declare I do not love you: I dislike you the worst of anybody in the world; and this book about the liar, you may give to your girl Georgiana, for it is she who tells lies . . . " '

That, of course, is from *Jane Eyre*. And the other, quite different, is shorter:

' "Me and my brother were then the victims of his feury since which we have suffered very much which leads us to the arrowing belief that we have received some injury in our insides, especially as no marks of violence are

"Purely for Love" by Joan Aiken from *Books: Journal of the National Book League* (Winter 1970): 9–21. Reprinted by permission of The National Book League.

visible externally. I am screaming out loud all the time I write and so is my brother which takes off my attention and I hope will excuse mistakes . . . " ' (Nicholas Nickleby).

I will leave those for the moment and go on.

I keep my gramophone records in old wooden coalboxes. Quite by chance a long time ago I discovered that old wooden coalboxes are exactly the right size and shape for keeping gramophone records in. Don't worry—there is a connection here: for someone who has been writing children's stories on and off for the last thirty years, the sudden rise to importance of children's literature has affected me rather in the same way that it would if I were to wake one day and find that university courses and seminars were being held on the necessity of keeping one's discs in old wooden coalboxes, and journals printed called *Wooden Coalbox News,* and even that an industry had sprung up for making imitation plastic wooden coalboxes. I do not wish to sound snide or ungrateful. In a way it's wonderful suddenly to find one's occupation so respectable, at least in certain circles. For it isn't yet with the general public. In most circles the confession that one writes children's books always produces the same response, and a very daunting response it is. I'll give an example.

A couple of months ago I went to a party with two friends. It was a very mixed party of all incomes, classes and professions, young and old; some guests were in TV, some in films or advertising, some wrote. The only common factor was that they were all very intelligent because the host was very intelligent. The friends with whom I went started off by introducing me as their friend Joan who wrote children's books. But they soon stopped that. Because at the phrase *children's books* an expression of blank horror would close down on every face, people would be unable to think of a single conversational topic, they obviously expected me to start reciting poetry about fairies in a high piping voice, they just could not wait to get away from that part of the room to somewhere safer and more interesting. My friends observed this phenomenon so they changed their tactics—they started introducing me as somebody who wrote thrillers. Instantly all was well, faces lit up. People love thriller-writers because everybody reads a thriller at one time or another, so they felt able to talk to me and I had a good time and came away from the party with a curious feeling of the relativity of identity. And wondering, too, who is a real adult—if anybody is, all the time, that is to say.

Obviously children's writing—writing for children—is regarded by society as a fairly childish occupation. But then it occurred to me that most people's occupations are pursued at a number of different levels—at varying mental ages. A man runs his business affairs with a 50-year-old intelligence, conducts his marriage on a pattern formed at age 20, has hobbies suitable to a 10-year-old, and a reading age that stuck at Leslie Charteris: is he an adult or not? And if he is not, how would you classify his reading-matter? There is a lot of what I would classify as non-adult reading: thrillers, funny books, regency romances, horror stories, westerns. Of course some of these, because of outstanding qualities, may fall into the adult sphere, but lots do not. And yet it is considered perfectly OK for a 45-year-old company director to read, say, Ian Fleming, whereas he would be thought odd if he read, say, Alan Garner, a much better writer. And there is the same ambivalence in the social attitude to the writers. If you say that you write books for children because you enjoy doing so, people instantly assume that you are retarded. Whereas, sad but true, if you say, "Of course I'd *rather* write adult fiction but writing for children is more paying," (not so, incidentally) people accept that as a perfectly logical, virtuous viewpoint. But to write children's books for pleasure—that, nine times out of ten, is considered almost as embarrassing as making one's money from the manufacture of contraceptives or nappy liners. And yet writing thrillers is OK. It's odd—because the really interesting point here is the strong similarity that in fact exists between thrillers and children's fiction: the moral outlook is the same, the pattern of mystery, danger, capture, escape, revenge, triumph of good over evil, is very similar indeed.

So society regards people who write for children as odd. And one can't help stopping from time to time and saying to oneself, "Maybe society is right about this. Why do people write for children? Is it a good thing that they should? Up to the nineteenth century children managed all right without having books specially written for them. Up to the nineteenth century children were not regarded as a different species, but were clothed, fed, and treated in most ways as adults of a smaller size. Are they, in fact, better off for being treated as a separate minority? And, turning to the people who write for children, ought they to indulge themselves in this way? And what started them doing so, in the middle of the nineteenth century? Was it the need of the children or the need of the writers to write in that particular way? And, if people are to be allowed to write for children, what ought they to write?"

I have started a lot of hares, some of which I do not intend to pursue. The last question is particularly silly—almost as silly as saying, "What ought people to write for adults?" But to go back to the first: Why do people write for children?

I am afraid there are quite a number who do it because it seems like easy money—especially in the present boom of children's literature. Their idea is that in children's fiction you can get away with a minimum of factual background, a skimpy story and a poverty-stricken vocabulary. But let's set all those on one side. If they found an easier racket, they would switch to it. Let's consider the ones who *like* to write for children—let's consider why, in spite of it being an embarrassing, ill-paid, guilt-producing and socially unacceptable thing to do, quite a number of people in fact *do* it, instead of writing adult novels or plays or TV scripts or biographies, or as well as these things. What sort of people are they?

Fairly soon we shall know the answers to some of these questions in detail, because Berkeley Department of Motivational Studies, University of California, is conducting a massive research project into the motivations of children's writers. They sent out a great questionnaire, which took a solid six hours to fill in going at top speed, and presently they will have the results all tabulated by computers. Though of course these results are bound to be an average only of the writers they selected—and who did the selecting, one wonders? Anyway, I'm going to guess ahead and predict that presently they will be able to say that most children's writers come from broken families, may have been ill when young, or handicapped, or misfits, or at least unsociably inclined. And when they do come up with this result, I'm not sure where it will get us; we have left behind the era when boys were castrated so they would always be sure of a part in opera; you would hardly break up your home in hopes your child might become a second Lewis Carroll. (It really is too bad that Berkeley started too late to send their questionnaire to *him*.)

However let's—rather sketchily—survey a few peaks sticking up out of the general landscape of children's literature. We can agree that Dickens (I include Dickens because, though not a children's writer, he has so many of the essential qualities of one: mystery, slapstick, simple emotion, intricate plots, marvellous language—and anyway, children enjoy him, and you could say he wrote for a mental age of 15) Dickens had a very unhappy childhood. So did Kipling and Masefield. Beatrix Potter had tyrannical, dominating parents, so did Charlotte Yonge. Ruskin and Lewis Carroll never entirely grew up. Hans Andersen's father died when he was small and his mother drank. Blake suffered from visions and was so gifted, *that* in itself must have made his childhood troubled. De la Mare was delicate, so was Robert Louis Stevenson who, moreover, had to endure a hellfire upbringing which caused him to have frightful nightmares and guilt fantasies. The theme certainly seems clear enough: writers who had unhappy childhoods tend to address themselves to children—not necessarily all the time, not necessarily their whole output—but, obviously, as a sort of compensation, to replace part of the childhood they lost, to return, perhaps, to the happier periods which may have seemed particularly radiant in retrospect compared with the black times. They address themselves to children because they need to, they are writing for the unfulfilled part of themselves. It would be invidious to talk about living writers in this context, but I can think of a couple among the top rank who were ill when young or suffered from broken homes. Here's an interesting thing, though—and in my list of classics it obtains too—this seems to apply to male writers more than to females. Plenty of well known women children's writers had stable happy childhoods and normal lives. Maybe women just take naturally to producing children's tales, it's an occupational occupation. They don't get such a complete break from childhood as men do, because they are likelier to be continually in contact with children between youth and middle age.

So we can guess that when Berkeley produces their profile of the children's writer, there will be a troubled childhood in the background. And here's where I'm going to put another question aimed at starting argument: is it a good thing that these disturbed, unhappy characters should be doing this particular job? Are the people who write for children the ones who *ought* to be writing?

There are quite a few professions—for instance, politics, the police, the prison service, maybe the civil service—which, one suspects, attract to them the very last people who ought to be in them. The very desire to be a prison warder or a prime minister should disbar one from eligibility. I dare say by the next century anybody expressing a wish to go into politics will be psychoanalysed and put through all kinds of vocational tests, as they ought before matrimony or being allowed to drive a car on the public roads. I know this is a shocking suggestion, verging on fascism, but we are moving into a more and more controlled way of living. Our environment has to be controlled. We are subject to restraints in many areas already: fluoridation, smokeless zones, no-parking areas, contraception, industrial regulations, the decision whether or not to die of nicotine cancer. Control is not enjoyable, it is just necessary because there are such a lot of us. Many industries already have their own personnel selection tests; before taking an advertising job in which I wrote copy for Campbells' soup tin labels I had to undergo a whole series of ability tests and finally a psychologist spent two hours trying to make me lose my temper. If one needs such stringent tests in order to write advertising copy, whose end-purposes may reasonably be regarded as frivolous—if not downright nefarious—how much more neces-sary might it not be thought to subject to some kind of psychological screening those people who are directing their energies into such a frighteningly influential area as children's books, material that can affect the outlook of whole generations to an incalculable degree? I know this is an outrageous suggestion: who would give the tests, what would they consist of, who would assess the results? The whole idea bristles with impossibili-ties. It certainly runs flat counter to the growing permissiveness in the adult field as to what can be written and published. I'm not suggesting it quite seriously. But it's worth talking around. After all, you need a licence to keep a dog, you need all kinds of official authority before you can adopt or foster a child or start a school or even run a playgroup—yet any paranoid can write a children's book. The only indirect control is the need to find a publisher and that's not too difficult.

Would not some control over the production of children's books be a good thing? I'm now going to stick my neck out a bit farther. I've heard that the average child in the course of childhood is estimated to have time to read six hundred books. Judging from myself and friends and children, it is probably less, because children read books over and over—which is a good thing: better read *Tom Sawyer* four times than four second-rate stories. So, six hundred or less. The book industry is unlike nearly all other industries in one marked particular: its products never perish. So those six hundred books have already been written. Without a shadow of doubt, any children's librarian could produce a list of six hundred titles, including all the classics and plenty of good modern books, enough to last any child right through. So where is the need to write any more? Particularly since writing for children is such a suspect, self-indulgent, narcissistic activity?

I'll leave that question in the air too and think a bit more about writers. Of course a troubled childhood in the background isn't the only contributory factor, or the world would be stuffed with children's writers. Plenty of people who suffer from childhood handicaps go on to become politicians or psychoanalysts or bank robbers. To be a writer you have to have the potential—to be a children's writer you have to have imagination, iconoclasm, a deep instinctive morality, a large vocabulary, a sense of humour, a powerful sense of pity and justice. . . . Besides that, I for one feel strongly that the ideal writer for children should do something else most of the time. Writing for children should not be a full-time job. Let me repeat that because it is probably the most important thing I have to say here: writing for children should not be a full-time job. And that's another thing Dickens, Masefield, de la Mare, Lewis Carroll, Ruskin, Kipling, Hans Andersen and William Blake had in common—children's writing was a sideline with them. (If indeed they were really writing for children at any time?) They had plenty of other professional interests. Which meant, first, that their writing was enriched by their other activities, knowledge, background—that it had plenty of depth; second, that they wrote, when they did write for children, purely for love. And that is the way children's writing should be done; it should not be done for any other reason.

Think of those six hundred books again—what a tiny total that is. It is frightful to think that a single one of them should have been written primarily to earn an advance of £250 on a 5 per cent royalty rising to 12 1/2 per cent—or to propagate some such idea as that it is a very enjoyable thing to be a student nurse. And I might as well add that I do not think any kind of fringe activity connected with children's literature should be a full-time occupation—editing, reviewing, publishing, anything—everyone connected with these professions ought to leave the children's field from time to time so as to get a different perspective. After all, children live in the world with the rest of us, they aren't a separate race. I'm a bit uneasy about this cult of treating children as creatures utterly divorced from adult life. In the BBC-2 TV series, *Family of Man,* which compared the social habits of different races, what struck me forcibly about the New Guinea tribesmen, the Himalayans, the Kalahari bushmen, the Chinese, is how very serene and well-adjusted their children seemed to be—because they had their established place in the adult world. And yet I'm ready to bet not a single one of them had a children's book. There's no need to point a moral here and anyway we can't reverse the course of civilisation. So I will go on to mention a danger that every children's writer is likely to encounter.

Most writers—most people—have at some point the idea for a good children's book. And maybe something fetches it out: an unresolved trauma from childhood to dispose of, or just the circumstance of having children and telling them stories which seem worth writing down—anyway, this person, due to some environmental factor, writes a good book, maybe two or three and then—although the formative circumstances no longer exist—is too caught up in the business to quit. Financial pressure, pressure of success, pressure of habit—it is easy to succumb. I can think of several people who wrote one or two good children's books and then their interests developed elsewhere in a natural progression and they stopped. I can think of several more who wrote one or two good children's books and should have stopped there but didn't. And I need hardly say, as my previous remarks will have made my opinion clear, but I will go on and say it again because I feel so strongly about it—writing anything for children unless one has a strong genuine impulse not only to write at all but to write that one particular thing—writing anything without such an impulse is every bit as wicked as selling plastic machine-gun toys, candies containing addictive drugs or watered-down penicillin.

Another reason why children's writers should have some other, predominant occupation, is simply because children have a greater respect for them if they do. Children, bless their good sound sense, are naturally suspicious of adults who devote themselves to nothing but children. For one thing, such adults are too boringly familiar—there aren't any mysteries about them. Don't you remember how at school the teachers who disappeared to their own pursuits after school were respected and how the ones who were always at hand doing things with the children as if they had nothing else to do, no better way of occupying themselves were despised? Elizabeth Jenkins, in her book *Young Enthusiasts,* says, "It is of course admirable to want to teach children, but the question all too seldom asked is: What have you got to teach them?" Parents, after all, are not occupied exclusively with their children—or heaven help them both. Surveys of distraught young mothers in housing estates who never have a chance to get away show what a very unnatural state of affairs this is, and how undesirable.

When I was a child, one of my greatest pleasures was listening to my elder brother play the piano. He was a lot older and he played pretty well. But the point was that he was playing for his benefit, not for mine. Part of my pleasure was the feeling that it was a free gift, that my brother and I were independent of one another. Another part was the understanding that some of the music was beyond my scope, which intensified my enjoyment of the easier bits. If my brother had said, "I'll play for you now, choose what you'd like," I would have been not only embarrassed and nonplussed, but also horribly constricted by such a gesture, it would have completely changed the whole experience. I think the essence of the very best children's literature is this understanding that it is a free gift—no, not a gift, a treasure trove—tossed out casually from the richness of a much larger store. Of course there are exceptions to this generalisation—I can think of several fine children's writers now at work who do nothing else at *present*—but my feeling is that they have the capacity to, and probably will do something else in due course.

I listened to a fascinating broadcast by Arthur Koestler recently, first delivered at the 1969 Cheltenham Festival. Its subject was literature and the law of diminishing returns, and Mr. Koestler first of all was discussing whether or not there is progress in art comparable with progress in science, where discoveries and the growth of knowledge can be continually recorded and tabulated. He came to the conclusion that there *is* progress in art but of a different kind—it proceeds by leaps and bounds instead of in a measurable upward graph, and it skips from one form to another; each art-form proceeds through four stages, a stage of revolution, a stage of expansion, a stage of saturation, when the audience has had enough of it, and the only way their attention can be held is by exaggeration or involution—and then a final collapse, as something else comes to the fore.

I suppose, judged in those terms, one could say that writing for children is just leaving its revolutionary stage, having been going for less than a hundred years, and is still expanding; just now, because it is expanding, it attracts people who fifty years ago would have been writing novels. I wonder what will have happened in, say, another twenty years? Maybe involution will have set in, there will be a kind of Kafka vogue in children's literature. I wouldn't be surprised. I believe one can see traces of it already.

I was thinking about this question of progress, after Koestler's talk—thinking that you cannot have progress without loss: you acquire nylon, you lose the spinning-wheel. You acquire colour photography, you lose Breughel. You acquire logic, you lose fairy tales. Our brains now have to contain such a frightening amount of *stuff,* just in order to carry on normal life: electronics, the decimal system, knowledge of what is happening all over the world, psychology, ecology, how to deal with parking meters and supermarkets and yellow tube tickets—when you think of all this information that has to be rammed in and stored at the front of our minds compared with, say, the necessary equipment for comfortable and rational living at the beginning of the nineteenth century, you can see why some people worry about what in the meantime may be trickling away at the back and being irretrievably lost. Sherlock Holmes, if you remember, had an idea that the brain's capacity was strictly limited. When Dr. Watson, rather scandalised, discovered that Holmes knew nothing about the solar system, and started telling him, Holmes brushed his proffered instruction aside, saying "I managed very well before, without this information, and what you have told me I shall now do my best to forget." I'm sure, whether or not this idea of the mind's limited capacity is correct, many people entertain it; consciously or unconsciously it forms part of their fear of progress: the feeling that if you acquire enough basic data about space flight to be able to understand what is going on in the lunar module, you will probably forget your wife's birthday or the theme of the first movement of the third Brandenburg concerto. I sometimes cheer myself up by remembering that in Peru they didn't learn about the wheel until bicycles were invented. I'm sure most children's writers are natural opponents of progress, unable to adapt to the world entirely, fighting a rearguard action, like people salvaging treasures in a bombardment; for growing up, of course, involves the severest loss of all, the one that is hardest to accept. Children's writers are natural conservatives in the sense that they want to *conserve.*

Earlier I was asking, not very seriously, if people are to be allowed to write for children at all, what should they be allowed to write?

The notion of any restraints or controls at all over writers is a horrifying one, I'm glad to think. And yet on the other side of the Iron Curtain such controls are in force. And in the field of children's literature, both in this country and America, I have come across educators who made fairly plain their feeling that some children's writers are a bunch of tiresome anarchists who could perfectly well be a bit more helpful if they chose, in the way of incorporating educational material and acceptable ethics into their writing. As if they were a kind of hot-drink vending machine and you had only to press the right knob to produce an appropriately flavoured bit of nourishment. I do not agree with this point of view. I do not think it is possible to exercise any control over what a creative artist produces, without the risk of wrecking the product. The only possible control is to shoot the artist. This view may seem inconsistent with what I have said before about who should be allowed to write for children. So it is. I don't pretend to have consistent views.

I would not dream of making suggestions to other writers as to what they should write. But I do have strong views as to the kind of intentions one should *not* have when setting out to write anything for children. Childhood is so desperately short, and becoming shorter all the time: they are reading adult novels at 14, which leaves only about nine years in which to get through those six hundred books—nearly two books a week, that means. Furthermore, children have so little reading-time, compared with adults, and that is growing less—there's school, there's bedtime, all the extra-curricular activities they have now. I am not decrying adventure playgrounds and drama groups and play classes and organised camp holidays, I think they are splendid—even television has its points—but all this means a loss of reading-time, and *that* means that when they do read, it is really a wicked shame if they waste any time at all reading what I am going to group under the heading of Filboid Studge. *Filboid Studge,* if you recall, was the title of a short story by Saki about a breakfast food which was so dull and tasteless that it sold extremely well because everybody believed that it *must* be good for them. (Really it is a pity we don't have an excretory system for mental waste matter as well as for physical. Children, at an age when their minds are as soft and impressionable as a newly tarred road, pick up such a mass of un-nourishing stuff and what happens to it? It soaks down into the subconscious and does no good there, or it lies around taking up room that could be used to better purpose.)

It is lucky that at least children have a strong natural resistance to phoney morality. They can see through the adult with some moral axe to grind almost before he opens his mouth—the smaller the child, the sharper the instinct. I suppose it's the same kind of ESP that one finds in animals—the telepathy that transmits to one's cat exactly which page of the Sunday paper one wishes to read so that he can go and sit on it. Small children have this to a marked degree. You have only to say, "Eat your nice spinach" for a negative reaction to be triggered off. You don't even have to add "because it's good for you." They pick that up out of the atmosphere. They sense at once when we want them to do something because it suits *us*. It's sad to think how much at our mercy children are: 90 per cent of their time we are organising them and guiding them and making them do things for utilitarian reasons—and then, the remaining 10 per cent, likely as not, we are concocting pretexts for getting rid of them. I can remember the exact tone of my mother's voice as she invented some errand that would get me out from under the grown-ups' feet for half an hour. And I now remember too with frightful guilt how pleased I was when my children learned to read. Apart from my real happiness at the thought of the pleasure that lay ahead of them, I looked forward to hours of peace and quiet.

On account of this tough natural resistance, I'm not bothered about hypocritical moral messages. That's where the Jane Eyre quotation comes in. It is a beautiful example of the calm and ruthless logic with which children bypass any bit of moral teaching they are not going to concern themselves with.

"What must you do to avoid going to hell?"

"I must keep in good health and not die."

It's an example of lateral thinking, anticipating Edward de Bono by one hundred and twenty years.

Unfortunately, as children grow older, this faculty becomes blunted because of education. So much of education consists of having inexplicable things done at one for obscure reasons, that it's no wonder the victims presently almost cease to resist. I can see that some education is necessary, just as the wheel is necessary. We have to learn to get into gear with the rest of the world. But it is remarkable how little education one *can* get along on. (This, incidentally, was a fact that emerged from a conference on the role of children's literature in education at Exeter last year—a large proportion of the writers there had had little formal education. And I don't think you could say of that group that they had taken to writing for children because they were unequipped to do anything else.)

It is a dangerous thing to decry education. But I feel there's something wrong with our whole attitude to it. The trouble is, we have taken away the role of children in the adult world. Instead of being with their parents, learning how: helping on the farm, blowing the forge fire, making flint arrowheads with the grownups, as would be natural, they are all shoved off together into a corner. And what happens then? We have to find them something to do to keep them out of mischief. I think too much—far, far too much—of education is still fundamentally just this: something cooked up to keep children out of their parents' hair till they are grown. I don't see how you can learn to have a spontaneous, creative, intelligent, sensitive reaction to the world when for your first six or twelve or eighteen years there is such a lot of this element of hypocrisy in how you are treated. And the worst of it is that this element is not only present in education, but in reading-matter too.

There's a whole range of it—from *The Awfully Sudden Death of Martha G—*, through *A Hundred and One Things to Do on a Wet Saturday and Not Plague Daddy,* and *Sue Jones Has a Super Time as Student Nurse,* to the novels, some of them quite good, intended to show teenagers how to adjust to the colour problem and keep calm through parents' divorce and the death of poor Fido. I even saw in a publisher's catalogue a series of situation books for *under-sixes.* I suppose they serve some purpose. But just the same I count them as Filboid Studge. And how insulting they are! Adults are not expected to buy books called *Mrs. Sue Jones—Alcoholic's Wife,* or *A Hundred and One Ways to Lose Your Job and Keep Calm.* Maybe some adults would be better adjusted if they did. It's true people will swallow things wrapped in this form of fictional jam. They will swallow it because they have been conditioned to it all their lives, because from the first primer their reading has become more and more impure—I'm not using impure in the sense of obscene, but in the sense of being written with a concealed purpose. In that same publisher's catalogue, advertising a series of basic vocabulary classics aimed at backward readers, the blurb said that in secondary schools a surprising number of children read nothing for pleasure except comics. Can you wonder, if the poor things have had nothing but situation books handed out to them? If you are bombarded with Filboid Studge, either you go on strike, or you become dulled, you cease to recognise propaganda when you hear it. I'm sure if children's reading were kept unadulterated, they would be quicker and clearer-minded as adults, more confident in making judgements for themselves.

I can see an objection coming up here—some of the greatest and best known children's books have a moral message. C. S. Lewis and George Macdonald: the Christian religion. Kipling: How to maintain the British Empire. Arthur Ransome: How to get along without parents just the same as if they were there. They had a moral message mostly because they were rooted in the nineteenth century when moral messages came naturally; everybody wore them like bustles. As we get farther and farther away from the nineteenth century the moral message has become more cautious and oblique, though it is still often there. Don't mistake me—I'm not opposed to a moral if it is truly felt—you can't have life without opinions, you can't have behaviour without character. I just don't like tongue-in-cheek stuff. Konrad Lorenz said somewhere that our intuitive judgements of people are partly based on their linguistic habits which is an interesting idea and I'm sure it is true. I certainly find it true in myself and not only on an intuitive level: from someone who uses sloppy secondhand phrases I would expect sloppy inconsiderate behaviour, whereas a person who uses vigorous, thoughtful, individual language will apply the same care to his behaviour— and this applies with double force to the written word. What I mean is that the author of a really well written book needn't worry about inserting some synthetic moral message—it will *be* there, embodied in the whole structure of the book.

Let's get back to the Dickens quotation a moment: "I am screaming out loud all the time I write and so is my brother which takes off my attention rather and I hope will excuse mistakes."

The reason why I love that so much is because it was plain that it was written with extreme pleasure. You can feel his smile as the idea came to him and he wrote it down. You can feel this smile in plenty of children's masterpieces—in *Jemima Puddleduck,* and in James Reeves's poem *Cows* and in Jane Austen's youthful history of the kings and queens of England—to pick a few random examples. And there's a serious counterpart of the smile—a kind of intensity—you feel the author's awareness that he is putting down *exactly* what he intended—in for instance, *The King of the Golden River,* and *A Cricket in Times Square,* and *Huck Finn,* to pick some more at random. Really good writing for children should come out with the force of Niagara, it ought to be concentrated; it needs to have everything that is in adult writing squeezed into a smaller compass. I mean that both literally and metaphorically: in a form adapted to children's capacities, and at shorter length, because of this shortage of reading-time. But the emotional range ought to be the same, if not greater; children's emotions are just as powerful as those of adults, and more compressed, since children have less means of expressing themselves, and less capacity for self-analysis. The Victorians really had a point with all those deathbed scenes.

Recently I had a home-made picturebook sent me from a primary school in Cornwall: it was about Miss Slighcarp, the villainess in one of my books. Each of the children had drawn a picture of her and written on the back why they hated her. And then under that their teacher had evidently suggested that each should write down his own personal fear: "In the kitchen, where the boiler is, the ventilator rattles and frightens me. I hate Mrs. Rance next door. Every time the ball goes in her garden she keeps it and I am frightened of her. I am frightened of the teacher and my mum and dad when they are angry." At first it was rather a worrying thought that my book had triggered off all this hate and fear, but then I thought, at least they are expressing their fears, and plainly they had an interesting time comparing their bogies and nightmares, maybe it was really a good thing for them.

This is another thing a children's story ought to do, I suppose, put things in perspective; if you think about it, a story is the first step towards abstract thought. It is placing yourself on one side and looking at events from a distance; in psychological terms, mixing primary mental process—dream-imagery, wish-fulfilling fantasy—with secondary process—verbalisation, adaptation to reality, logic. A story is like a *roux* in cookery: by the chemical process of rubbing fat into dry flour you can persuade it to mix with a liquid. So by means of a story you can combine dream with reality and make something nourishing. I think this mixing dream with reality, far from confusing children, helps them to define the areas of both.

I said something in my talk at Exeter last year which I would like to repeat here: it is about the texture of children's books. Children read in a totally different way from adults. It's a newer activity for them. To begin with they have to be wooed and kept involved. And then, when they are involved, reading isn't just a relaxation for them, something to be done after work. It's a real activity. (Children, after all, don't differentiate between work and non-work.) You see a child reading, he is standing on one leg, or squatting, or lying on his stomach, holding his breath, absolutely generating force. Children's reading-matter is going to be subjected to all sorts of strains and tensions, it needs to be able to stand up to this at every point. Children read the same book over and over, or just make for the bits they like best, or read the book backwards; there's a psychological explanation for all this re-reading, apparently it fulfills a need for security, a need to make sure the story is still there. (Or you could just call it love, of course.) And children may read very slowly or very fast; they gulp down books or chew them, they believe passionately in the characters and identify with them, they really participate. In order to stand up to all this wear and tear a book need almost be tested in a wind-tunnel before being launched. Furthermore, if it is going to be read and re-read, by the same child, over a span of perhaps ten years—my children certainly did this—it needs to have something new to offer at each re-reading. It is impossible to predict what a child's mind will seize on at any stage. Their minds are like houses in a staggered process of building—some rooms complete with furniture, others just bare bricks and girders. A lot of children will miss humour in a story at first reading while they concentrate on the plot. Richness of language, symbolism, character—all these emerge at later readings. Conversely anything poor or meretricious or cheap may be missed while attention is held by the excitement of the story, but sticks out like a sore thumb on a later reading. Reading aloud, of course, is the ultimate test—an absolutely basic one for a children's book—and I must add here that any adult who isn't willing to read aloud to a child for an hour a day I personally think doesn't deserve to *have* a child. I know this is probably an impossible ideal—both parents may be working, and there are so many counter-attractions and distractions— but just the same there is *nothing* like reading aloud for enjoyment and for building up a happy relationship between the participants.

Another factor which I think is of tremendous importance in this enrichment of texture is a sense of mystery and things left unexplained— references that are not followed up, incidents and behaviour that have to be puzzled over, language that is going to stretch the reader's mind and vocabulary. (Words, in themselves, are such a pleasure to children—and even the most deprived childhood can be well supplied with *them*.) Talking about mystery, I recently came across a fascinating analysis of Wilkie Collins's *Moonstone,* in psychological terms, by Dr. Charles Rycroft. (*Imagination and Reality,* Hogarth Press, 1968, 30s.) He begins his essay by saying that people who have a compulsion to read detective novels do so as a kind of fantasy defence against incomprehensible infantile memories connected with their parents—they, as it were, keep on solving the problem over and over to their own satisfaction and pinning the guilt firmly on to somebody else. It's a very ingenious theory, I'm not sure that I agree with it altogether, I can think of plenty of reasons for reading thrillers—but I daresay that is one of the reasons why we all love a mystery.

As I said before, there's a very close connection between writing thrillers and writing for children—I know two or three people who, like myself, do both. And since, presumably, a wish to keep solving the unresolved problems of childhood over and over characterises the writer of detective fiction, as well as the reader, this ties in neatly with our image of the children's writer as someone with a troubled past.

As for children themselves—it is not surprising they are fascinated by mysteries. An immense proportion of the world they live in, after all, must be mysterious to them, since they are expected to take most adult behaviour on trust, without explanations—not only adult behaviour but anything else that adults themselves can't explain or haven't time to account for. And there's no doubt that children do love mysteries; they are poets, too; they have a natural affinity for the crazy logic of magic. And they like open endings that they can keep in mind and ponder.

Since children's reading needs richness and mystery, and a sense of intense pleasure, and dedication, and powerful emotion, and an intricate story, and fine language, and humour—it is plain that only one lot of people are competent to write for children. They, of course, are poets—or at least people with the mental make-up of poets: writers who can condense experience and make it meaningful by the use of symbols.

Not surprisingly, the best children's writers *are* poets—I wonder if Berkeley will find that out?

I've said that I don't think children ought to be filled with Filboid Studge. And that the best children's writers should be mostly otherwise occupied, and should be poets. And I've ruminated a bit about what should be written or not be written. But—except insofar as what I've said may have been a conscious summing-up of unconscious processes—I can't claim to practise what I preach. There's a relevant fairy tale, which crops up in many folklores, so it must be a pretty basic message, the one about the helpful pixies. I expect you remember it. Mysterious little helpers do the farm-wife's work for her every night—spin the flax, collect the eggs, make the butter, and so forth; but when she watches and discovers who is helping her and, to reward them, makes all tiny suits of clothes, they put on the clothes, they are pleased, to be sure, and dance all about, but that's the end of them; they disappear and never return. That tale is a powerful warning against too much tinkering about with one's subterranean creative processes. I can't claim to write according to any of the lofty ideals I've put forward. But I said nobody should write for children unless it is with the whole heart. And I can claim to do that.

Happy Endings? Of Course, and Also Joy

Natalie Babbitt

Natalie Babbitt is both a writer and an illustrator, her first work being the drawings for her husband's The Forty-Ninth Magician *(1966) and her own* Dick Foote and the Shark *(1967). Her first story was the realistic picture-book,* Phoebe's Revolt *(1968), but her most noteworthy writing is in the fairy-tale tradition—*The Search for Delicious *(1969),* Kneeknock Rise *(a 1970 Newbery Medal honor book), and* Goody Hall *(1971).*

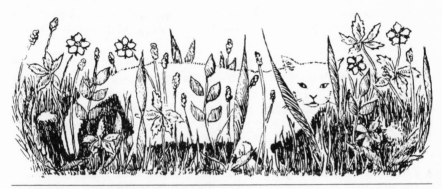

Illustration by Natalie Babbitt reprinted with the permission of Farrar, Straus & Giroux, Inc. and Curtis Brown, Ltd. from *Kneeknock Rise* by Natalie Babbitt, copyright © 1970 by Natalie Babbitt.

What in the world is a children's story anyway? What makes it different from a story for adults? Why does one writer choose to write for children and another for adults; or, if you will, what quality makes one writer's work appropriate for children while the work of another points in the other direction?

P. L. Travers has said, "There is no such thing as a children's book. There are simply books of many kinds and some of them children read. I would deny, however, that [they were] written for children." Well, perhaps. Sometimes. But someone must have the child in mind even if the author doesn't. Someone, editor or critic, must head a story in the right direction. As a rule, it isn't an especially difficult direction to find. Everyone can tell a child's book from one for adults, just as everyone knows hot water from cold. The difficulty lies in trying to define the essential nature of the difference.

The most common assumption, at least on the part of people who have had little to do with children's literature, is that books for adults are serious in intent while books for children are designed to amuse. But this is only an assumption and nothing more. There are indeed many serious stories for adults and truckloads of children's stories intended only for pleasure, but the reverse is just as true. Fluff, be it trivial or memorable, predominates in both worlds. However, you would be doing both an injustice if you tried to define their separate natures on the basis of fluff. There are no answers to be had by contrasting Jeeves to Winnie-the-Pooh, Hercule Poirot to Nancy Drew, Rhett Butler to the Grinch, or even the Yankee from Connecticut to Dorothy from Kansas. Dear friends all, each in his own place and time, but all members of the same unsubtle family. This leaves in each world an armful of books that are sometimes called classics (make your own list.) These are both serious in intent *and* entertaining, as all good stories should be; and it is only in these that any real definition can be found, if in fact it exists at all.

Well, then, perhaps you will say that the difference is still obvious, fluff or no, because adult books deal with adult emotions: love, pride, grief, fear of death, violence, the yearning for success, and so on. But why do we so often forget that children are not emotional beggars? They understand these feelings every bit as well as we do, and are torn by them as often. There is, in point of fact, no such thing as an exclusively adult emotion, and children's literature deals with them all. As for love, "Sleeping Beauty" and her sisters are nothing if not love stories of one kind, while "The Wind in the Willows" is another, and "Heidi" and "Hans Brinker" yet others.

Pride? Where is pride more gleefully exposed than in Toad of Toad Hall? For grief unsurpassed, try the closing chapters of "The Yearling." Fear of death begins in childhood and is dealt with supremely well in "Charlotte's Web," while its other side, the quest for immortality, is dealt with just as well in "Peter Pan." When it comes to violence, Ali Baba, Jack the Giant Killer, and the brave little tailor are only three of hundreds of inventive and bloody examples. And the yearning for success is a thread so common to all stories that I wonder why I even bothered to bring it up.

There is really no difference where emotional themes are concerned. There are only the subtleties, the nuances, the small ironies, of which adult fiction has made far more use but which are equally available to children's fiction, where their fitness is dictated exclusively by the writer's style and his attitude toward the perceptivity of his readers.

No difference in emotional themes? No—I will correct myself. There is one emotion which is found only in children's literature these years and for many years past, and that emotion is joy.

Next you will perhaps turn to range or scope or whatever you wish to call it. But even here, only at first glance does this appear to be genuine ground for defining a difference. While there was a time when the best adult fiction was timeless in nature and dealt at the core with Everyman, that is no longer true. Decade by decade, new books for adults have become more personal, more singular. It is a long and narrowing road from "Moby Dick" to "Portnoy's Complaint." More and more often we find ourselves making do with what Isaac Bashevis Singer has called "muddy streams of consciousness which often reveal nothing but a writer's boring and selfish personality."

Everyman has gone out of fashion for adults. What separates us has come to seem more pertinent than what draws us together. But Everyman is present still in the best children's stories, just as he always has been. All children can identify with and learn from characters like Peter Rabbit and Sendak's Max, in spite of the years between their creation; but many adults have trouble finding common coin with Henry Miller's Mona the way they could with Tolstoy's Natasha.

Content? Barring only graphic sex and other routine adult preoccupations (many of these dull to begin with), there is little difference. War, disability, poverty, cruelty, all the harshest aspects of life are present in children's literature. Daily banalities are there too, and the more subtle stuff of boredom, prejudice and spite. Where did we get the idea that a children's book is gentle and sweet? The only ones that are are those written by people who have been deluded by isolation or a faulty memory into thinking that children themselves are gentle and sweet.

A children's book is peopled with talking animals and other such fantastics? Sometimes, but by no means always. And anyway, adults are just as prone to attributing human characteristics to non-human things as children are, in life if not in their fiction. You need only mention the family dog or cat at a dinner party to find this out. And as for the dark world, children did not invent Martians, poltergeists, the seance or the Devil, or, I might add, the id and the ego, those goblins that out-goblin anything in the Brothers Grimm. If fantasy is absent from adult fiction, it is absent only because adults are too pompous to admit they still have a taste and a need for it.

A children's book uses simple vocabulary geared to the untrained mind? Compare a little Kipling to a little Hemingway and think again. Opening sentence of "A Farewell to Arms": "Now in the fall the trees were all bare and the roads were muddy." Opening sentence of "How The Rhinoceros Got His Skin": "Once upon a time, on an uninhabited island on the shores of the Red Sea, there lived a Parsee from whose hat the rays of the sun were reflected in more-than-oriental splendour." So much for that!

You might in desperation do something with size of type, seeing that children's books are usually printed in larger typeface; but this is really only because they shrewdly refuse to be bothered by anything less. Their eyes, after all, are by and large 20-20 per cent better than ours. You might also be reduced to bringing up length—children's books are usually shorter. However, I question whether, having said this, you have said much.

Not one of the above proposals will stand up. They are too arbitrary, too trivial, too riddled with exceptions. Perhaps it is possible only to settle for knowing the difference between the two literatures without being able to articulate it. And there are just enough stories that fall somewhere in between to cloud the issue further. Scrooge, Bilbo Baggins, Alice, Huck Finn, even Charlie Brown—for whom were these created? Ichabod Crane, William Baxter, Jason and Medea—on whose shelf do they belong? Perhaps P. L. Travers was right after all. Perhaps there is no such thing as a children's book once we are blessedly beyond the forgettable.

And yet it seems to me that there is a tangible difference when you apply one rather simple sieve to the mass. It does not work for every children's story, but perhaps it does apply to all that we remember longest and love best and will keep reading aloud to our children and our children's children as a last remaining kind of oral history, a history of the essence of our own childhood. I am referring, of course, to The Happy Ending.

Not, please, to a simple "happily ever after," or to the kind of contrived final sugar coating that seems tacked on primarily to spare the child any glimpse of what really would have happened had the author not been vigilant; not these, but to something which goes much deeper, something which turns a story ultimately toward hope rather than resignation and contains within it a difference not only between the two literatures but also between youth and age.

What, in the very simplest terms, is a child, after all, but an unrepressed adult? What is maturity, that supposed nirvana we seem never fully to achieve, but total emotional control learned from confrontation with that old apocalypt, experience, which teaches us the necessity for compromise? When one learns to compromise, one learns to abandon the happy ending as a pipe dream, or—a children's story.

When we envy our children, we envy them this first of all: "Oh," we say, "they have their whole lives ahead of them," and we believe with them and for them what we no longer believe for ourselves—that anything is possible. We believe that they may grow up to be another Sarah Bernhardt, a Madame Curie, a Jefferson, a Dickens—pick whichever giant you like. We believe that they may grow up happy, fulfilled, beyond pain. And when we pity our children, we pity them for this: "Oh," we say, "I wouldn't be young and have to go through all that again for anything."

By "all that" we really mean that we remember all too well the first hard lessons in compromise, the abandonment of the primary and then the secondary dream, and so on and on down to what we have at last settled on as possible. Alas, we have arrived and we are not unique after all. We are not beautiful, nor clever, nor even very good; and, no matter how well we do what we do, there is always someone who can do it better. The white house on the hill is lost to us forever, and all of our sweet tomorrows are rapidly becoming yesterdays which were almost (if we were lucky) but not quite.

But for the children, no matter how unpromising their circumstances, it is not too late. And we who write for them, or, if you must, we whose work seems appropriate for them, are perhaps those who, far from being glum, have a particularly tenacious view of life as an experiment in possibility without compromise. If we are not clever nor unique, we can at least recall without remorse how it felt to believe that we *might* be someday; probably despite plain and discouraging evidence, we are still not totally without hope; and so, in our stories—since, like it or not, every story comes out of the psyche of its author—Wilbur can escape an early death, Cinderella can be Queen, Bilbo can outwit the dragon, and the ugly duckling can become a swan. Not without pain, not without violence, not without grief; but in the end, somehow, everything will always be all right.

To be sure, there are stories for adults which end happily; but it is, in the stories that have lasted, a qualified happiness only, the quiet happiness of characters who have made their peace with their own compromises. So Natasha, at the end of "War and Peace" "had grown stouter and broader . . . her features . . . wore an expression of calm softness and serenity. Only on rare occasions now the old fire glowed in her again."

Not so with Ratty and Mole and Toad. Their story ends this way: "The . . . animals continued to live their lives . . . in great joy and contentment. Sometimes, in the course of long summer evenings, the friends would take a stroll together . . . and it was pleasing to see how respectfully they were greeted . . . : 'There goes the great Mr. Toad! And that's the gallant Water Rat . . . and yonder comes the famous Mr. Mole!' " Beauty established, nobility achieved, all obstacles overcome. A pipe dream, or—a children's story.

The Cry and the Creation

Meindert DeJong

Meindert DeJong came to the United States from The Netherlands as a young boy and after graduating from college worked at many occupations, from college teaching to farming. A number of his books have a Dutch background: Tower by the Sea *(1950),* Shadrach *(1953),* Far Out the Long Canal *(1964),* Journey from Peppermint Street *(1968), and* Wheel on the School, *the 1955 Newbery Medal winner. These are distinguished by a clarity of backgrounds, success in depicting children and their relationships with loving adults, and a liveliness of storytelling. The same compelling interest is aroused by his vivid characterizations of animals in* Hurry Home, Candy *(1953),* Along Came a Dog *(1958), and* Little Cow and the Turtle *(1955). Wartime experiences led to* House of Sixty Fathers *(1956), set in the Orient. As a writer for children DeJong has won the highest awards available: the International Hans Christian Andersen Medal in 1962 for the total body of his work, the first National Book Award for Children's Literature in 1969 for* Journey from Peppermint Street, *as well as the Newbery Medal.*[1]

I come from Michigan, and above Michigan lies Canada. Winter comes early to the northern vastness of Canada; summer falls into winter over a long, clear autumn night, and the geese begin to fly south. So it was that, just before coming here to Hamburg, early one morning I heard above my house the call of wild geese. I ran out of the house and stood watching them go over. A formation of well over a hundred geese were in all the cold grace and power of a perfect V flight. But already, as I planted myself in my yard, they were gone over the roofs of houses; and then their honking was gone, and in the surrounding city noises I could not hear the last disappearing cry of the geese. I jumped into my car and chased the formation until I found the geese again outside of town, winging away in all their magnificence of freedom of sky above a whole, still, early-morning earth.

Then the last cry came feathering back to earth and me, and in it was all of wildness and all of longing, thus all of living and all of loving. It struck me then, standing there in the loneness of the left-behind earthling, that what I had done is what the creative writer does all his life: run after, follow after, listen, live for a cry—not the cry specifically of winging wild geese, but for the cry of creativity.

However, the cry of the geese having brought forth, in this instance, the

"The Cry and the Creation" by Meindert DeJong from *Horn Book Magazine,* 39 (April 1963): 197–206. Reprinted by permission of Horn Book, Inc.

1. This paper accepting the Hans Christian Andersen Children's Book Award was given at the Congress of the International Board on Books for Young People in Hamburg, Germany, on September 28, 1962.

Illustration by Nancy Grossman from *Far Out the Long Canal* by Meindert DeJong. Copyright © 1964 by Meindert DeJong. Reprinted by permission of Harper & Row, Publishers, Inc. British edition published by Lutterworth Press.

creative cry in me—creating this speech—may I now examine creativity? For this question does not preoccupy the writer alone; it bemuses, puzzles, and intrigues everyone. I do not know of any question asked oftener of an author. Of course, no one asks concerning his creativity per se. The question, much more blunt and direct, is, "Where do you get your ideas?"

Everybody asks it. People that seldom open a book seem to be the first to ask it, but people in the deep know of books ask it even more insistently. Children ask it. In many of the children's letters that come to me are catalogues of questions. Have I any pets, have I any children, have I a wife? But the first question in any child's list inevitably seems to be, "Where do you get your ideas?"

Every author learns to dread this query. For, while it is easily tossed off, it always contains an element of earnest searching into a mystery, into the whence and where of the original germ idea, and into the how and why of the creative process that the original idea generates. The questioner wants to be led into the mystery of creation. The question probes the process of creation.

All right—where does one get his ideas? From where comes the creative, compulsive idea that is almost like a seizure when it strikes? It seems to come from somewhere and from nowhere; it comes *any* way, and in many strange ways—but it comes from within. It is wholly subjective.

That subjectivity immediately distinguishes the creative writer from the writing hack who jumps through every hoop of public need and demand and is, of course, a performing clown. The hack has his ear attuned to all public needs, fashions, changes, and demands; and thereby consciously and, no doubt, monetarily rewardingly, he gives the public what the public wants and dictates. He sways and swings in the greatest of ease with the changes and styles and fashions in books. If there is a shortage of a certain type of book, he dutifully rushes in to fill the vacuum. And there is need of him—I do not scorn him. But in doing what he does, he is the hack and not the creative writer.

To the creative writer there is one need, one challenge, and one duty, and it is completely subjective. His only duty is the duty of all art: to trap, as the Chinese philosopher Lu Chi put it, to trap heaven and earth in the cage of form. But before he can perform that duty of art, he has to listen for and to only one challenge: he has to listen to the cry of creativity. But he has to listen to it alone, somewhat the way I listened to the cry of the wild geese.

The creative writer has to walk alone. And at first he is quite alone in learning his creative art and trade. But even after he has achieved success, appreciation, understanding, and a following, still he walks alone. He walks ahead.

He walks ahead, paying little attention, creatively, either to the appreciative or the critical gabble of those who follow on behind, or to their needs, or their demands—not in any sense of superiority. He walks ahead, he has to walk ahead because still he has to walk alone, so that he can listen to the challenge—his only challenge—the cry of creativity.

He lives and has his meaning and his being in that cry. . . . The cry is in the shape of an idea that comes from somewhere or from nowhere, still best defined and expressed by the Hindu who said: "The artist takes a deep breath of blind assurance from some unimaginable source of certitude, and thereupon makes his utterance." Note that "deep breath of blind assurance." *Blind*—he doesn't know precisely where his ideas come from.

And then in making an utterance in the creative process—there the writer is, amidst the shuddering walls, holding that precious one live coal! He is practically a little god, creating, and at the same time immersed and swallowed up in his creation.

Let no man think that because I prate blandly about the creative, godlike state in this way that this is egotistic. I know of nothing that is more terrifyingly humbling than feeling oneself almost a god in one's own little creation while the walls shudder and the cry comes forth. For the walls may shudder as the artist holds the live coal of creativity, but always and at the same time he is palsied by the nearness and awareness of his flagrant and unnecessary body and of the animal hand so clumsy in its skill. For, whereas the heavens of creativity are high, the hells of it are deeper than the heavens are high.

I took comfort when recently I read that Tolstoy in creating *War and Peace*—writing it out in longhand seven times—even in the seventh stage of that book literally rolled on the floor in an agony of inadequacy before his own creation. It soothed me. If the great likes of him could roll on the floor, then I need not be ashamed of running through the house, practically climbing up the walls and shouting at those walls, "And what, you little so-and-so, makes *you* think *you* are a writer?"

Of course, here at the same time I have hastily and honestly to acknowledge that the agony and ecstasy of the creative process may have little bearing on the end product. While remembering Tolstoy, I also remember the woman hack writer who, in the midst of creating a slick little story for a woman's magazine, became aware that her apartment building was on fire; but still, with the fire crackling behind her study door, she had to go on, rushing the story to its end. Even though she knew, she said, that the story was of passing importance and would only end up in a magazine which today is and tomorrow is cast into the fire.

No, I guess for the hack as for the genius, the creative process contains the same ecstasy and agony, except that, when the vision is large and the creativity is large, the agony and ecstasy are, by that much, more terrible. The extent and intensity of the creative process may not have too much bearing on the end product. And only the creative writer himself knows the humiliating loss—the difference between what shook and possessed him and lived in him so perfectly and what finally transfers itself in words on paper. However, if he is truly creative, that loss interests him far less than the creative process among the shuddering walls.

What may here confuse and mystify the author's noncreative public is the failure of people to realize that the creative artist is a kind of schizophrenic. Or, to put it more charitably and take off its white coat and strait jacket, he is a split personality. He is a creator and he is a cabbage; and in between creations he is completely cabbaging it—waiting, listening for the creative cry to come when he can begin to live again, for really he only lives and is of interest and meaning to himself when he is creating.

Unfortunately, his public only meets him in his cabbage states as Cabbage Joe and not as Creative Joe; and he is either dull, entertaining, or annoying, according to the characteristics of the other half of his split personality. One thing is sure, he is not himself; and the picture his public may get of him is of an ordinary, mercenary, egotistic fellow, seemingly mostly interested in the popularity and sale of his latest book. Extraordinarily interested in himself and not too knowledgeable about much of anything outside his writing.

This exclusiveness is easily explained. Writing is, and by its very nature ought to be, a lonely job. The author writes alone, and between books he still walks alone, listening for the creative cry to come. In the throes of writing he has to be silent and alone; and between books, except for an occasional speech, the writer seldom meets his public, almost never creatively.

Then, too, being interested in and living only for the creative process, it is remarkable how little success and acceptance mean to him, egocentric and introverted as he is. Certainly success and acceptance have value for his security—the security of groceries he needs to write another book—and also for the self-assurance to help him write that next book, although to me past successes seem to help very little. It seems the creative process is never finished, never mastered, never even learned.

The last published book doesn't help a bit in easing the creative agonies of the next book. By this time the earlier book, public property now, has faded in your estimation, and the new book is the whole preoccupation.

It is amazing how subjective and possessive one is in the creative stage, and how objective and unconcerned in the public stage of his book. Its particular success may be welcomed or its particular failure bemoaned; but, at least in my case, the feeling toward it is much like the one toward that public, communal piece of property—the street before one's house. Fine if people use it, fine any use they want to put it to. It's their book now; but the artist is reaching toward the next book, listening for the next creative cry.

With me the unconcern over the public and its needs and wants and demands even reaches into the possessive, subjective, creative stage. I am not, and must not be, aware of my audience when I write my books. I must be wholly subjective, conscious only of the particular limiting cage of form of the children's book into which I must shape and compress my creation. Fortunately—as the British have so clearly seen—creative books for children are the nearest thing to that purest of all literary forms, the lyric poem. Now I doubt that the lyric poet ever gives a single thought to the state and condition and composition and needs of his eventual audience, and neither do I. After some twenty books, I still have no idea of the age, school grade, and state of literacy of the child for whom I write. I write not only out of myself but also for myself, necessarily shaping the work only to my particular cage of artistic form.

Thus, I have often been accused of writing only for the special, the gifted, the advanced and especially perceptive child. My impatient answer to that is—all children are special! But special or not, I know all will suck out of my story what they can use or handle, and spit out the bitter seeds of that which doesn't interest them or is still beyond them. Nevertheless, the bitter seeds ought to be there to make the child taste and stretch and reach, for by tasting he develops taste and by stretching and reaching he grows.

Up to this point, while I have examined the creative cry and explored the creative process, I have still—as always—avoided the direct answer to the direct question, "Where do you get your ideas?" The whole answer seems to be—*out of myself.* Out of myself by delving ever deeper into the subconscious where all creative material lies dormant until ready to respond to the creative cry and begin the creative process.

In talking to a friend recently about this digging into self and the subconscious, she asked, "But what are you going to do when you exhaust that mine?" Then she spoke of research and travel and being steeped in the life and facts of things about which one wants to write, thus garnering new material.

I've no quarrel with these research methods. How else is a writer to know? Certainly he can't know everything just from his limited experience. Experience is very circular, a round of repetitions. Certainly it is valid to become immersed in the locale and life of that about which one intends to write. But that method is not for me; I have to keep going back to the well of my subconscious. And I have been extraordinarily lucky in having had the childhood in the Netherlands that I left behind stay fixed in me forever, as if set in amber.

I left my native village of Wierum at the age of eight; thus I had some three or four years of conscious experiences there. Then in the great depression in the United States some twenty-five years later, for the first and last time in my life I lived on a farm, again for a period of about three years. But out of those two widely separated experiences all my books seem to have come, and, by way of the subconscious, I hope to return to these two wells again and again.

To the one—to my childhood village of Wierum, tight against the dike and the North Sea—I shall physically return now. And right here I must give my grave, deep thanks to the Council and to the Jury; and I must especially single out my perennial champion and enthusiastic defender, Miss Virginia Haviland—and my beloved editor at Harper & Row, Miss Ursula Nordstrom, the only one with the sense to know, some twenty years ago, that I was any good. In short, my thanks to all in this Congress of Books for Young People for awarding me the Hans Christian Andersen

Medal, and, in that, for making it possible for me to go back to my little childhood village of Wierum.

The winning of this great award somehow for me seems to be epitomized, made real and almost believable, by my going back to Wierum.

After this speech I am going by car through my native country, the Netherlands, of which I only know the village where I was born. I am going by car, but I am not going into Wierum by car—not by car. I want to walk toward Wierum. I want to walk alone along the dike until I see again the tower of Wierum. The tower rises out of Wierum right beside the dike, but it also rises out of all my books about my childhood village; it rises out of my childhood soul. I hope the sheep will still be on the dike as I walk along the sea. I remember the stupendous stupidity of sheep. Strange, over some fifty years, my irritation with those bare-faced Frisian sheep—an irritation, I guess, of having, when tending sheep with my older brothers, to risk my eight-year-young life to rescue sheep that just stood there stupidly drowning in the incoming tide in the sea. Somehow, loving all animals, I must have loved them, but I don't know; ever after, sheep, safely ensconced behind fences in safe American pastures, have had no interest for me. I must see how I feel toward those sheep on the dike.

The sheep may not be there, but whatever the changes brought to my village by nearly a half century, the dike will still be there, the sea will be there, and the tower. They will be there, because in the mind's eye, in the child's eye of an eight-year-old, they are there, strong and eternal, set forever.

Quakingly eager as I am to go, I will not go back to my village without trepidation, for now I will not see it with the child's giant eye of wonder and discovery. Now I will see it with the adult's knowing, measuring eye that reduces everything to size. And it could very well be that by going back I will lose this rich childhood well, out of which so many of my books have come.

Then there will be left only the three-year, forty-acre depression farm in Michigan to fall back on. I shall have to chance that; and if I lose Wierum by going back to Wierum, perhaps the farm will still be enough. For through the years that forty-acre farm, fertilized by imagination, has grown until now it covers at least a few counties. And of late I even seem to be growing a town on my farm and a village or two.

All that by way of a somewhat emotional aside, and hastily dismissing it, I am still not satisfied that, in probing into the source of ideas, I have isolated the germ idea that becomes a whole book. Certainly, its origin lies not in factual experience, even though such experience is used by the creative writer. I spoke earlier about being a little Creative Joe—God in the midst of the shuddering walls of a creation—but only a god can create out of nothing. So, of course, the human creator has to take the little grub of fact and transmute it—rather the subconscious does it for him—into creative, dramatic life.

A neighbor in Grand Rapids, Michigan, fills his cherry tree with tin cans on a rope and sits underneath to shake the tinny mess in a wild cacophony of rattlings to scare the birds away from his cherries. This grubby little fact becomes the dominating character of legless Janus in my Newbery Medal winner, *The Wheel on the School.* While fishing in a Michigan lake, I see a flight of lost bees come to rest on the boat. Some of them are helped out of the water with the blade of an oar, and the concern over some bees becomes little, scared, all-alone Davie in the book, *Shadrach,* trying to save a scary, monstrous bumblebee from drowning in a Dutch ditch.

However, these are merely incidents within books, based on miniscule life facts that, through the creative subconscious, have chrysalized and butterflied. But the genesis, the germ idea, the origin of any of my books I simply cannot find, try as I may. Even as that thimbleful of basic talent is a mystery, the germ idea veils itself and flits away in ghostly mystery after the book it produces has been written.

I remember the beginnings of my book, *Shadrach.* Just before going to bed one night, I was riffling through a magazine, reading some reviews of other people's books. And then a single line in one of those reviews struck fire. Instead of going to bed, I grabbed some paper and a pencil and, when morning came, there was *Shadrach,* a whole book all roughed out in the night. But later, in assiduously hunting through the whole magazine for the line that had caused a book in the night, I could not find it. I had forgotten it in writing the book.

The genesis of my book, *Dirk's Dog Bello,* was likewise somewhat startling. I had happened into the Grand Rapids Library. The librarian mentioned that there was a ten-thousand-dollar contest on for a children's book. The contest still had a month to go. With only a month to get ten thousand terrific dollars, I turned right around, rushed all the four miles home; when I got to my typewriter, there was exactly one opening line in my mind. Eight words: "The women of Wierum are on the dike." Well, I had my opening line, but that is all I had; not a sentence would follow. Instead, suddenly, as if out of nowhere, came the ecstatic, triumphant last chapter of the book. After that, it was simply a matter of writing the book. No, I didn't win the ten thousand dollars. Remember, the contest had a month to go and it took exactly a year to squeeze a book between that opening eight-word line and that ending chapter.

If only all beginnings and endings of books were so easy; they are not. *The House of Sixty Fathers* took two years of agonizing. The Newbery winner, *The Wheel on the School,* was a four-year agony. I am now working on a book that I have worried over for seven long years, yet I am *not* worried that it won't eventually come and that it will not be the better and the deeper for those seven years. Over the years of my writing I have learned to come in rapport with my subconscious. I simply assign it the task. I now know that, when the subconscious is at last ready, up will come the mass and mess that I have entrusted to it, transformed, transmuted in a creative metamorphosis that only the subconscious can perform. Of course, then still comes the struggle of the conscious creative intelligence—so limited, so clumsy in its skill.

No, I am not worried, not even after seven submerged years, that my book won't come; for the real proof of the tenacity of the subconscious lies in my latest book, *Nobody Plays with a Cabbage.* I wasn't aware of it in the actual writing of the book, but, in probing into the origins and germ ideas of my books, I suddenly came to the remembrance and realization that, back in college days some thirty years ago, I had once before written *Nobody Plays with a Cabbage.* I'd written it as doggerel for the college paper, a bad piece of doggerel at that.

Thirty years, and I forgot, but the subconscious never forgot that doggerel. Why? Simply because the subconscious was not finished with it, was not satisfied. Unbeknownst to me, it kept transmuting all the elements in that miserable piece of doggerel in its process of metamorphosis, until now, thirty years later, every element reappeared in what I consider my most graceful little book yet. Thirty years—but having rewritten the doggerel, now the creative subconscious could be at rest, and restlessly turn to the writing of the next book.

Here I cease, and here I stand. Because of you—gratefully here I stand. You have heard my speech. I heard the cry of the wild geese and in me it brought forth the creative cry needed to produce this speech. And, if now with me you have somewhat heard the cry, blessed be you. But I must go. I must go back now, back to Wierum, and the tower, and the dike—where it all began.

Chapter 5

Illustrators and Illustration

Strong forces have come to affect modern children's book illustration. Sophistication of technology, virtuosity of graphic art, and experimentation for new effects by commercial and other artists have paralleled an internationalism which has created a growing overseas exchange and new influences through coproduction and copublishing. Three decades after her *New York Times* critique reprinted here, Louise Seaman Bechtel stated that "The last twenty years have seen far greater changes in art and make-up of children's books than the thirty years preceding. This is the result of greater interest in modern art in adult painting and sculpture, as well as in book-making. Also in this period children have been much more encouraged in their own art of many sorts. The connection between their creative activities and what they read and look at has been more understood and emphasized."[1]

One wonders, however, whether all these changes have been beneficial. Are adults selecting for themselves and not for the child? Has a rich field become excessively opulent? Have pictures—as art—pushed texts into the background, beyond the necessity for illustrations to play their role in illuminating or extending the texts they accompany? Has the role of illustration thus changed, giving us a prodigality of art, the result of the European and Japanese output and cheaper color printing overseas?

Discussing the role of illustration in a book, Edward Ardizzone said in

---

1. Quoted from a letter to Virginia Haviland, 1970.

1959, ''The text can only give bones to the story. The pictures, on the other hand, must do more than just illustrate the story. They must elaborate it. Characters have to be created pictorially because there is no space to do so verbally in the text. Besides the settings and characters, the subtleties of mood and moment have to be suggested.''[2] Maurice Sendak, agreeing with Ardizzone on what the role of illustration should be, sees a recent change in that role. As a juror for an international competition of children's book illustration held in Eastern Europe in 1971, he saw there a tendency for illustrations to

> take on a dominance and importance which I, as an illustrator, do not approve of. The books become showcases for artists. You turn pages and there are extremely beautiful illustrations, but so far as I can see they could be taken out of one book and put into another. . . . [H]ere we are very much involved in making the illustrations work in a very specific way inside a book. A picture is there, not because there should be a picture there; there is a purpose for a picture—we are embellishing, or we are enlarging, or we are helping the author, or we are involving ourselves in some very deep way with the writer of the book, so that the book (when it is finally illustrated) means more than it did when it was just written[3]

Today's wealth in picture books derives in part from the great increase in reillustration of old stories and verses. In ''Mother Goose's Garnishings,'' reprinted in this chapter, Maurice Sendak traces the history of picturing Mother Goose, making clear the natural fascination of the classic rhymes for artists, so many of whom must depend for material to illustrate on the ready-made tales and rhymes available for reinterpretation. (For subsequent criticism, see the two reviews following Sendak's article.) However, the reillustration of certain classics is likely to raise the question of whether it is right to impose new illustration. Substitute pictures for those of Lear? Or Tenniel? Or Shepard? Brian Alderson in ''Non-sense and Sensibility'' notes: ''Lear was a marvelous draftsman and therefore able to fix for his 'nonsense' a unity in the presentation of words and pictures. . . . And, once fixed, this unity takes on a naturalness, an inevitability, that only a very daring or very stupid artist will attempt to disturb with intrusive ideas of his own.''[4] In agreement, artist Crispin Fisher evaluates Lear's followers in a group review included in this chapter; he confesses to ''a bit of a shock to be confronted with this colourful glut of re-interpretation. . . . Anything that creates a 'wider interest' in Lear is a good thing''—but ''Edward

---

2. ''Creation of a Picture Book,'' *Top of the News*, 15 (December 1959): 40–60.

3. ''Questions to an Artist Who Is Also an Author,'' *Quarterly Journal of the Library of Congress*, 28 (October 1971): 262–280.

4. ''Non-sense and Sensibility,'' *Children's Book News*, 5 (January-February 1970):9–11.

Illustration by William Steig reprinted with the permission of Farrar, Straus & Giroux, Inc. and Hamish Hamilton Ltd. from *Amos & Boris* by William Steig, copyright © 1971 by William Steig. *Amos & Boris* is a 1972 "Showcase" book.

Lear is still a vehicle whose engine generates more revs than their talent can ever aspire to.''

Another question related to children's book art concerns the tendency of many illustrators to repeat themselves—possibly the result of popular success—instead of renewing themselves and offering freshness and innovation. In 1957 Marcia Brown, an eminent spokeswoman for the illustrator,[5] analyzed in "Distinction in Picture Books"[6] modern picture-book production. Asking how we are to pick those works which are exceptional, she discussed elements which contribute to the making of a distinguished

---

5. See her articles in *Illustrators of Children's Books: 1946–1956*, compiled by Ruth Hill Viguers, et al. (Boston: Horn Book, Inc., 1957) and *Illustrators of Children's Books: 1957–1966*, compiled by Lee Kingman, et al. (Boston: Horn Book, Inc., 1968).

6. In *Illustrators of Children's Books: 1946–1956* and also *Horn Book Magazine*, 25 (September 1949): 383–395.

picture book. Pointing to the great variety of media and the fact that children enjoy equally books with little or no color and books in full color, she inquires, "Why is it that as we examine the output of many of our outstanding illustrators we find so few who have grown appreciably since their first books? . . . Their growth has been in perfecting what they already could do rather than in experimenting and reaching out into new fields. Perhaps we have directly or indirectly asked these artists to repeat themselves." Ten years later she somewhat more optimistically analyzed the preceding decade, noted new trends, experimentation, and technical advances, and wondered "if twenty or thirty years from now this middle of the century period of children's book illustration will not seem a spectacular flowering. . . . To look over the bulk of picture books and illustrated books for young children published in the past ten years is a stimulating, often exhilarating, chastening, saddening, and eventually numbing experience. . . . Some illustrators seem to have an inexhaustible capacity to renew themselves and maintain through many books a look of freshness."[7] She names Roger Duvoisin as one, perhaps more than any other, who can do this.

One question remains, however. How is the adult book selector to know what the child will like? Two selections in this chapter, Louise Seaman Bechtel's "The Art of Illustrating Books for the Younger Readers" and Roger Duvoisin's "Children's Book Illustration: The Pleasures and Problems," suggest some answers. By knowing some of the best contemporary illustrators and by knowing something about the art of children's book illustration, one can gain insights into how to select for children. Awards also offer some guidelines. The Caldecott Medal is awarded annually to the artist of the most distinguished American picture book published during the preceding year. In April 1972, the Children's Book Council's "Showcase" of illustrated books for children was initiated. A jury's choice of the outstanding illustrated books published in the preceding year is exhibited and also publicized in a catalog containing commentary by artists and designers (see Chapter 12).[8]

---

7. "One Wonders . . . ," in *Illustrators of Children's Books: 1957–1966*, pp. 2–28.

8. For further information on illustrators, see *Illustrators of Children's Books, 1774–1945*, compiled by Bertha Mahony Miller, et al. (Boston: Horn Book, Inc., 1947).

The Art of Illustrating Books for the Younger Readers

Louise Seaman Bechtel

Louise Seaman Bechtel has contributed in significant ways to advancing the cause of good children's books: as head of the first children's book department established by an American publishing house (Macmillan's), from 1924 to 1934; as editor of "Books for Boys and Girls" for the New York Herald Tribune Book Review, *1949–1956; as occasional reviewer for other important newspapers and periodicals; and as juror a number of times for the American Institute of Graphic Arts. She has served also as associate editor (1940–1957), director (1958–1969), and honorary director (1970–) of the* Horn Book Magazine.

Is there a special "art" for boys and girls? In our great wealth of American children's books have we found new ways of speaking to children pictorially? The answer is definitely no, not yet. Our artistic energies have been too widely diffused. Experiments have been too small and expensive. Fortunately or not, our norm of adult art appreciation stays on the level of the child. Not that of the untouched, truly poetic and creative small child, but that of the "normal," self-conscious twelve-year-old.

So, we lost Mr. Disney of the original Mickey Mouse and gained the technical wonders and artistic banalities of Snow White. So, our most popular art today is that of the photograph and the comic strip.

Some critics tell us that, especially in painting, there is a true renaissance of American art. If this is true, it must be reflected in our bookmaking, to which many of our best artists contribute. But I have a troubled feeling that the segregation of children's books, and therefore of their pictures, is a phase of an educational mood that will pass and should pass.

For many centuries children shared with the whole community whatever art forms existed, as they share today the movies and the comics. But today we have the special field of children's bookmaking. Relatively, it is a very small drop in the bucket of public expenditure. But we have reason to ask what artists are working specially for children, and whether they are running with the popular tide or saying something special.

These artists inherit a brief tradition that perhaps began with the illustrated books of the 1860's. Mrs. Gatty first did her own pictures, later saw her stories illustrated by Holman Hunt, Burne-Jones, Sir John Tenniel. Later came Walter Crane, Kate Greenaway, and Randolph

"The Art of Illustrating Books for the Younger Readers" from *Books in Search of Children* by Louise Seaman Bechtel. (New York, The Macmillan Company, 1969. London, Hamish Hamilton Ltd., 1970). Reprinted by permission of The Macmillan Company and Hamish Hamilton Ltd.

Caldecott. In America, we had the "parlor gift book" makers, but we also had Howard Pyle.

The happiest years for children's bookmaking came after the First World War, with the influx of books and also of artists from Europe. Then bookmaking stepped away from its tradition. It was a time of sufficient prosperity for American publishers and public to support experimental bookmaking. We found and brought from abroad and created here books whose artwork reflected the gaiety of the Czech peasant, the sophistication of French and Russian art, the best of varied work from many lands, including the U.S.S.R., Sweden, and the Orient. And an artist here doing a book about India or Egypt had the sense and taste either to copy or to imitate closely art forms from those far cultures.

So, within the last twenty years a great variety of beauty has flowered into American bookmaking for boys and girls. It accompanied a sudden expansion of purposeful study of "the child," and the new growth of children's work in public libraries. In spite of it all an overwhelming number of American children still see mostly and prefer the art of the comic strips, and such art as is purely photographic. Yet the audience for our better children's books may be wider than their limited sales figures. And in the schools some children may be reaching toward new conceptions as they paint and draw more freely.

With the swift progress of color lithography the lot of the freelance artist has not been easy. Many distinguished artists have given their whole time to bookmaking and their return has not been great. But never before has bookmaking been more friendly to them, or more eager to adapt itself and its improving processes to genius.

In black and white, we think first of three men: Robert Lawson (*Ferdinand*), James Daugherty (*Daniel Boone*) and Boris Artzybasheff (*The Seven Simeons*). Mr. Lawson works in a purely traditional style, with a superb mastery of exact draftsmanship, with a strong pattern delicately expressed. His own new book, *They Were Strong and Good,* is a fine bit of unusual Americana. Mr. Daugherty, much more modern, with his swirling, dynamic patterns and bold sweep of heavy line, is always more the painter as opposed to Lawson the etcher. Mr. Artzybasheff can be exquisite, as in *The Seven Simeons,* tonally restrained and realistic, as in *Nansen,* boldly forceful, as in the Aesop, and in the many books of folklore he has treated. Probably he is the most brilliant, powerful, competent artist in the bookmaking world today. But each of these men is a sincere artist, each has a keen sense of humor, of drama, of detail, none has ever turned out anything cheap or stupid. Also, none of them seems to be considering any special "age," or doing anything "childish."

This is not quite true of the three outstanding women artists I will mention next, who are possibly more popular, who work just as sincerely. Wanda Gág (*Millions of Cats*) has her own biography this fall, a surprise both in words and pictures, a remarkable artist's confession. Dorothy Lathrop (*Hitty, Animals of the Bible*) has a new story of a South American squirrel.

Helen Sewell (*A Head for Happy, A Round of Carols*) has a new picture book *Jimmie and Jemima*. These three are all distinguished for splendid black and white. Miss Gág's heavy line is flowing, rich, modern. Miss Lathrop has evolved a delicate realism within a bold design and has also done very beautiful color work. Miss Sewell, again more modern, has a most individualized sculptural treatment which has been widely imitated. It is most perfectly suited to the period pictures for Elizabeth Coatsworth's three Sally books.

If a child owned books illustrated by these six artists alone, what a wealth of inspiration he would have! What a high critical standard of bookmaking, what intelligent, varied suggestion for ways of visualizing life as well as words! How does a child react to these pictures? We cannot generalize, because their taste, even at the youngest ages, always surprises us. Most psychologists have not progressed beyond the fact that most small children like big spaces of bright color. One child may feel that Artzybasheff and Gág are "gloomy," Sewell "stiff," Daugherty "mixey," Lawson and Lathrop his favorites. The next of the same age, will say the last two are least interesting, and Gág makes him laugh, and he wishes he could draw like Artzybasheff. So, fortunately, we always dare to offer children the best and to continue to experiment. One thing we do know; they have little interest in each other's artwork, or in an artist's attempt to be naive in a child's way.

But this choice of six artists is rather arbitrary. So many others are doing splendid kinds of bookmaking. In color we have the Petershams, the D'Aulaires, the Haders. In black and white there are three famous printmakers: Thomas Handforth, Lynd Ward, Peggy Bacon. Then there are Clare Newberry, William du Bois, Zhenya Gay, Ludwig Bemelmans, Kate Seredy, Kurt Wiese, Valenti Angelo, N. C. Wyeth, Paul Brown, Hilda van Stockum. Robert McCloskey added a cheerful, truly American note this spring with his masterful, supersized comic, *Lentil*.

There are two new artists who step farthest away from traditional styles, who both in method and in imaginative approach are speaking to children in a somewhat new way. Both have a flavor of recent French and Russian bookmaking in their use of flat color combined with bold spaces of black and white. Both have a verve and simplicity which I think eventually will be widely approved by children. Clement Hurd showed himself a master of interpretation when he decorated Gertrude Stein's *The World Is Round*. He also did those gay panorama books of Town and Country, with their poster, toylike continued stories without words (only custom forced the editors to put in a few). Leonard Weisgard has a truly wonderful new *Punch and Judy*, a brilliant capturing of the essence of all puppet shows. Children can play with it too, just as they can release their energies in replying to his nonsense pictures for *The Noisy Book* and *The Country Noisy Book*.

If such a roll-call brings pictures to your mind's eye, think what a contrast they are to those of the many English illustrators we know so well. They are firmly in the old tradition, and also they are firmly entrenched in the hearts of American children, and will live on side by side with these other so much more varied American artists. What would our book world be without Arthur Rackham, Ernest Shepherd, Leslie Brooke, Beatrix Potter, F. D. Bedford? Yet, are we not lucky to have our own varied genius to contrast with them?

With so much that is very fine there is no need for a discriminating parent to spend money on poor bookmaking. I would even say there is no need for a child's fresh eyes to linger over comic strips or movies—but that is another subject, involving morals and literature. Let all that mass of dullness do its worst—at least there does exist a fine, strong store of art in books, always there to be looked at again if they have been bought and are waiting their turn.

Children's Book Illustration:
The Pleasures and Problems

Roger Duvoisin

Roger Duvoisin has had experience in many forms of artistic expression, including stage scenery, murals, posters, and textile design, as well as writing and illustrating children's stories. Among the many picture books he has illustrated are White Snow, Bright Snow *by Alvin Tresselt, which won the 1948 Caldecott Medal; and* The Happy Lion *(1954), written by his wife, Louise Fatio, which won the* Bilderbuchpreis *for its German edition. Among those books Duvoisin both wrote and illustrated are* The Three Sneezes and Other Swiss Tales *(1941) and the two picture-book series beginning with* Petunia *(1950) and* Veronica *(1961). Duvoisin has often served on juries for children's book illustration.*

When I was offered the honour of speaking here for "one full hour" about children's books, I worried a bit. The letter of invitation was clear: "We want you to speak for one full hour." This was flattering. To speak for one full hour without interruption is an opportunity never offered to most people. But it meant also, I took for granted, a formal *serious* talk. A formal serious talk, when "amusing and fun" is probably more appropriate to describe the making of children's books. In the actual work of making a child's book, the artist had better keep his sense of humour and pleasure about him: if he forgets to do so, he may well end up with a book which will bore children. Therefore, I will mix fun and seriousness in trying to tell about my personal pleasures and problems in this delightful occupation of illustrating children's books.

First, I must say I have a suspicion that more than a few artists who write and illustrate children's books have not deliberately chosen the occupation: they discovered its pleasures accidentally while doing some sort of stories with drawings as a form of play with their own children. It does not take long when playing in this fashion to have the rough form of a lively story, and all done with the participation of the children themselves. In executing this little feat the artist may be astonished to discover a previously unknown talent in himself.

Everyone who has improvised stories and pictures in the presence of a few children knows the fun one can have in that game. When this act has life and humour, the children's eager eyes and laughter are pleasant rewards. Even the bored looks which come to the children's faces when the story and the pictures lack inventiveness are part of the amusement. Bored looks spur one to higher feats of imagination in order to bring back the laughs.

"Children's Book Illustration: The Pleasures and Problems," by Roger Duvoisin from *Top of the News*, 22 (November 1965): 22–33. Reprinted by permission of the American Library Association.

The making of children's picture books is indeed like playing with children. The game is on even when the author-illustrator sits alone at his drawing table. For he is really not as lonely as he seems to be. He has his abstract public with him, as have artists in every field. In his case it is a public made up of two kinds of children. First, there is the child *he* was, a child who is very much present and who inspires him and helps him understand the other children. Second, there are the abstract children who are watching over his shoulder.

From his own childhood, he remembers the things, impressions, attitudes which impressed him most. He remembers his childhood conceptions of people, of animals, of scenes, and of books which were part of his world.

From the abstract children watching over his shoulder, he will have the fresh, unexpected, imaginative conceptions which they have expressed during games or conversations. In this give and take with his abstract public of children the illustrator will learn to let his imagination flow more freely.

There is in the maker of children's books what is in most adults in their relations to children: that little sneaking desire to teach and to moralize, to pass on to children what we think of our world. A picture book is such a fine medium for this exercise that it is difficult to resist the temptation. Even if these sentiments are carefully hidden in the book they are generally there, and so much the better. The children's-book maker has the added pleasure of believing that he has done more than merely entertain. Personally, I like to think that while children read my books they do not waste their time on the hundreds of toy trucks, cars, tractors, and bulldozers which fill most children's rooms nowadays, or on some of those books of useless facts.

The modern picture book with its large pages, its wealth of colour made possible by modern processes of reproduction, is a tempting invitation to the artist to play with his brush and pen. The fine books which have been published in recent years prove that more and more artists of talent are eager to join in the fun.

This fun is apparent to anyone who walks into public or school libraries or into bookstores. And it is fun which is spreading far and wide, for the modern picture book has invaded the world. I have seen picture-book stores all over Europe, east and west. I have seen a few in Iran. In an Iranian bookstore, a clerk brought out a book which he said was the outstanding picture book in Iran. I told him that I had seen two better ones in the office of a Teheran publishing firm. "I do not think that could be," he answered, "this one was chosen by the American Institute of Graphic Art for their book *The Children's Books of Asia.*" And indeed, he brought me the book which, until then, I had never seen. It was a most interesting book. This indicated that in Asia there were bookstores with children's-book departments such as the one I was visiting. There are very few of these stores in poor countries, however.

One might ask where all this is taking the children's-book creators. What standing have they won in our society? Who will take seriously artists who spend so much of their time playing with children and children's books? Not many people, in my own experience. Not even their own children. When I filled out an application for a passport last year, I wrote "Children's book illustrator and writer" in the space for "occupation." When the clerk saw this he looked up with a wink and a smile and said, "Hm, children's books, eh?" There was absolutely no doubt that he meant, "Hm, harmless fellow." Or at a party of serious business people, a lady friend is liable to introduce you to a grave-looking gentleman and say, "This is Roger Duvoisin; he is the author of *Petunia the Silly Goose*." This is sure to bring another wink and a smile. A third example is that of my granddaughter, who was asked when she was nine, "Well, Anne, do you write stories for children as does your grandfather?" "Oh yes," she replied, "I do write children's stories, but when I grow up I will write grownup stories."

Anne can be forgiven for she did not know that generally speaking one has to be a grownup to write and illustrate stories which children will enjoy. But as for those grave, practical grownups, I know it is they who are foolish, they who should be smiled and winked at. Their attitude does not give me the slightest inferiority complex. I have no apologies to offer for being part of a zoo of imaginary animals, geese, hippopotamuses, rabbits, lions, raccoons, bugs, crocodiles, and others. These animals are my loyal friends and my wife's too. We have much affection for them. Together we do our best to make the imaginative stories and fantasies which children need to develop their imagination and to learn about reality.

Instead of living in a zoo I could just as well live among fairies, dragons, dwarfs, and giants. They are just as necessary to children. But I love my zoo and I prefer to draw animals. Besides, animals have been used as symbols of men and to represent the gods and the world of magic ever since men could talk.

But there is also a serious aspect to the making of children's books, an aspect which at times demands very much hard work. This other aspect of children's books concerns the illustrations from an artistic point of view. That is to say that while the artist desires to communicate his own pleasure to children, he wants to do so with illustrations that are original in their conceptions, that are well composed in their designs and colours. In this he is driven by his own need to experiment and to try to improve his art, and he is encouraged by the importance the art in children's books has acquired as an art form.

The two aspects of illustrating children's books—the fun aspect and the serious artistic aspect—should not be separated really, for they are part of one overall effort to make a book as good and as beautiful as possible. But I will separate them here for the purpose of making it easier to explain, if I can, what an illustration is and what makes it beautiful.

The modern picture book, then, must be considered as more than a vehicle to carry stories and pictures to children in order to amuse them and give food to their imagination—and to amuse their authors at the same time. It is also a most interesting medium for artists to experiment in with colours and design—to invent to their heart's content. This is why many talented artists have been attracted to the picture book, not only for the fun of it but also for the opportunities it offers for their art. The result is that the best children's books have become art creations without losing the particular qualities which give pleasure to children.

Imagine a layman listening to one artist as he explains to another artist what he is trying to do in working on a new book. What he may hear will make him wonder whether the poor child has not been completely overlooked in the problems the artist is trying to solve. These problems may pertain only to the proportions of margins, to the interest of the white spaces and coloured shapes, to the inventiveness of the design, to the relationship of the various colours, and other such problems.

Where is the child in all these things? Has he been sent to bed to leave the grownups to discuss serious things without being disturbed? The answer is that the child is very much present indeed. One of the reasons for making a page which is well designed is to tell the story with more simplicity, more verve, clarity, and impact; to give importance to what is important; to eliminate what destroys the freshness, the originality of the page; in other words, to make a page which will be more easily read by the child. A well-designed page will also educate the child's taste and his visual sense. A beautiful book is a beautiful object which the child may learn to love.

The modern children's-book illustrator is not isolated from the turmoil of the art world around him. Instinctively or consciously, sometimes too consciously, he tries to swim in the current with varying degrees of success, depending on his talent. He wants to present to children books which reflect what he has learned from the new developments in art.

What these developments are everyone interested in painting and the graphic arts knows very well, but it seemed to me that it would be interesting to speak about them here and to tell how they are affecting the making of children's books.

Roughly, the extraordinary things which happened to painting during the nineteenth and twentieth century—its evolution away from representation and toward pure abstraction—have made the art of illustration what it is today. Illustration in some of its forms has long been confused with painting, and it is this evolution of painting toward abstraction which has helped clarify the difference between the two. However some confusion still exists. Illustration, in its narrow meaning, is an art whose purpose is to complement a text in a book or a magazine, to tell the story pictorially. But an illustration can tell a story without the help of a text. In this wider meaning, an illustration is a form of independent writing. It is pictorial literature.

It can even be said that illustration antedates the written word, for many of the prehistoric paintings or drawings were illustrations. For instance, those of the Tassili region in North Africa often describe scenes of the material or religious life of the people who made them: hunting, war, dance scenes, etc. The religious frescoes and paintings of the medieval period and the Renaissance were, for the people who could not read, what the illustrations in a picture book are for the child who has not yet learned to read. They told pictorially the stories and legends the people had heard.

A painting can be an illustration. A large painting which describes a battle scene can be merely a painted illustration and not a true painting. That is, its end may be strictly literary: to tell the story of a battle. Two well-known French painters of the nineteenth century—the historical painter Detaille and the great painter Delacroix—serve well as examples of this. When Detaille did a battle scene his purpose was simply to tell a highly sentimentalized, romanticized version of that battle. He painted the figures, the arms, and the uniforms down to the last button with a precise realism, like a storyteller who can't help putting in all the details. To Delacroix, however, the battle scenes he chose to paint were but subjects on which to work out abstract problems of painting. Even if, superficially, one will see only romantic pictures of battle scenes in the works of these two painters, the fact remains that Delacroix painted a painting while Detaille painted an illustration. This is how paintings can be confused with illustrations and illustrations with paintings.

Painting is the independent, abstract creation of an artist—abstract whether the subject which started it on its way remains or disappears in the process of creation, or whether there ever was any subject to begin with.

The arbitrary division between abstraction and representation in a painting has sometimes been explained by replacing a painting by a page of Chinese writing. To a person who cannot read Chinese, such a page is simply a beautiful abstract design. It means nothing, it only satisfies the visual senses. If, by some magic, the person admiring the abstract design of the page could suddenly understand the Chinese language and Chinese writing, the page would automatically cease to be a beautiful abstract design affecting the visual sense. It would become a poem about a lake, or a Chinese tale, or any other piece of writing. Only the trained artist may continue to admire the beauty of the abstract design.

Now, the point where a representational painting ceases to be a painting and becomes an illustration is not a well-defined one. The layman can take comfort in the fact that painters themselves do not always agree on the matter.

Up to the nineteenth century, no artist had left in writing his opinion of what makes a painting a true painting. We have only the opinions of writers who, for centuries, have considered that painting was an imitation of nature. In other words, a painting was a picture or illustration or literature.

The Greeks—for example, Aristotle—had expressed this opinion. The Greek paintings, the drawings on the Greek vases, all their art and sculpture were imitations of nature. They were representations of mythological figures or of everyday scenes. Unfortunately, we do not know what the artists thought of their art.

The paintings of the Romans reached an astonishing degree of realism. Many are pure illustrations painted on walls. They reveal to us the most intimate details of everyday life and the Roman's pictorial conceptions of their mythology.

The art of Byzantium was an interlude. Its almost abstract art ended realism and literature in art for several hundred years.

But toward the end of the thirteenth century the famous painter Giotto brought back realism and literature in painting. Whatever the value of his paintings as true paintings, their realism was the reason for his very success. People of his day flocked to see his paintings. Never before had the figures and scenes of the church seemed so alive to them. His realism and illustrative talent were highly praised by the writers of his day and of later periods. For them Giotto had liberated painting from the conventions of Byzantine art.

With the discovery of the laws of perspective in the fifteenth century, painting became more than ever illustration for most everyone, even for some painters. It is probable that most of the princes who ordered these paintings saw in them masterful illustrations of religious, mythological, or historical literature, and illustrations of their personal feats.

The problem went on during the next centuries and is well demonstrated in the art criticism which has been written all along. Paintings were almost continuously judged for qualities which were literary ones. A quotation from an eighteenth-century writer will give a good example. It was written about a painting by the French painter Greuze which was titled ''The Death of a Wicked Father'':

> The death of a wicked father, abandoned by his children, tears the soul of the spectator. It is hair raising. Everything expresses the despair of the dead, the disorder and horror of his condition. The strong, deep, revolting impression made by the painting repulsed many spectators. There is here a sublimity, as well as a beauty which few souls could bear.

In this case the painter was expressing human feelings which could be expressed in words. This made his painting a piece of literature. So we can forgive the writer for wanting to put it down in writing.

But the great painters of every period most certainly knew that the representation of a subject was not what mattered most in a painting even though they could not have discussed abstraction in the way it is discussed today.

It was in the nineteenth century that painters began to be articulate about the problem. Delacroix seems to have been the first to write on the subject. He was not only a great painter, he could also write well about painting. His diary and his letters make extremely interesting reading for artists. As far as we know, he was the first to express concern because people misunderstood paintings. When he painted he was not writing, he said. He had nothing to tell in mind. His paintings were only meant to reach the senses. In other words, what was of value in them was felt and could not be expressed in words. He also seems to have been the first to question the necessity of the subject. Its elimination was, of course, the most effective way to clear the misunderstanding. It is ironical that Delacroix ended up by being the victim of the subject. The subjects he chose for his paintings were so romantic that the paintings have not been popular in our century. But painters still see the true art in his paintings under their romantic dress.

More and more painters toward the end of the last century expressed the opinion that painting was a creation, an abstraction, not an imitation of nature, not literature. This led to twentieth-century painting, to pure non-representational art.

But painting also ceased to appeal to the layman. Spectators were so accustomed to considering painting as pictures or illustrations that their reactions were ones of revolt and anger when they first saw the paintings whose subjects were beginning to break up. They were frustrated at not recognizing their illustrations and accused the painters of mocking them. I remember the indignation that was created by a poster when I was a child. It represented a large horse done in stone lithography. The horse was not particularly distorted, but it was green. A green horse! Who had ever seen a green horse! That slight departure from realism was enough to bring a wave of protests.

While the painters were slowly effecting the divorce of illustration from painting, dismembering the subject, planning its final murder, the professional book illustrators had a good time.

Illustrated books were popular during the nineteenth century. There were many professional illustrators of talent who were often accomplished craftsmen in wood or copper engraving and in the new reproduction process of stone lithography. These illustrations were printed in black, but were sometimes coloured by hand. During the second half of the century the printing of colour overlays was perfected. But illustrators generally followed the tradition of realism and of closely following the text with exact literalness.

Children's-book illustrators were also busy during this time. What is remarkable is how some of these illustrators remained solidly wedded to the contemporary literature they illustrated. *Alice in Wonderland* and Tenniel comes to mind first as the classic example. When we think of Alice, we think of Tenniel's conception of her, and if we read the book without Tenniel's illustrations something is missing. At the turn of the century, *The Wind and the Willows* and Arthur Rackham is another example. We may not like now the mannered style of Rackham but his illustrations are well wedded to the story.

Even when an illustrator was not the contemporary of the author whose books he illustrated, his name could be closely associated with these books. Doré was such an illustrator. His drawings were not particularly distinguished, nor was he concerned with well-composed pages, but he had enormous verve and imagination. His name was for long identified with some of the classics he illustrated. Among these are masterpieces which are loved by children. They are Perrault's *Mother Goose Tales* and La Fontaine's *Fables*. In *Mother Goose Tales* Doré added to the fantasy of the tales; his forests were as dark, frightening, and mysterious as fairy-tale forests should be, and the romanticism of his castles lingered for a long time in the minds of readers.

But one of the most important things that happened to illustration during the nineteenth century was the interest that some major painters began to take in the work of illustrating books. It was a modest beginning at first, in the sense that few of these painters illustrated books. But it was the beginning of an interest which continued to grow and became extremely important during our century.

By a strange coincidence, the first of the major painters to express concern that his paintings were being mistaken for literary work was also the first to put his hand to the literary work of illustrating a book. He was Delacroix. Delacroix illustrated the *Faust* of Goethe on lithographic stones. It was, of course, the very personal creation of a great artist. Goethe himself was pleased with the vigour and power of these illustrations and was generous enough to say that they were superior to his text in the conception of some scenes. The book became a classic example of the combination in one book of a great writer and a great artist. Delacroix also illustrated *Hamlet* and other dramas.

A few more nineteenth-century artists, such as Turner, Manet, Rodin, did book illustrations. But it was in the twentieth century that their number really became important: Toulouse-Lautrec, Picasso, Matisse, Derain, Dufy, Miro, Redon, Juan Gris, Maillol, Klee, Chagall, even Calder and others. Recently, Rauschenberg did pages for Dante. Picasso himself illustrated a long list of books: poetry by his friends, novels, Greek classics, even Buffon's *Natural History*.

These painters who, little by little, led painting to non-figurative art also brought new conceptions to book illustration. They were often in their own art the equals, if not the betters, of the writers whose works they illustrated. With their creative powers, they could not simply see their illustrations as the servants of a text and illustrate with literalness and realism. They did away with these conceptions. They illustrated on their own terms though they kept within the spirit of the particular piece of literature they chose to illustrate.

What interested them in this literature was that it offered their creative imaginations a base from which to invent graphic ideas.

There has been much criticism expressing disapproval of the liberties these artists took with the literature they illustrated, but it was these liberties as well as the greatness of their art which make their work in book illustration valuable and defensible.

Literature is an art which has its own conceptions and its own means of expressions. It does not need help from another art, unless the writer himself has planned it that way. Illustrations which impose the artist's conception of a novel with definitiveness and precise literalness come like a screen between the author and his readers. The illustrations interfere in a very unpleasant way with the readers' own dreams.

But illustrations as done by the superior artists are related to the text in a free, loose, subtle way; they leave the reader free to interpret the writing with complete freedom. And he has the added pleasure of doing the same with the illustrations.

One can see the difference between the two conceptions by comparing the illustrations done for the same literary work by two artists. Doré illustrated an edition of Rabelais's *Gargantua* which had much success in his time. His illustrations had verve and boisterousness, but they fixed the scenes and personages of the book with such realism and definitiveness that the reader had no choice but to see Gargantua as Doré saw him. Derain's illustrations, half a century later, had much success also, but they are only free suggestions of Renaissance art and styles and of Rabelais's figures. They make fine pages which leave the reader free to see his own Gargantua. Thus, just as painters were extricating painting from illustration, they gave illustration some of the abstract features of painting.

It is worth saying here, also, that the pure abstract painters, that is the painters who have completely eliminated the subject in conceiving their paintings, have never illustrated books. Illustrative art and abstract art are too opposed to each other.

Now, after this very simplified history of the confusion between illustration and painting, we are back where we started: our modern picture book.

It may seem irrelevant to spend so much time speaking of the relationship between illustration and painting and of the evolution of painting toward abstraction in a talk about the minor art of children's-book illustration; it may also seem preposterous to imply that children's picture books have such noble ancestry. But all these things are what make our picture books what they are now.

In eliminating the representational from painting, painters were better able to examine what painting was. All the graphic arts profited from the discoveries the painters made.

Illustrators were able to learn the importance of the design which holds the narrative elements together in a page and gives order and visual qualities to that page. They could reflect over the conception that what makes a painting beautiful is not what it represents, a conception which to some extent is applicable to illustration. What makes an illustration beautiful is not its descriptive qualities but its underlying graphic inventions. Even in children's-book illustrations it is worth while to think of the narrative elements as materials with which to build a beautiful page instead of concentrating on them for their own sake.

Then there was the realization that literalness and realism were to the illustrator what the cage is to the bird. Having gotten out of the cage, illustrators found the most pleasant freedom in relating illustrations to a text, in composing pages, and in using colours.

Illustration profited much from abstract painting in spite of the opposition between the two. The treatments of surfaces, the use of space, the colour relations, the free, dramatic forms and lines, etc., of abstract paintings teach much to the illustrator.

However, the children's-book artist must think about all this within the very special art of picture books. Because making a picture book is like playing with children, the particular way children react to the world around them cannot be forgotten. This need not be a limitation; on the contrary, limitations are a challenge and a source of inventions.

With their uninhibited vision, children do not see the world as we do. While we see only what interests us, they see everything. They have made no choice yet. We do not see what sort of buttons a man we pass in the street has on his coat or how many there are, unless we are a button maker. But a child cares and will count the buttons if he can. He will care just as much about the tiny ladybug which falls accidentally on the dining-room table as about the grownups who sit around it. More, in fact. The child's interests are infinite and he sees the tiniest details of his world as well as the biggest forms. And he does not say, "I do not understand." He looks and sees. He lives among wonders and the children's book artist only has to take him by the hand, so to speak, to lead him toward the most imaginative adventures.

The child also has the tendency to enjoy this detailed world of his in terms of happenings, of things being done, in other words, in terms of stories.

In their own art, the children are not aware of abstract considerations. They are not concerned with colour harmony or colour contrast, with composition and design. Their art is only a sort of writing, however beautiful it might be sometimes. With it they tell a story. If a child is asked to explain a painting he has made, he will most likely tell what is happening in it. "This is a woman going to market to buy fruit. This is a truck driver climbing on his truck. This is the sea, full of fish which the fisherman will catch."

I still remember an experience I had with my elder son when he was four. It illustrates what I have just said. One day his mother took him up the Hudson River to Nyack. When they returned I asked him if he had liked the beautiful river with hills on both sides. He thought for a while and said, yes, he did. There was a boat on it which smoked and which had a little house in the middle. A door opened and a man came out of the house and went to look into the water. The only thing which struck him was an action, a little story. So let's give the child all the stories he wants.

Another quality children possess is their love and understanding of the humorous side of things. This also can be a rich source of ideas for the maker of children's books. Not only can he laugh with the child as he makes his books, but he can tell the most serious and important things while he laughs.

I have said enough, I think, to show that the artist and author cannot complain that the making of children's books has limitations. Those limitations rather resemble a jail whose windows and doors open wide into a beautiful paradise: The degree of talent of the children's-book maker may be the only limitation.

In the art itself, I think we will see artists taking more and more liberties. Even abstract art can have a place in a child's book under certain circumstances. If the artist is inclined to search for his page designs and for his colours by using the elements of the story in rough, free, almost abstract forms, he will be tempted to leave his page almost in the rough abstract condition. The forms, the bright colour surfaces which are not cut or soiled by details, the white spaces which remain pure have a freshness, a force, and an interest which they may lose when details and precisions are brought in. The artist may then be searching for a simpler and more ingenuous way of telling the necessary story.

When the artist writes his own story, he can conceive both his text and illustrations simultaneously, thus making the text and pictures help each other as they develop the story. He even can make his illustrations first with great freedom and get ideas for the text from them. In this case, the text may be like the threads the dressmaker uses to hold the pieces of material which will form the dress.

This matter of abstraction and illustration recalls to my mind a fascinating experience I had with a friend of mine, a well-known abstract painter. He wanted to illustrate a charming story he had invented for his children, but never having illustrated before, he came to live with us for a few days to work out the problem. In spite of his talent for drawing, making illustrations was for him like speaking the language of an unknown country. He could no longer see the story in literary terms when he tried to imagine the various scenes with his brush on the paper. To see visually the sequence of these scenes as they were described in his own story and translate them pictorially proved impossible for him. After several days a pile of nice miniature abstract paintings had been made, none telling any story. Yet when I think of this now, it seems to me that a few well-placed details drawn with the pen might have transformed the abstractions into story-telling pages. This experience demonstrates, however, how difficult it is to join two art conceptions which are so opposed to each other. It demonstrates also that in picture books, as in every art form, everything is worth trying.

As I come to the end of the "one full hour" I see that I could ramble on for another hour, but I think you can see now that the making of children's books can be as great a source of satisfaction for the artist as the finished book can be a source of pleasure for the child.

Mother Goose's Garnishings

Maurice Sendak

Singled out in many commentaries as the leading American children's book artist today, Maurice Sendak has been the subject of a number of articles and has himself written much about the business of illustrating. His reputation as a writer and illustrator of children's books is international and his books are widely republished. In 1970 he won the Hans Christian Andersen International Medal for illustration. Among the books created entirely by him are Where the Wild Things Are, *winner of the 1964 Caldecott Medal,* The Nutshell Library *(1962),* Higglety Pigglety Pop *(1967), and* In the Night Kitchen *(1970). His work for books written by others covers a wide range:* A Hole Is to Dig *(1952) by Ruth Krauss, the* Little Bear *series by Else Holmelund Minarik,* A Wheel on the School *(1954) by Meindert DeJong,* The Light Princess *(1969) by George Macdonald, and* The Animal Family *(1965) by Randall Jarrell, as well as many others.*

Only Mother Goose, that doughty old wonder bird, could have survived the assiduous attention of generations of champions and detractors, illustrators and anthologists. More than merely survive, she has positively flourished—younger, fresher, and more superbly beautiful than ever: witness the publication of Mother Goose books of every shape and size that has continued for generations, including the dozens now on the market in America. Among the most popular of this latter group is *The Real Mother Goose,* being issued this fall in a 50th anniversary edition by Rand McNally and bearing on its cover a commemorative gold seal. The name and the seal raise a basic and puzzling question: Is there a *real* Mother Goose? The answer lies in an exploration of the origins of Mother Goose and perhaps some assessment of the art that has illustrated them from their earliest editions.

It is fairly well agreed that the earliest use of the name Mother Goose in the English language dates from a translation of the Perrault fairy tales, *Contes de Ma Mere L'oye,* published in England in 1729. But the man who first took the name and gave it to a collection of traditional verses was John Newbery, who published his *Mother Goose Melodies* in 1791. After that the name was retained only in America; the English usually refer to the works of Mother Goose simply as nursery rhymes, songs, jingles or melodies. So any collection of Mother Goose rhymes confronting the bewildered purchaser is, strictly speaking, just as "real" as the Rand McNally edition, perhaps even more real, depending on the particular selection of rhymes and the perception of the illustrator.

"Mother Goose's Garnishings" by Maurice Sendak from *Book Week,* Fall Children's Issue (October 31, 1965): 5, 38–40. Reprinted by permission of Chicago Sun-Times.

Transmitted almost entirely by word of mouth, Mother Goose rhymes span an immense stretch of time, from the lovely "White Bird Featherless," which appears in Latin in the 10th century, up to "Horsey, Keep Your Tail Up," a popular commercial song of the 1920s. The origin of this potpourri of anonymous rhymes is described by Iona and Peter Opie, authors of the most authoritative collections of Mother Goose ever published, *The Oxford Nursery Rhyme Book* and the comprehensive *Oxford Dictionary of Nursery Rhymes,* from which I have borrowed much of my historical data. The *Dictionary,* a work of remarkable scholarship, is filled with a wealth of lore and generously sprinkled with some of the best examples of art illustrating Mother Goose.

The Opies note that the overwhelming majority of nursery rhymes were not originally composed for children, and that many would be *verboten* to children in the original wording. (The only "true" nursery rhymes, those specifically composed *for* children, are the rhyming alphabets, the lullabies and the infant amusements or poems accompanying a game created before 1800.) This genesis explains the earthy, ambiguous, double-entendre quality of so many of the verses—that lusty dimension too often missing in modern editions. The boring custom of passing over a witty, rambunctious, sometimes little-known verse ("I had a little husband, No bigger than my thumb," for example) in favor of a saccharine and pallid one such as "Mary Had a Little Lamb," adulterates the rich flavor of Mother Goose and undermines the value of any given collection.

Even before John Newbery officially credited them to Mother Goose, the rhymes had their detractors. Negative criticism began as early as 1641 and has continued ever since. William and Ceil Baring-Gould, in the introductory chapter to their informative and lively *Annotated Mother Goose* (Clarkson N. Potter), quote a Mr. Geoffrey Handley Taylor of Manchester, England, who condemns at least 100 of the rhymes for their unsavory elements. In 1952, Taylor listed a series of—in his estimation—ghastlinesses that occur in the typical collection: 1 case of death by shriveling, 1 case of body snatching, 1 allusion to marriage as a form of death, 9 allusions to poverty and want, and so inanely on. No comment from Mother Goose. That indefatigable lady has been too preoccupied in promulgating her poetry, busily adding to and enlarging her conglomerate collection with snatches of ballads, bits of political satire, snips of plays, folk songs, street cries, proverbs, and all manner of lampooneries.

The poets have repeatedly testified to the greatness of Mother Goose. Walter de la Mare wrote that many of the verses are "tiny masterpieces of word craftsmanship. Her rhymes free the fancy, charm the tongue and ear, delight the inward eye." Robert Graves claims the best of the older ones are nearer to poetry than the greater part of *The Oxford Book of English Verse.* G. K. Chesterton observed that so simple a line as "Over the hills and far away" is one of the most beautiful in all English poetry.

The powerful rhythms of the verses combined with their great strength and resonance account largely for their appeal to the child's inborn musical fancy. But there is more to the rhymes than music. Andrew Lang called them "smooth stones from the brook of time, worn round by constant friction of tongues long silent"—an image that suggests the subtle presence of elusive, mythic, and mysterious elements transcending the nonsense.

This elusive quality of the verses—that something more than meets the eye—partially explains the unique difficulty of illustrating Mother Goose. While it is true that the great children's literature is always underlaid with deeper shades of meanings which the perceptive illustrator must interpret, the Mother Goose rhymes stubbornly offer still further resistance. For a start, they have about them a certain baldness that betrays the unwary artist into banalities; the deceptively simple verse seems to slip just out of reach, leaving the illustrator with egg on his face. Another difficulty is related to that quality of the verses de la Mare described as "delighting the inward eye." Characteristic of the best imaginative writing, they evoke their own images, thus placing the artist in the embarrassing position of having to contend with Mother Goose the illustrator as well as the poet.

To make things more difficult, there is no room here for a mere show of sensibility, as some artists might get away with, for example, when illustrating the poetry of Robert Louis Stevenson or even the fairy tales of Andersen and Grimm. If the true measure of the rhymes isn't taken in the pictures, then the artist has failed Mother Goose. And her revenge is swift, for no other writing I know of so ruthlessly exposes the illustrator's strengths and inadequacies.

So it is with trepidation that the artist must approach this formidable muse. There are basically two approaches: First, the direct, no-nonsense approach that puts the facts of the case into simple, down-to-earth images. Miss Muffet, her tuffet, curds, whey and spider, all clearly delineated so as to erase all possible confusions in the child's mind. This kind of illustrating does not pretend to any profound leaps of the imagination or depths of interpretation. It simply translates the literal truth into literal images. It is respectful, honest, often beautiful and, I imagine, for the literal-minded child, the best possible accompaniment to the rhymes.

Blanche Fisher Wright's illustrations for *The Real Mother Goose* accomplish all this and a bit more. Despite a somewhat heavy-handed, humorless touch, they have great charm and vigor; best of all they manage to achieve that air of coziness and warmth so essential to the baby book. The sentimentalized art-nouveau style (the pictures date from 1916) helps to enhance the snug effect by ringing the pictures round the verses and locking them safely in. If these illustrations do not catch the spirited quality of the verses or perform in an imaginative counterpoint to them, if they obstinately face away from the dark side of the matter and maintain a too sunny disposition, they still have the virtue of simple, honest homeliness. This book is an excellent introduction to the rhymes (there are some 300 included).

For a more perceptive interpretation of Mother Goose one must look elsewhere. Not, I hope, at *The Little Mother Goose.* Jessie Willcox Smith's illustrations, which were done around 1912, are hopelessly alien to the spirit of the rhymes. Pudgy, prissy pictures, some in clotted colors that dissolve in soggy sentiment, make for a volume that sweetens rather than interprets the verses.

In the 1870s Walter Crane and the superb English color printer Edmund Evans (whose pioneer work also made possible many of the Caldecott and Greenaway books) collaborated on *The Baby's Opera,* an illustrated edition of nursery rhymes set to traditional music. Crane was a tireless, ingenious designer.

In Crane's hands a child's picture book became a matter of art. Everything is beautifully balanced in *The Baby's Opera,* from the busybody activities of the tiny drawings decoratively arranged around the music to the cleverly spaced full-page pictures. There are devilish bits of action going on in corners, an abundance of detail and subtle color throughout. But there is a flaw in this little book and it lies, ironically enough, deep within its superstructure of design. It is a breath too designed, thus fatally imprisoning the life within its pages.

Along about 1877 Randolph Caldecott began his illustrations for some of the nursery rhymes, and no artist since has matched his accomplishments. Caldecott breathed life into the picture book. The design of his books, so deceptively simple, allowed him the greatest possible freedom in interpreting the verses. I spoke earlier of two basic approaches to illustrating the rhymes, the first being the more literal, direct approach; the second is the way Caldecott chose. As in a song, where every shade and nuance of the poem is illumined and given greater meaning by the music, so Caldecott's pictures illuminate the rhymes. This is the *real* Mother Goose— marvelously imagined improvisations that playfully and rhythmically bounce off and around the verses without ever incongruously straying. If any name deserves to be permanently joined with that of Mother Goose, it is Randolph Caldecott. His picture books, published by Frederick Warne, should be among the first volumes given to every child.

Kate Greenaway, born the same month and year as Caldecott, was yet another contender for the honor of illustrating the real Mother Goose. Though probably more popular than Caldecott in her own time and certainly in our own, she can't hold a candle to him. When Caldecott's *Hey, Diddle Diddle* was about to be published, Miss Greenaway had an opportunity to see some of the originals, and in a letter to a friend she wrote: "They are so uncommonly clever. The dish running away with the spoon—you can't think how much he has made of it. I wish I had such a mind." Alas, she didn't and knew it. Her *Mother Goose or Old Nursery Rhymes* is, after Caldecott, an awful letdown. It is the great ancestor of the sentimental Mother Goose books, and it is hard not to blame Kate Greenaway for founding the line. For all its delicacy of design and exquisite color, for all its refinement of taste, there is little of the real Mother Goose in this lovely but antiseptic affair. The rhymes have been flounced out in a wardrobe of quaint Greenaway frocks, and they look stiff and inanimate;

Greenaway's surface charm does not mitigate the atmosphere of chilly Victorianism at the heart of her prim interpretation. See, for example, the two disdainful young ladies who seem to rush off in shocked distaste at the amusing verse they supposedly illustrate. All they lack are scented hankies to disguise the bad odor of Goosey, Goosey, Gander.

If Greenaway fails, perhaps it is due most of all to her error in tangling with Mother Goose, a doomed relationship that glaringly exposed her shortcomings. When Greenaway illustrates Greenaway, as in her perfect, tiny almanacks, she ranks with the best.

A spiritual descendant of Caldecott is L. Leslie Brooke (1862–1940) who illustrated, besides his more famous Johnny Crow books, a number of Mother Goose collections. The best of the lot is *Ring O' Roses*. Brooke's unabashed admiration for Caldecott is obvious in every aspect of this book, from the clever juxtaposition of black-and-white drawings and color pictures to the characteristically Caldecottian manner of animating the verses with a sequence of pictures that both amplify and enrich them. The Brooke illustrations convey a tremendous robustness and are very funny in the real old Mother Goose way. And *Ring O' Roses* is no mere pastiche Caldecott. The pictures are pure Leslie Brooke in flavor, the warm, homely, ample flavor that can only be English.

Brooke's nursery rhyme books are a wonderful swing up and away from the sentimental morass Mother Goose found herself wading in through the first quarter of the 20th century. Though the Blanche Fisher Wright pictures for *The Real Mother Goose* are far superior to most nursery rhyme illustrations of that time, their literalness and sentimentality are typical of the period. Mother Goose had to wait for a later generation to again take up her cause with genuine imagination. In the meanwhile, the rhymes suffered the abuses of oversentimentality, which, with virus-like tenacity, has nearly choked the life out of them. And the malady lingers on. Exponents in our own time are Marguerite de Angeli, Tasha Tudor and Joan Walsh Anglund. Miss de Angeli's *Book of Nursery and Mother Goose Rhymes,* a large, spacious book, chock full of rhymes and cheerfully illustrated, is by far the best of the three. The stifling, sweet atmosphere is at least partially relieved by the artist's quick appreciation of Mother Goose's go power. The pictures move, and thanks to the generously designed space, they have ample room to bounce about. The vision, however, of Mother Goose as baby-cute is a distortion that badly weakens the fiber of the verses.

Tasha Tudor deserves praise for including among the 77 verses in her *Mother Goose* some little known and extremely beautiful rhymes. Unfortunately, her illustrations convey nothing of the magic inherent in the verses. She manages warm, touching bits of observation throughout the book, but they barely survive the oppressive flood of sentimentality. Poorly designed pages and soupy, garish full-color pictures combine to deliver the rhymes a graceless *coup de grace.* Not as graceless, however, as the one accomplished by Joan Walsh Anglund's *In A Pumpkin Shell.* Mother Goose has more than met her match in Miss Anglund, who is famous for larding her works with pious sentimentalities. With the best intentions she decided to stand poor Mother Goose on her head, no easy trick, and the fact of her having achieved this astounding maneuver with far greater success than any other artist places Miss Anglund in a formidable light. One cannot help doubting the authenticity of some of the rhymes selected for this "Mother Goose ABC" (L for love and T for thank, naturally), they are so Anglundian in attitude and the banal illustrations adhere to the spirit of the book. Simply, Miss Anglund has managed the impossible—a saintly Mother Goose.

Philip Reed, Brian Wildsmith and Barbara Cooney have recently illustrated nursery rhyme books, each of them interestingly. Within the limits of its modest conception, Miss Cooney's version of *The Courtship, Merry Marriage and Feast of Cock Robin and Jenny Wren, To Which is Added the Doleful Death of Cock Robin* is a genuine *tour de force*. These animated and charmingly imagined pictures focus to marvelous effect on the minute details of the action. There is an amusingly jaded *joie de vivre* combined with a nice subtlety of discrimination in the characterization of Cock Robin and his seedy crew. Jenny Wren is the perfect portrait of the well-rounded, "getting on" type, who thought she'd never be asked; her simultaneous wedding and widowhood is all the more affecting for her air of I-knew-it-couldn't-be-true. Though artful, prankish and contemporary in mood and manner, these pictures never stray beyond the poetic logic of the verse.

This is not the case with Brian Wildsmith's *Mother Goose.* His full-blown, decorator-color images grossly underestimate the poetry by grossly overshooting the mark; such irreverent treatment of Mother Goose as a mere excuse for noisy posturing is irritating. On most pages the verses are scrunched down at the bottom, denoting only too clearly their unimportance in relation to the pictures. Mother Goose looks positively intimidated as in the rhyme, "Hickety, Pickety, My Black Hen," where she is literally sat upon. This pretentious book is Cinemascope Mother Goose, Mother Goose gone Wildsmith, and she has lost her identity in the process.

It is kept intact in Philip Reed's *Mother Goose,* which has been deservedly praised for its graphic excellence, for the setting of repose and naturalness it provides for the verses. His wood engravings, printed in six colors, bear comparison with the 18th-century woodcuts that first graced the nursery rhyme pages. Sadly, everything is here but the vivacity of those olden-day pictures; the repose is too reposeful, the quiet too quiet. The illustrations convey none of the nervy, nonsensical goings-on that beat through the verses. Reed's is an ambitious book that goes far, but I wish it had gone much further.

Joseph Low's *Mother Goose Riddle Rhymes* is a marvelously fresh, brilliantly colored, rebus Mother Goose which successfully captures the flavor of the racy old woodcuts. When executed with Mr. Low's wit, rhymes-into-picture-riddles is a happy device that neatly mirrors the quality of those verses devoted to puzzling or playing at games with the reader.

In Raymond Briggs' illustrations for three nursery rhyme collections (*The*

Illustration by Brian Wildsmith from *Brian Wildsmith's Mother Goose.* Reprinted by permission of Franklin Watts, Inc. and Oxford University Press.

White Land, Fee Fi Fo Fum and *Ring-a-Ring O' Roses),* a somewhat fussy technique does not detract from a genuinely funny, tongue-in-cheek literalness of interpretation. Charley Barley, after selling his poor dumb-founded wife for three duck eggs, really and truly does fly away, sanguine and blimp-like, with arms outstretched into a yellow green sky. All the Briggs books achieve, with varying degrees of success, a fresh, windy, out-o'-doors Mother Goose.

I am ignoring here masses of tasteless Mother Goose books—shiny, screeching banalities that culminate in *Walt Disney's Mother Goose* (Golden Press), where, as in some ghastly nightmare, Jack Sprat, Cross Patch, Jumping Joan and all our Mother Goose friends are rubbed out, and Mickey and Minnie Mouse and all those other egomaniacal Disney stars take over the nursery world (Donald Duck actually fills in for Humpty Dumpty and Minnie Mouse for Miss Muffet). The sorry rape of Mother Goose.

The Mother Goose book I like best, after the Caldecott books, is *The Only True Mother Goose Melodies,* a reproduction (published by Lothrop, Lee and Shepard in 1905) of an edition published in Boston in 1833 by Monroe and Francis, which, in turn was possibly a pirated edition of the John Newbery *Mother Goose Melodies* of 1791. The anonymous pictures are superb. Though badly reproduced, they are the very essence of Mother Goose—intensely alive, exceedingly droll ("to bed to bed says sleepy head," depicts a perfect moron type dropping turtles into a cooking pot). I agree with the Reverend Edward Everett Hale, who wrote in the introduction to this book that the artist who depicted the Man in the Moon (possibly Abel Bowen) ranks among "the original artists of the world." This picture graphically conceptualizes two aspects of nursery rhymes that, together, reveal a partial portrait of Mother Goose. A brick wall divides the picture through the center; on the right we see, vigorously drawn, a typical earthy Mother Goose buffoon slopping cold plum porridge over his head, while to the left—gracefully poised in mid-air, with one arm arched over the crescent moon and half his figure in mist—floats the ambiguous man in the moon, secret, magical and poetic. This is my favorite Mother Goose illustration.

What does Mother Goose have to say about her illustrators? Happily, nothing. But in the introduction to the 1833 edition of *The Only True Mother Goose Melodies*, she does have a bit to say about herself:

"Fudge! I tell you that all their [critics of her rhymes] batterings can't deface my beauties, nor their wise pratings equal my wiser prattlings; and all imitators of my refreshing songs might as well write a new Billy Shakespeare as another Mother Goose—we two great poets were born together, and we shall go out of the world together.

No, no, my melodies will never die,
While nurses sing, or babies cry."

Modesty never did become her.

Two Later Reviews of Mother Goose

Ruth Hill Viguers and Ethel L. Heins

Since Raymond Briggs' Mother Goose Treasury *(London: Hamish Hamilton; New York: Coward-McCann, 1966) was published too late to be included in the Sendak survey, the following review is provided. The review of* Brian Wildsmith's Mother Goose *(New York: Franklin Watts, Inc., 1965) is added because it presents an additional view of a widely enjoyed book.*

Mother Goose Treasury:

The artist's earlier illustrations for collections of rhymes give an idea of the verve, humor, and genius with line and color to be found in this one. . . . This book seems to have been illustrated exuberantly and continuously without pause for breath, so whole is it and so unified despite its comprehensiveness and the variety of approaches. . . . No other picture-book Mother Goose is so inclusive a treasury as this.

Ruth Hill Viguers

Brian Wildsmith's Mother Goose:

An impish Humpty Dumpty, blazing with luminescent color on the very first page, sets the tone for a wonderfully refreshing new edition of eighty-six traditional rhymes. . . . The artist's wholly original, sophisticated yet childlike interpretation of long-familiar material is revealed in his clever composition, unconventional humor, and characteristic water-color technique with its use of geometric patterns and brilliant chromatic modulations.

Ethel L. Heins

Review of Raymond Briggs' *Mother Goose Treasury* by Ruth Hill Viguers from *Horn Book Magazine,* 42 (October 1966): 558. Published by Horn Book, Inc. Review of *Brian Wildsmith's Mother Goose* by Ethel L. Heins from *Horn Book Magazine,* 41 (April 1965): 182–183. Published by Horn Book, Inc. London: Oxford University Press, 1964.

Illustration by Raymond Briggs reprinted by permission of Coward, McCann & Geoghegan, Inc. and Hamish Hamilton Ltd. from *Mother Goose Treasury*. Copyright © 1966 by Raymond Briggs.

A Load of Old Nonsense, Edward Lear Resurrected by Four Publishers

Crispin Fisher

Previously an art director for a publishing house in London, Crispin Fisher is presently a freelance artist-book designer. He is a naturalist as well and has illustrated his father's (James Fisher's) The Migration of Birds *(1966).*

Edward Lear. *The Quangle Wangle's Hat.* Heinemann 20s. Ill. Helen Oxenbury. 32 pp. $11\frac{1}{4} \times 8\frac{3}{4}$.
Edward Lear. *The Dong with the Luminous Nose and other poems.* Faber 18s. Ill. Gerald Rose. 32 pp. $7\frac{1}{2} \times 10$.
Edward Lear. *Incidents in the Life of my Uncle Arly and other nonsense.* Collins 16s. Ill. Dale Maxey. 32 pp. $11\frac{1}{4} \times 8\frac{1}{2}$.
Edward Lear. *The Owl and the Pussy-Cat and other nonsense.* Collins 16s. Ill. Dale Maxey. 32 pp. $11\frac{1}{4} \times 8\frac{1}{2}$.
Edward Lear. *The Jumblies.* Chatto and Windus 12s. Ill. Edward Gorey. 48 pp. $5\frac{3}{4} \times 9$.

I was brought up with a book of Nonsense with illustrations by Edward Lear himself, hanging together by a bit of luck, and its endpapers. So I accept these as the definitive illustrations, and I have formed my mental images of the Dong and others from these sources. It's a bit of a shock to be confronted with this colourful glut of re-interpretation. (All these books are in full-colour throughout, except Edward Gorey's.)

Of course this re-interpretation is desirable; it cannot after all subtract from the original. The "Introductory" to an edition published by Warne in 1900 expresses this as well as I can:

> In issuing this new edition of the 'Nonsense Songs' the Publishers desire to say that, feeling Mr. Lear had, contrary to his usual custom, presented these songs to the public illustrated in the slightest manner only, they have, with the assistance of Mr. L. Leslie Brooke['s pictures], endeavoured to create a wider interest in verses which for so many years have given unwonted pleasure to thousands of readers.

Anything that creates a "wider interest" in Lear is a good thing; the ringing of Lear's sumptuous adjectives isn't in our ears enough these days, so it's a jolly good thing that these four enlightened publishers are heaving

"A Load of Old Nonsense" by Crispin Fisher from *Growing Point*, 8 (November 1969): 1418–1420. Reprinted by permission of the author.

on the bell-ropes a bit. They've given their artists a wonderful opportunity: to be Lear's illustrator. It's no good asserting that Lear's own drawings were inseparable from the text, or indeed that they were necessarily the issue of a simultaneous conception. Nevertheless they were certainly attuned to it, and stand as a definition against which modern attempts may be compared.

Helen Oxenbury has all the ludicrous Lear ribbons, bibbons, loops and lace for her Quangle Wangle. Her Crumpetty Tree's tortured unearthly trunk and crumpet leaves are magnificent; her landscape is wide and magical, neither inviting nor repelling, but inexplicable—surely right for a Lear setting. I'm not happy with the characters who come to inhabit it, though. The Quangle Wangle itself is safe because you (rightly) never see his face; but the artist has got overexcited when confronted with unimaginables like the Fimble Fowl and the Attery Squash. I feel confused by the elaboration and decoration. Her Dong is a big mistake, a strange aardvark-like creature with a quasi-trunk. Lear meant the Dong to be humanised; he illustrated it as such. A detail within this particular poem, but a symptom of the excessive licence which Helen Oxenbury takes; perhaps she felt it was necessary to lay things on a bit thick for children. I don't agree with her.

Gerald Rose's consistently excellent work has been offered to children in many publications. He has a strong graphic sense, and his work is always enviable, impressive, flowing, varied beautifully in texture, medium, density. But sadly this is not Lear illustrated by Rose; it's paintings by Rose with captions by Lear. Judged by absolute standards the book is a sophisticated piece of graphic design whose overall elegance derives from the sensitive visual balance of areas of picture and areas of type. However, it has little of Lear's atmosphere—nothing of "the shade of the mountains brown" that the Jumblies saw—nothing of the "awful darkness and silence . . . Over the great Gromboolian plain" from the broodingly Wagnerian opening of "The Dong." Lear's stunningly descriptive word-use has been neglected in favour of Rose's own illustrative habits.

The "bold amusing pictures," say Collins on the jacket-flap of Dale Maxey's *The Owl and the Pussy-Cat,* "bring this adventurous pair vividly to life." But what a life! One can forgive Rose for imposing himself on Lear, because his work is delightful in its own right. But Maxey is patronising and facile. Colourful, cheerful these two books are; but they add nothing to encourage or consolidate an appreciation of Lear.

There is an awful stereotyping of characters: the two Old Bachelors, their Sage, Uncle Arly, the old man of Dumbree—they're all the same basic stock figure, with maybe different-coloured beards or clothes, identical fatuous visages. So, apart from the different Lear texts, these two titles are only slightly altered variations on the same theme. Uncle Arly sat on a heap of barley "Thro' the silent hours of night"; Maxey has supplied the same night for him as he has for the Owl and the Pussy-Cat when they "danced by the light of the moon." What a missed chance! sadly a conspicuous failing of these books. The "Tini-skoop-hills afar" aren't afar at all: they're twee little bumps with pretty flowers wallpapering them. The brambles aren't brambles. The Sage's "rugged rocks" turn out to be represented by a grassy knoll. Why?

A lazy ill-considered job. Wouldn't any illustrator exert and adapt himself a little for Lear?

Edward Gorey's *Jumblies* is a modest black-and-white book conceived close to my reading of Lear's spirit, even in the funny hand-lettered "typography"—not modern, not archaic, thoroughly "Lear." And the illustrations are as I think Lear himself would have drawn them, if he had illustrated "The Jumblies" more abundantly.

The drawings have been made in laboured pen-and-ink, and recall the technique of a nineteenth-century engraver. "Laboured" is not a criticism—this has been a labour of love; and "laboured" is not the visual result. Although I can visualise Gorey poring over his drawing-board scratching crampedly, the drawings don't look stilted; their very strongly constructed compositions are full of haunting atmosphere.

This differs from the others in that the artist has tried to fill the illustrative gap that Lear left. The author is the one who makes the pace and supplies the "briefing"—the artist carries out this briefing with craftsmanship.

Particularly, Gorey's Jumblies are characters. Here he has gone even one better than Lear. He hasn't found it enough to draw a quantity of similar individuals of the same species. Each one is a person, and is progressively identifiable as an individual in each picture that extends the story.

Oxenbury, Rose and Maxey have been greedy, imposing themselves and their own techniques on Lear. But Lear, his tradition and his vision, demand fidelity. Unless the artist is prepared to observe what is involved in

Illustration by Edward Lear from "The Dong with the Luminous Nose," from *The Complete Nonsense Book* by Edward Lear. Reprinted by permission of Dodd, Mead & Company. British edition published by Faber & Faber.

Illustration by Edward Gorey from *The Dong with the Luminous Nose* by Edward Lear. Illustrations © 1969 by Edward Gorey. A Young Scott Book. Reprinted by permission of Addison-Wesley Publishing Company. British edition published by Chatto & Windus.

such fidelity, it would be better to leave the visual interpretations of the poetry to the children themselves. (After all, the stimulation of a child's imagination is worth a hundred supplied solutions.)

Seen in isolation, these are colourful, well-executed and well-manufactured children's books. But it would have been so much more of a contribution if these artists had been original with the text too! We are asked to buy the results of a sort of Art-College-project: *Take a Lear poem and illustrate it,* rather than buy an underived creation. Lear has been grabbed, not as a master to be respected, honoured and pleased post-humously, but as a vehicle for their peculiar artistic styles.

What they have impertinently overlooked is that Edward Lear is still a vehicle whose engine generates more revs than their talent can ever aspire to.

Chapter 6

Folk Literature and Fantasy

In spite of the long and persistent attacks on fairy tales and folklore and the continuing fear that some are too frightening (see Chapters 1 and 3), there are many testimonies of the greatness and influence of classic inherited literature. In the first selection in this chapter, a paper delivered at an international library conference, Eileen Colwell points out the basic importance of folklore as an oral tradition, particularly for the storyteller who shares the tales with children. Following this, in a selection from "The Battle for the Fairy Tale," the beloved Russian children's poet, Kornei Chukovsky, conclusively states the value of folk tales for the young: "The fairy tale has . . . helped the child orient himself to the surrounding world, has enriched his spiritual life, has made him regard himself as a fearless participant in imaginary struggles for justice, goodness, and freedom; . . . up to the age of seven or eight, the fairy tale is for every normal child the most wholesome food—not just a tidbit but his nourishing daily bread, and no one has the right to deprive him of this health-giving, irreplaceable food." J. R. R. Tolkien, in "On Fairy-Tales," finds a somewhat different but equally positive value in fairy tales.

> The consolation of fairy-stories, the joy of the happy ending: or more correctly of the good catastrophe, the sudden joyous "turn" (for there is no true end to any fairy-tale): this joy, which is one of the things which fairy-stories can produce supremely well, is not essentially "escapist," nor "fugitive." In its fairy-

tale—or otherworld—setting, it is a sudden and miraculous grace: never to be counted on to recur. . . .

It is the mark of a good fairy-story, of the higher or more complete kind, that however wild its events, however fantastic or terrible the adventures, it can give the child or man that hears it, when the "turn" comes, a catch of the breath, a beat and lifting of the heart, near to (or indeed accompanied by) tears, as keen as that given by any form of literary art, and having a peculiar quality.

Even modern fairy-stories can produce this effect sometimes. It is not an easy thing to do; it depends on the whole story which is the setting of the turn, and yet it reflects a glory backwards. A tale that in any measure succeeds in this point has not wholly failed, whatever flaws it may possess, and whatever mixture or confusion of purpose.[1]

James Reeves, a reteller of famous German folk tales, also believes in the intrinsic value of the old tales:

Looking, then, at Grimm and at folk tales in general, we see that they have the quality of magic, of unexpectedness, of somehow being right and inevitable. I have been enjoying Grimm's *Tales* because I cannot understand at all what most of them are about, yet they seem to be absolutely inevitable. They are, in some ways, the most amazing novels I have read because they seem to have those qualities of rightness yet unexpectedness which one wants to look for in children's stories.[2]

Folklore and fantasy, viewed together as make-believe, can claim a large share of the credit for any golden years in children's literature. For creative poets, mystics, and storytellers—from Hans Christian Andersen, Walter de la Mare, and Eleanor Farjeon to Barbara Leonie Picard and Joan Aiken—ancient tales have formed a strong source of inspiration. Clearly, Tolkien has drawn from great traditional lore (the Norse sagas and the King Arthur legends) as have Alan Garner and Lloyd Alexander from the *Mabinogion* and other Welsh lore. A review of a modern fantasy (Ursula K. Le Guin's *A Wizard of Earthsea*) opens with a striking statement: "Any quick list of the outstanding books for the young of the past forty years or so will reveal that almost all have drawn on the extra dimension of magic or fantasy—Tolkien, White [T.H.], Lewis, Pearce, Garner, Hoban and the rest."[3] Equally obvious and arresting is the fact that those authors for adults who have

---

1. From "On Fairy-Stories," pp. 68–69, by J. R. R. Tolkien from *Tree and Leaf.* Copyright © 1964 by George Allen and Unwin Ltd. Reprinted by permission of George Allen & Unwin Ltd. and Houghton Mifflin Company.

2. "Writing for Children," *Proceedings, Papers and Summaries of Discussions at the Brighton Conference* (London: Library Association, 1958), p. 13.

3. "The Making of a Mage," *Times Literary Supplement*, Children's Books (April 2, 1971): 383.

written an occasional—or one—book for children have quite generally turned to fantasy. As poet John Farrar, editor of *The Bookman,* put it, "The great authors turn to the child mind in moods of gaiety and fantasy and, in those moods, create a very special type of book that often springs from the deepest inspiration."[4] C. S. Lewis was one who "fell in love" with the form of the fairy tale: "its brevity, its severe restraints on description, its flexible traditionalism, its inflexible hostility to the analysis, digression, reflection and 'gas'. . . . I wrote fairy tales because the Fairy Tale seemed the ideal Form for the stuff I had to say."[5]

Using ancient lore, however, presents its own problems for the writer. Alan Garner has discussed some of these problems in an introduction to an essay-appraisal of new fantasies:

> Fantasy has been for me a writer's tool (a crutch, if you like). . . . Myth has always been an attempt to come to terms with the world, not to avoid it. Of course we can each have our own ideas about Fantasy, but in order to exercise some control over himself and his material a writer must construct his terms of reference, and pursue them with bigotry. . . .
>
> . . . The modern, material world is the effective setting for Fantasy. An arbitrary time in a never-never-land softens the punch. For example, if we are in Eldorado and we find a mandrake, then OK, so it's a mandrake: in Eldorado anything goes. But, by force of imagination, compel the reader to believe that there is a mandrake in a garden in Mayfield Road, Ulverston, Lancashire, then when you pull up that mandrake it is really going to scream; and possibly the reader will, too.
>
> There is no doubt that traditional motifs are powerful ingredients in a modern story. A danger is that the writer will fall in love with legend and try to use it neat, with the common result that the source material sticks out of the text in raw lumps, making acute what is always a structural difficulty in Fantasy, namely its exposition. There comes a point when the fireworks have to make sense, where the action stops and some horny old wizard moans about the historical development of his situation and its philosophical implications. Given a modern, material setting it is the biggest single technical problem for the writer; to make clear, stay credible and not to clog the works. Not to clog the works: to keep the pages turning: that's what it's all about. If the serious writer can subject himself and his ideas to such a discipline the result, when successful, will be more effective than any tract.[6]

---

4. Quoted in Anne Carroll Moore, "The Reviewing of Children's Books," *The Bookman,* 61 (May 1925): 331.

5. "Sometimes Fairy Stories Say Best What's To Be Said," *New York Times Book Review,* pt. 2, v. 61 (November 18, 1956): 3.

6. From "Real Mandrakes in Real Gardens" by Alan Garner from *New Statesman,* 76 (November 1, 1968): 591–592. Reprinted by permission.

A discussion of fantasy must include a form which has become a distinct and important genre in children's literature: science fiction. Sylvia Engdahl, in an article included in this chapter, says, "The line between science fiction and fantasy has always been hard to draw; . . . both forms may, through the portrayal of a world other than our real world, express underlying truths about life as we now know it to be. . . . " She adds that "the role of science fiction in children's literature is a significant one indeed. . . . It has become so not because fictional speculations about moon landings have proven less fantastic than was formerly supposed, but because we live in an age when rapid change is both inevitable and, to the young, desirable." There are relatively few works of science fiction written specifically for children, but among the best are Robert C. O'Brien's *Mrs. Frisby and the Rats of NIMH* (the 1972 Newbery Award winner) and the novels of Andre Norton, Sylvia Engdahl, Ben Bova, Peter Dickinson, John Christopher, and the earlier titles of Robert Heinlein. And young readers addicted to science fiction also turn to the vast number of adult books in this field.[7]

7. On fantasy, see also Eleanor Cameron, *The Green and Burning Tree: On the Writing and Enjoyment of Children's Books* (Boston: The Atlantic Monthly Press, 1969); and "High Fantasy: Wizard of Earthsea," *Horn Book Magazine*, 46 (April 1971): 129–138. For folklore, see also Virginia Haviland and Margaret N. Coughlan, *Following the Folk Tales Around the World*, reprint from *Compton's Pictured Encyclopedia* (Chicago: F. E. Compton and Company, 1972).

Folk Literature: An Oral Tradition and an Oral Art

Eileen H. Colwell

Although retired from library and library school positions, Eileen Colwell is fully engaged in lecturing, storytelling, book reviewing, and writing. She is a founder member of the Youth Libraries Group of the Library Association, past chairman, children's librarians' section of the International Federation of Library Associations, an artist storyteller on TV and at international storytelling festivals, and editor of stories for children (A Storyteller's Choice *(1963) and its sequels and four Puffin collections of stories to be read to the very young), and in 1965 was chosen for the Queen's birthday honors. Because of her pioneer work in developing library service to children in England, she was requested to write* How I Became a Librarian *(1957). She has also written the monograph* Eleanor Farjeon *(1952). "Folk Literature" was an address given at the 1967 Toronto conference of the International Federation of Library Associations.*

The spoken word is the remembered word and the story that is *told* gains life and character from the teller. The survival of the folktale is the indisputable evidence of the strength of oral tradition. Generations of men and women of imagination and a feeling for the dramatic have given such life to ancient tales that today children can read printed versions of a story told centuries ago. Scholars have taken down folktales from oral recitals by storytellers who had themselves heard the stories told by a previous generation. Today these direct versions of the original story are in danger of being watered down and reduced to colorless narratives in their written forms because of modern theories of what is suitable for children.

How did it all begin? We can only surmise. It is certain that as men began to live in communities, they felt the desire to share their experiences. At first it was merely the telling of some personal exploit in hunting or war, but inevitably this simple narrative grew into what Arthur Ransome has called the "embroidered exploit." So embroidered did these adventures become that the storyteller could no longer presume to claim them as his own and so credited them to some ancestral hero, long since dead. Such stories gave pleasure and the man who could tell them was honored and given opportunity to tell more and more tales. Gradually stories came to embody the prowess of the tribal heroes, accounts of battles, the customs and ritual of the people. The storyteller was expected to keep important happenings in his memory and to reproduce them in story form. He became the historian, the genealogist, perhaps even the "medicine man" credited with

"Folk Literature: An Oral Tradition and an Oral Art," by Eileen Colwell from *Top of the News,* 24 (January 1968): 175–180. Reprinted by permission of American Library Association.

knowledge of magic. As time went on, the stories told were a mixture of hero tales, legends, mythology, and strange fragmentary memories of which no one knew the meaning any longer.

The Hero tales have always been a part of storytelling. The legendary hero's adventures, often the personification of national ideals, are full of action, courage, and even tragedy. So come to us the stirring stories of the Hound of Ulster and Finn McCool, the deeds of Robin Hood and Spain's El Cid, the stories of Charlemagne and his Paladins, the epics of the *Iliad* and the *Odyssey* set against the wine-dark seas of Greece. Every country had its heroic tales, not least Scandinavia. C. S. Lewis has said that on reading the words: "I heard a voice that cried 'Balder the beautiful is dead, is dead . . . ,' " he was uplifted "into huge regions of northern sky," and in following this story "again and again received the stab of joy." These stories and others like them, whether of the Finnish *Kalevala* or the thousand-year-old epic of *Beowulf*, were told for centuries before scholars printed them and such was their grandeur and wisdom that although they have passed through many hands since, they still retain the power of their original telling.

Mythology of a primitive kind was also part of the storyteller's material. The terrifying forces of Nature were outside his knowledge and he knew himself helpless before them. So in story form he gave his explanations of the creation of the world, the cause of thunder and storms and the relentless might of the seas. He credited supernatural beings with the power to rule such forces, man-made gods with more than human strength and wisdom, but vulnerable and with human frailties. Balder could be killed, the gods could take sides in the Homeric wars, goddesses could be jealous. But it was the Greek nature myths, above all, that through the centuries have had the most impact on the creative minds of artists and poets.

With the coming of Christianity, many tales were considered too pagan in their morality and imagery. As pagan feasts became Christian festivals, the popular tales were touched also with Christian mysticism, as, for example, in the ancient Irish tale of *The Children of Lir* in which the unhappy children in their swanforms find comfort in the teaching of a monk. But Christian tales of the deeds of saints became influenced in their turn and the legends that have been handed down to us often have more of the magical than devotional.

It was these kinds of stories and many others that the storytellers told and sang in the Middle Ages, the Golden Age of the professional storyteller. In the times of the Anglo-Saxons, "gleemen" were men of repute. Widsith, who lived in the fourth century, "could say and sing a story in the mead hall," was given a collar of gold, and had "travelled to the ends of the known world," seeking stories and telling them. Bede, the seventh-century historian, often had to use the oral memories of his contemporaries for accounts of old battles. "England was conquered to the music of verse and settled to the sound of the harp," says Stopford Brooke, a nineteenth-century writer. This was almost literally so, for it was a minstrel who rode out before the invading Norman host and sang *The Song of Roland* before riding into battle. With the Norman Conquest, the Saxon gleemen went "underground" to sing their stories of the heroic deeds of Hereward their champion, and the more sophisticated Norman minstrels took their place, singing in French and telling tales from Europe as yet unknown to England.

These minstrels were welcome visitors indeed in the dark, draughty baronial halls of the Middle Ages, as were their more humble counterparts in the marketplaces of towns and villages. Their racy stories, their gaiety, brought color to daily life, their warlike tales roused the martial spirit in times of unrest. They wore clothes of many colors and, with their instruments on their backs, traveled up and down England and on the continent, learning new stories as they went and passing on their native tales. A minstrel must have learning without pedantry, tact and insight into character, good humor and a trained memory for stories. How great a number of minstrels there were, we do not know, but we read that the King employed 426 minstrels at the wedding of Margaret of England in 1290, and that amongst the many minstrels on the payroll of Edward I there were two women with the intriguing names of Matill Makejoye and Pearl in the Egg.

The professional storytellers were not peculiar to England. They were to be found in every country. In Greece they chanted epics at the Olympic Games, in Scandinavia the *Skald* went with the King into battle and afterwards sang of his prowess—or composed his death song. In the Middle Ages—as Ruth Sawyer cites—the ransom of a storyteller taken in battle was 126 cattle! In Ireland the *Ollambs,* the master storytellers, had particular stories which they only could tell. In Germany the *Minnesingers,* members of guilds of music and poetry, told stories up and down the land.

It was the invention of printing in 1450 that gradually broke up the minstrel tradition as storytellers, although they still remained as musicians. Educated men could now read stories for themselves, and Caxton and other early printers produced books containing stories once known only orally— Reynard the Fox, King Arthur, Guy of Warwick, and Bevis of Southampton.

But these were for the rich and learned. Robert Burton in the sixteenth century says that the ordinary recreations in winter were "Merry tales of errant knights, queens, lovers, lords, ladies, giants, dwarfs, thieves, cheaters, witches, fairies, goblins, friars . . . which some delight to hear, some to tell, all are well pleased with." There was still an oral tradition in the country and an unwritten and vast store of folktales. Storytelling was a familiar feature of the social life of the people until the beginning of the eighteenth century.

The common people had a lore of their own, the folktales, which arose from the heart and were characteristic of the land from which they came. (As, for instance, the downright, compact English tale we find in Joseph Jacobs' collection, or the more sophisticated and witty Gallic tale from France.) Young and old listened to folktales and it was the storyteller who brought them to life. They had survived for centuries, through invasion and condemnation by the Church and educators. There are many theories as to their origin and the appearance of the same themes in variants all over the world. Three hundred and forty-five variants of the *Cinderella* theme have been noted and Joseph Jacobs once said that he had cited "an English version of an Italian adaptation of a Spanish translation of a Latin version of a Hebrew translation of an Arabic translation of an Indian original."

It is maintained that all folktales preserve remnants of nature myths, religious belief and ritual, ancient custom and incantations. Certain it is that in what Tolkien calls the "Cauldron of Story" and Dasent the "Soup," there are many queer ingredients. But whether *Red Riding Hood* is a sunrise and sunset myth, *Beauty and the Beast* a remnant of *tabu*, *The Frog Prince* an example of totemism, matters little. The important factor is the story content. It is only when the story is a good one that, however profound the basic association, it survives, and it is the individual storyteller who gives it life for his generation. The story is none the less enjoyable because we do not know its ingredients in the Cauldron of Story.

In speaking of folklore, I am thinking perhaps more of the Fairy story as in Tolkien's comprehensive definition in his *Tree and Leaf*. He says:— "Fairy-stories are not in normal English usage stories *about* fairies or elves, but stories about Fairy, that *Faerie*, the realm or state in which fairies have their being. *Faerie* contains many things besides elves and fays, and besides dwarfs, witches, trolls, giants, or dragons; it holds the seas, the sun, the moon, the sky; and the earth, and all things in it: tree and bird, water and stone, wine and bread, and ourselves, mortal man, when we are enchanted."

John Aubrey said, "The last fairy disappeared in the seventeenth century with a delicious perfume and a most melodious twang." And even Chaucer's Wife of Bath believed that the fairies had gone, although she admitted that in the "olde dayes of King Arthour," this land was "fulfild of fayereye." Fairies—or at least fairy stories in Tolkien's sense—are still with us and have something to say to both children and adults. Coleridge says that they habituate the mind to the Vast, the Great, and the Whole. Eleanor Farjeon once said, "Magic had its feet under the earth and its hair above the clouds" and "in the beginning Magic was everywhere and nowhere."

But this is a digression. Suffice it to say that it is the fairy story or folkstory that has been kept alive through the ages by being *told* and it is this type of story that has been most loved. Why did this oral tradition decline? Padraic Colum has a theory that it was due to a change in the rhythm between day and night, dark and light. Night was the time for telling stories and while the women were spinning and weaving, they could listen to a story. But with the coming of artificial light the day was prolonged, the night postponed. The newspaper took the place of the professional storyteller and there was no longer any need for one man to store local history, tradition, genealogy, and stories in his memory. One incident will serve to illustrate the tenacity of local memory possession from one storyteller to another. It was said that the ghost of a warrior wearing golden armor appeared at a cairn in Wales. In 1832 the cairn was investigated. Beneath it was the skeleton of a Roman wearing a golden breastplate. Tradition had kept this memory for over 1000 years.

It is possible also that as dialect was superseded by a more universal language, traditional stories tended to seem obscure. Grimm said that although a story gained in clearness when written in High German, it lost in flavor compared with the original oral version.

It was in Ireland and the outlying parts of the British Isles that storytelling lingered longest. The *Shanachies* still told their stories by the peat fires until quite recently. One of them knew two hundred stories and would tell them in his "singing voice," the sound and surge of the sea in the background. The storytelling of these men and women was distinguished by remarkable openings, effective pauses, notable climaxes. But the people who had the old tales, are all gone now.

Although the traditional art of storytelling has died out in many parts of the world, it is still an integral part of the daily life of people in areas where education is not universal and books are hard to come by. In Japan the arrival of the picture-showman with his wooden clappers calls the children to listen to his stories of the *Kappa,* those strange beings with webbed hands and shallow plates on the tops of their heads filled with water, the source of their life and strength. In India women can be found telling tales three thousand years old. As many as twenty storytellers have been seen practicing their art in the market place of Morocco. In Java the *Dalang* sings and chants the thousand-year-old stories of Ramayana, moving puppets against a screen to music. In Nigeria the storyteller is a welcome visitor with his stories of the cunning tortoise and of ghosts and witches, and many adults attend these storytelling sessions all the days of their life. In South Africa an old Bushman, exiled from his home, said:—"I sit waiting for the moon to turn back to me . . . that I may listen again to all the people's stories."

Much is being done to revive the art of storytelling. In Canada there is the John Masefield Festival, in the States there have been festivals both for adults and children. Librarians and teachers are telling stories everywhere. In our own century there have been notable storytellers—Gudrun Thorne-Thomsen, Marie Shedlock, Ruth Sawyer, Frances Clarke Sayers.

The present era has also seen the revival of storytelling through the medium of television and radio. In England we have two television programs directly concerned with storytelling, one for the preschool child, the other for children up to ten. The latter, *Jackanory,* has featured folktales from many countries told by natives of those countries.

Dr. John Masefield did much for storytelling in his long life, including his encouragement of storytelling in this very library.[1] He believed that,

---

1. Toronto Public Library's Boys and Girls House.

Illustration by Frederic Guirma from *Tales of Mogho: African Stories from Upper Volta* by Frederic Guirma. Copyright © 1971 by Frederic Guirma. Reprinted by permission of The Macmillan Company.

through storytelling, tradition and history could be preserved as in no other way for the young. He believed also that the folktale is a living thing, born out of the heart of the people, so that the history of today becomes the legend to tomorrow preserved in the popular tales. What matter if, in years to come, like Elsie Piddock's skipping, no one quite believes it ever happened! Dr. Masefield always hoped that storytelling could become once more a combination of all the arts, accompanied by music as it was in the Middle Ages.

Storytelling is a creative process, for the storyteller creates another world into which the hearer, if the storyteller has skill and sincerity, can enter with all his belief. How many generations of children and adults have listened entranced as some storyteller began with the magic words "once upon a time," those words which give the hearer the sense of a great unchartered world of time. In the best stories, too, there comes a place when, in Tolkien's words, the listener feels "a beat and lifting of the heart . . . a piercing glimpse of joy and heart's desire, as keen as that given by any form of literary art." And so to the ending—although no fairy tale really has an ending—"They lived happily ever afterwards."

There is an old Bushman tale which tells of a man married to a "woman of the sky." She brought with her a basket which her husband promised not to open without her permission. Needless to say, he opened it one day. When the Bushman's wife returned from the fields and knew what had happened, she asked:—

"You've looked in the basket, husband?"

"Why make such a fuss!" said the husband. "There was nothing in it after all."

"Nothing?" asked the wife with tears in her eyes.

"Nothing," answered her husband, and he laughed.

Weeping his wife walked away into the sunset and vanished.

She left him, not because he had broken his promise to her, but because he could not see what was really in the basket. It was full of beautiful things from the sky which she had cherished for them both to enjoy.

It is for storytellers everywhere to show children what there can be in the basket of ancient stories, beauty, fun and wisdom.

The Battle for the Fairy Tale:
Three Stages

Kornei Chukovsky

Russian "dean of children's poets," literary historian, critic, and translator, Kornei Chukovsky (1882–1969) brought translations of a number of classics to Soviet children, including The Adventures of Tom Sawyer, Kipling's Just So Stories, *and Lofting's* Doctor Dolittle. His *Doktor Aibolit, a free adaptation of* Doctor Dolittle, *became very popular and, interestingly, was brought back into English in 1967 by Richard Coe as* Doctor Concocter. *Poems by Chukovsky have been turned into English-language picture books:* Crocodile, *translated by Babette Deutsch, and* The Telephone, *translated and adapted by Marguerita Rudolph. Chukovsky's fame in the U.S.S.R. and abroad also rests upon his study of children and their imagination and creativity, about which he wrote in the widely translated* From Two to Five.

The well-known children's author, T. A. Bogdanovich, was brought up by another children's author, Aleksandra Annenskaia. Under the influence of the "enlightenment" of the sixties [of the nineteenth century], she so zealously protected the little girl from the *skazka* [the folk tale] that she even hesitated to hire a *niania* for her, fearing that the nurse would tell the child fairy tales. Only educational books were read to the child—mainly books on botany and zoology. But, at night, when the governess finally fell asleep, the child, at last free from the constant supervision, filled her room with all kinds of creatures. Monkeys scampered all over her bed. A fox and her babies suddenly appeared on her table. Strange birds nested in her clothes left folded near her bed, and she talked to these visitors for a long time.

She talked to them because every normal child talks to all creatures and objects and all creatures and objects seem to the child to speak to him. This nightly indulgence in fantasy and her nocturnal existence among imaginary animals gave the little girl immeasurable pleasure, because thus she satisfied a healthy and normal aspect of a child's nature. This child asserted her rights instinctively—her rights to the fairy tale—secretly giving herself up to that fantasy from which her adults shielded her as from typhus. All that her governess accomplished was to send the fairy tale underground and thus give it a much greater charm. Would it not have been better merely to read *Cinderella* or *Little Red Riding-Hood* to this child?

We have seen in an earlier chapter what a five-year-old child did when a

From "The Battle for the Fairy Tale: Three Stages" by Kornei Chukovsky, pp. 122–230 in *From Two to Five*, translated and edited by Miriam Morton. Originally published by the University of California Press, 1963; reprinted by permission of The Regents of the University of California.

too-clever Moscow mother (also an educator by profession), wishing to accustom him to the verities of life, told him too soon about the conception and birth of babies. After listening to her lecture, he at once changed the scientific facts to suit himself and told her that when he was inside her body he played in a little garden and drank tea with an uncle [*diadia*] who sojourned there, and that he saw there, as well, some salesmen selling all sorts of things.

This is what a five-year-old youngster did with the strictly scientific facts which were supplied to him too soon. He thus practically told his mother: "You can see for yourself that right now I need, not a lecture on embryology, but a fairy tale, so as to spend this most important period of my psychological development in a fuller, more marvelous, more sumptuous way. Don't be in too much of a hurry to condition me to adult thinking because every one of your adult truths, according to my nature, I shall, without delay, transmute into fantasy and shall scatter some sand, shall cultivate a garden, and shall set up a counter with salesmen behind it—even in your womb."

Deprived of the folk tale, of a Pushkin fairy tale, or a fairy tale written by a good contemporary poet, children are forced to rely on their own spontaneous compositions.

Deprived of *Munchausen, Gulliver, The Little Humpbacked-Horse,* the young child unconsciously compensates for this loss with countless "do-it-yourself" fairy tales. Therefore, the pedologists who snatched from him folk tales and fairy tales written by the great and the good writers, actually robbing him, committed this robbery without reflection and without, fortunately, even fulfilling their purpose.

The fairy tale continued to flourish in the child's world, except that instead of a folk tale or a tale by Pushkin, or a fairy tale by some living author, the children were obliged to serve themselves with their own fortuitous literary handiwork. Until recently, those in charge of setting standards for children's literature have given insufficient thought to children's demonstrated preference for fairy tales and to the value of such tales in developing, strengthening, enriching, and directing children's capacity for creative thinking and imaginative responses—a value that has been tested by classic works produced over the centuries.

Meanwhile, in our time, after witnessing the realization of the most amazing scientific and social "fantasies" which not so long ago seemed like senseless fairy tales, we must develop a generation of inspired creators and thinkers everywhere, in all fields of endeavor—in science, technology, agronomy, architecture, politics.

Without imaginative fantasy there would be complete stagnation in both physics and chemistry, because the formulation of new hypotheses, the invention of new implements, the discovery of new methods of experimental research, the conjecturing of new chemical fusions—all these are products of imagination and fantasy.

The present belongs to the sober, the cautious, the routine-prone, but the future belongs to those who do not rein in their imagination. Not without reason did the famous British physicist, John Tindale, champion fantasy:

"Without the participation of fantasy," he wrote, "all our knowledge about nature would have been limited merely to the classification of obvious facts. The relation between cause and effect and their interaction would have gone unnoticed, thus stemming the progress of science itself, because it is the main function of science to establish the link between the different manifestations of nature, since creative fantasy is the ability to perceive more and more such links."

Why, then, did our pedologists make the word "fantasy" a word of derision? In the name of what did they expunge it from the psyche of young children? In the name of realism? But there are different types of realism. There is the realism of a Bacon, or a Gogol, or a Mendeleev, or a Repin—and there is the realism of a teapot, a roach, or a 10-kopeck piece. Is it to advance the latter type of realism that we have taken such pains? And does it not seem that the actual name for this is—Philistinism? We must face the fact that many of our young children are even at present surrounded by Philistinism. We have not yet saved them entirely from the pettiness of narrow-mindedness. There are many among our children who are even more "adult" and more "practical" than their elders; and if we are to save them from anything, it is precisely from this horrible practicality instilled in them by old-fashioned and commonplace attitudes.

But the pedologists are worried and tremble at the thought that children will actually believe that shoes grow on trees. Some children are so suspicious of everything—even the most poetic, that is, the most unreal— that everything beyond the limits of the everyday and the ordinary they consider a bold-faced and senseless fabrication. For instance, once when someone tried to talk to a group of school children about sharks, one of them cried out:

"There is no such thing as a shark!"

Such children know of nothing rare or marvelous on the face of the earth; they know only of bread and cabbage, boots and rubles. To fear that some little fairy tale will turn them into romantics, into incompetents for practical living—this fear can possess only those bureaucratic contrivers who, attending meetings from morning till night, never see a live child.

Protecting little ones from folk songs, tall tales, fairy tales, these people are hardly aware of the banal fetish they make of practicality. As a result, they look upon every children's book as something that must immediately produce some visible, touchable, beneficial effect, as if a book were a nail or a yoke. They thus reveal the pettiness and the narrowness of their Philistine thinking. Their inventions about the harm of fairy tales are in themselves an insane fairy tale which overlooks all concrete facts. This is the only kind of fairy tale that we need to combat—the fairy tale of regressive pedologists about the fairy tale.

And we must say to these mystics: "Stop raving, get down to earth, become realists, look at the actual facts and you will cease trembling before Tom Thumb and Puss in Boots. You will see that by a certain age the fairy tale no longer charms the child so much (provided he lives in a healthy environment), and he then enters upon a period when he relentlessly "exposes" fantasy.

"But how could the Snow Maiden breathe if she had no lungs?"

"How could Baba-Yaga fly in the air on a broom if it had no propeller?"

The fairy tale has now accomplished its task. It has helped the child orient himself to the surrounding world, has enriched his spiritual life, has made him regard himself as a fearless participant in imaginary struggles for justice, goodness, and freedom; and now, when his need of the fairy tale has ended, the child himself does away with it.

But up to the age of seven or eight, the fairy tale is for every normal child the most wholesome food—not just a tidbit but his nourishing daily bread, and no one has the right to deprive him of this health-giving, irreplaceable food.

Formerly, it was precisely this kind of deprivation of the child which pedologists practiced. Not only did they take away from him the fairy tales of Pushkin and Ershov's *The Little Humpbacked-Horse,* and *Ali-Baba,* and *Cinderella,* but they demanded of us writers that we become their collaborators in this evil and senseless deed. And, of course, there were potboiling hacks who, to please the editors, diligently degraded in their writings the fairy tale and in every way mocked its wonders. This was done in the following pattern: a sly, inflexible boy was depicted, to whom all fairy tales were poison. A fairy would appear and would spread before him a magic carpet. But he—

> His hands
> In his pants
> He thrust,
> Snickered,
> Whistled,
> And said:
> "Auntie, you're fibbing—
> And how!
> Who needs you now
> And your magic rug?
> No one can you now fool
> With this or any humbug . . . "

And when someone told him the story of the ubiquitous *Humpbacked-Horse,* he again thrust his hands into his pockets and answered with equal depravity:

> Well, *I* find more jolly
> A long ride on a trolley.

The ill-bred, insolent urchin enjoyed the full admiration of the author.

There were many similar books, and one cannot claim that they did not influence children. Fortunately, not many were thus crippled. The large majority of four-year-old children saved their normal child-like psyche from these despoilers of childhood by means of their own imaginary games and their own fairy tales.

It does not follow from what I have just defended that I yearn for nothing else than that Soviet children should be bemused from morning till night by fairy tales. It is a matter of proportion, strictly observed. But we must not permit petty utilitarian theories of these wretched pedologists to deprive Soviet children of one of the greatest heritages of classical world folklore.

The dynasty of the above-mentioned defenders of the realistic education of children proved to be quite short-lived. In Moscow and in Leningrad and in other major cities there appeared a whole cohort of ardent defenders of the fairy tale, inspired and led by Maxim Gorki. The attackers retreated, not undamaged, and there came a time when everyone thought that they had disappeared forever.

IT WAS TIME TO GET WISE (1934)

There were many reasons for this illusion. As early as 1934, especially after the memorable appearance of Gorki at the First All-Union Congress of Soviet Writers, there appeared everywhere repentant educators, editors, and supervisors of kindergartens who had previously participated in the siege against the fairy tale with as much zeal as they were now showing in defending it. At that time the Young Guard Publishing House, and later the Children's State Publishing Bureau, began to put out huge editions of *Hiawatha, The Little Humpbacked-Horse,* and *Munchausen,* as well as Pushkin's tales, Russian folk tales, and all kinds of other works of fantasy.

But it was too soon to celebrate total victory. I was convinced of this through a personal experience. I had had occasion to publish that same year, in the magazine *Iozh [Hedgehog],* the story of the ancient myth about Perseus, Andromeda, and Medusa the Gorgon. The editorial office of this periodical promptly received a letter from an educator in Gomel:

"Esteemed Comrade Editor! Having read in your magazine, *Iozh,* the Greek fairy tale that appeared on page 24 of issue number 1, 'Brave Perseus,' the children in my school surrounded me and asked why such nonsense is being published in our Soviet magazines. . . . How can we explain to children all the absurdity and thoughtlessness of the episodes described in this story, so full of the most nonsensical and foolish superstitions? In my opinion, this fairy tale lacks all artistic and literary beauty. . . ."

This letter was signed: "School Director, A. Rappoport."

I felt like pointing out humbly to Rappoport that this very myth about Perseus, precisely because of its beauty and artistic merit, had attracted, over the centuries, first-rate sculptors, playwrights, poets—Ovid,

Sophocles, Euripides, Benvenuto Cellini, Corneille, Rubens, Titian, Heredia, and Canova.

I felt also like reminding him about Marx, who repeatedly stated that the ancient Greek epoch, with its ancient Greek art developed from mythology, "continues to offer us aesthetic pleasures and in a definite way safeguards the importance of quality and attainable standards."

But the Rappoports ignore both Euripides and Marx. And they try to justify themselves by attributing objections to the children. From the way school director Rappoport put it, one would think that the children in his charge were extremely enraged when they saw "Perseus" in the magazine, and that they at once voiced a collective protest against the publishing of ancient Greek myths.

I hope he will forgive me if I say that I do not believe this. It is impossible that there were no normal youngsters in his entire school who had a lively poetic sensitivity! It is also impossible that he had succeeded in thoroughly atrophying in all his pupils their natural attraction to fantasy! And if there were two or three children who did not understand this legend, it was Rappoport's duty to explain it to them.

Using "Perseus" as a starting point for a discussion in a school assembly, he could have talked with the students about the origin of myths, about the constellations of Cassiopeia, Andromeda, Perseus; he could have delivered a lecture on the saturation of Christian religion with myths of pagan antiquity, about the connection between the mother of Perseus and the Virgin Mary, about the resemblance between the dragon who was going to devour Andromeda and the whale who swallowed the Biblical Jonah, and so on. All this, of course, he would have done if he had been an educated man. However, since he was ignorant, he incited the children against the most treasured works of art and bothered editors of children's magazines with absurd and ludicrous complaints.

The absurdity of such complaints is seen, in my opinion, in the claim that a genuinely poetic work published for Soviet children—be it a legend about Ilia Muramets or Reynard the Fox, or Munchausen, or Perseus—is politically harmful; by means of such demagogy these people justify their obscurantism.

They consider the myth or the fairy tale a threat to Leninism!

The privileged classes of all lands have until now deprived the toiling multitudes of the opportunity to learn about Euripides, Sophocles, and Ovid, about Benvenuto Cellini; but now, precisely because of Leninism, these masses have made available to themselves the colossal cultural treasures that were previously not within their reach.

If thousands and tens of thousands of workers in the Soviet Union now delight in Shakespeare, Mozart, and Rembrandt, if their children now fill the music conservatories and the art academies—all this is owing to the victory of Leninism.

He must be a hopeless Tartuffe who pretends that the least harm will be done to Leninism if we offer the Soviet child intelligently the myth of

Prometheus, the poems about the flight of Icarus, the story about Odysseus, and the legend of Hercules.

I have deliberately quoted here Director Rappoport's letter because such as he are not unique even now. He has more than a few allies, and, although they no longer have the opportunity to display their narrow views in magazine and newspaper articles, they stubbornly follow the same theories in practicing their professions in the field of child education, and they keep from the young every work of art and genius if it is called a myth or a fairy tale. They thus reveal their shameless ignorance, which is usually equaled by their smug self-assurance.

I could understand it if my critic had taken objection to the interpretation I had given to the myth of Perseus. It would have been quite instructive to compare my version of it with those created for American and English children by Nathaniel Hawthorne and Charles Kingsley. But Rappoport was unable to undertake this task because it required thought and knowledge, and not merely the shaking of a fist.

I have given so much attention to Rappoport because these leftist educators still use quasi-revolutionary slogans to hinder and distort the literary development of Soviet children. They have quieted down in Moscow and in Leningrad, but in peripheral areas they still carry on as before. And every time the Children's Publishing Bureau or the Young Guard Publishing House puts out new editions of *Hiawatha,* or the tales of Pushkin or Munchausen, these enemies of childhood scream: "The Revolution is in danger"—and they save the Revolution from Pushkin. . . .

These "principled" opponents of the fairy tale use a typical method in their attacks—leftist slogans and the bravado of naked ignorance.

NARROW-MINDED METHODS OF CRITICISM (1956)

But the years passed, and all these obscurantists were overwhelmed by the forceful opposition of Soviet society. Articles began to appear more and more often extolling the great educational value of the fairy tale.

Now it is regarded as a generally recognized truth that the fairy tale develops, enriches, and humanizes the child's psyche, since the child who listens to fairy tales feels like an active participant and always identifies himself with those characters who crusade for justice, goodness, and freedom. It is in this active sympathy of little children with the high-minded and brave heroes of literary invention that lies the educational value of the literature of fantasy.

How can one help but be happy about the new generation of children! Finally they will be given, in abundant quantities, the nourishing, vitamin-filled, spiritual food that will ensure their normal and proper mental growth. It has been a long time since one encountered in print those "daredevils" who used to dare to come out openly against fairy tales and fantasy.

In our present way of life and in our present educational practice, the fairy tale no longer frightens anyone. Major and regional publishing establishments now provide children, unhindered, with Ukrainian, Azerbaidzhanian, Chinese, Hindu, Rumanian fairy tales, to say nothing of Danish, French, and German ones. The record of the writings about the general harm of fairy tales is now in archives—and forgotten. At present this question is considered in a much more circumspect way: Could specific fairy tales be harmful to children? Could a certain fairy tale inflict on them a grave trauma? This is a legitimate concern and one can only respect it.

The Novel and the Fairy Tale

John Buchan

John Buchan (1875–1940), 1st Baron Tweedsmuir, was an outstanding and versatile lawyer, journalist (correspondent for the Times *during World War I), statesman (Governor General of Canada, 1935–1940), and author. He wrote in a variety of genres, but was most famous for his secret-service thrillers, including* The Thirty-Nine Steps *(1915),* Greenmantle *(1916), Mr. Standfast (1919), The Three Hostages (1924), and John McNab (1925). His other works include biography (Sir Walter Scott, 1932, and Oliver Cromwell, 1934) and autobiography (Pilgrim's Way, 1940). "The Novel and the Fairy Tale" was a presidential address delivered to the Scottish Branch of the English Association on November 22, 1930.*

I want to invite you . . . [to] fling your mind back to the literature of your childhood. We have always had story-tellers and makers of fiction since the days of the cave-man. There is an eternal impulse in human nature to enliven the actual working life by the invention of tales of another kind of life, recognizable by its likeness to ordinary life, but so arranged that things happen more dramatically and pleasingly—which indeed is the familiar world in a glorified and idealized form.

That is the origin of what we call the folk tale or the fairy tale—we need not for our present purpose make any distinction between them. These tales come out of the most distant deeps of human experience and human fancy. They belong to the people themselves, not to a specially gifted or privileged class, and they are full of traces of their homely origin. They deal with simple and enduring things, birth and marriage and death, hunger and thirst, natural sorrows and natural joys. They sprang from a society where life was hard, when a man was never quite certain of his next meal, when he never knew when he arose in the morning whether he would be alive in the evening, when adventure was not the exception in life, but the rule. It was a dangerous world and a cruel world, and therefore those who dwelt in it endeavoured in their tales to escape from it. They pictured weakness winning against might, gentleness and courtesy against brutality, brains as against mere animal strength, the one chance in a hundred succeeding. Such things do sometimes happen, and the society where the folk tales were born clung fiercely to this possibility, because on it depended their hope of a better time. Like Malvolio, they "thought nobly of the soul." The true hero in all the folk tales and fairy tales is not the younger son, or the younger daughter, or the stolen princess, or the ugly duckling, but the soul of man. It was a world where a great deal of discomfort and sorrow had to

"The Novel and the Fairy Tale" by John Buchan from *The English Association Pamphlet No. 79* (July 1931): 6-16. Reprinted by permission of The English Association.

be borne, and where the most useful virtue was the passive virtue of
fortitude; but in the folk tales it is not this passive virtue that is exalted, but
daring, boldness, originality, brains—because the people who made them
realized that the hope of humanity lay not in passivity but in action.

The appeal of such stories has not been lessened by time. In one form or
other they have delighted youth for a thousand years and more. Poets and
artists have borrowed from them and made elaborate artistic creations out
of their simplicities. Their appeal is to every class and age; indeed they form
a kind of *corpus* of popular philosophy. But the particular point I want to
make is this: in a sophisticated society something more is wanted than the
simple folk tale, and that something is the novel. My argument is that only
in so far as the novel is a development of and akin to the folk and fairy tale
does it fully succeed, and that it is in this kinship that the virtue of the great
Victorian novels especially lies.

I observe about these novels that in the first place they tell a good
story—something which grips and enthrals the reader, with true drama and
wonder in it. In the second place they are full of characters recognizable as
real types, and they pass judgements on these characters; that is, the
story-teller regards some as definitely good and some as definitely bad. In
the third place, their method of reproducing reality is not that of an
inventory of details, but of a judicious selection. In the fourth place, the
story-teller is primarily interested in the events he has to tell of, and not in
what the jargon of to-day calls his "reactions" to them. He does not stop to
obtrude his own moods. Lastly, he has a dominant purpose, a lesson, if you
like, to teach, a creed to suggest, the nature of which we shall consider
later.

Now all these things the great Victorians had. Most of these things their
critics lack. All these things the folk tales possess. Let us look a little farther
into them.

First for the story. I believe that there are only a very limited number of
good plots in the world, though you have endless variations of them. That
was more or less the idea of the Greek dramatists; it seems to have been
more or less the idea of Shakespeare; and it is more or less the idea of the
great novelists. It is curious, if you consider the classic novels, how limited
is the number of motives. Moreover, I think you will find them all already
in the folk tales. Let us make a short list of them.

There is first of all what we may call the picaresque motive, the story
based on extension in space, on the fact that the world is very wide, and that
there are a great many odd things in it. A young man sets out to seek his
fortune; an ill-treated child runs away from its stepmother; a pretty girl is
driven into the forest. There are endless variations on the subject. The hero
may be the pure adventurer in the void, waiting to see what turns up; or he
may have a serious quest to find something or somebody that is lost, to
unravel a mystery, to marry a lady the fame of whose beauty has reached
him. And the thing may be done seriously or in a spirit of comedy. It may

stick close to earth or adventure into the clouds. The road may be a pleasant and bustling highway running past windmills and gardens and farms and little towns, or a mysterious path through enchanted forests. The one thing common to them all is the conviction that the world is full of surprising things and that anything may happen to the adventurer.

Open Grimm, or Perrault, or any of the great folk tale collections, and you will find a multitude of examples in this class. "Little Brother and Little Sister," "Hop o' my Thumb," "The Little Tailor," "The Two Brothers," "Puss in Boots," "The Sleeping Beauty" are a few of the most familiar. In fiction we have *Don Quixote* and *Gil Blas*; we have *Tom Jones* and *The Cloister and the Hearth*. When D'Artagnan rides to the sea he is doing what the people in folk tales did. So is Mr. Polly when he sets out on his travels, and so is Mr. Pickwick when he mounts the Rochester coach.

Next there is the motive which Aristotle said was one of the chief things in drama, and which he called *Peripeteia,* or Reversal of Fortune. It is the commonest subject of the folk tales. We can picture the peasant in the Middle Ages, groaning under the exactions of kings and nobles and churchmen and accustomed to see proud cavalcades drive him off the road into the ditch, consoling himself with tales which told how the mighty were brought low, and grace was given to the humble. And we can imagine the peasant's son, full of young ambitions which he sees no way to attain, being cheered by the tales of swineherds who became kings, and goose-girls who became princesses, and the plain fighting man who married the Sophy of Egypt's daughter. It is a very old motive and a very modern one. You will find it in the Bible, in the stories of Ruth and Saul and David, and of Nebuchadnezzar the King; you can find it in the latest trashy feuilleton, in which the beautiful kitchen-maid becomes a duchess. Very closely connected with it is another theme which Aristotle made the second staple of tragedy, and which he called *Anagnorisis* or Recognition. That is, so to speak, the proper climax of Reversal of Fortune, and you find it alike in the greatest and crudest of tales. Its crude form is the child changed at nurse, the missing heir with the strawberry mark on his arm, and all the business which concludes with "You are my long lost brother!" The mere fact that you find it in the most elementary literature which possesses any popular appeal seems to suggest that it is rooted in something very deep in human nature. The reason is obvious. It is the most dramatic form of happy ending. One look is given, one word is spoken, and the prince who has been a swine-herd is a prince again, while the usurper is cast out upon the world.

The folk tales based on Reversal of Fortune are among the best. At the top I should put one which is not a folk tale at all, but the invention of a modern writer, Hans Andersen's "Ugly Duckling." It is modern, but it is in the true folk tradition. Among the old stories I would cite "The Hut in the Forest," "The Goose Girl," and "Cinderella." If you want parallels from the great Victorians I would suggest *Guy Mannering* and *The Antiquary,* and *Ivanhoe* from the beginning of the era, and Thomas Hardy's *The Mayor of Casterbridge* from the close. Mr. Hardy is always very near the soil and the traditions of the soil, and the ascent of Donald Farfrae and the descent of Michael Henchard are in the true folk spirit.

The third theme is what I venture to call the Survival of the Unfittest, the victory against odds of the unlikeliest people. That is based upon the incurable optimism of human nature. The men who made the folk tales had no notion how it happened, so they were forced to bring in enchantments of all sorts to make it possible—fairy godmothers, benevolent old women, magic rings and swords and shoes and cloaks. But they had an unshakable conviction that it would happen and that it could happen, and they believed in happily fated people who had more luck than others, more courage, and more dexterity, who were somehow blessed by the gods, and were able to perform feats impossible for others. The popularity of certain film stars is a proof that human nature has not outgrown this belief.

The theme takes various forms. There is courage against impossible odds, as in the stories of the conquests of dragons and giants. "Jack the Giant-Killer" and "Jack and the Beanstalk" are familiar examples. Dumas is full of the same story, as in the deeds of D'Artagnan and the Three Musketeers, and the death of Bussy d'Amboise. Again, there is escape against all reasonable odds, as in "Blue Beard" and "Snowdrop" and "Rumpelstiltskin" and "Hansel and Gretel." Enchantments are unhappily denied to the modern novelist; he is not allowed to bring in fairies to help him out; but you will find the same situation when Dugald Dalgetty escapes from the dungeon at Inverary, and young Waverley is delivered from the hands of the Gifted Gilfillan by the Highlanders, and in Jeanie Deans's journey to London to see the King. The scale must be weighted against the hero in the folk tale; he must be the youngest son with no patrimony, the poor boy with no friends. His task must be made as difficult as possible, for how otherwise can we get the full drama—how otherwise can ordinary folk be persuaded that life has colour in it and a wide horizon?

One of the commonest varieties of this type is the story of the uncouth lover who at first sight has nothing to recommend him. You get it in "Bear-Skin," you get it in "The Frog Prince," in "Snow White and Rose Red," and in "Beauty and the Beast." The handsome swashbuckling gallant is all very well, but the folk mind did not think too highly of him. It suspected the obviously heroic and preferred to look deeper for quality. In this respect the folk tale has been followed in some of the greatest Victorian novels. What is the plot of *Vanity Fair*? It is the contest of two suitors for the hand of a very tiresome young woman—the dashing George Osborne and the cumbrous Dobbin, and the book is a record of the struggle of the homely worth of Dobbin against the glamour of his rival both in life and death, until at long last it is duly rewarded. In George Meredith's *Diana of the Crossways* it is Tom Redworth who wins the glittering lady, not Percy Dacier; and in Mr. Hardy's *Far from the Madding Crowd* Shepherd Oak, after many ups and downs, eventually is the accepted lover of Bathsheba Everdene. Truly the folk tale has august descendants.

So much for the plot and the theme of the story. The next thing to be noted about the great Victorian novelists is their handling of character. Now, in the folk tale there is never any mistake about the people. The characters are human beings, and represent humanity in its central region, and not in its remote suburbs. The old story-teller was not interested in freaks. He understood a great villain and a great hero, but above all things he understood ordinary men, and he makes them reveal their character in their deeds, and does not make any pother about describing it. "If you cannot get hold of my people," he seems to say to the reader, "by seeing the kind of thing they do, then you are past praying for." Now this seems to me to be the very essence of good fiction. I have read novels by able men and women in which the characters could not get started to do anything because of the meshes of analytic psychology with which their feet were clogged. Pages of torturous analysis had to be waded through before the hero could kiss his wife or eat his breakfast. The trick of dissecting a character before a reader's eyes seems to me abominably bad craftsmanship. The business of the novelist is to make men and women reveal themselves in speech and action, to play the showman as little as possible, to present the finished product, and not to print the jottings of his laboratory.

Another point. The makers of the folk tales were not afraid to pass judgement upon their characters. A man was brave or he was not; he was kind or he was cruel; he was foolish or he was wise. There is a school of fiction to-day which objects to passing moral judgements on anything or anybody. It derives principally from a really great man, the Russian Dostoievsky, and people have praised his divine humanity which finds surpassing virtues in the worst of rogues. Now, I have nothing to say against this impartiality, though I think it may as easily have its roots in moral apathy and intellectual slovenliness as in divine wisdom. Philosophically, it may have its justification, but I suggest that since fallible men must have their standards and stick to them, such detachment is rather for their Maker than for themselves. In any case it is no virtue in a novelist who can only get drama by strong contrasts. The moral molluscs of certain fiction of to-day, who spend their time, if I may borrow a phrase of the late D. H. Lawrence, in sinning their way to sanctity, would have puzzled the makers of folk tales, as they puzzle any ordinary man. The great Victorian novelists have the same clearness of moral outline. They realize that all of us are a compost of good and bad, but that the orientation of certain men and women is as clearly towards evil as that of others is towards good, and they do not scruple to say so.

One last word on the question of character. The folk tale is not afraid of greatness. It believes that humanity is not a drab collection of mediocrities, but that nearly everybody has some poetry in him, and that it can flower at times into something which leaves the earth altogether and strikes the stars. Because it believed in human nature it believed that human nature could transcend itself and become god-like. Its heroes are so full of vitality that no giant or dragon or wicked stepmother manages to hamper them in the long run. They go their appointed course with a divine carelessness. They are immortal until they have fulfilled their purpose.

Such a creed springs from optimism about human nature, and I do not think that any great imaginative writer has been without it. The power of creating a figure which, while completely human, seems to soar beyond humanity, is the most certain proof of genius. In such cases the creator seems to be dominated by his creation. It takes charge of him and has an independent life of its own over which he has no control. . . .

I will pass lightly over the other two characteristics of the great Victorian novels which I have cited, and in each of which they show their kinship with the folk tale. Both represent a world in which the selective power of art has been at work. The Victorian novel is often prolix but it is never confused. The main lines of development are always crystal clear. Scott, for example, is fond of pouring the contents of an antiquarian's memory into his pages, but when things begin to happen there is no prolixity. He selects infallibly the details which print a great scene eternally on the memory. So, too, with the folk tales. They never fumble. The right details are unerringly selected. A proof is their enduring power over the child's mind. Young people are gluttons for details and have an acute sense of what is fit and proper in that respect. They know that Robinson Crusoe found just the right number and kind of things at the wreck to satisfy the imagination, while they remember that that fearsome household, the Swiss Family Robinson, found so much that every scrap of interest goes out of the tale. And for generations youth has accepted the folk tale as never blundering in this vital matter.

Again, both the folk tale and the Victorian novel have the merit of being unselfconscious. The great Victorians did not lay bare their souls, apart from the souls of their characters. They were not concerned to preach a new metaphysic or a new morality. What they had to give in that respect must be implied. Their view of the universe is to be deduced from the drama unfolded; it is never given in set terms. Thackeray, indeed, has sometimes the air of a coy and sentimental showman, as in the last paragraphs of *Vanity Fair;* but this is a mere trick of his. His real views on the problems of life must be looked for in the fortunes of Becky Sharp and Dobbin and Pendennis and Colonel Newcome, and not in any irrelevant interpolations. The Victorian novelist at his best was as objective as Shakespeare, and as the anonymous folk tale.

I come lastly to the greatest of the links between the two—the fact that they have a dominant purpose and the same purpose. The Victorian novels and the folk tales are not mere transcripts of life—they are interpretations of life, and they are interpretations of life in a hopeful spirit. In the folk tale the plain man comforted himself in his difficulties by showing that the weak things of the earth can confound the strong; that nothing is impossible to the courageous and single-hearted; that the unfittest in the worldly sense can survive if he is the fittest in more important respects. They are a glorification of the soul of man, an epic of the resurgence of the divine in human nature. They make the world a happier place because they show it interpenetrated by hope and opportunity.

The great novelists do the same thing by subtler methods. With them it is not the good fairy that solves the problem, but something unconquerable in the human spirit. They make the world more solemn, for they show the darkest places in it. They show the capacities for evil in man's breast, the cruelty and callousness of life, the undeserved suffering of the good, and the undeserved fortune of the evil; they show the transience of human glory and the fragility of human hopes. But if they make life more solemn they also make it brighter. They enlarge our vision, light up dark corners, break down foolish barriers, and make the world more sunlit and more spacious. If they do not preach any single philosophy they, in Shelley's words, "repeal large codes of fraud and woe." They revive hope in humanity by revealing its forgotten graces and depths. They are optimists in the largest sense, for without optimism there can be no vitality. Thackeray, indeed, indulges often in a kind of gentle melancholy, but it is not to be taken too seriously. His gusto, his delight in his personages, gives the lie to his occasional pessimistic meditations, which indeed are only bits of self-humiliation designed to propitiate the gods.

The optimism of such novels and of the folk tale is a profound thing, for it is based upon a very clear and candid view of life. The folk tale knows only too well the stubborn brutality of things; and, knowing this, it is still prepared to hope. Such optimism is far more merciless than any pessimism. Also it is far closer to reality. A tale which describes any aspect of life and makes of it nothing but a pathological study in meanness and vice is more fantastic than any fairy tale. You remember Stevenson's fable of the *Lantern-Bearers*, where he pictures a camp of small urchins who carry their smelly tin lanterns buttoned under their overcoats, and reflects what asses such a group, sheltering in the cold sand on a bleak sea-shore on a dark autumn night, must have seemed to the spectator who could not understand their recondite pleasures. And from the picture he draws a profound moral.

"To miss the joy," he says, "is to miss all. . . . Hence the haunting and truly spectral unreality of realistic books. Hence, when we read the English realists, the incredulous wonder with which we observe the hero's constancy under the submerging tide of dulness, and how he bears up with his jibbing sweetheart, and endures the chatter of idiot girls, and stands by his whole unfeatured wilderness of an existence, instead of seeking relief in drink or foreign travel. Hence in the French, in that meat-market of middle-aged sensuality, the disgusted surprise with which we see the hero drift side-long, and practically quite untempted, into every description of misconduct and dishonour. In each, we miss the personal poetry, the enchanted atmosphere, that rainbow of fancy that clothes what is naked and seems to ennoble what is base; in each, life falls dead like dough, instead of soaring away like a balloon into the colours of the sunset; each is true, each inconceivable; for no man lives in the external truth, among salts and acids, but in the warm, phantasmagoric chamber of his brain, with the painted windows and the storied walls."

You have the same moral in a verse of Francis Thompson's:

> The Angels keep their ancient places—
>   Turn but a stone, you start a wing!
> 'Tis ye, 'tis your estranged faces,
>   That miss the many splendoured thing.

and in some delightful doggerel lines of Mr. Masefield:

> I have seen flowers come in stony places,
> And kind things done by men with ugly faces,
> And the Gold Cup won by the worst horse at the races,
>   So I trust, too.[1]

The folk tale belongs to no one country or age. Many go back to the ancientry of our race. They are part of the common stock of humanity and are closer to mankind than any written word. They are the delight of our childhood and they are part of our unconscious thought. I have a notion that things so long descended and prepotent are not likely to be forgotten. I have a notion, too, that any form of literature related to them, inspired by the same creed, close to the earth and yet kin to the upper air, will have the same immortality. To-day we are sometimes told that Scott and Thackeray and Dickens, and even Thomas Hardy, are back numbers, that they practised a superseded form of art, that the novel of the future will be a far more recondite thing, tremulous with meaning, profoundly "aware," surcharged with subtle psychology, and that the old crude business of story and character and moral preference and a cheerful philosophy is only for the amusement of children. I take leave to doubt that forecast. The other day I took up a book of essays on the "Eighteen-seventies," and I found these words by one of the truest of our living poets—Mr. Walter de la Mare:

> The distant rumour that thrills the air is not only the sound of Time's dark waters, but is mingled with the roar of our own busy printing presses. "As we are, so you shall be!" The very years that we now so actively occupy will soon be packed up in an old satchel, and labelled "The Twenties"; and our little hot, cold,

---

1. Reprinted by permission of The Macmillan Company and The Society of Authors as the literary representative of the Estate of John Masefield from *Poems* by John Masefield. Copyright 1951 by John Masefield.

violent, affected, brand-new, exquisite, fresh little habits of mind, manners, hobbies, fashions, ideals, will have thinned and vanished away, will steadily have evaporated, leaving only a frigid deposit of history; a few decaying buildings, a few pictures, some music, some machine-made voices, an immense quantity of print—most of it never to be disturbed again. In the midst of the battle maybe it is indiscreet to muse on the tranquil, moonlit indifference of the night that will follow.[2]

It is a salutary thing to remind oneself that the judgements of posterity may be different from our own. But it is permissible, I think, to claim endurance for things which have the qualities that hitherto have endured—things that are close to the tap-root of humanity. I believe that so long as youth ascends the beanstalk with Jack, and rides in the glass coach with Cinderella, and sets off with the youngest son to seek his fortunes—that so long all ages will continue to dance with Becky at the Waterloo Ball, and take the heather with Rob Roy, and mount the Rochester diligence with Mr. Pickwick.

---

2. Reprinted by permission of The Society of Authors as agent for the Walter de la Mare Estate.

Wanda Gág

Margery Fisher[1]

. . . In all her translations from Grimm, Wanda Gág shows how well she understands the basis of folk-tale—the humour of oddity, the casual acceptance of the marvellous, an intimate and rhythmical fireside prose to match homely settings. The stories that show her art at its best are domestic fables like *The Cat and the Fox* or *The Shoemaker and the Elves*. Like Hans Andersen himself, she can enjoy, and make children enjoy, the antics *and* the human attributes of spindle, straw and joint-stool.

> Once there was a tiny cottage, and in it lived no people, only a mouse, a bird and a sausage. There they had kept house most joyously together for many years, and had even been able to save some money besides.[2]

There is humanity here. There is also superb writing, selectively simple and with a varied, agreeable rhythm in it. Wanda Gág herself said that by simplification she did not mean "writing in words of one or two syllables" and that children could absorb long, even unfamiliar words "provided they have enough colour and sound-value." Lucky the child who meets a folk-tale with a relaxed, beautifully-turned opening like this:

> A tawny yellow cat with sea-green eyes, fine manners and a noble bearing, was taking an after-dinner stroll. What should he see but a mouse, a likable little mouse with handsome ears and big trusting eyes. The mouse was frightened and darted off but the cat called her back. Having just dined on two very plump mice, the cat did not feel like catching another, so he said: "Grey-mouse, my friend, somehow I like you well. Couldn't we be comrades and set up housekeeping together?"[3]

The humour that Wanda Gág finds in folk-tale may be occasioned by an accident, by incongruity, by mystery, by cunning overreaching itself: it may be related to people, objects or animals. Always it will be a good-hearted, utterly unmalicious humour, whether she renders it in a comic little drawing or in a descriptive paragraph. What a gift the Brothers Grimm brought to her cradle! She is not so much a translator as an interpreter of their writings, bringing to generations of children a lasting pleasure.

"Wanda Gág" by Margery Fisher from *Where*, Supplement 15, *Books for Children* (1969): 16. Reprinted by permission of the Advisory Centre for Education.

1. For biographical information about the author, see p. 126.

2. From "The Mouse, The Bird and the Sausage" from *More Tales from Grimm,* translated by Wanda Gág. Reprinted by permission of Coward, McCann & Geoghegan, Inc. and Faber and Faber, Ltd.

3. From "The Cat and Mouse Keep House" from *Tales from Grimm,* translated by Wanda Gág. Reprinted by permission of Coward, McCann & Geoghegan, Inc. and Faber and Faber, Ltd.

On Three Ways of Writing for Children

C. S. Lewis

Noted author, critic, and educator, C. S. Lewis (1898–1963) taught at both Oxford and Cambridge Universities, holding at the latter for the decade before his death the Chair of Medieval and Renaissance English Literature. Essays on children's literature in his Of Other Worlds, Essays and Stories *include "Sometimes Fairy Stories Say Best What's To Be Said,"[1] "On Juvenile Tastes,"[2] "It All Began with a Picture . . . "[3] (on how he came to write* The Lion, the Witch and the Wardrobe), *"On Science Fiction," and the essay reprinted below. Most celebrated of his works for children are the Narnia stories, beginning with* The Lion, the Witch and the Wardrobe *(1950). But Lewis has also written adult novels: the space trilogy* Perelandra *(1944),* Out of the Silent Planet *(1956), and* That Hideous Strength *(1965), and the philosophical* Screwtape Letters *(1944). Acknowledging the influence of and his admiration for poet and novelist George Macdonald, Lewis compiled* George Macdonald: An Anthology.

Illustration by Pauline Baynes from *The Horse and His Boy* by C. S. Lewis (copyright 1954 by The Macmillan Company). Reprinted by permission of The Macmillan Company and Collins Publishers.

I think there are three ways in which those who write for children may approach their work; two good ways and one that is generally a bad way.

I came to know of the bad way quite recently and from two unconscious witnesses. One was a lady who sent me the manuscript of a story she had written in which a fairy placed at a child's disposal a wonderful gadget. I say

"On Three Ways of Writing for Children" by C. S. Lewis from *Horn Book Magazine*, 38 (October 1963): 459–469. Reprinted by permission of Curtis Brown Ltd.

1. Also in *New York Times Book Review*, v. 7, pt. 2 (November 18, 1956): 3.

2. Also in *Church Times*, Children's Book Supplement (November 28, 1958).

3. Also in "Junior Radio Times" in *Radio Times* (July 15, 1960).

"gadget" because it was not a magic ring or hat or cloak or any such traditional matter. It was a machine, a thing of taps and handles and buttons you could press. You could press one and get ice cream, another and get a live puppy, and so forth. I had to tell the author honestly that I didn't much care for that sort of thing. She replied, "No more do I; it bores me to distraction. But it is what the modern child wants." My other bit of evidence was this. In my own first story I had described at length what I thought was a rather fine high tea given by a hospitable faun to the little girl who was my heroine. A man who has children of his own said, "Ah, I see how you got to that. If you want to please grown-up readers you give them sex; so you thought to yourself, 'That won't do for children; what shall I give them instead? I know! The little blighters like plenty of good eating!'" In reality, however, I myself like eating and drinking. I put in what I would have liked to read when I was a child and what I still like reading now that I am in my fifties.

The lady in my first example, and the married man in my second, both conceived writing for children as a special department of "giving the public what it wants." Children are, of course, a special public and you find out what they want and give them that, however little you like it yourself.

The next way may seem at first to be very much the same, but I think the resemblance is superficial. This is the way of Lewis Carroll, Kenneth Grahame, and Tolkien. The printed story grows out of a story told to a particular child with the living voice and perhaps *ex tempore*. It resembles the first way because you are certainly trying to give that child what he wants. But then you are dealing with a concrete person, this child who, of course, differs from all other children. There is no question of "children" conceived as a strange species whose habits you have "made up" like an anthropologist or a commercial traveler. Nor, I suspect, would it be possible, thus face to face, to regale the child with things calculated to please him but regarded by yourself with indifference or contempt. The child, I am certain, would see through that. In any personal relation the two participants modify each other. You would become slightly different because you were talking to a child and the child would become slightly different because he was being talked to by an adult. A community, a composite personality, is created and out of that the story grows.

The third way, which is the only one I could ever use myself, consists in writing a children's story because a children's story is the best art form for something you have to say: just as a composer might write a Dead March not because there was a public funeral in view but because certain musical ideas that had occurred to him went best into that form. This method could apply to other kinds of children's literature besides stories. I have been told that Arthur Mee never met a child and never wished to; it was, from his point of view, a bit of luck that boys liked reading what he liked writing. This anecdote may be untrue in fact, but it illustrates my meaning.

Within the species "children's story" the subspecies which happened to suit me is the fantasy or (in a loose sense of that word) the fairy tale. There are, of course, other subspecies. E. Nesbit's trilogy about the Bastable family is a very good specimen of another kind. It is a "children's story" in the sense that children can and do read it, but it is also the only form in which E. Nesbit could have given us so much of the humors of childhood. It is true that the Bastable children appear, successfully treated from the adult point of view, in one of her grown-up novels, but they appear only for a moment. I do not think she would have kept it up. Sentimentality is so apt to creep in if we write at length about children as seen by their elders. And the reality of childhood, as we all experienced it, creeps out. For we all remember that our childhood, as lived, was immeasurably different from what our elders saw. Hence Sir Michael Sadler, when I asked his opinion about a certain new experimental school, replied, "I never give an opinion on any of those experiments till the children have grown up and can tell us *what really happened.*" Thus the Bastable trilogy, however improbable many of its episodes may be, provides even adults, in one sense, with more realistic reading about children than they could find in most books addressed to adults. But also, conversely, it enables the children who read it to do something much more mature than they realize. For the whole book is a character study of Oswald, an unconsciously satiric self-portrait, which every intelligent child can fully appreciate; but no child would sit down to read a character study in any other form. There is another way in which children's stories mediate this psychological interest, but I will reserve that for later treatment.

In this short glance at the Bastable trilogy I think we have stumbled on a principle. Where the children's story is simply the right form for what the author has to say, then of course readers who want to hear that will read the story, or reread it, at any age. I never met *The Wind in the Willows* or the Bastable books till I was in my late twenties, and I do not think I have enjoyed them any the less on that account. I am almost inclined to set it up as a canon that a children's story which is enjoyed only by children is a bad children's story. The good ones last. A waltz which you can like only when you are waltzing is a bad waltz.

This canon seems to me most obviously true of that particular type of children's story which is dearest to my own taste, the fantasy or fairy tale. Now the modern critical world uses "adult" as a term of approval. It is hostile to what it calls "nostalgia" and contemptuous of what it calls "Peter Pantheism." Hence a man who admits that dwarfs and giants and talking beasts and witches are still dear to him in his fifty-third year is now less likely to be praised for his perennial youth than scorned and pitied for arrested development. If I spend some little time defending myself against these charges, this is not so much because it matters greatly whether I am scorned and pitied as because the defense is germane to my whole view of the fairy tale and even of literature in general. My defense consists of three propositions.

1. I reply with a *tu quoque.* Critics who treat "adult" as a term of approval, instead of as a merely descriptive term, cannot be adult them-

selves. To be concerned about being grown-up, to admire the grown-up because it is grown-up, to blush at the suspicion of being childish—these things are the marks of childhood and adolescence. And in childhood and adolescence they are, in moderation, healthy symptoms. Young things ought to want to grow. But to carry on into middle life or even into early manhood this concern about being adult is a mark of really arrested development. When I was ten, I read fairy tales in secret and would have been ashamed if I had been found doing so. Now that I am fifty I read them openly. When I became a man I put away childish things, including the fear of childishness and the desire to be very grown-up.

2.   The modern view seems to me to involve a false conception of growth. They accuse us of arrested development because we have not lost a taste we had in childhood. But surely arrested development consists not in refusing to lose old things but in failing to add new things? I now like hock, which I am sure I should not have liked as a child. But I still like lemon squash. I call this growth or development because I have been enriched: where I formerly had only one pleasure, I now have two. But if I had to lose the taste for lemon squash before I acquired the taste for hock, that would not be growth but simple change. I now enjoy Tolstoi and Jane Austen and Trollope as well as fairy tales and I call that growth: if I had had to lose the fairy tales in order to acquire the novelists, I would not say that I had grown but only that I had changed. A tree grows because it adds rings; a train doesn't grow by leaving one station behind and puffing on to the next. In reality, the case is stronger and more complicated than this. I think my growth is just as apparent when I now read the fairy tales as when I read the novelists, for I now enjoy the fairy tales better than I did in childhood: being now able to put more in, of course I get more out. But I do not here stress that point. Even if it were merely a taste for grown-up literature added to an unchanged taste for children's literature, addition would still be entitled to the name "growth," and the process of merely dropping one parcel when you pick up another would not. It is, of course, true that the process of growing does, incidentally and unfortunately, involve some more losses. But that is not the essence of growth, certainly not what makes growth admirable or desirable. If it were, if to drop parcels and to leave stations behind were the essence and virtue of growth, why should we stop at the adult? Why should not "senile" be equally a term of approval? Why are we not to be congratulated on losing our teeth and hair? Some critics seem to confuse growth with the cost of growth and also to wish to make that cost far higher than, in nature, it need be.

3.   The whole association of fairy tale and fantasy with childhood is local and accidental. I hope everyone has read Tolkien's essay on fairy tales,[4] which is perhaps the most important contribution to the subject that anyone has yet made. If so, you will know already that, in most places and times,

---

4. J. R. R. Tolkien, "On Fairy-Stories," *Essays Presented to Charles Williams* (Oxford University Press, 1947; o.p.)

the fairy tale has not been specially made for, nor exclusively enjoyed by, children. It has gravitated to the nursery when it became unfashionable in literary circles, just as unfashionable furniture gravitated to the nursery in Victorian houses. In fact, many children do not like this kind of book, just as many children do not like horsehair sofas; and many adults do like it, just as many adults like rocking chairs. And those who do like it, whether young or old, probably like it for the same reason. And none of us can say with any certainty what that reason is. The two theories which are most often in my mind are those of Tolkien and of Jung.

According to Tolkien the appeal of the fairy story lies in the fact that man there most fully exercises his function as a "subcreator"; not, as they love to say now, making a "comment upon life" but making, so far as possible, a subordinate world of his own. Since, in Tolkien's view, this is one of man's proper functions, delight naturally arises whenever it is successfully performed. For Jung, fairy tale liberates the archetypes which dwell in the collective unconscious, and when we read a good fairy tale we are obeying the old precept "Know thyself." I would venture to add to this my own theory, not indeed of the kind as a whole, but of one feature in it: I mean, the presence of beings other than human which yet behave, in varying degrees, humanly—the giants and dwarfs and talking beasts. I believe these to be at least (for they may have many other sources of power and beauty) an admirable hieroglyphic which conveys psychology, types of character, more briefly than novelistic presentation and to readers whom novelistic presentation could not yet reach. Consider Mr. Badger in *The Wind in the Willows*—that extraordinary amalgam of high rank, coarse manners, gruffness, shyness, and goodness. The child who has once met Mr. Badger has ever afterwards, in his bones, a knowledge of humanity and of English social history which he could not get in any other way.

Of course as all children's literature is not fantastic, so all fantastic books need not be children's books. It is still possible, even in an age so ferociously antiromantic as our own, to write fantastic stories for adults, though you will usually need to have made a name in some more fashionable kind of literature before anyone will publish them. But there may be an author who at a particular moment finds not only fantasy but fantasy-for-children the exactly right form for what he wants to say. The distinction is a fine one. His fantasies for children and his fantasies for adults will have very much more in common with one another than either has with the ordinary novel or with what is sometimes called "the novel of child life." Indeed the same readers will probably read both his fantastic "juveniles" and his fantastic stories for adults. For I need not remind such an audience as this that the neat sorting-out of books into age groups, so dear to publishers, has only a very sketchy relation with the habits of any real readers. Those of us who are blamed when old for reading childish books were blamed when children for reading books too old for us. No reader worth his salt trots along in obedience to a timetable. The distinction, then, is a fine one; and I am not quite sure what made me, in a particular year of my life, feel that not only a fairy tale, but a fairy tale addressed to children, was exactly what I must write—or burst. Partly, I think, that this form permits, or compels, one to leave out things I wanted to leave out. It compels one to throw all the force of the book into what was done and said. It checks what a kind but discerning critic called "the expository demon" in me. It also imposes certain very fruitful necessities about length.

If I have allowed the fantastic type of children's story to run away with this discussion, that is because it is the kind I know and love best, not because I wish to condemn any other. But the patrons of the other kinds very frequently want to condemn it. About once every hundred years some wiseacre gets up and tries to banish the fairy tale. Perhaps I had better say a few words in its defense as reading for children.

The fairy tale is accused of giving children a false impression of the world they live in. But I think no literature that children could read gives them less of a false impression. I think what profess to be realistic stories for children are far more likely to deceive them. I never expected the real world to be like the fairy tales. I think that I did expect school to be like the school stories. The fantasies did not deceive me; the school stories did. All stories in which children have adventures and successes which are possible, in the sense that they do not break the laws of nature, but almost infinitely improbable are in more danger than the fairy tales of raising false expectations.

Almost the same answer serves for the popular charge of escapism, though here the question is not so simple. Do fairy tales teach children to retreat into a world of wish fulfillment—"fantasy" in the technical psychological sense of the word—instead of facing the problems of the real world? Now it is here that the problem becomes subtle. Let us again lay the fairy tale side by side with the school story or any other story which is labeled a "Boy's Book" or a "Girl's Book," as distinct from a "Children's Book." There is no doubt that both arouse, and imaginatively satisfy, wishes. We long to go through the looking glass, to reach fairy land. We also long to be the immensely popular and successful schoolboy or schoolgirl, or the lucky boy or girl who discovers the spy's plot or rides the horse that none of the cowboys can manage. But the two longings are very different. The second, especially when directed on something so close as school life, is ravenous and deadly serious. Its fulfillment on the level of imagination is in very truth compensatory: we run to it from the disappointments and humiliations of the real world; it sends us back to the real world undivinely discontented. For it is all flattery to the ego. The pleasure consists in picturing oneself the object of admiration. The other longing, that for fairy land, is very different. In a sense a child does not long for fairy land as a boy longs to be the hero of the first eleven. Does anyone suppose that he really and prosaically longs for all the dangers and discomforts of a fairy tale?—really wants dragons in contemporary England? It is not so. It would be much truer to say that fairy land arouses a longing for he knows not what. It stirs and troubles him (to his lifelong enrichment) with the dim sense of something beyond his reach and, far from dulling or emptying the actual world, gives it a new dimension of depth. He does not despise real woods because he has read of enchanted woods; the reading makes all real woods a little enchanted. This is a special kind of longing. The boy reading the school story of the type I have in mind desires success and is unhappy (once the book is over) because he can't get it; the boy reading the fairy tale desires and is happy in the very fact of desiring, for his mind has not been concentrated on himself.

I do not mean that school stories for boys and girls ought not be written. I am only saying that they are far more liable to become "fantasies" in the clinical sense than fantastic stories are. And this distinction holds for adult reading too. The dangerous fantasy is always superficially realistic. The real victim of wishful reverie does not batten on the *Odyssey*, the *Tempest*, or *The Worm Ouroboros:* he (or she) prefers stories about millionaires, irresistible beauties, posh hotels, palm beaches and bedroom scenes—things that really might happen, that ought to happen, that would have happened if the reader had had a fair chance. For, as I say, there are two kinds of longing. The one is an *askesis*, a spiritual exercise, and the other is a disease.

A far more serious attack on the fairy tale as children's literature comes from those who do not wish children to be frightened. I suffered too much from night fears myself in childhood to undervalue this objection. I would not wish to heat the fires of that private hell for any child. On the other hand, none of my fears came from fairy tales. Giant insects were my specialty, with ghosts a bad second. I suppose the ghosts came directly or indirectly from stories, though certainly not from fairy stories, but I don't think the insects did. I don't know anything my parents could have done or left undone which would have saved me from the pincers, mandibles and eyes of those many-legged abominations. And that, as so many people have pointed out, is the difficulty. We do not know what will or will not frighten a child in this particular way. I say "in this particular way," for we must here make a distinction. Those who say that children must not be frightened may mean two things. They may mean (1) that we must not do anything likely to give the child those haunting, disabling, pathological fears against which ordinary courage is helpless: in fact, phobias. His mind must, if possible, be kept clear of things he can't bear to think of. Or they may mean (2) that we must try to keep out of his mind the knowledge that he is born into a world of death, violence, wounds, adventure, heroism and cowardice, good and evil. If they mean the first I agree with them, but not if they mean the second. The second would indeed be to give children a false impression and feed them on escapism in the bad sense. There is something ludicrous in the idea of so educating a generation which is born to the Ogpu and the atomic bomb. Since it is so likely that they will meet cruel enemies, let them at least have heard of brave knights and heroic courage. Otherwise you are making their destiny not brighter but darker. Nor do most of us find that violence and bloodshed, in a story, produce any haunting dread in the minds of children. As far as that goes, I side impenitently with the human race against the modern reformer. Let there be wicked kings and beheadings, battles and dungeons, giants and dragons, and let villains be soundly killed at the end of the book. Nothing will persuade me that this causes an ordinary child any kind or degree of fear beyond what he wants, and needs, to feel. For, of course, he wants to be a little frightened.

The other fears—the phobias—are a different matter. I do not believe one can control them by literary means. We seem to bring them into the world with us ready-made. No doubt the particular image on which the child's terror is fixed can sometimes be traced to a book. But is that the source, or only the occasion, of the fear? If he had been spared that image, would not some other, quite unpredictable by you, have had the same effect? Chesterton has told us of a boy who was more afraid of the Albert Memorial than anything else in the world. I know a man whose great childhood terror was the India-paper edition of the *Encyclopaedia Britannica*—for a reason I defy you to guess. And I think it possible that, by confining your child to blameless stories of child life in which nothing at all alarming ever happens, you would fail to banish the terrors and would succeed in banishing all that can enable him to endure them. For in the fairy tales, side by side with the terrible figures, we find the immemorial comforters and protectors, the radiant ones, and the terrible figures are not merely terrible, but sublime. It would be nice if no little boy in bed, hearing, or thinking he hears, a sound, were ever at all frightened. But if he is going to be frightened, I think it better that he should think of giants and dragons than merely of burglars. And I think St. George, or any bright champion in armor, is a better comfort than the idea of the police.

I will even go further. If I could have escaped all my own night fears at the price of never having known "faerie," would I now be the gainer by that bargain? I am not speaking carelessly. The fears were very bad. But I think the price would have been too high.

But I have strayed far from my theme. This has been inevitable, for, of the three methods, I know by experience only the third. I hope my title did not lead anyone to think that I was conceited enough to give you advice on how to write a story for children. There were two very good reasons for not doing that. One is that many people have written very much better stories than I, and I would rather learn about the art than set up to teach it. The other is that, in a certain sense, I have never exactly "made" a story. With me the process is much more like birdwatching than like either talking or building. I see pictures. Some of these pictures have a common flavor, almost a common smell, which groups them together. Keep quiet and watch and they will begin joining themselves up. If you were very lucky (I have never been as lucky as all that) a whole set might join themselves so consistently that there you had a complete story, without doing anything yourself. But more often (in my experience, always) there are gaps. Then at last you have to do some deliberate inventing, have to contrive reasons why these characters should be in these various places doing these various things. I have no idea whether this is the usual way of writing stories, still less whether it is the best. It is the only one I know: images always come first.

Before closing, I would like to return to what I said at the beginning. I rejected any approach which begins with the question "What do modern children like?" I might be asked, "Do you equally reject the approach which begins with the question 'What do modern children need?'—in other words, the moral or didactic approach." I think the answer is Yes. Not because I don't like stories to have a moral: certainly not because I think children dislike a moral. Rather because I feel sure that the question "What do modern children need?" will not lead you to a good moral. If we ask that question we are assuming too superior an attitude. It would be better to ask "What moral do I need?" for I think we can be sure that what does not concern us deeply will not deeply interest our readers, whatever their age. But it is better not to ask the question at all. Let the pictures tell you their own moral. For the moral inherent in them will rise from whatever spiritual roots you have succeeded in striking during the whole course of your life. But if they don't show you any moral, don't put one in. For the moral you put in is likely to be a platitude, or even a falsehood, skimmed from the surface of your consciousness. It is impertinent to offer the children that. For we have been told on high authority that in the moral sphere they are probably at least as wise as we. Anyone who *can* write a children's story without a moral had better do so—that is, if he is going to write children's stories at all. The only moral that is of any value is that which arises inevitably from the whole cast of the author's mind.

Indeed everything in the story should arise from the whole cast of the author's mind. We must write for children out of those elements in our own imagination which we share with children: differing from our child readers not by any less, or less serious, interest in the things we handle, but by the fact that we have other interests which children would not share with us. The matter of our story should be a part of the habitual furniture of our minds. This, I fancy, has been so with all great writers for children, but it is not generally understood. A critic, not long ago, said in praise of a very serious fairy tale that the author's tongue "never once got into his cheek." But why on earth should it?—unless he had been eating a seedcake. Nothing seems to me more fatal, for this art, than an idea that whatever we share with children is, in the privative sense, "childish" and that whatever is childish is somehow comic. We must meet children as equals in that area of our nature where we are their equals. Our superiority consists partly in commanding other areas, and partly (which is more relevant) in the fact that we are better at telling stories than they are. The child as reader is neither to be patronized nor idolized: we talk to him as man to man. But the worst attitude of all would be the professional attitude which regards children in the lump as a sort of raw material which we have to handle. We must of course try to do them no harm; we may, under the Omnipotence, sometimes dare to hope that we may do them good. But only such good as involves treating them with respect. We must not imagine that we are Providence or Destiny. I will not say that a good story for children could never be written by someone in the Ministry of Education, for all things are possible. But I should lay very long odds against it.

Once in a hotel dining room I said, rather too loudly, "I loathe prunes." "So do I," came an unexpected six-year-old voice from another table. Sympathy was instantaneous. Neither of us thought it funny. We both knew that prunes are far too nasty to be funny. That is the proper meeting between man and child as independent personalities. Of the far higher and more difficult relations between child and parent or child and teacher, I say nothing. An author, as a mere author, is outside all that. He is not even an uncle. He is a freeman and an equal, like the postman, the butcher, and the dog next door.

The Flat-Heeled Muse

Lloyd Alexander

Lloyd Alexander, author of books and articles for adults and translator of French literature, turned in 1963 to writing fantasy for children. His first children's book, Time Cat, *was followed by the five books of the Prydain cycle:* The Book of Three *(1964),* The Black Cauldron *(1965),* The Castle of Llyr *(1966),* Taran Wanderer *(1967), and* The High King *(1968). The last of this cycle won the 1969 Newbery Medal. He has also written two picture-story books set in the Land of Prydain:* The Truthful Harp *and* Coll and His White Pig. *In 1971* The Marvelous Misadventures of Sebastian, *a very different, amusing story about a court musician in an old Middle Eastern kingdom, won the National Book Award. Mr. Alexander has done much speaking and writing about the business of creating fantasy.*

The Muse in charge of fantasy wears good, sensible shoes. No foam-born Aphrodite, she vaguely resembles my old piano teacher, who was keen on metronomes. She does not carry a soothing lyre for inspiration, but is more likely to shake you roughly awake at four in the morning and rattle a sheaf of subtle, sneaky questions under your nose. And you had better answer them. The Muse will stand for no nonsense (that is, non-sense). Her geometries are no more Euclidean than Einstein's, but they are equally rigorous.

I was aware of the problems and disciplines of fantasy, but in a left-handed sort of way; because there is a difference between knowing and doing. Until I met the Muse in Charge of Fantasy personally, I had no hint of what a virago she could be.

Our first encounter was relatively cordial and came in the course of working on a book called *Time Cat.* I suspect I learn more from writing books than readers very likely learn from reading them, and I realize now that *Time Cat* is an example of a fantasy perhaps more realistic than otherwise. Basically, only one fantastic premise moved the story: that Gareth, a black cat, could take the young boy Jason into nine historical periods. The premise included some built-in and plausible hedges. Boy and cat could talk together during their journeys—but only when no one else was around to overhear them; after their return home they could no longer speak to each other, at least not in words. They enjoyed no supernatural protection or privilege; what happened to them, happened—indeed, if Gareth met with a fatal accident, Jason would be forever marooned in the past. They weren't allowed to interfere with or change the course of history, or do anything contrary to laws of the physical world and their personal capacities. Jason was a boy and Gareth was a cat.

Within those boundaries, the problem became one of straightforward historical research, with some investigation into how cats were regarded in various eras. Ichigo, the boy emperor in the Japanese adventure, really existed. His wanting to dress kittens in kimonos was valid; there was an extravagant preciousness in the Japanese court of that epoch, and historical records state that such things happened. In other adventures, only slight accommodations made it acceptable for Jason and Gareth to be where they were, doing what they were doing.

The creation of a fantasy that starts from the ground up is something else again. Melancholy men, they say, are the most incisive humorists; by the same token, writers of fantasy must be, within their own frame of work, hardheaded realists. What appears gossamer is, underneath, solid as prestressed concrete. What seems so free in fantasy is often inventiveness of detail rather than complicated substructure. Elaboration—not improvisation.

And the closer a self-contained imaginary world draws to a recognizably real one (Tolkien's Middle Earth instead of Carroll's Wonderland) the more likely its pleasant meadows are to conceal unsuspected deadfalls and man-traps. The writer is wise if he explores it thoroughly and eliminates them. His world must be all of a piece, with careful and consistent handling of background, implements, and characters.

I began discovering the importance of consistency as a result of some of the research for *Time Cat,* originally planned to include an adventure in ancient Wales. Surely everyone cherishes a secret, private world from the days of childhood. Mine was Camelot, and Arthur's Round Table, Malory, and the *Mabinogion.* The Welsh research brought it all back to me. Feeling like a man who has by accident stumbled into an enchanted cavern lost since boyhood, both terrified and awestruck, I realized I would have to explore further. Perhaps I had been waiting to do so all these years, and some kind of moment had come. In any case, I replaced the Welsh episode with an Irish one and later turned all my attention not to the beautiful land of Wales I knew in reality, but an older, darker one.

My first intention was to base a fantasy on some of the tales in the *Mabinogion,* and I started research accordingly. However, I soon found myself delving deeper and deeper into the legends' origins and significance: searching for what exactly I didn't know—to the despair even of the librarians, who must be among the most patient people on earth. A historical-realistic approach did not work. Unlike the Irish and Norse, the Welsh mythology has been irreparably tampered with, like so many pictures, old and new, cut apart and pasted every which way.

Sifting the material, hoping to find whatever I was groping for, I accumulated box after box of file cards covered with notes, names, relationships, and I learned them cold. With great pains I began constructing a kind of family tree or genealogical chart of mythical heroes. (Eventually I found one in a book, already done for me. Not the first book, but the fifteenth!) Nothing suited my purposes.

At that point, the Muse in Charge of Fantasy, seductive in extremely filmy garments, sidled into my work room. "Not making much headway, are you? How would it be," she murmured huskily, "if you invented your own mythology? Isn't that what you *really* want to do?"

She vanished. I was not to see her again in her aspect as temptress, but only as taskmistress. For she was right.

Abandoning all I had collected, I began once more, planning what eventually became *The Book of Three*. My previous labor had not been entirely in vain; it had given me roots, suggestions, possibilities. In addition, I was now free to do as I pleased. Or so I thought.

True enough, the writer of fantasy can start with whatever premises he chooses (actually, the uncomplicated ones work best). In the algebra of fantasy, A times B doesn't have to equal B times A. But, once established, the equation must hold throughout the story. You may set your own ground rules and, in the beginning, decree as many laws as you like— though in practice the fewer departures from the "real" world the better. A not-very-serious breach and the fantasy world explodes just as surely as if a very real hydrogen bomb had been dropped on it. With inconsistency (so usual in the real world), the machinery moving the tale grinds and screeches; the characters cease to be imaginary and become simply unreal. Truth drains out of them. Admittedly, certain questions have to be begged, such as "How did all these people get here in the first place?" But they are like the axioms of geometry, questioned only by metaphysicians.

Once committed to his imaginary kingdom, the writer is not a monarch but a subject. Characters must appear plausible in their own setting, and the writer must go along with their inner logic. Happenings should have logical implications. Details should be tested for consistency. Shall animals speak? If so, do *all* animals speak? If not, then which—and how? Above all, why? Is it essential to the story, or lamely cute? Are there enchantments? How powerful? If an enchanter can perform such-and-such, can he not also do so-and-so? These were a few of the more obvious questions raised by the Muse, now disguised behind steel-rimmed spectacles. Others were less straightforward.

"This person, Prince Gwydion," she said, "I presume, is meant to be a heroic figure. But what I should like to know is this," she added in an irritating, pedantic voice, "how is he different from an ordinary human being?"

I replied that I was prepared to establish that Gwydion, though not invincible, had a somewhat longer life span, greater strength and physical endurance. If he had powers of enchantment, these were to be limited in logical ways. I admitted, too, that he would nonetheless get hungry, thirsty, and tired.

"All very well," she said. "But is that the essential? Is he a human being with only a little more capacity? You must tell me how he is truly and rationally different."

I had begun to sweat. "He—he knows more? Experience?" I choked.

"He sees the meaning of things. Wisdom."

"I shall accept that," she said. "See that you keep it in mind."

On another occasion, I had planned to include a mysterious and menacing portent in the shape of a dark cloud. The Muse, an early riser, prodded me awake sometime well before dawn.

"I've been meaning to speak with you about that cloud," she said. "You like it, don't you? You think it's dramatic. But I was wondering if this had occurred to you: you only want a few of your people to see the cloud, is that not correct? Yet you have already established a number of other characters in the vicinity who will see it, too. An event like that? They'll do nothing but talk about it for most of the story. Or," she purred, as she always does before she pounces, "did you have something like closed-circuit television in mind?"

She clumped off in her sensible brogans while I flung myself from bed and ripped up all my work of the night before. The cloud was cut out.

Her subsequent interrogations were no gentler. Perhaps I should have foreseen all her questions and spared myself much revision. In defense, I can only say that I must often put something on paper and test the idea in practice. I did, gradually, grow more aware of pitfalls and learned to distinguish the telltale signs of mare's-nests.

The less fantastic it is, the stronger fantasy becomes. The writer can painfully bark his shins on too many pieces of magical furniture. Enchanted swords, wielded incautiously, cut both ways. But the limits imposed on characters and implements must be more than simply arbitrary. What does not happen should be as valid as what does. In *The Once and Future King,* for example, Merlyn knows what will happen in the future; he knows the consequences of Arthur's encounter with Queen Morgause. Why doesn't he speak out in warning? It is not good enough to say, "Well, that would spoil the story." Merlyn cannot interfere with destiny; but how does T. H. White show this in *specific* detail? By having Merlyn grow backwards through time. Confused in his memories, he cannot recollect whether he has already told Arthur or was going to tell him. No more is needed. The rationale is economical and beautiful, fitting and enriching Merlyn's personality.

Insistence on plausibility and rationality can work for the writer, not against him. In developing his characters, he is obliged to go deeper instead of wider. And, as in all literature, characters are what ultimately count. The writer of fantasy may have a slight edge on the realistic novelist, who must present his characters within the confines of actuality. Fantasy, too, uses homely detail, but at the same time goes right to the core of a character, to extract the essence, the very taste of an individual personality. This may be one of the things that makes good fantasy so convincing. The essence is poetic truth.

The distillation process, unfortunately, is unknown and must be classed as a Great Art or a Major Enchantment. If a recipe existed, it could be reproduced; and it is not reproducible. We can only see the results. Or hear

them. Of Kenneth Grahame—and the same applies to all great fantasists—
A. A. Milne writes: "When characters have been created as solidly . . .
they speak ever after in their own voices."

These voices speak directly to us. Like music, poetry, or dreams, fantasy
goes straight to the heart of the matter. The experience of a realistic work
seldom approaches the experience of fantasy. We may sail on the
Hispaniola and perform deeds of derring-do. But only in fantasy can we
journey through Middle Earth, where the fate of an entire world lies in the
hands of a hobbit.

Fantasy presents the world as it should be. But "should be" does not
mean that the realms of fantasy are Lands of Cockaigne where roasted
chickens fly into mouths effortlessly opened. Sometimes heartbreaking, but
never hopeless, the fantasy world as it "should be" is one in which good is
ultimately stronger than evil, where courage, justice, love, and mercy
actually function. Thus, it may often appear quite different from our own.
In the long run, perhaps not. Fantasy does not promise Utopia. But if we
listen carefully, it may tell us what we someday may be capable of achieving.

World Beyond World

P. L. Travers

P. L. Travers, the creator of the famous Mary Poppins, is a native Australian who has lived in London, the United States, and Ireland. In addition to writing the Mary Poppins stories, published between 1934 and 1952, she has written for magazines, lectured widely, and been writer-in-residence at Smith College and at Radcliffe College. Among her lectures on children's literature are "Only Connect,"[1] presented at the Library of Congress for National Children's Book Week in 1966, and "On Not Writing for Children," presented at the Amriswil, Switzerland, Congress of the International Board on Books for Young People in 1968.

Many are the times I have seen them lying in their pools, or under a cliff at the lacy edge of the tide, sea eggs that are neither rock nor wave and yet somehow compact of both, stones scribbled and shaped and brooded upon by wings and feathers of water.

But I never guessed—it took L. M. Boston, the author of the *Green Knowe* books, to teach me my biology—that one of them might possibly hatch out a Triton. Well, it has happened. And we owe our knowledge of the event to two of Mrs. Boston's sensible, ordinary little boys. When I say ordinary, I do so with intent, not at all meaning commonplace but giving this great word a ghostly capital letter, knighting it, as it were, and saying Arise! For it takes the ordinary to comprehend, even to be related to, the extraordinary, just as, in order to fly, you need firm ground to take off from. In airiness we lose all sense of air, let alone earth; in the poetic, poetry; in childishness, the child. It is solidity that gives us wings.

These two determined children in *The Sea Egg* (Harcourt Brace, Jovanovich, Inc., illustrated by Peter Boston, 94 pp., $2.50) pursue their adventure with far more concentration and maturity than is discernible in their parents and, as a result, the impossible happens. For a short time, or a long time—all is timeless here—we accompany them and the wonderful mer-boy through the moving ocean world, submerging, coming up for air, exploring the intestinal tunnels under islands, rubbing shoulders with seals, ourselves all but blowing the wreathed horn. Yet the children, even the Triton, are really supernumeraries. The true hero of the story is the sea itself. It is strange to me, as an islander, to remember that there are millions of people who have never looked upon the true skin of their planet, which is the sea. Never mind; in *The Sea Egg* they can drench themselves in it. The

"World Beyond World" (review of *The Sea Egg* by Lucy Boston) by P. L. Travers from *Book Week*, Spring Children's Issue (May 7, 1967): 4–5. Reprinted by permission of Chicago Sun-Times.

1. Published in *Quarterly Journal of the Library of Congress*, 24 (October 1967): 232–248.

book, indeed, might have been written by a seal, a relative, perhaps, of the Great Silkie in the Scottish ballad of Sule Skerry. The writer's element is here so manifestly water that at the end of the adventure the reader himself feels a stranger to land and listens nostalgically for the clamor of waves on the shore.

It is this ability to surrender himself to his own particular data, to the world beyond the visible world, the fact beyond the newspaper fact, that is the mark of the true storyteller. He creates—no, not creates—he harkens in to (as they call listening to the radio in Devon) and becomes an historian of the principality that interpenetrates and permeates our daily world, a country with laws and customs that are, within its own boundaries, valid and absolute. A reader given to splitting hairs—is this true, could it really happen?—will naturally not accept these laws. What matter? He is free to emigrate simply by closing the book.

The Sea Egg certainly comes from this kingdom and the *Green Knowe* books are already established there among the archives, existing not merely as literature but as an exact description, five volumes long, of one particular corner of its countryside. It would need far more space than any editor would give me to list the virtues of their author but there are three—apart from the flowing, flexible prose—that I must take note of, three crowns that must be offered. To begin with, one is never aware that any of the stories has either beginning or end. It has obviously existed long before we picked up the book and will go on long after we have put it down; all goes back to Deuteronomy and forward to who knows where. Then, the point of view is always mature, here ripeness is all; sadness and evil are not minimized, nothing is glossed over, nothing made sentimental. Best of all, the books do not have the air of having been written for children. They appear to have been set down—and this is another mark of the storyteller—simply to please L. M. Boston! If children read them, good; if grown-ups read them, good: if nobody reads them, good—they still have to be told. And to stories that *have* to be told, people cannot help listening.

And then, the characters are so perfectly balanced and juxtaposed, like those in the fairy tales—the very old woman who has dropped so much of life and the young boy who has not yet taken on the burden of it are brought together at the mutual moment when each can perceive, not merely the five fingers of the hand, but what lies in the space between. From this unknown invisible all the stories arise. Time and space are, as it were, pleated, they fold back upon themselves. The living child plays with the children who long ago were his ancestors, a lullaby is sung today and "four hundred years ago a baby went to sleep." Family blood, like time, is a long and winding river; who knows whom we shall meet when we set out to cruise along it?

In the first two *Green Knowe* books—*The Children* and *The Treasure*—it was the old house and its magic garden into which the author submerged. She became herself carved stone and tree walking until we knew the shape, size, and smell of each room and the prick of the thorns on the rose bushes.

Then came *The River* and there she was, waterily winding through the meadows, flowing among ghostly apparitions, bearing the reader along with the drowned reflected moon.

There was nothing here to suggest, however—though had I been asked I would have admitted to not putting it past her—that in the next book she would become (well, practically) a gorilla. Of all the books *The Stranger at Green Knowe* is my favorite. Where else, except, perhaps, in George Schaller's *Year of the Gorilla,* will you find a more exact, more poignant, more perceptive evocation of the great sad noble "man-animal?" As I read it, I imagined the writer standing day after day in front of that double-barred cage in the London zoo, watching, breathing in, and at last merging with the huge spread-eagled figure. And the description of the gorilla family's innocent, antique jungle life is masterly. The book is a paean to all lost children, to all creatures far from home, all things caged and prisoned. The refugee child, Ping, and Hanno, the gorilla—the one so weak yet outside the cage, the other so strong but behind bars—are two creatures of one kind; in some cosmic sense, brothers. When Hanno escapes it is inevitably Ping who finds, protects, and feeds him and by keeping the secret—not easy for a child—gives him three precious days of freedom before he dies. This is the whole theme of the book—simple, indeed, but never falling into oversimplification. We understand and accept that things must be as they are. When Hanno is killed we feel grateful, we experience the same catharsis as we do in Greek tragedy when the great heroes die. Better that than a newsboy crying "Zoo Gorilla Captured."

The last—though I prefer the word latest, as being less final—of the *Green Knowe* books, *The Enemy,* has none of Hanno's large simplicity. It is, indeed, the most complicated of them all, dealing as it does with magic, and black magic at that. Or perhaps it is truer to say that its theme is the struggle of black with white. We have, of course, met these elements before at Green Knowe, the statue of St. Christopher standing over against Black Ferdie, Old Petronella, and Green Noah himself. They seemed to me, thus, to be rightly opposed. We live, after all, between two worlds—it is our human condition—the one above and the one beneath, good and bad confronting each other and man with a Janus face for each. But the occult world—though this may well be purely subjective—seems to me to jut out at an angle to both and, for all its power, to have also a sense of unreality. *The Enemy* gives us—and very learnedly—spells spelt backwards, plagues comparable to those of Egypt, ominous writings on the wings of a dead bat, and all the coven's array of witchcraft. Yet the whole dreadful canon has not as much power as one syllable of "Binahel, O thou my love! Cherubim, be my strength in the name of Adonai!" so admirably declaimed by Mr. Pope, a character on the side of the gods. In life it is difficult not to make good seem sentimental, in books it is difficult not to make evil seem inadequate. But the earth has bubbles as the water has and without *The Enemy* we would never have known the tricky pleasure of seeing the iced cake, refused politely by Miss Powers, go sidling across the table under its own steam and land in the hand stretched to receive it behind her back. Nor would we have experienced the magic mirror, only equalled by Snow White's, which, having shown so much of ill throughout the book, redeems itself at the end by reflecting a happy image—Ping's father, thought to be dead, walking towards the house.

No old-fashioned recognition scene, no explanations, for nothing so banal could come from this writer.

"We have seen Ping's father and mine in the glass," says Tolly, "opening the garden gate."

"And so it was," the book ends.

And since, with L. M. Boston, nothing either begins or ends, so it still is and will be. We can go to bed happy. How fortunate!

British editions of books mentioned with their American publishers only in this article:

Lucy Boston. *The Sea Egg.*   Faber.
   The *Green Knowe* books. Faber.

The Changing Role of Science Fiction in Children's Literature

Sylvia Engdahl

Now a full-time writer, Sylvia Engdahl has in the past taught elementary school and worked as a developer and tester of programs for computer-systems. Her books include Enchantress from the Stars, *a 1971 Newbery Medal Honor Book,* Journey Between Worlds *(1970),* The Far Side of Evil *(1971), and* This Star Shall Abide *(1972).*

When casual acquaintances learn that I am a writer, they naturally ask what I write; and at my reply, "Science fiction for young people," they are apt to respond with surprise. I know what is going on in their minds. Being somewhat shy and formal, I do not seem the sort who would even read, let alone write, anything matching the average person's conception of science fiction. Those unfamiliar with the field of children's literature envision "teen-age" science fiction in particular as melodrama of the comic book and television variety, and I usually find myself at a loss for words to bridge the gap.

The situation is different when I appear on a panel of local authors, since the people to whom I then speak—both children and the adults who work with them—are aware that modern novels for teen-agers have a serious intent. Still, while a good many of the boys like science fiction, relatively few of the women and girls do. On several occasions I have been approached with the comment, "I didn't have any interest in science fiction until you started to talk about it." Though I am far from an effective speaker and my remarks had not been very inspired, I had aroused such an interest by making a seldom-recognized point: Not only is science fiction's potential appeal not confined to people who enjoy the type of adventure commonly thought of by that name, but neither is it limited to those who are interested in science.

Actually, I do not like the term "science fiction"; I never have—it is, I feel, rather misleading. Yet since no other term is available, I am obliged to use it. To be sure, *Enchantress from the Stars* (Atheneum) can also be classified as fantasy and may be enjoyed by fantasy enthusiasts who ordinarily would not choose a science fiction book; but it is not fantasy in a strict sense, for it has literal levels as well as symbolic ones. Its speculations about human evolution, like those of its sequel, *The Far Side of Evil* (Atheneum), are offered in all seriousness as theories that I myself consider tenable.

"The Changing Role of Science Fiction in Children's Literature" by Sylvia Engdahl from *Horn Book Magazine,* 47 (October 1971): 449–455. Reprinted by permission of Horn Book, Inc.

The line between science fiction and fantasy has always been hard to draw; it is defined in various ways. My personal view is that while both forms may, through the portrayal of a world other than our real world, express underlying truths about life as we now know it to be, science fiction also expresses ideas about things that are not yet known; and it does so without recourse to supernatural explanations—though it sometimes deals with phenomena normally thought to be "supernatural." The setting of the story plays no part in this distinction. C. S. Lewis's adult novels *Out of the Silent Planet* and *Perelandra* are often called science fiction because they happen to take place on Mars and Venus; yet to me they are no less pure fantasy than his Chronicles of Narnia, for their intent is equally allegorical. They present their author's vision of truth, as does all good fantasy, but it is not the same kind of truth as would be presented had Lewis chosen to portray Mars realistically. In other words, science fiction differs from fantasy not in subject matter but in aim, and its unique aim is to suggest real hypotheses about mankind's future or about the nature of the universe.

There is nothing inherently "scientific" in this aim, at least not unless "science" is defined in the broad but archaic sense of "knowledge." Indeed, like other works of imagination, science fiction is decidedly unscientific in that its hypotheses are based not upon systematic analysis, but upon free speculation. Fiction about the future must necessarily touch upon advances in science because new discoveries cannot fail to affect people's daily lives, but that does not mean that all of it must focus on technology. We read about automobiles without giving a second thought to the technology whereby they are produced; why should the same not be true of spaceships? Science fiction frequently does emphasize the technical aspects of future inventions, and this has great appeal for some children. Yet there are many others, especially girls, who have no interest in details of that kind and who therefore assume that science fiction is not to their taste. There is a feeling even among adults that anything connected with science is cold and inhuman, divorced from the realm of spiritual values— which is so, I think only when it is so presented. Science fiction's true scope encompasses far more than mere technological progress.

This fact, of course, is not news to dedicated fans, some of whom have been pointing out the social concern of the genre for years. But "fans" are an isolated group of people, for science fiction has been considered a separate genre in a more absolute sense than most other types of fiction, and with good reason. It has not been directed to the general public but has developed conventions and a jargon of its own that seem unreal or esoteric to the nonaficionado; and, in fact, novels with a less specialized appeal, even when set in the future, are sometimes not classed as science fiction at all. How often is Orwell's *Nineteen Eighty-four* placed in that category?

Nowadays, when so many subjects once wholly within the province of science fiction have emerged into that of everyday reality, it would seem that this separation between the genre and the mainstream of literature might be narrowing; and yet, by and large, this is not the case. Much current science fiction in its search for new themes and in response to the growing sophistication of its fans is becoming increasingly "far-out"—turning, for example, from speculation about human progress to less probable conjectures about the psychologies of nonhuman aliens. This is as it should be for this audience. It is happening in stories for young people as well as in those for adults, and when skillfully done, as in Andre Norton's books, it can greatly enrich the experience of those children with the background to comprehend it. But, at the same time, the advent of the space age has created a whole new audience: one attracted not so much by strange, bizarre, or exotic concepts as by the extension of the familiar and —to employ a much-overworked word—the relevant. With a few exceptions, notably some of Robert Heinlein's teen-age novels published in the fifties, even the best of "genre" science fiction leaves such readers cold.

It is for these people, people who are searching for touchstones in a rapidly changing world, that a different sort of science fiction is needed; and it is to them that I have directed my own books, sometimes to the confusion of the established fans. *Journey Between Worlds* (Atheneum), for instance, has been criticized by some for not being true "sci-fi"; yet the fact is that it was never intended to be, at least not in the fans' sense of the term. Nor was it aimed toward the readers to whom *Enchantress from the Stars* is most apt to appeal. *Journey Between Worlds* was written primarily for girls who like neither science nor fantasy, yet who wonder about what the future is going to bring. In exploring that question I feel there should be a wide variety of approaches; for the future is of interest to us all, whether we look to it with eagerness or with alarm, and whether or not we have any training or enthusiasm for science as such.

Yet, what are we to say of the future, and what, particularly, are we to say to children? We surely cannot provide a definitive description. Science fiction is not prophecy. It does not and cannot attempt to predict the precise form new developments will take. Moreover, like all art, it is selective; to create successfully a world with which readers will identify, the science-fiction writer must often ignore many of the changes that are likely to occur, concentrating on those pertinent to the story's theme while retaining a framework close enough to the reader's own background for him to supply the details that are not given. To be sure, science-fiction writers of the past have made some amazingly accurate forecasts; but stories about the future do not function as forecasts in the specific, literal sense. Rather, they serve to shape attitudes toward the future, and toward some of the possibilities the future may hold, as well as toward the universe that waits to be explored.

Considered in this light, the role of science fiction in children's literature is a significant one indeed. It has become so not because fictional speculations about moon landings have proven less fantastic than was formerly supposed, but because we live in an age when rapid change is both inevitable and, to the young, desirable. Many of today's children feel a closer kinship with the future than with the past; the popularity of historical fiction is declining, while that of science fiction is on the rise. Only through speculation about the future as related to the past can these readers gain the sense of continuity that their elders acquired through the study of history: the steadying realization that there is no jumping-off place, that past, present, and future are all part of one unbroken thread of time. Such a realization is essential if the problems of today are to be seen in any sort of perspective. We cannot tell the next generation what is going to happen; we do not know, and we will not be believed if we pretend otherwise—but we can and should suggest that whatever comes will be linked to some universal pattern, a pattern involving spiritual as well as physical principles into which further insight will someday be achieved.

Obviously, we cannot proffer these theoretical principles authoritatively except within the context of a given story, where the reader will be free to accept or reject them as he wishes. Yet, a science-fiction story, by its very nature, does present theory as fact, implicitly if not explicitly; and if it is well enough written for the action to seem convincing, the theories will be convincing, too. That is why the outlook of such stories is a matter of no small concern. I feel that anyone who writes science fiction for young people has a responsibility to consider carefully whether the outlook of the story is truly one that he wants to foster. An author who speaks to today's youth about the future must say what he believes about the future: not necessarily in regard to specific details (I do not, for example, believe that the peoples of other solar systems are as much like us in the physical and cultural sense as I portray them in my books) but certainly as far as philosophy is concerned. This is not always done in adult science fiction, and caution must therefore be used when that kind of fiction is given to children. Arthur Clarke prefaced his adult novel *Childhood's End* with the statement, "The opinions expressed in this book are not those of the author"; but even if such disclaimers were included wherever applicable, they would carry little meaning for young readers. The tour de force, the ingenious plot or concept that fascinates adult fans by virtue of its uniqueness and originality but that does not pretend to represent its author's actual opinions, is thus perilous fare in the hands of boys and girls who, consciously or unconsciously, may adopt its outlook as their own.

Perhaps this sounds so self-evident that it should not need to be said; still because comparatively few people draw a distinction between the impact of science fiction and that of other imaginative literature, its importance has rarely been taken into account. For instance, science fiction has traditionally depicted the more highly evolved beings of other planets either as hostile to less advanced people or as benevolent but presumptuous meddlers who think it their business to play God—traditions that in *Enchantress from the Stars* and *The Far Side of Evil* I have tried very hard to counteract. For is this how we want coming generations to view the hypothetical inhabitants of the universe? What is more, is this the conception of "advancement" we want them to form? We must not forget that what our own generation sees as pure allegory may not be dismissed as such by the young. There was a time when children thought "space people" to be in the same category as witches, fairies, and talking animals; they do not do so now. Today's children take the idea of an inhabited universe seriously, as do an increasing number of reputable scientists. Children know that the extraterrestrial aliens described in the books they read are as imaginary as the goblins in fairy tales, yet underneath they are forming basic attitudes about a topic to which they, or their descendants, may someday be required to give sober attention. Space travel was once imaginary too.

This is not to say that children should never be exposed to stories that deal with future invasion of Earth by hostile aliens; some such books—John Christopher's trilogy *The White Mountains, The City of Gold and Lead,* and *The Pool of Fire* (all Macmillan), for example—are of high quality and, on the symbolic level, contain much that is valid and worthwhile. Furthermore, perhaps hostile aliens do in fact exist. But if the theme of aliens as enemies were to predominate in the science fiction read by the first space-age generation, that generation would be bound to grow up with a somewhat different picture of the universe than the human race will eventually need to adopt. Thus, the body of science fiction as a whole must be judged not merely by its entertainment value nor even by its allegorical content, but also by the implications of any concepts that are subject to a literal interpretation. In fantasy we do not need to worry about the overall impression children will form of witches; witches can be presented as embodiments of evil without any effect on the evolving attitudes of mankind. With science fiction, however, the possibility of such an effect cannot be ignored.

Naturally, I am not suggesting that we should give children only science fiction having an outlook with which we as readers happen to agree. Opinions on what the future holds, or should hold, vary widely, and there is as much room for controversy in this area as in any other. The question to be posed is whether an author himself agrees with what his book is saying: not whether he really thinks that there is a planet somewhere inhabited by beings identical to those he has portrayed, for—of course—he does not; but whether his imaginative portrayal reflects his own real view of the universe. If it does, there will be no conflict between the various levels of the story; the symbolism, the underlying statement about life here and now, will not say one thing while the action, when taken at face value, says another. If, on the other hand, he is merely extrapolating from premises to which he does not subscribe—a common and accepted practice in adult science fiction—he runs the risk of inadvertently telling children something he does not mean to tell them.

All this, perhaps, makes science fiction sound very solemn and ponderous. I can hear people saying, "But shouldn't it be fun? Shouldn't it be read for pleasure instead of for deep, world-shaking philosophical messages?" Of course, it should! It should be romantic and exciting and, at times, humorous; and, certainly, philosophy should not outweigh story. But it will shape attitudes anyway. It will do so whether it is intended to or not, simply because children no longer assume that the future will be like the past. Critics sometimes claim that science fiction seeks to provide escape from reality; personally I feel that the reverse is true. I feel that it can offer a wider perspective on reality, leading young people to view the future not with our own era's gloom and despair, but with the broader realism of renewed hope.

British editions of books mentioned with their American publishers only in this article:

John Christopher. *The White Mountains.* Hamish Hamilton.
  The City of Gold and Lead. Hamish Hamilton.
  The Pool of Fire. Hamish Hamilton.

Chapter 7

Poetry

Evocative new editions of earlier poets, fresh volumes of the contemporary, anthologies of every form and subject, picture-poetry books with lavish illustration for the youngest, nonsense rhymes both original and traditional—the increased availability of poetry today for children and young people is striking. It has resulted naturally from the broadened interest in sharing poetry with the young and from the child's own increased delight in poetry which is presented attractively for pure enjoyment.

Children's interest in poetry is frequently awakened by hearing nursery rhymes. Nicholas Tucker, in "Why Nursery Rhymes," speaks of the delight in words to be found in them and notes that it "can lead to a direct short cut into poetry itself." Emile Cammaerts, the Belgian man of letters, in a discussion of nonsense, nursery rhymes, Lear, Carroll, and others, has written that "the technique of good nonsense verse is just as skilful and difficult as that of any other kind of verse. . . . If nonsense poetry is poetry run wild, it is a wildness which preserves and even emphasises its essential qualities. It is not necessarily the highest type of poetry, but it is the most poetical."[1]

However, some publishers and compilers are still offering the insipid, the deadening, and the sentimental in anthologies and textbooks. Critics have long inveighed against mistaken ideas of what children like. Andrew Lang in 1891 wrote in the introduction to his *Blue Poetry Book,* "It does not appear

---

1. "Nonsense and Poetry" from *"The Poetry of Nonsense,"* by Emile Cammaerts. Copyright 1925 by Emile Cammaerts. Reprinted by permission of Routledge & Kegan Paul Ltd.

to the Editor that poems about children, or especially intended for children, are those which a child likes best."[2] Agnes Repplier, in an article written in 1892 and reprinted here, offers surprisingly modern criticism: "It has been often demonstrated, and as often forgotten, that children do not need to have poetry written down to their intellectual level, and do not love to see the stately Muse ostentatiously bending to their ear." In agreement, a modern English poet, James Reeves, said in an address to a library conference:

> The qualities that one looks for in children's verse are still, I suppose, best shown in the things that do endure in children's poems—nursery rhymes and the best poems of Walter de la Mare, for example. These have almost the opposite qualities to those that one often associates with children's literature, which are provided by the numerous mistaken purveyors of children's verse who sentimentalize children by making the verse cosy and sloppy. . . . We must always provide poetry in such a way that it creates, and nourishes a continuing craving for poetry and does not kill it by making poetry seem something childish.[3]

And Scottish poet Edwin Muir advises, "The more genuine the imaginative quality of a poem, the deeper the enjoyment children will find in it." Poetry "should not be obviously moral in intention" or realistic or "contain, in short, anything that will weaken its purely imaginative force." It is Muir's conviction that an anthology of poetry for children "should contain nothing that is not the best of its kind. If the second-rate or fake is let in, it will discourage the natural love that children have for poetry, and the discouragement may last a lifetime."

Modern poets are injecting a fresh, invigorating impulse into children's book publishing, and the increased interest of children and young people in poetry has led to a revival in publication of poetry written by the young. Such voices as those of Eve Merriam and June Jordan and the ethnic poetry of American Indians, Eskimos, and blacks have not only awakened but sustained children's natural love of poetry.[4]

---

2. *The Blue Poetry Book* (London: Longmans, Green and Company, 1891), p. x.

3. "Writing for Children," *Proceedings, Papers and Summaries of Discussions at the Brighton Conference* (London: Library Association, 1958), p. 13.

4. For collections of ethnic poetry see John Bierhorst, ed., *In the Trail of the Wind* (New York: Farrar, Straus & Giroux, Inc., 1971) and Hattie Jones, ed., *The Trees Stand Shining; Poetry of the North American Indians* (New York: The Dial Press, Inc., 1971) for American Indian poetry; James Houston, *Ghost Paddles* (New York: Harcourt Brace Jovanovich, Inc., 1972) for Eskimo poetry; and June Jordan, *Some Changes* (New York: E. P. Dutton & Co., Inc., 1971) for black poetry. Collections of poems written by children include Richard Lewis, comp., *Miracles: Poems by Children of the English-speaking World* (New York: Simon & Schuster, Inc., 1966. London, Allen Lane, 1967) and Nancy Larrick, comp., *I Heard a Scream in the Street: Poems by Young People in the City* (New York: M. Evans & Co., Inc., 1970).

Why Nursery Rhymes?

Nicholas Tucker[1]

Nursery rhymes, as Andrew Lang once said, are like "smooth stones from the brook of time, worn round by constant friction of tongues long silent." The shapes and patterns that have finally emerged in what is probably the best-known literature of the English-speaking world have almost immeasurable possibilities for each generation of children.

In the field of linguistics, nursery rhymes, with their easily memorised rhymes, alliterative titles and infectious, foot-tapping rhythms, are ideally formed to help a baby master speech. Some of the first rhymes he will learn are those associated with jolly, knee-riding games, like "Trit trot to Boston, trit trot to Lynn," each word underlined by a hefty bounce. It will be a slow child who does not soon learn how to ask for a repeat performance of all this, especially as this particular rhyme, like so many other infant games, has the additional fun and mild tension of testing a child out against a common fear, in this case the idea of being dropped ("Look out, little boy, or you'll fall IN!").

Other rhymes familiarise themselves by carefully leaving a space for the baby's name ("And there will be plenty for . . . and me!") or by using a question and answer technique encourage a child to respond in an early form of dialogue. In all this, there is no trace of the deadening over-simplification that tends to run through literature that has been deliberately constructed for the use of children. Nursery rhymes, with their largely random origin, make use of some comparatively complex grammatical structures and certainly a wide vocabulary—of enormous help in the child's further linguistic development. For example, the frequent use of synonyms in nursery rhymes helps broaden the idea of language: we hear about a "cold and frosty morning," or a coat that is "flimsy and thin." Sometimes a whole riddle is given over to this:

> Elizabeth, Elspeth, Betsy and Bess,
> They all went together to see a bird's nest;
> They found a bird's nest with five eggs in,
> They all took one and left four in.

In the same way, some simple concepts are teased out into their smaller, constituent, parts. For example, we hear of dun-horses, cock-horses,

---

"Why Nursery Rhymes?" by Nicholas Tucker from *Where* (September 1969): 152–155. Reprinted by permission of the Advisory Centre for Education.

1. For biographical information about the author, see p. 104.

mares, colts, foals, donkeys, asses and ponies, who may amble, trot, gallop, prance or even dance, but still be whipped, slashed, lashed, beaten or walloped for their pains.

Many archaic words too, that would certainly not slip through any so-called scientific "word-frequency count" used to construct infant reading primers, still survive in nursery rhymes to fascinate and mystify parents and children alike:

As high as a castle,
As weak as a wastle
And all the king's horses
Cannot pull it down.
(*Answer, a pillar of smoke*)

Riddles like these also introduce the idea that words can be manipulated and played with, as in tongue-twisters, puzzles and catches too. On other occasions, reality itself is played with, in rhymes like:

The man in the moon
Came down too soon,
And asked his way to Norwich:
He went by the south,
And burnt his mouth
With supping cold plum porridge.

Such topsy-turvy rhymes can help a child in the most delightful way, to spot the difference between sense and nonsense—at a time when he still tends to be naturally confused between some fact and some fantasy. Once he has grown out of this muddle there are other nursery rhymes that invite him to suspend his new-found logic and speculate on such strange but enticing prospects as "If all the world were apple pie," or "If all the trees were bread and cheese."

DELIGHT IN WORDS

Other rhymes use nonsense in a different way, coining new words for the sheer pleasure of the sound they make, very much as a child will, particularly when he is stimulated by rhymes like:

Highty, tighty, paradighty, clothed all in green,
The king could not read it, no more could the queen.

This delight in words, as Walter de la Mare pointed out, can act as a direct short cut into poetry itself. G. K. Chesterton once said that "Over the hills and far away" is one of the most beautiful lines in English poetry, and there are many others from the same source that he could also have chosen. In another field, the lovely little songs we sing to nursery rhymes, often in fact taken from 18th-century tunes, can lead at the most formative years to a life-long feeling for music.

Of course, there is far more to nursery rhymes than their linguistic and musical genius alone. Their choice of themes tends also to echo the development of a child's main interests. For a baby, this will include learning to find his way around his own body, from head to toe, and he will enjoy the cuddling, tickling games that go with rhymes like "Here sits the Lord Mayor" or "This little pig went to market." Later, he will learn to recognise some of the immediate objects around him, like the shoes, cats, dogs and birds, flowers, the weather, or colours that also crop up in nursery rhymes, sometimes capturing the extraordinary vividness of these early first impressions:

> Daffy-down-dilly is new come to town,
> In a yellow petticoat and a green gown.

Other main interests are dealt with in numerous rhymes about cooking and eating every type of food, playing with other children, losing and finding things, and parental wrath, with the occasional moment of praise too. There are many rhymes about going to bed and sleep, and then getting up, willingly or unwillingly, the following morning. There is also some traditional wisdom to be picked up, on matters to do with the weather ("Red sky at night: shepherd's delight"); the amount of sleep each person needs; or the time to change from winter to summer clothes. Although some of this advice may be more traditional than wise, its effect is the same: to give the child some glimpse of a few of the rules, *mores* and predictions that go to bring some order and control into the booming, buzzing confusion of the world around him.

COMING TO TERMS WITH ADULTHOOD

Later, the child may be more interested in those rhymes that describe aspects of adult behaviour he may be curious about, like the adult world of work, courtship, motherhood, old age and death. Such themes are taken up by nursery rhymes in a way that a child can accept and understand. Courtship, for example, is described in terms of food, where Curlylocks is tempted into matrimony by the prospect of unlimited strawberries and cream. On the other hand, in "There was a little man," the little maid is altogether more mercenary, but still in the concrete terms a child can appreciate.

Although the more obvious sexual references, mostly dating from pre-Victorian times, have on the whole been dropped from anthologies now, physical relationships themselves are described, generally in terms of kissing, and there is a general awareness of sexual roles, just as in children's games around this subject.

NO TABOO ON DEATH

Death, so often ignored as a theme in children's literature, occurs frequently in nursery rhymes. It can happen casually, as in "Solomon Grundy," or be the central topic, as in "Who Killed Cock Robin?" which is also a beautiful description of the mourning process, that resolves the initial sadness of the verse. Once again, one can only be grateful to nursery rhymes for treating this subject in a way that a child can take. Death is usually met in terms of animals, and with an emphasis on acceptance rather than on morbid grief. Some tough old rhymes, coming from a rural society where the slaughtering of animals was an everyday sight, may still upset a few children, but once again even for the very young child it is almost certainly better for him to face up to things in this way, since the whole topic is bound at some time to come up in his own fantasy life.

At the same time, the child's growing imagination will also be stimulated by the more fantastic of the nursery rhymes: the galleries of kings and queens, lions and unicorns, and the references to silver and gold, or lands across the sea:

How many miles to Babylon?
Three score miles and ten.
Can I get there by candle-light?
Yes, and back again.

Many of the other old characters and strange, inconsequential little stories will always somehow defy logic, and continue, as Walter de la Mare once said, to "free the fancy, charm tongue and ear, delight the inward eye," in the way that they have always done in the past. A few rhymes have a darker meaning, sometimes mysterious and haunting, but a necessary part of the literature of childhood, however much we may neglect it now.

In other ways, nursery rhymes bring to the surface many of the important aspects of a child's emotional development. The very internal contradictions he may be experiencing—the sudden swings between violence and contrition, love and resentment—will all be mirrored in nursery rhymes, where pussy cats are both petted and drowned, and children beaten as well as kissed. When hearing about the girl with a curl right in the middle of her forehead, children will recognise the same mixture of the very, very good and the horrid within themselves.

VIOLENCE: RESOLVED, NOT MAGNIFIED

A statistical analysis of nursery rhymes has revealed that just about half of the old favourites contain a measure of violence, law-breaking or personal injury. Children, with their own fantasies of violence to cope with, welcome this open and "permissible" expression of it all in nursery rhymes since in this way violence is both recognised and also controlled. In the same way older generations have always turned to the arts to explore some of their particular conflicts. The rhyme, metre and song of a nursery rhyme all help to put its subject matter into an acceptable, stylised context, where violence is resolved rather than magnified.

There are only a very few nursery rhymes I can think of where the violence does get in any sense out of control: in the whole lugubrious saga of "The Babes in the Wood," for example, where a cruel story is realistically dwelt upon without rescue or relief. There are also one or two rather crude 'frighteners," aimed at giving the child an unpleasant start, or generally terrifying him into acquiescence at bed time, which I have already discussed (*Books for Children,* WHERE supplement 15).

With these very few exceptions, I find the violence in nursery rhymes to be one of their major assets. They help to present the child, at an early age, with a picture that makes sense both of himself and of some of his feelings, and also of aspects of the violent world around him. Attempts in some anthologies to prune back these rhymes, or on the BBC *Listen with Mother* programme to omit old favourites like "Goosey Goosey Gander," in case they encourage children to violence, seem to me to be quite wrong-headed. Children will always have ideas about throwing old men downstairs, hurting pussy cats or stealing things, whether they read nursery rhymes or not, and it may do them much more good to exorcise such feelings in print than to brood over them in private.

Indeed, nursery rhymes do much to link children to their inner selves, and also to their own age group and to the central archetypes of their own culture. Rhymes like "Simple Simon," for example, belong directly to an ancient tradition of "Silly son" stories, which can be traced in folk-lore all over the world. Other rhymes—on the perpetual warfare between cat and mouse, spider and fly—have similarly ancient roots, just as some of the rhymes about birds may go back as far as the very venerable idea of a parliament of fowls. The whole tradition of giants, witches and talking animals, with their different character stereotypes, have important links with a child's imaginative life as well as with antiquity. When two children, therefore, find they have an immediate common bond in being able to join hands and play "Ring-a-ring-a-roses," they are not just forming contacts with each other (another important function of nursery rhymes, of course) but also linking up with all the millions of children who have played such games centuries ago.

At their most mundane level, nursery rhymes can also teach the alphabet, counting, the days of the week, months and seasons, the difference between left and right ("Which finger did he bite? This little finger on my right") and even elementary reading (as Mr. and Mrs. Opie have pointed out, a child who knows a favourite rhyme by heart, and pretends to read it aloud, may in fact learn to do so). They are also full of historical references. These are not so much aimed at distinct historical figures, despite the thousands of ingenious but wrong speculations that have been made in this direction, but on the whole refer more generally to a distant, rural way of life—a time of different habits and beliefs. . . .

The Children's Poets

Agnes Repplier[1]

Now and then I hear it affirmed by sad-voiced pessimists, whispering in the gloom, that people do not read as much poetry in our day as they did in our grandfathers', that this is distinctly the era of prose, and that the poet is no longer, even as Shelley claimed, the unacknowledged legislator of the world. Perhaps these cheerless statements are true, though it would be more agreeable not to believe them. Perhaps, with the exception of Browning, whom we study because he is difficult to understand, and of Shakespeare, whom we read because it is hard to content our souls without him, the poets have slipped away from our crowded lives, and are best known to us through the medium of their reviewers. We are always wandering from the paths of pleasure, and this may be one of our deviations. Yet what matters it, after all, while around us, on every side, in schoolrooms and nurseries, in quiet corners and by cheerful fires, the children are reading poetry?—reading it with a joyous enthusiasm and an absolute surrendering of spirit which we can all remember, but can never feel again. Well might Sainte-Beuve speak bravely of the clear, fine penetration peculiar to childhood. Well might he recall, with wistful sighs, "that instinctive knowledge which afterwards ripens into judgment, but of which the fresh lucidity remains forever unapproached." He knew, as all critics have known, that it is only the child who responds swiftly, pliantly, and unreservedly to the allurements of the imagination. He knew that, when poetry is in question, it is better to feel than to think; and that with the growth of a guarded and disciplined intelligence, straining after the enjoyment which perfection in literary art can give, the first careless rapture of youth fades into a half-remembered dream.

If we are disposed to doubt the love that children bear to poetry, a love concerning which they exhibit a good deal of reticence, let us consider only the alacrity with which they study, for their own delight, the poems that please them best. How should we fare, I wonder, if tried by a similar test? How should we like to sit down and commit to memory Tennyson's Oenone, or Locksley Hall, or Byron's Apostrophe to the Ocean, or the battle scene in Marmion? Yet I have known children to whom every word of these and many other poems was as familiar as the alphabet; and a great deal more familiar—thank Heaven!—than the multiplication table or the capitals of the United States. A rightly constituted child may find the paths of knowledge hopelessly barred by a single page of geography or by a single sum in fractions; but he will range at pleasure through the paths of poetry,

"The Children's Poets" by Agnes Repplier from *Atlantic*, 69 (March 1892): 328–338.

1. For biographical information about the author, see p. 33.

having the open sesame to every door. Sir Walter Scott, who was essentially a rightly constituted child, did not even wait for a formal introduction to his letters, but managed to learn the ballad of Hardyknute before he knew how to read, and went shouting it around the house; warming his baby blood to fighting-point, and training himself in very infancy to voice the splendors of his manhood. He remembered this ballad, too, and loved it all his life, reciting it once with vast enthusiasm to Lord Byron, whose own unhappy childhood had been softened and vivified by the same innocent delights.

In truth, the most charming thing about youth is the tenacity of its impressions. If we had the time and courage to study a dozen verses to-day, we should probably forget eleven of them in a fortnight; but the poetry we learned as children remains, for the most part, indelibly fixed in our memories, and constitutes a little Golden Treasury of our own, more dear and valuable to us than any other collection, because it contains only our chosen favorites, and is always within the reach of reference. Once, when I was very young, I asked a girl companion—well known now in the world of literature—if she did not grow weary waiting for trains, which were always late, at the suburban station where she went to school. "Oh, no," was the cheerful reply. "If I have no book, and there is no one here to talk with, I walk up and down the platform and think over the poetry that I know." Admirable occupation for an idle minute! Even the tedium of railway traveling loses half its horrors if one can withdraw at pleasure into the society of the poets, and, soothed by their gentle and harmonious voices, forget the irksome recurrence of familiar things.

It has been often demonstrated, and as often forgotten, that children do not need to have poetry written down to their intellectual level, and do not love to see the stately Muse ostentatiously bending to their ear. In the matter of prose, it seems necessary for them to have a literature of their own, over which they linger willingly for a little while, as though in the sunny antechamber of a king. But in the golden palace of the poets there is no period of probation, there is no enforced attendance upon petty things. The clear-eyed children go straight to the heart of the mystery, and recognize in the music of words, in the enduring charm of metrical quality, an element of never-ending delight. When to this simple sensuous pleasure is added the enchantment of poetic images, lovely and veiled and dimly understood, then the delight grows sweeter and keener, the child's soul flowers into a conscious love of poetry, and one lifelong source of happiness is gained. But it is never through infantine or juvenile verses that the end is reached. . . .

Too often . . . the poet strives to adjust himself to what he thinks is the childish standard. He lowers his sublime head from the stars, and pipes with painstaking flatness on a little reed, while the children wander far away, and listen breathlessly to older and dreamier strains.

"She left the web, she left the loom,
She made three paces thro' the room,

She saw the water-lily bloom,
She saw the helmet and the plume,
    She looked down to Camelot.
Out flew the web and floated wide;
The mirror crack'd from side to side;
'The curse is come upon me,' cried
    The Lady of Shalott.''

Here is the mystic note that childhood loves, and here, too, is the sweet constraint of linked rhymes that makes music for its ears. How many of us can remember well our early joy in this poem, which was but as another and more exquisite fairy tale, ranking fitly with Andersen's Little Mermaid, and Undine, and all sad stories of unhappy lives! And who shall forget the sombre passion of Oriana, of those wailing verses that rang through our little hearts like the shrill sobbing of winter storms, of that strange tragedy that oppressed us more with fear than pity!

"When the long dun wolds are ribb'd with snow,
And loud the Norland whirlwinds blow,
    Oriana,
Alone I wander to and fro,
    Oriana.''

If any one be inclined to think that children must understand poetry in order to appreciate and enjoy it, that one enchanted line,

"When the long dun wolds are ribb'd with snow,''

should be sufficient to undeceive him forever. The spell of those finely chosen words lies in the shadowy and half-seen picture they convey,—a picture with indistinct outlines, as of an unknown land, where the desolate spirit wanders moaning in the gloom. The whole poem is inexpressibly alluring to an imaginative child, and its atmosphere of bleak despondency darkens suddenly into horror at the breaking off of the last line from visions of the grave and of peaceful death,—

"I hear the roaring of the sea,
    Oriana.''

The same grace of indistinctness, though linked with a gentler mood and with a softer music, makes the lullaby in The Princess a lasting delight to children, while the pretty cradle-song in Sea Dreams, beginning,

"What does little birdie say
In her nest at peep of day?''

has never won their hearts. Its motive is too apparent, its nursery flavor too pronounced. It has none of the condescension of Minnie and Winnie, and grown people can read it with pleasure; but a simple statement of obvious truths, or a simple line of obvious reasoning, however dexterously narrated in prose or verse, has not the art to hold a youthful soul in thrall.

If it be a matter of interest to know what poets are most dear to the children around us, to the ordinary "apple-eating" little boys and girls for whom we are hardly brave enough to predict a shining future, it is delightful to be told by favorite authors and by well-loved men of letters what poets first bewitched their ardent infant minds. It is especially pleasant to have Mr. Lang admit us a little way into his confidence, and confess to us that he disliked Tam O'Shanter, when his father read it aloud to him; preferring, very sensibly, "to take his warlocks and bogies with great seriousness." . . .

"Poetry came to me with Sir Walter Scott," says Andrew Lang; with Marmion, and the Last Minstrel, and The Lady of the Lake, read "for the twentieth time," and ever with fresh delight. Poetry came to Scott with Shakespeare, studied rapturously by firelight in his mother's dressing-room, when all the household thought him fast asleep, and with Pope's translation of the Iliad, that royal road over which the Muse has stepped, smiling, into many a boyish heart. Poetry came to Pope—poor little lame lad—with Spenser's Faerie Queene; with the brave adventures of strong, valiant knights, who go forth, unblemished and unfrighted, to do battle with dragons and "Paynims cruel." And so the links of the magic chain are woven, and child hands down to child the spell that holds the centuries together. I cannot bear to hear the unkind things which even the most tolerant of critics are wont to say about Pope's Iliad, remembering as I do how many boys have received from its pages their first poetic stimulus, their first awakening to noble things. What a charming picture we have of Coleridge, a feeble, petulant child, tossing with fever on his little bed, and of his brother Francis, stealing up, in defiance of all orders, to sit by his side and read him Pope's translation of Homer. The bond that drew these boys together was forged in such breathless moments and in such mutual pleasures; for Francis, the handsome, spirited sailor lad, who climbed trees, and robbed orchards, and led all dangerous sports, had little in common with his small, silent, precocious brother. "Frank had a violent love of beating me," muses Coleridge, in a tone of mild complaint (and no wonder, we think, for a more beatable child than Samuel Taylor it would have been hard to find). "But whenever that was superseded by any humor or circumstance, he was very fond of me, and used to regard me with a strange mixture of admiration and contempt." More contempt than admiration, probably; yet was all resentment forgotten, and all unkindness at an end, while one boy read to the other the story of Hector and Patroclus, and of great Ajax, with sorrow in his heart, pacing round his dead comrade, as a tawny lioness paces round her young when she sees the hunters coming through the woods. As a companion picture to this we have little Dante Gabriel Rossetti playing Othello in the nursery, and so carried away by the passionate impulse of these lines,

> "In Aleppo once,
> Where a malignant and a turban'd Turk
> Beat a Venetian and traduced the state,
> I took by the throat the circumcised dog,
> And smote him, thus,"

that he struck himself fiercely on the breast with an iron chisel, and fainted under the blow. We can hardly believe that Shakespeare is beyond the mental grasp of childhood, when Scott, at seven, crept out of bed on winter nights to read King Henry IV, and Rossetti, at nine, was pierced to the soul by the agony of Othello's remorse. . . .

Mr. Stevenson is one of the few poets whose verses, written especially for the nursery, have found their way straight into little hearts. His charming style, his quick, keen sympathy, and the ease with which he enters into that brilliant world of imagination wherein children habitually dwell make him their natural friend and minstrel. If some of the rhymes in A Child's Garden of Verses seem a trifle bald and babyish, even these are guiltless of condescension; while others, like Travel, Shadow March, and The Land of Story-Books, are instinct with poetic life. I can only regret that a picture so faultless in detail as Shadow March, where we see the crawling darkness peer through the window pane, and hear the beating of the little boy's heart as he creeps fearfully up the stair, should be marred at its close by a single line of false conception:—

> "All the wicked shadows coming, tramp, tramp, tramp,
> With the black night overhead."

So fine an artist as Mr. Stevenson must know that shadows do not tramp, and that the recurrence of a short, vigorous word which tells so admirably in Scott's William and Helen, and wherever the effect of sound combined with motion is to be conveyed, is sadly out of place in describing the ghostly things that glide with horrible noiselessness at the feet of the frightened lad. Children, moreover, are keenly alive to the value and the suggestiveness of terms. A little eight-year-old girl of my acquaintance, who was reciting Lord Ullin's Daughter, stopped short at these lines,

> "Adown the glen rode armed men,
>   Their trampling sounded nearer,"

and called out excitedly, "Don't you hear the horses?" She, at least, heard them as if with the swift apprehension of fear, heard them loud above the sounds of winds and waters, and rendered her unconscious tribute of praise to the sympathic selection of words. . . .

The question at issue . . . is not so much what kind of poetry is wholesome for children as what kind of poetry do children love. In nineteen cases out of twenty that which they love is good for them, and they can guide themselves a great deal better than we can hope to guide them. I once asked a friend who had spent many years in teaching little girls and boys whether her small pupils, when left to their own discretion, ever chose any of the pretty, trivial verses out of new books and magazines for study and recitation. She answered, Never. They turned instinctively to the same old favorites she had been listening to so long; to the same familiar poems that their fathers and mothers had probably studied and recited before them. Hohenlinden, Glenara, Lord Ullin's Daughter, Young Lochinvar, Rosabelle, To Lucasta on Going to the Wars, the lullaby from The Princess, Lady Clara Vere de Vere, Annabel Lee, Longfellow's translation of The Castle by the Sea, and The Skeleton in Armor,—these are the themes of which children never weary; these are the songs that are sung forever in their secret Paradise of Delights. . . .

We adults pass our days, alas, in the Town of Stupidity,—abhorred of Bunyan's soul,—and our companions are Mr. Worldly Wiseman, and Mr. Despondency, and Mr. Want-wit, still scrubbing his Ethiopian, and Mr. Feeble-mind, and the deplorable young woman named Dull. But it is better to be young, and to see the golden light of romance in the skies, and to kiss the white feet of Helen, as she stands like a star on the battlements. It is better to follow Hector to the fight, and Guinevere to the sad cloisters of Almesbury, and the Ancient Mariner to that silent sea where the death-fires gleam by night. Even to us who have made these magic voyages in our childhood there comes straying, at times, a pale reflection of that early radiance, a faint, sweet echo of that early song. Then the streets of the Town of Stupidity grow soft to tread, and Falstaff's great laugh frightens Mr. Despondency into a shadow. Then Madeline smiles on us under the wintry moonlight, and Porphyro steals by with strange sweets heaped in baskets of wreathed silver. Then we know that with the poets there is perpetual youth, and that for us, as for the child dreaming in the firelight, the shining casements open into fairyland.

A Child's World Is as a Poet's

Edwin Muir

A Scottish poet, critic, translator, novelist, and prose writer, Edwin Muir (1887–1959) achieved a well-deserved fame. As a critic he was scrupulously fair and independent in judgment, and his criticism was regarded by T. S. Eliot as the best of our time. Among his critical works are Transition *(1926),* The Structure of the Novel *(1928),* Essays on Literature and Society *(1949), and* The Estate of Poetry *(1962). Muir's best prose work,* An Autobiography, *was published in 1954 and his collected poems came out in 1960.*

When he is most lucky, the poet sees things as if for the first time, in their original radiance or darkness; a child does this too, for he has no choice. He is new in the world, and everything in the world is new to him. He does not ask or know, in that first state, whether the objects he sees are useful or not. They are, as they are to the poet, of complete novelty and hidden meaning; and if the child stretches out his hand for them, that is because he wants to bring them close and discover what they really are.

Later he will wish to own them, but that means that he has already set out on the road of experience; and the things he is so determined to own he will never see again as if for the first time. They no longer exist for themselves in their own world, but have become a part of his. He looks at them with affection and the jealousy of the proprietor; he never tires of examining them and fondling them; and his devotion to them is partly a discipline in the art of loving things, and partly an assertion of his absolute rule over his own small province. He is an arbitrary ruler, can pull the cat's tail or smother it in caresses, or kiss or abuse the doll. He becomes awkward, torn between these two desires: the very image of the adolescent, and often of the grown-up.

There are a great number of things which he still cannot own, which still exist for him in their own world, and these for a few years he will continue to see as if for the first time: men and women, horses, trees, trains, automobiles. The orient corn still stands for him from everlasting to everlasting, as it did for the child Traherne, and the colored world has still a radiance which habit later will steal away. Poets such as Traherne, Vaughan, Blake and Wordsworth testify to the reality of this childish vision. What kind of poetry is likely to be taken most naturally into that early world which renews itself with every generation and is a world of its own within the greater world?

"A Child's World Is as a Poet's" by Edwin Muir from *New York Times Book Review*, v. 60, pt. 2 (November 13, 1955): 1, 44. © 1955 by The New York Times Company. Reprinted by permission.

The child not only sees with this unique clarity the things around him; he also wishes to know how they came to be there; this takes him into the past, and he demands to hear the story. I remember as a child how eager I was to learn all about the life of my father and mother, and how strange their lives were to me; and the things which happened to them before I was born filled me with wonder. They had many stories of witches and fairies, and of good and evil deeds; I believed everything, and enjoyed the evil as much as the good, as I think all children do; and the bad witch, the good minister, the kind man and the cunning man, all seemed to have a natural place of their own in the world. The pattern of life seemed to become clear as I listened to the stories and the songs, all of them quite simple even when they told of marvels, and all without a single didactic note.

When my father said descriptively, "He was a good man," or "He was a bad man," I accepted his words merely as a necessary classification, not as an occasion for moralizing. After I went to school I encountered the didactic poem with a moral lesson or a comforting ending, and like most of my playmates I recognized it as false, and though professing an outward respect, was inwardly bored. I suppose I felt, without knowing it, that childhood was regarded by grown-ups as an artificial state for which this artificial verse had to be fabricated. The magic which had delighted me in the old songs and ballads sung in our house was not to be found in these improving poems.

As for the sort of poetry that appeals to children, one has to go on what one can remember of one's own experience, and on the general experience which is attested by the lasting popularity among children of such things as Grimm's and Andersen's fairy tales. I think that children can be enchanted by any poem which opens their minds to the world of imagination, and it does not matter whether the things they find there are terrifying or delightful. The more genuine the imaginative quality of a poem, the deeper the enjoyment children will find in it. The more wonderful the events it describes, the greater the credulity that will rise to meet it. The poem should tell of the past, and make the child aware of the strangeness of time, about which he speculates, in any case, as soon as speculation is given him.

The poem should not be obviously moral in intention, else it will kill imagination to make a point. It must not be realistic, for realism is learned from experience. It should not, on any account, deal with relations between parents and children; that must be left to parents. It must not exhort children to be kind to other children or to animals, on pain of encouraging sentimentality; more practical means are needed for that. It must not contain, in short, anything that will weaken its purely imaginative force.

On the other hand, the poem may legitimately be a mere nonsensical jingle, for children are intensely interested in words, and often make up a secret language of their own. So that

Hey diddle diddle,
The cat and the fiddle,
The cow jumped over the moon;

is perfectly acceptable, and needs no explanation. But these jingles must not be self-consciously quaint or facetious, or they will be immediately detected.

It is for these reasons that an anthology of poetry for children should be chosen, like other anthologies, with a high respect for its audience, and should contain nothing that is not the best of its kind. If the second-rate or the fake is let in, it will discourage the natural love that children have for poetry, and the discouragement may last a lifetime. Every poem in the anthology should be of such quality that the experienced lover of poetry will find pleasure in it when he has long since left childhood behind. It may be thought that this sets an impossibly high standard. But there is in fact a superabundance of great poetry which a child can spontaneously enjoy and understand in his own way: the ballads, both sad and happy, the carols, the folk-songs, songs in Elizabethan plays, Shakespeare's above all, Blake's songs, and in them can appear the tiger as well as the lamb, such poems as "The Ancient Mariner" and in general anything that sings; and on a lower plane the fantastic rhymes of Lewis Carroll and Edward Lear. Children can enjoy what they do not understand. There was a play-rhyme once sung by young girls:

Water, water, wall-flower,
Growing up so high.
We are all maidens,
And we must all die.

It has the very dying fall of melancholy, and yet it was sung with sorrowful delight by generations of children. Such verses nourish the child's sense of wonder, and that is perhaps the best thing a child's anthology can do; for without encouragement wonder is likely to pine in the routine of life, and with it imagination.

Chapter 8

Fiction and Realism

A discussion of fiction and realism raises many questions regarding the most persistent controversial issues surrounding contemporary literature for young people. Is the "new realism" in books dealing with social and psychological problems reverting to the old didacticism? Would it be better to present such problems in nonfiction? Could writing with a purpose become a form of propaganda? Does an emphasis on the current, including the latest new vocabulary, seriously limit the life of a book? Does *realism* mean only the identifiably current? Does it mean only the unpleasant or tragic, as it apparently does to some? Can fantasy have realism as well as the "true" story?

There are, of course, varying definitions of realism. Elizabeth Enright has identified it as "less that which is current, factual, a part of known life, than that which is universal in the personality, action, and reaction of the characters, whether they are people, animals, or even objects."[1] In "The Long Life of Jane Cares," reprinted in this chapter, she reviews the work of an author who does present children realistically, commenting, "Not many writers of children's books dare to make children as real as they are. . . . "
Another kind of realism is recognized by a reviewer of Meindert DeJong's work. He feels it is the "exact and entertaining social observation," the "deep feeling for the life of a community" which creates excitement in DeJong's stories.

But the new realism of today, the realism which emphasizes themes reflecting current social problems and unrest, has raised in some the fear that honesty has simply become a mask for didacticism. Paula Fox, considering "the new kind of children's fiction," with its intention to deal

---

1. "Realism in Children's Literature," *Horn Book Magazine,* 43 (April 1967): 165–170.

with things as they really are, says, "We imagine that reality fairy tales are morally superior to fantasy fairy tales. We offer simulacra of truth to escape truth."[2] Mary Q. Steele, in "Realism, Truth, and Honesty," examines the current crop of "tell it like it is" novels and finds that in spite of the liberal sprinkling of neurotics, lushes, potheads, illegitimate pregnancies, abortionists, and pimps, they lack honesty. "I would define honesty," she continues, "as the open acknowledgment that a writer writes to be writing; he does not write to be heard. This is the real honest-to-God nitty-gritty: A writer who puts his audience's reaction before his own is dead."

Many other authors and critics agree that an author's honesty and freedom are of primary importance. Robert Burch writes in "The New Realism": "I have tried to use [grim] details for a purpose, the purpose not being to shock but to give as accurate a picture as possible of the events taking place in a story and of the time and place in which it is set. . . . [A] story should entertain the reader, in the sense of holding his attention and making him care about it; and I feel it is more apt to do this, that the characters and the action are more likely to ring true, if the person writing the story can discuss whatever matters most to him." Margery Fisher, in her Arbuthnot Honor Lecture, cautioned "We should not *expect* children's stories to be sermons or judicial arguments or sociological pamphlets. As independent works of art they must be allowed to appeal to the imagination, the mind, the heart on their own terms. . . . If a writer cannot say what he really feels, if he cannot be serious in developing a theme relevant to life today, if he has in any way to minimize, then he should surely not cast his material in the mould of a story for adolescents. [A book should not] be recommended because it delivers a strong message on an important question. This approach to books for the young must eventually dilute their quality as mainstream literature."[3] Finally, novelist Nat Hentoff writes of the weaknesses in books for young people:

> To read most of what is written for young readers is to enter a world that has hardly anything to do with what the young talk about, dream about, worry about, feel pain about. It is indeed a factitious world, and that kind of writing for teen-agers is not worth doing, because it is not worth their reading. But there may be a place in writing for the young for those authors of whatever age who have not forgotten the exultancy and the fear that are intertwined in possibility, who are neither didactic ('I was young once myself') or lost in the illusion that they can *be* young again. Who, in sum, are still struggling themselves with the question of what life is—and who feel there are things they can still learn along with the young.[4]

---

2. "Bitter-Coated Sugar Pills," *Saturday Review*, 53 (September 19, 1970): 34.

3. "Rights and Wrongs," *Top of the News*, 26 (June 1970): 373–391.

4. "Tell It Like It Is," *New York Times Book Review*, v. 72, pt. 2 (May 7, 1967): 3, 51. See also Sheila Egoff, "Children's Books: A Canadian's View of the Current American Scene," *Horn Book Magazine*, 46 (April 1971): 142–150.

The Long Life of Jane Cares

Elizabeth Enright[1]

Not too many years ago I was asked to read a number of manuscripts of children's stories in order to help form an opinion on which ones were publishable. I read dutifully and doggedly. I read three fairy tales, all dead as mutton; a story about live dolls who somehow never came to life; a pre-teen-age romance of sorts in which the conversation had all the spirited quality of cement. There was a competent tale of early life on the Great Plains, and rather a pleasant one about a truant and his dog; but I must confess a lot of sighing and yawning accompanied my reading.

Then I came to a manuscript called *A Lemon and a Star* by E. C. Spykman. "On her tenth birthday," I read, "Jane Cares was walking up the west end of the Summerton Village road back to the Red House. She was taking slow and careful steps so that her new sneakers would make clear, complete patterns in the soft gray dust. All the way from the old gate of the Big Field, where she had slipped out onto the road, they were perfect, and she was praying—lightly and without much hope—that the watering cart would not come by this afternoon and spoil them."

I pricked up my ears or my eyes—at any rate, my attention. Jane Cares, on a sunny summer day in 1907, was still energetically alive. As I read on, I discovered that she was carrying a small suitcase because she had every intention of leaving home forever and living in a tree. Her older brother, Theodore, had threatened to kill her after she has basted him in the neck with a mud pie of excellent, adhesive quality.

"If he caught you I guess he'd do it, too, Jane," her younger brother, Hubert, had assured her. It seemed prudent to retire from family life.

However, Jane's sanctuary had proved to be a failure. "Living in a tree was quite impractical. Nothing would stay where you put it."

As I went on, increasingly enchanted, I made the acquaintance of these brothers: thirteen-year-old Theodore, lordly, courageous, and impatient; eight-year-old Hubert, entirely, comfortably himself. And then the little sister, Edie, five years old, the thorn in everybody's flesh.

There were others: Father, a brisk, Teddy Rooseveltish type (Mother, as in so many children's books, was dead and nicely out of the way); the terrible-tempered Cook; the kindly parlor maid, Gander; eventually a beautiful and understanding stepmother; and others. But the four children were the important ones: the heart of the matter.

Each of these children, like Jane herself, lived with an almost electrical reality. I should say *live;* they do. Not many writers of children's books dare

---

"The Long Life of Jane Cares" by Elizabeth Enright from *Book Week,* Spring Children's Issue (May 8, 1966): 22. Reprinted by permission of Chicago Sun-Times.

1. For biographical information about the author, see p. 78.

to make children as real as they are; not many know how. Here was a writer who did. The Cares children fight, feud, laugh, cry, hate, enjoy, adventure, are bad as can be, magnanimous on occasion, loyal to each other in their own way, interesting always. And *funny*. I laughed out loud many times as I read. When I came to the end, I was sorry and felt deprived that there was no more.

Fortunately, there was another book before too long, and then another, and another, each one maintaining the pace and quality of the first.

The setting of the stories in itself is interesting. The era, the early 1900s, seems now as remote, as different from ours today as the era of Jane Austen. For people of means, like the Cares family, it was a fine era, fine to read about: a time of ample comfort, large, prosperous farms and fields, plenty of servants, horses, carriages, fat cattle, and above all, on the part of the adults, the absolute belief that they knew what they were doing and that what they were doing was *right;* a very comforting ambiance for a child.

Against this splendid background of total security (no wars, no hardships, plenty of aunts and uncles, a pleasant grandfather, pets, bicycles and horses to ride, a wide domain to wander in) the Cares children create their own dangers, dramas, and warfares. They are ardently individual, each one, and original to the core: fascinating to read about.

As for the dialogue, here are two examples. The first concerns Hubert, who cannot see the sense in fighting, a characteristic that exasperates Theodore into trying to explain.

"'Your honor, you ass,' Theodore had often told him. 'You fight for your honor.'"

"'I haven't got any,' said Hubert frankly.

"And what was worse, Hubert thought this was a good thing. 'If I had, with you and Jane around, I'd a been dead long ago.'"

And here are Edie and her friend Susan having an argument about North and South.

"What Susan did was to say out loud on the Main Street without any excuse except that her grandfather lived in Cambridge, Maryland, that she was for the South.

"'Do you want slaves?'" Edie had asked, shocked.

"'I wouldn't mind a slave or two,' said Susan carelessly.

"'Well, the South got beaten, so you can't have them,' said Edie, turning to walk backwards so she could see how Susan liked that.

"'The Southerners were a lot better-looking anyway,' said Susan, pushing her hair back.

"'Not than Abraham Lincoln,' said Edie quickly."

All their talk is bright, real, contentious, touching: *children's* talk. Never cute or bookish-virtuous. They, and their conversations, are tough, in the sinewy sense of the word. Vital. Alive.

There are only four of these precious books about the Cares children: *A Lemon and a Star; The Wild Angel; Terrible, Horrible Edie;* and *Edie on the Warpath.* In *Edie on the Warpath,* Mrs. Spykman's last book, 11-year-old

Edie, the Cares child who is oftenest in trouble, embarks upon a bitter battle to vindicate her sex. Scathing remarks by her worldly eldest brother, Theodore, as to the obvious inferiority of all girls, are emphasized by the new public spectacle of lady suffragettes in a struggle for their rights. Added to this is the rejection by ridicule of the one male object of her adoration: Greg Robinson.

Edie, rebellious, bad, bright and interesting (one could add lovable, though she probably wouldn't like it) wages ingenious and dedicated warfare, resentful of all males including God until almost the end of the story. Then the understanding of her stepmother, the wise, sympathetic words of a father who is not always sympathetic; but her own prized, dramatic, and utterly unnecessary display of courage restore Edie to a sense of proportion and a knowledge of happiness. A highly satisfactory conclusion to a highly satisfactory book.

Like the immortal stories of Louisa May Alcott, these by Mrs. Spykman possess an enduring vitality, an integrity that never wears thin; and like the stories of Louisa Alcott, there will be no more, for Mrs. Spykman died last year. Alas.

When Once a Little Boy . . .

Times Literary Supplement

> The pile of hay exploded under her. In paralysed surprise the hen
> sat sunken in hay, looking glassy-eyed at the huge black dog that
> had burst up from the hay. The dog looked strangely at the
> chicken. For a moment they stood motionless before each other.
> Then a single alarmed cluck welled up in the chicken. She began
> clucking, clucking—and as if the clucking wound her up, she
> marched again, stalked again, ran. Ran, flew, flew up in a wild
> welter of cacklings, as if propelling herself up on great squalls of
> cackles. She landed on a big crossbeam, high against the peaked
> roof. She paced there, head bobbing, clucking—telling herself
> hysterical things about the scary huge dog in this strange, silent,
> huge place.

There are now many readers in this country who, told that this passage
came from a children's book, would guess at once that it was written by
Meindert DeJong. They would recognize the vigour and spontaneity of it,
the sympathetic characterization of the bird; the repetitions that make the
passage alive with the runnings and cacklings of the hen, and that contrive
to have the hugeness of the dog shared with the hugeness of the place. Even
the absence of care to avoid an unmeaningful repetition, as in those three
"hays" in the first two sentences, is a habit of writing unmistakable to the
admirer.

Four books by this native of Holland who has lived all his adult life in
America have now been published over here. The first—and best—was the
Newbery Medal winner, *The Wheel on the School*, which accompanied a
headlong ardour of style with a most unusual theme, a splendid dramatic
shape, and a jubilation in character unusual in children's literature. On this
side of the Atlantic we have paid honour to it by demanding, in the three
years since it appeared, six impressions.

Probably the most striking quality of Mr. DeJong's work is the enormous
excitement he generates in all his books. This is not only quite distinctive: it
is also a matter of controversy. Those who cannot admire him call it
hysteria. It is there, at once, in *The Wheel on the School*. From the moment
that Lina, the only girl among the six schoolchildren in the little village of
Shora, reads out her composition, "Do You Know about Storks?" the
excitement begins. Why do no storks nest in Shora? A passionate tension is
the mood in which the children examine this question. And when they
resolve that it is because the roofs are too sharp, and that they must find a
cartwheel to put on the roof of their school, the excitement becomes

tremendous. In the search for the wheel each of the children has his own adventure, and all the adventures explode together in a roaring climax of discovery and rescue: which takes us only halfway through the book, with another series of adventures, blown at us by one of Mr. DeJong's superb outbursts of bad weather, sweeping down upon us and whirling us towards yet another climax. The whole thing trembles with impatience and anxiety.

Similar excitement is generated in *The House of Sixty Fathers*; the search of a little Chinese boy for his parents, from whom he has been separated during the Japanese invasion, becomes boundlessly passionate and insistent. *Shadrach* is full of the trembling expectancy of a little boy waiting for a black rabbit he has been promised: and it, too, when the rabbit is lost, has its agonizing search. The latest book, *Along Came a Dog,* has a climax of quite astonishing tension, the last-minute rescue by a dog of a little red hen and her chicks being attacked by a hawk.

Illustration by Maurice Sendak from *Shadrach* by Meindert DeJong. Copyright 1953 by Meindert DeJong. Reprinted by permission of Harper & Row, Publishers. British edition published by Lutterworth Press.

To those who are cool about Mr. DeJong's work, these exhilarations and tremblings and throbbings of intense excitement appear excessive. To an admirer, there seem to be two answers to this charge. The first is that the excitement is an aspect of Mr. DeJong's skill as a storyteller and of his sheer high spirits as a writer. The second is that it is essentially of a degree that a child, and only a child, feels. Little Davie's impatience as he waits for the coming of his rabbit, in *Shadrach,* for instance, is a drumming impatience, and we are made to feel every aching moment of it: and the adult, who has accustomed himself to be suspicious of unmeasured emotion, may begin to feel as he would if a real little boy were at his elbow, growing feverish and pettish with expectation. But—and this is the point—this tension that drives all the books is exactly the tension a child feels, immoderate and sometimes alarming. To an admirer it would seem to be one of the things that distinguish Mr. DeJong's work from nearly everything else being written for children today. His writing is close, in a way that the writing in ninety-nine out of a hundred children's books is not, to the impetuous, overbrimming quality of a child's emotions.

Mr. DeJong simply has a wonderful memory for what it is to be a child. He is hardly to be matched when he is writing of children, alone, thinking. There is a passage in *The Wheel on the School* where Pier, out searching for the wheel, suddenly thinks of old Janus, a legless man living in the village, and tries to imagine what it would be like to have no legs.

> In a scary sort of way, he was enjoying the numb feeling in his legs which he imagined had been cut off. He looked around him in the stillness. How was he going to get home—legless? He pictured himself crawling home along the winding road, his stumps of legs dragging on behind. He moaned. He hastily tried to make it a little laugh, but it sounded like a groan in the deep country silence. "Hey, cut it out!" he told himself.

Again, in *Shadrach* there is a scene where little Davie creeps out into the countryside to pick clover for his rabbit, still six days off. Down by the canal he finds the clover but he finds bees, too, swarms of big bees, and he is frightened; but he moves among them, cajoling them, placating them, and eventually becoming ridiculously and touchingly implicated with one of them. One can say of such scenes only that this indeed was what it was like to be a child, alone, so easily and so utterly alone and at the mercy of such ready and preposterous fantasies and fears.

And the fact is that all these fears and fevers and excitements that mark Mr. DeJong's books are rooted in exact and entertaining social observation. In the wide world of America Mr. DeJong has not forgotten the small world of Holland. He has a deep feeling for the life of a community, his books are full of grandparents and elders of all kinds and his children are firmly placed in a hierarchy of age. Again this is seen at its best in *The Wheel on the School,* where the search for the wheel is made a sort of catalyst, precipitating all kinds of enhanced relationships within the community.

By the end of the story the children have not only found their wheel and their storks: they have found their village, too. They have discovered, for example, the legless old man, Janus, whom the search draws out of the closed garden in which for years he has sat brooding over his mutilation, a pile of stones at hand to throw at boys or birds trying to rob his cherry tree. He, the children find, is not at all as they thought he was; and some of the most exhilarating passages in the book are those which describe how, at first incredulous, they are urged by Janus to push him in his wheelchair, faster and faster, on errands of rescue or discovery.

One would like room to discuss, or simply to illustrate, Mr. DeJong's powers of humorous observation (his books are funny in the way that life is funny): his brilliant eye for relationships between children (for example, that, in *Shadrach,* of little Davie with his elder brother Rem, comforter and betrayer at once). One would like to say a great deal about Maurice Sendak, who has illustrated all the books and who shares his author's view of people entirely. There can be few illustrations anywhere more affectionate and enchanting—and absolutely appropriate—than those in which he draws his, and Mr. DeJong's, tiny, touching Dutch people.

But there is space only to speak of the latest DeJong, *Along Came a Dog*, which is a *tour de force* of a new kind for the author. In it there are only two human characters, and they are both grown men. The world of this book is the world of the farmyard hens and the big, homeless dog who hides among them. But Mr. DeJong has not deserted children, for these animals are the children of the story, with (on the part of the dog) a child's longing for love, and (on the part of the chickens) a child's touching grotesquerie of behaviour. Not that the animals here are merely children on all fours, or with wings. They are indubitably animals, beautifully characterized. More than once in his earlier books Mr. DeJong must have reminded adult readers, in his style and especially in his sympathetic understanding of animals, of D. H. Lawrence. The thought may have been put away with an embarrassed shrug, but, though it remains an excessive thought, there is something in it: for Mr. DeJong has some of Lawrence's power to convey, by a special use of vocabulary and a special movement of his prose, the essential character of any animal. It is so here, with his hens and his preposterous, ill-fated rooster: and the effect, as in so much that Mr. DeJong does, is not only very exciting but beautiful, touching, and most warmly and eagerly alive.

The New Realism

Robert Burch

Robert Burch has produced a series of stories for children which treat characters and background with clarity and sensitivity. They are set in Fayetteville, Georgia, his home. Other than two picture books, Joey's Cat *(1969), illustrated by Don Freeman, and* Hunting Trip *(1971), illustrated by Susanne Suba, he has written stories for children above the picture-book level:* Tyler, Wilkin, and Skee *(1963);* Skinny *(1964);* D. J.'s Worst Enemy *(1965);* Queenie Peavy *(1966), a winner of many honors;* Renfroe's Christmas *(1968); and* Simon and the Game of Chance *(1970).*

I do not know what is so new about the New Realism. It would seem to me that realism dates back as far as mankind itself. And sometimes we get ourselves in trouble if we fail to take the past into consideration. Sometimes we get ourselves in trouble if we do. For instance, during 1970 Southern Baptists voted in Nashville to give sex-education courses in their churches, based on "a sound Biblical approach"; and one newspaper columnist could not resist pointing out the kind of Sunday School discussions that could possibly result from such an approach. He could visualize a poor teacher fielding questions from children about some of the stories that appear in the Bible, giving as examples: Abram lending his wife to the Pharaoh, the account of Lot and his daughters, and the way Moses and his band slew the men of Midian and many of the women, but kept thirty-two thousand virgins for themselves. The columnist added that there would be some people who would contend that such material has no place in our nation's churches, and he hoped the Baptists would not get themselves arrested.

But realism, whether new or not, is being discussed nowadays. In an article for the *New York Times,* Mr. Isaac Bashevis Singer[1] said that "Stories for children are now being written without a beginning, middle or end." It bothered him, and it bothers me—but not much, because I agree with him that children probably will reject them. His way of putting it was that from his own experience, he[2] knew "that a child wants a well constructed story with clear language and strict logic. . . . " I am glad that variety is offered children, but I am also glad that they do not accept everything that is offered them.

I have never found those slice-of-life stories, or whatever they are called now, very satisfactory reading experiences. And I do not care much for slice-of-life plays either. I remember the first one I saw; I was living and

"The New Realism" by Robert Burch from *Horn Book Magazine,* 47 (June 1971): 257–264. Reprinted by permission of Horn Book, Inc.

1. Isaac Bashevis Singer, " 'I See the Child as a Last Refuge,' " *New York Times,* Book Review Section 7, Part II (November 9, 1969), p. 66.
2. Ibid.

working in New York at the time. The playwright was gifted, with a keen ear for the speech patterns of New Yorkers; and the actors were enormously talented. During the first act I said to myself, "This is wonderful. The characters on stage are so real! Why, they sound exactly like my neighbors arguing." It continued, nothing much happening—no rising action and, as far as I could tell, no character development—but still with realistic dialogue. And by the third act I was saying, "I might as well have stayed home and listened to my neighbors." But the show was "in" at the moment, it was being talked about at parties, and I wanted to know about it, so I would have gone, even if I had known that it would bore me. We adults are like that. I am glad children are not. Mr. Singer[3] says "it's a lot easier to hypnotize grown-ups than children. . . . easier to force . . . [us] to eat literary straw and clay than an infant in kindergarten."

Mr. Singer's article did a great deal to renew my faith in the state of children's books, for, the previous season, one of the special newspaper supplements on children's books had worried me. You will probably consider me the biggest prude you ever met when I tell you that it was a review of a picture book that bothered me. It mentioned the "New Realism," a phrase which caught my eye. The book, by a talented team and published by a fine firm, was *Bang Bang You're Dead* (Harper). In one comment on it, the reviewer[4] said: "[S]ome parents may not relish reading to a 4-year-old such luscious lines as 'Give up, puke-face. You don't have a chance,' to which the dainty rejoinder is 'Up your nose you freak-out.'" Well, I hope there are some parents who would not relish reading it. That is how square I am. Some parents will approve, while others may not, but will accept it rather than be labeled old-fashioned.

A woman I know, an authority in the book field, defended *Bang Bang You're Dead*. She said that in using such words as puke-face in picture stories, we let the child know that we know that he knows and uses such words, helping to strengthen our lines of communication. I am not sure she is right. I do not know what a child thinks, but neither am I sure that when I was young I would have been wildly pleased that adults knew that I knew and used certain words. Would the words not have become respectable somehow, and we children have been put to the trouble of finding new ones—new till some well-meaning adult got around to making them respectable, too? I do not know that children want us to communicate with them to such an extent.

Another argument for that particular book is that our language is changing, and, of course, it is—constantly. In a *Look* magazine article[5] on language, I read that "so much irrational emotional baggage has been heaped on so many words that our ability to voice a gut-felt notion is

---

3. Ibid.

4. Nora L. Magid, "Picture Books," *New York Times*, Book Review Section 7, Part II (May 4, 1969), p. 53.

5. William Hedgepeth, "Growl to Me Softly And I'll Understand," *Look* (January 13, 1970), p. 48.

stifled." Perhaps so. But I do not know that I am quite ready for gut-felt picture books. The same article[6] also stated:

> Speech doesn't have to be linear; it can come out as a compressed overlay of facts and sensations and moods and ideas and images. Words can serve as signals, and others will understand. The way a man feels can be unashamedly expressed in sheer sound, such as a low, glottal hum, like the purring of a cat, to indicate contentment.

Are you ready for that? If not, I am ahead of you. It has already come to our house. One of my nephews, a high-school junior, often answers me with something of a grunt or a groan, and occasionally a more contented sound. I had accused him of being lazy in his speech, but I suppose he is merely advanced. He is not mumbling; he is giving me a compressed overlay of facts and sensations and images.

But I want to discuss the trend toward the so-called "New Realism." I have defended realism in children's books for a long time. You might say I have had to defend it, since I have been criticized at times for some of the grim details I have used in stories for the young. I have tried to use such details for a purpose, the purpose not being to shock but to give as accurate a picture as possible of the events taking place in a story and of the time and place in which it is set. If a story set in the Depression years tells only of church suppers or of all-day sings, what sort of picture of the times would that be? On the other hand, stories can be overloaded with details of a period. If my main purpose were to give the reader facts about the Depression, then I would write a nonfiction book.

I believe that Flannery O'Connor once said that in the South we like to write stories because we have the Bible and a little bit of history. In several books, I have used a little bit of that little bit of history, drawing background material from the Great Depression itself. However, my most recent book is a modern-day story, *Simon and the Game of Chance* (Viking), much of which is based on the premises found in Ecclesiastes. I have been accused of presenting in it a negative view of Bible-belt Christianity, but I hope that I did not. I tried to show the misuse of dogma and its effect upon the lives of those touched by it. In any event, I believe in realism in stories for the young and favor the trend toward what May Hill Arbuthnot[7] called "a frank treatment of the grave and often tragic social problems [young people] are encountering and talking about today."

Since I am primarily interested in junior novels with realistic settings, I am vitally concerned about the changes that are taking place in this kind of novel, and I find the trend toward stronger realism healthy. I do not think we should scare children, but on the other hand we should not lie to them

---

6. Ibid., p. 50.

7. May Hill Arbuthnot, *Children's Reading in the Home* (Illinois, Scott, Foresman and Company, 1969), p. 174.

by pretending that the world is entirely safe. C. S. Lewis[8] said it better than I can. He said that we need not try to keep out of a child's mind "the knowledge that he is born into a world of death, violence, wounds, adventure, heroism and cowardice, good and evil . . . ," which he says would be "to give children a false impression and feed them on escapism in the bad sense."

If we could guarantee children that the world out there would be completely safe, then fine, we could afford to give them only stories that leave that impression. But until we can, in whatever we present as being realistic, is it not cheating for it to be otherwise? No doubt, there are some books that still distort or mislead, but there are an increasing number each year that do not.

One I enjoyed recently was *Where the Lilies Bloom* (Lippincott) by Vera and Bill Cleaver. A fourteen-year-old girl in the mountains of North Carolina struggles to keep the children in the family together in ways that are sometimes sad and sometimes hilarious, but she always does so with a fierce dignity and the rejection of charity. This book has a strong impact, an impact I think right for the children of today. If they are so far removed from poverty themselves, why should they not see that it does exist?

Another of my favorite books of recent years is Theodore Taylor's *The Cay* (Doubleday). It says more about loving our neighbor than any sermon I have heard in a long time, although it does not preach. Good stories never do. I suppose *The Cay* could be called an adventure story—there is a shipwreck, an attempt by two people, a man and a boy, to survive on a coral island. The boy is blind; the man is black. The man dies before there is any sign of rescue. While reading *The Cay*, I forgot that I was reading it—so to speak—as homework, finding myself thoroughly engrossed in it, and I thought of another comment by C. S. Lewis,[9] who said that he was "almost inclined to set it up as a canon that a children's story which is enjoyed only by children is a bad children's story."

Another book I especially like is *Let the Balloon Go* (St. Martin's) by Ivan Southall. It is not perfect in every way, but what book is? It tells of a sad situation, the central character being spastic, but young people can read the book as a tale of challenge and excitement—because it is that, with a great deal of suspense—and if they get a glimpse at the same time of what it is like to be a spastic, then so much the better. I know that I felt involved in it to that extent. And no brochure from the March of Dimes campaign, or anything else, has made me feel that the cause is as urgent as I consider it since reading *Let the Balloon Go*. It is a simple story of a twelve-year-old boy and his longing to do something other boys his age take for granted: to climb a tree.

Such situations are sad, but it does not hurt the child to read about them

---

8. C. S. Lewis, "On Three Ways of Writing for Children," *Of Other Worlds: Essays and Stories* (New York, Harcourt Brace Jovanovich, Inc., 1966), p. 31.

9. Ibid., p. 24.

unless his gradual development of a concern for others is considered wrong. Tragedies in literature do not depress any of us in a really harmful way. Lloyd Alexander[10] has reminded us in the *Horn Book Magazine* of a comment attributed to De La Rochefoucauld, which was: "We all have sufficient strength to endure the misfortunes of others." I am not sure but that we draw strength from such misfortunes. Occasionally, we all need to escape into a fantasy world, but perhaps it is good also to escape at times from our own real world into someone else's real world.

Maybe it is the same with children, and it does not matter whether a story teaches them anything or not. Mr. Singer[11] in his article in the *New York Times* said that not everyone would agree with him, "but that we are living in a time when literature aspires more and more to be didactic and utilitarian. It doesn't seem to matter what lesson it teaches—a sociological, psychological or humanistic one—as long as it teaches." He also said that he did not know "of a single work of fiction in our time which has contributed much to psychology or sociology, or helped the cause of pacifism."

I do not know if any of the children's books of recent years will seriously contribute to these areas, but I have been interested to hear of one college that is using some of them in child and adolescent psychology courses. The students read from a list of junior novels and discuss them in class each Monday. The only drawback, it has turned out, is that they have become so interested in the experiment that book discussions run over into midweek when other ground is supposed to be covered. I think it speaks well for today's realism that the professor saw these books as a basis—or as a springboard—for discussions, and that the students were enthusiastic about them, whether or not we agree that works of fiction should teach anything.

We would all agree, however, that a story should entertain the reader, in the sense of holding his attention and making him care about it; and I feel it is more apt to do this, that the characters and the action are more likely to ring true, if the person writing the story can discuss whatever matters most to him. Maybe this is why I am excited about the New Realism. While C. S. Lewis[12] said that "Anyone who *can* write a children's story without a moral, had better do so—that is, if he is going to write children's stories at all"; from my standpoint I cannot see how anyone could put the required amount of time and energy into a book unless he is holding it together, or trying to hold it together, with a theme of importance to himself. And I cannot imagine a theme in a children's story strong enough to hold anything together that does not, in the final analysis, turn out to be moral, or at least morally sound. Stronger stories in every sense are likely to result when the writer is free to tackle whatever is meaningful to him. And if it is to find a

---

10. Lloyd Alexander, "No Laughter in Heaven," *Horn Book Magazine* (February 1970), p. 14.

11. Singer, op. cit., p. 66.

12. Lewis, op. cit., p. 33.

young audience, it must be with material meaningful to young people—no matter what the subject.

But subjects alone, no matter how important, do not make a good story. However timely and appropriate they may be, unless they are fleshed out with believable characters—I would go so far as to say with at least some characters the reader cannot only believe in but care about—and unless something resembling a plot is provided, the finished item is not likely to be a good junior novel. John Rowe Townsend,[13] the British author and critic, said that "you can't turn a bad novel into a good one by filling it with pregnancy, pot and the pill." A story should never be merely a platform from which to discuss a topic, although I admit that the themes of my stories are figurative soapboxes or platforms from which to express my own outlook on life. But a soapbox and nothing else is a rather dismal sight.

For the fun of it, I have looked back to what people were saying not so very long ago—five or ten years or thereabouts—about realistic stories for children. C. S. Lewis,[14] who was discussing fantasy, touched on realism in an essay, saying:

> I think what profess to be realistic stories for children are far more likely to deceive them [than fantasy]. I never expected the real world to be like the fairy tales. I think that I did expect school to be like the school stories. The fantasies did not deceive me: the school stories did.

He went on to say that "All stories in which children have adventures and successes which are possible . . . , but almost infinitely improbable, are in more danger than the fairy tales of raising false expectations," and I agree with him. But today, the kind of realistic stories he had in mind are not as likely to find a publisher—or, if they do, a reader. Surely not as many of them nowadays raise false expectations about the world in which we live, and there are school stories now that are like school.

Another quote, this one by Elizabeth Enright,[15] whom I admired so much and whose death was a loss to all of us. She said this seven or eight years ago about realism in children's books: "It is apt to be kinder than the real thing; also neater, more just, and more exciting. Things turn out well in the end." Today, not always. Sometimes they do; sometimes they do not. She went on to say,

> But unlike life, the end of the story comes at the high point. We do not have to go on with these people through high school, college, marriage, mortgage payments, child rearing, money

---

13. John Rowe Townsend, "It Takes More Than Pot and the Pill," *New York Times,* Book Review Section 7, Part II (November 9, 1969), p. 2.

14. Lewis, op. cit., pp. 28–29.

15. Elizabeth Enright, "Realism in Children's Literature," *Horn Book Magazine* (April 1967), p. 168.

worries, dental problems . . . or any of the rest of it. It is our privilege to leave them in their happiness forever. . . .

I am glad that there are still books that end happily. I hope there will never be a brand of realism that rules out happy endings. But I somehow get the feeling that realism to some people has come to mean only the harsher side of life. Surely, in life there are as many happy endings as sad ones, so to be truly realistic, should books not average out accordingly?

For all children, whether they face the world as gradually as we would have them, or have to face it earlier, I think that when it comes to realism in their stories, honesty is what we owe them. Is it too much to ask that anything we present as being realistic be realistic?

British editions of books mentioned with their American publishers only in this article:

Vera and Bill Cleaver. *Where the Lilies Bloom*. Hamish Hamilton.
Theodore Taylor. *The Cay*. Bodley Head.
Ivan Southall. *Let the Balloon Go*. Methuen.

Realism, Truth, and Honesty

Mary Q. Steele

Under her own name and the name Wilson Gage, Mary Q. Steele has produced a number of award-winning books for children. She lives, with writer-husband William O. Steele, in Tennessee, the background of much of her writing. Wilson Gage's books reveal a deep interest in nature: Big Blue Island *won the American Library Association's Aurianne Award for "the best children's book of 1964 on animal life which develops a humane attitude." Other stories by Wilson Gage include* Dan and the Miranda *(1962),* Miss Osborne-the-Mop *(1963), and* Mike's Toads *(1970). Under her real name, she wrote* Journey Outside, *a 1970 Newbery Medal honor book. The following paper was presented in 1970 at the annual seminar on Excellence in Children's Literature sponsored by the Library School of the University of California, Berkeley.*

Truth? What is truth? asked Pilate and sent for a basin of water in which to wash his hands.

Honesty? What is honesty? asked the artist and sent for a bottle of gin in which to drown his sorrows.

Realism? What is realism? asked the children's book author and sent for a royalty statement in which to soak his head.

Realism. Oddly enough when I think of realism in children's fiction, what pops into my head is the loving and lovingly detailed description of the parlor of the Misses Matilda and Louisa Pussycat. No photograph could realize that room more completely, nor could it be so evocative. It could not, for instance, take the head of the owl snuff box and reveal that its contents were pins and buttons, not snuff.

Other things come to mind: the ring of authenticity in the historical appointments of *Hitty* (Macmillan); the uncompromising inexorability of the spank on Ping's back; the terrible dilemma of Huck Finn confronted by the question, in one of seven genuine dialects, "Is your man white?"; the perfectly normal and completely detestable pomposity of Oswald Bastable. Are these things not representative of excellence in realism?

Yet, several years ago Andy Warhol showed us what was the absolute perfect excellent end of realism—a Brillo box, or an eight-hour movie of a man realistically experiencing a realistic eight-hour night's sleep. Mr. Warhol was kidding and pulling our legs and making a serious statement to the effect that realism is impossible to achieve in art without reducing art and life to absurdities.

By and large, the authors of children's books are a little less ambitious or a little more sanguine than Mr. Warhol. The illusion of reality is surely within our capabilities. Life can be reflected in other ways than by simply

"Realism, Truth, and Honesty" by Mary Q. Steele from *Horn Book Magazine,* 46 (February 1971): 17–27. Reprinted by permission of Horn Book, Inc.

holding up a mirror. Dealing as we do with minds less sophisticated, more sparsely furnished, more impressionable if you will, we can hold that bold, bright strokes may be effective, may in fact convey better and more immediately what we are trying to say than the finer brushwork of specifics and naturalism. Certainly, tradition has allowed the bold, bright stroke, has allowed the writer of children's books license to ignore some aspects of life, including for instance most physiological processes.

In fact, this kind of omission has not been merely "allowed"; it has been mandatory. The children's book editor has a long list of "don'ts" handed to her—or him?—by librarians, teachers and parents, which she hastily hands on to the writer, whether or not editor or writer is altogether convinced of their validity. From my own experience and that of people close to me I can remember that children were not allowed to stick their tongues out at one another, that immature ten-year-old twins were barred from sharing a room ("Build a wing on the house if you have to, but get those kids in separate bedrooms!" my editor wired frantically), that mild hecks and darns were deleted, and that brotherly smacks and sisterly pinches were hastily blue-penciled out of existence.

In 1955 my husband was writing a book called *The Lone Hunt* (Harcourt), an intensely realistic book in every sense of the word, for it was a piece of historical fiction based on recorded facts, figures, dates, and statistics, which offered to the tough-minded of the younger generation an exposition of the harsh old Spanish proverb: "Take what you want and then pay for it." In a dramatic and tragedy-shadowed scene a mad old Indian speaks of his gun as "no damn good." My husband's editor with adamant eraser expunged that expletive, whose actual loss would have meant the reduction by half of the vocabulary of the Indian as well as of the white man of the time. Librarians and parents would object strenuously, the editor explained.

A year or so later, I myself wrote a book which made no claim to starkness or to an unvarnished portrait of a bloody era or of disordered lives or uneasy souls. Quite the contrary. It aspired to be realistic only in what I considered its natural picture of ordinary present-day reasonably happy family, and in particular of the mother, a confirmed bird watcher. Here is the response from a lady who lives in California: "There is a continual run of ridicule, through the story, toward brother and sister, instead of respect towards each other. Throughout this book, also, the children show a slight sarcasm towards the mother for her interest in birdlore. From the tone of this book the children are more or less top people while their parents are what is currently called 'squares.' Therefore, apart from the story material this book is poorly written and neglects to teach children to be thoughtful, respectful and loving toward the family unit." (Please remember that the syntax is hers, not mine.)

In 1964 I published a book which looked at an altogether different kind of child under altogether different circumstances, a boy so lost and forlorn, so frightened and battered and troubled that I could scarcely think of him without tears. I made a horrendous effort to deal with this boy realistically, to view his situation as it might be viewed in the hard actual light of fact; not to sentimentalize him or his surroundings or his chance at life; not to make him, in spite of my sympathy for him, a better or wiser or soberer boy than he might truly be; and at the same time not to minimize or gloss over the things he was up against; and not to allow my own feelings to color his, even though I did love the physical setting in which he found himself.

This book was appreciatively received by most people, but the *New York Times* said caustically that it supposed an anti-hero in the children's book field was inevitable. Also a school librarian told me that she sometimes read the book aloud to her classes, stopping often to exclaim, "Isn't this boy a real stinker?," thus collapsing my bubble with a word.

That was yesterday. Today, in keeping with the world's present swift pace the gap between the time when "damn" was barred and Anglo-Saxon interjections were permitted has been very narrow. It is urged that we should call a spade a spade or even worse, that mothers should be neurotic, that fathers should be lushes, brothers potheads, sisters five months illegitimately pregnant, and everybody's acquaintances liberally sprinkled with pimps, dealers, abortionists, and members of the Mafia. Sex, death, and taxes are considered the proper subjects for today's young people's novels, and woe betide the writer who is irrelevant.

Well, I for one am glad to see the change in many ways. Things can be a bit easier for the writer when they are less restricted and more natural, closer to what he hears and sees with his own ears and eyes. If editors and teachers, parents and librarians, can recognize and concede that children are apt to be a bit scornful of a bird-watching mother, are likely in moments of anger to bestow on each other what used to be termed in my family "a good hard smack," are inclined to use language that makes "darn" and "heck" rather pale substitutes, and tend to be, in fact, completely human, then I think that is great. I like to think that though I write for children, I am as free to write about anything I please as the next writer. I like to think that we respect our children's intelligence enough to suppose that the world need be presented to them in no rosy light, but as it is—as most of us know it is—a hard road strewn with stones and bordered with thorns, ending where, it is claimed, the paths of glory do but lead. The world has not spared children hunger, cold, sorrow, pain, fear, loneliness, disease, death, war, famine, or madness. Why should we hesitate to make use of this knowledge when writing for them?

Not too long ago, an editor came to see me—a person of great charm and intelligence, a friend of long standing. She said to me: "Today many people are writing about the present-day teen-ager in terms of his own problems and in his own images. You seem to have enjoyed your own children and their friends so much" (at that time I had one child still technically a teen-ager) "why don't you write about this age group living in today's world? Surely you have something to say?"

"Surely I do," I said with something less than complete self-confidence.

And having so far committed myself, I went to the library to look over the crop of books that purported to "tell it like it is." Books that aspired to deal with the problems of the real world, with the things that cause our young people to be disturbed and alienated, to show them how to cope with these problems, how to meet the future without a "confrontation," how to change the world in ways other than burning it down and inviting it to throw tear-gas bombs in retaliation.

It seemed to me that many of these books failed sadly in this high aim. It was not so much that they reaffirmed Establishment values, for these are legitimate values and certainly the Establishment almost always wins. It was that they do this so patently, without any real exploration of what the anti-forces had to offer, without any real interest in these forces. The trappings were there, but not the spirit.

It was not so much that they ended on an upbeat note—humanity is almost always hopeful and especially young humanity. It was that the upbeat was too often achieved by putting down and discounting the young, the new, the different.

It was not just the feeling that many of these books were written to be fashionable; it was, worst of all, I think, that they were written out of expediency, that we rushed in to convince our children that we too were concerned and interested, not perhaps because we *were* concerned but because we suddenly discovered we ought to be. As though, indeed, we were telling them not what we honestly believed but too often what we thought it was easiest and safest and most convenient to have them believe.

A question occurred to me: Who are these books written for? Twelve- to sixteen-year-olds? Ten- to fourteen-year-olds? Young adults? Who is this fourteen-year-old who is interested and mature and concerned enough to want to investigate today's dilemma at length? *And why isn't this person reading something else?* Why not *Been down So Long It Looks like up to Me?* Why not *Slaughterhouse Five* or *The Fire Next Time?* How about *I Ain't Marchin' Anymore* or *The Sidelong Glances of a Pigeon Kicker.*

Have we indeed aimed for a sort of Cherry Ames mentality which has suddenly become imbued with a notion to get it together? Is it possible that we are really adding to our troubles by a pretense of doing what we do not do, thereby offending those who would honestly like a little light shed and who would welcome the thought that the older generation was making an effort to meet them on their own grounds in coping with a world gone apparently mad? And reinforcing the type of mind that much prefers not to acknowledge or even notice the symptoms?

And another question: In these realistic and liberated new books, may we now have for hero or anti-hero—at any rate, protagonist—a dope dealer, a member of the Weathermen faction of SDS, or any member of SDS, a white racist or, for that matter, a black racist? May we on the other hand write a book in which a black boy or girl turns out to be a thoroughly unmitigated villain? Or a member of the Christian Athletes? Or Tricia Nixon? Or the leader of the noble Sioux tribe?

The quality I missed in these books and have missed in far too many children's books reaching far back into the dim beginnings, is an abrasive quality called, at least by me, honesty. And I would define honesty in a writer as the open acknowledgment that a writer writes to be writing; he does not write to be heard. This is the real honest-to-God nitty-gritty: A writer who puts his audience's reaction before his own is dead.

Truth is a great and slippery beast. Few people are capable of cramming it between the pages of a book. The writer can only hope that he has at best left some room to accommodate a particular piece, left some space in which the reader may walk around and perceive the general outline of some part of some vastness, seen stereoscopically through his own and the writer's eyes. Realism, contrariwise, is a small creature, almost moribund and suffering from partial paralysis, depending on how it was captured and in what net. It is never going to be a unicorn, a wild and graceful beast of the forest. But it can be a serviceable and sturdy beast of burden, provided you can drench it with sufficient honesty to save its life.

I am not suggesting a new school of naturalism for the kiddies. I do not propose Zola in the third grade and Céline in the fifth; aside from other considerations I think children would be bored out of their minds. But what I would hope for is that books for children were more often written by people who wanted to write a book—not people who importuned an audience. What I would hope for is books written out of the heart, out of that strange generosity of the heart of the writer who is determined to speak and let who wishes hear.

At the time I am writing, the country is in a state of turmoil and unrest. The aching frustration and agony of some of us, the heartchilling fear and distrust of many of us, the anger, the despair, the ever-widening chasms are possibly unique in the world's history. For one thing, the dangers have never been so great; and for another, the means of conveying the news of our disease are so efficient. The world has trembled on the brink of disaster before, but only recently has it balanced on the ledge and listened to the siren invitation to jump.

I think perhaps teachers, librarians, writers, and editors might take some moments to ponder the fact that it is today's young people, and quite often the best of today's young people, who are most anguished, most disaffected, most despairing. I cannot suppress the persistent notion that we of an older generation are somehow and to some extent to blame.

When I was a child, my readers were illustrated with black and muddy orange silhouettes of children dressed in Empire clothes. Nobody pretended that anything in those readers reflected life or anything like it.

My children, on the other hand, learned to read from those smug suburbanites, Dick and Jane. This is *life,* said text and pictures; this is the way things are—repeating it so often and so positively and in such happy and naturalistic colors that most of us were ashamed to question it or to point out that it was not so. Most of us had known or seen people who either lived like Dick and Jane or ardently aspired to. The brainwashing was not too subtle, but it was thorough. This is indeed the way things are in certain places and with certain people. It came as a nasty shock to many young people to discover that they had been left unaware of the fact that the lives of Dick and Jane might not even be anything nearly approaching an ideal existence.

> "I said to Heart: 'How goes it?' Heart replied:
> 'Right as a Ribstone Pippin!' But it lied."

In the eyes of youth, hypocrisy is as it should be—the sin against the Holy Ghost, the half-truth worse than the outright lie. It is traumatic to discover that this is indeed a nation under God but that often enough the god is Mammon, that the land that seems to lie before us like a land of dreams is really made of plastic, designed by Walt Disney, and bought and sold for green stamps.

It is not that those of us over thirty—and over forty, and even over fifty, are so much more hypocritical than we have ever been before. It is that we protested overmuch about our truth-telling. It is that we allowed ourselves to be half-way convinced, more than half-way convinced, that what we were talking about was fact and not a sort of documentarized fiction.

I think we are still continuing our unhappy progress. I think that all too often we still fail to level with our children; I think too many of the present-day spate of so-called problem novels continue the old mechanisms in different ways. "I beseech you," cried Oliver Cromwell, "bethink you that you may be mistaken." We didn't think, and often we still don't. And what we failed to do our children did for us. I think that our children are discovering what we are doing, and are going to be once again bitter about the discovery. If your child asks for bread and you give him a stone, sooner or later he is going to get indigestion. Perhaps we should spend more time reading Ecclesiastes aloud, not only to children but to ourselves and to each other.

Let us return now to my lovely and talented editor and her arm-twisting. She has returned to New York and left me staring at my typewriter. What have I done? I am now committed. What is worse, a book is there in my head clamoring to be let out. I now have to face up to all those hard things I have said. And I have to face up to myself. Here I am a middle-aged amateur natural historian, author of a number of light-hearted entertainments for eight- to eleven-year-olds, and what do I have to say to today's Now Generation? I am a most thoroughgoing old-fashioned square, who still reads Beatrix Potter. My motto has ever been, "Live pure, speak true, right wrong, and follow the king," and nobody has been more astounded than I to discover myself up against the wall, with the long hairs, the freaks, the revolutionaries.

I have perforce had to learn the names of a couple of honest bondsmen, though my own record is pure as the driven snow. I have learned to differentiate between a hash pipe and a roach clip, but I have never used either. I have learned to love the Beatles, the Credence Clearwater Revival, and Jimi Hendrix, but I cannot recognize George Harrison for the soul of me, and the thought of attending a Rock Festival causes me to come all over funny and have to lie down. Still, I have in some bewilderment attended a fund-raising picnic on the banks of the Charles for the SDS and paid a stupendously large sum of money for a series of stickers depicting a clenched black fist against a red-and-white ground. Willy-nilly, I have collected enough underground and radical newspapers to fuel a whole neighborhood of hibachis. If I have not been of this generation, I have certainly been with it—in the older sense.

And yet, in truth, I remained a white Anglo-Saxon Protestant middle-aged middle-class middle-brow housewife living in a small Tennessee town and washing a lot of dishes. And I knew it. And I began to wonder if in speaking to an audience older than was my wont I was going to be able to avoid sounding like Arthur Fiedler and the Boston Pops playing "Strawberry Fields Forever."

And yet, what I had in mind was something I believed and something I wanted to talk about and something I had a perfect right to say: that life is difficult and that most of the time, however hard we try, we are on the wrong track and might as well get used to it. That the choices that we must make at the cost of heartbreak are seldom between black and white but between almost indistinguishable shades of gray. That to most questions there is not one answer but seven or a thousand or even none at all.

When I wrote my book, I spoke in the oblique Swahili of fantasy. It is not after all such a bad way. It has been since the beginning of time a valid way to express verities—witness all mythologies and the Bible. Any writer has to admit that a piece of fiction worth its while is just that—fiction, an extended and elongated metaphor, tangential to reality at only the most infrequent points. The reader has always demanded the right to ignore what the writer was saying when he chose to do so. It is one of the rules of the game.

And in some ways I must say it required of me more discipline than I had supposed it would. A writer can be a little too comfortable in a country so purely of his own invention. He can easily resort to devices that are not fair. I was grateful for the inspiration that brought my young hero out of darkness into light for the first time in his life and gave him a secure tie to common earth and gave me a unique opportunity to observe that common earth and how remarkably uncommon it is.

I told the story (*Journey Outside* [Viking]) of a boy who found his own life smothering and pointless and so found a way to leave it behind and come out into the open day. To come out and discover other ways of living and that each had its uniquely pleasant advantages and yet each was as flawed as what he had left behind; and to travel the world until he eventually came upon a man with sufficient objectivity to tell him his choices: to point out that having left the straight world behind he could either retire to Vermont and raise rhubarb and rhetoric or return whence he came to try to convince his family and friends that their way was not the only way and perhaps a less happy way than some others. The decision must be his alone, based not on experience or logic, for neither will tell him what to do. Something else must identify for him his own thing and that is what he will do, conscious of the fact that what he does is neither "right" nor "wrong," but simply what he must do if he is not going to think of himself as having failed.

I tried to be honest as I wrote, though I was not what is in general termed realistic. If I was dishonest in putting something over on my readers, I certainly did not stack the cards; I simply did a little finessing. I am used to doing it, for I have been doing it right along in all of my books, however mundane and however frivolous they may have been. For I have my own bit of truth to leave room for and to speak of sotto voce. I have had to walk around it a bit warily, for I have an idea it is not exactly a popular bit of truth. But what I have tried to say in all my books I do most honestly believe: that it is our differences, not our likenesses that matter. It is our dissimilarities that give life its astonishing richness and wonder and make life rewarding. Concede a spider its inalienable right to eight legs as it has never for a moment doubted your right to two, and you have gone a long way toward being truly human. A universe which has produced a quarter of a million species of beetles must have great respect for and put great value on differentiation. I think it is arrogance for us not to do the same.

I would like to say, then, that I may be very wrong in everything I have written here. There are many sorts of people, and they need many sorts of books. There may be some who need the sort of books I write and others who need the kind of book I would not be caught dead writing. One man's realism is another man's science fiction.

The people who write the kind of book I have deplored may in fact be writing as well and as honestly as they know how. Or they may have some sort of casuistical reasoning for what they are doing which has eluded me, but which certainly seems to them to be sufficient. There may be numbers of readers for whom condescension is a sort of necessity. There may be many children who might suffer real trauma at being presented with a set of values not their own, so that however often the old values were restored to them they could not really lay claim to either one; who need reinforcing over and over again in what they have once learned so that they will not drift away into chaos. And there may be a multitude of young people who are simply lacking in the facility of mind to make a choice, who are going to be forced always to prefer the older or more simplistic or easier idea because it is the only one they can comprehend. Books should most surely be written for these people, books surely are written for these people, perhaps these books are actually better and more serviceable than the ones I prefer.

And yet, perhaps most unrealistically, I could suppose that these people are fewer in number than we seem to imagine. I, for one, would go on the assumption that our children are brighter and better than we have ever imagined them to be. Perhaps wrongly I would proceed on the premise that young minds like young bodies could profit by a little exercise. Perhaps unwisely I would put more trust in our children to choose wisely when given a choice.

Foolishly perhaps, I am hopeful of today's dissident young. There may be much to condemn about them, but there is much to condemn about all of us. I stand in something like awe of the courage that has dared to question authority on every topic from the length of hair to the inevitability of war. I rejoice at the vitality that did not hesitate to put traditions to the test and the intelligence that was unafraid to say they needed testing and to offer alternatives. And we certainly need some alternatives. Years ago a transmogrified poet and cockroach observed: ''the human race is doing the best it can but hells bells thats just an explanation not an excuse. . . . '' This observation is worth thinking about. I would like to think that some of today's realistic writers are encouraging some of today's young readers to do just that kind of thinking.

British editions of books mentioned with their American publishers only in this article:

Rachel Field. *Hitty.* Routledge.
William O. Steele. *The Lone Hunt.* Macmillan.
Mary Q. Steele. *Journey Outside.* Macmillan.

Chapter 9

The Creative Use of History and Other Facts

Writing based on research might be said to have four criteria for excellence: accuracy, judicious selectivity, organization, and an imaginative and lively use of facts. All of these criteria are, of course, interrelated, but it is the last which has been emphasized by authors and critics. To physicist Max Born presenting a scientific subject is an "artistic task" comparable to that of a novelist, while the distinguished biographer, Catherine Drinker Bowen, says "History is, in its essence, exciting; to present it as dull is to my mind, stark and unforgivable misrepresentation. And . . . biography should prove, intrinsically, more exciting even than history. Biography is more immediately comprehensible." [1]

What contributes to the creation of excitement and involvement in the young reader? The selections in this chapter present some important answers. Margery Fisher, in a selection reprinted from *Matters of Fact*, says it is the writer's ability to convey his own enthusiasm and attitudes. And although here, speaking about writing natural history, she stresses the writer's responsibility to choose words which convey scientific truth, in *Intent Upon Reading*, speaking about writing historical fiction, she would subordinate accuracy to imagination. "Without imagination and enthu-

---

1. "The Business of a Biographer," *Atlantic Monthly,* 187 (May 1961): 50–56.

siasm, the most learned and well-documented story will leave the young reader cold, where it should set him on fire. . . . Fact used imaginatively—this is what children look for in historical stories—a good story and a full, even a crowded background."[2] Hester Burton, an author of prize-winning historical fiction, suggests that the writer must research the period of the story so well that he sees the background and feels a part of it. Yet, "The prime object of writing an historical novel is an exercise of the heart rather than the head. It is an exploration of the imagination, a discovery of other people living at other times and faced with other problems than our own. In other words, it is an extension of the author's human sympathies." Rosemary Sutcliff supports this view in "History Is People." Mary K. Eakin, however, suggests another way of creating excitement and involvement in the young reader: by presenting the controversies and conflicts of history, by opening the readers' minds to the facts of change and leading them to ask Why? and Why not?, by meeting the challenge of a changing world.[3]

2. Margery Fisher, *Intent Upon Reading: A Critical Appraisal of Modern Fiction for Children* (New York: Franklin Watts, Inc., 1962. Leicester: Brockhampton Press, 1961.)

3. See also Miriam Selsam, "Writing About Science for Children," in *A Critical Approach to Children's Literature,* ed. by Sara Innis Fenwick (Chicago: University of Chicago Press, 1967), pp. 96–99.

The Writing of Historical Novels

Hester Burton

After earlier experience as a teacher and editor, Hester Burton turned to writing, her first book being published in 1959. The ensuing sequence of historical novels has won her substantial recognition. Castors Away *was a 1962 Carnegie Medal honor book and* Time of Trial *won the Carnegie Medal in 1963. Later titles include* No Beat of Drum *(1967);* The Great Gale, *published in the United States as* The Flood at Reedsmere *(1968);* In Spite of All Terror *(1969); and* Thomas, *published in the U.S. as* Beyond the Weir Bridge *(1970), also an honor winner. The following article is adapted from a paper read at the International Summer School on* Current Trends in Children's Books *at the Loughborough School of Librarianship in August 1968.*

Historical novels—like most mixed marriages—are frowned upon by the Establishment. Historians look upon them with contempt, feeling sure that their authors must have tampered with, or at least distorted, historical fact. The straight novelist regards them as unfortunate aberrations—at best, as a misuse of their writers' talents. A novelist's duty, he thinks, is to portray life as he *knows* it—namely, in the contemporary scene. Anything else must be false, for how can a writer living in the twentieth century really put himself into the mind, say, of a Roman centurion or a fifteenth-century wool merchant or one of Lord Nelson's powder monkeys? He may well learn every detail concerning the centurion's armor and the wool merchant's trade and the powder monkey's duties on board a man-of-war, but how can the most fertile imagination living today re-create the secret fears and unrecorded hopes of people living in times past?

The purpose of this article is to explain how one historical novelist—myself—answers these very serious questions.

Sooner or later, the writer of historical fiction has to make quite clear to himself where history ends and where fiction may legitimately begin. If his books are to appear on the shelves of a school library, I think it is his duty to indicate in an introduction where this dividing line comes.

I have been writing historical novels for nine years, and during this time I have formulated certain other rules for myself.

First, I must acquaint myself as thoroughly as I possibly can with the historical period and the event I am describing. Ideally, I should be so knowledgeable that I have no need to turn to a book of reference once I have actually started writing the book. I should be able to see clearly in my mind's eye the houses in which my characters live, the clothes they wear, and the carts and carriages and ships in which they travel. I should know

"The Writing of Historical Novels" by Hester Burton from *Horn Book Magazine*, 45 (June 1969): 271–277. Reprinted by permission of the author.

what food they eat, what songs they sing when they feel happy, and what are the sights and smells they are likely to meet when they walk down the street. I must understand their religion, their political hopes, their trades, and—what is most important—the relationships between different members of a family common to their particular generation. Moreover, I must carry this knowledge as lightly as the contemporary novelist carries his knowledge of the contemporary scene.

My second rule is never to use a famous historical person as the pivot of my story and never to put into his mouth words or sentiments for which there is no documentary evidence. The reason for this rule is my conviction that it is legitimate for a writer such as myself to try to re-create an historical situation or event, such as the Fire of London, the Battle of Trafalgar, or the Agrarian Revolt of 1829, and then to place fictional characters in this situation and describe how they behave. It is *not* legitimate to reverse the order: namely, to take an actual historical personage and plunge him into fictional adventures.

My last rule is really more of a warning than a rule. When I come to describe the historical situation which I have chosen, I try to view it through the limited vision of a single character or group of characters. I am not all-wise or all-knowing as the historian is; but neither, it is well to remember, were the people actually taking part in the historical event I am describing. They had no access to state papers; they could merely use their eyes. Not only is it a wise caution for the writer of historical novels to limit his range of vision but it is also much better art. I first realized this when I read Stendhal's *The Charterhouse of Parma.* In an early chapter, a young man riding through the Flanders countryside strays by accident into the middle of the Battle of Waterloo. His ensuing feelings of surprise and horror at the muddled and brutal engagements going on all about him made me realize for the first time the utter bewilderment of war. It is a fictional treatment of a great battle which seems utterly right. Thackeray does the same thing in *Vanity Fair*; he views Waterloo through the eyes of the womenfolk waiting anxiously for news in Brussels. Tolstoy, too, in *War and Peace* limits his view of Borodino and so achieves the most vivid effects. In my very humble way, I applied this rule to my account of the Battle of Trafalgar in *Castors Away!* I described it through the eyes of a boy of twelve running almost nonstop from the lower deck down through the orlop deck to the powder magazine and back again, bringing powder for the gunners. The battle comes to him as a series of salvos, cries, shouts, jolts, and the grinding of wood as the ships run each other down and are grappled together.

It is much more difficult to try to answer the strictures of the contemporary novelist upon historical novels. Why, he asks, with an exciting, familiar world going on all about us, do writers, such as myself, plunge themselves into a past which they cannot hope to know as well as they know the middle of the twentieth century?

Each writer has to answer for himself. I am conscious of two reasons why I have chosen to write historical novels. The first is extremely simple and mundane. The second is more complex. The simple reason is this: As a novelist, I am primarily interested in one kind of story; it is the story of young people thrown into some terrible predicament or danger and scrambling out of it, unaided. The first book I wrote, *The Great Gale* (published in the United States as the *Flood at Reedsmere*), was not an historical novel. The predicament was the sudden flooding of the children's village in Norfolk on the night of January 31, 1953. The incidents in the story were based on what really happened all along the east coast on that night. *The Great Gale* is, in fact, what one American reviewer has delightfully called "documentary fiction." When I came to search for another real-life predicament set in modern times upon which I could base a second story, I could not find one. The reasons are obvious: In England, we do not suffer from the natural hazards of earthquake, tornado, or bush fire; and against all other dangers we surround our children with loving parents, schoolteachers, and policemen. For a novelist, such as myself, life is far too safe for the young in the twentieth century. Therefore, I looked back in time to the beginning of the nineteenth century, when it was not at all safe to be young, when boys like Nelson himself were sent to sea at the age of eleven and might very well take part—as my Tom Henchman took part—in a battle as bloody as Trafalgar. The truth is that English history—all history for that matter—is full of robust, exciting plots for novelists who, like myself, wish to subject their characters to the test of danger.

The more complex reason why my imagination finds refuge in history was not at first apparent to me. Now, with every passing year, I am coming to realize more and more clearly how little I understand this present age. I do not understand its poetry or its art or its music. I do not understand why the young take drugs or become "hippies." I am bewildered by the multiplicity and contradictions of the facts, figures, fashions, and opinions which are presented to me daily in the newspapers. I am lost in the fog. If I look back at a past age, however, the fog clears; the facts and figures fall into place. Not only have the accidents of time selected the evidence but historians have interpreted that evidence for us and taught us to see the past in perspective.

What is complex about the situation is that though the past is better signposted than the present, I, the traveler, carry with me the anxieties and preoccupations of the twentieth century. I am quite conscious that I choose an event or theme in history because it echoes something I have experienced in my own life. For example, when I described the autumn of Trafalgar in *Castors Away!*, I consciously relived the summer of 1940. Both seasons were a time of great national danger, stress, and joy; in both we were threatened by invasion and were fighting for our lives. In the courage of Nelson, I felt again the inspiration of Winston Churchill, a personal experience of feeling which I have tried to recapture in my book *In Spite of All Terror*. In a quieter way, the themes of *Time of Trial* and *Thomas* echo a contemporary experience, namely the growing concern of many of us at the encroachment of the State upon the rights of the individual; while the theme of *No Beat of Drum* is perhaps the most insistently modern of all, since it is concerned with the bitter misery of the poor in a world of the rich. Whether it is right to use history in order to explore one's own problems, I do not know; but it certainly adds a deep and adult pleasure to storytelling.

In further reply to the contemporary novelist's criticism, I would add that having chosen a historical event in which one can hear one's own heart beat, it is not so impossible to imagine oneself living a hundred and sixty years ago—or more; for so much in England is still the same. Large parts of the Suffolk coast are the same, and the line of the South Downs, and the Cotswold villages, and a field of standing wheat undulating in the wind, and the weather. By concentrating on the sameness, one can gradually slip into what is different. The most important sameness, of course, is human nature. Men and women and children have always known happiness, felt terror, been angry, felt irritable, known despair. The emotions are the same; it is what evokes them that changes down the ages. Remembering our own everpresent terror of the nuclear bomb, it is not so impossible to imagine a seventeenth-century Puritan's terror of hell-fire. The courage of the three astronauts circling the moon is matched by the courage of Drake sailing round the world—and our response to both is the same.

Every novelist finds joy and an extension to his life in the characters which he creates in his stories, but the writer of historical fiction has yet another pleasure, which is his alone. It is the pleasure of discovery. The results of the research necessary before the writing of any historical novel open up for the author a new and absorbing world. I can only compare this experience with that of looking through a microscope at a number of formless blobs on one's slide and then twiddling with the knobs until, suddenly, the blobs come into focus and an intricate network of cells and nerves and structures is clearly revealed.

When I came to write *Time of Trial*, it was necessary for me to find out as much as possible about life in London in the year 1801. The little that I already knew was vague and formless. In search of information, I went to the Bodleian Library in Oxford and read as much contemporary material as I could discover in the catalogue. This, among many other books, included *A Guide to Visitors to London Newly Come Up from the Country*. In this guidebook, I learned which coffeehouses were patronized by what profession or political party, where the best tea gardens were, in which church I could hear the best sermon, and how I ought to behave when I visited that most popular attraction of sight-seers—Newgate Prison—in order to stare at the prisoners. I discovered, too, various street maps, a ground plan of the prison known as Poultry Compter (to which I sent my unfortunate bookseller-hero, Mr. Pargeter), and a book of etchings of the most noteworthy buildings in the metropolis. I looked also at contemporary cartoons and had the good fortune to light upon a little six-penny book published especially for children. This consisted of colored plates illustrating the many street vendors in the city, with their particular street cry printed below; for example, a boy carrying a flat basket of fish on his head with the caption "Mackerel. Fresh Mackerel," and a dustman with his cart crying "Dust O! Bring out your dust!" From oddly assorted material such as this, a strange, exciting, rather savage city gradually came into focus. I could lie in bed and listen—as Margaret Pargeter lay and listened in the first chapter of the book—to the countless church bells, the harsh grinding of iron wheels over the cobbles, the street cries, and the mutter of angry, half-starved men and women living in the terrible attics and cellars of the dark courts. The London of 1801 had mysteriously burst into life for me.

If writing historical novels has its own special pleasures, it also has its own special difficulties—especially if one knows that one's books are going to be read primarily by children. Children are not less intelligent than grownups. The problem is that they *know* less. In particular, they know less history. The first difficulty, then, is to give the historical setting of one's story and to impart the necessary historical facts without appearing to teach or to preach and—what is more important—without slowing up the pace of the narrative. Both the child and the writer want to hurry on to the action of the story. Yet, if the historical background is not firmly painted in, both child and author come to grief. The characters in the story move in a kind of featureless limbo, and both reader and writer lose interest in them. For this reason, I find the writing of the first chapter of every novel extremely difficult. There is so much to do all at the same moment: there are the characters to describe, the geographical setting to depict, the plot to be introduced, and, on top of all, the problem of history. I know from children themselves that I have not entirely mastered this difficulty, for I sometimes receive letters which begin: "I liked your story except for the beginning which I found boaring [sic]."

Another difficulty lies in children's susceptibilities: their capacity to be frightened or appalled. Yet, if one is drawn to write historical novels, what is one to do? History is not pretty. The Nazi concentration camps aside, I think people were far more cruel to each other in times past than they are today. The law was certainly more cruel. So was poverty. So was the treatment of children. How then is the writer to deal honestly with history and show sympathetic understanding toward his reader? One certainly does not want to cosset children in their reading. In my own case, the kind of story I like writing precludes such softness and emotional coziness. Yet, the difficulty remains: The brutality of times past may shock the oversensitive.

If one can only overcome these difficulties, both the writing and the reading of historical novels bring great rewards. The writer acquires much factual information from his researches which, if he is skillful, he can pass on pleasurably to his readers. Yet this, happily, is not his chief aim. The prime object of writing an historical novel is an exercise of the *heart* rather than the head. It is an exploration of the imagination, a discovery of other people living at other times and faced with other problems than our own. In other words, it is an extension of the author's human sympathies.

Writing my historical novels has made me far more understanding of human nature. I feel that it is not I who brought compassion to the writing but the actual writing that gave it to me. And if I have in any measure passed on this experience of sympathy to my readers, then I am indeed rewarded as a writer.

History Is People
Rosemary Sutcliff

A Sussex author who early became a writer for adults as well as for children, Rosemary Sutcliff writes historical fiction and has retold hero tales. In evaluating her literary stature after she won the Carnegie Medal in 1959 for The Lantern Bearers, *Marcus Crouch says:*

> *The Carnegie Medal Committee must have been inclined to honour Rosemary Sutcliff in each year since this most distinguished writer made her debut in 1950. . . . [Indeed, she was commended four times before winning the medal.] It is part of Miss Sutcliff's singular excellence as an historical novelist that she commands the reader's deep and personal identification with her characters . . . it is this passionate intensity of feeling which puts her in the forefront of post-war children's novelists.[1]*

Among her books are The Eagle of the Ninth *(1954),* The Outcast *(1955),* The Shield Ring *(1956),* Warrior Scarlet *(1958),* Rudyard Kipling *(1962),* Beowulf *(1962), and* Tristan and Iseult *(1971).*

Illustration by Charles Keeping from *The Lantern Bearers* by Rosemary Sutcliff, © 1959 by Rosemary Sutcliff. Reprinted by permission of Henry Z. Walck, Inc. and Oxford University Press.

"History Is People" by Rosemary Sutcliff is a previously unpublished paper distributed at a conference on Children's Literature in Education, Exeter, England, 1971. Reprinted by permission of the author.

1. *Chosen for Children*, ed. by Marcus Crouch (London: The Library Association, 1967), pp. 97, 98.

All writers with an interest in their work that goes beyond the bread-and-butter level, are aware of some kind of aim, something that they feel they are doing or trying to do. And this I think is, or at any rate should be, especially true of writers for the young. You, reading this, have formed your reading tastes, or had them formed for you; you have also done your growing up (well, most of it; I suppose one never quite finishes until the day one dies) and become the sort of people, more or less, that you are going to be for the rest of your lives, allowing for the natural differences between, say, eighteen and eighty. At any rate, in writing for you, nobody has to feel responsibility for helping to form you, or your tastes. But the reading child is liable to absorb ideas from books which may remain with him for the rest of his life, and even play some part in determining the kind of person that he is going to become. Along with most of my fellow writers, I *am* aware of the responsibilities of my job; and I do try to put over to the child reading any book of mine some kind of ethic, a set of values beyond the colour-television-two-cars-in-the-garage variety. I keep well clear of the treasure-hunt theme (with its under-tones of something for nothing) which in one form or another does seem to rather dog children's literature; I try to show the reader that doing the right/kind/brave/honest thing doesn't have to result in any concrete reward (help an eccentric old lady across the road and she will send you to ballet school), and that this doesn't matter; the reward lies in having *done* the right/kind/brave/honest thing, in having kept faith with one's own integrity—and probably in being given a more difficult thing to do next time.

Another responsibility of the writer for children which I try my best to fulfil is simply to supply them with words. This may sound trivial and obvious. But the words are man's means, not only of communicating, but of giving shape and manageability to his own thoughts and ideas. I have heard really tragic stories of children and young people failing in all-important exams or in interviews for jobs, not for any lack of intelligence, knowing perfectly well the answers to questions put to them, knowing what they wanted to say, but simply lacking the vocabulary with which to communicate in plain English. Since children learn their English from story books for pleasure as well as from lesson books in school, this is an appalling indictment of their reading matter, and one which we who write books for them must do something about. America has of late years begun the scientific production of books with graded vocabularies, two hundred words, four hundred words and so on. You match the size of vocabulary to the age of the child and it all sounds perfectly splendid. But this is to rob children of the beckoning splendour of words they do not yet understand (It matters remarkably little to a child that he does not understand a particular word; it's the flavour that counts.) and possibly of all curiosity as to words later. This is the eighth Deadly Sin, and I don't care how scientific it is!

My kind of book, the historical novel, is sometimes looked on as being an easy retreat from the complications and restrictions inherent in writing a modern story for the young. This is unfair! It is true that one has greater freedom in some ways. In Roman Britain or Norman England a boy of fourteen or fifteen can play a man's part, which is unlikely in the modern world; and the writer can make use of situations which would be far-fetched or even impossible in the present day; and there's a kind of safety barrier which makes it possible to deal with harsher realities than most children can take in their stride, if one were writing of people and events in their own world as they know it. The safety barrier is, I think, becoming less important, both to children themselves and to parents, teachers and librarians; but I don't believe that I could make my hero kill himself, as I did in *The Mark of the Horse Lord,* in a modern story set in everyday England. (One might get away with it in a story set in a far-off and very "different" place, say New Guinea, but this would merely be to substitute distance of place and culture for distance of time, as a safety barrier.

This is all true, but greater freedom is not in itself a bad thing; and there are plenty of extra problems to set against it, beside the obvious ones of research and historical accuracy. There is the ever-present danger of spilling over into cloak-and-dagger. There is the necessity to keep the people from being engulfed in the trimmings. (This can happen very easily, especially if the garnered results of the writer's research have not been properly digested before being used—nothing is worse for a historical story than undigested fragments of historical background!) There is the problem of making the people as real and individual as their modern counterparts, while at the same time not turning them into modern men and women in fancy dress. There is the problem, too, of the spoken word. Victorian writers, and even those of a somewhat later date, had no difficulty. They saw nothing ludicrous in "Alas! fair youth, it grieves me to see thee in this plight. Would that I had the power to strike these fetters from thy tender limbs." Josephine Tey, whose death I shall never cease to lament, called this "Writing forsoothly." A slightly different variant is known in the trade as "Gadzookery." Nowadays this is out of fashion; and some writers go to the other extreme and make the people of Classical Greece or Mediaeval England speak modern colloquial English. This is perhaps nearer to the truth of the spirit, since the people in question would have spoken the modern colloquial tongue of their place and time. But, personally, I find it destroys the atmosphere when a young Norman Knight says to his Squire, "Shut up, Dickie, you're getting too big for your boots." Myself, I try for a middle course, avoiding both Gadzookery and modern colloquialism; a frankly "made up" form that has the right sound to it, as Kipling did also. I try to catch the rhythm of a tongue, the tune that it plays on the ear, Welsh or Gaelic as opposed to Anglo-Saxon, the sensible workmanlike language which one feels the Latin of the ordinary Roman citizen would have translated into. It is extraordinary what can be done by the changing or transposing of a single word, or using a perfectly usual one in a slightly unusual way: "I beg your pardon" changed into "I ask your pardon." . . . But I would emphasize that this is not done by any set rule of thumb; I simply play it by ear as I go along.

I seem to have written the word "people" a great many times; and this I think must be because I feel so strongly that history *is* People—and people not so very unlike ourselves. This is a favourite thumping-tub of mine, and I now propose to thump it for a while.

The way people act is conditioned by the social custom of their day and age—even the way they think and feel with what one might call their outer layers. To take a very simple and obvious example: The men of the first Elizabethan age (and, Heaven knows, they were a tough enough lot!) cried easily and without shame in public. The rising generation of this second Elizabethan age are returning to much the same feeling, that one's emotions are not for hiding; but the men of my generation, my father's and grandfather's, were so conditioned in their extreme youth to the idea that men simply *didn't*, that by the time they were fifteen or sixteen they *couldn't*, even in private, except for such things as the death of a wife or child. But that's not to say that they feel, or felt, any less about the things they would have cried about, four hundred years ago.

I know there are two schools of thought about whether or not human nature actually changes, some maintaining that it does, some—me amongst them—that it doesn't. I believe most strongly that People Don't Change, that under the changing surface patterns of behaviour, the fundamental qualities and emotions and relationships remain the same. —Very much the qualities and emotions and relationships, incidentally, that one finds in Westerns; which is one reason why I like Westerns, and why most of the people in my own books would be perfectly at home in Laramie, while I would have no hesitation in sending The Virginian north of Hadrian's Wall to recover the Eagle of a lost Legion.

But even the surface patterns don't alter perhaps so much as one tends to think; and it is possible, sometimes, through a letter or a line of ancient poetry or some small object held in the hand, to catch glimpses of people separated from us by two hundred or two thousand years, so like ourselves that for the moment it is almost frightening because for that moment it makes nonsense of time.

About ten years ago, on a Hellenic cruise, I visited the museum at Heraklion, and spent a happy afternoon among the treasures excavated from the Palace of Knossos: octopus and dolphin jars, inlaid weapons, jewellery of intensely yellow gold, ivory bull-dancers in mid-leap. In the corner of one room was a case of little ornaments and children's toys; amongst them a tiny pottery tree with five or six branches, each ending in a fat little bird. It was painted in stripes, pale and pretty as an old-fashioned peppermint stick, the most completely charming thing. My first feeling on seeing it was a small sharp shock of delight, and my first thought, "*How* I should have loved to have that when *I* was a little girl!" It wasn't until the moment after, that I remembered that the little girl who must have loved it, and felt that same shock of delight on first seeing it, had been dead for three thousand years or so.

Then Homer has that lovely bit in the *Iliad,* just before Hector goes out from beleaguered Troy on the final sally that ends in his death. He is saying goodbye to his wife and baby son, and

> . . . as he spoke, Hector held out his arms for his boy, but the boy shrank back into the nurse's bosom, crying and scared at the sight of his father, for he was afraid of the gleaming metal and the horsehair crest when he saw that dreadful thing nodding from the top of the helmet. Father and mother laughed aloud, and Hector took off the helmet and set it down on the ground, shining and flashing. Then he kissed his son and dandled him in his hands and prayed aloud to Heaven. . . .

How many infants since Homer's day must have been terrified by the sight of father in an over-splendid hat? I know one myself, when we were both about five. He was supposed (though he turned brilliant later) to be slightly retarded; and for this, his Nannie held his parents to be entirely responsible. They had taken him to see his Grandfather—known throughout the Navy as "Monkey" Domville, for reasons which were painfully obvious—in full dress for some Court function; and the poor child, who was quite used to his Grandfather in the usual way, had taken one look at him under a gold-laced cocked hat, screamed wildly, and according to Nannie, fallen in a fit and never been the same child since.

There's another tiny story about Hector and his son which I like: that the boy's real name was Astyanax, but Hector called him Scamander after the river which ran through the Plain of Troy. No reason is given for the father's choice of name, and one can only assume that Astyanax was a wet baby. The small family joke may be Homer's rather than Hector's, but it is still of respectable antiquity, and it's a joke that might quite easily have been made this morning.

In Britain, very early letters, etc., have little chance to survive the climate and conditions; but everyone knows how long papyrus holds together in the dry air of Egypt; and there is in existence a delightful letter dating from Roman times, from a young officer of the Legions stationed at Alexandria, to his mother. (To this day, it is generally to the mother rather than the father that a boy turns when he wants a bit extra.) "I hope you are well as I am. Please send me two hundred Drachmae. I've bought a mule cart and that has taken all my money; so dear Mother, *do* please send me my month's allowance. Valarius' mother sent him plenty of olive oil and a parcel of meat and two hundred drachmae! Please send me some money and don't leave me like this. My brother wrote to me but he only sent me a pair of drawers. Please answer this letter quickly. Give my Greeting to all at home. Your loving Son."

From Mediaeval times onwards, of course, many English letters have survived. I cherish extracts from three in particular: one Mediaeval, one dating from Tudor times, and one from the Civil War.

The first is a lovely piece of husbandcoaxing, written in 1443 when scarlet gowns were the height of fashion. On September 28th of that year, Margaret Paston, wife of a Country Knight, wrote to her husband who was in London and suffering from a bad leg of some kind: "I would ye were at home, if it were for your ease, and your sore might be as well looked to here as it is where ye be now; liefer than a gown, though it were of scarlet."

History doesn't record whether the good knight took the hint; but I hope so much that he did.

The Tudor one is from Catharine Parr to Tom Seymour, Lord High Admiral of England. One tends to think of her as dull and middle-aged; in fact, she was a woman of great charm and intelligence, and she was only thirty-six when she died. She was married off to old men and widowed twice, and was already engaged, for the first time by her own choice, to Tom Seymour when Henry VIII cast his eye on her. And after his death she went to her own house at Chelsea; and Tom came courting her again. They were married, and when their child was born, she died. The recent T.V. serial, "The Six Wives of Henry VIII" did less than justice to her relationship with Seymour, suggesting that after the King's death she had no longer any wish to marry him, and was forced into it for reasons of State. Reasons of State there were, for the marriage, and entanglements with the Princess Elizabeth too; but whatever the Lord Admiral's feelings for the ex-Queen (my own guess is that he was one of those men capable of being genuinely in love with two different women at the same time), her letters to him, written from Chelsea in the months before their wedding, are the letters of a woman serenely and very happily in love.

> I would not have you think that this, mine honest goodwill towards you, proceeds from any sudden passion. For as truly as God is God, my mind was fully bent the *other* time I was free, to marry you before any man I know. However, God withstood my will therein most vehemently for a time; and through His grace and goodness made it possible for me to do what I did not think possible, to utterly renounce mine own will and follow His willingly. It would take too long to write all the story of this matter. If I live, I shall tell it to you myself. I can say nothing; but as My Lady of Suffolk saith, 'God is a Marvellous Man!'
>
> Katryn the Queen.

And again she writes a note to Tom, who was in the habit of walking across from Westminster through the fields in the early summer mornings. "I pray you let me have knowledge overnight at hour you will come, that your portress may wait at the gate to the fields for you."

Last of all, the Civil War letter. Edward Spencer, Earl of Sunderland, declared for the King, and five letters which he wrote home from the Royalist army to his young wife are still in existence; the last written just four days before the second battle of Newbury. His adored little three-year-old daughter must have sent him a "Scribble" letter of the kind so often enclosed with a mother's letter to her husband away from home—to

Heaven knows how many servicemen in Heaven knows how many wars since then—for he sends her this message: "Pray bless Poppet for me, and tell her that I would have written to her but that, upon careful consideration, I find it to be uncivil to return an answer to a lady in other characters than her own, which I am not yet learned enough to do."

Four days later he was killed in action.

Forgive me if I have meandered too long among my favourite bits and pieces; thumping my favourite tub. It is important to me, all this, because History *is People* and I try to teach history. The man's eye view of history, not the God's eye view. It is because history books must of necessity take the God's eye view, that they can so often and so easily become dull; that, and because they so often break it up into set, static pictures, each, as it were, separately framed (often by the reigns of succeeding monarchs), instead of treating it as a living and continuous process, of which we are a part, and of which our descendants (supposing that we haven't blown the world up) will be a part also. I feel it to be enormously important that the young should be given this sense of continuity, that they should be given the feeling of their roots behind them. To know and really understand something of where one came from helps one to understand and cope better with where one is now—and where one is going to. And as we today are standing too near our own particular stretch of history to be able to make out the pattern and "see how the story ends," so I feel that history can best be brought to life for children through people in the like situation with regard to their own stretch of history, people standing too close to see the pattern, and who, like us, "don't know how the story ends." That's my justification for being a historical novelist and not a historian. But they must be people with whom the children can identify through the fundamental sameness—like calling to like under the changing surfaces.

Some years ago, I was struck by a *Sunday Times* article putting forward the theory that the ability to write for children is the result of an unlived pocket of childhood left over in the writer. I think this is very probably true, —it was certainly true of Rudyard Kipling and Beatrix Potter, and it is certainly true of me. But I think also that it draws heavily on a feeling for the primitive and fundamental things of life. The young have this feeling very strongly. It is why myths and legends, certainly not meant for children, have been taken over by them. It is one of the reasons why children like Westerns; and why—as I said before—I like them too. Legends and Westerns and my sort of historical novel are all alike in dealing in the big basic themes, comradeship between men, loyalty and treachery and divided loyalty, love and hate, the sense of property, revenge for slain kinsfolk; and of course the age-old struggle between good and evil. As I say, the instinct for this is strong in children; in most adults it has been pushed down, sometimes only a little way, sometimes almost entirely, into the subconscious; but it is always *there,* forming a common ground on which children's books can appeal to adult readers. Which is why it is not only unnecessary, but wrong, to write down for children; instead, the child should be drawn out and up. This is why books can play such a great part in a child's development, enlarging him and giving him a broader and deeper awareness—and why we who write for children carry such terrible responsibility on our shoulders.

So—I have said what I wanted to say. I hope it makes sense to you. It is all true; but in case you think it all sounds too earnest and didactic, I will add one thing more:—that basically, fundamentally, and at the beginning of all things, I merely find, or am found by, a story which I want to tell, which seems to me worth telling, and above all, which I want to *hear*, and tell it to the very best of my ability. All the rest, if I'm lucky, is added unto me in the course of the telling.

Matters of Fact

Margery Fisher[1]

It is the writer's business to provide a book which a child *can* use himself, whether in private or in the atmosphere of a classroom, to discover something new or to confirm what he already knows. The fact that the reader is young will impose certain limitations and responsibilities. Beyond the literary obligations which any writer faces in regard to any kind of readership—obligations to be accurate, to be clear in explanation, to be stimulating, to pursue a logical arrangement of his material—he must be aware of the age and aptitude of his readers in a broad way, just as a teacher or a parent selecting books must take into account in a relative way a writer's choice of vocabulary and of facts, as well as the illustration and design of a book as a whole.

But there is more to an information book than its technical aspect. Each one should contain fact, concept and attitude. Any book that is not a mere collection of facts (and many of them are only this) has an end in view, a generalisation towards which the facts are arranged. This final concept might be a statement of the result of victory or defeat, in a book of historical fact, or the definition of the end-product of a process and its use, in a book of technology; it might be the summing-up of the purpose of an institution or a public service, or the pronouncement of an abstract idea.

Behind the generalisation that concludes, or should conclude, an information book lies the attitude of the writer. In some cases this may be a visible partisanship—as for instance in Frank Knight's *The Dardanelles Campaign* or Bruce Catton's study of the American Civil War, *This Hallowed Ground*. The enthusiasm of an expert discernible in a book on a sport, a pastime, a hobby, is in itself an attitude. Flatness of style, perfunctory writing, flabbiness in generalisation, all denote the lack of an attitude and promise ill for any book. A writer's conviction has an immediate effect on the reader, whether it is to invigorate and stimulate interest or to communicate a prejudice.

A writer's attitude is often revealed in his terminology. Natural history books provide a useful example here. In any index of this category certain words are likely to recur—Wonderful, Marvellous, Oddities, Miracle, Secrets. What attitudes do these indicate and how should we regard them?

Anyone who chooses to write about natural history has the responsibility for communicating a scientific attitude. To indicate that nature is "wonderful" is to suggest that to the writer the world of nature, in which he

1. For biographical information about the author, see p. 126.

properly includes his own existence, is something that excites him and something that he feels could excite the reader. The child's sense of wonder is two-fold. He notices with a lively interest and he also wonders—that is, he wants to know and he asks questions. Whether his interest is stimulated by reading a book or by using his eyes when he is walking in city or country, "wonder" implies an attitude that is potentially active. It leads to discovery and knowledge. "Wonderful" is a word that denotes the observer and his state of mind, not the observed; it need not interfere with a scientific attitude.

But—"marvellous"? What does this imply? Surely, that there is something inexplicable in nature, something involuntary, something different. Such an attitude is basically unscientific. Whether it is devoted to a single subject (spiders, a cat having kittens) or to a region of behaviour (animal navigation), the business of a natural history book is to relate facts to a pattern of life in which humans participate as animals and which they should understand because they are part of it. However informal the approach, however simple, a natural history book for the young belongs to the science of biology. To suggest that the food-catching mechanism of a mussel or the egg-depositing behaviour of a cuckoo is "marvellous" is to make nonsense of the whole process of evolution. This pre-Darwinian attitude is discernible today also in the words "miracle" and "creature," though these may be used without any conscious intention. Words like this are enough to lead a young reader to accept the author's anthropomorphism as a matter of course.

An equally dangerous attitude may be detected in the *avoidance* of certain words. Scientific principles and terminology need not be daunting to young readers. It does not make it easier to see the natural world in perspective, for instance, if the term "animal" is used for "mammal," as it almost invariably is in information books. Alan James in *Animals* (1969) even goes so far as to explain that "usually when we say 'animals' we are talking only about *Mammals*" but he still decides "we shall use the word 'animal' all through the book." His reasoning eludes me. It is not pedantic to suggest that the proper terms should be used in the simplest book. Children read books like this to sort information, and to sort properly they must be given the proper categories and terms to work with.

Formally or informally, an information book sets out to teach. To conceal this entirely natural aim, authors writing in many categories use the ubiquitous word "fun" as a smoke-screen. In this respect, trends in non-fiction have followed trends in education, not always with advantage. The move away from a captive audience and set classroom lecturing, healthy though this move certainly is, can lead to trivial studies as easily as to original and exciting work. A superficial permissiveness in the classroom is reflected in the throw-away manner of some information books. An advertisement for a junior travel series announces "a series of guides for young people with a completely original approach. The books are fun to read and the authors have concentrated on amusing the reader, while the educational aspect is left to look after itself."[2] The book advertised on this occasion was *Let's Look at Austria* by Gwynneth Ashby. I wonder how the partition of Austria in the past or her fate in World War II could be made to seem "amusing"; in fact, the author does not try to fulfill this promise except by being evasive at this stage of her survey.

Children are invited to have fun with coloured paper and with time, with collage and with palaeontology. How disconcerting for them to discover that a book recommends them to *use* mind or hands, and how surprising, too, to open a book like *Mr. Budge Buys a Car* and to find that Gareth Adamson has made technicalities into fun without saying so and without demeaning himself or his readers.

Learning has always been fun in the sense of exciting, invigorating, stimulating and entertaining, but it has never offered to be effortless. The delight in discovery goes far deeper than "fun." A title that uses the word "quest" or "discover" or "look at" picks up and uses the energy which boys and girls are ready to exercise if they are helped to do so. The writer who respects his readers will call upon them to exercise their minds as well as their hands; no better exercise-machine for the intellect has yet been devised than a book. . . .

2. *The Bookseller*, no. 3158 (2 July 1966), p. 28.

The Changing World of Science and the Social Sciences

Mary K. Eakin

Mary K. Eakin is a teacher of children's literature and former editor of the Bulletin of the Center for Children's Books. *While editor, she was compiler of* Good Books for Children, Nineteen Fifty-Nineteen Sixty Five *(3rd ed., 1966). She is also the compiler, with Albert C. Haman, of* Library Materials for Elementary Science *and editor of* Subject Index to Books for Intermediate Grades *(3rd ed., 1963) and* Subject Index to Books for Primary Grades *(3rd ed., 1967). The following paper was presented in Bologna, Italy, at the 1970 Congress of the International Board on Books for Young People.*

The poet-anthropologist, Loren Eiseley, tells a story in his book, *The Firmament of Time,* which seems especially pertinent to any consideration of the effects of today's changing world on matters of science and the social sciences; whether these effects pertain to future needs in children's books, to implications for all of education, or to re-assessments of their own roles by scientists and social scientists.

"There is a story about one of our great atomic physicists—a story for whose authenticity I cannot vouch, and therefore I will not mention his name; I hope, however, with all my heart that it is true. If it is not, then it ought to be, for it illustrates well what I mean by a growing self-awareness, a sense of responsibility about the universe.

This man, one of the chief architects of the atomic bomb, so the story runs, was out wandering in the woods one day with a friend when he came upon a small tortoise. Overcome with pleasurable excitement, he took up the tortoise and started home, thinking to surprise his children with it. After a few steps he paused and surveyed the tortoise doubtfully.

'What's the matter?' asked his friend.

Without responding, the great scientist slowly retraced his steps as precisely as possible, and gently set the turtle down upon the exact spot from which he had taken him up.

Then he turned solemnly to his friend. 'It just struck me,' he said, 'that perhaps, for one man, I have tampered enough with the universe.' He turned, and left the turtle to wander on its way.

The man who made that remark was one of the best of the modern men, and what he had devised had gone down into the whirlpool. 'I have tampered enough,' he said. It was not a denial of science. It was a final recognition that science is not enough for man. It is not the road back to the

"The Changing World of Science and the Social Sciences" by Mary K. Eakin from *Bookbird*, v. 8, no. 2 (1970). Reprinted by permission of the International Institute for Children's Juvenile and Popular Literature.

waiting Garden, for that road lies through the heart of man. Only when man has recognized this fact will science become what it was for Bacon, something to speak of as 'touching upon hope.' Only then will man be truly human."

At a recent graduation convocation, the Dean of the College of Natural Sciences at the University of Northern Iowa, spoke on the topic: "A Winter of Discontent." In reference to the upsurge of interest in science within the schools and universities which came about through the development of the first atomic reaction and, later, through the launching, by Russian scientists, of the first man-made satellite to successfully penetrate outer space, circle the earth, and return safely, he says:

> Stimulated some by the activity going on in the physical sciences and engineering laboratories and classrooms, and even more by their scholastic concerns, the social scientists and the scholars of the humanities became emboldened. In literature, in art and music, and in social constructs, they reminded us in striking fashion of our human predicament and of our social nature. Although modern physics has pronounced great revolutions in the interpretation of our physical universe, the teacher of physics seldom attracts questions of propriety in discussing such revolutionary ideas. But a teacher of humanities, asking his students to study and react to social ideas expressed with language that has not been commonly used in the public exhibitions of life, finds he may be charged with irresponsibility as a scholar and especially as a teacher. If he protests the charge, he is an enemy of the people because the people are made uncomfortable, and he realizes there has been a misunderstanding as to what really is his commission and responsibility.

The problem is basically one of our attitude toward change; what one scientist has described as "the crisis of transformation." Traditionally, we have tended to accept, even to welcome, changes brought about by discoveries in science and their application in technology, but have been hesitant to accept, sometimes to even discuss, changes brought about by discoveries in the social sciences. To quote again from Dean McCollum: . . . "there must be developed in our time a willingness to accept change. As we accept and welcome technological change, so we must eagerly invent and try out new social structures and procedures. . . . There must be abroad in our world, in our time, a restless yearning or aspiration for improvement in our human endeavor."

Yes, we may say, but we are here to talk about children and children's books, and these are adult problems suitable for adult consideration only. Adults have long assumed that children cannot understand such complex problems; that the important thing is to give them the facts first so that when they become adults they can then grapple with matters such as these men are talking and writing about. There is, of course, a grain of truth to this observation, but then we face the question: Which facts? Or, more importantly, What are facts?

In the past, children's education, as children's books, has tended to be carefully compartmentalized. When the child is studying "reading," he is not studying "science." When he is studying "history," he is not studying "literature." When he studies "government," he is not studying "astronomy." Is it any wonder, then, that adults find it difficult to make casual relationships between the scientific and technological "progress" of which they are so proud, and the ever-increasing social problems with which they are "plagued"?

Heretofore, children's books have reflected the ideas, the mores, the customs of the period in which they were written. Thus they have tended in two directions. Many times they have dealt with the past, but with the past as it was interpreted by the current generation. Books purporting to deal with present times have tended to defend the status quo. Seldom have we seen children's books, with the possible exception of a few pieces of science fiction, which projected into the future. Even science fiction, for younger children, tends to be science fantasy and to deal with the mechanics of travel, communication, and conflict in the future rather than with the effects of those new means of travel, communication, and conflict on human relationships.

Since change creates anxieties, and we are imbued with the idea that childhood is and must be kept a carefree time, therefore free of anxieties, we have tended to give our children books of scientific and social "facts," but facts which have been carefully selected to exclude any ideas which might possibly disturb the child and make him begin to look more critically and more questioningly at the world around him. It is much easier for the child of today to learn the basic principles of atomic fission than the equally available and clearly understandable facts about the effects of modern technology on the pollution of air and water.[1] Much less do we give him any of the tools needed to begin to project what a future will be like when there is no clean air or water left in the world.

After most of the major forests of the United States were destroyed, the people of that country established Arbor Day to commemorate the need for nurturing the trees and forests which were left; but the reader of science or social science books for children would look long and fruitlessly to find anywhere an objective discussion of the efforts of lumbering companies to take over the last of the great redwood forests. Geography books tell a student much about the places around the globe where oil is found; astronomical figures as to the amounts that are taken from the wells each year; even more astronomical figures as to the monetary value of these wells—but nothing of the off-shore oil slicks which are destroying wildlife, ruining beaches, and disrupting the lives of many people who live near the

---

1. [This was written before many books were published on the subject, 1970 and after—Editor's note.]

drilling areas; nothing of the exploitation of other countries by major powers whose economic and educational aid to those countries is expressed in terms of better roads (to the oil fields), better technology (for such refining and storage plants as will provide the least expensive handling and transporting of oil), better education (to the point of providing semi-skilled labor for the oil industries); but little real concern for what such activities do to the country as a whole.

It is an encouraging sign of a possibly more honest and healthy approach to children's books that we have today a conference dedicated to the theme: "A Changing World, the Challenge of Children's Books" (in my own mind, I paraphrase that: "the Challenge to Children's Books"), and that the planners of the conference would assign a paper in which science and social studies books are to be dealt with together.

Perhaps we have reached a point where we can turn from the *Pippa Passes* ("God's in his heaven. All's right with the world") attitude of past writing for children, to the more mature and more relevant attitude expressed in Yevtushenko's *Lies:*

> Telling lies to the young is wrong.
> Proving to them that lies are true is wrong.
> Telling them that God's in his heaven
> and all's well with the world is wrong.
> The young know what you mean. The young are people.
> Tell them the difficulties can't be counted,
> and let them see not only what will be
> but see with clarity these present times.
> Say obstacles exist they must encounter,
> sorrow happens, hardship happens.
> The hell with it. Who never knew
> the price of happiness will not be happy.
> Forgive no error you recognize,
> it will repeat itself, increase,
> and afterwards our pupils
> will not forgive in us what we forgave.[2]

What are some of the areas of science and of the social sciences in which we have failed children in the past and hopefully will do better in the future? There is the idea that the world is static; that evolution was something which took place entirely in the past. Some books seem to imply that evolution stopped at the point where Darwin "discovered" it. But to quote again from Loren Eiseley, "The world is fixed, we say: fish in the sea, birds in the air. But in the mangrove swamps by the Niger, fish climb trees and ogle uneasy naturalists who try unsuccessfully to chase them back to the

---

2. "Lies" by Yevgeny Yevtushenko from *Yevtushenko: Selected Poems*, translated by Robin Milner-Gulland and Peter Levi, S. J. (Harmondsworth: Penguin Books, 1969). Translation Copyright © Robin Milner-Gulland and Peter Levi, 1962.

water. There are things still coming ashore." Perhaps the idea that man is the final end-product of evolution is one of those errors which we need to see today and explain to the children, through their books, so that they will have no cause to face us, tomorrow, with an accusing and unforgiving, "Why did you lie to us?"

Children may need books to make them fully aware of the danger of losing a part of their natural heritage. So along with the books of beautiful color photographs of nature, in its smallest manifestations—insects, hummingbirds, a single flower, let them also see picture books of the devastated earth, of lumbered and burned over areas; of birds dying in the oil slicks along the coasts; of fish gasping for air in lakes so polluted that they can no longer sustain any life except algae; of skies lost to sight in the smog over cities, and children in those same cities wearing gas masks.

Some people will say that such subjects are too grim, too disturbing, and too strong fare for young children. That they will create fears which will cause children unnecessary anxiety and possibly even result in some children becoming so depressed about the future of the world and of their own lives that they will completely withdraw, emotionally or through suicide. It is, of course, true that problems created by science and technology can be presented to children in such a manner that there seems no hope for the world. However, it does seem that writers should be able to achieve a balance between the Pollyanna attitude of the past (All is for the best in this best of all possible worlds) and complete resignation to a future of such insurmountable problems that no one will be able to solve them. Until we have more science writers with a social conscience—such as the man in Loren Eiseley's anecdote—perhaps it should become the responsibility of every publishing house to have science and social science editors work as pairs to make certain that every science and technological publication of the future contains at least one section devoted to the social implications of the discovery or the new technique being described.

Science books published during the past decade have tended more and more to be open-ended in that theories are carefully labeled as theories, rather than having one preferred theory (preferred by the author, that is) stated as a proven fact, and they have tended to leave the reader with the feeling that there is still more to learn about the subject under discussion. Books in the natural sciences make use of the ecology approach, showing each plant and animal in relation to the other plants and animals of its natural habitat rather than describing it in an isolated setting which gives the reader little understanding of its place in the balance or the continuum of nature. Seldom does a writer of science books for children any longer state that mankind has gone as far as possible in any field of endeavor or has learned all there is to learn about any aspect of the physical world. This same quality of open-endedness might be used to start children thinking about some of the after-effects of scientific discoveries.

Many of the same criticisms which are raised regarding the tendency of science books of the past to ignore the implications of scientific discoveries for the social side of man's existence may also be leveled at books in the areas of the social sciences themselves, especially history. The primary purpose of informational books for children should be to stimulate them to ask questions—to ask questions which grow out of a desire for more information than the book gives them, and to ask questions about the validity of what the book tells them. We applaud the inquiring mind of a child that causes him to take a piece of machinery apart and see what makes it run; we should equally applaud and encourage the inquiring mind of a young person that takes a social institution, an account of history, a religious belief, or a human relationship apart and seeks to find out why they are as they are and if they need to always remain as they are now. We need to not only applaud such inquiries when they happen to appear, but also to provide books which will stimulate children to raise questions in these areas.

All too often our social studies books have been devoted to perpetuating the status quo instead of sending young people seeking new ideas and new, creative ways of facing problems of human relationships; which, after all, is what social science is all about. It is true histories change from time to time, but the changes are, more often than not, instituted for the purpose of justifying a present action or attitude of the government rather than to stimulate a young mind to seek out more accurate information about events of the past. Even when new information is available regarding events and famous figures of the past, such information is usually made available to children only in so far as it enhances those events or figures; seldom is it included when it reveals a weakness or error of judgement. No country has ever had a history of perfection; always there has been good balanced against evil; failure against success; yet, in all too many books for children the evil and failures are selected out, leaving only a dull and wholly unbelievable account of continuous success and well-being.

Controversy needs to become a positive factor in children's social studies books of the future, if these books are to help children adjust to a changing world; for changes, almost without exception, imply controversy. Not everyone is going to agree on the direction in which governments should move, social institutions should evolve, or values and mores should alter. Even among those persons who feel that there is nothing to be gained from a simpleminded attempt to cling to the present or return to the past, there is little agreement as to the goals toward which changes should be aimed or the best means of achieving those goals. To pretend to children that such conflicts are not a part of the world today is to leave them in as difficult and vulnerable a position as results when parents pretend to their children that no problems or conflicts exist within a family that is on the verge of divorce or financial disaster. Children have always been more perceptive than adults are usually willing to credit them with being and, with the advent of television and other forms of mass communication, are ever more acutely aware of the changes and conflicts taking place in their world today. Instead of trying to hide the world's controversies, we need to let children examine them, find out as much as they can about the causes, discuss the possible consequences of a variety of courses of action, and thus be prepared to understand the problems with which they will one day be faced.

If books are to meet the challenge of a changing world we must begin to give children histories of their own countries written from the point of view of countries with which their own has been in conflict. (It is, for example, wonderfully salutary for children in the United States to read a British historian's account of the American Revolution.) There must be books which show the way in which history itself changes from one generation to the next as new information and new understanding become available. There must be books on government which admit to the weaknesses of each form of government as well as to the strengths of each—and this for the accounts of governments with which a given country is on unfriendly terms as well as for the accounts of the governments of its allies. There must be books of science and technology which concern themselves with the social implications of discoveries in these fields. We need books which relate mankind to the on-going process of evolution; which show him as being *of* the total environment and the total universe, rather than merely being *in* an environment or in the universe. Most importantly, we need books which open the child's mind to the facts of change; to the challenges of change; and to the part he can play in determining the direction of future changes; books which lead him to ask: Why? and Why not?; books which will open for him the way to becoming truly human; and which will create within him that restless yearning for improvement in our human endeavor. When children's books of science are written with an awareness of the responsibility of science for its contribution not only to technological progress but also for the social problems that technology creates; when books of social studies are written with an awareness of mankind's responsibility for insuring the wisest use of science's discoveries, then we can truly say that children's books are meeting the challenge of a changing world.

The Prose Imagination

Irving Adler

Irving Adler is a college teacher and author of many books on science and mathematics, most of them illustrated by his wife Ruth Adler. The titles of his books for young people indicate the range of his scientific interests: Energy *(o.p.),* Time in Your Life *(1958),* Seeing the Earth from Space *(rev. ed., 1962),* Oceans *(1962),* Numerals *(1964),* Electricity in Your Life *(1965),* Magnets *(1966), and* The Sun and Its Family *(rev. ed., 1969).*

> "Physics is not a collection of 'facts' which can be learned; it is a highly imaginative intellectual structure of concepts that gives a meaningful and creative picture or model . . . of man's experience of the world." —Organization for Economic Cooperation and Development, "A Modern Approach to School Physics"

> "To present a scientific subject in an attractive and stimulating manner is an artistic task, similar to that of a novelist or even a dramatic writer." — Max Born, in "Bulletin of the Atomic Scientists," November 1965

Several years ago I was invited by the late Richard Banks of Yale University to appear on his television interview program, "The Opinionated Man." Mr. Banks had brought in for the same program the poet Brother Antoninus, so that he might have an opportunity to develop through our conversation the *contrast* between the scientific and the artistic points of view. However, what emerged clearly in the course of our conversation was an important *resemblance* between scientific and artistic production: they both involve creative acts of the imagination.

The resemblance between science and art is not adequately appreciated. There is a common misconception about the work of scientists and science writers. People think of a scientist as someone who gathers *facts* like a clerk taking inventory in a hardware store. And they think the work of the science writer is like recording the inventory in a hardware catalog. To see the error in this view, let us examine briefly the work of the scientist and science writer.

The scientist bases all his work on *observation* of some segment of reality. But his observation is not like taking inventory of objects already neatly arranged in piles on a shelf. It is more like taking inventory of things jumbled in a heap on the floor. He must first separate them, identify them, and classify them according to some pattern of organization. This pattern

---

does not flow automatically out of the things themselves; it has to be created by the scientist.

However, there is an important way in which scientific observation is not at all like taking inventory. The *facts* of science are not simply lying around exposed to view and waiting to be seen. They have to be looked for, and, in many cases, they first have to be produced. Scientific observation is not a mere passive viewing of phenomena. It involves active intervention in the phenomena. The scientist does not merely say, "Let me see what is happening." He says, "Let me see what happens if I do this and what happens if I do that." In short, observation is closely linked to experimentation.

When he performs an experiment, the scientist is asking nature a question, and he creates conditions under which nature will give him a clear answer. Before he performs the experiment, the scientist must first decide what question he wants nature to answer. Choosing a good question is neither simple nor automatic; it requires knowledge, insight and imagination. Getting an answer to the question is equally difficult. Nature is often reluctant to reveal her secrets. She keeps them hidden in "a riddle wrapped in a mystery inside an enigma." It requires skill, insight, and inventiveness to be able to create the conditions under which nature stops talking in riddles and starts giving clear-cut answers to a question. Thus, the design of a successful experiment, from asking a significant question to obtaining a clear answer, involves acts of creative imagination.

Observation and experiment are the foundations of science, but it is important to note that they are only the foundations, and not the whole structure. Scientific knowledge is not merely a list of results obtained from experiment and observation. As the British scientist J. D. Bernal has put it, "If it were, science would soon become as unwieldy and as difficult to understand as the Nature from which it started. Before these results can be of any use, and in many cases before they can even be obtained, it is necessary to tie them together, so to speak, in bundles, to group them and to relate them to each other." The scientist puts together and relates the results of his experiments and observations to form a *theory,* which is a mental picture of the phenomena he is studying.

The formulation of a scientific theory is sometimes compared to solving a jigsaw puzzle. But it is a puzzle with most of the pieces missing. The scientist has to use his imagination to fill in the gaps and produce a whole picture. Actually, the jigsaw puzzle analogy is somewhat misleading, because the relationship of observed facts to scientific theory is not that of part to whole. The relationship, on the contrary, is really that of conclusion to premises in a deductive system of propositions. The scientist says in his theory that if we make certain assumptions or hypotheses, then we can deduce from them conclusions that correspond to the observed facts. What a scientist does when he formulates a theory is better expressed by the closed box analogy: Nature is like a closed box containing a mechanism which controls some observable events that occur outside the box. The scientist cannot see what is inside the box. So, instead, he *imagines* what the inside mechanism must be like in order to produce the outside effects that he observes. Thus, the formulation of a scientific theory is a creative act of the imagination. Of course a theory is a creation of a special kind, whose consequences must stand up under the rigorous tests of experience.

The science writer has the job of transmitting to the layman an understanding of the vast, complex, and growing body of scientific knowledge. He cannot do this by merely recording scientific knowledge and then playing it back like a tape recorder. The form in which scientific knowledge is reported to the community of scientists is not the same as the form in which it may be introduced to the uninitiated. Before he can present scientific knowledge to the child or to the general reader, he must rework the material in a special way. He must first select from the great mass of scientific knowledge certain key ideas that can serve to convey to the reader an understanding of the problems, the methods, and the ever-changing conclusions of science. He must break these ideas down into their constituent parts, so that when the parts are presented in the proper sequence, each is easy to understand. He must organize this sequence, so that the reader is led step by step from simple ideas to more and more complex combinations. By the use of appropriate analogies and images, he relates new ideas to familiar ideas in the reader's experience. And finally, while doing this, he must convey to the reader some feeling of the excitement of science as an exploration of unknown regions of the universe; an appreciation of the beauty of the imaginative structure produced by scientists; and a grasp of the significance of science in man's efforts to control his environment for human purposes.

To do these things is no routine job that can be performed in a perfunctory manner. Successful science writing is, as Max Born says, "an artistic task." Like the discovery of new scientific knowledge or the writing of poems, plays or novels, it requires the play of a creative imagination, which, no less than artistic constructs, illuminates the structure of reality.

Chapter 10

The International Scene

Since internationalism (through publication of translations) has become an increasingly important aspect of modern children's literature, a consideration of what is happening abroad is now a significant part of the study of children's books. Greater attendance at international congresses, book fairs, and seminars on children's literature is evidence of interest. A number of the papers in this volume were presented first in such gatherings. They reveal developments in children's literature in only a sampling of geographical areas.[1]

In addition to being significant for their literary revelations, these selections incidentally accomplish to some degree what F. J. Harvey Darton achieved in *Children's Books in England:* they reveal some elements of the social life of certain countries. Helga Mach begins her Czechoslovakian survey by saying, "To speak about children's books in Czechoslovakia means also to speak about political events in this country." Miriam Morton, in the introduction to her *Harvest of Russian Children's Literature,* states that one of its purposes is the provision of insight into "an important aspect of

---

1. For information on children's literature in some other countries, see Sheila A. Egoff, *The Republic of Childhood: A Critical Guide to Canadian Children's Literature in English* (Toronto, London: Oxford University Press, 1968), and Mary Ørvig, "A Survey of Children's Books in Sweden" (Stockholm: Swedish Institute on Children's Books, rev. ed. in press). For a general view see Paul Hazard, *Books, Children, and Men,* trans. by Marguerite Mitchell (Boston: Horn Book, Inc., 1944). *Bookbird Magazine* also occasionally publishes survey articles on international literature.

Russian child culture—its literature—and to show how it reflects modern Russia's ideas and ideals." And Shigeo Watanabe remarks that the development of children's literature in Japan has paralleled changes in social thought and behavior.

In the field of children's literature, as in many other matters, nations are truly interconnected and interdependent. The literature of Japan, for example, has been greatly enriched by a translations program, but it is important to add that the production of distinctive picture books in Japan has, through translation and republishing, significantly enriched the picture-book field in Western countries. Many other articles in this chapter also note the importance of a translations program to the development of a nation's children's literature.

Another important factor in the development of the literature is the state of criticism of children's books. Bertha Mahony Miller stated concisely a principle few, if any, would disagree with: "Arts flourish where there is sound critical judgment to examine and appraise."[2]

---

2. *Horn Book Magazine*, 22 (June 1946): 175.

A New Internationalism

Virginia Haviland[1]

In this age of internationalism, marked by a growing number of international congresses of interest to professionals in the children's book world and an increased flow of children's books between countries, the creators, publishers, selectors, and distributors of children's books do well to gain whatever knowledge they can of what is outstanding in a country's writing and illustrating for children. And they must keep in mind that it is not always the best book which is translated and republished, just as it is not always the best book which is a big seller or a selection for children's reading.

In 1966, Mildred L. Batchelder, then Executive Secretary of the Children's Services Division of the American Library Association, became concerned with the question of translation. On a half-year's sabbatical in Europe, she talked with librarians, critics, and those who produce books, to learn whether Europeans were happy with what they saw from the United States and with our selection of their books. This made clear certain failings in the world of children's books to achieve the best possible in the exchange. When she retired from the ALA, it seemed appropriate to establish in her honor an annual award. The Mildred L. Batchelder Award was first presented in 1968 to the American publisher of the best juvenile book originally published abroad in another language. Selection is made from a list of nominees by members of the ALA Children's Services Division. Presented each April 2nd, Andersen's birthday, it has been given for Erich Kästner's *The Little Man,* translated by James Kirkup (Knopf); Alki Zei's *Wildcat Under Glass,* translated by Edward Fenton (Holt); Hans Baumann's *In the Land of Ur,* translated by Stella Humphries (Pantheon); and Hans Peter Richter's *Friedrich,* translated by Edite Kroll (Holt). (Andersen's birthday is also celebrated as International Children's Book Day, sponsored by the International Board on Books for Young People, or IBBY.)

Congresses, book fairs, exhibitions, and competitions which bring together librarians, publishers, and others interested in children's literature provide both a formal platform and informal occasions for the exchange of information and the promotion of excellence in children's literature. The last decade and a half—or the postwar years—have seen a variety of new efforts to foster such an exchange.

It is not a new idea, of course, that children's books should become recognized across the sea. In 1884 *Heidi* was published in English, both in

"A New Internationalism" by Virginia Haviland from *De Openbare Bibliotheek,* v. 14, no. 9, (1971). Reprinted by permission of NBLC.

1. For biographical information about the author, see pp. 88 and 436.

England and the United States, four years after it appeared in German. It took *Little Women* from 1868 to 1871 to travel from Boston to London, but by a curious circumstance of Miss Alcott's travel abroad, in 1871 *Little Men* was published in London one month earlier than it was released in the United States. There was communication then, too, even if publishers and their agents, and book selectors and jurors, could not fly back and forth over the Atlantic to each others' publishing houses, international congresses, seminars, and book fairs.

Internationalism developed significantly in the 1950s. The first general assembly of IBBY was held in 1953 and the International Federation of Library Associations (IFLA) established a Sub-section of Library Work for Children in 1955. IBBY brings together publishers, librarians, educators, critics—anyone working with children's books. An organizing meeting had been called in Munich, November 1951. It was attended by 250 persons, from whom a committee was formed—representing Austria, Germany, Holland, Norway, Sweden, and Switzerland—to draw up the documents of organization. The first general assembly, held in 1953, was visible culmination of the idea proposed by IBBY's founder, Jella Lepman.[2] She felt that the most important aim for IBBY was that it should be established as a world conscience for international children's literature, and among its goals would be the awarding of international prizes.

What has happened in IBBY since 1953? In 1956 IBBY's first Hans Christian Andersen Medal for writing (sometimes called the "Little Nobel") was awarded to Eleanor Farjeon and two years later to Astrid Lindgren. Today the conditions for this "Little Nobel" prize have changed; an author is recognized for the entire body of work, not just one book. The Andersen jury knew that—although unofficially—they were actually recognizing Astrid Lindgren for all her writing, not just for *Rasmus På Luffen;* and Eleanor Farjeon for more than *The Little Bookroom;* and Erich Kästner for *Emil and the Detectives,* more than for *When I Was A Little Boy.* In 1962, however, Meindert DeJong was officially saluted for all his writing, and in 1964 René Guillot was celebrated for the total body of his work.

Then in 1966 came another innovation: the first Hans Christian Andersen Medal was awarded to an artist, to Alois Carigiet. The companion medal for literature went to Tove Jansson for her Moomin stories. Now there are four illustrator medalists, for Carigiet was followed in 1968 by Jiří Trnka, the famous Czech puppeteer-artist, in 1970 by Maurice Sendak, and in 1972 by Ib Spang Olsen.

You may well ask how a jury for an international award judges fairly the work of authors and illustrators of other countries. Let me say that the jury members generally understand each other and that deliberations are conducted in English. Nominees for the medals are usually those writers

---

2. This and several other inspirations developing out of her work as director of the International Youth Library in Munich, founded in 1949, are described in her book, *Kinderbuchbrucke*, or *A Bridge of Children's Books*, trans. by Edith McCormick (Chicago: American Library Association, 1969).

Illustration by Tove Jansson from *Moominvalley in November* by Tove Jansson, © 1971 by Tove Jansson. Reprinted by permission of Henry Z. Walck, Inc. and Ernest Benn, Ltd.

whose works have been widely translated, and there is a fairly good comprehension of at least some of the creator's work. The illustrator award poses a different problem—whether, as some believe, illustration in picture books should be judged first as art and then as illustration; or should most of all be considered as successful art only as it truly illustrates, enhances, and is integral with the text, forming a picture book with unity.

One of the happiest privileges of serving on the jury is the gaining of an awareness that whatever one's own country of origin or profession within the children's book world, we speak a common language in regard to the literary and artistic qualities in children's books and the child's understanding. I can hear Bettina Hürlimann, Jo Tenfjord, Carla Poesio, Jan Cervenka, and others speaking in terms that we as children's librarians understand wherever we are. It is stimulating to discover that in spite of differences in the national literatures there is a common denominator in criticism.

There is no doubt that the selection of winners of the Andersen Medals and the biennial congress have continued to be major affairs of IBBY, but for a wider audience there is *Bookbird Magazine*. Also reaching many more of the children's book world are the activities of national sections of IBBY. Today, from the small cluster of Europeans who formed the board in 1953, there are some 30 national sections (there had been 12 national sections represented in reports in the 1958 congress; 22 in 1964). These range from Japan through Africa, the Middle East, West and East Europe, North and Latin America. Their national activities have included the publishing of periodicals, book lists, and reviews; the conduct of seminars and book weeks; and the awarding of prizes. The Arbeitskreis für Jugendschrifftum in West Germany since 1953 has determined choices for the annual Kinderbuchpreis, the Jugendbuchpreis, and the Bilderbuchpreis. Finland's section also awards a prize, the Anni Swan Medal given every three years for the best children's book of the period. The Swedish national section has created an award to recognize annually an outstanding contribution to the field of children's books. The Swiss section publishes Das Buch für Dich, an annual attractive free booklist distributed widely to school children; its colorful cover is a reproduction of the year's poster, painted by such artists as Celestino Piatti and Brian Wildsmith.

The United States national section, which comprises jointly the Children's Services Division of the American Library Association and the Children's Book Council, made up of the publishers of children's books, does not of itself try to stimulate the publishing and distribution of children's books through such activities as these, because the two organizations it represents have been doing this. However, it does plan meetings held at national library conferences, and it has arranged for the deposit of 11 small collections of outstanding American children's books in centers abroad, as a memorial to Margaret Scoggin, a former coordinator of work with young adults at the New York Public Library who was active on behalf of the International Youth Library in its earlier years.

In 1955, as mentioned above, the Sub-section for Library Work with Children was formed within the Public Library Division of the International Federation of Library Associations. In the early 1960s, the sub-section began to publish compilations of articles and bibliographies. *Translations of Children's Books*[3] includes five printed IFLA and other conference papers on the translation of children's literature and a list of best books submitted by 16 member countries. Thus the sub-section hopes, like IBBY, to promote an exchange of information about the best books of member countries. It aims to stimulate children's librarians to continue to compile such lists annually. Among the countries doing this are Denmark, Sweden, England, West Germany, France, The Netherlands, and the United States. The Lenin State Library in Moscow sends out an annual list, compiled by the children's reading specialist for the Ministry of Culture. In addition to its committee-chosen annual "Notable Children's Books," the Children's Services Division of the American Library Association through its Interna-

---

3. Distributed by the ALA, 1963.

tional Relations Committee regularly compiles a list entitled *Children's Books of International Interest,* which is widely distributed abroad.[4]

Succeeding publications of the IFLA children's library group include three volumes of *Library Service to Children.*[5] Each of the first two (1965 and 1966) contains articles written by children's librarians about their country's library services for children, important professional publications and prizes, and trends and developments related to book production—for African countries, the Middle East, Latin America, and the East, as well as nations of Europe and North America. The third volume is a compilation of papers on training for children's librarianship first presented at a working seminar in Frankfurt in 1968. In revision now is *Professional Literature About Children's Literature,* originally published in 1966.

At all congresses it is the informal exchanges that take place between formal conference sessions, and later through correspondence, as well as the content of lectures and discussions that provide vivid, convincing views of what is excellent in children's literature and give us the pleasure of meeting people behind the books. At IBBY we have been happy to meet such well-known creators of books as Aimée Sommerfelt, Brian Wildsmith, Tove Jansson, P. L. Travers, James Kruss, and many others. We are delighted here for the opportunity to meet Annie Schmidt, about whom Annie Moerckerken van der Meulen told us in 1961 at the children's librarians' gathering in Keele, England. We know and delight in her highly original fantasy *Wiplala* (Abelard, o.p.). It is delightful to see again Miep Diekmann whom some of us met at the IBBY congress in Luxembourg, when one of her books was on the Andersen Honors List. Her story *The Haunted Island* (Dutton, o.p.) was published in the United States in 1962 and this year (1970) another book, *Slave Doctor* (Morrow) has been translated for publication there. And of course we are delighted to meet A. Rutgers van der Loeff, several of whose books have meant much in the United States, from *Avalanche* and *Oregon at Last* to *Vassilis on the Run* (all Morrow).

I have spoken of meetings and projects in which children's librarians find their chief international involvement. But I should add that one who is truly concerned goes beyond the confines of a congress to become acquainted with the reference and bibliographical activities on behalf of children's literature that are carried on in international children's literature centers. First, of course, is the International Youth Library in Munich, established in 1949. Two of its most welcome publications are *Preisgekrönte Kinderbücher,* a catalog of its children's book prizes,[6] and *Die Besten der Besten (The*

---

4. An edited summary of these annual lists has been issued by the ALA: *Children's Books of International Interest: Selected from Four Decades of American Publishing,* ed. by Virginia Haviland (Chicago: ALA, 1972).

5. Volumes 2 (1966) and 3 (1968) distributed by the ALA; volume 1 (1965) available from Bibliotekstjänst, S-223 63 Tornavägen 9, Lund, Sweden.

6. Distributed in the U.S. as *Children's Prize Books* (New York: R. R. Bowker Co., 1969).

Best of the Best).[7] This will spread the news of national and international prizewinners to publishers as well as to those who select books for libraries and do research in children's literature.

Here among national book awards one can see that some titles have already traveled between countries. Annie Schmidt's *Wiplala* won the Austrian State Award, which since 1966 has admitted translated books. In West Germany the Arbeitskreis für Jugendschrifftum has many times selected a work of foreign origin for one of its awards. Thus its winners have included Pauline Clarke's *The Return of the Twelves* (first published in England), Meindert De Jong's *Wheel on the School* (Harper), Scott O'Dell's *Island of the Blue Dolphins* (Houghton), Louise Fatio's and Roger Duvoisin's *The Happy Lion* (McGraw), and Leo Lionni's *Swimmy* (Pantheon). In Italy, the Premio Bancarellini (an award determined by the votes of teen-agers) went in 1968 to Hugh Lofting's *Story of Dr. Dolittle* (Lippincott). In communist countries, also, awards have sometimes been given to books from the West. In Czechoslovakia, the Marie Majerova Prize has a regular category for translation, and has been presented for *Winnie the Pooh* and earlier classics. In 1962, the U.S.S.R. gave an award for a new edition of *Huckleberry Finn.*

National centers usually turn out to be international, as well, in many services—such as those of the Bureau Boek and Youth in The Hague (1951), the Swedish Institute for Children's Books in Stockholm (1965), The International Institute for Children's and Popular Literature in Vienna (1965), and the Children's Book Section of the Library of Congress (1963). "All national libraries must be international at the same time" said Sir Frank Francis, President of IFLA. At the Library of Congress the first supplement to *Children's Literature: A Guide to Reference Sources* has over a third of its annotations related to foreign-language works about children's literature and libraries. The Library of Congress regularly acquires such works and its reference work relates to them. It is aware that the *Guide* has found its way to reference shelves around the world. For the first supplement, Helga Mach from West Germany worked on items in German, Czech, and Polish, and Lisa-Christina Persson from the Bibliotekstjänst in Sweden on Scandinavian works.

The copublishing of today is facilitated by the meetings of editors at international displays: the annual Frankfurt Book Fair in September and the Bologna Children's Book Fair in April. At the former in 1968 I saw a copublishing arrangement made by Judy Taylor of London for Maurice Sendak's *Where the Wild Things Are* (Harper) to be printed in English, French, German, Swedish, and Danish editions. The Bologna fair has grown in importance as increasing numbers of exhibitors have participated from all sides of the world. Now also there is the Biennale of Illustration in Bratislava, Czechoslovakia, scheduled in the odd-numbered years, alternating with IBBY congresses.

---

7. Distributed in the U.S. by R. R. Bowker Co., 1971.

Through the best of exchanges children's literature has indeed been enriched. Aware not only of the active Anglo-American exchange, any children's librarian in the United States recognizes many other standard successes in their libraries as having foreign-language origins. But if an English-language book gets belatedly to the other shore, the librarian or critic can only wonder whether it was missed by accident or succeeded on a second publisher offer after the author had a later success. Just as children's interest in folk tales has no boundaries, many other modern tales—whether realistic, fanciful, or historical—transcend barriers of language and geography. There is nothing new in this—but the channels for communication are more numerous and open today.

British editions of books mentioned with their American publishers only in this article:

Erich Kästner. *The Little Man.* Cape.
Alki Zei. *Wildcat under Glass.* Gollancz.
Hans Baumann. *In the Land of Ur.* Oxford University Press.
Hans Peter Richter. *Friedrich.* Longman/Kestrel.
Annie Schmidt. *Wiplala.* Abelard-Schuman.
Miep Diekmann. *The Haunted Island.* Methuen.
Rutgers Van der Loeff. *Avalanche.* University of London Press.
    Oregon at Last. University of London Press.
    Vassilis on the Run. University of London Press.
Pauline Clarke. *The Twelve and the Genii.* (published in U.S.A. as *The Return of the Twelves.*) Faber.
Meindert DeJong. *The Wheel on the School.* Lutterworth Press.
Scott O'Dell. *Island of the Blue Dolphins.* Longman/Kestrel.
Louise Fatio and Roger Duvoisin. *The Happy Lion.* Bodley Head.
Leo Lionni. *Swimmy.* Dobson.
Hugh Lofting. *The Story of Doctor Dolittle.* Cape.
Maurice Sendak. *Where the Wild Things Are.* Bodley Head.

British Children's Books
in the Twentieth Century

Frank Eyre

Frank Eyre has been a designer, editor, and publisher of children's books. He was in charge of children's book publishing for the Oxford University Press in London and now directs general publishing for the Australian office. He has served as vice president and president of the Children's Book Council of Victoria and as president of the Federal Australian Children's Book Council. With committees of librarians he has compiled the Council's selective book lists.

A new generation of children's editors began to emerge [in the post-war years] and it slowly became respectable for intelligent adult critics to take a serious interest in books written for children. But efforts at improvement were for a time thwarted by the operation of a children's book variant of Gresham's Law. The commercial success of a type of book allegedly written for children but in fact produced to a formula by cynical opportunists discouraged publishers from risking capital on a different kind of book. Once again the type of book produced for children was being dictated by commercial considerations.

A few publishers continued to produce occasional exceptional books, chosen by editors of quality for reasons which were not purely commercial, but publishers' sales staffs (and accountants) remained resistant to change. To break this barrier two things were needed: a publisher prepared to risk capital on a new kind of children's book list, and intelligent reviewing, reaching a wider public, to make parents aware of the existence of these better books. The introduction in 1949 of a special *Children's Books Supplement* as a periodic feature of *The Times Literary Supplement* was the most encouraging development of this period. Not only because it introduced literate parents to a type of children's book of which many had previously been unaware, but also because it did much to improve the status of the children's writer of integrity, who had in the past to plough a lonely furrow, often with inadequate reward and always without recognition outside a small circle of specialists.

Publishers were finally found willing to risk capital on better books and reviewing continued to improve. By 1950 British children's books were entering a new phase. It is not easy, looking back, to establish just when the change occurred, but it was well on the way at the turn of the half-century. Almost overnight writers who had seemed on a pinnacle of commercial

Excerpts from "Historical Survey" and "Fiction for Children" from *British Children's Books in the Twentieth Century* by Frank Eyre, pp. 26–30, 35, 77–79. Copyright © 1971 by Frank Eyre. Reprinted by permission of Longman Young Books, now Kestrel Books.

success became disreputable. Their books continued to sell, but at a different level—the steadily increasing population making it possible for their sales to be maintained at this lower level although the majority of educated parents and most libraries ceased to buy them. In their place a new kind of children's book emerged and at the same time a new kind of critic and professionally interested person appeared to admire and write about them. The two developments followed each other so closely that it is difficult now to tell which most influenced the other, but their mutual interdependence is undeniable, for neither could have been so successful without the other.

For the next ten years there was so much good and constructive writing about children's books that the critical situation is now completely transformed. By the 'sixties there were so many good critics that it would be impossible to list them all, but everyone interested in British children's books will acknowledge the pioneer work of such writers as Margery Fisher, whose *Growing Point,* founded in 1962, was the first periodical in this new field of independent critical reviewing for parents rather than librarians (*The Junior Bookshelf* had tended always to be librarian influenced and slanted), and Anne Wood whose *Books for Your Children* was founded in 1965. The intelligent parent who is interested in what his children read no longer has to search for himself or, alternatively, trust blindly to a single opinion. He has a wide range of journals and critics to choose from and can compare one critic's view with another's and form his own opinion, just as he has long been accustomed to do for his own reading, or theatre- or film-going.

The critical journals have come of age, and so have the critics. The writer for children can now confidently expect informed reviewing and intelligent debate about his books, and for the first time may be able to derive profit from criticism, because the critics know what they are talking about.

Inevitably such a climate of opinion encouraged a new breed of children's publishers and editors. When the first edition of this book was written there were less than a dozen publishers who maintained editorial departments specially for children's books, and not more than five or six specialist children's editors. In 1970 there are some sixty publishers actively engaged in children's books and The Children's Book Circle, an informal group of men and women working in the children's book departments of publishing firms, has ninety members.

Other developments emphasised the improved status of children's books in Britain. In 1966, after a one-day conference at the Holborn Library, a Joint Committee for Children's Books was formed. Three years later, in 1969, this was enlarged to create a more formal committee to be known by the impressive-sounding title of The Joint Consultative Committee on Children's Books (how far away the Sunday School reward days seem!). Membership consisted of two representatives each from the Library Association, the Booksellers' Association, the Publishers' Association, the National Book League, the Society of Authors and the School Library

Association, with a single representative from the British Museum. What, if anything, the Committee actually accomplishes is not known, but that so many important bodies, between them representing all the interests involved in children's books (except children and parents!) should have come together is indicative of the new importance of writing for children.

This was also emphasised by the remarkable success of a conference held, in August 1969, at St. Luke's College, Exeter, on "Recent Children's Fiction and its Role in Education." No less than two hundred and twenty people attended, including teachers, lecturers from colleges of education and university departments of education, and writers. A second conference followed in August 1970 which was notable for some lively discussion between authors and audience, and for a provocative piece of special pleading by Peter Dickinson, "A Defence of Rubbish." Most of the papers given at these conferences, and some of the discussions, are reprinted in a new journal, *Children's Literature in Education*. . . .

It was only to be expected that such a dramatic change in public opinion towards children's books should produce a corresponding change in the policies of publishers. Once a few publishers had been able successfully to demonstrate that it was possible to sustain a list from books of the highest quality only—and to make money from them—others soon followed. By the middle 'sixties the better-class children's book, the type of book that became known as a "librarian's book," had become a standard to which the shrewd and successful could repair. There were, naturally enough, insufficient authors of real stature to supply all publishers with books, but the formula could be followed and the distinctive production style that a few publishers had evolved for this new type of children's fiction could be fairly easily copied. It was interesting to see publishers who had for so long regarded with disdain the methods and styles of others now following them in production style, editorial treatment and even the tone of their advertising.

The book to succeed became the "better book for children"; to succeed it must carry on its face and on its pages the recognisable stamp of such a book, so as to be identifiable by the right kind of parent or librarian; and so publisher after publisher followed the pattern. Inevitably, imitation dilutes the overall level of quality and that has to some extent now occurred with children's books. But the improved quality of reviewing has compensated for this (though even in this field success is beginning to produce imitators) and the general level of new children's books is now astonishingly high.

What this new type of late-twentieth-century British children's book was concerned with will be examined in detail later. Some general developments should, however, be noted. No one looking for the first time at the books of the past twenty years could fail to notice the curious contradiction between two parallel trends. On the one hand we find critics, librarians, teachers, writers, preaching the need for an ever-increasing social realism—and authors doing their best to meet this need. On the other, an extraordinary revival and re-creation of folk-tales, fairy stories, fantasies, allegories, myths and legends which combine to produce an escape from reality, or a turning to a simpler kind of truth, so massive that it must surely indicate a profound need by present-day children. . . .

The age at which children read particular kinds of books has continued to contract during the past twenty years and in the last decade publishers and writers have been taking a good hard look at teenage reading. One approach to this problem has been a deliberate seeking after realism, and the effects of the permissive society are beginning to find their way into this sort of book for children. A more interesting, and more genuine develop- ment has been the introduction of what appears to be the beginning of an altogether new kind of writing for children. One publisher has described these books as "novels for new adults," others call them "novels for older children" and there are several variations on these themes. Some of these books are little more than a normal children's book with a love interest added, but the best of them have enlarged the range of children's literature by creating a kind of book which although no longer in any sense a "children's book" by any earlier definition of that phrase is nevertheless not written for adults and is in some undefinable way recognizably different from a book written for adults. But it is already obvious, from their reception by critics, that books of this kind are read and enjoyed by adults, and it may well come about that such books will form a new category that can be read with equal enjoyment by both children and adults. . . .

Most authors in the late 'twenties and 'thirties had to limit themselves to conventional stories of various kinds—school stories, adventure stories, horse stories—and the writing of these was made increasingly difficult by the reduction in the age at which a particular type of book was read. Harvey Darton had already noted this trend, but it increased steadily throughout the century and by 1950 school and adventure stories which twenty years ago would have been read at fourteen or sixteen were being read at ten or even nine.

The problems posed by such a rapidly reducing age level to writers of children's fiction were obvious, and were partly responsible for the wild improbability of the plots of so many of the stories of the time. Children like to imagine themselves in the situations they are reading about, so authors were driven progressively to reduce the ages of their heroines and heroes, with results that put an impossible strain on credulity. For adventures which can by a stretch of imagination be conceived as just possible for a boy of sixteen become ludicrous for one of nine or ten.

Children had also in the first half of the century begun to read adult fiction much earlier, with the result that it largely replaced the better type of adventure story for boys which had been popular at the end of the last and the beginning of this century. . . .

Children's fiction was thus read at an earlier age, and for a shorter time, and this reduction of both the range and extent of such reading brought about a drastic reduction in quality. The more intelligent a child is, the more likely he is to turn sooner to adult reading, unless the children's books with which he is provided give him something to get his intellectual teeth into, and stimulate his imagination. . . .

The difficulties facing a writer for children in the 1970s are of a very different kind. If he is a writer of integrity—and the most encouraging and rewarding aspect of a study of contemporary children's books is the discovery that so many of them are by such writers—he will be increasingly concerned with problems that are intellectual, emotional, moral and social, rather than the practical ones that confronted his counterpart in the 1930s or '40s. He will find himself and his work being critically examined by all sorts of people who would previously have been unlikely to take writing for children seriously. Librarians, reviewers in distinguished periodicals, teachers, lecturers, even university professors, will all assess it and give judgement on it. He will be called to many different Bars to give an account of himself, and to explain why his books fail in this or that particular. He will discover (to his surprise and concern if he is one kind of writer, to his gratification if he is another) that his work is regarded as of great social and educational significance; that it is being taken seriously because of the effect it may have on the future development, intellectually and morally of his readers. He will be asked to address learned and consequential seminars on such topics as "The Importance of Social Realism in Writing for young Children," and may be surprised to discover that educational authorities are at last finding out for themselves something that everyone seriously interested in children's books has known for the past century—that the stories children read play a vital part in their total education. A part that may be at least as important as their formal studies.

An Indigenous Children's Literature

Barbara Buick

Barbara Buick is children's book editor for the Cheshire Publishing Company in Australia and a former children's librarian. She has served as president of the children's libraries section of the Library Association of Australia and is a research assistant at the Australian National University.

It is not surprising, perhaps, that the development of Australian and American children's literature should show traceable parallels, for the histories and ways of life and outlook of both countries and peoples obviously motivated the choosing of similar themes. Imaginative literature best illustrates this rather than factual writing for obvious reasons.

Books for children about Australia began in 1841 when *Mother's Offering to Her Children,* by a Lady Resident in New South Wales, was published in Sydney. British stalwarts of children's adventuring such as W. K. Kingston, William Howitt, B. L. Farjeon, G. A. Henty, George Manville Fenn, and Gordon Stables wrote a number of sagas of Australia during the 19th Century, though few of them visited Australia. The virtues of pioneering and exploration, their hardships and rewards, the extraordinary fauna and flora, unbeautiful to European eyes, the Aborigine, subhuman to these upholders of Empire, were recurring subjects in these British published books.

Rosemary Wighton points out:

> The fact that most of the early Australian children's books were published overseas, and directed to overseas readers, may seem too obvious to mention, but it did have an effect on the books themselves. The emphasis is very much on the presentation of a new country to children who did not already know about it—its physical strangeness, the differences in social behavior, the dangers and difficulties. And not only did most of the Australian children's books of the last century tend to tell their readers what they *ought* to know about Australia, but also they told them again and again what they *wanted* to hear—the particular things that were popularly connected with this new country, such as pioneering, bushrangers, marauding blacks, bushfires and so on. Accounts of the particular qualities that were most likely to help the new arrival . . . frequently appear, and are undoubtedly connected with the fact that most of the readers did not live in Australia.[1]

1. Wighton, Rosemary. *Early Australian Children's Literature.* (New York: Sportshelf, 1963. Melbourne: Oxford University Press, 1967).

For all this, underlying attitudes can be compared closely with American children's books both of the 19th and 20th Centuries. The New Land, the New Life, Opportunity; the force of the democratic dream—your antecedents could be convict born or free: these beliefs were stated of the two countries repeatedly in children's books, and still are. Life on the land was the Real Life; children born and bred there were healthier, more virtuous and more likely to succeed than unfortunate towny cousins. The romanticism of Outbackery can be compared with the frontier novel.

Australian writing for adults, however, by more observant authors such as Henry Lawson and Joseph Furphy (Tom Collins) had underlying pessimism, showing the tragedy that drought and fire brought, the loneliness and squalor of bush life, but this scarcely spilled over into children's books. In them, horse riding, mustering sheep, fighting bushfires and mateship were still presented as the noble life, to be hankered for by the majority of children who were in increasing numbers city bred and raised. Children were able to cope with all situations, and perhaps this is why the school story had few ardent practioners, though one book which can be considered outstanding in any literature, was published in 1911: Henry Handel Richardson's *The Getting of Wisdom,* about the painful process of growing up of individualist Laura in a 19th-Century Melbourne boarding school. The station, i.e. ranch, property was self-sufficient in people and supplies, and John Rowe Townsend has shown that the typical school story had just this appeal of secure self-containment.[2]

Another book of interest was Ethel Pedley's *Dot and the Kangaroo,* 1899, which is remarkable today only for the fact of its inexplicable republishing, even in 1965. It is a strange mixture of twisted anthropomorphism, but with a genuine love for the beauty of the bush and its creatures.

Ethel Turner, probably the dominating figure of Australian children's literature, published 40 books from 1894 to 1928, far too many for consistency of quality. Nevertheless, the richness of her thinking is unmatched. Starting with *Seven Little Australians* and its sequels, through to the sensitively realized study of inadequate adolescence in *The Cub;* of the grind of poverty in overlarge, underearning families in *The Little Larrikin,* Ethel Turner examined and probed the attitudes and foibles of her time and place. Her books were written with immense vitality and were immediately popular through wide translation. Yet there is not one respectable edition of any of her books in print today, though several titles are available with a dreary 19th Century appearance. Her books have a vividness, for many of them speak with force to children of the 1960's. To compare Ethel Turner with her contemporary Louisa May Alcott is to place Turner on a higher rung of literary achievement. Judy in *Seven Little Australians* is as vital a character as Jo, but Bunty, Loll and the Cub make Laurie and other male characters seem pale mish-mash of boys.

The mantle of Ethel Turner's success, in Australia at least, but not her

---

2. Townsend, John Rowe. *Written for Children.* (London: Miller, 1965. New York: Lothrop, Lee and Shepard Company, 1967). Revised edition, Kestrel Books, 1974.

ability, then fell to the writer of the greatest Australian cliché of all time, Mary Grant Bruce. She wrote 12 books in her Billabong series, in which no station life was ever so idyllic, no people so true blue as Norah, Jim and Wally, and no stories so myopic of the struggles of life on the land during those drought and depression years. The Billabong books today represent a major headache for librarians fighting to preserve the quality of their collections from the pressures of rose-spectacled parents.

There was however, one other writer of significance at this time, and this was Louise Mack. Now out of print, *Teens* (1897) was an imaginatively written school story with an urban setting, and was followed by *Girls Together* in 1898. Louise Mack wrote more of the relationship of children with each other than conventional school stories.

It is impossible to go further with this survey without pointing to the paucity of books worth mentioning compared with those from the U.S. at this time. It is understandable if only on a population basis—assuming that talent can be measured by such things! Hack writers flourished from 1900 to the present day. One or two writers showing promise were unmeasured against the best of world children's literature and so were not encouraged to develop. The climate of critical appreciation so necessary to development did not begin to appear until the end of the Second World War. [There was] the influence of librarians and their migrations to other states from such institutions as the State Library of South Australia, which probably stands in relation to children's libraries in Australia as does the Enoch Pratt Library, Baltimore (albeit a poverty relationship in terms of comparative resources) to the U.S. Children's Book Council was established, and the Council offered an annual award for the best children's books of the year. It is a reflection of the juvenility of the publishing industry that from the beginning, most publishers entered in the award competition *every* children's book produced, however meretricious. Professionals found overseas reviewing of Australian books je-jeune; they were generally approvingly reviewed as exotica, even the most spurious. But gradually standards rose.

Serious reviewing began with the establishment of the *Australian Book Review* in 1961. Dennis Hall, formerly a children's librarian in South Australia, has dominated the reviewing in this journal. Often so fiercely denunciating that authors and publishers shudder at his shadow, he writes, nevertheless, from as fine a set of principles for critical evaluation as anyone in the English-speaking world. The national newspaper, the *Australian,* began regular reviews of children's books in 1965, as did the *Australian School Librarian,* published by the School Library Association of Victoria. The State Library of South Australia and the Children's Book Council of Victoria compile fairly regular and carefully evaluative selection guides. Until all this happened there were many who claimed with some potency that it was necessary to have a double standard for selection for libraries, and that to encourage the writing and publishing of children's books, still usually under 100 titles each year, one had to evaluate Australian books at a lower level than their U.S. or British counterparts, the latter forming the main reading diet of Australian children. Today such double standards are both unjustified and unnecessary.

The small publishing industry was encouraged to think seriously about its children's book programs by the arrival of Frank Eyre, author of *Twentieth Century Children's Books,* as manager for the Oxford University Press, in the 1950's.[3] It is not surprising that under his careful guidance such writers as Nan Chauncy and Eleanor Spence developed. During the 1960's two of the largest and most influential indigenous publishing houses, Angus and Robertson's and Cheshire, appointed their first children's book editors. Although the lists of these firms are still in their infancy, both promise to provide an opportunity for local authors to receive the individual attention impossible when the publisher lives 12,000 miles away, and is not in intimate contact with the country's cultural climate.

The visit to Australia, in 1964, of Sara Fenwick of the University of Chicago's Graduate Library School was a rare stimulus to professional thinking. Her interest in Australian children's literature, and her surprise to find how little it was known and appreciated by children and teachers, was another spur.[4] As a result of all these influences, but chiefly because several writers of rich ability were now reaching the height of their powers, Australian children's literature is coming of age. There are still deplorable gaps; we have produced no picture book worthy of the name since Norman Lindsay's *The Magic Pudding,* that glorious gutsy fount of knockabout humor, written and illustrated by a fine draughtsman, which is probably the one and only true classic of Australian children's literature. Year after year no award has been possible for the picture book category of the Book Council competition, perhaps because until 1967, artists have not been encouraged to consider children's book illustration a stream worthy of creative effort. The Cheshire Company is deliberately setting out to alter this with its Authors and Artists for Young Australians series, where the best literary and artistic creators are to combine in producing beautiful books for young children.

Trends in contemporary thematic writing still show close parallels with American children's literature. Themes such as assimilation into a new society in the books of Eleanor Spence, Frank Kellaway, L. H. Evers reflect the huge postwar migration when Australia's population jumped by one sixth. The plight of the dispossessed Aborigines, their ways of life, parallel American writing of the Indians. Nan Chauncy has written a superb book on this in *Tangara,* and A. Poignant, F. D. Davison, K. Langloh Parker, Tindale and Lindsay have written with varying effectiveness also. Man against a harsh environment, children facing responsibility, and the effect of country life on character have been illuminated again by Nan Chauncy, our major writer, Reginald Ottley, Joan Phipson, Ivan Southall, Betty Roland

---

3. Eyre, Frank. *Twentieth Century Children's Books.* (Cambridge University Press, 1953).

4. Fenwick, Sara Innis. *School and Children's Libraries in Australia.* (Melbourne: Cheshire, 1966).

and Colin Thiele. Family stories have able practitioners in Eleanor Spence, Joan Phipson, Celia Syred, and Patricia Wrightson. Poverty has been tellingly told by Mavis Thorpe Clare, Alan Marshall and Joan Phipson. The regional story is poorly represented, but Colin Thiele and Nan Chauncy have written memorable books reflecting richly a segment of country and people. Humor is hardly evident, though Colin Thiele again has a delightful touch, while Dal Stivens with his tall tales, told in dry laconic Australian style, is more reflective of the traditional bush yarn. Stories for teen-agers have been perceptively written by Patricia Wrightson, and to a lesser extent by H. F. Brinsmead, whose work, though popular, is indicative of a similar trend in American writing for children, when writers tend to see their characters from the outside in terms of psychological case study progression, rather than from within deeply realized characters. Many subject fields are still untouched, as are fine historical writing and fantasy—we can make no real claim to P. L. Travers who reveals no hint of her Australian background in the Mary Poppins books. So we await an Australian L'Engle, L. M. Boston or even a Tolkien with hopeful anticipation.

Appreciation of the best contemporary writers caused Geoffrey Trease in the *New Statesmen* to speak of "the recent flowering of children's books in Australia," and observers of the scene are hopeful that this blossoming will find the appreciation it deserves in American libraries.

Across the Rhine: Juvenile Literature in German-Speaking Countries

Walter Scherf

Walter Scherf is Director of the International Youth Library in Munich, German Federal Republic. Before taking that position in 1957, Dr. Scherf worked in publishing and translated many books for young people into German; he recently translated a new edition of Treasure Island. *He has written many articles and edited publications for the International Youth Library. Among these are* Preisgekrönte Kinderbücher *(Children's Prize Books, 1969) and* Die Besten der Besten *(The Best of the Best, 1971)—both published in Munich by Verlag Dokumentation and distributed in the U.S. by R. R. Bowker. He has been active in the work of international organizations, serving as a vice president of the International Board on Books for Young People. In 1971 he made an extensive lecture tour in the United States. The following paper has been revised and updated from a lecture presented at the 1969 Loughborough Summer Seminar in International Children's Literature.*

PICTURE BOOKS

While England at the end of the last century produced an admirable and still lively renaissance of picture books thanks to Walter Crane, Kate Greenaway, and Randolph Caldecott, the German-speaking countries witnessed a similar but more differentiated renaissance. The reform educationalists became so enthusiastic about impressionism and the impressionistic way of looking at the world that they transmitted their enthusiasm to a long line of artists and publishers who produced a previously unknown abundance of picture books. People also discovered through stimulation from England the colored Japanese woodcut, the personification of nature and an entirely new ornamentation, no longer copying historical patterns but living by virtue of the line (Ernst Kreidolf and many others). This was joined by a strong element of education, a downright missionary zeal, which tried to provide even the simplest citizen with art. The results were issues of art books for children, picture-book experiments that ranged from Holbein and Dürer to Adolf von Menzel and Moritz von Schwind.[1]

"Across the Rhine: Juvenile Literature in German-Speaking Countries" by Walter Scherf is revised and updated from a lecture presented at Loughborough, 1969, and published in *Top of the News*, 26 (January 1970): 180–187, 205. Reprinted by permission of the author.

1. See the chapter on picture books (pp. 9–77) in Hermann Leopold Köster, *Geschichte der deutschen Jugendliteratur in Monographien (History of German Children's Literature in Monographs)*, 4th ed. 1927, 2nd reprint of the International Youth Library with annotations (Weinheim: Pullach, 1971) and Horst Kunze, *Schatzbehalter (Treasure of German Children's Literature)*, with illus. (Berlin: 1965).

The second picture-book renaissance, which has occurred in the last ten years, is comparable in its extraordinarily broad effect. But the tendencies and the impulses which aroused its development were different.

For the first ten years after the war the best German picture books were Swiss: from Hans Fischer, Alois Carigiet, and Felix Hoffmann. At the same time the Golden Books from Simon & Schuster flooded the market. Today you may think it was rather strange but the generous scale, the experienced naiveté and the robust coloring were fresh and fascinating, so that everyone started picture book collections of them. Real stimulation came from Babar and Madeline.[2]

The first more important accomplishments we owe to Beatrice Braun-Fock with her charming illustrations of fairy tales; to Katharine Maillard, who cut colored paper and glued the different figures into a Noah's ark frieze; to Marianne Scheel with her impressionistic nature and landscape picture books; and to Lieselotte Schwarz, who created very solid leporellos (folding picture books) for the smallest children.

PICTURE BOOK AWARD WINNER

With that the second renaissance was introduced, and Marlene Reidel, one of the pioneers, was the first picture book artist to earn the German children's book award. The large scale of her lively lino-cut planes not only convinced the judges but touched the general public. Kasimir's trip round the world (*Kasimir's Journey*) has been translated several times. Later she created still more lino-cut books, several with her own texts (for example, *Jacob and the Robbers*), some with traditional nursery rhymes. The most outstanding one was the Bavarian folk ballad of robber Kneissl (*Der Räuber Kneisse*); the illustrations have a power of expression that may be compared with Masereel's woodcuts of the twenties.

Then three tendencies became clearly visible; the pleasure of experimenting, the psychological interest in children, and finally the turn toward the old treasures.

The pleasure of experiment, of which the picture books of Günther Stiller, Winfried Blecher, Franz Haacken, Klaus Winter, and Helmut Bischoff are typical,[3] is explained by the following fact. For graphic artists who like to publish shapes in color for a wide public, only posters and picture books are

---

2. Bettina Hürlimann, *Three Centuries of Children's Books in Europe,* with illus. (New York: The World Publishing Company, 1967. London: Oxford University Press, 1967).

3. The most outstanding exhibitions are to be seen at the Klingspor Museum, Offenbach. Its director, Hans Halbey, is one of the first promoters of modern picture-book experimenting. See also the richly illustrated collection of articles about the modern picture book: Alfred Clemens Baumgärtner, *Aspekte der gemalten Welt (Aspects of the Painted World* (Weinheim: 1968). The best survey is given by the illustrated systematical catalog, *Das Bilderbuch (The Picture Book),* 3rd ed. (Munich: German Section of IBBY [Munich 22, Kaulbachstrasse 40], 1970).

possible. Art folders for an adult public have a very limited market. And who will publish illustrated belles lettres for adults? Nobody. Certainly that is an important reason why artists who like experiments devote themselves to children's books. That kind of picture book has its connoisseurs and collectors with their own aesthetic interests, and it is bought often without regard to children.

On the other hand, *the regard for children* is often of visible importance. When Reiner Zimnik with his *Bear on the Motorcycle* celebrates the performance of some previously misunderstood being; when Lilo Fromm with Christa Duchow's text lets a primitive tyrant be defeated by a kind and charming little hare who develops new forces in his misery (*Oberpotz und Hoppelhans*); and when Ali Mitgutsch shows the fear and triumph of a bright boy who is caught by a wild and fantastic robber band (*Der Kraxenflori*), we witness in all these titles a loving understanding of the child's psyche. Indeed this interest goes so far that certain types of books which are a real need for smaller children but which had met only a little interest on the side of the publishers, have been excellently developed in the last years. I am thinking of Eva Heyduck's picture books for the smallest children; of the leporellos by Lieselotte Schwarz, and of Ali Mitgutsch, who paints pictures without text but with an abundance of details which provoke creative fabrication. I'm also thinking of the challenge to read which is presented by the little colored symbol shapes among the text lines in Sigrid Heuck's *Buffalo Man and Eagle King*.

Generally speaking, the whole attitude has changed. There are no schools, there is no pressure for one all-encompassing style of the epoch. The different styles, attitudes, views, ways of thinking coexist equally: from the creative impudence of Janosch to the graphic finesse of Gerhard Oberländer, from the naive drawing and coloring of Wanda Zacharias to the mannerisms of Eva Johanna Rubin's artificial world of toys and Monika Laimgruber's rediscovering of art nouveau's magic, from Hap Grieshaber's elementary expressionism to Binette Schröder's surrealistic dreamland.[3]

The third and latest tendency can be seen in *the growing interest in traditional subjects, collections, classics, and hidden treasures*. Editions of legends and folk tales are flourishing, old nursery rhymes and song are becoming the basis of picture books, and the inexhaustible household reading-aloud collection plays a more and more important part in the family. The presentation, the illustration, and the choice of texts as well as the prefaces, annotations, and biographical notes efface the limits between books for children and books for adults.

The most beautiful fairy-tale illustrations we owe to Lilo Fromm: her magically glowing colors emerge from dream scopes (Brothers Grimm: *The Golden Bird*). As a new name Peter Beste should be introduced; with a magical fascination of detail he has created an extraordinarily rich Gulliver illustration. On the other hand, it is annoying that one of our most prominent fairy-tale illustrators, Horus Engels, has not yet been discovered in publishers' circles.

Illustration by Janosch from *Dear Snowman* by Janosch. Copyright © 1969 by Parabel Verlag, Munich. Reprinted by permission of The World Publishing Company. British edition published by Dennis Dobson.

POETRY

To speak abroad about our poetry for children, about playing with rhyme and poetical nonsense, one can only begin by apologizing. Our primers and readers are subjected to the dictatorship of school inspectors—or have been subjected, for something is changing, I think. Now poems are taken which by no means fit the patterns of the classics from Schiller to Uhland.

For one decade James Krüss from Heligoland has furnished rhymes with incredible skill. But he not only rhymes, he also teaches how to rhyme; he spread the pleasure of poetical games,[4] and what is more, he edited the best anthology of German poems.[5] Today he is no longer isolated. The unsophisticated Josef Guggenmos is broadcasting on the old wave-length of Joachim Ringelnatz and the tradition of terse witty folk rhymes is also being continued. Even our critics have noticed learnedly the "importance of being poetic" and they are beginning to measure prose texts on the scales of poetry. The best examples to show how strong the new creative wave really is and what its roots and aims are can be found in Hans-Joachim Gelberg's collection of recent children's poetry: *Die Stadt der Kinder (The Children's Town)*. Two names should be noticed especially: Christine Busta from Austria *(Die Sternenmühle/The Star Mill)* and Peter Hacks from the German Democratic Republic *(Das Turmverliess/The Dungeon)*.

REALISTS

The new children's literature could be divided at first glance into two camps; fortunately they have not yet started to quarrel with each other. In the first camp there are the realists. Several books tell of childhood memories. The puppet player Heinrich Maria Denneborg recalls his Westphalian childhood in *Jan und der Wildpferd (Jan and the Wild Horse)*. Another excellent example is Benno Pludra from the German Democratic Republic who gave a masterly report of a little Mecklenburg fisherboy with big griefs trying to emulate his beloved father and set aside the shoes of his childhood *(Little Matthias)*. Masterly too are the memories of Erich Kästner's childhood *(When I Was a Little Boy)*, where he draws a picture of his beloved mother and, a sensitive and humorous observer, describes the middle-class life of the old art-loving Saxonian capital. But speaking about realism in children's literature, we cannot forget the classical narrator of boys' pranks, Ludwig Thoma from Bavaria, with his terse, understated language in *Lausbubenstreiche (Stories of Saucy Boys)* and Erich Kästner's detective story, *Emil and the Detectives,* which influenced a whole generation of authors, not least of whom is Henry Winterfeld with his transformation to old Rome in *Detectives in Togas.*

FANTASY

In the other camp there are, thanks to English stimulation of yesterday and today, writers of the fantastic novel—above all Erica Lillegg, who lives in Paris, with *Vevi,* and Otfried Preussler, from Bohemia, with *The Little*

---

4. There are two translations of *My Great-Grandfather and I* available: In American English by Edelgard von Heydekampf Brühl (New York: Atheneum Publishers, 1964) and in British English by James Kirkup (London: University of London Press, 1964).

5. A book everyone should have for pleasure as well as for basic study: *So viele Tage, wie das Jahr hat (As Many Days as a Year Has),* ed. by James Krüss (Gütersloh, 1959).

Water Sprite. The fantastic element in *Vevi,* which increases to a pervading surrealistic atmosphere, lies in the division of the little heroine into two beings: a good girl and a bad girl. The fantastic element in *The Little Water Sprite* is the transformation of a loving human family into the mysterious world below the surface of a pond. In that masquerade, adventures as well as the possibility of going home can be tasted fully. During recent years Preussler has become more and more fascinated by Slavic legends, his last books dealing with the Sorbian sorcerer Krabat and his apprentice.

To Katherine Allfrey, who lives in England, German children's literature owes an important contribution, a book in which the old legends shine through modern everyday life in a Greek village (*Golden Island*). Meanwhile, Michael Ende has followed his own fantastic associations on a grotesque trip around the world with a very old-fashioned railway engine (*Jim Knopf and Lukas the Engine Driver*). Henry Winterfeld, whose books are well known in the States, transformed a Gulliver adventure into one set in our modern world—*Castaways to Lilliput.*

Because of its more abstract style Gina Ruck-Pauquet's *Joschko* cannot be classified either as a realistic or a fantastic novel. A lonesome boy leaves his village on the shore of some southern country, roaming from landscape to landscape; his series of adventures gives him the opportunity to understand other people and their ways of life and finally to find himself. Odd and charming in its two-level humor are Friedrich C. Heller's prose texts which pretend to give dream explanations to children, but which in fact are a most amiable modern Viennese poetry of the nursery—accompanying Franz Schmögner's nonsense pictures in *Traumbuch für Kinder.*

The most important work in narrative prose is Reiner Zimnik's *The Bear and the People* in which text and drawings form a unit. With his bear a juggler is traveling on the high roads. He holds dialogues with his bear and with God and he is involved in conflict with the evil in our world. I don't like giving forecasts, but I think this book will last. And if it happens that there are good translations, it will be world literature.

SCHOOL LIBRARIES

You may wonder why I have not mentioned non-fiction for children. Indeed nothing of lasting value has been produced, although a long row of very interesting experiments could be studied. But comparison is not possible with English and American non-fiction for children. The reason is to be found in the hopelessly underdeveloped school libraries. German school libraries are no factor on the market, they fail to be considerable purchasers. What is more, the few teachers who succeed in building larger school libraries understand their main task to be lending books for home reading and sometimes discussing problem literature. The much more important specific functions of a school library, to complement and supplement teaching, to educate students in library use, and to give reference aid, have not yet been discovered.[6]

On the other hand, in the field of non-fiction for teen-agers and young adults, much has been done, which is evident in the special non-fiction "best" list and recently in an extra non-fiction award.[7] However, I cannot maintain that in the German language some extraordinary genius of non-fiction writing is at work, who by virtue of his style or by virtue of his particular method of explaining the subject has created international patterns. We also must keep in mind that free development of non-fiction writing was, ridiculously enough, paralyzed by those super-intelligent critics with their preconceived opinion that every subject must be adapted from a story, must be transformed into action. That's bare theory, surely, but they stated that it was not enough to give action in some narrative framework, the book must make clear the essential human relation to the respective subject.

That theory is responsible for a legion of "uncle" tales, in which some omniscient man offers instruction in dialogue with the "hero" of the story, who, naturally, listened with respect, in order not to disturb the readers. Only one author became master of such a construction, relating a story from the early cave paintings. Only he succeeded in interlacing with inner necessity the experience and the adventure of a long-ago way of life and religion, and the psychological development of boys. I'm speaking of Hans Baumann and his *The Caves of the Great Hunters*. This book is a considerable contribution to international youth literature. I would also like to mention the systematical work of Heinrich Pleticha, who edited his anthologies *History from First Hand* and *Modern History from First Hand* from text sources and authentic eyewitness reports which in a glance make clear the historical or political state of the case.

YOUNG ADULT LITERATURE

What remains is a word on the books for teen-agers and young adults. Certain West German papers and broadcasting programs have tried to deprive these of their right to exist. This criticism on the one hand surely is nothing but some fashionable attitude. On the other hand it is an attempt to

6. See the investigation which has been done under the International Youth Library's mentorship, to compare the situation in Germany with the school library systems of the United States, Great Britain, and Scandinavia: Ulrich Mallmann, *Theorie und Praxis der Schulbücherei (Theory and Practise of the School Library)*, (Munich: 1966). See also: *Die Moderne Schulbibliothek (The Modern School Library)*, ed. by Klaus Doderer (Hamburg: 1970).

7. The official German children's book award was divided in four ways until 1970: picture books, children's books, youth books, and non-fiction for all age groups. Now, with a slight change, children's and youth books share one of the prizes and the fourth prize is given to a pioneer creation. Each year a best list appears in a German as well as in an English version: *Die besten Jugendbücher* (Munich: 1967–1969). There is also published a cumulative edition with several articles and other information: *Zehn Jahre Deutscher Jugendbuchpreis (Ten Years of the German Children's Book Award)*, (Munich: 1966). Since the beginning, the award has been international. About 50 percent of the prizes have been given to foreign authors or illustrators. The International Youth Library's *Preisgekrönte Kinderbücher (Children's Prize Books)*, (Munich: Verlag Dokumentation, 1969/New York: R. R. Bowker Co., 1969), and its supplements gives the complete picture.

introduce youth as early as possible to literary sensibility. But what is the use of all that? Young people must have a very intensive experience of adventure and that is at least one reason why adventure has become a classic category of world literature. Meanwhile the other aspect has also proved to be true.

The best youth books of the last years are at the same time first-class books for adults: the successful translation from the Czech of Jan Procházka's *Long Live the Republic!* and the literary, convincing, anti-authority novel of Cecil Bødker, *Silas,* translated from the Danish.

Where are the internationally valuable contributions to the field of teen and young adult literature? The best adventure books in my opinion are those written by Fritz Mühlenweg and Kurt Lütgen. The great influence of *Big Tiger and Christian* I realized several years ago when I met some scout groups who lived playing in that world. Not only did they identify themselves with their heroes, but they also assumed the ritual of that free life in the steppes in order to create a background and a support for their dreams of boyhood, outside of our benumbed, over-civilized adult society.

Kurt Lütgen's books reflect quite another world, an adult rather than a boy's adventure world. His most important work is *No Winter for Wolves,* which has an extraordinary structure. A rescue march across Alaska leads through difficult and dangerous situations. But into this dramatic line are blended several separate tales, which reflect the inner development of the actors and which change them.

Equally well depicted are the inner discussion between father and son, a young man's part in the community, and the problems of social acceptance and prestige in the outstanding Dakota-trilogy of Liselotte Welskopf-Henrich from East Berlin. She not only has an original gift of narration, but also solid knowledge of the American and Canadian Indians. Finally, we should mention Kurt Held's gang novel which has already become a classic: *Red Zora.* Kurt Held, who died several years ago in Switzerland, was always interested in social youth problems. (He was married to the folk-tale narrator Lisa Tetzner to whom we owe not only lively reports of her storytelling wanderings in the twenties but a long series of fairy-tale collections and fiction of her own.)

Historical novels are also at home in German youth literature, which can be traced back to Walter Scott and his rich influences on contemporary German authors. These influences proved to be stronger than Alexandre Dumas and his late romanticism on the one hand and Mark Twain's anti-heroism and anti-romanticism on the other. There are many classic editions on the German market, new editions of old historical novels and a great number of new ones—to begin with Fritz Halbeck in Vienna and to end with Hans Baumann and Ingeborg Engelhardt; to go back to Martin Luserke, with his fascinating descriptions of the North Sea coast and the realm between land and sea; and finally to come to Ludwig Renn, the pacifist and former commander of an international brigade in Spain, who confines himself to socialist revolution themes.

POLITICAL INFLUENCES

And here we encounter political interest. There is no youth literature in the world—except that of several socialist states—which is engaged so extensively with social criticism, race problems, and modern historical facts as Germany's. Taking for granted that most of this interest is temporary and will be forgotten, at the end the only survivor may be Hans Leip's great novel *Der Nigger auf Scharhörn Island* which has the poetry of childhood and the smell of the sea, developing sharp social observation and psychology; perhaps Kurt Held's *Giuseppe and Mary* will remain as a picture of war's end and post-war social problems; and maybe Herbert Kaufmann's monument to that Negro king who was defeated by the brutality of European merchants in the 1860's (*The King's Crocodile*). In order to describe horror and cruelty, Winfried Bruckner, the young Austrian trade-union secretary, introduced expressionistic elements of style (*The Dead Angels*) and the Swiss journalist and commentator Lorenz Stucki edited a solid and objective modern history with general European aspects: *The Genesis of Present Time*. The list of names which should be enumerated if I were to give titles suitable for translation would be very long. I should speak of Auguste Lazar and her book about a concentration camp's death march; of Hans Peter Richter and his realistic self-accusation in *Friedrich*; of Peter Berger, who described in a rather drastic manner the growing political radicalism before 1933.[8] And there is the Austrian Karl Bruckner's *Sadako will leben (Sadako Will Live)*.

CONCLUSION

The history of children's and youth literature in the German language is long. A good deal of German folk tradition and its early accounts is worthy of being discovered, retold, adapted. Naturally many of these tales and rhymes are also suitable for translation. The question is only that we should not send routine workers into these mines, but real experts in folklore and psychology. What is more, a strong tendency is evident toward starting a similar treasure hunt in far-away literature and folk traditions. This shows that German children's literature could make an important second-hand contribution as well: by means of translations it could be a mediator of languages which are accessible to it, as is the case already with the Slavic literatures.

These tasks are proposed to every literature. We must further the public's interest systematically. It should be said that there is unlimited exchange between Austria, Switzerland, and the German Federal Republic.

---

8. See Walter Scherf, *Politische Bildung durch das Jugendbuch? (Political Education by Means of Youth Literature?)*, (Munich: 1963); continued in "Zeitgeschichte und Jugendbuch," *Der Schweizer Buchhandel* (Bern), 26 (1968): 793–800.

An attempt to draw literary borderlines would lead to artificial results. Only Switzerland is doing more for its native regional literature in dialects. As to the German Democratic Republic, there are still reservations about average production, whereas the top literature is thoroughly appreciated, even when its social analysis proves to have another base.

To come to the end: is it possible to characterize in a few sentences the actual German contribution of original children's literature which succeeds in being effective beyond national borders? It is not easy. But it can be said that the roots of that contribution are to be found in the traditional narrative treasure; in the mysticism, poetry, and fantasy of the romantic art and way of life; and in the expressionistic human ideal and the parallel educational reform policy of the golden twenties. As always, romanticism and realism are in opposition and even become manifest in extremes, but at the same time they supplement each other. The strongest influence from outside Germany has been from England, and, during the last twenty years, Sweden and America: but French influences still remain lively. All the other literatures fall back completely, though a new interest is growing in the Slavic literatures.

What has become visible from the new experiments are the picture books and, hopefully not to remain in the shadow of graphic artificiality, the real, psychologically founded, modern picture book *culture;* a new, just developing poetry for children; prose texts originating from reading aloud and from storytelling, partly realistic, partly fantastic;[9] a new type of book which is interesting to the family as a whole; adventure and gang novels; and finally, political discussion. But right here it must be stated that overnight the interest in political questions arising from contemporary history has shifted. The historical aspect has dropped completely, political interest faces the actual situation of our society. From students' communities and now even from really established publishing houses a new production has arisen already of anti-authority picture books for small children.

But all this is generalization and I confess that I fear generalizations and standardizations of criticism. German children's book production is far too much oriented towards the opinions of its critics, and the critics on the other hand stick far too firmly to what they have assiduously learned. If they meet something unusual and original they give what proves to be a preconceived opinion: or, in their insecurity, they decline to give way to the fashionable new waves. To continue with generalizations you could say that the average level is quite high[10]—but all that is unusual and original must struggle very hard to make its way. But that has been the fact in every age and in every country!

---

9. The best survey of actual writing can be found in the following anthology, with its appendix: *Kinderland, Zauberland (Land of Childhood, Land of Magic),* ed. by Jans-Joachim Gelberg, illus. by Günther Stiller (Recklinghausen: 1967).

10. See that very useful tool from the International Institute for Children's Literature in Vienna: *Lexikon der Jugendschriftsteller in deutscher Sprache,* compiled by Lucia Binder (Vienna: 1969).

Children's Literature in France

Isabelle Jan and Geneviève Patte

Translated by Patricia M. Lafferty

Isabelle Jan is experienced in many areas of work with children's literature: as a librarian in L'Heure Joyeuse (a children's library in Paris), a teacher of children's literature in teacher-training schools, and as publishing assistant to Père Castor and selector of titles for Fernand Nathan's Bibliothèque International *(a series of translated world classics). She has translated* It's Like This, Cat; Little House in the Big Woods; Finn Family Moomintroll; *and other works and is the author of* Essai sur la litérature enfantine *(Paris: Editions ouvrieres, 1969) and many articles on children's literature.*

Formerly children's librarian at the New York Public Library (1961–1963), Geneviève Patte has been Director of the modern children's library, La Joie par les Livres, in Clamart, France, since 1964. She has lectured on children's literature and contributed to and edited Bulletin d'Analyses, *a quarterly publication of La Joie par les Livres containing articles on and reviews of children's literature. Mlle Patte is also a member of the Executive Committee of the International Board on Books for Young People (1970–   ).*

In examining the recent production of imaginative literature for children in France, one is immediately struck by some principal characteristics, the most noticeable of which is uniformity: uniformity in presentation, in illustrations, in format, in subjects and themes. This uniformity of presentation in fiction contrasts strongly with the quality of picture books and nonfiction. The latter are, in general, more carefully done, better researched, and freer in both conception and realization than the endless parade of monotonous novels in which interchangeable illustrators promenade from story to story the same silhouettes of stereotyped children, well suited to the grey and boring typography. These novels are formal and stilted in style and totally without charm. The uniformity of presentation is due partly to the fact that most publishers of collections for children are also publishers of school books, but there is also a uniformity in subjects and themes. Dull book covers conceal the same stories everlastingly repeated: a certain group is perplexed by a mystery; a gang of children is investigated; two children separated by everything—race, religion, rivalry—meet and a great friendship is born; or, a quiet, dreamy-eyed preadolescent is rejected by his class or gang and again friendship triumphs.

These plots are not new, but like any other subject they can be the point of departure for a discovery rich in surprises. They do not contain, in themselves, their own condemnation: the imagination which stimulates emotion, which conveys to thought, can vivify the simplest structures. It is necessary, then, for us to examine whether this first impression of repetition, of monotony, is verified by the reading. We must ask ourselves what kind of writing appears in children's books.

Two tendencies clearly arise: the didactic concern on the one hand and literary nostalgia on the other. There are informational novels which are set in a definite time and place and give the reader, at the same time, a lively plot and a certain amount of information; these one can call, without exaggeration, documentary novels. There are novels in which the plot depends essentially on the psychology of the characters—psychology proclaimed, improved, and abundantly described by means of more or less complicated, but easily identifiable, stylistic figures which seem to be repeated from one novel to another and even from one author to another. Between these two types of literature, "the document-novel" and "the novel-too-well-written," one might detect a contradiction. In reality they correspond with and complement each other, for they both express the same tendency—a tendency, certainly, seldom conscious to their authors, but which an adult reader cannot fail to notice and which will mark, unconsciously, even a young reader. Although masked by the importance given to the document or by implicit reference to a certain type of literature, there is a preoccupation with escape from the immediate, from everyday life, and above all, from the real problems of the world today. French children's literature is an unrealistic literature, oriented toward the past. It is a literature of escape.

One could invoke neutrality here and certain critics will not fail to do that. In the desire to not take sides, to not judge, one can see, in fact, a concern with objectivity which would reflect accurately enough the ideal of the nondenominational school of the Third Republic (a school which was open to all and in which each was allowed to live without being annoyed by a too noticeable ideology and to keep his opinons, his beliefs, and his inconsistencies to himself). But this nondenominational neutrality is very often a double-edged sword. By not taking sides, one simply evades approaching the essential problems and, when it concerns literary expression, one can produce no more than a sclerotic and, consequently, sterile work.

There are certain attempts to modernize children's literature in France, but they are merely a matter of modernization, that is, of adjustment, of adaptation of out-of-date structures so that they are again usable, rather than a true reexamination. Certainly authors are conscious of the need to abandon the old themes, to approach life as it is and not as they would wish it to be for children. But conviction is not there. Therefore, they modernize the story, that is, they make it fashionable, to the taste of the day, by applying a veneer of lifeless documentation. Indeed, when the problems of today are treated, it is superficially: the setting changes, but the contents remain the same.

Two recent examples can illustrate this double movement, which can be described as a desire for renovation, an impetus, which is immediately controlled and, hence, rendered ineffective by excessive scruples. Emotion is stifled in spite of all the good intentions of the authors. Thus, a novel on the Vietnamese war presents impartially the good and the bad: for each sympathetic character in one camp there is an equally sympathetic character in the adverse camp, and it is the same for the unsympathetic characters. Only horror and pity abide—the horror of the war, of war in general, of all war viewed as an inevitable calamity, and pity for the victims of a catastrophe comparable to an earthquake. Another novel describes the life in the shanty-towns of the Parisian region. Here it is not false objectivity which is at fault, but excessive use of documentation to explain the problem. When one compares such works to a whole segment of recent American children's literature which reflects the current preoccupations and obsessions of the American people, it becomes clear that in these two works the authors wanted to be truthful, but without committing themselves. They worked in all good conscience and did their moral duty toward the publisher, here a substitute for that figure so important in the collective mentality of the French, the professor. But any subject involving social issues—whether written for adults or for children—must be dictated by a very strong inner need; or it will only exploit disorder and misery, which then become new subjects in themselves, and the original issue loses all true meaning.

If, on the one hand, current problems are rarely treated or treated in a timorous manner, on the other hand, writers try to remove the child from his natural sphere. The majority of French novels for children in the past ten years, whether historical or exotic, are set in the most distant time or space possible—often, both at the same time.

REMOVAL IN TIME: THE HISTORICAL NOVEL

It is interesting to ask ourselves what periods of history writers prefer. The answer is easy: the great majority choose very distant times. The first choice is antiquity, the early history of the peoples of the Mediterranean basin and the Near East. Then the Middle Ages, European likewise. There is, of course, a very simple explanation for this. These novels correspond exactly to the history syllabus of students in sixth or fifth grade,[1] that is, between eleven and thirteen years old, the age at which they are ready to read such books. This demonstrates once again that children's literature is considered, more or less consciously, a scholastic complement which helps one to better assimilate history courses. But it should be noted also that the more distant the events, the less involved the reader might feel. Perhaps this is a way to neutralize history, to make it innocuous by reviving a past of

---

1. The first and second years of secondary school, in the French school system.

which only traces exist in museums instead of retelling a past still present in our lives, capable of exciting and stirring deep interest.

Antiquity

Certain French children's authors are truly specialists in this period. The most prolific author is L. N. Lavolle, for whom one can remember two titles among a very abundant production: *Les clés du désert* and *L'acrobate de Minos*. Pierre Debresse *(La ville aux sept collines, Les larmes d'Isis)* and Marcelle Lerme-Walter *(Les enfants de Pompéi)* use detailed documentation in a more lively and more interesting way. From this mass of works devoted to the most remote times emerges a novel by Nicole Vidal *(Les jours dorés de K'ai Yuang)*[2] which is as striking for its innovation in using remote settings as for its powerful prose. Set in eighth-century China, it will perhaps make French children aware of the fact that all civilization was not born on the shores of the Mediterranean.

The Middle Ages and Contemporary History

Novels set in the Middle Ages are also very numerous. The author most representative and most worthy of esteem is Georges Nigremont, who describes with great realism and sensitivity the life of ordinary people: *L'oiselier du Pont-au-Change* and *Jean Parizet, tapissier d'Aubusson*. On the historical events themselves, the novels of Jacqueline Dumesnil *(Les compagnons du Cerf d'Argent, Le combat du Cerf d'Argent)* are also lively and well-constructed. Production gradually decreases as one approaches our time.

It is necessary to note here that the historical novel is seldom historical. It appears, rather, as a chronicle, more or less moving, of the manners and customs of past times. In this regard, the narratives set in the fifteenth, sixteenth, and seventeenth centuries are very significant: customs, old crafts, costumes, festivals, and modes of transportation—all is re-created with a thread of plot which, itself, could just as well happen in our day. But the events themselves and especially the great political and social upheavals are not mentioned, as if the novel could record only the peaceful periods of history. Thus, one does not find any novel which has either the French Revolution or the Napoleonic period for a background. The religious wars are better represented with some good novels: particularly *La ville déchirée* by Georges Nigremont, *Le mystère de l'abbaye brûlée* by Renée Aurembou, and *Temps d'orage* by Alice Piguet. On the life and customs of the seventeenth century, one can cite Pierre Debresse's *Les sept J chez le Roi Soleil;* the series by Alice Piguet, *Tonio,* which unfolds the adventures of a child of a silk worker from Lyon; and very recently, Jean-Paul Nogues' *Mon pays sous les eaux,* an interesting book because it is told from the viewpoint

---

2. Published in English as *Ring of Jade* (London: Mayflower, 1969).

of the adversary at the time of the invasion of the Netherlands by the armies of Louis XIV. But the most striking point is that on contemporary history there is complete silence. The nineteenth century with its national and social struggles, the war of '70, that of '14 to '18, and the discoveries of modern times do not inspire the writers for children. One can name only a very charming book by Colette Vivier on the 1900 era, *La grande roue,* and only one testimony on the life of child laborers of the nineteenth century, Georges Nigremont's *Jeantou, maçon Creusois.* This is all the more paradoxical because it is in the nineteenth century that the condition of children became hazardous because it was entrusted to the fluctuations of rising industry, which ought to touch readers of today. One should not be astonished, then, if children continue to read the great classics of popular literature of the nineteenth century, in which they find the echo of these still recent struggles: Victor Hugo, George Sand, Eugène Le Roy. Nor should one be astonished if they are still enraptured by the novels of Alexandre Dumas, enlivened and related in a different manner than those that are invented today for their enjoyment.

The Second World War

One problem is, however, amply treated: the Second World War and the Resistance. The Resistance is too often seen as a detective story. In general, the authors strive not to take sides, not to politicize, on the period of Franco-German union. But in thus neutralizing the problem, they sometimes end up with some real aberrations, as much on the historical plane as on the moral plane. It is no longer the Resistance as it was, but as one might see it today, in a perspective of pardon and reconciliation. The most striking example of a negative and disputable cooperation is the book by G. Fonvilliers, *L'enfant, le soldat et la mer,* which ends by denying the deeds of the occupation troops in France and, all told, justifying the collaboration. The best novels are probably those which were written immediately after the events: that of Yvonne Meynier, *Un lycée pas comme les autres,*[3] an autobiographical story; Colette Vivier's *La maison des quatre-vents,*[4] a true story of a group of unyielding Parisians; and Marianne Monestier's *C'est déjà Midi,* a description of the Resistance in the country and in the course of which a child is killed in a maquis. One is reminded that books which avoid traumatizing the child by scenes of violence and death are, to that extent, simply false to the reality of actual events.

REMOVAL IN SPACE: THE EXOTIC NOVEL

When authors approach contemporary life, in most cases, they write about very remote countries and different civilizations—which, in effect,

---

3. *A School with a Difference* (New York: Abelard-Schuman Limited, 1963).
4. *House of the Four Winds* (New York: Doubleday & Company, Inc., 1969).

removes the child from what he knows. The initiator of this genre of novels is René Guillot, for whom one can name, at random from a superabundant production, *L'extraordinaire aventure de Michel Santanrea.* But the exotic novel is represented mainly by Jacqueline Cervon and Francois Balsan. Balsan invariably develops the same theme: that of tribal conflict resolved by friendship. And the encounter between two children of different races or of hostile countries is also the main theme of the novels of Jacqueline Cervon. She shows a certain talent as storyteller when she addresses herself to the very young, between eight and ten years old, as in her first novel, *Ali, Jean-Luc et la gazelle,* which remains one of her best. For older children one remembers her *Le naufragé de Rhodes.*[5] Many other authors try their hand at this difficult genre. Among the good books that one has been able to read these last few years is *Lady Bengale* by Elsie, who makes the poetry of distant countries and its influence on Europeans understandable. And surely Andrée Clair exposes most honestly the relations between the whites and the blacks of Africa in an already old novel, *Moudaïna.*

On the whole, all of these are as poor and as artificial as the historical novel, and the fundamental problem of the relations between different civilizations is not really presented, but merely evaded by an idealistic solution: all is resolved thanks to the friendship of two children. What is most remarkable in this category of books is, sometimes, a certain scientific pretension which is supposed to make up for the absence of real experience. The success of the reports of Haroun Tazieff or of Norbert Casteret prove that children turn away from these artificial pseudoromantic and pseudodocumentary stories to read true stories.

REMOTENESS BY LITERARY NOSTALGIA

Literature for the young in France was strongly influenced by Alain Fournier's *Le Grand Meaulnes,*[6] but, it must be said, not always favorably. Many authors for children dream of writing a new *Grand Meaulnes* and it is more Augustin Meaulnes' adolescence than their own that they strive to regain by calling up a certain climate of childhood—its difficulties of adjustment, its psychological problems, and the gulf which separates daily reality from the aspirations and dreams of a wandering imagination. For *Le Grand Meaulnes,* for the majority of French people, has sketched a satisfying portrait of adolescence; it has without doubt defined it for a long while. It is a privileged period, a golden age propitious for the quest for a paradise lost. Naturally, this is not false in itself, but can be frozen into a set literary pattern by the writing.

The quest for paradise lost, forbidden except to childish innocence, is

---

5. *Castaway from Rhodes* (London: The Bodley Head, 1967. New York: Franklin Watts, 1973).
6. *Grand Meaulnes* (London: Methuen, 1968).

certainly one of the major themes of all literature. To the foreigner, it finds its most natural expression in books about animals, such as *The Wind in the Willows*. Works with such appropriate and poignant poetry do not exist in France, where any kind of book on animals is rare enough. But those which do exist do not lack interest. Besides Babar (which continues to be successful and which expresses, with a clarity and precision that is very French, a peaceful utopia), there is one of the very first French successes in this field: the series of picture books by Lida (published under the name of "Père Castor"): *Le roman des bêtes*. In these the scientific facts are presented honestly but with emotion, allowing the child to accept them as a story. Other authors devoted to showing stories of a child with an animal are René Guillot (*Grichka et son ours)*[7] and Michel-Aimé Baudouy (Bruno, roi de la montagne[8] and *Le seigneur des hautes buttes,* two well-written books). But of all these endeavors, the most interesting and the most successful is, unquestionably, *Le lion*[9] by Joseph Kessel. In it we see the power of innocence against the forces of evil and its possibilities of communication with the mysteries of nature, better expressed than in the two most famous French novels which exploit the same theme, Saint-Exupéry's *Le petit Prince*[10] and Maurice Druon's *Tistou les pouces verts.*[11]

André Dhotel, upon whom Alain Fournier has had a striking influence, is also oriented toward childhood and its magic. And Henri Bosco and, very recently, Michel Tournier in *Vendredi ou la vie sauvage*[12] write on the same theme. These authors, very different in many ways, have in common a sort of complaisance toward miracle, fruit of the nostalgia for a world which is closed to them forever and which, by inventing, they have lost the ability to see. The stories of Bosco—and even more of Michel Tournier—lack airiness and can only redeem themselves by their purity of style. But one can also see how a poetic necessity can introduce into this literature an absolutely antiquated writing, encumbered with cliché-images. The most striking example of this style of writing is that of Minou Drouet.

Aberrations of writing often express a false psychology which chooses children, marked as "strange" beings, and makes of them pathological cases who, however, enhance the highest fantasy. The principal characteristic of this literature is thus to start not from reality, but from a bookish experience. This is, after all, what Tournier has done in a conscious, thus controlled, manner, but which remains more or less subconscious in most of those who, believing they are writing an original work, elicit in the reader an impression of artifice.

---

7. *Grishka and the Bear* (New York: Criterion Books, Inc., 1960. London: Oxford University Press, 1959).
8. *Bruno, King of the Mountain* (New York: Harcourt Brace Jovanovich, Inc., 1960). *Bruno, King of the Wild* (London: The Bodley Head, 1962).
9. *The Lion* (New York: Alfred A. Knopf, Inc., 1962).
10. *The Little Prince* (New York: Reynal & Hitchcock, 1943. London: Heinemann, 1945).
11. *Tistou of the Green Thumbs* (New York: Charles Scribner's Sons, 1958).
12. *Friday and Robinson* (New York: Doubleday & Company, Inc., 1969. London: Aldus Books, 1972).

Illustration by Jacqueline Duhème from *Tistou of the Green Thumbs* by Maurice Druon.
Reprinted by permission of Charles Scribner's Sons.

THE REALISTIC CURRENT

Happily, there exists a whole realistic tradition which comes, in part,
from the Comtesse de Ségur. It may seem paradoxical, but it was in fact the
most reactionary writer of our literature who made French writers for
children aware of the needs of children and who initiated a language which
could speak directly to them.

The most interesting French writers are those who write about daily reality: the family, the school, and children's relations with other children. Novels centered on school life describe, in general, schools in the country. Their authors are teachers who rely upon their experience, like Pierre Gamarra (*Le mystère de la Berlurette*) or Léonce Bourliaguet (*Quatre du Cours moyen*). In the good humor and familiarity in these books one can see the influence of Louis Pergaud's famous *Guerre des boutons*,[13] which is a chronicle on the life of students rather than a book for children. But in spite of the success of *La guerre des boutons* and of the stir it caused, such books are rather rare.

School work inspires few, and yet work in general is indeed the principal theme of realistic French novels. One must see this as the expression of a whole social morality strongly anchored in the French consciousness since the time of the craft guilds—a morality taken up again by the lay school and of which one finds echoes through all the literature from the eighteenth century to our day and in writers as diverse as Péguy or Charles Vildrac. Labor is presented positively in so far as it results in work well done and satisfying to the worker. The unpleasant and especially the frustrating side of work is hidden and the worker, whatever he does, is presented as an artisan. The novel most representative of this state of mind is Charles Vildrac's *Milot*. A child hero would naturally not know how to be a workman, but it seems important, in order to fulfill this implicit moral, that he be an active person. Thus the heroes of these novels are constantly doing; they never enjoy a moment of rest, and every idea, every initiative, every manifestation of their personality is immediately realized in action. They are directed wholly toward doing. For them, vagabondage and reverie hold no possibilities for self-expansion, for invention and creation. This is clearly evident in the little stories that Albertine Delataille has composed for Père Castor's picture books and in the novels of Michel-Aimé Baudouy, such as *Mick et la P. 105* and *Le garçon du barrage*.[14] In Georges Nigremont's writing, however, work is not idealized but shown in its harsh reality.

It remains, nonetheless, that the best French writers for children are the realistic novelists: Pierre Gamarra, Andrée Clair, Georges Nigremont, Madeleine Gilard, Paul Berna, and, surpassing all by the appropriateness of her style, the acuity of her observation, the naturalness of her dialogues, Colette Vivier. Realism becomes truly interesting when it uses humor to achieve some distance from its object, which is sometimes the case with Gamarra and often with Colette Vivier. But purely humorous books remain an exception. One can, however, name Léopold Chauveau's *Les deux font la paire;* Maud Frere's *Le journal de Véronique;* and Sempe and Goscinny's *Le petit Nicolas*. *Le petit Nicolas* addresses itself to all, the youngest and the oldest, but its success with children shows clearly the need for humor. It is,

---

13. *The Boy Who Belonged to No One* (New York: Harcourt Brace Jovanovich, Inc., 1967). *The Boy on the Dam* (Leicester: Brockhampton, 1970).
     More than Courage (New York: Harcourt Brace Jovanovich, Inc., 1961). *Mick and the Motorbike* (London, The Bodley Head, 1961).
14. *The War of the Buttons* (New York: Walker & Company, 1969).

in fact, humor alone which can give to French children's literature what it so much lacks: the sense of the marvellous, poetry. This is why Marcel Aymé's *Les contes du Chat Perché*[15] seems always so lively and so precious to us. That is certainly the true classic for children, pure in form and free from all didactic concern. These narratives, which border between tale and novel and give free rein to the imagination without forcing the style, do not always penetrate easily to French children. Those which, like *Contes du Chat Perché*, obtain their approval are, without doubt, the best children's literature. Let us name, for example, Claude Aveline's *Baba-Diène et Morceau-de-Sucre*, André Maurois' *Patapouf et Filifer*,[16] Micheline Maurel's *Les contes d'Agathe*, and, very recently, Marcelle Lerme-Walter's *Les Voyageurs sans soucis*. Such books which have incontestable qualities of charm and fantasy are very rare in France. And as far as the tale is concerned, it would be better to go to the true folklorists.

The glory of Perrault has made the work of the folklorists pass into the background. And yet France possesses a rich folklore, which has been collected from the nineteenth century. Among the most interesting collectors, besides Perrault, one must mention Bladé for the stories of Gascogne; Deulin for the French Flanders (*Contes du Roi Gambrinus* and *Contes d'un buveur de bière*); and Henri Pourrat, who, in the *Trésor des contes*,[17] is especially attached to the midland region.

This rich folklore, which is often splendidly manifested in the tale, has not revived popular poetry. This explains, perhaps, the scantiness of poetry for children. Poetry draws its inspiration naturally from the child's playsong, such as "London's Bridge," but it can also remain a prisoner of it. Madeleine Ley and Marie Noel knew how to detach themselves from it in order to create a poetry directly accessible to children by starting with sensation. The poets who reign in the nursery, Robert Desnos and Maurice Careme, are more interested in play upon words. But one must note that surrealism has stamped its mark on most of the poets whom children read today: Jacques Prevert, Philippe Soupault, Raymond Queneau, Ionesco, and René de Olbadia. But we are extrapolating and leaving children's literature properly so called.

Any kind of description that we can construct quickly of the situation of children's literature as it is today is abstract and limited. It does not take into account the general context in which children read, and, in particular, it omits the translations which hold a considerable place and play a primary role in the general policy of publication for children in France.

---

15. *Tales of the Perching Cat,* published as *The Wonderful Farm* (New York: Harper & Row, Publishers, 1951. London: The Bodley Head, 1952). *The Magic Pictures* (New York: Harper & Row, Publishers, 1954). Also called *Return to the Wonderful Farm* (London, The Bodley Head, 1954).
16. *Fattypuffs and Thinifers* (New York: Alfred A. Knopf, Inc., 1969. London: The Bodley Head, 1968).
17. *A Treasury of French Tales* (Boston: Houghton-Mifflin Company, 1954. London: George Allen & Unwin, 1953).

Czech and Slovak Children's Literature

Helga Mach

Helga Mach is a lecturer at the South German Library School in Stuttgart, German Federal Republic. Born in Prague, she is fluent in Czech, Slovak, Polish, German, and English. In 1970 she served as a special consultant to the Children's Book Section at the Library of Congress, working on bibliographical reference sources in these languages. She has also been an active participant in international library conferences. The following paper was first presented at the international course in children's literature held in Lochem, The Netherlands, in 1970.

To speak about children's books in Czechoslovakia means also to speak about political events in this country. Its geographical situation, political history, and cultural connections with other countries are determinants in its literature and therefore also in children's literature, because children's books show in a special way the mind of a nation.

Czechoslovakia within its present borders is a rather small country (about 13 million inhabitants) almost in the middle of Europe, with neighbors speaking many different languages: German, Polish, Hungarian, Roumanian, Serbo-Croatian, and Russian. Minorities of all these population groups are living in Czechoslovakia today. The two main languages are Czech (spoken in Bohemia and Moravia) and Slovak (spoken in Eastern Czechoslovakia). Most of the inhabitants grew up and still grow up with two, often with three languages. Such a multilingual situation is not without influence on the development of culture, especially of literature.

Furthermore, it is hard to understand the present state of this country without knowing the historical changes. Being under German and Austrian government for more than 900 years, and being a small part of an empire covering very different populations, the inhabitants gained a continent-wide view of life. The first republic, established in 1918, was the result of national consciousness that arose during the nineteenth century. One of its chief problems remained the adaption of minorities. To consider Czechoslovak children's literature today it is necessary to look at the influences which are still efficient in politics and in literature—from the years of German occupation and World War II with all the harm and pain known all over Europe; and since 1945 the existence of the second republic, its connection to the socialistic part of the world, not without conflicts and confounding results, and, not least, the Russian intervention in 1968.

"Czech and Slovak Children's Literature" by Helga Mach from *De Openbare Bibliotheek*, v. 14, no. 9, (1971). Reprinted by permission of NBLC.

THE NINETEENTH CENTURY TO WORLD WAR I

The importance of tradition in literature is revealed in the authors and books of the nineteenth century, not only for their influence on the development of children's literature but also on publication today, which includes, to a great extent, reprints of classics. An example is *Babička* (*Grandmother*)[1] by Božena Němcová, regarded as the most popular prose work in Czech literature and besides that as the first Czech contribution to literature of worldwide recognition. These "pictures from the country-side" (subtitle) show the life of the poor and oppressed country people in the nineteenth century, living in a kind of slavery in their dependency on landowners. It is Grandmother's silent, warmhearted, and wise activity that provides a place of rest and security for her family.

Among innumerable reprints and translations there are editions available today as children's books. In others of her work Němcová struggled for a recognition of women in the social structure, and she collected folk tales and nursery rhymes. Evidence of the high esteem held for this author by her nation is the fact that her grave is situated in the Prague cemetery for national heroes and—as I saw during my last visit—is still adorned with flowers.

Together with the works of Němcová, books from Jan Neruda and Alois Jirásek have survived as classics for both adults and children. From the former came *Malostranské Povídky (Stories from the "Small Side")*,[2] which has witty sketches about the life of middle-class townspeople, and *Dětem (For Children)*,[3] a collection of poetry for children. The latter's works meet the nineteenth-century interest in history in *Staré Pověsti České (Old Czech Legends)*[4] and *Psohlavci ("Dogheads"*—the name of a resistance group),[5] which shows the resistance of farmers against landowners in former times.

From this time on, three important characteristics of children's literature prevail.

1. Almost all authors of children's books are also authors of books for adults; in other words, there seems to be no shame in writing children's books and no barrier therefore between the writing for children and the entire national literature. The high standards of children's books and the criticism of them may be due to this.

---

1. Božena Němcová (1820-1862), *Babička*, 1855. *Die Grossmutter* (Zurich: Manesse, 1959).

2. Jan Neruda, *Malostranské Povídky (Stories from the "Small Side")*, 1878 (Prague: SNDK, 1959). *Kleinseitner Geschichten* (Munich: Winkler, 1965).

3. Jan Neruda, *Dětem (For Children)*, (Prague: SNDK, 1963).

4. Alois Jirásek (1851-1930), *Staré Pověsti České (Old Czech Legends)*, 1894, illustrated by Jiří Trnka (Prague: SNDK, 1961). *Böhmens alte Sagen* (Prague: Artia, 1963).

5. Alois Jirásek, *Psohlavci ("Dogheads")*, 1884, (Prague: SNDK, 1952).

2. The aspect of social problems as subjects.

3. The close connection between folklore traditions and illustration in children's books.

The first important book especially for small children is Jan Karafiát's *Broučci (Glowworms)*.[6] Here is the first in what would become a long line of stories for children in which the events and feelings of children's lives are transfigured into the world of animals and thus resemble fairy tales or—twenty years later—the comics. Here is the story of a glowworm-boy bearing a lantern; he awakes in the spring; he has his first flight on St. John's night in midsummer and then exciting adventures exploring the world by himself. He marries a handsome glowworm-girl, and when winter comes they put their ten children to bed, consoling them with, "After your long sleep there will be St. John's night for you."

The value of this story lies not only in its caressive view of the child's world, but also in its poetic prose. The story belongs in the first reading of almost every child even today. Many editions with different illustrations came to be produced, including the most congenial art work by Jiří Trnka, whom I will mention later.

Before considering the uprooting change brought by World War I, we must note the first work by Marie Majerová, an author of great importance for Czech children's literature in this century, not only because of her own works but through her influence on criticism. An important Czech prize for children's books bears her name. *Čarovný Svět (Magic World)*,[7] her collection of folk tales from different countries, has had a wide influence on later such anthologies.

THE FIRST REPUBLIC AND WORLD WAR II

The end of World War I in 1918 brought political independence for the Czech and Slovak nations and the first Czechoslovak republic. Soon afterward appeared another famous contribution to world literature: *Osudy Dobrého Zojáka Švejka za Světové Války (The Good Soldier Shvejk in the World War)*[8] by Jaroslav Hašek. More than any other work of national literature, perhaps, it shows a special Czech view of life—a sense of humor and the practical joke even in oppressive social situations, a way of outwitting totalitarian governments by a special kind of mother-wit and common

---

6. Jan Karafiát (1864-1929), *Broučci (Glowworms)*, 1895, illustrated by Jiří Trnka (Prague: SNDK, 1961). *Leuchtkäferchen*, retold by Max Bollinger (Zurich: Artemis, 1969).

7. Marie Majerová (1882-1967), *Čarovný Svět (Magic World)*, 1913, illustrations by Karel Svolinský (Prague: SNDK, 1958). *Zauberwelt des Märchens* (Prague: Artia, 1963).

8. Jaroslav Hašek (1883-1923), *Osudy Dobrého Zojáka Švejka za Světové Války (The Good Soldier Shvejk in the World War)*, 1921-1923, illustrated by Josef Lada. *Die Abenteuer des braven Soldaten Schwejk* (Reinbek: Rowohlt).

sense, a way of surviving by turning orders to contrary meanings and, by doing so, unmasking them as phrases.

Even if such a view of life could be a help also for children, Hašek's Shvejk stories with all their sometimes funny, sometimes rough, sometimes cruel details are not for children. However, their influence on children's literature cannot be overlooked. A selection of Hašek's *Veselé Povídky (Cheerful Stories)*[9] produced for children has formed the political mind of resistance against totalitarian systems of at least one.

Hašek found his congenial illustrator in Josef Lada who, with his special technique of drawing and painting, created a new style of illustration for children, closely related to folklore but with cartoon-like features which can show the working of intellect. His own writing has the same style. His story *Mikeš, o Kocourovi Který Mluvil (Speaking Tom-Cat Mikesh)*[10] has a mixture of fairy-tale details, incidents from country life, and wit. In *Nezbedné Pohádky (Funny Fairy Tales)*[11] he creates fun by converting fairy tales to the opposites of their well-known situations—not quite parodies, but a way of giving distance to facts that are perhaps too familiar.

Most authors of this time wrote in a similar style, whether for adults or for children. So Josef Čapek's *Povídání o Pejskovi a Kočičce (Stories from a Puppy and a Cat)*,[12] with his own illustration for amusing episodes, became as famous as his brother, Karel Čapek's, stories in *Devatero Pohádek (Nine Fairy Tales)*.[13] Neither book can be taken as straight fairy tale.

Quite another line of tradition begins with František Langer's adventures of a group of boys in *Bratrstvo Bílého Klíče (The League of the White Key)*.[14] The white key opens the door to a forgotten small garden amidst the city, a paradise for the boys' games. The influence of Erich Kästner, especially his *Emil und die Detektive,* which is quoted several times by the boys, is evident. It shows the same insight into children—their feelings, actions, and outlook on life; but, moreover, Langer has a larger proportion of sense in his nonsense than Kästner shows in his stories about children. A bit of this nonsense distinguishes also the illustrations by Oldřich Sekora.

One cannot discuss illustration without mentioning the most famous Czech illustrator, Jiří Trnka, whose first work for children was published in

---

9. Jaroslav Hašek, *Veselé Povídky (Cheerful Stories)*, illustrated by Josef Lada (Prague: SNDK, 1953).

10. Jaroslav Hašek, *Mikeš, O Kocourovi Který Mluvil (Speaking Tom-Cat Mikesh)*, 1935, illustrated by the author (Prague: SNDK, 1956). *Kater Mikesch* (Aarau: Sauerländer, 1962).

11. Jaroslav Hašek, *Nezbedné Pohádky (Funny Fairy Tales)*, 1946, illustrated by the author (Prague: SNDK, 1958).

12. Josef Čapek (1887-1945), *Povídání o Pejskovi a Kočičce (Stories from a Puppy and a Cat)*, 1929, illustrated by the author (Prague: SNDK, 1965). *Schrupp und Schlipp* (Stuttgart: Union, 1965).

13. Karel Čapek (1890-1938), *Devatero Pohádek (Nine Fairy Tales)*, 1931, illustrated by Josef Čapek (Prague: SNDK, 1959).

14. František Langer (1888-1965), *Bratrstvo Bílého Klíče (The League of the White Key)*, 1934, illustrated by Ondřej Sekora (Prague: SNDK, 1964). *Der weisse Schlüssel* (Prague: Artia, 1958); *Der silberne Schlüssel,* shortened (Stuttgart: Herold, 1968).

Illustration by Jiří Trnka from *The Fireflies* by Max Bolliger, copyright © 1969 by Artemis Verlag, Zurich. Used by permission of Atheneum Publishers.

1936. Here is quite another, highly original style. His puppet plays and puppet films revealed a most individual art. His puppets, with their rather weak outlines and almost unfeatured faces, which obtain their liveliness from change of light, become his special type of figures for his children's book illustration.

The tradition of Božena Němcova's *Grandmother* is followed, but with some change, in Josef Věromír Pleva's *Malý Bobeš (Little Bobesh)*.[15] This novel (first published in three volumes) describes the fate of a country family and shows the downward career of poor farmers to positions of proletarians in towns—a bitter accusation of social facts, especially in the latter part of the book. The first part shows the early childhood of Bobesh and his world, seen through the eyes of a child. It can be regarded as the first valuable example of socialistic writing in children's literature.

Here again is Maria Majerová, who also wrote short stories with socialistic subjects. But her *Robinsonka (The Robinson-girl)*[16] establishes a new tradition: girls' books without sentimentality. The story of a lonely motherless girl, who must leave school to keep house for her father, and who tries to manage this work while finding a middle way between a child's dreaming and reality, has justifiably been reprinted frequently. Its influence on later authors of girls' books, especially on Helena Smahelová, is easily seen. *Robinsonka* was Marie Majerová's last publication before the prohibition of her entire work under the German government, in the same manner that the work of many other authors was forbidden. Karel Čapek, whose adult novel *Válka s Mloky (The War Against Salamanders)* was a prophetic vision of the consequences of Nazi government, died before the German occupation and before the prohibition of his entire work. His brother Josef Čapek came to death in a concentration camp.

THE SECOND REPUBLIC AFTER 1945

The scene changed after 1945. The second republic started with optimistic consciousness of renewed national freedom, of new political tasks, and new problems of education. The main subjects in literature for adults and children were events from the shorter past and possibilities for a better future. But almost all of these stories had only temporary value.

The political change in 1948, establishing a socialistic government, also brought a change in literature. The demand for totalitarian education through every means, including channels of literature, led to the literary scheme of socialistic realism. The new publishing law in 1949 established a strict censorship by government. For children's literature there remained only two publishing houses: *Státni Nákladetelstvi Dětské Knihy* (SNDK, later

---

15. Josef Věromír Pleva, *Malý Bobeš (Little Bobesh)*, 1931-1934 (Prague: SNDK).
16. Maria Majerová, *Robinsonka (The Robinson-girl)*, 1940 (Prague: SNDK, 1953).

named simply Albatros) in Prague for the Czech, and Mladé Letá at Bratislava for the Slovak production.

From this point on, there has been disagreement and discussion between demands for political education and socialistic realism on the one hand, and, on the other, a demand for children's literature to accord with literary standards and children's interests.

The Albatros series *Edice Střelka* (Compass Edition) includes stories about children in the socialistic youth group, Pioneers—about their camp life, heroic exploits, unmasking of spies, etc. But after 1956, with its anti-Stalinistic program, even in this series books appeared which sustain comparison with accepted, good writing. Moreover, it must be recognized that membership in the Pioneers *is* a part of children's life in Czechoslovakia and it cannot be omitted, but, hopefully, be given a realistic relationship to other aspects of contemporary life.

A few examples can include Jan Mareš's *Bracha a Já (My Brother and I)*,[17] the story of twin brothers and their adventures with an older friend, a journalist. Helena Smahelová's *Karlínská Číslo 5 (Karlín Street Number 5)*[18] describes the amusing experiences of children who try to renovate the apartment of a comrade whose mother is in the hospital. This writer proves herself a talented author for children, evidently influenced by Marie Majerová.

Rudo Moric and his *Pri Zaklatiej Rieka (At the Cursed River)*[19] can be taken as an example of political education. Its impressive report of a journey to Vietnam reveals literary talent, but also the strict political mind of its author. Mr. Moric is a Slovak author. Czech and Slovak, though similar, each show a special national consciousness. Most outstanding books of Czechoslovakia are published in both languages. Publishing in Slovak represents the problem of small nationalities, for it is spoken by only about four and a half million people. During recent years, however, Slovak children's books have gained the level of the best literature for children in other countries.

It is possible now to point out authors who are not limited to rules of government and who are appreciated also in nonsocialistic countries.

Striking attention has been given to illustration and graphic art in children's books, the best tradition developing from before World War I and being carried on today. In 1958 SNDK won the Grand Prix for illustrations at the Brussels Exposition.

Picture books are notably important. Old nursery rhymes are few, but since the nineteenth century poetry for children has been a rich contribution, continuing to today. This, however, is hard to translate.

A tradition for criticism of children's literature, since the beginning of the century, has been closely connected to similar efforts in Germany. A

---

17. Jan Mareš, *Bracha a Já (My Brother and I)*, (Prague: SNDK, 1961).
18. Helena Šmehelová, *Karlínská Číslo 5 (Karlín Street Number 5)*, (Prague: SNDK, 1961).
19. Rudo Moric, *Pri Zaklatiej Rieke (At the Cursed River)*, (Bratislava: Mladé letá, 1958).

revival in 1956 came with the issuance of *Zlatý Máj (Golden May)*,[20] a periodical with critical reviews of books for children, essays on special subjects, illustration, and portraits of authors.

The fantastic stories popular before World War II have appeared again, whether they describe the adventures of a little chalk man scrawling on a wall—Václav Čtvrtek's *Čárymáry na Zdi (Chalk Scrawling on the Wall)*[21]—or Ota Šafránek's *Slon v Domácnosti (An Elephant in the Household)*,[22] a grotesque situation of having a baby elephant as a family member, fascinating play completed by excellent illustration.

Ota Šafránek's *Bosi Rytíři (The Barefooted Knights)*[23] mingles boys' adventures with fantastic details; it tells the story of two boys following a kidnapper and can be taken as a parody of detective stories. *Z Deníku Kocoura Modroočka (The Diary of a Cat with Blue Eyes)*[24] by Jiří Kolář gives an entertaining view of the world through the eyes of a cat. His *Nápady Pana Aprila (The Odd Ideas of Mr. April)*,[25] in the same manner as Miloš Macourek's surrealistic story *Mravenečník v Početnici (The Ant in the Arithmetic Book)*,[26] is another tale of wit and nonsense in the tradition of Karel Poláček—nonsense with its own rules of logic and therefore again not without meaning.

Of special importance within the contemporary book production are everyday stories about children and teen-agers which are outside of that literature which tries to induce a lasting effect in political education. Here again are efforts to carry on the best tradition, to keep the doors open for children's individuality, to write and publish stories set in real surroundings, which show children as children and teen-agers with their individual problems, and not as part of an imposed social structure.

Bohumil Říha's *Honzíkova Cesta (Little Johnny's Way)*,[27] a story for younger children, with bright illustrations, may be regarded as an attempt to find a middle way between extreme views.

The children portrayed by Jaroslava Blažková could have had their adventures in almost any country. Whether, as in *Ohňostroj pre Deduška*

---

20. *Zlatý Máj (Golden May)*, ed. by Kruh Prátel Detské Knihy, 1956 ff., monthly.

21. Václav Čtvrtek, *Čárymáry na Zdi (Chalk Scrawling on the Wall)*, illustrated by Olga Cechová (Prague: SNDK, 1961). *Die Geschichte vom Kreidemännlein* (Vienna, Stuttgart: Braumüller, 1967).

22. Ota Šafránek, *Slon v Domácnosti (An Elephant in the Household)*, (Prague: SNDK, 1965).

23. Ota Šafránek, *Bosi Rytíři (The Barefooted Knights)*, 1947 (Prague: SNDK, 1958). *Die barfüssigen Ritter* (Nuremberg: Sebaldus, 1963).

24. Jiří Kolář, *Z Deníku Kocoura Modroočka (The Diary of a Cat with Blue Eyes)*, (Prague: SNDK, 1965). *Kater Schnurr mit den blauen Augen* (Stuttgart: Thienemann, 1969).

25. Jiří Kolář, *Nápady Pana Aprila (The Odd Ideas of Mr. April)*, illustrated by V. Fučík (Prague: SNDK, 1961). *Die Weisheiten des Herr April* (Prague: Artia, 1963).

26. Miloš Macourek, *Mravenečník v Početnici (The Ant in the Arithmetic Book)*, illustrated by Miroslav Stepánek (Prague: SNDK).

27. Bohumil Říha, *Honzíkova Cesta (Little Johnny's Way)*, illustrated by Helena Zmatlíková (Prague: SNDK, 1960).

(Fireworks for Grandfather),[28] they try to create a celebration honoring a beloved grandfather, culminating with fireworks of sprinkling lights saved from their last Christmas tree; or whether, as in *Ostrov Kapitána Hašašara (The Island of Captain Hashashar)*,[29] they find a forgotten garden and make it the romantic island of Captain Hashashar (who is in fact merely a picture from a Chinese teabox)—there are real children and parents and teachers who accept them as children.

Helena Šmahelová's *Dobrá Mysl (Good Mind)*,[30] the story of an idealistic girl's experiences with her father who renovates paintings in an old castle and with a young stork fallen out of its nest, is closely related to Marie Majerová's *Robinsonka*, except in its rural surroundings.

In Klára Jarunková's *Hrdinský Zápisník (Diary of Heroes)*[31] the "heroes" of the diary are again similar to František Langer's boys with the white key and even to Erich Kästner's boys and girls. Her *Brat' Mlčanlivého Vlka (The Brother of the Silent Wolf)*,[32] a story of outstanding literary quality, gained in translation a West German Book Award for 1970. Its story of a boy in the High Tatra, whose adored elder brother loses his girl friend in an avalanche accident, presents well the maturation of a boy into an adult. Her *Jediná (The Only Daughter)*[33] also shows literary quality, but the main problem here is not a search for an individual way but for a place within a group of young people. This book led to the group of girls' books mentioned before, those without sentimentality, and new attempts toward a special literature for young adult girls: books which show new possibilities and effects by breaking with tradition. *Ai Žije Republika (Long Life for the Republic)*,[34] the experiences of a young boy at the end of World War II, won a West German Book Award in 1969.

Such books are responses to the demands for an adequate literature for young adults—a literature which does not present strict rules for "right or wrong" in a simplistic way, nor pretend to have the truth as its own possession, but which shows the world as it is, and leaves decisions to the reader. The special value of the book last mentioned, it seems to me, is that it presents its story without prejudice and hate, and points out for everyone who is willing to accept it that freedom—every kind of freedom—is not at all a self-evident fact.

---

28. Jaroslava Blažková, *Ohňostroj pre Deduška (Fireworks for Grandfather)*, (Bratislava: Mladé letá, 1962). *Feuerwerk für den Grossvater* (Stuttgart: Herold, 1964).

29. Jaroslava Blažková, *Ostrov Kapitána Hašašara (The Island of Captain Hashashar)*, (Bratislava: Mladé letá, 1962). *Mein Freund ist Käpten Haschaschar* (Stuttgart: Herold, 1965).

30. Helena Šmahelová, *Dobrá Mysl (Good Mind)*, (Prague: SNDK, 1964). *Störche mögen keine Orangen* (Cologne: Schaffstein, 1966).

31. Klára Jarunková, *Hrdinský Zápisník (Diary of Heroes)*, (Bratislava: Mladé letá, 1965).

32. Klára Jarunková, *Brat' Mlčanlivého Vlka (The Brother of the Silent Wolf)*, (Bratislava: Mladé letá, 1967). *Der Bruder des schweigenden Wolfes* (Hamburg: Oetinger, 1969).

33. Klára Jarunková, *Jediná (The Only Daughter)*, (Bratislava: Slovenský spisovatel, 1963).

34. Jan Procházka, *Ai Žije Republika (Long Life for the Republic)*, (Prague: SNDK, 1966). *Es lebe die Republik* (Recklinghausen: Bitter, 1968).

A Harvest of Russian Children's Literature

Miriam Morton

An authority on Russian children's literature, Miriam Morton has translated many works into English. She compiled and wrote the critical commentary in A Harvest of Russian Children's Literature *(1967). She has also selected, translated, and edited* Voices from France; Ten Stories by French Nobel Prize Winners *(1969). The excerpts reprinted here are from the Introduction to the former book.*

The undeniable evidence that basic Soviet ideology is generally unaccepted in America gave rise to many quandaries in choosing material. Ideology, however, is pervasive in almost all Russian literature and, in fact, has been part of its strength and inspiration. The Russian people have never known a time without extreme social stress, without turbulent political events and disturbing currents and undercurrents of protest. As Russians have also traditionally ascribed to literature a guiding and teaching role, it is not surprising that their leading authors reflect in their work the social as well as the human condition of the people.

Russian children's literature, for the child of about nine and up, has shared not only the superior quality of its adult counterpart, but also its concern with the social problem—with the woes of the underprivileged and their strivings for a better life and a new social order. Great care has therefore been taken to strike an objective balance: to include among the selections some that reflect universal values and measure up to acknowledged literary criteria, as well as some that elucidate evolving Russian social and political ideals. . . .

A number of the unique features of Russian children's literature are reflected in the works chosen for this volume.

The pervasive humanist tradition and the basically optimistic realism of Russia's nineteenth-century literature, so richly endowed by Russia's master writers, are also present in the works of the same period written expressly for the young. This tradition has been carried over in large measure to books written and published for children in the Russia of the twentieth century, including, of course, Soviet Russia.

The Soviet child, especially the schoolchild and the adolescent, has been doubly fortunate. He has inherited his country's nineteenth-century masterpieces, and he has had enlightened and courageous Soviet children's authors—men and women of artistic conscience and unusual creative

Excerpts from pp. 3, 4–7, 8 of the "Introduction" to *A Harvest of Russian Children's Literature*, edited by Miriam Morton. Originally published by the University of California Press; reprinted by permission of The Regents of the University of California.

abilities—write expressly for him. Some Soviet writers have safeguarded children's literature from the limiting and corroding effects of the excesses of socialist didacticism of the Stalin era. Notable among these crusaders have been Kornei Chukovsky and Samuel Marshak, champions of the child's need and right to experience the whole range of literary genres from nonsense verse and fantasy, folktales and fairy tales, to social satire. The careers of these two poets for the very young have spanned five of the six decades of the twentieth century. Marshak began to write for children in the 1920's, and died in 1964. Chukovsky published his first animal tale in verse in 1916; he is now eighty-six.

These two poets and literary critics, together with Sergei Mikhalkov and Agnya Barto, founded an excellent literature in verse for the preschool child. (In the Soviet Union, this means the child from three to seven, for kindergarten begins at the age of three and ends at the age of seven. The age categories used in classifying children's books are somewhat different in Russia; in addition to the more extended preschool age, young people are considered as children through the age of seventeen. In America, the child over fourteen is now considered a young adult, at least in the libraries and by publishers.)

Little attention was given to the literary needs of the very young prior to the 1920's. A "Great Literature for Little Folk" was developed by the energetic quartet named above. Maxim Gorky, though noted for his realistically grim novels and plays, an important part of Russia's "literature of accusation" against the oppressive czarist autocracy, was paradoxically also the leading spirit in establishing the principle that the very young need happy as well as artistically sound verse, and jolly stories and folk literature for their mental and emotional growth. He exerted much effort and influence, over a period of years following the Revolution of 1917, in founding in the new Soviet Republic a uniquely felicitous literature for the very young. English nursery literature served as a model for Chukovsky, Marshak, Mikhalkov, and Barto. Chukovsky and Marshak have provided excellent translations of English nursery rhymes.

In Russia, to a greater degree than perhaps in any other country, literary masters have written deliberately for the older child reader. More masterpieces have been adopted by the young. There has been a coherent and purposeful effort since the 1860's to enrich children's reading with the works of the great Russian writers. Important stories and novels have often been published in children's editions at the same time or soon after they appeared for grown-ups. These gifts from the masters have been made fully available to the Soviet child, for Soviet publishers issue them constantly and in mammoth editions, with helpful and appropriate commentary by educators, critics, and even academicians. Soviet children thus have in their libraries and on their bookshelves at home works by writers who have immeasurably enriched world literature: the poets Zhukovsky, Ershov, Pushkin, Lermontov, Nekrassov, Tuitchev, Fet, Blok, Essenin, Mayakovsky, and others, and the prose writers Pushkin, Leskov, Aksakov, Turgenev, Leo Tolstoy, Korolenko, Chekhov, Gorky, Paustovsky, Aleksei Tolstoy, Sholokhov, Kataev, Fadeev, and more.

The genre of the short story has been highly respected and developed in the whole body of Russian literature. Many short stories by the past masters of the medium and by more recent writers of great talent are part of the literature for Russian children. This is a happy circumstance for the anthologist.

The earnestness and the serious goals of Russian writings for children are another unique feature of this literature; such goals are stressed more than similarly serious goals in children's literature of Western countries. Russian works, particularly for the older child, do not merely or primarily seek to entertain him. The bitter past of Russian life is not sweetened or hidden from him in what he reads. The following words of Maxim Gorky are therefore often quoted in connection with reading material for the young: "Lead them into the future by teaching them to know and value the past." Professor Marc Slonim, literary historian and critic, in the introduction to his book, *The Epic of Russian Literature* (New York: Oxford University Press, 1950), touches upon the same theme: "For centuries the search for truth, the ideological controversies, the political longings of the Russian people found expression in the literature. It would be futile to attempt to separate Russian writers from the spirit of their times and the various trends of national thought." Those in Russia who have concerned themselves with literature for the young have deemed attempted separation of writers from the spirit of their times not only futile, but also undesirable. Such a separation would diminish the enlightening and inspiring force of their literature and would render the young less prepared when they become adults to enjoy and value their literary heritage.

The serious intent of Russian children's literature has been expressed in writing of excellent quality, encompassing a wide spectrum of human aspirations and experience. The child can enjoy, understand, respond to, and identify with the people and events in his books. The recurring themes have been the moods and delights of nature, the love of country, issues of social justice, love of one's fellowman, love of work, peace, adventure and discovery, faith in the goodness of man, hope for the future, courage, the importance of knowledge, and the fascinations of science. These themes are treated with perspective and with careful regard for the child's nature. Humor, satire, and optimism lighten the solemnity. Sensationalism and excitement for their own sake are conscientiously avoided.

Because of the long tradition of viewing literature as enlightenment, and because of the noncommercialized methods of Soviet publishing, Russia's literature for children, despite its diversity, is exceptionally coherent in standards and purpose. It constitutes an integral part of the child's education. Moreover, it is common practice to refrain from abridging important works, distorting classics, softening folktales and fairy tales, or in other ways violating the integrity of artistic literary works.

Most of the fare for preschool children and young schoolchildren is free from solemnity; it is remarkably gay and full of fantasy, humor, and light satire. The wealth of folk literature is also made amply available to these children. It now includes the folktales of many peoples of non-European Russia. There are 167 distinct nations and ethnic groups in Russia, and 60 different languages. The esoteric and exotic folk literature of these peoples, who since the Revolution of 1917 have gradually acquired cultural identity, is translated and published for Russian-speaking children. The folktales in this anthology include examples from some of these folk literatures. Violence and grimness are not a basic characteristic of these folktales; shrewdness, tenacity, kindness, forgiveness, and courage, as well as a healthy and unequivocal condemnation of evil, put violence and grimness in their proper place.

Books read by the older child, however, often reveal life in the raw. The harshness of Russian life in the past is not glossed over. Reality is not expurgated, although it is leavened with optimism and faith in human nature. The Russian youth finds in his reading no sharp transition from a romanticized view of human existence to an extremely pessimistic one—a transition that the young reader in the West has to make and still manage not to feel a deep disillusionment in his world. The beat generation of the West is suffering, among other things, from a letdown induced by the nihilism and negation of contemporary literature.

The Russian thinking behind the unexpurgated realism offered to the older child reader is not new. It goes back to the middle of the nineteenth century when the intelligentsia, seeking to lead the people to a better life, affirmed that the young have to know and understand the evils of their society to be spurred on to a dedicated resolve to improve it. . . .

An omnipresent aspect of unexpurgated realism in contemporary Soviet children's literature is the political and social theme, the truth about war. When I asked Leo Kassil, a prominent Soviet children's author, how Soviet educators and cultural leaders justify exposing children to these realities, he repeated to me his reply to a similar question put to him by a group of American educators: "How is it that in the West you expose children from practically nursery school age to the complexities of religion and the tragic story of Christ and the Christian Martyrs?"

I asked another children's author, Boris Polevoy, how the theme of possible nuclear warfare is dealt with in Soviet literature for the young. His answer was that the children are assured that nuclear war is an impossibility because of the basic sanity of humanity. The subject is not stressed, but the theme of victory over the Germans in the last war, the defeat of such formidable past invaders as the Mongolians of the Golden Horde and as Napoleon, and the legendary courage of the Russian people in times of war are everywhere emphasized. Mr. Polevoy pointed out that 73 million Russians lived in the territory invaded by the Nazis in World War II Children's books celebrate, in fiction and biography, the many adult and child heroes of those years.

Other heroes in Russian works for children are the political leaders, foremost among them Lenin; but there is also the writer hero who faced persecution, exile, and at times the firing squad or the hangman's noose for the sake of writing the truth; or the revolutionary, the great scientist, the scholar, the dedicated physician, the poet, the explorer, the naturalist, the outstanding musician or painter. But the victim of social injustice is the greatest hero of all.

There is a trend now, after the discrediting of the personality cult, to bring a new type of hero into literature for the child—the boy, girl, or adult who tries against great odds, to cope with a personal or a family problem. A new villain is the adult who is inflexible, authoritarian, and self-seeking, particularly in his attitude toward youth.

Post-War Children's Literature in Japan

Shigeo Watanabe

Shigeo Watanabe is a professor in the School of Library and Information Science, Faculty of Letters, Keio University, Tokyo. He is deeply involved in children's book activities in Japan, both as an author of children's books and of articles on children's literature and as a lecturer. In 1956–1957 he worked in the children's rooms of the New York Public Library and was a guest participant in the 1956 storytelling festival in Miami, Florida, sponsored by the American Library Association. The following paper first appeared in the International Library Review *(1970) and has been revised and updated for this reprinting.*

Illustration by Toba Sojo reprinted by permission of G. P. Putnam's Sons from *The Animal Frolic* by Toba Sojo. Copyright © 1954 by the Temple of Kozanji.

"Post-War Children's Literature in Japan" by Shigeo Watanabe from *International Library Review*, no. 2, (1970): 113-124. Reprinted by permission of the author and Academic Press Inc. (London) Limited.

It is not easy to trace the development of children's literature in Japan during the past 20 years. It has been a crowded period, deeply influenced by the effects of World War II, and made confused by changes in the social structure and in the life of the country. These facts, while causing an increase in the number of children's books and in the number of readers, created many problems for writers, artists and publishers as well as for educators, teachers, librarians and parents.

However, some broad lines of development can be discerned, and it is interesting to notice how closely they parallel changes in social thought and behaviour. When World War II ended, the pendulum of society swung wildly from one extreme to the other. Militaristic and nationalistic ideas were cast aside together with a large number of the country's traditions, and a flood of new democratic ideas overwhelmed the Japanese people.

Between 1946 and 1947 more than a dozen children's magazines were published. Among those may be listed *Akatombo* (The Red Dragonfly), April 1946–October 1947, *Kodomo no Hiroba* (Children's Plaza), April 1946–March 1950, *Ginga* (The Galaxy), October 1946–August 1948, *Dowa Kyoshitsu* (The Classroom of Fairy Tales), January 1948–March 1949, *Kodomo no Mura* (Children's Village), February 1947–?, *Shonen Shojo* (Boys and Girls), January 1948–December 1950. These magazines were conceived and published with "good" and serious intentions to enlighten the children of the new Japan. They sold quite well for a short period of time as the public up to the end of the war had had no reading material that had not been censored. The publishers' intentions appealed to adults too as the themes of the stories, such as rebellion against militarism and totalitarianism, hatred of war and hope for peace, criticism against non-scientific and non-logical thought, etc. were sincerely felt by all. Yet there was a fatal flaw in the stories contributed to those magazines, i.e., most of the writers forgot what the children liked to read and concentrated on what they ought to read. It was not exactly the same didacticism which spread during the eighteenth and nineteenth centuries in Europe and in North America. But the idea that a children's book of whatever type should have a "purpose", had a very strong influence on the Japanese writers. Almost no children's story could stand exclusively on its own artistic or entertaining value: it had to have a "purpose", or moral.

No wonder Japanese children could no more stand those stories of "good" intention than did European children their "goody books" in the past two centuries. All such magazines had to disappear from the children's world during the following few years, though other causes of this phenomenon could be found. In fact, by the end of 1950, all the above mentioned children's magazines ceased to exist. Instead the pendulum swung wildly backward and cheap adventure stories by hack writers and comics of vulgar nature took their places.

But just before the quality of children's books was to be at the mercy not only of hack writers but also of unscrupulous publishers, a few outstanding works were offered to the public—the word "public" being intentionally used here because adult readers enjoyed and appreciated these works no less than children did—by non-professional and unconventional writers. *Biruma no Tategoto (A Harp of Burma)*, 1947 by Michio Takeyama and *Non-chan Kumo ni Noru (Non-chan Rides a Cloud)*, 1947 by Momoko Ishii are the best examples.

War and Peace can be the greatest and most difficult subject to be treated in any kind of literature. Michio Takeyama proved that the subject was worth being tried in the realm of children's literature. The theme was played on the delicate strings of the harp carried by a young Japanese soldier over the embattled fields of Burma. Beautiful yet very dramatic incidents in the story captivated the minds of the children while the underlying philosophy of the story touched their hearts as well as those of the adult readers. *A Harp of Burma* has been in a sense the most controversial issue among the works of post-war children's literature in Japan. While some critics praised the work as a masterpiece for its humanitarian approach against destructions and tragedies the war brought about, others criticized the work by saying that the author had viewed the war as a fatal happening in the human world and had looked for salvation only in a spiritual way. The author, Mr. Michio Takeyama, formerly a professor of German Literature in Tokyo University, is a well-known commentator on world affairs. His outspoken hatred, in his professional view, against Nazism, and now his firm stand against Communism may induce some kind of prejudice among critics and adult readers, but in my opinion the literary value of *A Harp of Burma* has not lessened irrespective of criticisms about the author's political views.

A Harp of Burma was translated into English a few years later.

Miss Momoko Ishii is probably the best-known author and translator of children's books in Japan at present. Through her facile and delicate pen and excellent knowledge of both the Japanese and English languages, such famous classics as Beatrix Potter's *The Tale of Peter Rabbit*, A. A. Milne's *Winnie the Pooh*, and Kenneth Grahame's *The Wind in the Willows* and Eleanor Farjeon's *The Little Bookroom*, have become very popular among Japanese readers. Her reputation as the author of such outstanding original stories for children as *Non-chan Kumo ni Noru (Non-chan Rides a Cloud)*, *Yama no Tomu-san (Tom of the Mountain Village)*, *Maigo no Tenshi (Stray Angels)*, *Sangatsu Hina no Tsuki (The Doll's Day for Yoshiko)*, place her among the best authors of books for children. Yet, until *Non-chan Kumo ni Noru (Non-chan Rides a Cloud)*, her first original story had been published, Miss Ishii was little known as an author. In fact she had been better known as an editor and a translator. "Non-chan," a small second-grade schoolgirl, climbed up a tree and while holding out her hands, she fell down and fainted. There the story starts. She meets an old man with a long white beard who lived up on a cloud. This story could be called a dream-fantasy according to the definition made by Miss Smith, the author of *The*

Unreluctant Years.[1] In her story, dream and reality are so naturally blended that few readers notice that her work follows the well-defined pattern of great works of fantasy. "Non-chan" has been translated into Chinese, English and German. Almost 20 years later the same author wrote *Sangatsu Hina no Tsuki (The Doll's Day for Yoshiko)*. In this realistic story the author portrays a traditional Japanese Doll's Festival for girls through which warm yet conflicting feelings between a mother and a young daughter are delicately expressed. This work has also been translated into English, and published by Oxford University Press in England and Follet in America.

The third author who can be put in the same category as the other two writers is Mrs. Sakae Tsuboi. She did not start as a children's author yet became our best realistic storyteller. She wrote *Kaki no Ki no Aru Ie (A House with a Kaki Tree)*, *Haha no Nai Ko to Ko no Nai Haha to (Mothers without Children and Children without Mothers)*, *Sakamichi (A Sloping Road)*, and her best-known work *Niju-shi no Hitomi (Twenty-four Eyes)*.

None of her work is intrinsically dramatic. Apart from their literary value, her novels, rather than being stories for young readers have come to interpret and reconstruct for them the fabric of the society of the author's times. *Twenty-four Eyes* faithfully mirrors some aspects of the period between 1928 to the end of World War II through social changes undergone by a young woman-teacher and her 12 schoolchildren at a small country school. In this work the war itself plays an important role yet it does not dominate the story. The peace-loving nature of the common people and the difficulty of living in a human society are her main themes throughout all of her works. *Twenty-four Eyes* since it appeared in 1952, reached a larger public than any other story written for children. The sustained popularity confirms that her books make a lasting impact on the reader; they are all close to reality and with the passage of time acquire value as social history.

These three works by three different authors won the Ministry of Education "Prizes for Fostering the Arts" in 1951 and 1952.

It should be noted that these authors were not originally professional writers of books for children. *A Harp of Burma, Non-chan Rides a Cloud*, and *Twenty-four Eyes* have become new classics of the post-war period although conventional and professional children's writers were reticent in saying what they thought of these works by outsiders and what they themselves were doing. They were reticent perhaps, because by children's stories they had meant, traditionally, only short fairy-tales so that they had nothing to say about long novels written for children. Or perhaps because they were given no chance to publish in any form their original works for almost all children's magazines had discontinued publication during that period.

It may be significant to note that there was a lone star up above the barren field of children's literature. It was Takeji Hiratsuka, the author of *Uma Nusubito (A Horse Thief)* written in 1955. Takeji Hiratsuka was a student of

---

1. Lillian H. Smith (1953). *The Unreluctant Years; a critical approach to children's literature*, p. 160. Chicago: A.L.A.

Miekichi Suzuki, an author and a promoter of the children's literature of the period, and began his career by contributing short stories to "Akai Tori" *(The Red Bird)* before the war. Since his first book *Kaze to Hanabira (The Wind and Flower Petals)* was published in 1942 he has written a dozen works among which *Tamamushi no Zushi no Monogatari (The Story of an Iridescent Shrine)*, 1948 and *Uma Nusubito (A Horse Thief)* 1955 have gained reputation as works of high literary standard. The author in *The Story of an Iridescent Shrine* portrayed a young furniture apprentice who, while looking for a new design for a miniature shrine, was inspired by the colour of a small insect and in the end found the spirit of nature that ever exceeds artificial efforts.

In *A Horse Thief* the hero stole the horse that belonged to the lord of the country not only for his personal affection for the horse but also because of his philosophy that the horse should belong to nature. The author states that children's literature is a labour of good intention but a number of authors use it as an invisible cloak to hide their inner selves " . . . their voices are pretentious and too sweet . . . "

With the exception of this "lone star" while most authors of children's books remained silent, student writers with adult editorship put out collections of their diaries. Some of these became best-sellers and were translated into foreign languages. *Yamabiko Gakko (The Echo of Mountain School)* and *Genbaku no Kora (Children of the Atomic Bomb)* were the best examples.

Both *Yamabiko Gakko (The Echo of Mountain School)* and *Genbaku no Kora (Children of the Atomic Bomb)* put extremely controversial questions to the public in many ways.

The collection of students' diaries based on their isolated life in a mountain village and compiled by their young teacher, Seikyo Muchaku, who is a leading educationalist, then an utterly unknown young man, was highly praised as the best result of democratic and free education and enthusiastically supported by a progressive group of young teachers and educators, while strong objections were raised by the conservatives and the conformists.

Children of the Atomic Bomb spread like wildfire over the dried-up realm of human justice and sympathy. It put the fire of hatred against the manufacturers of atomic bombs and the people who dropped them. At the same time it urged men's hearts to long for peace. A critic in the coming centuries may comment that this book led to the peace movement in Japan as *Uncle Tom's Cabin* may be said to have led to the anti-segregation movement in the U.S.A. Be that as it may, apart from its literary value *Children of the Atomic Bomb* is and will always be a witness to the misuse of scientific inventions.

These contradictory reactions to the same works were reflected by the unstable social conditions. While adults were seriously concerned with a lack of school facilities, the teacher union movement was torn by ideological struggle; strong opposition was made by the Zengakuren (Student

Union) against the MSA (American Military Aid) in a bloody fight against the police. The economic depression, and many other problems gave rise to new types of sensational, barbaric and sentimental comics and magazines put forth in large quantity by unscrupulous publishers. These publications almost dominated the world of children's literature in Japan in those years. Because of the depression, a number of small publishers went out of business. Only a few experienced publishers with large capital barely managed to survive by repeatedly putting out coarse editions of the same favourite classics, most of them translated from foreign languages. Even these few large publishers might have had to close their children's book departments, had not school-teachers started setting up a great number of school libraries.

In 1950 the Japanese Library Law was promulgated. This law authorized prefectural governments and local authorities to establish public libraries in their communities. At that time the Supreme Commander of Allied Powers Cultural Information Education libraries had strong influence and gave suggestions for setting up new public libraries and for improving pre-war library facilities.

It should be noted that the outstanding leadership and constructive advice offered during the following ten years by Dr. Robert L. Gitler and by other visiting professors from libraries and library schools in the U.S.A. to the Japan Library School, Keio University, and to all types of Japanese libraries played an impressive role in the development of our libraries.

In February of that year the Japan School Library Association was created, the first of its kind in Japan's history. With the strong support and advice of the United States Education Commission to Japan which matched the enthusiastic requests for new school library services made by Japanese school teachers and librarians, the School Library Law was passed by Japanese Diet in 1953. Under the School Library Law each school had the legal obligation to establish a school library. In fact, starting in 1954 the Ministry of Education subsidized more than 40,000 public schools to help them build their library facilities and book collections. The subsequent development of the Japanese school libraries and the changes which have taken place in the library world are such a large topic that a separate essay would be necessary to cover it. Here I can only relate a fact, namely, that the development of school libraries increased the need for great numbers of children's books and allowed the publishing houses to make large profits while possibly raising the standards of children's literature in Japan.

The number of children's books being published increased dramatically during those years and continued to increase steadily up to now.

At about the same time it was clear that school librarians were increasingly dissatisfied with the cheap and ephemeral editions of the favourite classics then on the market. The publishers thus found they could no longer sell such books in large quantities. To replace partially these cheap editions, new works by twentieth-century children's authors of high reputation in various countries began to be translated into Japanese. Hugh

Lofting, Hendrich Van Loon, Hans Baumann, Meindert DeJong, Dola DeJong, Eleanor Estes, Eleanor Farjeon, Erich Kästner, E. Nesbit, Astrid Lindgren, to name a few, were thus made accessible to Japanese readers.

In 1957, Paul Hazard's *Books, Children and Men* was translated from the original French edition into Japanese and met with great success. *The Unreluctant Years* by Lillian H. Smith was translated in 1964 and is becoming one of the best authorities for students of children's literature.

Another important trend relating to the development of the school libraries was the wide variety of children's books which had been published in these ten years. Retellings of folktales and myths, biographies (not only of famous people but also of individuals of merit who had distinct personalities), books of history and geography, books of discoveries and explorations, and picture books, have proved to be very popular. And yet, during this period of time Japanese librarians did not have enough influence on authors and publishers to make them produce good children's books. As for original works by Japanese authors, this period seems to have mainly served to advance the reputation of those few pre-war authors who were favoured by grown-ups for some sentimental reasons and whose books they bought for their children. Lack of intelligent criticism and reviewing was one of the principal reasons which prevented so many parents and teachers from realizing the need for better books.

In 1960 *Kodomo to Bungaku (Children and Literature for Them)* written jointly by six authors created a great controversy because of its critical approach. The six writers who had in one way or another something to do with children's reading—Miss Momoko Ishii, author and translator, Miss Tomiko Inui, author and editor, Mr. Shinichi Suzuki, editor, Mr. Teiji Seta, editor and translator, Mr. Tadashi Matsui, editor, and myself—had started a study group several years earlier. They intended to compare Japanese children's literature and foreign children's literature, especially books by European and North American authors. What the group wanted to prove was simple enough. No force in the world can compel children to read what they do not want to read. Only books of value should be put into the children's hands—books of honesty, integrity and vision—books which would help them mature emotionally and intellectually. Following this approach, six of the most representative Japanese authors were re-evaluated. As a result, a somewhat negative criticism was made of Mimei Ogawa, Joji Tsubota and Hirosuke Hamada; at the same time the works of Kenji Miyazawa, Shozo Chiba, and Nankichi Niimi were praised. By evaluating the works of these six authors an indication of what was lacking in the Japanese children's literature was attempted.

Ever since there have been books written for children in Japan, there have been many interpretations of what an ideal children's book should be. Emphasis was alternately placed on making children polite, well-informed on every subject, or aware of some social or economic problems with which the adults of the time were preoccupied. And I am afraid this is still true to a great extent. But fortunately this situation has gradually been improved by a host of younger writers. Tomiko Inui's first long story, *Nagai Nagai Pengin no Hanashi (A Long Long Story of Penguins)*, was published in 1954. In Japan, stories for younger children and schoolchildren of the intermediate grades have consisted mostly of fairy tales, usually rather short stories. *A Long Long Story of Penguins* was the first attempt to offer the young a long story written for them. *Kokage no Ie no Kobitotachi (Little Men in the House under a Tree)* was her second work meant for older children. *Hokkyoku no Mushika Mishika (Mushika and Mishika at the North Pole)*, her third work was on the "runner's-up" list of the Hans Christian Andersen Award for 1964. Tomiko Inui worked energetically with double capacities as author and editor of children's books. As an author she has added a few more works on the list that includes *Umineko no sora (The Sky for Seagulls)*, 1965, *Bokura wa Kangaroo (We are the Kangaroos)*, 1966, *Midori no Kawa no Ginshokishoki (Ginshokishoki in the Green River)*, 1968 and others. Though she started her author's career as a writer for young children most of her recent works are for older children. It is true that a long experience of editing more than 200 titles, mostly translations from outstanding foreign children's titles, at Iwanami Shoten, the most renowned publishing house in the nation, gave her a wide background of worldwide children's literature, but her talent for creating original stories, and her keen eye for observing the human world and her power of interpreting problems for children through her story-telling are far above those average authors of the same generation. In most of her stories animals and fairy-sort-of-creatures take the main parts and these are blended into a realistic world built into her stories without any misfit.

Chibikko Kamu no Boken (Adventures of Tiny Kam), 1961 is another work of fantasy of a type rarely written by a Japanese author. The author, Mrs. Toshiko Kanzawa, has that rare gift for creating dramatic episodes in a fantastic world. The giant who lives on the top of a volcanic mountain and tends the fire and the smoke of the volcano, the lake of magic water, a huge bear with supernatural powers, etc. may be conventional tools for tellers of fantastic stories in the English-speaking countries but among the Japanese young writers they indicate a rare quality, one to be praised and cultivated as it would spur the imagination of our children.

Another work of fantasy written by an author of the same generation is a trilogy by Satoru Sato—*Dare mo Shiranai Chiisana Kuni (The Tiny Country Nobody Knows)*, 1959 and its sequences *Mametsubuhodo no Chiisana inu (A Little Dog as Tiny as a Pea)*, 1962 and *Hoshikara ochita chiisana hito (A Tiny Man Who Dropped from a Star)* 1965. The author has brought into his stories a Japanese native dwarf rather like a fairy god of the Ainu legend. Like E. Nesbit's Psammead or sand fairy his *Koboshisama (The Ainu Fairy)* takes an active role along with a group of children and their adult friends in the present day set-up of his stories.

Tatsunoko Taro (Dragon Taro) written by Miyoko Matsutani and placed on the honour list of the Hans Christian Andersen Award for 1962 is another masterpiece written by a young, post-war author. The folktale on which

Dragon Taro is based was very little known until it was discovered by Mrs. Matsutani and her husband in the mountain region of Shinshu of central Japan. But their discovery would have meant just one more folktale among the few that have been recently offered to the public had not Mrs. Matsutani rewoven the tale into an adventure story of real fantasy. A few years later she wrote another work of the same nature, *Maegami Taro (Taro, the Young)*, 1965, which was well accepted by readers of the former. She has written a few original stories for younger children but her retellings of folktales in picture books from which the pictures were in most cases drawn by the Grand Prize Artist Yasuo Segawa, have been more widely read by children. She has certainly initiated a new movement of retellings and re-creatings of folktales for the present-day children in Japan.

If "cute" is a wrong word for praising a children's book, "very pretty and vivid portrayal of children behaving naturally and yet fancifully" is a good definition of Mrs. Reiko Nakagawa's *Iya Iya En (The Naughty Nursery)*, 1962, its sequels, *Kaeru no Eruta (Eruta, the Frog)*, 1964, and *Momoiro no Kirin (A Pink Giraffe)*, 1965.

In the field of realism a large number of stories has been written by authors whose themes were based upon world peace, on the contrast between rich and poor, and other social and economic aspects of our society and of the world in general. Their intentions are good and sincere. However, it is difficult to see how these works, based as they are on political and social situations which may last for a short time only, can keep on appealing to the children, once the events which simultaneously prompted their authors to write them have become a thing of the past. Though an appraisal of these works may take time some of the works by such contemporary authors as Nobuo Ishimori, Yoshitomo Imae, Taruhi Furuta, Yasuo Maekawa and Sukeyuki Imanishi have proved to be worthy to be assessed by their sustained popularity.

The post-war period has produced many such writers and books, for it is one of the surprises of publishing children's books in Japan that, despite all that has been said against certain aspects of it, a high proportion of the best children's books of the century has in fact been first published in Japan including a large number of translations of foreign children's books.

The bookshelf of the Japanese child has been greatly enriched by translations of literature from Europe and America. The main influx has been from countries where they have had a long history of children's literature such as England, the United States, Germany, France, Denmark, Russia and to a lesser extent from Italy, Spain, Scandinavian countries other than Denmark and such East European countries as Poland and Czechoslovakia.

Charles Perrault, the Grimm Brothers, Hans Christian Andersen, Carlo Collodi, Jules Verne, Selma Lagerlof, Lewis Carroll, Oscar Wilde, A. A. Milne, Louisa May Alcott, Mark Twain and a host of other authors of the classics have been known for a long time among the Japanese reading public and after World War II the works of these authors have been repeatedly included in encyclopedic compilations of children's books.

As time goes by, the Japanese children's appetite for new foreign dishes has never flagged. Just to name a few: Arthur Ransome, Eleanor Farjeon, Walter de la Mare, Richard Armstrong, Mary Norton, Pamela Travers, C. S. Lewis, Philippa A. Pearce, Rosemary Sutcliff, Lucy M. Boston, William Mayne (England); Hugh Lofting, Robert Lawson, Robert McCloskey, James Thurber, Will James, Ruth Sawyer, Armstrong Sperry, Lois Lenski, William Pène du Bois, Eleanor Estes, Ann Nolan Clark, Meindert DeJong, Scott O'Dell, Madeline L'Engle (America); Paul Berna, René Guillot (France); Erich Kästner, Hans Baumann, James Kruss (Germany); Astrid Lindgren, Tove Jansson (Scandinavian countries); and many others.

I do not know whether we should be proud of translating so many foreign works, but it is true that our children have never had so rich an opportunity for international orientation and understanding through their reading as they have now.

Yet these books in Japan came out, not as a part of a consciously planned publishing programme or from any preconceived idea of what constitutes a good children's book, but seemingly in a haphazard fashion put out by a number of indifferent and strongly competing publishing houses. Some of them set the fashion for a time. Multi-volume anthological publications are the best example. Others were lonely stars like Fukuinkan's picture books, and still others are best mentioned as works which stand on their own, rather than being representatives of a brief historical period.

This brief survey is far from complete nor is it a comprehensive essay; it is only a short report which, I hope, can take the place of individual replies to the many inquiries from abroad about recent trends in children's literature in Japan.[2]

---

2. Translations of books mentioned in this article:
Ishii, Momoko, *A Doll's Day for Yoshiko*, Follett. Oxford University Press (U.K.)
Ishii, Momoko, *Non-chan Rides a Cloud*, O.P.
Matsutani, Miyoko, *Taro, the Dragon-Boy*, Kodansha (Japan). Ward Lock (U.K.)
Muchaku, Seikyo, *Echoes of a Mountain School*, Kenkyusha (Japan)
Osada, Arata, *Children of the Atomic Bomb*, Putnam (U.S.A.). Peter Owen (U.K.)
Takeyama, Michio, *A Harp of Burma*, Tuttle (U.S.A.)
Tsuboi, Sakae, *Twenty-Four Eyes*, Kenkyusha (Japan)

The Finnish Juvenile Book in the 1960's: A Summary

Maija Lehtonen

Assistant Professor of Comparative Literature at the University of Helsinki, Maija Lehtonen lectures mainly on French and German literature and in 1970 gave the first course in children's literature at the University. Professor Lehtonen is also a reviewer, lecturer, and researcher in the field of children's literature. She is the author of "Finnish Children's Literature in the 19th Century," Anni Swan (a monograph on this outstanding Finnish writer, 1958), and "Art-Knowledge-Wishful Dreaming?" (an article on the problems of children's literature, in the Finnish review Aika, February 1971). The following paper is a summary of an address presented at the Scandinavian congress on children's literature, 1970.

During the sixties the so-called "teen-age novel", which deals with the development of the young person and his entry into the world of grown-ups, came to flourish in Finland. The image of society in these books has become more versatile. Descriptions of the middle-class milieu are no longer so dominant as before; a great many books deal with children of working-class parents. Manual work is described expertly.

A critical attitude toward the parents has become quite fashionable in juvenile books. The father may be an unsociable hermit or tyrant, a drunkard who maltreats his children. The mother usually is of the traditional quiet, self-sacrificing type, especially in working-class families; the busy and ambitious middle-class woman is observed ironically. If Father has died, Mother has to go to work; otherwise she should stay at home with the family. In this respect the writers tend to be rather conservative. The so-called sex-role-thinking is very obvious in the descriptions of the hobbies and the plans for the future of boys and girls; a girl's world is much more limited than a boy's.

Psychological description is richer than before, and neurotic features are accentuated in both boys and girls. Love has become an important factor even in boys' books. The changes in the sexual behaviour of the young are reflected in juvenile literature, but erotic descriptions are rather discreet. The young person is seeking safety and contact; on the other hand, he is also trying to find an answer to the question "who am I?" Other central themes are death and religious questions.

Social problems, like alcoholism and unemployment, are dealt with in a few of the books; at the end of the sixties, discussions appear in some books about topical political and social problems: Vietnam, pacifism, welfare

"The Finnish Juvenile Book in the 1960's: A Summary" by Maija Lehtonen from *Bookbird*, v. 9, no. 1, (1971): 11–12. Reprinted by permission of Bookbird.

society and hunger. Unfortunately these discussions sometimes seem like rather loose appendages. The juvenile book has always more or less consciously taught attitudes and values; during the last few years it seems to have become even more didactic.

Urbanisation is pictured in books. Previously juvenile books were most often placed in a rural setting; now they almost always are set in a city or another densely populated area. Motorization is obvious; cars have an important part in the development of the plot. A car accident is a frequently occurring theme. Other scenes and situations found in many books are dances (especially country barn dances where young people get together), listening to records and, in boys' books, fighting and the first experience being drunk.

The juvenile book has, of course, been influenced by adult literature as far as subject matter, language and narrative technique are concerned. According to a Swedish critic, juvenile literature does not even form a special category of literature, the only difference being that a book which is meant for young readers must be simpler in structure and style than a book for adults. The juvenile book has adopted some characteristics of modern fiction; the "know-all" storyteller has vanished, the events are seen from the point of view of the protagonist, first person narratives are popular. The writers are experimenting with the stream-of-consciousness technique and even more complicated structures. The language has come closer to colloquial speech, a trend we can see in adult literature as well; however, in the juvenile book slang often has too prominent a place.

It is a pleasure to see that writers have discarded many old, conventional patterns in the juvenile book; although, on the other hand, a new kind of formalism is threatening it already. We have reason to hope that the juvenile book of the 'seventies will seek new paths.

Chapter 11

Criticism and Reviewing

Creators of books as well as book selectors recognize the importance of the criticism and reviewing of children's books. Ivan Southall, distinguished Australian writer, addressing critics and librarians in an award-acceptance speech, goes so far as to state that "The conscientious critic may contribute as much to the literature of a country as the conscientious writer. . . . " His point of view has been echoed in many countries, in respect to the importance of a sound body of criticism for the development of literature.

Book selectors who must lean on reviews have a practical interest in criticism. Specialists who are wholly involved in appraising children's literature feel it is imperative to view children's books as a part of the mainstream of literature, using the same standards as are applied in the criticism of books for adults. They worry about a lack of sufficiently critical comment and the failure of literary and general magazines and newspapers to provide enough space for criticism of children's books. They ask why the exceptional children's book is not reviewed among adult books rather than held for a semi-annual or annual summary.

What makes a good review and marks the true critic? Many well-known critics have emphasized such essentials as a wide knowledge of literature and life and the ability to make aesthetic judgments and to stimulate interest in the reviewed book. Siri Andrews, critic and former children's book editor, says:

There are many book reviewers, and many are competent. But true book *critics* are rare. It is the gift of the critic to make each book distinct from all others, partly through recognition of the exceptional, partly by means of clear characterizations which apply to that book and to no other. Both come from the critic's maturity, zest, openmindedness, life experience, command of English, as well of course as from a background of wide reading in both adult and children's books.

One of the rather few critics of children's books was Miss Anne Carroll Moore. Out of her years of living and of wide and thoughtful reading Miss Moore had developed an almost intuitive feeling for the truly new and creative writers and artists. And then put that feeling into words so alive and so sharp that one could hardly wait to see the book, which is one of the qualities of a good critic. One did not always agree with Miss Moore's verdict but the book was read and it generated thought and an opinion; the first objective of a critic was achieved. . . . [1]

In *The Three Owls, Book Three,* Anne Carroll Moore herself speaks of her approach to reviewing:

Next to writing for children nothing is more difficult than writing about children's books. One must view the books as books in their changing relation to the general stream. One must also keep in living touch with childhood by natural ways of communication. There is no short cut to first-hand knowledge of books of any kind and children's books are not an exception. One learns to know them only by reading them in the light of all the other books one has read. To the extent that one shares the reading interests of children one revises and enlarges his own impressions of the relative value of books at different stages of experience. . . .

Next to the pure joy of creating a thing one's self is the discovery of something created by another. The instant recognition and detachment of a piece of original work from a mass of ready-made writing and the presentation of one's findings and conviction constitute the reviewer's main chance. His function is to declare the book's quality and give it a place in association with other books. To the degree that the review stimulates the desire of the reader to read the book to confirm or to differ with the critic it will be contributory to thought, discussion, criticism, fresh creative work. And this, as I see it, is the true objective for the reviewer of children's books no less than for the reviewer in the general field. [2]

---

1. Siri Andrews, "Criticism and Reviewing of Children's Books," in *The Hewins Lectures, 1947–1962* (Boston: Horn Book, Inc., 1963), pp. x, xi.

2. Anne Carroll Moore, *The Three Owls, Book Three* (New York: Coward-McCann, Inc., 1931. London: Hamish Hamilton, 1973). See also Frances Clarke Sayers, *Anne Carroll Moore* (New York: Atheneum Publishers, 1972).

Critic, writer, and librarian Frances Clarke Sayers describes the qualities of reviewer and librarian Anne Thaxter Eaton:

> It was the wealth of background and experience, as well as knowledge of books and of children's reactions to them, which A. T. E. brought to the reviewing of books. . . . For fourteen years Anne Eaton's book reviews sharpened the appreciation of children and adults alike. Looking back upon that spacious and golden era of reviewing, one marvels at the scope of A. T. E.'s mind. Here were no snippets of reviews in seven lines. New books were discussed in relation to the old, and a family's reading course might well be charted and steered by the light of the wisdom to be found in these fortnightly pages. How enduring and timeless they were is proved by the fact that the articles that appeared in the *Times* are the basis for her book *Reading with Children,* which, with its supplementary volume *Treasure for the Taking,* is recognized as a lasting source of sound advice, enjoyment, and inspiration. One feels the response of actual children on every page.[3]

Three later critics have demanded an emphasis on literary values in reviewing. Lillian Smith, whose *Unreluctant Years* is the outstanding American work on the criticism of children's books, stresses that "The qualities which are basic in good writing are literary values: that is, they do not concern the subject matter so much as how it is presented." (See "An Approach to Criticism of Children's Literature" in this chapter.) Paul Heins and John Rowe Townsend, from two sides of the Atlantic, also see literary values as most important in criticism. Heins, in "Out on a Limb with the Critics," says "Actual—one should even dare to say serious— criticism will occur only when judgments are being made in a context of literary knowledge and of literary standards." In his Arbuthnot Honor Lecture (1971) Mr. Townsend remarked:

> When we look for individual assessments of actual books (as distinct from general articles on children's literature and reading) we find that most of what is written comes under the headings of (a) overwhelmingly, reviews, (b) aids to book selection, and (c) general surveys. There is little writing that I think would be dignified with the name of criticism, a point to which I will return later. While examining reviews, selection aids, and surveys, in both the United States and Britain and in relation to imaginative literature, I asked myself not whether they were sound and perceptive or whether I agreed with them, but what they were actually doing and what their standards appeared to be. . . .
> What the reviewers and selectors were largely concerned with, more often than not, it seemed to me, was telling you what the story was about: a necessary activity, but not an evaluative one. I

---

3. *Summoned by Books* (New York: The Viking Press, Inc., 1965), pp. 81–82.

came to the conclusion that where they offered judgments the writers always concerned themselves with one or more of four attributes, which I do not place in order of importance or frequency. These were (1) suitability, (2) popularity, or potential popularity, (3) relevance, and (4) merit. [4]

On the other hand, Margaret Meek, review editor and contributor of critical reviews to *The School Librarian,* points out the need for an awareness of children.

Many successful children's authors have been indifferent to children and their needs, claiming that they wrote for themselves alone. Critics cannot, dare not be so. Whereas children will select from what is available to them, reading the bad if the good is not at hand, those who buy children's books in great numbers, teachers and librarians for example, have to like children and children's books enough to read, *with adult discrimination,* great numbers of them. They know too that the best children's books are reserved for the comparative few who have the ability and the desire to read. Thus there is a strong didactic element in choosing for children as it includes an assessment of the kind of satisfaction the books offer children at a given stage in their development.[5]

Librarians, parents, and teachers have many occasions for exerting critical judgments—whether in the selection of children's books for purchase or for citations of distinction, or in writing reviews. These judgments should be based upon both critical values and an awareness of the child's needs.

Book selectors often must judge not only the literary content but the illustrations. The layman is generally less familiar with criteria for book illustrations. One new source of criticism in this area is the Children's Book Council's "Showcase" exhibition, initiated in 1972. The printed catalog for the exhibition contains general statements of criteria and comments on the selection of books of the previous year deemed outstanding for their illustration. The jury consists of two artists and two book designers; in 1972 the artist jurors were Marcia Brown and Maurice Sendak.[6]

---

4. "Standards of Criticism for Children's Literature," *Top of the News,* 27 (June 1971): 373–387.

5. "Choosers for Children," *Books,* Journal of the National Book League (May-June 1965): 86–90.

6. For more information on the criticism and reviewing of children's literature, see Richard L. Darling, *The Rise of Children's Book Reviewing in America, 1865–1881* (New York: R. R. Bowker, 1968). Anne Carroll Moore, "Creation and Criticism of Children's Books," *American Library Association Proceedings, 1934* (Chicago: American Library Association, 1934). Anne Carroll Moore, "The Reviewing of Children's Books," *The Bookman,* 61 (May 1925): 325–331. Anne Carroll Moore, *My Roads to Childhood: Views and Reviews of Children's Books* (Boston: Horn Book, Inc., 1961). Elizabeth Nesbitt, "The Critic and Children's Literature," *A Critical Approach to Children's Literature,* edited by Sara Innis Fenwick (Chicago: University of Chicago Press, 1967). Zena Sutherland, "Current Reviewing of Children's Books," also in *A Critical Approach to Children's Literature.*

An Approach to Criticism of Children's Literature

Lillian H. Smith

Lillian H. Smith was librarian of the Boys and Girls House of the Toronto Public Library from 1912 until her retirement in 1952. At the 1964 dedication of the new quarters of this children's library she was paid tribute for establishing an unpatronizing, unsentimental tone and for keeping the library free of the "mawkish and spinsterish approach" often found in other children's libraries and in children's literature. The selection reprinted below is a condensed version of Chapter 3 of her study of children's books and children's reading, The Unreluctant Years *(1953). Miss Smith also compiled the early editions of the annotated catalog,* Books for Boys and Girls *(1st ed., 1927).*

Many factors help to produce numbers of children's books that are not literature. The publishing of children's books has become a profitable field as we see when we find it stands second only to fiction in the number of books of all classes of literature published in any year. When we consider the number of children's books arriving from the press the matter becomes fundamental. There is a real possibility that the fine book may pass unnoticed, simply because serious attention to children's books is all but absent in contemporary criticism. The fine children's book in which literature is attained is as valid and as worthy of serious criticism as any other good book.

The development and use of a personal yardstick gained from and based on the classics of children's literature, if applied to any newly published book, will help us to recognize those books which share, in varying degrees, the ingredients of the books which have shown enduring qualities. The need for such a yardstick is obvious, in order that we shall be able to recognize those qualities which are basic in good writing. Children have wide individual differences in taste and preference; but the recognition of an underlying soundness or unsoundness in writing, theme, and content will serve to keep in the field of children's books those that will bring a deeper and more lasting pleasure to children.

The qualities which are basic in good writing are literary values: that is, they do not concern the subject matter so much as how it is presented. The subject matter of a book may be eminently sensible, and the presentation of it preeminently dull. In other cases, the subject matter may be nonsense, yet the presentation of it suggests the most profound truths. The success of *Robinson Crusoe,* for instance, revealed that the subject matter of shipwreck

"An Approach to Criticism of Children's Literature" by Lillian H. Smith from *School Activities and the Library* (1956): 1–3. Reprinted by permission of American Library Association.

on a desert island was one of great interest to the reading public, especially to children. A host of imitators seized on the idea and stories of castaways appeared in great numbers. Most of these have fallen by the wayside and passed into oblivion, while *Robinson Crusoe,* after over two centuries, continues to be "the best desert island story ever written." Defoe created in *Robinson Crusoe* a fundamental and universal conception which his imitators never achieved.

A clear understanding of the fundamental principles of good writing should underlie all informed book criticism and selection, whatever kind of book is being judged. There is not one set of values for one class of book and another set for another group; there are certain basic principles which apply to all. They are best discovered by the critic or reviewer who asks such questions of a book as: What did the author intend to do? What means did he employ? Did he succeed? If his success was partial, where did he fail? That is to say, the reviewer's approach to the book he is reviewing will be an analytical one.

The analysis of a book helps us to arrive at certain conclusions. But the validity of these conclusions depends on the qualities the reviewer brings to the book as well as on those of the book itself. To learn to evaluate and analyze is to learn to read with mind and heart, with interest and sympathy. To read this way brings excitement to the discovery of the idea of the writer behind the writing and of his use of language to express his idea. On the other hand, while one book may arouse enthusiasm, to another our response may be disappointment. In either case it will be wise to analyze the causes of each reaction.

The qualities a reviewer brings to a book are important. A sincere critic makes an effort to separate his personal opinions from his literary judgments and to have a reason for the faith that is in him. It is the *why* of criticism that is the test of our judgment of a book: why do we like it, or why do we not? When we know this, then only can we claim to have penetrated beneath the surface of a book. Otherwise our opinion is no more considered than that of any casual or superficial reader. "To like and dislike rightly," Bosanquet wrote, "is the goal of all culture worth the name." It is also the goal of the sincere critic of any form of literature.

A fine book has something original to say and says it with style. Originality and style are words that are used loosely by many reviewers of books; but, quite simply, an original idea is one that has its origin in the truth as one person sees it, which is never quite the same as anyone else's truth, and so is "original"; a word that is not to be confused with mere novelty. An original writer will know what he is trying to say because his idea comes from within; it is a fusion of experience, observation, and the creative mind.

Style, on the other hand, describes the different ways writers have of expressing what they want to say. Each one of us forms his sentences differently and the personality of the writer is woven into the manner of his expression. When a writer forms his sentences so that the order and choice of the words is distinguished, he attains literary style. His style, or use of language, is thus both personal and revealing of the quality of the writer.

Choosing a subject for a book is perhaps the least difficult of a writer's problems. He can say, "I will write a book about a circus" or "about a trip to the moon" or "about kindness to animals." The variety of subjects that present themselves seems inexhaustible, and almost any subject may be presented from a variety of points of view. If the writer has nothing of his own to say about the subject, if he has arrived at no personal viewpoint, the book will lack the individuality that only a writer's personal expression can lend it. The result will be a pointless account that lacks impact and challenge, and we say it has no center.

For the subject matter chosen by the writer is there for the purpose of developing his idea, his theme; and takes shape or form as he uses it to construct his book, whether it be fiction or any other form of writing. Variety is one of the characteristics of children's literature. Whatever form a book may have, whether a fairy tale, a book about animals, or the life of a hero, or whatever it may be, it must have some of the qualities inherent in good writing of any kind if it is to deserve serious consideration.

There is an attitude that has some prevalence among adults that informational books are more *valuable* to a child than other kinds because they provide him with the materials of knowledge which will help him to get on in life, forgetting that a child's own curiosity and desire to know and understand make him turn readily and of his own accord to all the sources of information about the things that interest him.

But books of imagination also furnish the mind, if not in so purely utilitarian a fashion. They give it scope and awareness, beauty and growth. Growth comes only through contact with what is larger and greater than oneself—something to "stretch" the mind and give direction to the imagination. Because the books in which the imaginative content is greatest are more closely akin to pure literature and are richer in the qualities that we find in great writing, let us consider from the standpoint of construction, idea, and expression, those books in which the subject matter is treated imaginatively. Of these, the greatest number are fiction. Fiction is also the most difficult of all forms of writing in which to distinguish between what is good and what is not good; between what is significant and what is trivial.

We have said that the writer's idea, the structure he builds, and his power to express his idea in language will to a great extent determine the literary quality of his book. Let us examine these determining qualities in this order, as they apply to fiction for children. In an analysis of fiction, the idea behind the story is our first concern. No story can carry itself unless there is an idea at the back of it, even though it is an obvious or hackneyed one such as "be kind to animals, they are our friends."

Ever since there have been books written for children there have been fashions in concepts of what children's books should be. Looking back at the history of forgotten children's books we can recall the emphasis that was placed on making children polite, or pious, or well-informed on every subject, or even on some social or economic aspect of the period with which adults of the time were preoccupied. This was a well-intentioned and sincere effort on the part of those writers whose names are now as forgotten as their books. But their ideas were based on uncritical standards of the nature of literature, and on a complete misconception of the nature of children.

When a new children's book is acclaimed by adults, not because of its creative conception, its imaginative treatment, its values in the art of writing for children, but merely because the subject matter confirms an adult interest in some ephemeral phase of adult problems or experience, it is time to ask oneself whether a new book is being praised for right reasons, or because of mistaken ideas of what constitutes a suitable theme for a good children's book.

The immediate interest of children is in the action of the story the author tells. If it is not a good plot, no matter with what skill or art it is presented, it will not hold their interest for long. At the same time, children recognize a difference in the stories they read, and are aware of other values, when they are present, than those of pure entertainment.

There are stories for children which are purely objective, which rely for their interest on the quick-moving action of the tale. These stories create an atmosphere of suspense. Their interest is centered on the outcome of the imagined events, and, once this is known, the interest drops. The excitement, for the reader, is in proportion to the skill with which the plot is handled, but if suspense is all the book has to offer, there is little pleasure in rereading it since the suspense disappears in a second reading.

There are other objective stories in which, while the action is their immediate attraction, the characters of the story take on life and individuality until they live in the reader's imagination long after the events of the story fade from the mind. A child, for instance, may read a number of stories about pirates and find them more or less equally entertaining. They will leave practically the same impression. But when he reads Stevenson's *Treasure Island* he carries away a distinct idea of having met a terrifying, although somewhat likeable pirate, a living character who, by the alchemy of Stevenson's imagination, will always be to him Long John Silver, the pirate of pirates.

In these stories the writer uses an objective approach to his subject. Everything is there for the sake of the story—the imagined events, the characters who are affected by the events or who bring them about, the setting, or the time and place, in which the events happen. Their place in literature is determined, not by the suspense of the story, but by other factors; the writer's ability to create memorable and living characters, not just puppets or types who are necessary to the action; the writer's sense of place and time which makes the "climate" of the story a pervasive influence within which the reader feels the illusion of reality, not mere scene painting but giving the tale added depth and subtlety; and finally, there is the writer's power of language.

But there is another way of writing for children than the purely objective. There is the story in which we hear overtones and which has values other than those of the events of the story. We feel that the writer is remembering his own childhood and is bringing his mature understanding and experience of life to illuminate an imaginary experience of childhood. His approach is subjective rather than objective. He has something he wants to say to children and charms them into listening through his ability to tell a story.

Paul Hazard asks that children's books contain a profound morality; that they set in action certain truths worthy of lasting forever, that maintain in their own behalf faith in truth and justice. To write for children in this way demands a great deal from the writer; a sense of the importance of universal moral and spiritual values, creative and imaginative powers, and strength of expression, of language.

The ability to distinguish a good book from a poor one, to know when the spirit of literature is present and when it is not, requires the sensitive feeling and reasoning of the reader which tells him, "This is right" and "this is real," or that it is not. There is no formula we can apply which will infallibly tell us whether what we are reading is good or bad. Familiarity with and understanding of the books which have been proved to have permanent value will give a bedrock of reasoning and feeling which one can work from, and go back to, in the evaluating of contemporary writing for children.

Out on a Limb with the Critics

Paul Heins

A former secondary-school English teacher and editorial adviser for his school's magazine, Paul Heins turned to editing the Horn Book Magazine *in 1968. He is also a reviewer for its Booklist. The following essays on criticism were first presented as conference talks.*[1]

To be a critic—a literary critic—is almost, by definition, to be out on a limb. In addition to being in a precarious position, one never knows whether one will be top-heavy and crack the limb because of his weight or whether somebody will come along with a saw. Either way, the position is fraught with danger. Yet, since critics rush in where angels fear to tread, there must be some justification or explanation for their existence.

I do not think we have to be concerned about the criticism of what might be called adult literature. Aristotle started the business long ago, and it is enough to mention Coleridge and Goethe, Dr. Johnson and Matthew Arnold, I. A. Richards and Allen Tate, to show that whenever literature is produced, critics are sure to follow. What does concern us, however, is the criticism of children's literature—a formidable task, and much more difficult than the criticism of adult literature.

Children's literature—for good or for bad—is not the concern of children alone. Parents, teachers, and librarians as well as authors, illustrators, and publishers are potential judges of books for children. Questions of suitability and vocabulary jostle with personal likes and dislikes, and there is always the question of whether a particular book written for children will appeal to children. We have also been made painfully aware of the fact that we are dealing with a generation conditioned by television; and we are being told that children's literature should be realistic and should absorb, in some form or other, the social and psychological problems of the day.

Even a philosopher can say something—at times—that has a bearing on children's literature. In 1957, Suzanne K. Langer, in *Problems of Art: Ten Philosophical Lectures,* made a number of statements worth considering:

> Every generation has its styles of feeling. One age shudders and blushes and faints, another swaggers, still another is godlike in a

---

"Out on a Limb with the Critics" by Paul Heins from *Horn Book Magazine,* 46 (June 1970): 264–273. Reprinted by permission of Horn Book, Inc.

1. Expanded from a talk entitled "Scratching the Surface, or Some Random Thoughts on the Reviewing and Criticism of Children's Books," first given on April 24, 1969, at a meeting of the Children's Book Guild, Washington, D.C. Delivered in its present form on June 18, 1969, at the Fifth Intermountain Conference on Children's Literature, the University of Utah, Salt Lake City, Utah.

universal indifference. These styles in actual emotion are not insincere. They are largely unconscious—determined by many social causes, but *shaped* by artists, usually popular artists of the screen, the jukebox, the shop window, and the picture magazine. (That, rather than incitement to crime, is my objection to the comics.)

Furthermore, she comes to a rather stringent conclusion about what she calls "art education"; and if we think about children's literature at all, it does not seem too farfetched to consider it in the category of the arts.

According to Mrs. Langer, "Art education is the education of the feeling, and a society that neglects it gives itself up to a formless emotion. Bad art is corruption of feeling." How many of us are willing to say that the moving-picture versions of *Mary Poppins* and *Dr. Dolittle* were bad art? Some of us will, because we believe that each picture version failed to capture the spirit of the book on which it was based. How many of us would go so far as to say these cinematic productions were not only bad art, but—because they were bad art—were corrupt in feeling? I, for one, am willing to say so.

Incidentally, critics of children's literature have frequently spoken up against shoddy methods and shoddy productions. Perhaps three of the most famous *Horn Book* articles represented this kind of frontal attack on mediocrity: "Walt Disney Accused" (Frances Clarke Sayers, *Horn Book,* December 1965), "Not Recommended" (Ruth Hill Viguers, *Horn Book,* February 1963), and "An Imaginary Correspondence" (Rumer Godden, *Horn Book,* August 1963), which delightfully accomplished its aim indirectly—by satire, humor, and irony. The chief value of this kind of criticism—of debased classics, of vocabularized texts—consists of clearing the decks for a more positive kind of criticism.

It has been said that people who insist that they have no philosophy or no religion will ultimately, in the course of conversation or discussion, reveal their explanation of the universe or of the beliefs which guide their lives. We are all critics whether we know it or not; and every time we pass judgment on a book or express enthusiasm for it, we are engaging in a critical act.

In her recent amusing book *The Girl on the Floor Will Help You,* Lavinia Russ speaks of "that crashing bore of a question which inevitably totters into any discussion of children's books, 'Are they written for children or for adults?' " Now, Mrs. Russ is naturally entitled to her opinion, not to say to her emotions; but she immediately follows up her condemnation by adding two statements: "She [E. Nesbit] didn't write for adults; she didn't write for children; she wrote for herself. Not her adult self, but to please and delight the child in herself—the child she remembered with fondness." In spite of her boredom, in spite of her initial outburst, Mrs. Russ was drawn into an act of criticism; and although she did not develop a point of view at length—as did Eleanor Cameron in her article "Why *Not* for

Children?'' (*Horn Book,* February 1966)—Mrs. Russ was actually delivering herself of an opinion on a topic which—as she herself states—unavoidably crops up in many discussions concerning children's literature. Mrs. Russ is a critic in spite of herself.

Children's books and authors, naturally, are not exempt from the random impressions and evaluations of readers. Perhaps the time has come for the criticism of children's literature to be more conscious than ever before of its existence—and better still of its function. It should learn to speak with precision and to qualify its enthusiasms. There is certainly available a large body of worthwhile children's books that invites critical consideration. As a matter of fact, because of the proliferation of good books for children during the last fifty years, the era has been termed a "golden age."

Incidentally, the term "golden age" is not without its difficulties. It can be a confusing term, for it seems that there are two golden ages. Both of them are mentioned in John Rowe Townsend's brief but excellent literary history *Written for Children: An outline of English children's literature.* In it we find an interesting summary of the last years of the first golden age:

> In children's literature at least, the opening years of the century were the last of a golden age. . . . the shortest of short lists . . . must include nearly all of E. Nesbit's work and much of Kipling; the play of *Peter Pan; The Wind in the Willows; The Secret Garden;* and—Beatrix Potter's splendid little books for small children.
> The Victorian-Edwardian era ended gloriously.

Elsewhere in Townsend's book, the two golden ages are brought into focus:

> The half century before 1914 was the first golden age of children's literature. The second golden age is now.

In *A Critical History of Children's Literature,* Part Four is entitled The Golden Age 1920–1950.[2] In this book, the term is applied to children's literature in both the United States and England, and Ruth Hill Viguers naturally discusses both American and English books. In "The Book and the Person" (*Horn Book,* December 1968), Mrs. Viguers names more than two dozen men and women who during the twentieth century have written outstanding books that "give pleasure to children"; and in her list of ". . . Twentieth-century Children's Books Every Adult Should Know" she supplies titles by thirty authors. Although voices are occasionally raised deploring what the uninitiated call the inadequacy of children's literature, students of children's literature and people working with books and children know that there is almost an embarrassment of riches.

---

2. In the Revised Edition of *A Critical History of Children's Literature* (1969) this section is entitled Golden Years and Time of Tumult 1920–1967.

Along with the growth in the number of outstanding books for children, there has crystallized a feeling—to use Eleanor Cameron's words—that "children's literature does not exist in a narrow world of its own, but is enmeshed in a larger world of literature. . . . " Moreover, this perception of the locus of children's literature carries with it a further consequence. To quote again from Mrs. Cameron: "the highest standards of the one hold good for the other." And more than twenty years ago Bertha Mahony Miller wrote in a *Horn Book* editorial (May-June 1946):

> Arts flourish where there is sound critical judgment to examine and appraise. The critic must, first of all, have a real point of view about his subject. The essential point of view grows out of acquaintance with the best children's books past and present, and also with the world's best literature for everyone.

This high standard for the criticism of children's literature may be seen exemplified in such works as *Books, Children and Men* and *The Unreluctant Years*. It continues with unabated significance in Mrs. Cameron's recent volume *The Green and Burning Tree*.

About the relationship between children's literature and literature in general, John Rowe Townsend also has made some clear and definite statements:

> I believe that children's books must be judged by much the same standards as adult literature. A good children's book must not only be pleasing to children: it must be a good book in its own right.
>
> Where the works of the past are concerned, I have much faith in the sifting process of time—'time' being the shorthand for the collective wisdom of a great many people over a long period of time. . . . Survival is a good test of a book. . . . With present-day books, the sifting process is incomplete and judgments [Townsend is modestly referring to his own] are provisional.

But what of reviewing? Is reviewing criticism, or should it be criticism? Actually, criticism cannot be kept out of reviewing. Even the short capsulelike review cannot avoid making some critical comment, and a long review tends to become a critical essay.

What is the function of reviewing? I know of no better discussion of the subject than is found in a pamphlet published by the Hogarth Press in England in 1939. Entitled *Reviewing,* it was written by Virginia Woolf, some of whose previously unsigned reviews have recently been identified and republished in the London *Times Literary Supplement.* She states her observations in a definitive manner. When reviewing rose in importance at the beginning of the nineteenth century, "Its complex task was partly to inform the public, partly to criticize the book and partly to advertise its existence." During the present century, "The critic is separate from the reviewer; the function of the reviewer is partly to sort current literature; partly to advertise the author; partly to inform the public." Present-day authors will doubtless acquiesce in her opinion that "it is a matter of very great interest to a writer to know what an honest and intelligent reader thinks about his work." And when Virginia Woolf states that "It is impossible for the living to judge the works of the living," one recognizes the confession of an honest reviewer, who was also a critic in her own right.

Although a review serves the practical purpose of giving information and of advertising—using the word in its Woolfian sense—it cannot avoid making certain critical gestures. To consider only children's books: Of the thousands published yearly, how many of them is it physically possible to review? If a journal, like *The Horn Book Magazine,* reviews only books considered worthy of mention, the very task of selection is, by its very nature, a task of criticism—of judgment. Any form of literary classification, comparison, or evaluation must also be considered a form of criticism. Actual—one should even dare to say serious—criticism will occur only when judgments are being made in a context of literary knowledge and literary standards. If a reviewer perceives clearly the intention of the author and states it, the author will surely appreciate the intelligence—that is, the critical acumen of the reviewer. If the reviewer tries to indicate how well the author has succeeded in accomplishing his intention, the reviewer— once again—assumes the role of the critic.

Reviewing, however, is only concerned with what is imminent in publishing, with what is being produced at the present time; and does its job well by selecting, classifying, and evaluating—evaluating for the time being. Criticism deals with literature in perspective and places a book in a larger context—be it historical, aesthetic, psychological, or what you will. I deliberately say "what you will" for there are—as we all well know— Marxian critics, Thomistic critics, and psychoanalytical critics, who concern themselves with evaluations which are not always purely literary.

As I have suggested before, the reviewing and criticism of children's literature is more complex and more fraught with misconceptions than any other kind of reviewing and criticism. If children's literature—at its best—is worthy of consideration with the rest of literature, if the understanding and appreciation of children's literature is to lead to the development of relevant and reliable criticism, one must never forget that the term *children's* remains a specifying term and, willy-nilly, must be respected.

It is certainly important and necessary at times to consider children's literature purely as literature. Questions of style, structure, and technical subtlety are as applicable to children's literature as to any of the other branches of literature. Julia Cunningham's *Dorp Dead* (Pantheon) may be considered as an exemplar of the Gothic novel; and one could learn much by comparing the structure of her story with that of *Jane Eyre.* Incidentally, a good reviewer's critical apparatus should obviously include a wide knowledge of universal literature. The reviewer of Scott O'Dell's *The Dark Canoe* (Houghton) who confessed to an ignorance of—that is, of having never read—*Moby Dick* could scarcely begin to do justice to Mr. O'Dell's book, whatever its ultimate literary significance or value may be.

However, even if children's literature should be considered as literature, it does not cease to be children's literature. But, unfortunately, there is no simple, or clear and easy way by which to determine the proper relationship between the term *children's* and the term *literature.* The most one can do is to consider a few varying points of view.

To ask a child invites defeat. Often his response is primitive or rudimentary; a child's enthusiasm for a book is a much better indication of what the book means to him and does for him than any direct answer to a question posed at him. Jean Karl, editor of children's books, Atheneum, has stated the child's case with great common sense:

> No book is for every child and no book should be made to appeal to every child. A book is made to be loved and cherished by the child it is right for and rejected by those who prefer others.

Or one may consider the point of view of the literary purist, as in Brian Alderson's article "The Irrelevance of Children to the Children's Book Reviewer" (*Children's Book News,* London, January-February 1969). One may agree with Alderson that such remarks as "My Euphemia loved the tasteful blue and yellows" does not get one very far; but when he states that

> It may be objected that to assess children's books without reference to children is to erect some absolute critical standard relating neither to the author's purpose or the reader's enjoyment. To do much less, however, is to follow a road that leads to a morass of contradictions and subjective responses, the most serious result of which will be the confusion of what we are trying to do in encouraging children to read.

I wonder whether Mr. Alderson has not sidetracked one of the chief problems in the consideration of children's literature—literary merit—by speaking of "encouraging children to read," which is a pedagogical point of view and therefore should also be irrelevant to the children's book reviewer.

Interestingly enough, John Rowe Townsend looks upon "acceptability to a child as a preliminary hurdle rather than a final test." Personally, I question whether Mr. Townsend has not put the cart before the horse. In discussions of recently published children's books, generally after a discussion of a book of rare value, one often hears the voice of the devil's advocate: "But, will children like it?" or more pessimistically, "What child will read it?" Surely the question of acceptability to a child is a question concerning book selection and not a fundamental critical question—not a question of literary criticism.

A conciliatory point of view is found in the editorial by Bertha Mahony

Miller previously referred to. In it, she modified her statement about the criticism of children's literature by adding an important qualification. "This point of view—this measuring stick—"(by which she meant literary standards) "must also bear some relation to children themselves and their reaction to books today." The word "some" is significant. Mrs. Miller's chief accomplishment was to have considered the child and the book together, not in an intellectually critical way, but appreciatively—one may say, intuitively. Some of her intuitions still bear repeating:

> Who can say what is the right book for the right child? That, thank God, is the child's own adventure (*Horn Book* editorial, November 1933).

> . . . it is foolish to say 'we ought only to give the child conceptions it can understand.' His soul grows by wonder over things it cannot understand (*Horn Book* editorial, January 1934).

These statements may seem both inspirational and idealistic in form and utterance, but in essence they show a deep respect for the child as a person.

Except by taking polls and by compiling statistics, one could not determine the frequency of appeal of William Mayne's *Earthfasts* (Dutton) or Alan Garner's *The Owl Service* (Walck) among children. But popularity is only a descriptive, not a critical term. Among mature readers, how many are there who read *Paradise Lost* or *Finnegan's Wake* for the sheer pleasure of it? There are some, of course, who do; and if children's literature has so developed in richness and scope as to have produced a number of recondite masterpieces, these works should first be respected and treated as works of literature before one goes through the agony of deciding: To how many, to what kinds of children will these works appeal?

Finally, reviewers and critics are but readers; and if they function properly, should simply be better readers than most. Perhaps they should try to be humble rather than clever. Lewis Carroll once managed to be both in a letter that was disarmingly simple and devastatingly logical:

> As to the meaning of the Snark (he wrote to a friend in America), I'm very much afraid that I didn't mean anything but nonsense. Still, you know, words mean more than we mean to express when we use them; so a whole book ought to mean a great deal more than the writer means. So whatever good meanings are in the book, I'm glad to accept as the meaning of the book. The best that I've seen is by a lady (she published it in a letter to a newspaper), that the book is an allegory on the search after happiness. I think this fits in beautifully in many ways—particularly about the bathing machines:[3] when people get weary of life, and can't find

---

3. Bathing machine—a small bathhouse on wheels, to be driven into the water, for bathers to undress, bathe, and dress in (*Webster's New International Dictionary of the English Language,* Second Edition, Unabridged, 1943).

happiness in towns or in books, then they rush off to the seaside to see what bathing machines will do for them.[4]

One of Carroll's statements—"whatever good meanings are in the book, I am glad to accept as the meaning of the book"—invites speculation. He does not consider a possible logical loophole—the possible bad meanings. I am sure that Freudian critics have already taken care of the loophole. As for the lady's idea that "the book is an allegory on the search after happiness," Carroll delightfully and logically destroys her interpretation by pursuing it to its absurd extreme. And yet, Maurice Sendak was to give creative vitality to a very similar bizarre situation in *Higglety-Pigglety Pop!* by transforming nonsense into allegory. During the past year, the editor of *The Horn Book Magazine* received a letter from a student of children's literature who was planning to investigate symbolism in Beatrix Potter. She was— unfortunately—unacquainted with Lewis Carroll's letter.

In *Notes Towards the Definition of Culture,* T. S. Eliot stated what he considered to be "the three permanent reasons for reading: the acquisition of wisdom, the enjoyment of art, and the pleasure of entertainment." It is certainly the third of these reasons which is the most nearly universal. Most children become aware of words at an early age and advance naturally to the more complicated pleasure of listening to stories. If conditions are favorable, children will discover that the world of books can still further augment their verbal pleasures. The prime function, then, of the reviewer and even of the critic of children's books is to signalize those books which appealing at present to children will seem even better when they are reread by those same children in their adulthood.

British editions of books mentioned with their American publishers only in this article:

Julia Cunningham. *Dorp Dead.* Heinemann.
Scott O'Dell. *The Dark Canoe.* Longman/Kestrel.
William Mayne. *Earthfasts.* Hamish Hamilton.
Alan Garner. *The Owl Service.* Collins.

---

4. Quoted by Bertha Mahony Miller from *The Life and Letters of Lewis Carroll* by Stuart Dodgson Collingwood in a *Horn Book* editorial, February 1932.

Coming to Terms with Criticism[1]

Paul Heins

If we are going to come to terms with criticism, especially the criticism of children's literature, we should state the terms. Actually, "Out on a Limb with the Critics" (*Horn Book,* June 1970) was an attempt to suggest some of the critical problems worthy of exploration and, if possible, of clarification. Let us now spell out what these problems are, perhaps indicate certain areas of discussion, or—better still—list certain topics worthy of consideration.

1. Children's literature is a part of general literature; and even at the risk of overemphasizing the notion of branches, children's literature may be said to be a branch on the tree of literature. There have been authors like Stevenson, Mark Twain, and Kipling who in the past have written for both children and adults, as well as more recent writers like Thurber, C. S. Lewis, and E. B. White. And in pursuing the relationship further, one could discover that perhaps Long John Silver, despite his lovable traits, is a distant cousin of schizophrenic Dr. Jekyll; and that C. S. Lewis' Christianity is reflected in his Narnia stories.

It is obvious that the folk tales and hero tales of children's literature are descended from literary forms that were created to entertain whole strata of society and that the minstrels who sang and told of Odysseus and Beowulf would have been surprised to learn that their works would one day be recast for children. Contemporary children's books, also, often suggest analogies with books for adults. The proportions of the world of *The Borrowers* (Harcourt) or of *The Return of the Twelves* (Coward) suggest the relativity of big and small found in the first two voyages of *Gulliver's Travels.*

2. If children's literature is a part of all literature, then the criticism of children's literature becomes a part of the criticism of all literature. A children's book deserves to be probed as much as an adult book for general questions of diction, structure, significance of detail, literary integrity. Not for the purpose of what is often called "dry" analysis, but for the joy of discovering the skill of the author.

3. A much more difficult area to localize is found in the attempt to decide what distinguishes a children's book from an adult book. Thus far, discussions have led to a violent taking of sides—in such articles as John Tunis's "What Is a Juvenile Book?" (*Horn Book,* June 1968) or in Eleanor Cameron's, "Why *Not* for Children?" (*Horn Book,* February 1966). Perhaps it would be wise to distinguish, on the one hand, between books written for adults and books written for children, and to distinguish, on the other hand, between books read by adults and those read by children.

"Coming to Terms with Criticism" by Paul Heins from *Horn Book Magazine,* 46 (August 1970): 370–375. Reprinted by permission of Horn Book, Inc.

1. Delivered on June 19, 1969, at the Fifth Intermountain Conference on Children's Literature, the University of Utah, Salt Lake City, Utah.

If children made *Robinson Crusoe* one of their own books long ago, adults have since adopted *Alice in Wonderland* for themselves. In the 1968 Commencement Address at Colby College (Waterville, State of Maine), the poet David McCord listed what he called "good" books, "wise" books—and included *Alice* along with *The Tempest, The Oregon Trail,* and *War and Peace.* The literary essays of Graham Greene include a discussion of the writings of Beatrix Potter—a discussion which the creator of Peter Rabbit and Jemima Puddleduck did not approve of, because she considered the critic's point of view to be unnecessarily Freudian. Even in serious philosophical criticism, a writer will occasionally draw from children's literature for examples. In *The Mind of the Maker* (Harcourt), Dorothy L. Sayers discusses, among other things, writers whose "work and every part of it can be referred to as a coherent and controlling unity of Idea." Along with Blake, Aquinas, and Euclid, she mentions Lewis Carroll and the Alice books.

4. The child as reader. Is what a child reads significant from the point of view of criticism? Spontaneous young readers may be devoted to one kind of book, may read indiscriminately, or may be inspired to read certain books as the result of the suggestions of teacher, librarian, or any other kind of miscellaneous adult. A knowledge of what they read, however, is essentially valuable for an understanding of their personal or intellectual development, and will naturally always be interesting to those of us concerned with children's books. But it is a subject only occasionally related to literary criticism.

Edward Fenton, in an article entitled "Mystery" which appeared in the June 1968 *Horn Book Magazine,* presented an author's point of view about one possible relationship:

> Children's interests are as broad as the horizon. They are interested in practically everything—with the exception of sexual love, which bores them, being beyond their experience. They know that grownups fall in love and marry, but it is a convention they accept without caring about the details. As for all the other problems related to life (including death), it is impossible to overestimate the capacity of children to feel, suffer, understand, and share them all if properly presented. But they must be in terms of action and plot.

The proper presentation to children of these "problems related to life" does concern criticism, and Mr. Fenton does specifically emphasize the primacy of action and plot.

5. The child as critic. Generally it is not a child's reasoned opinion—after all, he is not ready for that—but his reactions that are significant. Ranging from the lukewarm tolerance of calling a book "all right" to positive dislike or enthusiasm, his reactions are generally worth considering for their emotional overtones, which—again—are only indirectly related to critical judgments. The statistical approach, also, is not particularly signifi-

cant: I know of one community in which children do not care to read Lloyd Alexander's fantasies and of another in which the children were very anxious to purchase for themselves paperback copies of *The Book of Three* and *The High King* (both Holt/Dell Yearling).

6. The apologetics of children's literature is a very important branch of criticism. Just as romantic poets and realistic novelists have had in the past to defend their positions, just as fiction itself and drama have had to withstand puritanical and other kinds of religious attacks and criticism, children's literature—especially the quality of present-day children's literature—needs constant defending. The June 1968 editorial of *The Horn Book Magazine* touched on the situation. "Recently, some voices have been raised—generally those of psychologists and educators—in protest against the inadequacies of children's books. Books for children are accused of being condescending, out of touch with the reality of a child's life, and superficially optimistic." Although other champions of children's books may have at times spoken more eloquently, the editorial proffered a simple suggestion: "Before carping about the quality of literature for children, the dissenters should become more familiar with it." If we are living in the midst of a golden age of literature for children, many people are not aware of the fact. The existence of the term "kiddy lit" shows that crusaders still have enough left to do.

7. A topic closely related to the defense of children's literature is concerned with the castigation of inferior literary productions intended for children. "Walt Disney Accused" (*Horn Book*, December 1965), "Not Recommended" (*Horn Book*, February 1963), and "An Imaginary Correspondence" (*Horn Book*, August 1963) are important examples of this kind of criticism.

8. The trends of the age. This very important topic, although historical in nature, is closely interlinked with critical problems. In recent years the subject matter of children's books has expanded considerably to include social problems, questions of prejudice, urban and academic situations, and psychological dilemmas; in addition, there has been a greater stress than ever before on realism of presentation; and the vocabulary of children's books is beginning to reflect the spirit of the times. Even though we have left far behind us what George Santayana once called the "genteel tradition" of American literature (and life), the problems of literary criticism remain constant. After we have absorbed new kinds of subject matter and new points of view, we still have to ask not only what a book tries to do, but how well it does it.

9. Although something has already been said about reviewing and criticism, at least one further comment is necessary. Reviewers do not sift for eternity; they are kept busy selecting the best or the most significant of the books available during a given period of time. Incidentally, a similar method is followed by judges of book awards; the Newbery Award, as we all know, considers the contributions to children's literature during a given year. But time alone is the ultimate judge of the value of a book. Age in a

book is not necessarily a sign of decay; it may indicate what in the book has resisted decay. Even a review may—after the passing of time—emerge triumphant: During the 1920's *The New York Times Book Review* called Joyce's *Ulysses* "the most important contribution that has been made to fictional literature in the twentieth century."[2] A reviewer does not have to be a prophet, but merely a sensitive reader who is able to perceive the quality of a new book. If the reviewer is in tune with literature, he may often make an uncanny judgment that will be justified by time.

10. In an era that has been made increasingly aware of the interrelation-ships of the various branches of knowledge, criticism can serve as a borderline service by stressing excellence. Teachers of history have long used historical novels and other forms of literature to vivify the background of their subject; and at the present time, the link between literature and the teaching of language is being stressed. I shall only mention in passing the excellent article "Helping Children Claim Language Through Literature" by Bill Martin, Jr.

I should like to quote, however, from Hester Burton's novel *In Spite of All Terror* (World):

> Then, too, there was the problem of the way she talked.
>
> Liz, like most of her friends at the Weavers Green Grammar School, was bilingual in two kinds of English. In Nile Street and in the school playground she spoke cockney. . . . One recited Shakespeare and read the New Testament lesson in Assembly in "posh," and one always addressed the teachers in this way. . . .
>
> The trouble now, however, was that [her] quick ear told her that the vowel sounds of Weavers Green "educated" English differed in some respects somewhat embarrassingly from that of the Breretons.

The quotation casts an interesting sidelight on the relationship between language and literature, which is obviously a universal problem. But the critic's ultimate responsibility is to judge any book on its own—its literary—merit.

The listing of ten areas of possible discussion from the point of view of the criticism of children's literature, especially from that of the literary criticism of children's literature, was not intended to be exhaustive. The number is an arbitrary one; but the listing was intended to demonstrate the complexity of the problems of judging children's books: to show that there is a lot going on—at one and the same time.

"Out on a Limb with the Critics" attempted to give one an idea of the currents and crosscurrents, the jostling but dynamic contradictions, and the interplay of the various phases found in discussions of children's books.

---

2. From *"The Story of The New York Times Book Review,"* an essay by Francis Brown, editor of *The New York Times Book Review,* appearing as the introduction to the bound volumes for the years 1896–1968.

"Coming to Terms with Criticism" tries to isolate the various phases, and suggest the value or the importance of each. But these phases, in reality, are coexistent and react on one another, so that the whole subject of the criticism of children's books may be visualized as a huge mobile consisting of many parts delicately and effectively balanced.

Perhaps one should distinguish, in the long run, between the two different ways of approaching children's books: (1) the criticism of these books as they concern the different kinds of people who use and work with these books and (2) the literary criticism of children's literature. But I still feel that a conscious and enlightened literary criticism should direct and govern our whole approach to children's literature. Whether it rules as a constitutional monarch or as a duly elected president makes little difference.

British editions of books mentioned with their American publishers only in this article:

Mary Norton. *The Borrowers.* Dent.
Pauline Clark. *The Twelve and the Genii* (published in U.S.A. as *The Return of the Twelves*). Faber.
Dorothy L. Sayers. *The Mind of the Maker.* Methuen.
Lloyd Alexander. *The Book of Three.* Heinemann.
Hester Burton. *In Spite of All Terror.* Oxford University Press.

A Critique of Children's Book Reviewing

Ivan Southall

An Australian, Ivan Southall is well-known in the Anglo-American children's book world where he has traveled as a lecturer. Three of his many books for the young have won the Australian annual Book of the Year Award: Ash Road *(1966),* To the Wild Sky *(1968), and* Bread and Honey *(1970). Of the third, which also appeared as* Walk a Mile and Get Nowhere, *the Judges' Report in the* Australian Book Review *(Winter 1971: 123-124) says: "In many ways this book is ahead of its time." The following extracts are from his acceptance speech for the Australian Children's Book Council's Book of the Year Award for* To the Wild Sky.

This is a very happy occasion for me—I make no bones about that—and I would rather not dignify it with ostensibly wise words that may tire us all, particularly me, because the responsibility is mine to produce them, but I suppose it will have to happen because the occasion demands it and you're a captive audience too well-bred to walk away.

Let me assure you, as if you didn't know, that the agony, however jealously enjoyed, of creating a book that means something to the adult who writes it and not significantly less to the boy or girl who reads it, is enough for one person to live with. But in this age of proliferating sources of criticism the agony does not end there any more.

Beyond the writer, between him and the child, has grown a barbed wire entanglement through which his book, beating with his own blood, must thrust its way. Sometimes the book breasts the entanglement and drives on joyfully to meet the child; sometimes the book falls half-way, all bloodied and torn. Usually, if it falls, it has earned its fair reward, but mistakes can be made. Sometimes the book that breasts the entanglement is not the one that deserves to live and afterwards promptly dies, just to prove it, and the other fights on and breaks through and lives for a generation.

You people here represent the citadel of enlightened adult opinion—in all its variety of points and purpose—that the writer of serious intent for children in this country must eventually conquer. You may not, of course, have been described as a citadel before, or even as a barbed-wire entanglement, and may not care for it very much. Forgive me. I am speaking from my desk, from the two square yards of polished oak upon which so many anguished metaphors have been born. Here anything can happen; even handsome people may become citadels or barbed wire entanglements; even six children may be cast by chance to the mercies of *The Wild Sky.*

"A Critique of Children's Book Reviewing" by Ivan Southall from St. Martin's Press Catalog, 1969, pp. 24–25. Reprinted by permission of Ivan Southall.

As members of a critical body, as a body of assessment, as guardians of standards, as the ultimate of all barbed wire entanglements, you can help to break the writer or help to make him and this is not an activity to be lightly, casually, or carelessly undertaken. This accounts for your serious demeanor, and for the slight sinking sensation your presence generates in the hearts of valiant authors.

There are critics not associated with the Children's Book Councils of the various States, but not many. I think it is reasonable to say that most of the serious critics in this country whose interests centre on books for children are represented directly or indirectly in this place and it is to you all that I would address myself. I am well qualified. Critics have flogged me up and down the village square for eighteen years since Simon Black in all his manly splendor arrived by rocket ship on the scene. But I would not speak to the critic as a collective body; I would speak to each as a person.

Remember that in the critical exercise of your generosity you may encourage a writer who has entirely mistaken his direction and would be better working elsewhere. The good children's book belongs to a field of particular application. And remember that in the critical exercise of your wit you may, I say *may*, break the spirit of another who is stumbling in a wilderness only a year or two short of power. When you make your mistakes, let them be honest. The writing of a book, however ill-conceived, is a labor at least of months; the writing of a criticism is rarely the labor of more than a few days. I know; I have written a couple of hundred myself.

There are writers who assure me that the views expressed by critics mean nothing to them. In the long view I suspect this to be a defence for wounded souls. My own painful evolution as a writer for children has laid me open to a great deal of criticism and I believe at different times I have said that sticks and stones break the body but criticism bounces off. But, believe me, it has worried me; at times bewildered me. Some of it has been lazy, masses of it have been useless, but a significant residue has made me think, has helped me to grow, has modified even at this moment tendencies to get stuck in a rut.

The conscientious critic may contribute as much to the literature of a country as the conscientious writer, an obvious sort of thing to say, I know; but something that needs to be repeated a little more often.

A writer cannot thrive in a destructively hostile environment, nor can the critic. A writer bares his soul at some personal risk to produce a significant work; the critic in his own way must go equally as far if he is to enjoy the satisfaction of fulfilling a constructive function.

Integrity, no matter what the cost, is the ultimate truth for the writer and for the critic. Don't go soft on those who have attained temporary eminence nor, for that matter, murder them unnecessarily. These writers, with two or three good books behind them, need your honest and courageous judgement as much as the new writers; all need more than patronage or a rehash of the blurb if they are to fulfill their promise.

Chapter 12

Awards

To recognize distinction and express appreciation for creative work in children's literature, judges for medals and other prizes expend much energy, generate great excitement, and become involved in many controversies. In countries with a large and competitive book production, awards are needed less for the purpose of stimulating publishing than to call attention to distinguished work, but in countries where few books are produced, the establishment of an award is likely to be one of the first steps taken to publicize the importance of writing for children.

Awards have increased in number over the years. Illustration is now recognized, and there is a great range of regional, international, ethnic, and subject categories. It has become important to understand the criteria for selection and the bases on which the awards are administered in order to comprehend the heights of distinction offered.[1]

---

1. See also *Children's Books: Awards and Prizes* (New York: Children's Book Council, pub. annually).

Newbery and Caldecott Awards

Elizabeth Burr

Elizabeth Burr is Consultant in Children's and Young People's Services for the State Department of Public Instruction, Madison, Wisconsin. As such, she is responsible for the Cooperative Children's Book Center and its bibliographical, reference, and research services. It is this center that chooses annually the Lewis Carroll Shelf Awards—"books worthy to sit on the shelf with" Lewis Carroll's writing. In 1959 she was chairman of the Newbery-Caldecott Committee.

The Newbery and Caldecott medals for distinguished children's books are awarded each year by the American Library Association. It was June 21, 1921, at Swampscott, Massachusetts, that Frederic G. Melcher proposed a medal for children's books and suggested it be named to honor John Newbery, 18th century London bookseller and publisher. On June 24, 1937, in the ballroom of the Waldorf-Astoria at the business meeting of the American Library Association Section for Library Work with Children, the children's librarians "accepted with enthusiasm the generous offer of Frederic Melcher" of a picture book medal to be named the Caldecott Medal in honor of Randolph J. Caldecott, 19th century English illustrator. The medals, donated by Mr. Melcher, were designed by René Paul Chambellan.

From their beginnings, the awards have had a significant influence in stimulating publication and appreciation of outstanding children's books. They have also stimulated children's librarians in school and public libraries throughout the U. S. to read children's books critically and to participate in selection of the award winners by nomination of books to be considered.

The Newbery Medal is "awarded annually to the author of the 'most distinguished contribution to American literature for children,' the award being made to cover books whose publication in book form falls in the calendar year last elapsed. The award is restricted to authors who are citizens or residents of the United States. Reprints and compilations are not eligible for consideration. There are no limitations as to the character of the book considered except that it be original work. It need not be written solely for children; the judgment of the librarians voting shall decide whether a book be 'a contribution to the literature for children.' The award considers only the books of one calendar year and does not pass judgment on the author's previous work or other work during that year outside the volume that may be named." (November 9, 1922, Mr. Melcher's agreement with ALA Executive Board.)

"Newbery and Caldecott Awards" by Elizabeth Burr from *Top of the News*, 15 (December 1959): 67–70. Reprinted by permission of American Library Association.

The Caldecott Medal "shall be awarded to the artist of the most distinguished American picture book for children published in the United States during the preceding year. The award shall go to the artist, who must be a citizen or resident of the United States, whether or not he be the author of the text. Members of the Newbery Medal Committee will serve as judges. If a book of the year is nominated for both the Newbery and Caldecott awards, the Committee shall decide under which heading it shall be voted upon, so that the same title shall not be considered on both ballots." (Voted June 24, 1937, ALA Section for Work with Children Business Meeting.)

The purpose of the Newbery Medal stated by Mr. Melcher in his formal agreement with the ALA Executive Board in 1922 applies also to the Caldecott Medal.

"Purpose of the John Newbery Medal: To encourage original and creative work in the field of books for children. To emphasize to the public that contributions to the literature for children deserve recognition as do poetry, plays, or novels. To give to those librarians who make it their life work to serve children's reading interests an opportunity to encourage good writing in this field."

Selection of the books to receive the medals is delegated by the American Library Association to its Children's Services Division. The Division assigns to the Newbery-Caldecott Awards Committee responsibility for making the final choice. The committee is made up of twenty-three division members and represents all kinds of libraries serving boys and girls. It is composed of the officers of the division (president, vice-president, past-president, and treasurer), the Book Evaluation Committee (five members), eight members selected from sixteen candidates in the annual CSD spring election, and six members appointed by the CSD president. The chairman of the committee is the CSD vice-president.

The committee is charged with reviewing, clarifying, and redefining the terms which govern selection of the books to receive the awards, as well as serving as the jury for selection of the award-winning books. The terms have been changed three times by official action, two of those cancelling each other out. In April, 1932, two resolutions were adopted by the Section for Library Work with Children and approved by ALA Executive Board: (1) "To be eligible for the Newbery Medal, books must be original, or, if traditional in origin, the result of individual research, the retelling and reinterpretation being the writer's own. (2) Since the Newbery Medal is intended to encourage an increasing number of authors to devote their best efforts to creating children's literature, the book of a previous recipient of the Newbery Medal shall receive the award only upon unanimous vote of the Newbery Committee."

In January, 1958, the Board of Directors of the Children's Services Division voted that "In view of the fact that a unanimous vote in the case of a previous winner of the Newbery-Caldecott awards was first instituted to encourage new authors and illustrators at a period when such encouragement was needed, and since such need is no longer apparent, the restriction of a unanimous vote for winning either award more than once be removed from the terms for selection of the Newbery-Caldecott awards.''

For the Caldecott Medal, additional qualifications have grown out of committee deliberations. The text need not be the work of the artist, but must be worthy of the book. There are no limitations on the character of the illustrations. There is no limitation as to age level of the book, although it is recognized that most picture books are intended for young children. The award is made for a picture book in which the pictures rather than the text are the heart of the book.

Procedures used in selection have been worked out over the years. Changes have been made only after careful study by the committee. Basic to the selection process are the nominations by mail ballot made by the members of the Children's Services Division. From early October until the decision is reached, Newbery-Caldecott Awards Committee members are hard at work reading and rereading books which are proposed for consideration.

During the midwinter American Library Association meeting in Chicago at the end of January each year, the Newbery-Caldecott Awards Committee holds a series of meetings at which the books which have been nominated are fully discussed. Committee voting is done by written, secret ballot and often several ballots are necessary before the final decision is determined. On each ballot committee members indicate a first, second, and third choice. A point system, which assigns four points to first choice, three to second, and two to third, is used in the ballot count. To receive the award, a book must have at least twelve first-choice votes, or a count of forty-eight.

Public announcement of the two award-winning books is made in mid-March[1] by the chairman of the Newbery-Caldecott Awards Committee from the New York office of the donor of the medals, Frederic G. Melcher.

Presentation of the two medals is made at a gala banquet during the American Library Association annual conference. At these colorful dinners, more than a thousand librarians and others interested in encouraging the best in writing, illustrating, and publishing for children gather in recognition of the significance of the Newbery and Caldecott medals in achieving that goal.

In the years since 1922, when the Newbery Medal was instituted, and since 1938, when the Caldecott Medal was first presented, these two awards have helped parents, teachers, and children as well as librarians and publishers to gain a realization of the qualities which make a book distinguished. They have contributed to the recognition of children's books as an important part of current literature and art. Librarians and teachers have contributed to the prestige and the continuing value of the awards by

---

1. Beginning in 1970, the announcement is made in January on the day following the decision, in the midwinter meeting of the American Library Association—Editor's note.

their widespread promotion and introduction of the books which have received them. Bookstores have made the winning books readily available for their customers, and parents have learned to seek them for birthday and holiday additions to the home library shelves of books worth many readings.

Newbery and Caldecott medal winners have also gained prestige from the special contribution which Bertha Mahony Miller and Horn Book, Inc., have made by publishing the acceptance speeches in *The Horn Book Magazine* each August and by publication of the two[2] handsome volumes which bring together the results of the beginning years of each award and, in addition, include outstanding articles on distinguished literature and illustrations for children—*Newbery Medal Books: 1922–1955* (1955); *Caldecott Medal Books: 1938–1957* (1957). Both books are edited by Mrs. Miller and Elinor Whitney Field. A further useful book for background on the medals is *A History of the Newbery and Caldecott Medals* by Irene Smith. (Viking 1957).

Complete lists of the award-winning books are available in school and public libraries, are found in recent editions of children's encyclopedias, and may be obtained on request from the American Library Association. Bookmarks listing titles which have received each award may be purchased in quantity from the Children's Book Council, 175 Fifth Avenue, New York 10, N. Y.

---

2. Now three volumes—Editor's note.

Winners and Runners-Up for the Newbery and Caldecott Awards

1. NEWBERY AWARDS: 1922-1974

1922 Award: *The Story of Mankind,* Hendrik Willem van Loon. Liveright. (London: Harrap)

Honor books: *The Great Quest,* Charles Hawes. Little, Brown. (London: Heinemann)
Cedric the Forester, Bernard Marshall. Appleton-Century.
The Old Tobacco Shop, William Bowen. Macmillan.
The Golden Fleece and the Heroes Who Lived Before Achilles, Padraic Colum. Macmillan.
Windy Hill, Cornelia Meigs. Macmillan.

1923 Award: *The Voyages of Doctor Dolittle,* Hugh Lofting. Lippincott. (London: Cape)

Honor books: No record (Chairman, Elva Smith, Carnegie Library, Pittsburgh. C.L.S. voted by section membership.)

1924 Award: *The Dark Frigate,* Charles Hawes. Little, Brown. (London: Heinemann)

Honor books: No record (Saratoga Springs, N. Y. A.L.A. established special selection committee.)

1925 Award: *Tales from Silver Lands,* Charles Finger. Doubleday. (London: Heinemann)

Honor books: *Nicholas,* Anne Carroll Moore. Putnam.
Dream Coach, Anne Parrish. Macmillan.

1926 Award: *Shen of the Sea,* Arthur Bowie Chrisman. Dutton. (London: Hamish Hamilton)

Honor books: *Voyagers,* Padraic Colum. Macmillan.

1927 Award: *Smoky, the Cowhorse,* Will James. Scribner.

Honor books: No record.

1928 Award: *Gayneck, the Story of a Pigeon,* Dhan Gopal Mukerji. Dutton. (London: Angus and Robertson)

Honor books: *The Wonder Smith and His Son,* Ella Young. Longmans.
Downright Dencey, Caroline Snedeker. Doubleday. (London: Heinemann)

1929 Award: *The Trumpeter of Krakow,* Eric P. Kelly. Macmillan. (London: Chatto)

"Winners and Runners-Up for the Newbery and Caldecott Awards," originally prepared by Bonita E. Stecher, Cooperative Children's Book Center, Madison, Wisconsin, for *Newbery and Caldecott Medal Books, 1956–1965,* edited by Lee Kingman and published by Horn Book, Inc. in 1965. The list is herein brought up-to-date. Reprinted by permission of Horn Book, Inc.

Illustration by Lynd Ward from *The Cat Who Went to Heaven*, by Elizabeth Coatsworth. Copyright © 1930, 1958 by *The Macmillan Company*.

Honor books: *Pigtail of Ah Lee Ben Loo*, John Bennett. Longmans.
                Millions of Cats, Wanda Gág. Coward-McCann. (London: Faber)
                The Boy Who Was, Grace Hallock. Dutton. (London: Dent)
                Clearing Weather, Cornelia Meigs. Little, Brown.
                Runaway Papoose, Grace Moon. Doubleday.
                Tod of the Fens, Elinor Whitney. Macmillan.
1930 Award: *Hitty, Her First Hundred Years*, Rachel Field. Macmillan. (London: Routledge)
Honor books: *Daughter of the Seine*, Jeanette Eaton. Harper.
                Pran of Albania, Elizabeth Miller. Doubleday.
                Jumping-off Place, Marian Hurd McNeely. Longmans.
                Tangle-coated Horse and Other Tales, Ella Young. Longmans.
                Vaino, Julia Davis Adams. Dutton. (London: Dent)
                Little Blacknose, Hildegarde Swift. Harcourt.
1931 Award: *The Cat Who Went to Heaven*, Elizabeth Coatsworth. Macmillan. (London: Dent)

Honor books:	Floating Island, Anne Parrish. Harper. (London: Benn)
	The Dark Star of Itza, Alida Malkus. Harcourt.
	Queer Person, Ralph Hubbard. Doubleday.
	Mountains Are Free, Julia Davis Adams. Dutton.
	Spice and the Devil's Cave, Agnes Hewes. Knopf.
	Meggy MacIntosh, Elizabeth Janet Gray. Doubleday.
	Garram the Hunter, Herbert Best. Doubleday. (London: Dent)
	Ood-le-uk the Wanderer, Alice Lide and Margaret Johansen. Little, Brown.
1932 Award:	*Waterless Mountain*, Laura Adams Armer. Longmans.
Honor books:	*The Fairy Circus*, Dorothy Lathrop. Macmillan.
	Calico Bush, Rachel Field. Macmillan.
	Boy of the South Seas, Eunice Tietjens. Coward-McCann.
	Out of the Flame, Eloise Lownsbery. Longmans.
	Jane's Island, Marjorie Allee. Houghton Mifflin.
	Truce of the Wolf and Other Tales of Old Italy, Mary Gould Davis. Harcourt.
1933 Award:	*Young Fu of the Upper Yangtze*, Elizabeth Lewis. Winston. (London: Harrap)
Honor books:	*Swift Rivers*, Cornelia Meigs. Little, Brown.
	The Railroad to Freedom, Hildegarde Swift. Harcourt. (London: Bodley Head)
	Children of the Soil, Nora Burglon. Doubleday.
1934 Award:	*Invincible Louisa*, Cornelia Meigs. Little Brown.
Honor books:	*The Forgotten Daughter*, Caroline Snedeker. Doubleday.
	Swords of Steel, Elsie Singmaster. Houghton.
	ABC Bunny, Wanda Gág. Coward-McCann. (London: Faber)
	Winged Girl of Knossos, Erik Berry, *pseud.* (Allena Best). Appleton-Century.
	New Land, Sarah Schmidt. McBride.
	Big Tree of Bunlahy, Padraic Colum. Macmillan.
	Glory of the Seas, Agnes Hewes. Knopf. (London: Cassell)
	Apprentice of Florence, Anne Kyle. Houghton Mifflin.
1935 Award:	*Dobry*, Monica Shannon. Viking. (London: Harrap)
Honor books:	*Pageant of Chinese History*, Elizabeth Seeger. Longmans.
	Davy Crockett, Constance Rourke. Harcourt.
	Day on Skates, Hilda Van Stockum. Harper.
1936 Award:	*Caddie Woodlawn*, Carol Brink. Macmillan. (London: Collier-Macmillan)
Honor books:	*Honk, the Moose*, Phil Stong. Dodd, Mead. (London: Harrap)
	The Good Master, Kate Seredy. Viking. (London: Harrap)
	Young Walter Scott, Elizabeth Janet Gray. Viking. (London: Nelson)
	All Sail Set, Armstrong Sperry. Winston. (London: Bodley Head)
1937 Award:	*Roller Skates*, Ruth Sawyer. Viking. (London: Bodley Head)
Honor books:	*Phebe Fairchild; Her Book*, Lois Lenski. Stokes.

Whistlers' Van, Idwal Jones. Viking. (London: Selwyn and Blount)

Golden Basket, Ludwig Bemelmans, Viking.

Winterbound, Margery Bianco. Viking.

Audubon, Constance Rourke. Harcourt. (London: Harrap)

The Codfish Musket, Agnes Hewes. Doubleday.

1938 Award: *The White Stag*, Kate Seredy. Viking. (London: Harrap)

Honor books: *Pecos Bill*, James Cloyd Bowman. Little, Brown.

Bright Island, Mabel Robinson. Random House. (London: Hutchinson)

On the Banks of Plum Creek, Laura Ingalls Wilder. Harper. (London: Methuen)

1939 Award: *Thimble Summer*, Elizabeth Enright. Rinehart. (London: Heinemann)

Honor books: *Nino*, Valenti Angelo. Viking.

Mr. Popper's Penguins, Richard and Florence Atwater. Little, Brown. (London: Bodley Head)

"Hello the Boat!", Phyllis Crawford. Holt. (London: Harrap)

Leader by Destiny: George Washington, Man and Patriot, Jeanette Eaton. Harcourt. (London: Harrap)

Penn, Elizabeth Janet Gray. Viking.

1940 Award: *Daniel Boone*, James Daugherty. Viking.

Honor books: *The Singing Tree*, Kate Seredy. Viking. (Leicester: Brockhampton)

Runner of the Mountain Tops, Mabel Robinson. Random House.

By the Shores of Silver Lake, Laura Ingalls Wilder. Harper (London: Lutterworth Press)

Boy with a Pack, Stephen W. Meader. Harcourt.

1941 Award: *Call It Courage*, Armstrong Sperry. Macmillan. (London: Bodley Head. Published as *The Boy Who Was Afraid)*

Honor books: *Blue Willow*, Doris Gates. Viking. (London: Muller)

Young Mac of Fort Vancouver, Mary Jane Carr. Crowell.

The Long Winter, Laura Ingalls Wilder. Harper. (London: Lutterworth Press)

Nansen, Anna Gertrude Hall. Viking.

1942 Award: *The Matchlock Gun*, Walter D. Edmonds. Dodd, Mead.

Honor books: Little Town on the Prairie, Laura Ingalls Wilder. Harper. (London: Lutterworth Press)

George Washington's World, Genevieve Foster. Scribner.

Indian Captive: the Story of Mary Jemison, Lois Lenski. Lippincott. (London: Coach House Press)

Down Ryton Water, Eva Roe Gaggin. Viking.

1943 Award: *Adam of the Road*, Elizabeth Janet Gray. Viking. (London: Black)

Honor books: *The Middle Moffat*, Eleanor Estes. Harcourt. (London: Bodley Head)

"Have You Seen Tom Thumb?", Mabel Leigh Hunt. Lippincott.

1944 Award: *Johnny Tremain,* Esther Forbes. Houghton-Mifflin. (Harmondsworth: Longman/Kestrel)
Honor books: *These Happy Golden Years,* Laura Ingalls Wilder. Harper. (London: Lutterworth Press)
Fog Magic, Julia Sauer. Viking. (London: Woodfield)
Mountain Born, Elizabeth Yates. Coward-McCann.
Rufus M., Eleanor Estes. Harcourt. (London: Bodley Head)
1945 Award: *Rabbit Hill,* Robert Lawson. Viking.
Honor books: *The Hundred Dresses,* Eleanor Estes, Harcourt.
The Silver Pencil, Alice Dalgliesh. Scribner.
Abraham Lincoln's World, Genevieve Foster. Scribner.
Lone Journey; the Life of Roger Williams, Jeanette Eaton. Harcourt.
1946 Award: *Strawberry Girl,* Lois Lenski. Lippincott. (London: Oxford University Press)
Honor books: *Justin Morgan Had a Horse,* Marguerite Henry. Rand McNally.
The Moved-Outers, Florence Crannell Means. Houghton Mifflin.
Bhimsa, the Dancing Bear, Christine Weston. Scribner. (London: Macmillan)
New Found World, Katherine Shippen. Viking.
1947 Award: *Miss Hickory,* Carolyn Sherwin Bailey. Viking.
Honor books: *Wonderful Year,* Nancy Barnes. Messner.
Big Tree, Mary and Conrad Buff. Viking.
The Heavenly Tenants, William Maxwell. Harper.
The Avion My Uncle Flew, Cyrus Fisher, *pseud.* (Darwin L. Teilhet).
Appleton-Century.
The Hidden Treasure of Glaston, Eleanore Jewett. Viking. (London: Dobson)
1948 Award: *The Twenty-One Balloons,* William Pène du Bois. Viking. (Kingswood: World's Work)
Honor books: *Pancakes—Paris,* Claire Huchet Bishop. Viking.
LiLun, Lad of Courage, Carolyn Treffinger. Abingdon.
The Quaint and Curious Quest of Johnny Longfoot, Catherine Besterman. Bobbs Merrill.
The Cow-tail Switch, and Other West African Stories, Harold Courlander. Holt.
Misty of Chincoteague, Marguerite Henry. Rand McNally. (London: Collins)
1949 Award: *King of the Wind,* Marguerite Henry. Rand McNally. (London: Collins)
Honor books: *Seabird,* Holling C. Holling. Houghton Mifflin. (London: Collins)
Daughter of the Mountain, Louise Rankin. Viking. (London: Bodley Head)
My Father's Dragon, Ruth Gannett. Random House. (London: Macmillan)

Story of the Negro, Arna Bontemps. Knopf.

1950 Award: *The Door in the Wall,* Marguerite de Angeli. Doubleday. (Kingswood: World's Work)

Honor books: *Tree of Freedom,* Rebecca Caudill. Viking.

The Blue Cat of Castle Town, Catherine Coblentz. Longmans.

Kildee House, Rutherford Montgomery. Doubleday. (London: Faber)

George Washington, Genevieve Foster. Scribner.

Song of the Pines, Walter and Marion Havighurst. Winston.

1951 Award: *Amos Fortune, Free Man,* Elizabeth Yates. Aladdin.

Honor books: *Better Known as Johnny Appleseed,* Mabel Leigh Hunt. Lippincott.

Gandhi, Fighter Without a Sword, Jeanette Eaton. Morrow.

Abraham Lincoln, Friend of the People, Clara Ingram Judson. Wilcox and Follett.

The Story of Appleby Capple, Anne Parrish. Harper.

1952 Award: *Ginger Pye,* Eleanor Estes. Harcourt. (London: Bodley Head)

Honor books: *Americans Before Columbus,* Elizabeth Baity. Viking.

Minn of the Mississippi, Holling C. Holling. Houghton Mifflin.

The Defender, Nicholas Kalashnikoff. Scribner. (London: Oxford University Press)

The Light at Tern Rock, Julia Sauer. Viking.

The Apple and the Arrow, Mary and Conrad Buff. Houghton Mifflin.

1953 Award: *Secret of the Andes,* Ann Nolan Clark. Viking.

Honor books: *Charlotte's Web,* E. B. White. Harper. (London: Hamish Hamilton)

Moccasin Trail, Eloise McGraw. Coward-McCann.

Red Sails to Capri, Ann Weil. Viking.

The Bears on Hemlock Mountain, Alice Dalgliesh. Scribner. (London: Epworth Press)

Birthdays of Freedom, Vol. I., Genevieve Foster. Scribner.

1954 Award: *. . . and now Miguel,* Joseph Krumgold. Crowell.

Honor books: *All Alone,* Claire Huchet Bishop. Viking.

Shadrach, Meindert DeJong. Harper. (London: Lutterworth Press)

Hurry Home Candy, Meindert DeJong. Harper. (London: Lutterworth Press)

Theodore Roosevelt, Fighting Patriot, Clara Ingram Judson. Follett.

Magic Maize, Mary and Conrad Buff. Houghton Mifflin.

1955 Award: *The Wheel on the School,* Meindert DeJong. Harper. (London: Lutterworth Press)

Honor books: *Courage of Sarah Noble,* Alice Dalgliesh. Scribner. (London: Hamish Hamilton)

Banner in the Sky, James Ullman. Lippincott. (London: Collins)

1956 Award: *Carry On, Mr. Bowditch,* Jean Lee Latham. Houghton Mifflin.

Honor books: *The Secret River,* Marjorie Kinnan Rawlings. Scribner.

The Golden Name Day, Jennie Lindquist. Harper.

Men, Microscopes, and Living Things, Katherine Shippen. Viking. (London: Phoenix House)

1957 Award: *Miracles on Maple Hill,* Virginia Sorensen. Harcourt.

Honor books: *Old Yeller,* Fred Gipson. Harper. (London: Hodder)

The House of Sixty Fathers, Meindert DeJong. Harper. (London: Lutterworth Press)

Mr. Justice Holmes, Clara Ingram Judson. Follett.

The Corn Grows Ripe, Dorothy Rhoads. Viking.

Black Fox of Lorne, Marguerite de Angeli. Doubleday. (Kingswood: World's Work)

1958 Award: *Rifles for Watie,* Harold Keith. Crowell. (London: Oxford University Press)

Honor books: *The Horsecatcher,* Mari Sandoz. Westminster. (Leicester: Brockhampton)

Gone-Away Lake, Elizabeth Enright. Harcourt. (London: Heinemann)

The Great Wheel, Robert Lawson. Viking. (London: Angus and Robertson)

Tom Paine, Freedom's Apostle, Leo Gurko. Crowell.

1959 Award: *The Witch of Blackbird Pond,* Elizabeth George Speare. Houghton Mifflin. (London: Gollancz)

Honor books: *The Family Under the Bridge,* Natalie S. Carlson. Harper.

Along Came a Dog, Meindert DeJong. Harper. (London: Lutterworth Press)

Chicaro: Wild Pony of the Pampa, Francis Kalnay. Harcourt. (London: Macmillan)

The Perilous Road, William O. Steele. Harcourt. (London: Macmillan)

1960 Award: *Onion John,* Joseph Krumgold. Crowell. (London: Lutterworth Press)

Honor books: *My Side of the Mountain,* Jean George. Dutton. (London: Bodley Head)

America Is Born, Gerald W. Johnson. Morrow.

The Gammage Cup, Carol Kendall. Harcourt. (London: Dent. Published as *The Minnipins)*

1961 Award: *Island of the Blue Dolphins,* Scott O'Dell. Houghton Mifflin. (Harmondsworth: Longman/Kestrel)

Honor books: *America Moves Forward,* Gerald W. Johnson. Morrow.

Old Ramon, Jack Schaeffer. Houghton Mifflin. (London: Deutsch)

Cricket in Times Square, George Seldon, *pseud.* (George Thompson). Farrar, Straus. (London: Dent)

1962 Award: *The Bronze Bow,* Elizabeth George Speare. Houghton Mifflin. (London: Gollancz)

Honor books: *Frontier Living,* Edwin Tunis. World.
The Golden Goblet, Eloise Jarvis McGraw. Coward-McCann.
(Harmondsworth: Longman/Kestrel)
Belling the Tiger, Mary Stolz. Harper.

1963 Award: *A Wrinkle in Time,* Madeleine L'Engle. Farrar, Straus. (Harmondsworth: Longman/Kestrel)

Honor books: *Thistle and Thyme: Tales and Legends from Scotland,* Sorche Nic Leodhas, *pseud.* (Leclaire Alger). Holt. (London: Bodley Head)
Men of Athens, Olivia Coolidge. Houghton Mifflin. (London: Bodley Head)

1964 Award: *It's Like This, Cat,* Emily Neville. Harper. (London: Angus and Robertson)

Honor books: *Rascal,* Sterling North. Dutton. (Leicester: Brockhampton)
The Loner, Ester Wier. McKay. (Harmondsworth: Longman/-Kestrel)

1965 Award: *Shadow of a Bull,* Maia Wojciechowska. Atheneum.
Honor book: *Across Five Aprils,* Irene Hunt. Follett. (London: Bodley Head)

1966 Award: *I, Juan de Pareja,* Elizabeth Borton de Treviño. Farrar. (London: Gollancz)

Honor Book: *The Black Cauldron,* Lloyd Alexander. Holt. (London: Heinemann)
The Animal Family, Randall Jarrell. Pantheon. (London: Hart-Davis)
The Noonday Friends, Mary Stolz. Harper.

1967 Award: *Up A Road Slowly,* Irene Hunt. Follett. (London: Macdonald)
Honor books: *The King's Fifth,* Scott O'Dell. Houghton-Mifflin. (Harmondsworth: Longman/Kestrel)
Zlateh the Goat and Other Stories, Isaac Bashevis Singer. Harper. (Harmondsworth: Longman/Kestrel)
The Jazz Man, Mary Hays Weik. Atheneum.

1968 Award: *From the Mixed-Up Files of Mrs. Basil E. Frankweiler,* E. L. Konigsburg. Atheneum. (London: Macmillan)

Honor books: *Jennifer, Hecate, Macbeth, William McKinley and Me, Elizabeth,* E. L. Konigsburg. Atheneum. (London: Macmillan)
The Black Pearl, Scott O'Dell. Houghton. (Harmondsworth: Longman/Kestrel)
The Fearsome Inn, Isaac Bashevis Singer. Scribner.
The Egypt Game, Zilpha Keatley Snyder. Atheneum.

1969 Award: *The High King,* Lloyd Alexander. Holt.
Honor books: *To Be a Slave,* Julius Lester. Dial. (Harmondsworth: Longman/Kestrel)
When Shlemiel Went to Warsaw and Other Stories, Isaac Bashevis Singer. Farrar. (Harmondsworth: Longman/Kestrel)

1970 Award: *Sounder,* William Armstrong. Harper. (London: Gollancz)
Honor books: *Our Eddie,* Sulamith Ish-Kishor. Pantheon.

The Many Ways of Seeing: An Introduction to the Pleasures of Art, Janet Gaylord Moore. World.

Journey Outside, Mary Q. Steele. Viking. (London: Macmillan)

1971 Award: *The Summer of the Swans,* Betsy Byars. Viking.

Honor books: *Kneeknock Rise,* Natalie Babbitt. Farrar.

Enchantress from the Stars, Sylvia Louise Engdahl. Atheneum.

Sing Down the Moon, Scott O'Dell. Houghton-Mifflin. (London: Hamish Hamilton)

1972 Award: *Mrs. Frisby and the Rats of NIMH,* Robert C. O'Brien. Atheneum. (London: Gollancz)

Honor books: *Incident at Hawk's Hill,* Allan W. Eckert. Little, Brown. (London: Hamish Hamilton)

The Planet of Junior Brown, Virginia Hamilton. Macmillan.

The Tombs of Atuan, Ursula K. Le Guin. Atheneum. (London: Gollancz)

Annie and the Old One, Miska Miles. Little, Brown.

The Headless Cupid, Zilpha Keatley Snyder. Atheneum.

1973 Award: *Julie of the Wolves,* Jean Craighead George. Harper. (London: Hamish Hamilton)

Honor books: *Frog and Toad Together,* Arnold Lobel. Harper. (Kingswood: World's Work)

The Upstairs Room, Johanna Reiss. Crowell.

The Witches of Worm, Zilpha Keatley Snyder. Atheneum.

1974 Award: *The Slave Dancer,* Paula Fox. Bradbury Press. (London: Macmillan)

Honor Book: *The Dark is Rising,* Susan Cooper. Atheneum/A Margaret McElderry Book. (London: Chatto & Windus)

II. CALDECOTT AWARD: 1938-1974

1938 Award: *Animals of the Bible, A Picture Book.* Illustrated by Dorothy P. Lathrop. Text selected by Helen Dean Fish. Lippincott. (London: Woodfield)

Honor books: *Seven Simeons: a Russian Tale.* Retold and illustrated by Boris Artzybasheff. Viking. (London: Cassell)

Four and Twenty Blackbirds ... Illustrated by Robert Lawson. Compiled by Helen Dean Fish. Stokes. (London: Hutchinson)

1939 Award: *Mei Li.* Illustrated and written by Thomas Handforth. Doubleday. (Kingswood: World's Work)

Honor books: *The Forest Pool.* Story and pictures by Laura Adams Armer. Longmans.

Wee Gillis. Illustrated by Robert Lawson. Text by Munroe Leaf. Viking. (London: Hamish Hamilton)

Snow White and the Seven Dwarfs. Freely translated and illustrated by Wanda Gág. Coward-McCann. (London: Faber)

Barkis. Story and pictures by Clare Newberry. Harper. (London: Hamish Hamilton)

Andy and the Lion. Written and illustrated by James Daugherty. Viking.

1940 Award: *Abraham Lincoln.* Written and illustrated by Ingri and Edgar d'Aulaire. Doubleday.

Honor books: *Cock-a-doodle Doo . . .* Story and pictures by Berta and Elmer Hader. Macmillan. (London: Collier-Macmillan)

Madeline. Story and pictures by Ludwig Bemelmans. Viking. (London: Deutsch)

The Ageless Story. Illustrated by Lauren Ford. Dodd Mead.

1941 Award: *They Were Strong and Good.* Written and illustrated by Robert Lawson. Viking.

Honor books: *April's Kittens.* Story and pictures by Clare Turlay Newberry. Harper. (London: Hamish Hamilton)

1942 Award: *Make Way for Ducklings.* Written and illustrated by Robert McCloskey. Viking. (Oxford: Shakespeare Head Press)

Honor books: *An American ABC.* Text and pictures by Maud and Miska Petersham. Macmillan.

In My Mother's House. Illustrated by Velino Herrera. Text by Ann Nolan Clark. Viking.

Paddle-to-the-Sea. Written and illustrated by Holling C. Holling. Houghton Mifflin. (London: Collins)

Nothing At All. Story and pictures by Wanda Gág. Coward-McCann. (London: Faber)

1943 Award: *The Little House.* Written and illustrated by Virginia Lee Burton. Houghton Mifflin. (London: Museum Press)

Honor books: *Dash and Dart.* Story and pictures by Mary and Conrad Buff. Viking.

Marshmallow. Story and pictures by Clare Turlay Newberry. Harper. (London: Hamish Hamilton)

1944 Award: *Many Moons.* Illustrated by Louis Slobodkin. Written by James Thurber. Harcourt. (London: Hamish Hamilton)

Honor books: *Small Rain: Verses from the Bible.* Illustrated by Elizabeth Orton Jones. Verses selected by Jessie Orton Jones. Viking.

Pierre Pidgeon. Illustrated by Arnold E. Bare. Text by Lee Kingman. Houghton Mifflin.

The Mighty Hunter. Story and pictures by Berta and Elmer Hader. Macmillan. (London: Collier-Macmillan)

A Child's Good Night Book. Illustrated by Jean Charlot. Text by Margaret Wise Brown. W. R. Scott.

Good-Luck Horse. Illustrated by Plato Chan. Text by Chih-Yi Chan. Whittlesey. (London: Collins)

1945 Award: *Prayer for a Child.* Illustrated by Elizabeth Orton Jones. Written by Rachel Field. Macmillan.

Honor books: *Mother Goose.* Illustrated by Tasha Tudor. Walck.

In the Forest. Story and pictures by Marie Hall Ets. Viking. (London: Faber)

Yonie Wondernose. Written and illustrated by Marguerite de Angeli. Doubleday.

The Christmas Anna Angel. Illustrated by Kate Seredy. Written by Ruth Sawyer. Viking. (London: Cassell)

1946 Award: *The Rooster Crows . . .* Illustrated by Maud and Miska Petersham. Macmillan.

Honor books: *Little Lost Lamb.* Illustrated by Leonard Weisgard. Text by Golden MacDonald, *pseud.* (Margaret Wise Brown). Doubleday.

Sing Mother Goose. Illustrated by Marjorie Torrey. Music by Opal Wheeler. Dutton.

My Mother Is the Most Beautiful Woman in the World. Illustrated by Ruth Gannett. Retold by Becky Reyher. Lothrop.

You Can Write Chinese. Text and illustrations by Kurt Wiese. Viking.

1947 Award: *The Little Island.* Illustrated by Leonard Weisgard. Written by Golden MacDonald, *pseud.* (Margaret Wise Brown). Doubleday. (Birmingham: Combridge)

Honor books: *Rain Drop Splash.* Illustrated by Leonard Weisgard. Story by Alvin Tresselt. Lothrop.

Boats on the River. Illustrated by Jay Hyde Barnum. Text by Marjorie Flack. Viking.

Timothy Turtle. Illustrated by Tony Palazzo. Written by Al Graham. Robert Welch Pub. Co.

Pedro, the Angel of Olvera Street. Text and illustrations by Leo Politi. Scribner.

Sing in Praise: a Collection of the Best Loved Hymns. Illustrated by Marjorie Torrey. Stories of hymns and musical arrangements by Opal Wheeler. Dutton.

1948 Award: *White Snow, Bright Snow.* Illustrated by Roger Duvoisin. Written by Alvin Tresselt. Lothrop.

Honor books: *Stone Soup.* Told and illustrated by Marcia Brown. Scribner.

McElligot's Pool. Written and illustrated by Dr. Seuss, *pseud.* (Theodor Seuss Geisel). Random House.

Bambino the Clown. Text and pictures by George Schreiber. Viking (London: Woodfield)

Roger and the Fox. Pictures by Hildegard Woodward. Text by Lavinia Davis. Doubleday.

Song of Robin Hood. Designed and illustrated by Virginia Lee Burton. Selected and edited by Anne Malcolmson. Houghton Mifflin.

1949 Award: *The Big Snow.* Written and illustrated by Berta and Elmer Hader. Macmillan.

Honor books: *Blueberries for Sal.* Written and illustrated by Robert McCloskey. Viking. (London: Angus and Robertson)
All Around the Town. Illustrated by Helen Stone. Text by Phyllis McGinley. Lippincott.
Juanita. Written and illustrated by Leo Politi. Scribner.
Fish in the Air. Story and pictures by Kurt Wiese. Viking.

1950 Award: *Song of the Swallows.* Written and illustrated by Leo Politi. Scribner.

Honor books: *America's Ethan Allen.* Pictures by Lynd Ward. Story by Stewart Holbrook. Houghton Mifflin.
The Wild Birthday Cake. Illustrated by Hildegard Woodward. Written by Lavinia R. Davis. Doubleday.
The Happy Day. Pictures by Marc Simont. Story by Ruth Krauss. Harper.
Bartholomew and the Oobleck. Written and illustrated by Dr. Seuss, *pseud.* (Theodor Seuss Geisel). Random House.
Henry Fisherman. Written and illustrated by Marcia Brown. Scribner.

1951 Award: *The Egg Tree.* Written and illustrated by Katherine Milhous. Scribner.

Honor books: *Dick Whittington and His Cat.* Told and illustrated by Marcia Brown. Scribner.
The Two Reds. Illustrated by Nicolas, *pseud.* (Nicolas Mordvinoff). Written by Will, *pseud.* (William Lipkind). Harcourt.
If I Ran the Zoo. Written and illustrated by Dr. Seuss, *pseud.* (Theodor Seuss Geisel). Random House.
The Most Wonderful Doll in the World. Illustrated by Helen Stone. Written by Phyllis McGinley. Lippincott.
T-Bone, the Baby Sitter. Story and pictures by Claire Turlay Newberry. Harper.

1952 Award: *Finders Keepers.* Illustrated by Nicolas, *pseud.* (Nicolas Mordvinoff). Written by Will, *pseud.* (William Lipkind). Harcourt. (Kingswood: World's Work)

Honor books: *Mr. T. W. Anthony Woo.* Story and pictures by Marie Hall Ets. Viking.
Skipper John's Cook. Written and illustrated by Marcia Brown. Scribner.
All Falling Down. Illustrated by Margaret Bloy Graham. Written by Gene Zion. Harper.
Bear Party. Written and illustrated by William Pène du Bois. Viking.
Feather Mountain. Written and illustrated by Elizabeth Olds. Houghton Mifflin.

1953 Award: *The Biggest Bear.* Written and illustrated by Lynd Ward. Houghton Mifflin. (London: Scholastic)

Honor books: *Puss in Boots.* Illustrated and translated from Charles Perrault by Marcia Brown. Scribner.

One Morning in Maine. Written and illustrated by Robert McCloskey. Viking.

Ape in a Cape: An Alphabet of Odd Animals. Text and pictures by Fritz Eichenberg. Harcourt.

The Storm Book. Illustrated by Margaret Bloy Graham. Written by Charlotte Zolotow. Harper.

Five Little Monkeys. Story and illustrations by Juliet Kepes. Houghton Mifflin.

1954 Award: *Madeline's Rescue.* Written and illustrated by Ludwig Bemelmans. Viking. (London: Deutsch)

Honor books: *Journey Cake, Ho!* Illustrated by Robert McCloskey. Text by Ruth Sawyer. Viking.

When Will the World Be Mine? Illustrated by Jean Charlot. Written by Miriam Schlein. W. R. Scott.

The Steadfast Tin Soldier. Illustrated by Marcia Brown. Story by Hans Christian Andersen, trans. by M. R. James. Scribner.

A Very Special House. Illustrated by Maurice Sendak. Written by Ruth Krauss. Harper.

Green Eyes. Story and pictures by A. Birnbaum. Capitol Pub.

1955 Award: *Cinderella, or the Little Glass Slipper.* Illustrated and translated from Perrault by Marcia Brown. Scribner.

Honor books: *Book of Nursery and Mother Goose Rhymes.* Illustrated by Marguerite de Angeli. Doubleday.

Wheel on the Chimney. Illustrated by Tibor Gergely. Written by Margaret Wise Brown. Lippincott.

The Thanksgiving Story. Illustrated by Helen Sewell. Text by Alice Dalgliesh. Scribner.

1956 Award: *Frog Went A-Courtin'.* Illustrated by Feodor Rojankovsky. Text retold by John Langstaff. Harcourt. (Kingswood: World's Work)

Honor books: *Play With Me.* Story and pictures by Marie Hall Ets. Viking.

Crow Boy. Written and illustrated by Taro Yashima. Viking.

1957 Award: *A Tree Is Nice.* Illustrated by Marc Simont. Written by Janice May Udry. Harper. (Kingswood: World's Work)

Honor books: *Mr. Penny's Race Horse.* Written and illustrated by Marie Hall Ets. Viking. (London: Woodfield)

1 Is One. Story and pictures by Tasha Tudor. Walck.

Anatole. Illustrated by Paul Galdone. Written by Eve Titus. McGraw-Hill. (London: Bodley Head)

Gillespie and the Guards. Illustrated by James Daugherty. Written by Benjamin Elkin. Viking.

Lion. Written and illustrated by William Pène du Bois. Viking.

1958 Award: *Time of Wonder.* Written and illustrated by Robert McCloskey. Viking.

Honor books: *Fly High, Fly Low.* Story and pictures by Don Freeman. Viking.
Anatole and the Cat. Illustrated by Paul Galdone. Written by Eve Titus. McGraw-Hill. (London: Bodley Head)

1959 Award: *Chanticleer and the Fox.* Adapted from Chaucer's *The Canterbury Tales* and illustrated by Barbara Cooney. Crowell. (Harmondsworth: Longman/Kestrel)

Honor books: *The House that Jack Built: La Maison Que Jacques A Batie.* Text and illustrations by Antonio Frasconi. Harcourt.
What Do You Say, Dear? Illustrated by Maurice Sendak. Written by Sesyle Joslin. W. R. Scott. (London: Faber)
Umbrella. Story and pictures by Taro Yashima. Viking.

1960 Award: *Nine Days to Christmas.* Illustrated by Marie Hall Ets. Written by Marie Hall Ets and Aurora Labastida. Viking.

Honor books: *Houses from the Sea.* Illustrated by Adrienne Adams. Written by Alice E. Goudey. Scribner.
The Moon Jumpers. Illustrated by Maurice Sendak. Written by Janice May Udry. Harper.

1961 Award: *Baboushka and the Three Kings.* Illustrated by Nicolas Sidjakov. Written by Ruth Robbins. Parnassus Press.

Honor books: *Inch by Inch.* Written and illustrated by Leo Lionni. Ivan Obolensky, Inc. (London: Dobson)

1962 Award: *Once a Mouse.* Retold and illustrated by Marcia Brown. Scribner.

Honor books: *The Fox Went Out on a Chilly Night; an Old Song.* Illustrated by Peter Spier. Doubleday. (Kingswood: World's Work)
Little Bear's Visit. Illustrated by Maurice Sendak. Written by Else H. Minarik. Harper. (Kingswood: World's Work)
The Day We Saw the Sun Come Up. Illustrated by Adrienne Adams. Written by Alice E. Goudey. Scribner.

1963 Award: *The Snowy Day.* Story and pictures by Ezra Jack Keats. Viking. (London: Bodley Head)

Honor books: *The Sun is a Golden Earring.* Illustrated by Bernarda Bryson. Text by Natalia M. Belting. Holt.
Mr. Rabbit and the Lovely Present. Illustrated by Maurice Sendak. Written by Charlotte Zolotow. Harper. (London: Bodley Head)

1964 Award: *Where the Wild Things Are.* Written and illustrated by Maurice Sendak. Harper. (London: Bodley Head)

Honor books: *Swimmy.* Story and pictures by Leo Lionni. Pantheon. (London: Dobson)
All in the Morning Early. Illustrated by Evaline Ness. Text by Sorche Nic Leodhas, *pseud.* (Leclaire Alger). Holt. (London: Bodley Head)
Mother Goose and Nursery Rhymes. Illustrated by Philip Reed. Atheneum. (London: Hamish Hamilton)

1965 Award: *May I Bring a Friend?* Illustrated by Beni Montresor. Written by Beatrice Schenk de Regniers. Atheneum. (London: Collins)

Honor books: *Rain Makes Applesauce.* Illustrated by Marvin Bileck. Written by Julian Scheer. Holiday House.

The Wave. Illustrated by Blair Lent. Written by Margaret Hodges. Houghton Mifflin.

A Pocketful of Cricket. Illustrated by Evaline Ness. Text by Rebecca Caudill. Holt.

1966 Award: *Always Room for One More.* Illustrated by Nonny Hogrogian. Written by Sorche Nic Leodhas, *pseud.* (Leclaire Alger). Holt.

Honor books: *Hide and Seek Fog.* Illustrated by Roger Duvoisin. Written by Alvin Tresselt. Lothrop. (Kingswood: World's Work)

Just Me. Written and illustrated by Marie Hall Ets. Viking. (London: Angus and Robertson)

Tom Tit Tot. Illustrated by Evaline Ness. Edited by Joseph Jacobs. Scribner.

1967 Award: *Sam, Bangs and Moonshine.* Written and illustrated by Evaline Ness. Holt. (London: Bodley Head)

Honor books: *One Wide River to Cross.* Illustrated by Ed Emberley. Adapted by Barbara Emberley. Prentice. (London: Chatto)

1968 Award: *Drummer Hoff.* Illustrated by Ed Emberley. Adapted by Barbara Emberley. Prentice. (London: Bodley Head)

Honor books: *Frederick.* Written and illustrated by Leo Lionni. Pantheon. (London: Abelard-Schuman)

Seashore Story. Written and illustrated by Taro Yashima. Viking.

The Emperor and the Kite. Illustrated by Ed Young. Written by Jane Yolen. World.

1969 Award: *The Fool of the World and the Flying Ship: A Russian Tale.* Illustrated by Uri Shulevitz. Retold by Arthur Ransome. Farrar.

Honor books: *Why the Sun and the Moon Live in the Sky: An African Folk Tale.* Illustrated by Blair Lent. Retold by Elphinstone Dayrell. Houghton-Mifflin.

1970 Award: *Sylvester and the Magic Pebble.* Written and illustrated by William Steig. Windmill/Simon. (London: Abelard-Schuman)

Honor books: *Goggles!* Written and illustrated by Ezra Jack Keats. Macmillan. (London: Bodley Head)

Alexander and the Wind-up Mouse. Written and illustrated by Leo Lionni. Pantheon. (London: Abelard-Schuman)

Pop Corn and Ma Goodness. Illustrated by Robert Andrew Parker. Written by Edna Mitchell Preston. Viking.

Thy Friend Obadiah. Written and illustrated by Brinton Turkle. Viking.

The Judge: An Untrue Tale. Illustrated by Margot Zemach. Written by Harve Zemach. Farrar. (London: Bodley Head)

1971 Award: *A Story, a Story: An African Tale.* Retold and illustrated by Gail E. Haley. Atheneum. (London: Methuen)

Honor books: *The Angry Moon.* Illustrated by Blair Lent. Retold by William Sleator. Little, Brown.

Frog and Toad Are Friends. Written and illustrated by Arnold Lobel. Harper. (Kingswood: World's Work)

In the Night Kitchen. Written and illustrated by Maurice Sendak. Harper. (London: Bodley Head)

1972 Award: *One Fine Day.* Illustrated and retold by Nonny Hogrogian. Macmillan. (London: Hamish Hamilton)

Honor books: *If All the Seas Were One Sea.* Written and Illustrated by Janina Domanska. Macmillan.

Moja Means One: Swahili Counting Book. Illustrated by Tom Feelings. Written by Muriel Feelings. Dial.

Hildilid's Night. Illustrated by Arnold Lobel. Written by Cheli Duran Ryan. Macmillan. (Harmondsworth: Longman/Kestrel)

1973 Award: *The Funny Little Woman.* Illustrated by Blair Lent. Retold by Arlene Mosel. Dutton. (Harmondsworth: Longman/Kestrel)

Honor books: *Anansi the Spider.* Adapted and illustrated by Gerald McDermott. Holt. (London: Hamish Hamilton)

Hosie's Alphabet. Illustrated by Leonard Baskin. Written by Hosea, Tobias and Lisa Baskin. Viking.

Snow White and the Seven Dwarfs. Illustrated by Nancy Ekholm Burkert. Translated by Randall Jarrell. Farrar. (Harmondsworth: Longman/Kestrel)

When Clay Sings. Illustrated by Tom Bahti. Written by Byrd Baylor. Scribner.

1974 Award: *Duffy and the Devil.* Illustrated by Margot Zemach. Retold by Harve Zemach. Farrar, Straus and Giroux. (Harmondsworth: Kestrel)

Honor books: *Three Jovial Huntsmen: A Mother Goose Rhyme.* Adapted and illustrated by Susan Jeffers. Bradbury Press. (London: Hamish Hamilton)

Cathedral: The Story of Its Construction. Written and illustrated by David Macauley. Houghton-Mifflin. (London: Collins)

The Laura Ingalls Wilder Award

Harriet G. Long

Harriet G. Long has been a professor in the library school of Case Western Reserve University and has written much on children's library service. Among her books are Rich the Treasure, Public Library Service to Children, *and* Wider Horizons in Library Service to Boys and Girls. *She is also the joint author of the frequently revised list,* Books Too Good To Miss, *published by Case Western Reserve University Press.*

The Wilder Award differs from the long established Newbery-Caldecott awards in several respects. First, the idea originated among children's librarians themselves. Second, the candidates are not only nominated, but are voted on, by the entire membership of the Children's Services Division. Third, the award is given not for one book considered in relationship to other books published that year, but is granted to an author or illustrator for his full work over a period of years. And, finally, it is not made annually, but every five years.

Children's librarians had long wished to express in some significant way their deep appreciation to Mrs. Wilder. This desire grew in intensity upon the publication, in 1953, of the beautiful new edition of the author's eight books, with illustrations by Garth Williams. The section for work with children of the California Library Association took the lead and appointed the Committee for Laura Ingalls Wilder.

On January 22, 1953, this committee sent a report to the Children's Library Association concerning recognition of Mrs. Wilder's place in the field of children's literature. The purpose was to determine what ideas might develop, or what steps might be taken on a nation-wide basis, "so that we, who work so closely with boys and girls and their books, and are most acutely aware of the debt of gratitude owed to Laura Ingalls Wilder, may seize the opportunity before it is too late, and have no occasion in the future to regret any possible inaction and procrastination." Among the ideas proposed was the establishment of an award in her name.

A year later, in February 1954, the Executive Board of the Children's Library Association "concluded with unanimity of feeling, based on widespread expression of hope and conviction from the membership, that it was important to honor Laura Ingalls Wilder." A Committee on the Laura Ingalls Wilder Award was appointed to draw up plans. Its members were Helen Kinsey and Effie Lee Morris, with Virginia Haviland as chairman. A draft of the committee's ideas was submitted to the membership of the Children's Library Association at the June 1954 business meeting, enthu-

"The Laura Ingalls Wilder Award" by Harriet G. Long from *Top of the News*, 21 (Jan. 1965): 131–133. Reprinted by permission of American Library Association.

siastically approved, and then sent through the Committee on Awards to the Executive Board of the American Library Association. All went well and the award became an actuality.

The terms of the award gradually took form; ideas were suggested and some abandoned. The final statement is as follows:

> The Laura Ingalls Wilder Medal shall be awarded to an author or illustrator whose books, published in the United States, have over a period of years made a substantial and lasting contribution to literature for children.

The Executive Board of the Children's Library Association decided to pay tribute to Mrs. Wilder at the June meeting in 1954 "for the lasting contribution which your books have made to literature for children. In future years the award shall be made in your name and be called the Laura Ingalls Wilder Award." Then eighty-seven years of age, the author regretted that her health would not permit a trip to Minneapolis, but sent a letter of appreciation in which she wrote: "When writing those memories of my long-ago childhood I had no idea they would be so well received and it is a continual delight to me that they should be so well loved." The medal, designed by Garth Williams, illustrator of the new edition of the Wilder books, was sent to Mrs. Wilder.

It was decided that in the future the award would be made each five years beginning with June 1960, thus bringing the event into easily remembered years—1960, 1965, etc. Thus, in 1958, a new Wilder Award Committee was appointed to prepare for awarding the second medal in 1960. Rosemary Livsey was the chairman, and the other members were Mary K. Eakin, Marion Herr, Isabella Jinnette, Georgianna Maar, and Effie Lee Morris. Since the first award to Mrs. Wilder had been a spontaneous expression of appreciation, no vote had been required. Consequently, it became the responsibility of this new committee to work out the time schedule and the many details for securing nominations by stimulating the participation of all members of the Children's Services Division. Eighty-three candidates were nominated. Six names appeared over and over, and these made up the ballot, which was prepared for membership vote.

The winner, Clara Ingram Judson, was not to be announced until the book awards banquet in Montreal, June 21, 1960. However, the news was released after the death of Mrs. Judson, on May 24, at the age of eighty-one. Fortunately, Mrs. Judson had known of the award in February and had written her acceptance speech, which was published in *The Horn Book Magazine*. Her daughter was present at the awards banquet to accept the medal.

The following procedures are used in the selection of a Laura Ingalls Wilder Award winner. A Wilder Award Committee of six members is appointed by the incoming president of the Children's Services Division to serve during the two years before the award is made. The first year the committee mails to the membership information about the Wilder Award with a request for nominations. In the second year, the committee prepares the ballot from the nominations, and then submits the ballot to the membership for a final vote.

The present committee, appointed in 1963, after having solicited nominations, is presenting three candidates to be voted on by members of the Children's Services Division. The names on the ballot which will be mailed to all members in late 1964 are: Ruth Sawyer, Katherine Shippen, and Elizabeth Yates. Frances Sullivan is the present chairman, and the other committee members are: Laura E. Cathon, Christine B. Gilbert, Harriet G. Long, Donna Secrest, and Ruth Hill Viguers.

Laura Ingalls Wilder Award Winners

1954:   Laura Ingalls Wilder
1960:   Clara Ingram Judson
1965:   Ruth Sawyer
1970:   E. B. White

Illustration by Garth Williams from *Little House on the Prairie* by Laura Ingalls Wilder. Copyright 1953 as to pictures by Garth Williams. Reprinted by permission of Harper & Row, Publishers. British edition published by Methuen.

The New National Book Award for Children's Literature

Virginia Haviland

Virginia Haviland has been chairman of the Newbery-Caldecott Committee (1953–1954), a member of the first National Book Award jury (1969), and president of the Hans Christian Andersen international awards jury (1972, 1974). For further biographical information, see p. 88.

Another award. . . .

Among the quick responses to news of the establishment of the National Book Award for Children's Literature—from veteran book selectors, sometime Newbery-Caldecott jurors, and other critics in the children's book world—one kind of remark has been prevalent and uncontested. It stresses the fact that the addition of an award for creative excellence in children's literature to the thousand-dollar awards already administered by the National Book Committee for important categories of adult literature firmly places children's books in the realm of literature as a whole—where thoughtful spokesmen on the subject have long argued it belongs.

A second reverberation, but one not reaching any consensus, has been the questioning of what another major children's book award based on recognition of creative writing would mean to the prestige of the American Library Association's annual Newbery Medal. Since the establishment of the latter by bibliophile Frederic G. Melcher in 1922, it has stood as the most significant, most coveted American citation for children's books. If there is any truth in the old cry that every new award somewhat diminishes the prestige of each of the other awards, then subject to such criticism are the Spring Book Awards, the Globe-Horn Book Awards, and any of the prizes open to a specific category of writing for children within a given period of time (we do note that for these just mentioned the publishing period under consideration differs in each case from that for the Newbery Medal). On the other hand, we have not heard (not loudly, at least) a clamoring for the elimination of awards; instead, there has come a demand for more, and more—for poetry, nonfiction, teen-agers' books, and illustration (not just for picture-book art). But the more opportunity for public attention to be directed to children's books, the better—whether for publishers' promotion, or for occasions provided for libraries to publicize special books, or for critics to wave their banners with an extra flourish.

The evidence is clear that the National Book Committee and the Children's Book Council, a co-sponsor of the new award, command the

"The New National Book Award for Children's Literature" by Virginia Haviland from *Horn Book Magazine*, 49 (June 1969): 283–286. Reprinted by permission of Horn Book, Inc.

ultimate in resources for promoting awards. I believe we must welcome this opportunity for publicity rather than worry about any parochial qualms as to competition. Because of the recognition of the importance of children's book departments in publishing houses, because of modern technical developments in bookmaking and illustration, and because of support from the vast selective purchasing by libraries and schools, the world of children's books has become a huge one, with the general level of quality rising over the years. Actually, in most years there appears no single "best" or "most"; from the long years of jury arguments I have been a part of I can attest to this.

The announcement of five nominees six weeks in advance of the final selection gives the new award a fresh image and a different send-off.[1] Presenting five titles allows for a range of recognition and broadens the scope of honors given. To make early announcement of the five is somewhat like offering five prizes to begin with—stirring up an increasing interest in anticipation of a final single winner.

To be one of the five is indeed significant. For the six weeks, these writers have equal status, and their publishers can make a great deal of the distinctions achieved. Always, in arriving at one top book a jury dealing with a year's or a season's titles has the formidable task of shifting from one genre to another: from fantasy to historical fiction, to a here-and-now story, to nonfiction of a creative kind—around and around the circle. How to compare? There is no way other than to measure the distinction of any one book against the total of its kind, present-day and earlier, and then to determine the levels of distinction.

Let us conclude with a look at the first year's National Book Award. Here among the five contenders in children's literature was 1969's Newbery Medal winner, *The High King* (Holt), Lloyd Alexander's fifth book in a cycle of tales about the mythological land of Prydain. The Newbery Medal's two runners-up—*When Schlemiel Went to Warsaw and Other Stories* by Isaac Bashevis Singer (Farrar) and *To Be a Slave* by Julius Lester (Dial)—were not among the five nominated. Instead there were Esther Hautzig's moving autobiographical account *The Endless Steppe* (Crowell)—about her years from ten to fifteen when her family was shipped from Poland to exile in Siberia; Patricia Clapp's *Constance* (Lothrop), a vivid historical romance set in early Plymouth Colony; Milton Meltzer's *Langston Hughes* (Crowell), a biography of the Negro poet; and the winning book, Meindert DeJong's *Journey from Peppermint Street* (Harper), which adds one more award to his long record of honors, including the Newbery Medal in 1955 for *The Wheel on the School* and the international Hans Christian Andersen Medal in 1962 for the total body of his work.

The award ceremonies on March 12 in Philharmonic Hall in New York City demonstrated the significance of the new regard for children's literature. The citation to Mr. DeJong reads: "To Meindert DeJong for

---

1. In 1972 the number of nominees was 10—Editor's note.

Journey from Peppermint Street, a recreation of the strange sweet world of a nine-year-old Dutch boy. Mr. DeJong has the gift of summoning child-marvelous experiences to his narrative, yet of containing them in his sure sense of childhood. His management of the interplays between child and adult is especially notable. The quality of his perceptions transforms this simple tale into a full experience of a small boy's unfolding world.

In his speech of acceptance the author stated:

> . . . The separate world of the child is a brief world because it is a world of wonder.
>
> Come into any afternoon of a child and into the simple wonder of the curl of smoke out of a chimney, or the agony of seeing a crippled bird wing-dragging across a lawn, or the loveliness seen in the curl of a sleeping cat that needs to be cradled in small arms and held tight. Or if that is too pleasant, the eternity of twenty minutes of a child's life as he waits before a closed door, desolate, alone and bereft.
>
> What can be more alone than a child? What separates this world from the adult world is, as I have said, wonder. But where does wonder go? In a few brief years it is stultified into adulthood. And its duration is shortened all the more because adults are eternal-ly—maybe necessarily—busy making the child adult and like unto themselves.
>
> One wonders why when one sees the mess the world is in. One wonders all the more because all the adult seems to have as a substitute for wonder is experience—the dreary convoluting round of the same thing repeating itself over and over. And that, woefully, seems to be the only superiority the adult holds over the child—experience—repetition with the wonder gone.
>
> And few seem to realize that it is precisely that wonder and that intensity of sensation (which are lost in adult stultification) that the child must draw on in order to grow and gain acceptance, assurance and security.
>
> Certainly, in terms of adult experience, the child's world and the world of children's literature are limited worlds. But it is in that very limitation that the writer for children finds his joy and his challenge and his untrammeled creativity. Braque said it right for painting; I say it after him for children's literature: "Limitation of means determines style, engenders form and new form, and gives impulse to creativity."
>
> These absolutes must be kept in mind when reaching as an adult author into the important separateness of the child's world. I am not, and must not be, aware of my audience when I write my books. I must be wholly subjective, conscious only of the particular limiting cage of form of the children's book into which I must shape and compress my creation. After some twenty books, I still have no idea of the age, school grade, and state of literacy of the child for whom I write. I write not only out of myself but also

for myself, necessarily shaping the work only to my particular cage of artistic form.

It does strike me, a bit impertinently and tongue in cheek, that while all these adult-writing colleagues of mine are today achieving one-sixth of an award, to children's literature you have given a whole seven-sevenths award . . . since children's literature comprises all six categories you are separately honoring here—from fiction through poetry to science. . . . [2]

British editions of books mentioned with their American publishers only in this article:

Isaac Bashevis Singer. *When Schlemiel Went to Warsaw and Other Stories.* Longman/Kestrel.

National Book Award Winners

1969: *Journey From Peppermint Street,* Meindert DeJong. Harper. (London: Lutterworth)

1970: *A Day of Pleasure: Stories of a Boy Growing Up in Warsaw,* Isaac Bashevis Singer. Farrar.

1971: *The Marvelous Misadventures of Sebastian,* Lloyd Alexander. Dutton.

1972: *The Slightly Irregular Fire Engine, or The Hithering, Thithering Djin,* Donald Barthelme. Farrar.

1973: *The Farthest Shore,* Ursula K. Le Guir. Atheneum. (London: Gollancz)

1974: *The Court of the Stone Children,* Eleanor Cameron. E. P. Dutton.

2. Reprinted by permission of Harper & Row, Publishers, Inc.

Looking for a Winner

Peggy Heeks

Peggy Heeks is an English children's librarian who has been active in serving the Youth Library Group of the Library Association, including chairmanship of its Carnegie-Greenaway Committee. Her professional writing, in addition to book reviews, includes: The Administration of Children's Libraries, *(1967),* Books of Reference for School Libraries *(2nd ed., 1968), and* Eleven to Fifteen: A Basic List of Non-Fiction for Secondary School Libraries *(3rd ed., 1963).*

The fact that this year I have been one of the Carnegie/Greenaway sub-committee is largely irrelevant, serving merely to concentrate the mind. Each year the Library Association invites all its members to submit suggestions for medal-winning books, so in the early spring many other than the selection committee are trying to spot the winners from the children's books of the previous twelve months. The suggestions from members are tabulated and provide a starting point for those making the final choice. The awards are not, however, decided by ballot. The decisions rest with the selection committee and some members feel that, in these circumstances, theirs is an empty exercise. Perhaps they will take heart from knowing that their views are a very real help and that this year these views and the committee's decisions were closely parallel. An article last year complained of the secrecy of the selection procedure. The committee's discussions are confidential, rightly so I believe: the names of the committee and their method of operation are not. Since 1967, when the role of Youth Libraries Group was increased, the selection committee has consisted of four representatives of the Publications Committee of the Library Association and four of Youth Libraries Group. The latter have a double task: they sit on the final selection committee and they also draw up the short-list which forms the basis of the discussions.

What are librarians looking for when choosing the award winners? By now a kind of mythology has grown up around the awards: they can never be awarded to the same person twice,[1] the Carnegie medal can be given either for an individual book or for a corpus of work, the Greenaway medal is for a picture-book, and so on. In fact, the terms are set out clearly. The Carnegie medal is "for an outstanding book." The Greenaway is given for "the most distinguished work in the illustration of children's books during the preceding year." It will be seen that the word "best" is carefully avoided. It would need bravery, and presumption, indeed to declare

---

1. In 1971 John Burningham became the first to receive a second medal.

unequivocally "This is the best book of the year," but one is looking for books which excel. Beginning by considering all the children's books published in the year, one reaches ɩ plateau of finely written, beautifully designed books and from this rise the peaks, the books which it is appropriate to judge by the highest standards. We are not looking for the most popular book, the most promising book, the most socially useful book—although all these have been suggested in the past as desirable aims. Books of this kind may merit recognition, but what the Library Association has decided to recognize is quality, and quality full-grown, not in the bud.

Looking for books of this kind, what do the selection committee find? Usually, a winner for each award. No book was considered worthy of the Carnegie medal last year—a matter of controversy—but otherwise the award has always been made except for two lean war years; the Kate Greenaway medal has been withheld twice. Usually a story wins the Carnegie medal, a picture-book the Greenaway: of twenty-nine Carnegie awards only four have gone to non-fiction, and a betting person would quickly see that the odds on fantasy are high. Walter Hodges stands out among the Greenaway winners as the one who did not illustrate a picture-book for young children. We also notice, looking at the list of Carnegie medallists since 1936, when the award was instituted, that the books do not all reach the same standard. To us today they do not all seem outstanding.

Let us make sure that we draw the right conclusions from these observations. We could say that the awards are made by people sold on fantasy and antipathetic to non-fiction, interested in picture-books rather than book illustration generally. This would ignore the selectors' dependence on the literary output of each year. The awards show where the best work tends to fall and which areas need attention. One of the disappointments to me this year is that no non-fiction book appears on the Carnegie honours list. We tried to find non-fiction which reached the standard of the many fine novels of the year: we did not find it and rarely have our predecessors. To suggest reasons for this would need an article on its own, but we have here an indication that we need to look critically at the state and status of information books. The choice of award winners must reflect the quality of the selectors and as the team changes so may the standard of the books chosen. It is no secret that some results have caused surprise and disappointment. It would be destructive to offer too much criticism. Finding fault with the selection committee's choice, like finding fault with other people's bibliographies, is a popular game: most of us play it, but it should be played with good will. Choosing the outstanding among contemporary writing is, and always has been, a risky business. What a let-down Henry James is on the writers of his own time, how shrewd on those of the past; how narrow Eliot appears confronted with the living: what a record this century can show of authors misjudged. Then we must realize what the selection committee is trying to do: it is marking the publication of work outstanding in its year, not selecting children's classics of the future.

We look at some of the early award winners and think "small beer"; we look at later ones and feel at home. We should not therefore decry the former but rather see the list as a mirror of the advance which children's books—and children—have made in the past thirty years.

What are the difficulties in this annual selection? There is the obvious fear that one may have completely overlooked the finest book of the year, a fear that haunts one irrationally however carefully one checks and rechecks. There is the problem of choosing between the top two or three books of the year. It is often very difficult to measure the distance between an award winner and a commended book, and this makes it particularly important to enhance the status of all the books which appear on the Library Association's honours list.

What is the value of the awards? The originators hoped that they would encourage the production of better children's books and that winners would "receive a hallmark of excellence which would have considerable publicity value." Brave hopes, perhaps not fully realized. Children's books have certainly improved since 1936 and book illustration has advanced since 1955 when the Greenaway medal was established, but it would be silly to see these changes as resulting solely from the Library Association's actions. The publicity value of the awards has never been very great: it is still the unusual parent or teacher who knows what they are. The need for more publicity has been a cry reiterated through the years. Each year we progress a little, and now that we have more outlets for news of children's books than ever before, and a growing realization that they are big business, we can hope to spread the interest further. But surely the significance of the awards goes beyond the official statement. They are the Library Association's recognition of the outstanding work of authors, illustrators, publishers; they are our annual celebration of the healthy state of children's literature in England; they are our thanks to those who give us the tools for our work. Thinking of them, I recall two sentences from *The Owl Service,* "Mind how you are looking at her," and "She wanted to be flowers and they made her owls." The awards are the Library Association's bouquets: let us mind how we look at them and keep them flowers.

Children's Book Medals

Times Literary Supplement

In future the Library Association's Carnegie and Kate Greenaway Medals will not be confined to British subjects. The field of choice is to include all children's books written in English and having their original publication in the United Kingdom during the year preceding the presentation of the awards. It is now clearly stated that the awards can be made to the same person more than once. Furthermore, the final selection is to be delegated entirely to the Youth Libraries Group of the Library Association, and a sub-committee, under the Chairmanship of Mrs. Peggy Heeks, is currently considering not only the composition of the selection committee, but also possible changes and improvements in procedure.

The Carnegie and Kate Greenaway Medals

The Carnegie Medal has been awarded annually since 1936 for an outstanding book for children written in English and published initially in the United Kingdom during the preceding year. At the end of each year recommendations for the award are invited from members of the Library Association, who are asked to submit a preliminary list of not more than three titles from which the Committee of the Youth Libraries Group makes a final selection. While it is not possible to lay down criteria applicable to every category of book, the following criteria for fiction and information books may act as a general guide: choice of works of fiction is based upon consideration of (1) plot, (2) style, (3) characterization; choice of information books is based upon (1) accuracy, (2) method of presentation, (3) style, and (4) format. The medal can be awarded to an author more than once.

The Kate Greenaway Medal, named after one of the nineteenth-century artists who had created a new kind of picture-book for children, has been awarded annually since 1955 to recognize the importance of illustrations in children's books. It is awarded to the artist who, in the opinion of the Library Association, has produced the most distinguished work in the illustration of children's books initially published in the United Kingdom during the preceding year. Recommendations for the award are invited from members of the Library Association, who are asked to submit a preliminary list of not more than three titles. Books intended for older as well as younger children are included, and reproduction will be taken into account. The medal can be awarded to an illustrator more than once.

"The Library Association Carnegie Medal" by the Secretary. Reprinted by permission of The Library Association.

"The Library Association Kate Greenaway Medal" by the Secretary. Reprinted by permission of The Library Association.

Carnegie Medal Winners

1936: *Pigeon Post.* Arthur Ransome. Jonathan Cape.

1937: *The Family from One End Street.* Frederick Muller. (New York: Vanguard Press)

1938: *The Circus is Coming.* Noel Streatfeild. J. M. Dent.

1939: *The Radium Woman.* Eleanor Doorly. William Heinemann.

1940: *Visitors from London.* Kitty Barne. J. M. Dent.

1941: *We Couldn't Leave Dinah.* Mary Treadgold. Jonathan Cape. (New York: Penguin Books)

1942: *The Little Grey Men.* "B.B." (D. J. Watkins-Pitchford). Eyre & Spottiswoode.

1943: Award withheld as no book considered suitable.

1944: *The Wind on the Moon.* Eric Linklater. Macmillan.

1945: Award withheld as no book considered suitable.

1946: *The Little White Horse.* Elizabeth Goudge. Brockhampton Press. (New York: Coward, McCann and Geoghegan)

1947: *Collected Stories for Children.* Walter de la Mare. Faber and Faber.

1948: *Sea Change.* Richard Armstrong. J. M. Dent.

1949: *The Story of Your Home.* Agnes Allen. Faber and Faber. (New York: Transatlantic Press)

1950: *The Lark on the Wing.* Elfrida Vipont. Oxford University Press.

1951: *The Wool-pack.* Cynthia Harnett. Methuen

1952: *The Borrowers.* Mary Norton. J. M. Dent. (New York: Harcourt Brace Jovanovich)

1953: *A Valley Grows Up.* Edward Osmond. Oxford University Press.

1954: *Knight Crusaders.* Ronald Welch. Oxford University Press.
Commended
The Children of Green Knowe. Lucy M. Boston. Faber and Faber. (New York: Harcourt Brace Jovanovich)
Over the Hills to Fabylon. Nicholas Stuart Gray. Dennis Dobson. (New York: Hawthorn Books)
The Horse and His Boy. C. S. Lewis. William Collins. (New York: Macmillan)
Lady of the Linden Tree. Barbara Leonie Picard. Oxford University Press. (New York: Criterion Books)
English Fables and Fairy Stories. James Reeves. Oxford University Press. (New York: Henry Z. Walck)
The Eagle of the Ninth. Rosemary Sutcliff. Oxford University Press. (New York: Henry Z. Walck)
Special Commendation
Lavender's Blue. Kathleen Lines. Oxford University Press.

"Honours List, The Carnegie & Kate Greenaway Medals." Reprinted by permission of the Kent County Library.

1955:   *The Little Bookroom.* Eleanor Farjeon. Oxford University Press. (New York: Henry Z. Walck)
        Commended
        Man Must Measure. Lancelot Hogben. Macdonald.
        Candidate for Fame. Margaret Jowett. Oxford University Press.
        The Story of Albert Schweitzer. Jo Manton. (New York: Abelard-Schumann)
        A Swarm in May. William Mayne. Oxford University Press.
        Minnow on the Say. Philippa A. Pearce. Oxford University Press.
1956:   *The Last Battle.* C. S. Lewis. Bodley Head. (New York: Macmillan)
        Commended
        The Fairy Doll. Rumer Godden. Macmillan. (New York: The Viking Press)
        Chorister's Cake. William Mayne. Oxford University Press.
        The Member for the Marsh. William Mayne. Oxford University Press.
        Ransom for a Knight. Barbara Leonie Picard. Oxford University Press. (New York: Henry Z. Walck)
        The Silver Sword. Ian Serrailler. Jonathan Cape. (New York: S. G. Phillips)
        The Shield Ring. Rosemary Sutcliff. Oxford University Press. (New York: Henry Z. Walck)
1957:   *A Grass Rope.* William Mayne. Oxford University Press. (New York: E. P. Dutton)
        Commended
        The Warden's Niece. Gillian Avery. William Collins.
        Songbird's Grove. Anne Barrett. William Collins.
        Falconer's Lure. Antonia Forest. Faber and Faber.
        The Blue Boat. William Mayne. Oxford University Press. (New York: E. P. Dutton)
        Story of the Second World War. Kathleen Savage. Bodley Head. (New York: Henry Z. Walck)
        The Silver Branch. Rosemary Sutcliff. Oxford University Press. (New York: Henry Z. Walck)
1958:   *Tom's Midnight Garden.* Philippa A. Pearce. Oxford University Press. (New York: J. B. Lippincott)
        Commended
        The Chimneys of Green Knowe. Lucy M. Boston. Faber and Faber. (New York: Harcourt Brace Jovanovich)
        Warrior Scarlet. Rosemary Sutcliff. Oxford University Press. (New York: Henry Z. Walck)
1959:   *The Lantern Bearers.* Rosemary Sutcliff. Oxford University Press. (New York: Henry Z. Walck)
        Commended
        The Load of Unicorn. Cynthia Harnett. Methuen.
        The Borrowers Afloat. Mary Norton. J. M. Dent. (New York: Harcourt Brace Jovanovich)

The Rescuers. Margery Sharp. William Collins. (Boston: Little, Brown)

Friday's Tunnel. John Verney. William Collins. (New York: Holt, Rinehart and Winston)

Quiet as Moss. Andrew Young. Hart-Davis. (New York: Dufour Editions)

1960: *The Making of Man.* Ian W. Cornwall and Howard M. Maitland. Phoenix House. (New York: E. P. Dutton)

1961: *A Stranger at Green Knowe.* Lucy M. Boston. Faber and Faber. (New York: Harcourt Brace Jovanovich)

Commended

Peter's Room. Antonia Forest. Faber and Faber.

Miss Happiness and Miss Flower. Rumer Godden. Macmillan. (New York: The Viking Press)

Ragged Robin. James Reeves. William Heinemann. (New York: E. P. Dutton)

February's Road. John Verney. William Collins. (New York: Holt, Rinehart and Winston)

1962: *The Twelve and the Genii.* Pauline Clarke. Faber and Faber. (New York: Coward, McCann and Geoghegan)

Commended

The Greatest Gresham. Gillian Avery. William Collins.

Castors Away. Hester Burton. Oxford University Press. (New York: World)

Armour and Blade. S. E. Ellacott. Abelard-Schumann.

The Summer Birds. Penelope Farmer. Chatto and Windus. (New York: Harcourt Brace Jovanovich)

The Story of John Keats. Robert Gittings and Jo Manton. Methuen. (New York: E. P. Dutton)

Windfall. K. M. Peyton. Oxford University Press.

1963: *Time of Trial.* Hester Burton. Oxford University Press. (New York: World)

Commended

The Latchkey Children. Eric Allen. Oxford University Press.

Kings, Bishops, Knights and Pawns: Life in a Feudal Society. Ralph Arnold. Longman/Kestrel. (New York: W. W. Norton)

Castaway Christmas. M. J. Baker. Methuen. (New York: Farrar, Straus and Giroux)

The Thursday Kidnapping. Antonia Forest. Faber and Faber. (New York: Coward, McCann and Geoghegan)

Hell's Edge. John Rowe Townsend. Hutchinson. (New York: Penguin Books)

1964: *Nordy Bank.* Sheena Porter. Oxford University Press. (New York: Roy)

Commended

London's River. Eric de Mare. Bodley Head. (New York: McGraw-Hill)

The Three Brothers of Ur. J. G. Fyson. Oxford University Press. (New York: Coward, McCann and Geoghegan)

The Namesake. C. Walter Hodges. G. Bell. (New York: Coward, McCann and Geoghegan)

The Maplin Bird. K. M. Peyton. Oxford University Press. (New York: World)

1965: *The Grange at High Force.* Philip Turner. Oxford University Press. (New York: World)

Commended

The Journey of the Eldest Son. J. G. Fyson. Oxford University Press. (New York: Coward, McCann and Geoghegan)

Elidor. Alan Garner. William Collins. (New York: Henry Z. Walck)

The Bus Girls. Mary K. Harris. Faber and Faber. (New York: W. W. Norton)

The Orchestra and Its Instruments. Christopher Headington. Bodley Head. (New York: World)

The Plan for Birdsmarsh. K. M. Peyton. Oxford University Press. (New York: World)

One is One. Barbara Leonie Picard. Oxford University Press. (New York: Holt, Rinehart and Winston)

1966: Award withheld as no book considered suitable.

Highly Commended

The Bayeux Tapestry: The Story of the Norman Conquest. Norman Denny and Josephine Filmer-Sankey. William Collins. (New York: Atheneum)

Commended

The Wild Horse of Santander. Helen Griffiths. Hutchinson. (New York: Doubleday)

Thunder in the Sky. K. M. Peyton. Oxford University Press. (New York: World)

Marassa and Midnight. Morna Stuart. William Heinemann. (New York: McGraw-Hill)

1967: *The Owl Service.* Alan Garner. William Collins. (New York: Henry Z. Walck)

Commended

The Dream Time. Henry Treece. Brockhampton Press. (New York: Meredith)

The Piemakers. Helen Cresswell. Faber and Faber. (New York: J. B. Lippincott)

Smith. Leon Garfield. Longman/Kestrel. (New York: Pantheon)

Flambards. K. M. Peyton. Oxford University Press. (New York: World)

1968 *The Moon in the Cloud.* Rosemary Harris. Faber and Faber. (New York: Macmillan)

Honors List

Whispering Mountain. Joan Aiken. Jonathan Cape. (New York: Doubleday)

When Jays Fly to Barbmo. Margaret Balderson. Oxford University Press.

Black Jack. Leon Garfield. Longman/Kestrel. (New York: Pantheon)

1969: *The Edge of the Cloud* (for the Flambards trilogy). K. M. Peyton. Oxford University Press. (New York: World)

Honors List

The Nightwatchman. Helen Cresswell. Faber and Faber. (New York: Macmillan)

The Intruder. John Rowe Townsend. Oxford University Press. (New York: J. B. Lippincott)

1970: *The God Beneath the Sea.* Edward Blishen and Leon Garfield. Longman/Kestrel. (New York: Pantheon)

Honors List

The Devil's Children. Peter Dickinson. Victor Gollancz. (Boston: Little, Brown)

The Drummer Boy. Leon Garfield. Longman/Kestrel. (New York: Pantheon)

Ravensgill. William Mayne. Hamish Hamilton. (New York: E. P. Dutton)

1971: *Josh.* Ivan Southall. Angus & Robertson. (New York: Macmillan)

Highly Commended

A Likely Lad. Gillian Avery. William Collins. (New York: Holt, Rinehart and Winston)

Up the Pier. Helen Cresswell. Faber and Faber. (New York: Macmillan)

Tristan and Iseult. Rosemary Sutcliff. Bodley Head. (New York: E. P. Dutton)

1972: *Watership Down.* Richard Adams. Rex Collings. (New York: Macmillan)

Commended

The Dancing Bear. Peter Dickinson. Victor Gollancz. (Boston: Little, Brown)

No Way of Telling. Emma Smith. Bodley Head. (New York: Atheneum)

1973: *The Ghost of Thomas Kempe.* Penelope Lively. William Heinemann. (New York: E. P. Dutton)

Commended

Bongleweed. Helen Cresswell. Faber and Faber. (New York: Macmillan)

Carrie's War. Nina Bawden. Victor Gollancz. (New York: J. B. Lippincott)

The Dark is Rising. Susan Cooper. Chatto and Windus. (New York: Atheneum)

Julius Lester. *To Be a Slave.* Longman/Kestrel.

Esther Hautzig. *The Endless Steppe.* Hamish Hamilton.

Kate Greenaway Medal Winners

1955: Award withheld as no book considered suitable.

1956: Edward Ardizzone. *Tim All Alone.* Oxford University Press. (New York: Henry Z. Walck)

1957: V. H. Drummond. *Mrs. Easter and the Storks.* Faber and Faber.

1958: Award withheld as no book considered suitable.

1959: William Stobbs. *Kashtanka* and *A Bundle of Ballads.* Oxford University Press. (New York: J. B. Lippincott)
Commended
Edward Ardizzone. *Titus in Trouble.* Bodley Head. (New York: Henry Z. Walck)
Gerald Rose. *Wuffles Goes to Town.* Faber and Faber.

1960: Gerald Rose. *Old Winkle and the Seagulls.* Faber and Faber.

1961: Antony Maitland. *Mrs. Cockle's Cat.* Longman/Kestrel. (New York: J. B. Lippincott)

1962: Brian Wildsmith. *Brian Wildsmith's ABC.* Oxford University Press. (New York: Franklin Watts)
Commended
Carol Barker. *Achilles the Donkey.* Dennis Dobson. (New York: Franklin Watts)

1963: John Burningham. *Borka: The Adventures of a Goose with No Feathers.* Jonathan Cape. (New York: Random House)
Commended
Victor G. Ambrus. *The Royal Navy* and *Time of Trial.* Oxford University Press. (New York: World)
Brian Wildsmith. *The Lion and the Rat* and *The Oxford Book of Poetry for Children.* Oxford University Press. (New York: Franklin Watts)

1964: C. Walter Hodges. *Shakespeare's Theatre.* Oxford University Press. (New York: Coward-McCann)
For their work in general: Victor G. Ambrus and William Papas.
Raymond Briggs. *Fee Fi Fo Fum.* Hamish Hamilton. (New York: Coward-McCann)

1965: Victor G. Ambrus. *The Three Poor Tailors.* Hamish Hamilton. (New York: Harcourt Brace Jovanovich)

1966: Raymond Briggs. *Mother Goose Treasury.* Hamish Hamilton. (New York: Coward-McCann)
Commended
Doreen Roberts. *The Story of Saul the King.* Oxford University Press. (New York: David White)

1967: Charles Keeping. *Charley, Charlotte and the Golden Canary.* Oxford University Press. (New York: Franklin Watts)
Commended
Brian Wildsmith. *Birds.* Oxford University Press. (New York: Franklin Watts)

William Papas. *The Church* and *No Mules.* Oxford University Press. (New York: Coward-McCann)

1968:   Pauline Diana Baynes. *Dictionary of Chivalry.* Longman/Kestrel. (New York: T.Y. Crowell)
Honors List
Gaynor Chapman. *The Luck Child.* Hamish Hamilton. (New York: Atheneum)
Shirley Hughes. *Flutes and Cymbals.* Bodley Head. (New York: T.Y. Crowell)
William Papas. *Taresh the Tea Planter; A Letter from Israel* and *A Letter from India.* Oxford University Press.

1969:   Helen Oxenbury. *The Quangle-Wangle's Hat* (New York: Franklin Watts) and *The Dragon of an Ordinary Family.* William Heinemann.
Honors List
Charles Keeping. *Joseph's Yard.* Longman/Kestrel. (New York: Franklin Watts)
Errol le Cain. *The Cabbage Princess.* Faber and Faber.

1970:   John Burningham. *Mr. Gumpy's Outing.* Jonathan Cape. (New York: Holt, Rinehart and Winston)
Honors List
Charles Keeping. *The God Beneath the Sea.* Longman/Kestrel. (New York: Pantheon)
Jan Pienkowski. *The Golden Bird.* J. M. Dent. (New York: Franklin Watts)
Krystyna Turska. *Pegasus.* Hamish Hamilton. (New York: Franklin Watts)

1971:   Jan Pienkowski. *The Kingdom Under the Sea and Other Stories.* Jonathan Cape.
Highly Commended
Victor G. Ambrus. *The Sultan's Bath.* Oxford University Press. (New York: Harcourt Brace Jovanovich)
Brian Wildsmith. *The Owl and the Woodpecker.* Oxford University Press. (New York: Franklin Watts)

1972:   Krystyna Turska. *The Woodcutter's Duck.* Hamish Hamilton. (New York: Macmillan)
Commended
Carol Baker. *King Midas and the Golden Touch.* Franklin Watts.
Pauline Baynes. *Snail and Caterpillar.* Longman/Kestrel. (New York: McGraw-Hill)
Antony Maitland. *The Ghost Downstairs.* Longman/Kestrel. (New York: Pantheon)

1973:   Raymond Briggs. *Father Christmas.* Hamish Hamilton. (New York: Coward-McCann)
Commended
Fiona French. *King Tree.* Oxford University Press. (New York: Henry Z. Walck)
Errol Lloyd. *My Brother Sean.* Bodley Head.

Hans Christian Andersen Medal Winners

The Hans Christian Andersen Medal has been presented biennially since 1956 to an author whose works have made an outstanding contribution to children's literature. An artist's medal has been awarded as well since 1966. The Hans Christian Andersen Awards are sponsored by the International Board on Books for Young People. Each National Section of the International Board proposes one author and one illustrator as nominees for the Awards. The Awards Jury selects the Andersen Medal winners from among the nominees.

1956:   Eleanor Farjeon (Great Britain)
1958:   Astrid Lindgren (Sweden)
1960:   Erich Kästner (Germany)
1962:   Meindert DeJong (U.S.A.)
1964:   René Guillot (France)
1966:   Author: Tove Jansson (Finland)
        Artist: Alois Carigiet (Switzerland)
1968:   Author: James Krüss (Germany) and José Maria Sanchez-Silva (Spain)
        Artist: Jiří Trnka (Czechoslovakia)
1970:   Author: Gianni Rodari (Italy)
        Artist: Maurice Sendak (U.S.A.)
1972:   Author: Scott O'Dell (U.S.A.)
        Artist: Ib Spang Olsen (Denmark)

Index